The
International Critical Commentary

on the Holy Scriptures of the Old and
New Testaments.

UNDER THE EDITORSHIP OF

THE REV. SAMUEL ROLLES DRIVER, D.D., D.LITT.,
Regius Professor of Hebrew, Oxford;

THE REV. ALFRED PLUMMER, M.A., D.D.,
Late Master of University College, Durham;

AND

THE REV. CHARLES AUGUSTUS BRIGGS, D.D., D.LITT.
Professor of Theological Encyclopædia and Symbolics,
Union Theological Seminary, New York.

THE JOHANNINE EPISTLES

Rev. Canon A. E. BROOKE, D.D.

The International Critical Commentary

A

CRITICAL AND EXEGETICAL COMMENTARY

ON THE

JOHANNINE EPISTLES

BY

Rev. Canon A. E. BROOKE, D.D.

FELLOW, DEAN AND DIVINITY LECTURER, KING'S COLLEGE
CAMBRIDGE

EDINBURGH
T. & T. CLARK, 38 GEORGE STREET

PRINTED IN GREAT BRITAIN BY
MORRISON AND GIBB LIMITED
FOR
T. & T. CLARK, EDINBURGH
NEW YORK: CHARLES SCRIBNER'S SONS

FIRST PRINTED . . . 1912
LATEST IMPRESSION. . 1971

PREFACE.

———

THE following Commentary is an attempt to apply to the Johannine Epistles the method of historical interpretation, the only method of exegesis which can claim to be scientific. I do not mean by historical interpretation a series of ingenious attempts to fit the Epistles into the scheme of known facts, dates, and places of early Christian history, and to assign them, or their constituent parts, to definite persons, places, and decades. A more modest, but equally difficult task has been attempted, that of determining, in the light of our knowledge of Christian life and thought at the end of the First and beginning of the Second Century, what the writer seems to have intended his readers to understand by the words which he addressed to them. When that has been done we may permit ourselves to draw conclusions, or hazard conjectures, about the author's theology, or the value of his words for later generations. The process is possible, even, if we do not know the writer's name, or the exact place and date of his activity. The question of authorship has been deliberately avoided. It cannot be profitably discussed apart from the wider question of the date and authorship of the Fourth Gospel. But we can, I believe, determine what it was that the writer wanted to say to definite groups of men and women whom he knew, as a spiritual father to his own children in the Faith, and whose circumstances he enables us to depict, at least in outline. The method attempted carries with it one necessary result, a prominence given to matters connected with exhortation and edification which may seem out of proportion in a Critical Commentary. But is any other method of interpreting the Johannine Epistles scientific, or even possible? The writer may or may not have been a Theologian. Undoubtedly he *was* the Pastor of his Flock. His chief interest is the cure of souls. He teaches and discusses only in order that his readers " may believe, and believing have life." The meaning of his words can only be determined by the sympathetic recollection of this obvious fact. Rothe's Commentary on the First Epistle is by far the most illuminating book which has been written on the subject, even though in points of detail his explanations of particular phrases and passages are often unsatisfactory and unconvincing. Jülicher's patronising appreciation of its value is somewhat amusing, " Der wertvollste, trotz seiner erbaulichen Tendenz." The supreme merit of Rothe's really remarkable work is that his " tendency to edify " has given him sympathetic insight into the meaning and aims of a writer at least as guilty as himself of the crime of 'erbaulichen Tendenz.' He has seen, as Jülicher has not, that the writer knows to whom he is writing, and knows them well.

The preparation of this Commentary has been the παρέργον of several years in such intervals as could be spared from Septuagint and College Work. Spasmodic efforts, frequently interrupted, lead to uneven results. This is the only excuse I have to offer for want of completeness and consistency in interpretation, as well as for the late date at which the book appears.

My sincerest thanks are due to Dr. Plummer for the kind liberality with which he has interpreted the duties of Editor, and the invaluable help which I have in consequence received from him, during the period of writing as well as that of passing the sheets through the Press.

July 1912.

CONTENTS.

———

			PAGE
INTRODUCTION TO THE JOHANNINE EPISTLES	.	.	i–xc
§ 1. THE EPISTLES AND THE GOSPEL	.	.	i
§ 2. THE AIM	. . . .	·.	xxvii
§ 3. DESTINATION	. . .	.	xxx
§ 4. ANALYSIS	. . .	.	xxxii
§ 5. THE FALSE TEACHERS	. .	.	xxxviii
§ 6. LITERARY HISTORY	. .	.	lii
§ 7. THE TEXT	. . .	.	lxii
§ 8. COMMENTARIES, ETC.	. . .	.	lxxi
§ 9. AUTHORSHIP OF THE SECOND AND THIRD EPISTLES	. . .	.	lxxiii
§ 10. THE SECOND EPISTLE	. .	.	lxxix
§ 11. THE THIRD EPISTLE	. .	.	lxxxi
§ 12. HISTORICAL BACKGROUND OF THE TWO SHORTER EPISTLES	. .	.	lxxxiv
NOTES ON THE FIRST EPISTLE	. .	.	1
NOTES ON THE SECOND EPISTLE	. .	.	166
NOTES ON THE THIRD EPISTLE	. .	.	181
APPENDIX—THE OLD LATIN VERSION	.	.	197
INDICES	. . . .	.	225–242
A. GENERAL	. . .	.	225
B. AUTHORS AND WORKS	. .	.	226
C. GREEK WORDS AND PHRASES EXPLAINED	.	228
D. GREEK WORDS USED IN THE EPISTLES	.	229
E. WORDS USED IN GOSPEL BUT NOT IN EPISTLES	.	235

INTRODUCTION.

———◆———

§ 1. The Epistles and the Gospel.

(a) *Identity of Authorship.*

THE discussion of the question whether the First Epistle and
the Gospel are by the same author may seem to many to be
almost a waste of time.   The view which at first sight must
seem obvious has always been maintained by the majority of
scholars who have investigated the subject.   The list includes
men of widely divergent views, among whom Eichhorn, Credner,
De Wette, Lücke, Ewald, Keim, and Huther may be mentioned.
And the patent similarity of style, language, and ways of thinking
between the two writings might reasonably be regarded as leaving
no room for doubt.   But the views of a minority of competent
scholars cannot be ignored, especially as the number of those
who reject the traditional view has been largely increased in
modern times.   Baur's view, that the explanation of the obvious
connection between the two writings is to be found in imitation
rather than in identity of authorship, meets with an increasing
number of supporters who have a right to be heard.

   The most careful and exhaustive discussion of the question
is contained in H. Holtzmann's article in the *Jahrbuch für
Protestantische Theologie*, 1882, p. 128, which forms the second
of his series of articles on the " Problem of the First Epistle of
S. John in its relation to the Gospel."   He has collected, and
stated with absolute fairness, all the evidence on the subject
which can be derived from the vocabulary, style, and content of
the Epistle, as compared with the Gospel.   In the present section
the freest use has been made of his article, and most of the lists
are practically taken from his.

   The list of phrases common to the two writings is very
striking.   An attempt has been made to bring out its true

significance by a fuller quotation of the Greek in the passages which Holtzmann has collected.

EPISTLE.

GOSPEL.

v. 20. ἵνα γινώσκωμεν τὸν ἀληθινόν.

xvii. 3. ἵνα γινώσκωσίν σε τὸν μόνον ἀληθινὸν θεόν.

iv. 9. τὸν υἱὸν αὐτοῦ τὸν μονογενῆ ἀπέσταλκεν.

i. 14. ὡς μονογενοῦς παρὰ πατρός.

i. 18. μονογενὴς θεός (v. l. ὁ μονογενὴς υἱός).

iii. 16. τὸν υἱὸν τὸν μονογενῆ ἔδωκεν.

iii. 18. τοῦ μονογενοῦς υἱοῦ τοῦ θεοῦ.

iv. 6. τὸ πνεῦμα τῆς ἀληθείας.

xiv. 16 f. ἄλλον παράκλητον ... τὸ πνεῦμα τῆς ἀληθείας (cf. xv. 26).

xvi. 13. ἐκεῖνος, τὸ πνεῦμα τῆς ἀληθείας.

i. 6. οὐ ποιοῦμεν τὴν ἀλήθειαν.

iii. 21. ὁ δὲ ποιῶν τὴν ἀλήθειαν.

i. 8. ἡ ἀλήθεια οὐκ ἔστιν ἐν ἡμῖν.

viii. 44. οὐκ ἔστιν ἀλήθεια ἐν αὐτῷ.

ii. 4 ἐν τούτῳ ἡ ἀλήθεια οὐκ ἔστιν.

ii. 21. ἐκ τῆς ἀληθείας οὐκ ἔστιν.
iii. 19. ἐκ τῆς ἀληθείας ἐσμέν.

xviii. 37. πᾶς ὁ ὢν ἐκ τῆς ἀληθείας.

iii. 8 ἐκ τοῦ διαβόλου ἐστίν.

viii. 44. ἐκ τοῦ πατρὸς τοῦ διαβόλου ἐστέ.

iii. 10. οὐκ ἔστιν ἐκ τοῦ θεοῦ (cf. iv. 1–4, 6, v. 19).

viii. 47. ὁ ὢν ἐκ τοῦ θεοῦ.

iv. 7. ἡ ἀγάπη ἐκ τοῦ θεοῦ ἐστίν.

vii. 17. περὶ τῆς διδαχῆς, πότερον ἐκ τοῦ θεοῦ ἐστιν.

ii. 16. ἐκ τοῦ κόσμου ἐστίν (cf. iv. 5).

viii. 23. ὑμεῖς ἐκ τούτου τοῦ κόσμου ἐστέ (cf. xviii. 36).

xv. 19. εἰ ἐκ τοῦ κόσμου ἦτε (cf. xvii. 14, 16).

ii. 29. ἐξ αὐτοῦ γεγέννηται.

i. 13. οἳ ... ἐκ θεοῦ ἐγεννήθησαν (v. l. qui, ... natus est).

iii. 9. ἐκ τοῦ θεοῦ γεγέννηται (cf. iv. 7, v. 1).

Cf. iii. 8. ὁ γεγεννημένος ἐκ τοῦ πνεύματος.

v. 4. πᾶν τὸ γεγεννημένον ἐκ τοῦ θεοῦ.

v. 18. ὁ γεγεννημένος ἐκ τοῦ θεοῦ ὁ γεννηθεὶς ἐκ τοῦ θεοῦ.

iii. 1. ἵνα τέκνα θεοῦ κληθῶμεν.

i. 12. ἔδωκεν αὐτοῖς ἐξουσίαν τέκνα θεοῦ γενέσθαι.

iii. 2. νῦν τέκνα θεοῦ ἐσμέν (cf. iii. 10, v. 2).

xi. 52. τὰ τέκνα τοῦ θεοῦ τὰ διεσκορπισμένα.

ii. 11. ἐν τῇ σκοτίᾳ περιπατεῖ.

viii. 12. οὐ μὴ περιπατήσῃ ἐν τῇ σκοτίᾳ.

i. 6. ἐν τῷ σκότει περιπατῶμεν.

xii. 35. ὁ περιπατῶν ἐν τῇ σκοτίᾳ (cf. xi. 9, 10).

iv. 20. τὸν θεὸν ὃν οὐχ ἑώρακεν.

vi. 46. οὐχ ὅτι τὸν πατέρα ἑώρακέν τις.

iv. 12. θεὸν οὐδεὶς πώποτε τεθέαται.

i. 18. θεὸν οὐδεὶς ἑώρακεν πώποτε.

EPISTLE.

GOSPEL.

xiv. 9. ὁ ἑωρακὼς ἐμὲ ἑώρακεν τὸν πατέρα.

iii. 16. ἐκεῖνος ὑπὲρ ἡμῶν τὴν ψυχὴν αὐτοῦ ἔθηκεν.

x. 11. τὴν ψυχὴν αὐτοῦ τίθησιν ὑπὲρ τῶν προβάτων (cf. ver. 15).

x. 17. τίθημι τὴν ψυχήν μου, ἵνα πάλιν λάβω αὐτήν.

x. 18. ἐξουσίαν ἔχω θεῖναι αὐτήν.

xiii. 37. τὴν ψυχήν μου ὑπὲρ σοῦ θήσω (cf. ver. 38, xv. 13).

i. 8. ἁμαρτίαν οὐκ ἔχομεν.

ix. 41. οὐκ ἂν εἴχετε ἁμαρτίαν (cf. xv. 22, 24, xix. 11).

v. 13. ἵνα εἰδῆτε ὅτι ζωὴν ἔχετε αἰώνιον.

iii. 15. ἵνα πᾶς ὁ πιστεύων ἐν αὐτῷ ἔχῃ ζωὴν αἰώνιον (cf. vv. 16, 36, v. 24, vi. 40, 47, 54).

v. 39. δοκεῖτε ἐν αὐταῖς ζωὴν αἰώνιον ἔχειν.

iii. 14. μεταβεβήκαμεν ἐκ τοῦ θανάτου εἰς τὴν ζωήν.

v. 24. μεταβέβηκεν ἐκ τοῦ θανάτου εἰς τὴν ζωήν.

Cf. xiii. 1. μεταβῇ ἐκ τοῦ κόσμου τούτου πρὸς τὸν πατέρα.

v. 4. νικᾷ τὸν κόσμον (cf. ii. 13). ἡ νίκη ἡ νικήσασα τὸν κόσμον.

xvi. 33. ἐγὼ νενίκηκα τὸν κόσμον.

v. 5. τίς ἐστιν ὁ νικῶν τὸν κόσμον;

v. 9. εἰ τὴν μαρτυρίαν τῶν ἀνθρώπων λαμβάνομεν.

iii. 33. ὁ λαβὼν αὐτοῦ τὴν μαρτυρίαν (cf. iii. 11).

v. 34. ἐγὼ δὲ οὐ παρὰ ἀνθρώπου τὴν μαρτυρίαν λαμβάνω.

iii. 5. ἐκεῖνος ἐφανερώθη ἵνα τὰς ἁμαρτίας ἄρῃ.

i. 29 ὁ αἴρων τὴν ἁμαρτίαν τοῦ κόσμου.

v. 6. ὁ ἐλθὼν δι᾽ ὕδατος καὶ αἵματος (cf. v. 8).

xix. 34. ἐξῆλθεν εὐθὺς αἷμα καὶ ὕδωρ.

iii. 9. οὐ δύναται ἁμαρτάνειν.

viii. 43. οὐ δύνασθε ἀκούειν.

iv. 20. οὐ (v.l. πῶς) δύναται ἀγαπᾶν.

v. 44. πῶς δύνασθε...πιστεῦσαι;

xiv. 17. ὁ κόσμος οὐ δύναται λαβεῖν.

iii. 20. μείζων ἐστὶν ὁ θεὸς τῆς καρδίας.

iv. 4. μείζων ἐστὶν ὁ ἐν ὑμῖν.

x. 29. ὁ πατήρ μου ὃ δέδωκέν μοι πάντων μεῖζόν ἐστιν (v.l ὃς ... μείζων).

v. 9. ἡ μαρτυρία τοῦ θεοῦ μείζων ἐστιν.

xiv. 28. ὁ πατὴρ μείζων μού ἐστιν.

viii. 53. μὴ σὺ μείζων εἶ τοῦ πατρὸς ἡμῶν Ἀβραάμ;

v. 36. ἔχω τὴν μαρτυρίαν μείζω τοῦ Ἰωάνου.

ii. 6. ὁ λέγων ἐν αὐτῷ μένειν (cf. ii. 27, iii. 6, 24, iv. 12, 13, 15, 16).

xv. 4. ἐὰν μὴ ἐν ἐμοὶ μένητε.

ii. 24. ἐὰν ἐν ὑμῖν μείνῃ ὃ ἀπ᾽ ἀρχῆς ἠκούσατε.

xv. 7. καὶ τὰ ῥήματά μου ἐν ὑμῖν μείνῃ.

ii. 28. μένετε ἐν αὐτῷ.

vi. 56. ἐν ἐμοὶ μένει κἀγὼ ἐν αὐτῷ (cf. xiv. 10).

iv. 12. ὁ θεὸς ἐν ἡμῖν μένει (cf. vv. 13, 15, 16).

b

EPISTLE.	GOSPEL.
iii. **4.** πᾶς ὁ ποιῶν τὴν ἁμαρτίαν (cf. iii. 8, 9).	viii. **34.** πᾶς ὁ ποιῶν τὴν ἁμαρτίαν.
iv. **16.** καὶ ἡμεῖς ἐγνώκαμεν καὶ πεπιστεύκαμεν τὴν ἀγάπην κ.τ.λ.	vi. **69.** καὶ ἡμεῖς πεπιστεύκαμεν καὶ ἐγνώκαμεν ὅτι σὺ εἶ κ.τ.λ.
ii. **3.** ἐὰν τὰς ἐντολὰς αὐτοῦ τηρῶμεν (cf. ii. 4, iii. 22, 24, v. 3).	xiv. **15.** τὰς ἐντολὰς τὰς ἐμὰς τηρήσετε.
ii. **5.** ὃς δ' ἂν τηρῇ αὐτοῦ τὸν λόγον.	xiv. **21.** ὁ ἔχων τὰς ἐντολάς μου καὶ τηρῶν αὐτάς (cf. xv. 10).
iii. **23.** καθὼς ἔδωκεν ἐντολὴν ἡμῖν.	xiv. **31.** καθὼς ἐντολὴν ἔδωκέν μοι ὁ πατήρ (v.l. ἐνετείλατο).
	xii. **49.** ὁ . . . πατὴρ ἐντολὴν δέδωκεν τί εἴπω.
	xiii. **34.** ἐντολὴν καινὴν δίδωμι ὑμῖν.
	xi. **57.** δεδώκεισαν δὲ οἱ ἀρχιερεῖς . . . ἐντολάς.
ii. **11.** οὐκ οἶδεν ποῦ ὑπάγει.	iii. **8.** οὐκ οἶδας . . . ποῦ ὑπάγει.
	viii. **14.** οἶδα . . . ποῦ ὑπάγω (cf. xiii. 33).
	xiii. **36.** ποῦ ὑπάγεις ; (cf. xiv. 5, xvi. 5).
v. **6.** οὗτός ἐστιν ὁ ἐλθών.	i. **33.** οὗτός ἐστιν ὁ βαπτίζων.
	(? Cf. i. **15.** οὗτος ἦν ὁ εἰπών—v.l. ὃν εἶπον.)
ii. **17.** μένει εἰς τὸν αἰῶνα.	viii. **35.** ὁ υἱὸς μένει εἰς τὸν αἰῶνα.
	xii. **34.** ὁ χριστὸς μένει εἰς τὸν αἰῶνα (not confined to Johannine books).
ii. **27.** οὐ χρείαν ἔχετε ἵνα τις διδάσκῃ ὑμᾶς.	ii. **25.** οὐ χρείαν εἶχεν ἵνα τις μαρτυρήσῃ.
	xvi. **30.** οὐ χρείαν ἔχεις ἵνα τίς σε ἐρωτᾷ (cf. xiii. 10, οὐκ ἔχει χρείαν νίψασθαι).
iii. **3.** ἁγνίζει ἑαυτόν.	xi. **55.** ἵνα ἁγνίσωσιν ἑαυτούς.
ii. **6.** (ἐκεῖνος = Christ) καθὼς ἐκεῖνος περιεπάτησεν (cf. iii. 3, 5, 7, 16, iv. 17).	ii. **21.** ἐκεῖνος δὲ ἔλεγεν περὶ τοῦ ναοῦ τοῦ σώματος αὐτοῦ.
	iii. **30.** ἐκεῖνον δεῖ αὐξάνειν.
	iv. **25.** ὅταν ἔλθῃ ἐκεῖνος.
	ix. **37.** ὁ λαλῶν μετὰ σοῦ ἐκεῖνός ἐστιν.
	(?) xix. **35.** καὶ ἐκεῖνος οἶδεν ὅτι ἀληθῆ λέγει.

With regard to the use of ἐκεῖνος of Christ, Holtzmann quotes Jn. i. 8, which is obviously a mistake. The last passage from the Gospel, not quoted by Holtzmann, is the only exact parallel, if it is to be interpreted in this sense, to the usage of the Epistle. In all the other instances there is some sort of antecedent which determines the meaning of ἐκεῖνος. But, at any rate, it is possible to see in the Gospel, if it is earlier than the Epistle, a growing tendency to use ἐκεῖνος of Christ, almost as a proper name, a use which has become fixed in the Epistle.

The attempt has been made to show how each phrase is used

in the Gospel and the Epistle. The connection is obvious. In explaining it the choice has to be made between an imitator and a writer repeating, *not without significant variations*, his common phrases and methods of expression. The usage of these phrases seems on the whole to support the latter hypothesis. But the question can only be determined after considering the other evidence.

It will be noticed that in the phrases quoted above the similarity is not confined to actual phrases used, but extends to common types, in which the same outline is variously filled up. Other, and perhaps clearer, instances of this have been noticed. Compare 1 Jn. v. 10 with Jn. iii. 18 (the upper line gives the words of the Epistle, the lower of the Gospel) ὁ μὴ πιστεύων

τῷ θεῷ ψεύστην πεποίηκεν αὐτόν $\genfrac{}{}{0pt}{}{ὅτι\ οὐ}{ἤδη\ κέκριται\ μὴ}$ πεπίστευκεν εἰς τὴν μαρ-

τυρίαν ἣν μεμαρτύρηκεν ὁ θεὸς περὶ τοῦ $\genfrac{}{}{0pt}{}{υἱοῦ\ αὐτοῦ}{τὸ\ ὄνομα\ τοῦ\ μονογενοῦς\ τοῦ\ θεοῦ}$; or 1 Jn. i. 2

with Jn. i. 1, $\genfrac{}{}{0pt}{}{(ἡ\ ζωή)}{ὁ\ λόγος}$ ἥτις ἦν πρὸς τὸν $\genfrac{}{}{0pt}{}{πατέρα}{θεόν}$; 1 Jn. iii. 8 with

Jn. viii. 41, τὰ ἔργα $\genfrac{}{}{0pt}{}{τοῦ\ διαβόλου}{τοῦ\ πατρὸς\ ὑμῶν}$; 1 Jn. iv. 5 with Jn. iii. 31,

$\genfrac{}{}{0pt}{}{αὐτοὶ}{ὁ\ ὢν\ ἐκ\ τῆς\ γῆς}$ ἐκ $\genfrac{}{}{0pt}{}{τοῦ\ κόσμου\ εἰσίν.}{τῆς\ γῆς\ ἐστίν}$ διὰ τοῦτο ἐκ $\genfrac{}{}{0pt}{}{τοῦ\ κόσμου}{τῆς\ γῆς}$ $\genfrac{}{}{0pt}{}{λαλοῦσιν}{λαλεῖ}$; 1 Jn. iv. 13 with Jn. vi. 56, ἐν αὐτῷ μένομεν καὶ αὐτὸς

ἐν ἡμῖν, ἐν ἐμοὶ μένει κἀγὼ ἐν αὐτῷ; 1 Jn. v. 4 with Jn. iii. 6, τὸ

γεγεννημένον ἐκ τοῦ $\genfrac{}{}{0pt}{}{θεοῦ}{πνεύματος}$; 1 Jn. iii. 15 with Jn. v. 38, οὐκ ἔχει

ζωὴν αἰώνιον ἐν αὐτῷ μένουσαν, τὸν λόγον αὐτοῦ οὐκ ἔχετε ἐν ὑμῖν

μένοντα; 1 Jn. ii. 21 with Jn. viii. 32, $\genfrac{}{}{0pt}{}{οἴδατε}{γνώσεσθε}$ τὴν ἀλήθειαν. It

would be easy to make the list a long one. But these examples serve as illustrations. Again, the usage suggests a writer who varies his own phrases, rather than a mere copyist. If it is a question of copying, there has at least been intelligent use and not slavish imitation.

The following points of similarity of style have often been noticed :

(1) The infrequent use of the relative. The thought is carried on by means of

(a) οὐ . . . ἀλλά. This use is very frequent. Cf. Jn. i. 8, 13; 1 Jn. ii. 2, 16, 21.

(*b*) Disconnected sentences. Cf. 1 Jn. i. 8 (ἐὰν εἴπωμεν), 9 (ἐὰν ὁμολογῶμεν), 10 (ἐὰν εἴπωμεν); Jn. iii. 18, ὁ πιστεύων . . . ὁ μὴ πιστεύων. Frequent in Gospel and Epistle.

(*c*) Positive and negative expression of a thought. Cf. 1 Jn. i. 5, ὁ θεὸς φῶς ἐστὶν καὶ σκοτία οὐκ ἔστιν ἐν αὐτῷ οὐδεμία : Jn. i. 3, πάντα δι' αὐτοῦ ἐγένετο καὶ χωρὶς αὐτοῦ ἐγένετο οὐδὲ ἕν.

(**2**) The emphasizing of a thought by introducing it with a demonstrative, ἐν τούτῳ, αὕτη, etc., followed by an explanatory clause introduced by ἵνα, ἐάν, or ὅτι, or by a clause added in apposition.

EPISTLE.	GOSPEL.
v. 4. αὕτη ἐστὶν ἡ νίκη . . . ἡ πίστις ἡμῶν.	
iii. 11. αὕτη ἐστὶν ἡ ἀγγελία . . . ἵνα ἀγαπῶμεν.	xv. 12. αὕτη ἐστὶν ἡ ἐντολή . . . ἵνα ἀγαπᾶτε.
	vi. 29. τοῦτό ἐστι τὸ ἔργον . . . ἵνα πιστεύητε.
v. 9. αὕτη ἐστὶν ἡ μαρτυρία . . . ὅτι μεμαρτύρηκεν.	iii. 19. αὕτη ἐστὶν ἡ κρίσις ὅτι τὸ φῶς ἐλήλυθεν κ.τ.λ.
iv. 9. ἐν τούτῳ ἐφανερώθη ἡ ἀγάπη . . . ὅτι . . . ἀπέσταλκεν.	ix. 30. ἐν τούτῳ γὰρ τὸ θαυμαστόν ἐστιν ὅτι ὑμεῖς οὐκ οἴδατε.
ii. 3. ἐν τούτῳ γινώσκομεν . . . ἐὰν . . . τηρῶμεν.	xiii. 35. ἐν τούτῳ γνώσονται . . . ἐὰν ἀγάπην ἔχητε.
ii. 6. ἐν τούτῳ γινώσκομεν . . . ὁ λέγων . . . ὀφείλει.	iv. 37. ἐν τούτῳ ὁ λόγος ἐστὶν ἀληθινὸς . . . ἐγὼ ἀπέστειλα κ.τ.λ.
iii. 24. ἐν τούτῳ γινώσκομεν . . . ἐκ τοῦ πνεύματος.	
iv. 17. ἐν τούτῳ τετελείωται . . . ἵνα παρρησίαν ἔχωμεν.	xv. 8. ἐν τούτῳ ἐδοξάσθη . . . ἵνα καρπὸν φέρητε.
v. 2. ἐν τούτῳ γινώσκομεν . . . ὅταν . . . ἀγαπῶμεν.	
iii. 1. διὰ τοῦτο οὐ γινώσκει . . . ὅτι οὐκ ἔγνω.	v. 16. διὰ τοῦτο ἐδίωκον . . . ὅτι ἐποίει.
iii. 8. εἰς τοῦτο ἐφανερώθη . . . ἵνα λύσῃ.	xviii. 37. εἰς τοῦτο γεγέννημαι . . . ἵνα μαρτυρήσω.

In most of these instances the reference of ἐν τούτῳ, etc., to what follows is undoubted, though some of them are often, if not usually, interpreted otherwise. Again, the impression left by studying them is not that of slavish copying.

(**3**) Several other small points may also be noticed :

The use of πᾶς ὁ with a participle : cf. 1 Jn. iii. 4, πᾶς ὁ ποιῶν : Jn. iii. 16, πᾶς ὁ πιστεύων. Frequent in both writings.

πᾶν (τὸ) with the participle, where πάντες might have been used.

Cf. 1 Jn. v. 4, πᾶν τὸ γεγεννημένον ἐκ τοῦ θεοῦ νικᾷ: Jn. vi. 37, πᾶν ὃ δίδωσίν μοι . . . πρός με ἥξει.

The repetition of emphatic words, especially κόσμος, θεός, πνεῦμα.

The frequent use of καὶ . . . δέ: cf. 1 Jn. i. 3, καὶ ἡ κοινωνία δὲ ἡ ἡμετέρα: Jn. vi. 51, καὶ ὁ ἄρτος δέ.

The elliptic use of ἀλλ' ἵνα: cf. 1 Jn. ii. 19, ἀλλ' ἵνα φανερωθῶσιν ὅτι οὐκ εἰσὶν πάντες ἐξ ἡμῶν: Jn. ix. 3, ἀλλ' ἵνα φανερωθῇ τὰ ἔργα τοῦ θεοῦ: Jn. i. 8, ἀλλ' ἵνα μαρτυρήσῃ περὶ τοῦ φωτός.

The use of καθὼς . . . καί: cf. 1 Jn. ii. 18, καθὼς ἠκούσατε . . . καὶ νῦν . . . γεγόνασιν: Jn. xiii. 15, ἵνα καθὼς ἐγὼ ἐποίησα . . . καὶ ὑμεῖς ποιῆτε.

The elliptic use of οὐ καθώς: cf. 1 Jn. iii. 11, 12, ἀγαπῶμεν ἀλλήλους· οὐ καθὼς Καὶν ἐκ τοῦ πονηροῦ ἦν: Jn. vi. 58, οὗτός ἐστιν ὁ ἄρτος ὁ ἐξ οὐρανοῦ καταβάς, οὐ καθὼς ἔφαγον οἱ πατέρες καὶ ἀπέθανον.

Some of these are worth noticing in view of the assertion that the similarities of style and expression are mostly in the case of obvious points, which are easily imitated.

(4) Attention must also be drawn to the limited vocabulary of both writings, and the very small number of ἅπαξ λεγόμενα (*i.e.* words not found elsewhere in the New Testament) which they contain in common. Of words common to both writings but not found elsewhere in the New Testament we have only ἀνθρωπόκτονος and παράκλητος. The First Epistle gives us four ἅπαξ λεγόμενα (ἀγγελία, ἱλασμός, νίκη, χρίσμα). If the three Epistles are taken together the list is increased by the following words, ἀντίχριστος, ἐπιδέχομαι, κυρία, φιλοπρωτεύω, φλυαρέω, χάρτης. The number in the Gospel is far larger, and does not offer any striking contrast to the other Books of the N.T. But its longer list, as compared with the Epistles, is adequately explained by the character of the words which it contains.

The importance of N.T. ἅπαξ λεγόμενα has naturally decreased in consequence of the discoveries of Papyri in the last quarter of a century, which have taught us the danger of treating N.T. Greek as an isolated phenomenon, even if the actual words in question are not among those of which our knowledge has been substantially increased by better acquaintance with vulgar Greek. It may also be doubted whether the author's vocabulary is really so limited as the perusal of his writings at first suggests. He can say most of what he has to say by the careful use of a few words, and prefers to vary his forms of expression rather than his vocabulary. He has no love for synonyms which have no difference in meaning. He does not care to show his command of language by the use of many σημαίνοντα to express the same σημαινόμενον. He is altogether free from the artificialities of the later literary κοινή. He does not, however seem to be at loss for a word to express his meaning. But however this may be, the limited range of normal vocabulary is a feature common to both writings.

The similarity is not confined to style and vocabulary, extends to ideas, both as regards doctrine and ethics.

(1) The general ideas which form the basis of the Johannine teaching are common to both.

The incarnation of the Son of God:

1 Jn. iv. 2. Ἰησοῦν Χριστὸν ἐν σαρκὶ ἐληλυθότα.

Jn. i. 14. ὁ λόγος σὰρξ ἐγένετο.

The life which has its source in Him:

1 Jn. v. 11. αὕτη ἡ ζωὴ ἐν τῷ υἱῷ αὐτοῦ ἐστιν.

Jn. i. 4. (ὃ γέγονεν) ἐν αὐτῷ ζωὴ ἦν.

vi. 35. ὁ ἄρτος τῆς ζωῆς (cf. ver. 48).

vi. 33. ζωὴν διδοὺς τῷ κόσμῳ.

And which is identified with Him:

1 Jn. i. 1, 2. ὃ ἦν ἀπ' ἀρχῆς . . . περὶ τοῦ λόγου τῆς ζωῆς . . . καὶ ἡ ζωὴ ἐφανερώθη.

Jn. v. 26. οὕτως καὶ τῷ υἱῷ ἔδωκεν ζωὴν ἔχειν ἐν ἑαυτῷ.

xi. 25. ἐγώ εἰμι . . . ἡ ζωή.

(In 1 Jn. v. 20, οὗτός ἐστιν ὁ ἀληθινὸς θεὸς καὶ ζωὴ αἰώνιος probably refers to the Father, the God who has been made known by Jesus Christ; cf. Jn. v. 26a.)

Abiding in God: being in Christ, the means of abiding in God:

1 Jn. ii. 24. ἐν τῷ υἱῷ καὶ ἐν τῷ πατρὶ μενεῖτε.

iii. 6. πᾶς ὁ ἐν αὐτῷ μένων.

Jn. vi. 56. ἐν ἐμοὶ μένει κἀγὼ ἐν αὐτῷ.

xv. 4–7. (ὁ μένων ἐν ἐμοὶ κἀγὼ ἐν αὐτῷ).

1 Jn. v. 20. ἐσμεν ἐν τῷ ἀληθινῷ ἐν τῷ υἱῷ αὐτοῦ Ἰησοῦ Χριστῷ.

Jn. xiv. 20. ἐγὼ ἐν τῷ πατρί μου καὶ ὑμεῖς ἐν ἐμοὶ κἀγὼ ἐν ὑμῖν.

xvii. 21. ἵνα καὶ αὐτοὶ ἐν ἡμῖν ὦσιν.

God's word abiding in us:

1 Jn. ii. 14. ὁ λόγος τοῦ θεοῦ ἐν ὑμῖν μένει.

ii. 24. ὃ ἠκούσατε ἀπ᾽ ἀρχῆς ἐν ὑμῖν μενέτω.

Jn. v. 38. τὸν λόγον αὐτοῦ οὐκ ἔχετε ἐν ὑμῖν μένοντα.

God's love proved by the sending of His Son:

1 Jn. iv. 9. ἐν τούτῳ ἐφανερώθη ἡ ἀγάπη τοῦ θεοῦ ἐν ἡμῖν ὅτι τὸν υἱὸν αὐτοῦ τὸν μονογενῆ ἀπέσταλκεν.

Jn. iii. 16. οὕτως ἠγάπησεν ὁ θεὸς τὸν κόσμον ὥστε τὸν υἱὸν τὸν μονογενῆ ἔδωκεν.

The command to love the brethren, which is the result of this:

1 Jn. iii. 23. καὶ ἀγαπῶμεν ἀλλήλους καθὼς ἔδωκεν ἐντολὴν ἡμῖν (cf. iii. 11, 16, 18).

Jn. xiii. 34. ἵνα ἀγαπᾶτε ἀλλήλους καθὼς ἠγάπησα ὑμᾶς (cf. xv. 12, 17).

Believers the children of God:

1 Jn. v. 1. πᾶς ὁ πιστεύων . . . ἐκ τοῦ θεοῦ γεγέννηται.

Jn. i. 12, 13. ἔδωκεν αὐτοῖς ἐξουσίαν τέκνα θεοῦ γενέσθαι, τοῖς πιστεύουσιν εἰς τὸ ὄνομα αὐτοῦ.

The great stress laid on " witness ":

1 Jn. v. 6. τὸ πνεῦμά ἐστιν τὸ μαρτυροῦν (cf. vv. 9–11).

Jn. v. 36, 37. ἐγὼ δὲ ἔχω τὴν μαρτυρίαν μείζω τοῦ Ἰωάνου κ.τ.λ. Cf. viii. 17 f.

(2) Certain pairs of opposites common to both writings: Light and Darkness, Life and Death, Love and Hate, Truth and Falsehood, The Father and the World, To be of the World, To be not of the World, God and the Devil, The children of God and the children of the Devil, To know and not to know God, To have seen and not to have seen Him, To have life and not to have life.

It would be very easy to extend largely those lists of similarities between the two writings. Many more are noticed in the Commentary. To quote all that exist would involve printing practically the whole of the Epistle and a large part of the Gospel. Schulze's statement, quoted by Holtzmann (p. 134), can hardly be denied, " In the whole of the first Epistle there is hardly a single thought that is not found in the Gospel."

No one would dispute Holtzmann's judgment, that these similarities are closer than those which connect the Third Gospel and the Acts, "whose common authorship is un-doubted." In the Pauline literature the case of Ephesians and Colossians is analogous. We ought perhaps to add that of (part of) the two Epistles to the Thessalonians. And it must be admitted that these analogies raise the question of imitation. The question may well be asked whether a writer of such undoubted power and originality as the author of the Fourth Gospel[1] would be likely "only to copy himself." It is quite possible that a writer who had steeped himself in the thought of the Fourth Gospel might produce the First Epistle. And it is by no means impossible that we have a similar case, perhaps the work of the same imitator, in the twenty-first chapter of the Gospel.

The answer to the question may prove to be discoverable only in the light of the writer's circumstances. The author of the Epistle certainly does not aim at literary effect. The edification of his children in the faith is his sole purpose in writing. And he is intensely in earnest. He is convinced that he knows what truths will meet their needs. He is fully aware that he has nothing new to say. They must learn to use what they already possess, even that which they had been taught from the beginning, by himself or by another. These are circumstances under which repetition was almost inevitable, especially in the case of a man whose nature led him to ponder deeply over a few ideas rather than to produce new thoughts every day.

There is another point which must be considered in this connection. In what sense is the author of the Fourth Gospel original? Few would venture to deny the depth of thought and spiritual insight of the Fourth Gospel. How far is this due to the author's originality? How much has he learnt from others, or from Another? There will probably always be differences of opinion as to whether he is most indebted to S. Paul or to the Lord Himself. The Fourth Gospel has a large part to play in the controversy which rages round the question Jesus or Paul? But whether we accept or reject the paradox of Wernle, "It is S. Paul who is original, S. John is not," as a solution of the Johannine problem, we can hardly escape the impression which the study of the Fourth Gospel leaves with us, that its author meditates and transforms rather than originates. The process may have reached a further stage of development in the Epistle. We may be nearer to the writer's own thoughts, or rather the process of assimilation may be more complete, whereas in the Gospel we can trace more clearly his debt to another. But such a writer as the author of the Gospel might well "repeat himself," especially if he were fully conscious that he had already said or taught his readers all that they required to meet the circumstances in which they found themselves placed. Ὑμεῖς ὃ ἠκούσατε ἀπ' ἀρχῆς ἐν ὑμῖν μενέτω is the burden of his message. His chief object in writing is to remind them what it was.

It cannot, therefore, be said that the absence of new matter

[1] If, for present purposes, we may so describe the man who has given it to us in its present form.

in the Epistle is *necessarily* suspicious. But this view would, of course, have to be modified if convincing evidence were forthcoming that the resemblance between the two writings is mainly confined to obvious points which could be easily caught and imitated, while there are real differences in minor points of style and expression where conscious imitation would be less easy, and where the peculiarities of the imitator would be most likely to show themselves. The following points are cited in support of such a hypothesis:

Ἔχειν ἐλπίδα ἐπί τινι. This is said to be "contrary to the general usage of the N.T. (Ro. xv. 12 being a quotation from the O.T.), and also to that of Jn. v. 45 (ἐλπίζειν εἰς τινα)." The "usage of the N.T." is surely rather difficult to decide. As to ἔχειν ἐλπίδα we have Ac. xxiv. 15, ἐλπίδα ἔχων εἰς τὸν θεόν, and the passage in question from the Epistle with ἐπί. As to ἐλπίζειν we find εἰς ὅν, Jn. v. 45 ; ἐπ᾽ αὐτῷ, Ro. xv. 12 (= Is. xi. 10) ; ἐν Χριστῷ, 1 Co. xv. 19 ; ἐπὶ θεῷ, 1 Ti. iv. 10, vi. 17 ; ἐπὶ [τὸν] θεόν, 1 Ti. v. 5 ; ἐπὶ πλούτου ἀδηλότητι, 1 Ti. vi. 17 ; ἐπὶ τὴν . . . χάριν, 1 P. i. 13 ; εἰς θεόν, 1 P. iii. 5. It is unnecessary to illustrate or quote its use with the accusative, or ὅτι, or the infinitive, or its use absolutely. The evidence is clearly insufficient to establish a N.T. use for or against any particular construction.

We must next consider the use of ἀπό with the verbs ἀκούειν, αἰτεῖν, λαμβάνειν (cf. also ἔχειν, ii. 20, iv. 21), as against the usual construction with παρά which is found in the Gospel. With regard to ἀκούειν the usage is clear, so far as it goes, though it may be noticed that ἀκούειν ἀπό occurs only once in the Epistle, where it probably has a slightly different shade of meaning, emphasizing the ultimate rather than the immediate source of the hearing, that both constructions, ἀπό and παρά, are found in Acts (ix. 13, x. 22), and that Gospel and Epistle share the commoner construction, *i.e.*, with a genitive of the person. Λαμβάνειν occurs twice, αἰτεῖν once in the Epistle, with the construction ἀπό τινος. In the Gospel λαμβάνειν παρά is found four times, αἰτεῖν παρά once. There is not very much ground here for a theory of separate authorship.

The following differences are also noticed, which for convenience may be tabulated:

EPISTLE.	GOSPEL.
κοινωνία.	The Holy Spirit.
ἔχειν τὸν υἱόν.	Birth from above.
ἀγάπη τετελειωμένη.	
θεὸς ἀγάπη.	θεὸς πνεῦμα.
ἀγάπην ἀγαπᾶν.	ἀγάπην διδόναι.
πεπιστεύκαμεν καὶ ἐγνώκαμεν.	ἐγνώκαμεν καὶ πεπιστεύκαμεν.
ποιεῖν τὴν δικαιοσύνην.	ποιεῖν τὴν ἀλήθειαν.

So far the list is perhaps more striking for its resemblances than its differences. There are, however, undoubtedly many words and phrases which are peculiar to each. Some of them remind us that the vocabulary of the author or authors is not quite so limited as is generally assumed. In any case, can we say that the peculiarities are greater than can be naturally explained by differences of time, circumstances, and subject?

The Index has been arranged so as to give with rough accuracy the full facts of vocabulary. It will be sufficient here to notice the differences to which Holtzmann has called attention.

The following words are quoted from the Gospel which are absent from the Epistle: δόξα, δοξάζειν, χάρις, πλήρωμα, οὐρανός, ἀνιστάνειν, ἀναστῆναι, ἀνάστασις, ἐγείρειν, οἱ νεκροί, ἄνωθεν, βασιλεία τοῦ θεοῦ, τὰ ἐπίγεια (ἐπουράνια), ὑψοῦσθαι, ἀπολλύναι, σώζειν, ἐργάζεσθαι (used in the shorter Epp.), σωτηρία, ὁ πέμψας, κρίνειν, κρίμα, διακονεῖν, διάκονος, ἐμφανίζειν, εἰρήνη. Of these words some are so rare, comparatively or absolutely, that their absence in the Epistle would be more probable than their presence. There are not many which we should even expect to find, though the absence of δόξα, ὁ πέμψας, κρίνειν, ἄνωθεν calls for notice. There is perhaps not one of which we can say that the author of the Gospel *must* have used it if the Epistle were his.

The list of phrases is larger. A few facts as to usage, which go far to modify the significance of the list, have been noted in brackets: τὸ πνεῦμα τὸ ἅγιον (*once* in Gospel, cf. also xx. 22, πνεῦμα ἅγιον, whereas τὸ πνεῦμα is the common usage in both), γεννηθῆναι ἐκ πνεύματος, ἐξ ὕδατος καὶ πνεύματος (confined to the conversation with Nicodemus, while γεννηθῆναι ἐκ θεοῦ is common to both writings), ἀγαπᾶν τὸ φῶς, τὸ σκότος (*once* in Gospel), φαῦλα πράσσειν (*twice*), μαρτυρία, of God (? cf. 1 Jn. v. 9, 10), ὁ κύριος, of Christ (*six* times, of which three are in ch. xxi.; xiii. 14, 16 have not been included), ἡ ὀργὴ τοῦ θεοῦ (*once*, cf. Apoc.), ἰδεῖν ζωήν (*once*), προσκυνεῖν ἐν πνεύματι καὶ ἀληθείᾳ (*twice*, in ch. iv.), τιμᾶν τὸν πατέρα, υἱόν (*thrice* in one verse, besides which only viii. 49, τιμῶ τὸν πατέρα μου, cf. xii. 26, τιμήσει αὐτὸν ὁ πατήρ), ποιεῖν τὰ ἀγαθά (*once*), ἀνάστασις ζωῆς, κρίσεως (*once* each), μαρτυρεῖν τῇ ἀληθείᾳ (*twice*, cf. 1 Jn. v. 6, καὶ τὸ πνεῦμά ἐστι τὸ μαρτυροῦν, ὅτι τὸ πνεῦμά ἐστιν ἡ ἀλήθεια), ἐραυνᾶν τὰς γραφάς (*once*), οὐκ ἀποθνῄσκειν (*twice*, in ch. xxi., but cf. μή, οὐ μή twice or thrice) ἀποθνῄσκειν ἐν τῇ ἁμαρτίᾳ (*thrice*, in one context), ῥήματα τοῦ θεοῦ, ζωῆς αἰωνίου (*twice* and *once*), φῶς τοῦ κόσμου, τῆς ζωῆς (*thrice* and *once*), εἶναι ἐκ τῶν ἄνω, κάτω (*once* each), μένειν ἐν τῷ λόγῳ (*once*, cf. 2 Jn. 9, μένειν ἐν τῇ διδαχῇ: the corresponding ὁ λόγος . . . μένει . . . ἐν is common to Gospel and Epistle), ὁ λόγος χωρεῖ (*once*), ἐλευθεροῦν (*twice*); and ἐλεύθερος γενέσθαι (*once*, in same context), θεωρεῖν θάνατον, γεύεσθαι θανάτου (*once* each), ὁ ἄρχων τοῦ κόσμου (*once*, τούτου *twice*), υἱοὶ τοῦ φωτός (*once*), ὁ υἱὸς ἐν τῷ πατρί (?), ὁ πατὴρ ἐν τῷ υἱῷ (*once*, ὁ πατὴρ ἐν ἐμοί, etc., fairly common), φιλεῖν, μισεῖν τὴν ψυχήν (*once* each), ἔχειν εἰρήνην (*once*), ἔχειν τὸ φῶς (*twice*), πιστεύειν εἰς τὸ φῶς (*once*), ἐτοιμάζειν τόπον (*twice*, in same context), αἰτεῖν ἐν τῷ ὀνόματι (Χριστοῦ) (*five* times, cf. 1 Jn. v. 14, κατὰ τὸ θέλημα), μονὴν ποιεῖν παρά τινι (*once*), καρπὸν φέρειν (*eight* times, of which *six* are in xv. 2–8), φανεροῦν τὸ ὄνομα (*once*, the use of φανεροῦν is characteristic of both), ἓν εἶναι (*four* times). If this list is at all complete, or representative, it certainly affords very little evidence of the presence in the Gospel of *characteristic* phrases not to be found in the Epistle. It consists mostly of phrases which are found only once or twice, or which, if they occur more frequently, are generally confined to a special context. There are very few of them of which we can say that their absence from the Epistle is significant.

It may be worth while to go through in the same way the fifty "peculiarities" which Holtzmann has noted for the Epistle.

(1) ὁ with the Present Participle. (Found *eight* times in Jn. xiii.–xvi., but certainly more frequent in the Epistle.)

(2) ἐὰν εἴπωμεν ὅτι, περιπατῶμεν, ὁμολογῶμεν (ἐάν with each of these verbs occurs in the Gospel, and the use of ἐάν is fairly frequent in both writings ; naturally opportunities for the use of the 1st person plural are far less in the Gospel than in the Epistle).

(3) ἔκ τινος γινώσκειν (*twice*). Cf. 1 Jn. ii. 18 (ὅθεν).

(4) ὑμεῖς followed by a relative sentence, which becomes the subject of the main sentence (ὑμεῖς ὃ ἠκούσατε . . . ἐν ὑμῖν μενέτω, ii. 24, cf. 27). (May we not compare Jn. x. 29, ὁ πατήρ μου ὃ δέδωκέν μοι πάντων μεῖζόν ἐστιν?)

(5) κοινωνία, with God, Christ, the brethren. (The teaching about κοινωνία in the Epistle is surely the natural sequel of Jn. xiv.–xvii.)

(6) ἀγγελία, ἐπαγγελία, ἐπαγγέλλειν. (It may be noted that ἀγγέλλειν is a N.T. ἅπαξ λεγόμενον in the Gospel.)

(7) ἑαυτὸν πλανᾶν. (The *verb* is common to both.)

(8) ὁμολογεῖν τὰς ἁμαρτίας. (The verb is, of course, common to both. Its use with ἁμαρτία is peculiar, in the N.T., to the one passage 1 Jn. i. 9 ; cf. ἐξομολογεῖσθαι, Mt., Mk., Ja.)

(9) πιστός, of God. (*Once*. The word is used *once* in the Gospel.)

(10) ἡ ἀγάπη τετελείωται. (Cf. Jn. xvii. 23, ἵνα ὦσιν τετελειωμένοι εἰς ἕν . . . καὶ ἠγάπησας αὐτοὺς καθὼς ἐμὲ ἠγάπησας.)

(11) διάνοια (*once*).

(12) παράγειν. (More correctly παράγεσθαι. The active παράγειν occurs twice in the Gospel, in a different sense.)

(13) ἀγαπᾶν τοὺς ἀδελφούς. (The phrase of the Gospel, ἵνα ἀγαπᾶτε ἀλλήλους, quoted as a *contrast*, is perhaps a sufficient parallel.)

(14) σκάνδαλον, ii. 10 (cf., however, with the context, ἐν τῇ σκοτίᾳ περιπατεῖ οὐκ οἶδεν ποῦ ὑπάγει: Jn. xi. 9, ἐάν τις περιπατῇ ἐν τῇ ἡμέρᾳ οὐ προσκόπτει.)

(15) ἀφέωνται ὑμῖν αἱ ἁμαρτίαι διὰ τὸ ὄνομα αὐτοῦ. (Cf. Jn. xx. 23, ἄν τινων ἀφῆτε τὰς ἁμαρτίας ἀφέωνται αὐτοῖς.)

(16) ψευδοπροφῆται, ἀντίχριστοι. (Cf. Jn. v. 43.)

(17) ἀγαπᾶν τὸν κόσμον. (Should we compare Jn. xxi. 15, ἀγαπᾷς με πλέον τούτων? At any rate the resemblance of the two writings in their use of κόσμος is far more striking than the absence of a particular phrase from one of them.)

(18) ἀλαζονεία (*once*).

(19) βίος (*twice*).

(20) ἀγαπητοί. (*Six* times; cf. 3 Jn. ἀγαπητέ thrice. The doctrine of ἀγάπη contained in the Gospel would certainly account for the frequency of this form of address in the Epistle.)

(21) τὸ χρίσμα. (*Thrice*; cf. Jn. iii. 34, δίδωσιν τὸ πνεῦμα: cf. vii. 39.)

(22) ἀρνεῖσθαι, ὁμολογεῖν, τὸν υἱόν. (Cf., however, Jn. i. 20, ὡμολόγησεν καὶ οὐκ ἠρνήσατο.)

(23) ἔχειν τὸν πατέρα, τὸν υἱόν. (Cf., perhaps, Jn. iii. 29, ὁ ἔχων τὴν νύμφην.)

(24) παρρησία πρὸς τὸν θεόν. (The *word* is fairly common in the Gospel.)

(25) αἰσχύνεσθαι (ii. 28, αἰσχυνθῶμεν ἀπ᾽ αὐτοῦ. (Cf. Jn. iii. 20, οὐκ ἔρχεται πρὸς τὸ φῶς, ἵνα μὴ ἐλεγχθῇ τὰ ἔργα αὐτοῦ.)

(26) παρουσία (*once*).

(27) ὅμοιοι αὐτῷ ἐσόμεθα. (? Cf. Jn. ix. 9, ὅμοιος αὐτῷ: viii. 55, ἔσομαι ὅμοιος ὑμῖν.)

(28, 29) Omitted apparently by mistake.

(30) ἐλπίς. (*Once*. The word does not occur in any of the Gospels. Cf., however, Jn. v. 45, εἰς ὃν ἠλπίκατε, with the passage in the Epistle, iii. 3, ὁ ἔχων τὴν ἐλπίδα ταύτην ἐπ᾽ αὐτῷ.)

(31) ἁγνός. (*Once*. But ἁγνίζειν, which occurs in the same verse, is common to both.)

(32) ἀνομία. (*Twice*. In the same context.)

(33) ἐφανερώθη ὁ υἱὸς τοῦ θεοῦ. (Cf. Jn. i. 31, ἀλλ' ἵνα φανερωθῇ τῷ Ἰσραήλ.)

(34) λύειν τὰ ἔργα τοῦ διαβόλου. (Cf. Jn. vii. 23, ἵνα μὴ λυθῇ ὁ νόμος : viii. 41, τὰ ἔργα τοῦ πατρὸς ὑμῶν.)

(35) τὸ σπέρμα τοῦ θεοῦ, ὁ γεννήσας (of God). (Cf. Jn. i. 13, ἐκ θεοῦ ἐγεννήθησαν : viii. 33, σπέρμα Ἀβραάμ.)

(36) ἐν τούτῳ φανερά ἐστιν. (Φανεροῦν is characteristic of both writings.)

(37) καταγινώσκειν. (*Twice.* Elsewhere only in Gal. ii. 11.)

(38) ὁ ἐν ὑμῖν, ὁ ἐν τῷ κόσμῳ. (The contrast is characteristically Johannine, though the actual phrases do not occur in the Gospel.)

(39) μένειν ἐν τῷ θανάτῳ. (A phrase cast in a thoroughly Johannine mould. Cf. also Jn. iii. 36, ὁ δὲ ἀπειθῶν τῷ υἱῷ οὐκ ὄψεται ζωήν, ἀλλ' ἡ ὀργὴ τοῦ θεοῦ μένει ἐπ' αὐτόν.)

(40) πιστεύειν τῷ ὀνόματι τοῦ υἱοῦ (iii. 23. If we complete the phrase, αὐτοῦ Ἰησοῦ Χριστοῦ, we may compare Jn. xx. 31, ἵνα πιστεύητε ὅτι Ἰησοῦς ἐστιν ὁ Χριστὸς ὁ υἱὸς τοῦ θεοῦ, καὶ ἵνα πιστεύοντες ζωὴν ἔχητε ἐν τῷ ὀνόματι αὐτοῦ).

(41) τὸ πνεῦμα τῆς πλάνης. (Cf. τὸ πνεῦμα τῆς ἀληθείας, which is common to both. The one phrase suggests the other.)

(42) δοκιμάζειν τὰ πνεύματα (*once*).

(43) κλείειν τὰ σπλάγχνα. (The verb is common to both.)

(44) πείθειν τὰς καρδίας ἡμῶν. (Cf., perhaps, μὴ ταρασσέσθω ὑμῶν ἡ καρδιά.)

(45) ἁμαρτία πρὸς θάνατον. (Cf. Jn. ix. 41, ἡ ἁμαρτία ὑμῶν μένει : viii. 24, ἀποθανεῖσθε ἐν ταῖς ἁμαρτίαις ὑμῶν.)

(46) τηρεῖν ἑαυτόν, ἑαυτὸν φυλάσσειν. (The former is probably not the true text, αὐτόν having better support. With τηρεῖ αὐτόν, cf. Jn. xvii. 12, ἐγὼ ἐτήρουν αὐτοὺς ἐν τῷ ὀνόματί μου. For φυλάσσειν cf. xvii. 12, καὶ ἐφύλαξα.)

(47) ὁ κόσμος ὅλος ἐν τῷ πονηρῷ κεῖται. (Cf. Jn. xvii. 15, ἵνα τηρήσῃς αὐτοὺς ἐκ τοῦ πονηροῦ.)

(48) φόβος, as the opposite of ἀγάπη, the Gospel having only φόβος τῶν Ἰουδαίων. Perhaps it is not altogether fanciful to see some recollection of the fear which kept men from open confession, in the love issuing in confidence, which "casts out fear."

(49) ἔχειν τὴν μαρτυρίαν ἐν ἑαυτῷ. (Perhaps we may compare Jn. iii. 33, ὁ λαβὼν αὐτοῦ τὴν μαρτυρίαν ἐσφράγισεν).

(50) κόλασις (*once*).

Thus on closer inspection a considerable number of the phrases which are actually peculiar to the Epistle remind us so strongly of similar phrases and thoughts in the Gospel that it is again the resemblance rather than the difference that is brought into prominence. The phenomena are not inconsistent with the theory of imitation, but they do not find their most natural explanation in it. The variations in phrase suggest common authorship rather than servile, or even intelligent, copying. Both writings show the same characteristics, a small vocabulary used and used up; reiteration with slight variations, generally conveying some correspondingly slight difference of meaning; and no more new words than the differences of subject and circumstance call for, and are amply sufficient to explain.

Is there any difference in the ideas and conceptions expressed in this similar but not identical phraseology, sufficiently marked to compel us to assume a corresponding difference in authorship?

Such a difference can hardly be found in the λόγος of the Gospel Prologue as compared with the vaguer λόγος τῆς ζωῆς of the Epistle. No doubt the one phrase describes a difference of Person, while the other is impersonal. But the personal distinction of υἱός and πατήρ is as clearly marked in the Epistle as in the Gospel. It is possible that the more definite λόγος has been avoided in agreement with the growing Monarchian tendencies of a later stage of doctrine, but the pre-existent personality of Him who "came in flesh" is as definitely taught in the Epistle as in the Gospel.

In the Epistle the sum of the ἀγγελία which the writer has to announce is said to be that *God* is light. In the Gospel, light is used as a description of the pre-existent and the Incarnate Logos. And in general it has been maintained that the Christ of the Epistle is more definitely separated from God and brought nearer to the believing Christian. The Christ of the Epistle is only Prophet, Example, Advocate, Reconciler. He is separated from us by sinlessness rather than by Divinity.

It is probably true that in the Gospel Christ is always represented as the connecting point between God and the world. As God is to Christ, so is Christ to "His own," whereas in the Epistle this relation is "simplified." Commentators are divided as to whether this is brought about by setting God on the one side, Christ and His own on the other, or whether the Epistle goes further than the Gospel in the direction of glorifying the Christ. The number of passages in the Epistle in which it is extremely difficult to decide whether God or Christ is the subject, certainly point in the latter direction. But it is doubtful whether the differences between Gospel and Epistle are as great as is assumed by those who maintain the theory of different authorship. In the Gospel it is natural that the relation of Christ to God on the one hand, and to His followers on the other, should be dwelt upon; while in the Epistle the relation of the Brethren to the Father should be more prominent. But this relationship is always conceived of as realized in and through Christ. "Our fellowship is with the Father, and with His Son Jesus Christ." We may compare Jn. xvi. 27, "the Father Himself loveth you"; "I do not say that I will ask the Father concerning you." The difference exists, but it is a difference of standpoint and of expression, not a fundamental difference of conception. And it is a difference specially noticeable in certain forms of expression which are used, rather than in the general teaching of the Epistle as a whole. The Gospel taught who and what the Christ is. The Epistle is written to assure those who had learned its lesson that, if they will but remember it, they can feel sure confidence as to the relationship in which they stand to God in His Son Jesus Christ. The differences correspond to the different objects of the two writings.

If this view of the general teaching of the two writings is correct, it will explain the similar phenomena which are traceable with regard to the ideas of life and love. In the Gospel it is Christ who came that they might have life—in the Epistle we read ζωὴν αἰώνιον ἔδωκεν ἡμῖν ὁ θεός : but the author hastens to add, "this life is in His Son." So with love. In the Gospel "the love wherewith God loves the faithful is always grounded in the love wherewith He loves the Son." They must abide in the Son's love, as He abides in the love of the Father. In 1 Jn. iv. 9–11 the stress is laid on the love of God for the world and for us. But the intimate connection of this passage with Jn. iii. 16 certainly suggests that the writer of the Epistle is conscious of no fundamental difference of view. Again, in the Gospel it is the Logos who gives power τέκνα θεοῦ γενέσθαι—in the Epistle it is "a direct proof of the love of the Father ἵνα τέκνα θεοῦ κληθῶμεν, καὶ ἐσμέν." But in all these points it is hardly too much to say that a real difference can be established only by ignoring the expressions and thoughts in either document which tell the other way. It may also be true that in the Gospel the unity of the Son with the Father is the type of the union of the faithful with the Son, and *therein* with the Father (cf. xiv. 20, xvii. 23); whereas the Epistle speaks more directly, "We are in God," "God in us"; and the same difference can be traced in the use of μένειν. Christ's command in the Gospel to exercise mutual love may be expressed in the Epistle as an ἐντολὴ τοῦ θεοῦ. But such differences are not mutually exclusive. To the mind of the writer or writers of Gospel and Epistle it is doubtful if they would present themselves as differences at all. The emphasis falls differently. But the final summary of the Epistle, if naturally interpreted, points to fundamental unity of conception. "We are in the true God, in His Son Jesus Christ." "This (the God revealed in Jesus Christ) is the true God and eternal life." The same is true of the conception of the death of Christ as propitiatory. Ἱλασμός occurs only in the Epistle. The idea is more prominent in the Epistle. It is not absent from the Gospel. It is to be found both in what the Evangelist puts into the mouth of others, and also in his own comments.

So, too, with the conception of the Parousia. In both we find the spiritual idea of an abiding presence, and the more popular conception of a day of judgment, a last day, a last hour. The difference is one of emphasis. In the Epistle, as well as in the Gospel, eternal life is a present possession, and also an object of promise. The many Antichrists and many false prophets of the Epistle are its peculiar form of expression, but there is room for them in the sufferings of the Disciples which are foreseen in Jn. xvi. 2–4, even if we refuse to see in the warning of the Gospel, "If another come in his own name, him ye will receive," a historical reference to Bar-Kochba. Popular conceptions may be more prominent in the Epistle, though we are not justified in ignoring the "spiritualizing" of the conception of Antichrist as fulfilled in many forms of anti-Christian teaching. But fundamental difference can be maintained only by ignoring parts of the evidence.

The differences of thought and expression make it probable that some interval of time should be placed between the composition of the two writings. In view of such differences it is difficult, if not impossible, to accept Lightfoot's view, that the Epistle was intended to serve as an Introduction to the Gospel written to accompany it.[1] The evidence does not justify the conclusion that they *could* not have been written at the same time by the same writer. It does, however, make such a view extremely improbable. On the other hand, it is not enough to compel us to assume different authors. In most cases of a similar kind, certainly in this particular instance, it is practically impossible to *prove* common authorship, as against imitation, or similarity produced by common education in the same school of thought. We are always on safer ground when we speak of the "Ephesian Canonical Writings" than when we assign them definitely to S. John, Apostle or Elder. But there are no adequate reasons for setting aside the traditional view which attributes the Epistle and Gospel to the same authorship. It remains the most probable explanation of the facts known to us.

---

[1] Unless, indeed, the Epistle was written to accompany its publication sometime after it was written.

The further conclusion that the theory of common authorship can be maintained only on the hypothesis that the Epistle
is earlier than the Gospel, is still more precarious.   It is really
based on the assumption that one who had reached the heights
of the Gospel could never have descended to the more common-
place conceptions of the Epistle.   And this ignores the fact that
whatever his own highest achievements may have been, the
author is practically limited by the intelligence and spiritual
capacity of his readers.   The more the Epistle is read and
studied, the more fixed becomes the impression that we have in
it an attempt to make plainer, for practical purposes of spiritual
and religious life, the profound teaching contained in the
Gospel, which the author had tried to convey to his fellow-
Christians in all his dealings with them, but which they had in
large measure failed to make their own.   The results of the
Gospel, or of the teaching which it contained, had not realized
his expectations.   To use one of the expressions of that Gospel,
its message οὐκ ἐχώρει among those with whom the author dwelt
and for whom he worked.   He had to descend to a lower plane.
But the question of priority must be discussed more fully, and
in a separate section.

(b) *Priority.*

The discussion of the identity of authorship has at least
established clearly the close connection which exists between
the Gospel and the Epistle.   The view of the priority of either
document can be reasonably held in conjunction with that of
imitation or of identity of authorship, though Holtzmann regards
the latter view as tenable only on the assumption that the Epistle
represents an earlier stage in the development of the writer's
theological position.   At any rate the question can be discussed
independently of that of authorship.
   The priority of the Epistle has been maintained on the following grounds :
   (1) The introductory verses (1–4), which show many points
of close connection with the Prologue of the Gospel, are said to
present an earlier stage of the Logos doctrine.   It does not go
beyond the "personification of abstract categories, ζωὴ αἰώνιος,
λόγος τῆς ζωῆς," and the concrete conception of the Personal
Logos has not yet been reached.   It is only in the Gospel that the
Monarchianism, common to the Epistle and other second century
writings, is met by a clear differentiation of the Person of the
Father and the Son.
   If our evidence were confined to the Prologue and the Introduction, this statement might be regarded as satisfactory so far

as the facts of doctrine contained in the two are concerned. But what is perhaps true of the prefatory verses cannot be so clearly established for the whole of the Epistle as compared with the whole of the Gospel. There are many passages in the Epistle where the "personal differentiation" of the Father and the Son is presented as clearly as in the Logos doctrine of the Gospel (cf. ii. 22 f., iv. 2, v. 10, etc., even if we do not quote the third verse of the Epistle), though the relation of Christ to the Father is not so prominent a subject of teaching, or speculation, in the Epistle as in the Gospel, and the author's insistence on the fact that the fellowship of Christians with God is realized in and through their union with Jesus Christ often makes it difficult to decide whether particular statements are meant to refer to Christ or to God. And even if this statement of the relations between the prologues is true, they lend themselves equally well to another explanation. It is at least as probable that in the Epistle there is a further accommodation to the Monarchian ideas which came into greater prominence as time went on. As Réville and others have shown, the doctrine of the Gospel was probably far in advance of the general Christian opinions and feeling of its date. Some accommodation to the average faith of Christendom would not have been unnatural.

And the general impression left by a comparison of the two passages is that the Preface to the Epistle presents a summary of the various points contained in the Prologue, and distributed throughout the Gospel, upon which the writer wishes to lay stress in the new circumstances that have arisen. Style and structure and vocabulary all point clearly to a close connection between the two. To those who had been taught on the lines of the Prologue to the Gospel the opening expressions of the Epistle would be intelligible and full of meaning. It is far more difficult to explain the Prologue as an expansion and development of what is contained in the Epistle.

(2) It has been thought that the ἄλλος παράκλητος of Jn. xiv. 16 was suggested by the doctrine of the Epistle, which presents Christ as the Paraclete (ii. 1). The two ideas are quite different, and neither of them excludes the other. In the Epistle, Christ's advocacy is exercised in heaven. He pleads the cause of His followers with the Father, to whose presence His "righteousness" gives Him, so to speak, the right of entry. In the Gospel, the sphere of the Spirit's advocacy is on earth, and is consequent on the withdrawal of the bodily presence of the Speaker. The "advocacy" consists in calling to the remembrance of the Disciples the real import of the Lord's words, in convicting the "World" of the mistakes they have made with regard to the Christ, and in leading the Disciples into all the truth. A com-

parison of the use of παράκλητος in the Epistle with that found in the Gospel yields no indication as to which document is the earlier.

(3) Eschatological teaching.   The writer of the Epistle, it is said, expects the Parousia in the immediate future.   The last hour has struck.   Antichrist is already at work, or at least the work of his subordinates proclaims his near approach.   The Evangelist has given up this expectation.   The "coming" has been refined into the symbolical expression of a spiritual presence.   Here again it may be quite true that the Epistle represents average Christian feeling more closely than the Gospel.   If it is so, modification of more original, and perhaps unpopular, views is quite as probable an explanation as growth out of the stage of ordinary Christian opinion.   In reality, however, the difference between the two has been greatly exaggerated.   Serious divergence can perhaps be maintained only by the convenient, but arbitrary, process of eliminating from the Gospel all the evidence which tells the other way.   The language of Jn. v. 26–29, vi. 39, 40, shows that the Evangelist had not given up the popular expectation of a "last day" and a final judgment.   There are many expressions in the farewell discourses which point in the same direction.   And even if there is any real difference, it is not improbable that the events in which the writer of the Epistle saw the signs of the approach, or the actual advent, of Antichrist may have led to a nearer approach, at a later period, to the average Christian expectation, which at the time when the Gospel was written, though never actually repudiated, was less prominent in the writer's view.   It should also be noticed that the "spiritualization" of the idea of Antichrist in the Epistle is at least as complete as the spiritualization of popular eschatology in the Gospel.   The Parousia, which the writer of the Epistle expected, perhaps more eagerly than when he wrote the Gospel, was nevertheless a spiritual fact rather than an apocalyptic display.

(4) The Epistle is said to come nearer to the Pauline teaching than the Gospel, on the subject of propitiation.   In i. 9, God's justice is put forward as the motive for the forgiveness of sins. Christ is spoken of as ἱλασμὸς περὶ τῶν ἁμαρτιῶν ἡμῶν: cf. Ro. iii. 25, ὃν προέθετο ὁ θεὸς ἱλαστήριον διὰ πίστεως ἐν τῷ αὐτοῦ αἵματι.   The Evangelist, it is said, conceives of Christ's work from a wholly different standpoint,—the glorifying of the Father by the Son in making His name known among men (Jn. xvii. 4–8).   Again it is a question of proportion rather than of fundamental difference.   The expiatory character of Christ's work is not specially prominent in the Fourth Gospel, but it is clearly recognized, both in the saying ascribed to the Baptist, Ἴδε ὁ

ἀμνὸς τοῦ θεοῦ ὁ αἴρων τὴν ἁμαρτίαν τοῦ κόσμου, and in the prophecy assigned to Caiaphas (Jn. xi. 51 f.), and the Evangelist's comment upon it, in which some have seen, perhaps rightly, a literary connection with 1 Jn. ii. 2.   Even if a real difference could be established, it would have little bearing on the question of priority.

(5) Some have found in the record of the piercing of the side (Jn. xix. 34 f.) a reminiscence of 1 Jn. v. 6, involving a misunderstanding of that passage.   In the Epistle the "water" refers to the Baptism, and has nothing to do with the death of Jesus.   It should not, it is said, have been introduced in that connection.   Most scholars will agree with Holtzmann's judgment, "nur schwer lässt sich das Missverständniss beweisen." It would certainly be difficult to prove the misunderstanding. It may be added that the connection between the two passages is probably not so close as has often been supposed.   The meaning of the "coming by water and blood" is discussed in the notes on the passage, and need not be considered at length here.   It is far more probable that the incident, real or reputed, which the Evangelist records, suggested to the writer of the Epistle the significance of water and blood in the Messianic work of the Son of God.   And this is true whatever relation we assume to exist between the Gospel and Epistle.

(6) Some have detected an improvement in the Greek style in the Gospel as compared with the Epistle.   The argument would no doubt appeal to those who have detected the difference. To the ordinary student it is certainly not obvious.   It has, of course, no force or bearing on the question of priority for those who do not accept the common authorship of the two writings. And by those who do, Holtzmann's judgment may again be quoted, "es giebt auch Rückschritte."

(7) Stress has also been laid on the fact, if it is a fact, that the Epistle was used by Papias and Polycarp at a time when certain traces of the Gospel are wanting.   It may be sufficient to answer, with Holtzmann, that the Gospel was certainly known in Justin's time, and it is not unnatural that the more popular writing which gave less offence to traditional Christian opinion should have become known first.   The argument, however, such as it is, loses most of its force if we accept, with Bishop Lightfoot on the one hand, or Dr. Schwartz on the other, the more probable view that Papias knew and used the Fourth Gospel.

A considerable portion of the evidence which has been put forward in favour of the priority of the Gospel is as little conclusive as most of what has been considered on the other side. The following points need consideration :

(1) Many passages in the Epistle seem to need the help of

the Gospel in order to become intelligible. They could only have been addressed to those who knew the Gospel, or, at least, the teaching which it contains. The following passages are cited by Holtzmann:

ii. 2. καὶ αὐτὸς ἱλασμός ἐστιν περὶ τῶν ἁμαρτιῶν ἡμῶν, οὐ περὶ τῶν ἡμετέρων δὲ ἀλλὰ καὶ περὶ ὅλου τοῦ κόσμου.

Jn. xi. 51 f. . . . ἐπροφήτευσεν ὅτι ἔμελλεν Ἰησοῦς ἀποθνήσκειν ὑπὲρ τοῦ ἔθνους, καὶ οὐχ ὑπὲρ τοῦ ἔθνους μόνον, ἀλλ᾽ ἵνα καὶ τὰ τέκνα τοῦ θεοῦ τὰ διεσκορπισμένα συναγάγῃ εἰς ἕν. It is possible to see in the words of the Epistle, especially οὐ . . . ἀλλὰ περὶ ὅλου, an echo of the language, and still more of the thought, of the Gospel. But the instance does not carry us very far.

ii. 23. πᾶς ὁ ἀρνούμενος τὸν υἱὸν οὐδὲ τὸν πατέρα ἔχει· ὁ ὁμολογῶν τὸν υἱὸν καὶ τὸν πατέρα ἔχει.

Jn. xv. 23 f. ὁ ἐμὲ μισῶν καὶ τὸν πατέρα μου μισεῖ. . . . νῦν δὲ καὶ ἑωράκασιν καὶ μεμισήκασιν καὶ ἐμὲ καὶ τὸν πατέρα μου.

There is nothing here to determine the question of priority, though the similarity of thought is obvious.

ii. 27. καὶ ὑμεῖς τὸ χρίσμα ὃ ἐλάβετε ἀπ᾽ αὐτοῦ μένει ἐν ὑμῖν, καὶ οὐ χρείαν ἔχετε ἵνα τις διδάσκῃ ὑμᾶς· ἀλλ᾽ ὡς τὸ αὐτοῦ χρίσμα διδάσκει ὑμᾶς περὶ πάντων . . .

Jn. xiv. 26. ὁ δὲ παράκλητος, τὸ πνεῦμα τὸ ἅγιον . . . ἐκεῖνος ὑμᾶς διδάξει πάντα καὶ ὑπομνήσει ὑμᾶς πάντα ἃ εἶπον ὑμῖν ἐγώ.

iii. 8. ὁ ποιῶν τὴν ἁμαρτίαν ἐκ τοῦ διαβόλου ἐστίν, ὅτι ἀπ᾽ ἀρχῆς ὁ διάβολος ἁμαρτάνει. Cf. 1 Jn. iii. 15.

Jn. viii. 44. ὑμεῖς ἐκ τοῦ πατρὸς τοῦ διαβόλου ἐστὲ καὶ τὰς ἐπιθυμίας τοῦ πατρὸς ὑμῶν θέλετε ποιεῖν. ἐκεῖνος ἀνθρωποκτόνος ἦν ἀπ᾽ ἀρχῆς, καὶ ἐν τῇ ἀληθείᾳ οὐκ ἔστηκεν.

iv. 6. ὁ γινώσκων τὸν θεὸν ἀκούει ἡμῶν, ὃς οὐκ ἔστιν ἐκ τοῦ θεοῦ οὐκ ἀκούει ἡμῶν.

Jn. viii. 47. ὁ ὢν ἐκ τοῦ θεοῦ τὰ ῥήματα τοῦ θεοῦ ἀκούει· διὰ τοῦτο ὑμεῖς οὐκ ἀκούετε, ὅτι ἐκ τοῦ θεοῦ οὐκ ἐστέ.

v. 12. ὁ ἔχων τὸν υἱὸν ἔχει τὴν ζωήν· ὁ μὴ ἔχων τὸν υἱὸν τοῦ θεοῦ τὴν ζωὴν οὐκ ἔχει.

Jn. iii. 36. ὁ πιστεύων εἰς τὸν υἱὸν ἔχει ζωὴν αἰώνιον· ὁ δὲ ἀπειθῶν τῷ υἱῷ οὐκ ὄψεται ζωήν.

v. 14. καὶ αὕτη ἐστὶν ἡ παρρησία ἣν ἔχομεν πρὸς αὐτόν, ὅτι ἐάν τι αἰτώμεθα κατὰ τὸ θέλημα αὐτοῦ ἀκούει ἡμῶν.

Jn. xiv. 13. καὶ ὅτι ἂν αἰτήσητε ἐν τῷ ὀνόματί μου, τοῦτο ποιήσω . . . ἐάν τι αἰτήσητέ με ἐν τῷ ὀνόματί μου ἐγὼ ποιήσω.

In none of these instances do we find any thought or expression in the Epistle which is obviously, and beyond all doubt, borrowed from the Gospel. But there is no mistaking the general impression which they convey. Originality and force is always in the Gospel rather than in the Epistle, where the thoughts are, as a rule, derived and generalized. The writer would seem to be choosing from a larger store what he can most usefully apply to the circumstances with which he is dealing. He has but little, if anything, to add to what his readers have already been taught. Assume that they have been taught the content of the Gospel, and his language is nearly always seen to be intelligible and pertinent.

It must, of course, be remembered that, even if this is true, it does not amount to proof of the priority of the Gospel in actual composition. The author had, in all probability, taught its contents for some time before he committed them to writing. It may well have been that in the course of teaching they gradually took shape. Even if we need the Gospel to explain the Epistle, the readers of it may have had their necessary commentary in the author's oral teaching.

Attention has been called to the proportion of the closest parallels between Gospel and Epistle which are found in chs. xiii.–xvii. of the Gospel. The proportion is certainly large, if the length of these chapters be compared with that of the whole Gospel. The situation depicted in the last discourses, where the Christ gives His last instructions to the Disciples whom He is about to leave, naturally offers more points of contact with that of the Pastor committing, perhaps, his last words to writing for the sake of his "children," than the earlier chapters of the Gospel which show the Christ disputing with the Jews. The aim of the Epistle is far more to encourage and to build up than to warn and destroy, though the critical examination of its contents tends to bring the passages devoted to controversy into greater prominence than those which deal with edification. But the point has really no bearing on the question of priority.

The supposed direct references to the Gospel which are to be found in the Epistle must be considered next. It has been maintained that the ἀπαγγελία announced in the Epistle (i. 3, 5), that God is light and there is no darkness in Him at all, is not really carried out in the Epistle itself; and that the reference must therefore be to the Gospel. This is doubtful, especially in view of the identification of Christ with the "Light" in the Gospel as compared with the announcement of the Epistle that God is light. There is much about light and darkness in both, as Dionysius of Alexandria saw: but it can hardly be said that the announcement "God is light" is the message of the Gospel as a whole more than of the Epistle. And the idea which the phrase is introduced to emphasize, that fellowship with God is possible only for those who, so far as in them lies, strive to make themselves like Him, is one of the leading thoughts of the Epistle. It is true that the Epistle does not deal with the whole message about life, as detailed in the first verse, "that which was from the beginning, that which we have heard and seen," etc., and

that in a sense the Gospel might be said to include it all.[1]   But
there is no necessary reference to the Gospel.   The whole of the
witness which their Christian teachers had borne to them, and
the whole of the teaching which they had received from them,
and especially from the writer of the Epistle, is a more natural
explanation.

The other direct reference, as has been supposed, is found in
ii. 14 (ἔγραψα ὑμῖν, παιδία κ.τ.λ.), where the triple ἔγραψα has
been thought to refer to the Gospel.   The change from present
to aorist is difficult to explain.   Perhaps no thoroughly satisfactory explanation can be offered.   At first sight the reference
to the Gospel is tempting.   But the reference must have been
made more explicit if it was to be intelligible, unless, indeed, the
Epistle was written to accompany the Gospel, in which case the
difference between γράφω and ἔγραψα has less point.   And the
reasons given for writing are not specially applicable to the Gospel,
either in themselves or as distinguished from the almost identical
reasons given for the three statements introduced by γράφω.

The theory that the Epistle was written as a *Begleitungs-*
schrift, when the Gospel was published, deserves consideration.
The case has been best stated by Ebrard, who tries to show that
the false teaching of Cerinthus is really combated in the
Gospel—written to prove the identity of Jesus with "the
Christ, the Son of God" and God's agent in Creation, as
contrasted with "an inferior power," ignorant of the Supreme
God—as well as in the Epistle.   The theory was held by Bishop
Lightfoot, who refers to it three times in his lectures on S. John,
but apparently never gave his reasons in full.   It must stand or
fall with the identity of aim and content of the two writings.   The
differences in vocabulary, style, and thought, which have been
discussed in the previous section, lead to no definite conclusion.
They merely make it difficult to suppose that the two writings
are of exactly the same date.

The connection between the introductory verses and the
Prologue of the Gospel has already been mentioned.   If the
whole is most easily explained as presupposing the Prologue, a
closer examination of ver. 2 almost compels us to take this view.

καὶ ἡ ζωὴ ἐφανερώθη (taking up the λόγος τῆς ζωῆς)	ἐν αὐτῷ ζωὴ ἦν, καὶ ἡ ζωὴ ἦν τὸ φῶς τῶν ἀνθρώπων.
καὶ ἑωράκαμεν	καὶ ὁ λόγος σὰρξ ἐγένετο καὶ ἐθεασάμεθα τὴν δόξαν αὐτοῦ.
καὶ μαρτυροῦμεν.	ἀλλ' ἵνα μαρτυρήσῃ, Cf. καὶ ὑμεῖς μαρτυρεῖτε, ὅτι ἀπ' ἀρχῆς μετ' ἐμοῦ ἐστε (xv. 27)

---

[1] Perhaps the phrase καὶ ταῦτα γράφομεν of ver. 4 implies that vv. 1–3
contain something more than a summary of the contemplated letter.

καὶ ἀπαγγέλλομεν ὑμῖν τὴν ζωὴν τὴν
αἰώνιον (. . . ἵνα καὶ ὑμεῖς κοινωνίαν ἔχητε κ.τ.λ.)
ἥτις ἦν πρὸς τὸν πατέρα
καὶ ἐφανερώθη ἡμῖν.

Cf. ταῦτα δε γέγραπται . . . ἵνα
πιστεύητε . . . καὶ ἵνα πιστεύοντες
ζωὴν ἔχητε ἐν τῷ ὀνόματι αὐτοῦ.
οὗτος ἦν ἐν ἀρχῇ πρὸς τὸν θεόν.
καὶ ἐσκήνωσεν ἐν ἡμῖν καὶ ἐθεασάμεθα.

There can be no doubt on which side the originality lies. The Epistle presents a summary, not a first sketch.

The exact interpretation of the ἐντολὴ καινὴ καὶ παλαιά of ii. 7, 8 is doubtful. But in the language used in these verses there is an almost certain reference to the "new commandment" of Jn. xiii. 34. Cf. especially ὅ ἐστιν ἀληθὲς ἐν αὐτῷ καὶ ἐν ὑμῖν. The Lord had made a new commandment of the old legal precept, "Thou shalt love thy neighbour as thyself." It becomes new again in each Christian who fulfils it by obedience.

The expressions used in ii. 10 f., of love and light, hatred and darkness, appear to be a summary of the teaching contained in different passages of the Gospel (cf. xi. 9, 10, xii. 35 ff.).

The "promise which He promised, even eternal life" (ii. 25), is most naturally explained by reference to Jn. x. 28 (κἀγὼ δίδωμι αὐτοῖς ζωὴν αἰώνιον, καὶ οὐ μὴ ἀπολῶνται εἰς τὸν αἰῶνα). Should we also compare xiv. 19, ὅτι ἐγὼ ζῶ καὶ ὑμεῖς ζήσετε?

The section iii. 8–15, with its distinction of those who are born of God and those who are "of the Devil," who sinneth from the beginning, and its denunciation of the murderous character of hatred, recalls the passage of the Gospel (viii. 40–44) where the Jews are proved to be "of the Devil" by the murderous hate with which they pursue the Lord, so closely that we are compelled to see dependence on its substance if not on its text. Again it is the Gospel that is "original," though we may hesitate to follow Wellhausen in making use of the Epistle to rewrite the Gospel in its original form as presupposed by the Epistle (ὑμεῖς ἐκ τοῦ πατρὸς τοῦ Καίν ἐστε) in order to get a simpler explanation of ὁ πατὴρ αὐτοῦ in ver. 44. In the Epistle we find again the generalization of thoughts first struck out in the heat of controversy.

The "coming by water and blood" is not to be explained as a direct reference to the incident recorded in Jn. xix. 35. But it is almost certain that the record of that incident suggested to the writer of the Epistle the significance of "blood" and of "water" in the Messianic work of the Redeemer.

These instances could easily be multiplied, but they are representative. None of them amount to proof positive of the writer's actual dependence on the text of the Gospel. But their evidence, such as it is, all points in the same direction. The

Epistle presupposes in its readers acquaintance with "a compact body of teaching like that which we find in the Fourth Gospel," to use Dr. Sanday's phrase.[1] And the general impression gained from studying the two writings is convincing. The impression left—the more clearly the longer the Epistle is studied—is that it was written to help and to warn those for whom the teaching of the Gospel, or "a body of teaching like" it, had not accomplished all that the writer had hoped. Throughout it is an appeal to the readers to use that which they already possess. It never should have been necessary, the writer seems to say, for him to write the Epistle. They needed no further instruction, if they would but make use of what had been theirs ἀπ' ἀρχῆς. Their own experience should be able to do the rest. He writes to them not because they do not know, but because they know. They have received sufficient instruction and full illumination. They "all know." But knowledge has not been adequately translated into corresponding action and conduct. It has not been realized in life. And so there is doubt and hesitation in the face of new difficulties and changed circumstances. The whole aim of the Epistle is to recall to mind and to supplement what has long ago been fully given, but not adequately grasped. It is not the earnest of things to come. It owes its existence to the failure to make the most of the abundance that has been given. It is the aftermath, not the first-fruits, of the writer's message to the Church.

These considerations, if they accurately represent the facts, determine with certainty the question of priority, so far as the substantial content of the two documents is concerned. They do not perhaps preclude the possibility of a later date for the actual composition, or publication, of the Gospel. But in view of them such hypotheses are extremely unlikely

§ 2. The Aim.

The more definitely polemical aim of the Epistles is discussed in another section, where the passages which contain clear references to the tenets of the opponents are fully considered, as well as the extent to which the writer has them in view in other passages not so directly controversial in tone, and indeed throughout the Epistle. It is probably true that the writer never loses sight altogether of the views of his opponents in any part of the Epistle. But it is important to emphasize the fact that, in spite of this, the real aim of the Epistle is not exclusively, or even primarily, polemical. The

---

[1] *Recent Criticism of the Fourth Gospel*, p. 245.

edification of his "children" in the true faith and life of Christians is the writer's chief purpose. The errors of the opponents do not constitute the only danger. The victory has been won, if only after a hard-fought battle, and the opponents, whose errors have been unmasked, "have gone out from among us," or at least the leaders of the movement have withdrawn or been expelled. But there is still strong sympathy with their views, and perhaps acute danger of their return in power. The real danger is the attitude of the "children" themselves towards the Christian faith and life. The enthusiasm of the early days of the Faith is no longer theirs. Many of them had been brought up as Christians, and did not owe their faith to strong personal conviction or experience. Their Christianity had become largely traditional, half-hearted and nominal. They found the moral obligations of their religion oppressive. The "world" had great attractions for them. They wished to be on better terms with it than their Faith allowed. They were only too ready to welcome elements of religious and philosophical speculation foreign to the Faith and really destructive of it. They could not tolerate a sharp distinction between Christian and Unchristian in belief and practice. And therefore they were easily deceived by specious novelties. They had lost their instinctive feeling for what was of the essence of the Faith which they had received, or lay on the line of true development, and what was antagonistic to it. And another consequence of this "loss of their first love" was doubt and uncertainty as to their position as Christians. This is clearly seen if the verses introduced by ἐν τούτῳ γινώσκομεν or similar phrases are studied. Nine times at least the writer offers his readers tests by which they may assure themselves about the truth of their Christian position (ii. 3, ἐν τούτῳ γινώσκομεν ὅτι ἐγνώκαμεν αὐτόν: 5, ἐν τούτῳ γινώσκομεν ὅτι ἐν αὐτῷ ἐσμεν: iii. 16, ἐν τούτῳ ἐγνώκαμεν τὴν ἀγάπην: 19, ἐν τούτῳ γνωσόμεθα ὅτι ἐκ τῆς ἀληθείας ἐσμέν: 24, ἐν τούτῳ γινώσκομεν ὅτι μένει ἐν ἡμῖν: iv. 2, ἐν τούτῳ γινώσκετε τὸ πνεῦμα τοῦ θεοῦ: 6, ἐκ τούτου γινώσκομεν τὸ πνεῦμα τῆς ἀληθείας: 13, ἐν τούτῳ γινώσκομεν ὅτι ἐν αὐτῷ μένομεν: v. 2, ἐν τούτῳ γινώσκομεν ὅτι ἀγαπῶμεν τὰ τέκνα τοῦ θεοῦ). The writer's aim in this ninefold "hereby we know" cannot be only to set forth the true knowledge in opposition to the false "Gnosis" of his Gnostic opponents. Clearly his readers had felt the doubts which had grown in force in proportion as the enthusiasm of earlier days had waxed cold.

This view of the circumstances and condition of the Church or Churches addressed has been maintained by several writers, among whom Lücke and Rothe may be especially mentioned. It is presupposed in the words in which the author expresses the aim of his writing, before summing up the chief points of his message, ταῦτα ἔγραψα ὑμῖν ἵνα εἰδῆτε ὅτι ζωὴν ἔχετε αἰώνιον, τοῖς πιστεύουσιν εἰς τὸ ὄνομα τοῦ υἱοῦ τοῦ θεοῦ. Cf. also i. 4, ii. 1. Rothe's words are worth quoting : " Der Apostel denkt sich also seine Leser als solche, in denen die ursprüngliche Klarheit des eigenthümlichen christlichen Bewusstseins verdunkelt, sein sciherer, scharf alles Unchristliche unterscheidender Tact abgestumpft, in denen die Frische des eigenthümlichen geist-lichen Lebens ermattet, die Lauterkeit desselben verunreinigt ist."[1] Huther's rejection of this view on the ground of such passages as ii. 13, 14, 20, 21, 27, iii. 5, 14, iv. 4, 16, v. 18–20, meets with Holtzmann's approval. The picture which they present of the readers' state is too favourable to admit of such dark shortcomings. In reality it is just these passages which prove the point. The writer appeals to their privileged position and past victories. They are of those whose sins have been forgiven, who have known the Eternal, who have won the victory, in whom the Word of God abides. On these grounds he can appeal to them. But if they had been true to their privileges and their knowledge, it would not have been necessary to make the appeal. Those of whom ii. 13, 14 were true ought not to have needed the warning of ver. 15, Μὴ ἀγαπᾶτε τὸν κόσμον μηδὲ τὰ ἐν τῷ κόσμῳ. They have the unction of the Spirit, knowledge is the possession of them all. He wrote to them not because of their ignorance, but their knowledge of the truth. He would recall to new life what is in danger of dying away. They do not need teaching, if only they will use the powers which they possess (20, 21, 27). He would not write thus, unless they had in some measure failed to do their part. The extent of the failure must be measured by the gravity of the danger. They are of God, and have won a notable victory over the opponents (iv. 4). But they have to be reminded of the facts to urge them to the needed effort. The summary in v. 18–20 of what they know, and ought to use, has to be com-pleted by the warning of ver. 21, φυλάξατε ἑαυτὰ ἀπὸ τῶν εἰδώλων.

Holtzmann has done good service towards the interpretation of the Epistle by showing how clearly Gnostic ideas are reflected throughout the Epistle. The writer always makes it his aim to set forth the true "knowledge" of Apostolic Christianity in its opposition to the false gnosis for which such great claims were made. And it is of primary importance to realize the undoubted polemical aim of much of its contents, and the modifications in his statement of what he believes to be positive truth, which are due to the fact that he never loses sight, in anything that he

[1] Rothe, *Der erste Brief Johannis*, p. 4.

says, of the false teaching and unchristian conduct of his opponents. But it is at least as important to remember that his primary objects are to exhort and to edify. He is a pastor first, an orthodox theologian only afterwards. He cannot separate doctrine from ethics. But it is the life which he cares about. For him the Christian Faith is a life of fellowship "with the Father and with His Son Jesus Christ." His first object in writing is to help his fellow-Christians to lead this life of fellowship, that his joy and theirs may be fulfilled. And no interpretation of the Epistle is likely to elucidate his meaning satisfactorily if it fails to realize where the writer's interest really lies. The nature and character of the false teaching denounced in the Epistle is a fascinating problem. But even a satisfactory solution of it would fail to provide an adequate explanation of the Epistle. Those methods of exegesis are unscientific which lay too exclusive stress on the doctrine which it teaches or the heresy which it seeks to refute. They tend to obscure rather than to elucidate the author's meaning. The polemical and controversial aims of the Epistle are considered at length elsewhere. Here it is only necessary to insist on the importance, for the right understanding of the Epistle, of fully recognizing the writer's other aims.

§ 3. DESTINATION.

The general character of the Epistles, even of the First, show that they are almost certainly addressed to a definite Church, or group of Churches, the circumstances and difficulties of which were well known to the writer, or writers, of the Letters. The author of the First Epistle writes to Christians whom he knows, with whose needs he is fully acquainted, whom he has the right to help, and who acknowledge his right. The τεκνία are *not* the whole body of Christians dispersed throughout the world. But we have nothing to help us in determining the destination of the Epistles beyond the universal tradition which connects them with Ephesus, or at least Asia Minor, the earliest traces of their appearance, and the undoubted connection of some of the Johannine literature with the Roman province of Asia.

In the "antiqua translatio" of Cassiodorus (*Instit. Div. lit.* 14) all three Epistles apparently bore the title "ad Parthos," and in his *Complexiones* (ll. 1370) the First Epistle is so designated.[1] This attribution was not uncommon in the West. It is first found in Augustine, in the title of his ten *Tractatus* ("in

[1] Cf. Zahn, *Forschungen*, iii. 92, etc., from whom most of the information in this paragraph is taken.

epistolam Ioannis ad Parthos") and also in his *Quaest. Ev.* ii.
39. 1.[1] Vigilius (? Idacius Clarus) in the *Contra Varimadum*
introduces the gloss of the heavenly witnesses with the words
"Item ipse ad Parthos." The title found in a Genevan MS
(Sabatier), "incipit epistola ad Sparthos," suggests a Greek
origin for the title (πρὸς πάρθους, the ς of the preposition having
been dittographed), or at least a Greek archetype for the title
as it occurs in that MS. According to Bede the title was found
in "many ecclesiastical writers," including Athanasius. The
title Ἰωάννου ἐπιστολὴ β΄ πρὸς πάρθους is found in the Greek
minuscule, Oxford, Bodleian. Misc. 74 (Scr. 30, von Soden
α 111),[2] and in the Florentine MS, Laur. iv. 32 (Scr. 89), both
of the eleventh century. It appears also as colophon in a
Paris MS of the fourteenth century (Reg. Gr. 60, olim Colb. ;
Scr. 62).

The title would therefore appear to have originated in the
East, from whence it may well have reached the West as early
as the time of Athanasius. Various explanations of the title
have been suggested. (1) It has been supposed to be a
corruption of πρὸς παρθένους (cf. "Clement" quae ad uirgines
scripta). Its reference to the First Epistle has been explained
as the result of mistaking the title of the Second for the
colophon of the First. (2) Zahn suggests that the real explanation is to be found in the next phrase of Clement's *Adumbrationes*, "Scripta uero est ad quandam Babyloniam, electam
nomine." Clement takes the "Babylonian" lady for a real
person, whose children are mentioned later in the Epistle. He
cannot, therefore, have written πρὸς παρθένους, which must be a
corruption of πρὸς πάρθους, which his translator read as παρθένους
and translated accordingly. If a title corresponding to πρὸς
Γαλάτας, Ἑβραίους, and the like was to be found for the Babylonian lady and her children, πρὸς πάρθους would be the natural
title to use in the time of Clement. There is no tradition of
relations between S. John and Babylon or Parthians. The
title must have been suggested by the name of the recipient, and
not *vice versa*. Zahn further suggests that Clement must have
identified the ἐκλεκτῇ κυρίᾳ of the Second Epistle with the ἡ ἐν
Βαβυλῶνι συνεκλεκτή of 1 P v. 13. The difficulty raised by the
passage in Eus. *H. E.* ii. 15, which apparently makes Clement
interpret that phrase allegorically of Rome, Zahn meets by
pointing out the uncertainty of how much of the Eusebian
passage can be rightly referred to Clement. (Cf. ἦν καὶ συντάξαι
φασὶν ἐπ᾽ αὐτῆς Ῥώμης.)

---

[1] "Secundum sententiam hanc etiam illud est quod dictum est a Ioanne
in epistola ad Parthos."
[2] Cf. Mill, p. clx.

Zahn's explanation of the origin of the title is certainly the most ingenious which has been suggested. It offers an adequate explanation of the opening sentences in the Latin summary of Clement's comments on the Second Epistle. If the explanation of the title of the First Epistle, or of all three, is to be sought in this passage of Clement, Zahn's hypothesis offers the most probable solution of the question. But our knowledge is too scanty to enable us to attain to certainty in the matter.

(3) Lücke has accepted the suggestion which, according to him, was first made by Gieseler, that πάρθους has arisen out of a misunderstanding of the title πάρθενος which was given to S. John (cf. *Pistis Sophia*, ed. Petermann, p. 45, εὖγε Johannes παρθένος, qui ἄρξεις in regno lucis, quoted by Zahn, *Acta Johannis*, p. ci, who traces back the probable origin of the tradition of John's "virginity" to the Leucian Acts).

But whatever may be said for these ingenious conjectures, there is no reason to suppose that the title which we find in Augustine, and which may have been used by Clement of Alexandria, rests on any trustworthy tradition about the destination of the Epistles. We have nothing but internal evidence to guide us in determining the question. Nothing in the Epistles themselves affords any clear guidance in the matter; but the evidence, such as it is, gives us no reason to distrust the tradition which connects them with Asia Minor, and especially Ephesus. The Apocalypse is clearly connected with Ephesus, and we are certainly justified in attributing all the Johannine Books to the same school, though not to the same author. The question cannot really be discussed apart from the Gospel. The district of Asia Minor meets all the known requirements of the case, and the literary history of the Epistles, as well as of the Gospel, shows that it is in this region that we first meet with traces of their existence. It is natural, therefore, to suppose that the origin and destination of the Epistles are to be found in this region.

§ 4. ANALYSIS.

While some agreement is found with regard to the possible division of the First Epistle into paragraphs, no analysis of the Epistle has been generally accepted. The aphoristic character of the writer's meditations is the real cause of this diversity of arrangement, and perhaps the attempt to analyse the Epistle should be abandoned as useless.

According to Von Soden (*Die Schriften des NT.* i. 1, p. 459), the commonest system of κεφάλαια and ὑποδιαιρέσεις is as follows:

Κεφαλαια Ιωαννου επιστολης πρωτης

α.   (i. 1) επαγγελικη θεολογια περι Χριστου, **εν ω.**
           (i. 6) περι εξομολογησεως και προσοχης
                εις το μη αμαρτανειν.
           (ii. 3) οτι η τηρησις εντολων θεου την
                γνωσιν βεβαιοι.

β,   (ii. 7) περι αγαπης ης ανευ ασεβεια, εν ω.
           (ii. 12) παραινεσις περι χαριτος εκαστου καθ
                ηλικιαν και περι αποτροπης της
                προς τον κοσμον αγαπης.

γ.   (ii. 18) περι ψευδαφελφων αρνησιθεων και οτι η εις
                Χριστον ευσεβεια πατρος ομολογια, η γαρ του
                πατρος δοξολογια του υιου εστι θεολογια, εν ω.
           (ii. 26) περι θειου και πνευματικου χαρισματος εν
                αγιασμω επ ελπιδι εις γνωσιν θεου.
           (iii. 2) οτι πας ο εν Χριστω εκτος αμαρτιας.
                ο γαρ αμαρτανων εστιν εκ του διαβολου.

δ. (iii. 9 or 10b) περι αγαπης της εις τον πλησιον και διαθεσεως
                μεταδοτικης, εν ω.
           (iii. 19) περι συνειδησεως αγαθης της **εν** πιστει
                Ιησου Χριστου.
           (iv. 1) περι διακρισεως πνευματων εφ ομολογια
                της του Χριστου ενανθρωπησεως.

ε.   (iv. 7) περι φιλαδελφιας εις θεοσεβειαν.

5. (iv. 15 or v. 1) περι θεολογιας υιου εν δοξη πατρος **και περι**
                νικης της κατα του πονηρου δια πιστεως
                Ιησου Χριστου εις ζωην.

ζ.   (v. 16) περι αντιληψεως του αμαρτανοντος αδελφου δια
                προσευχης και περι του μη αμαρτανειν, εν ω.
           (v. 18) περι αποχης δαιμονικου σεβασματος.

Κεφαλαια Ιωαννου επιστολης δευτερας.

α.   (i. 4) μετα το προοιμιον περι ορθου βιου **εν** αγαπη
                θεου δια πιστεως ευσεβους αμεταθετου, εν ω.
           (i. 10) οτι ου δει αιρετικον εισοικιζειν η χαιρετι-
                ζειν εφ αμαρτια

β.   (i. 12) επαγγελια παρουσιας αυτου επ ελπιδι προς
                ωφελειαν.

Κεφαλαια Ιωαννου επιστολης τριτης.

α.   (i. 2) ευχη υπερ τελειωσεως και ευχαριστιας **εφ**
                ομολογια φιλοξενιας των αδελφων δια Χριστον,
                εν ω.
           (i. 9) περι της **Διοτρεφους** φαυλοτητος **και**
                μισαδελφιας.

β.   (i. 12) περι Δημητριου, ω μαρτυρει τα καλλιστα.

γ.   (i. 13) περι αφιξεως αυτου προς αυτους επ ωφελεια εν
             ταχει.

By far the most successful attempt to analyse the Epistle in
such a manner as to show that there is a real underlying sequence
of thought which can be represented, at least to some extent, in the
form of analysis, is that of Theodor Häring (" *Gedankengang und
Grundgedanke des ersten Johannesbriefs*," Theol. Abhandlungen,
Carl von Weizsäcker gewidmet, Freiburg i. B., 1892, Mohr). He
finds in the Epistle a triple presentation of two leading ideas,
which may be called an Ethical and a Christological Thesis.
(1) The ethical thesis is developed in the sections i. 5–ii. 17,
ii. 28 (?)–iii. 24, iv. 7–21, "without walking in light," more
specially defined as "love of the brethren, there can be no
fellowship with God." (2) The Christological thesis is found in
the sections ii. 18–27, iv. 1–6, v. 1 (or 5)–12, "beware of those
who deny that Jesus is the Christ." In the first part (i. 5–ii. 27)
these ideas are presented, the one after the other, without any
indication of their connection with each other. In the second
(ii. 28 (?)–iv. 6), they are again presented in the same order, but
vv. 23, 24 of ch. iii., which form the transition from the one to
the other, are so worded as to bring out clearly the intimate
connection which, in the author's mind, exists between the
two. In the third (iv. 7–v. 12), they are so intertwined that it is
difficult, if not impossible, to separate them.

As Häring's analysis has generally been followed in the notes
of this edition, it may be convenient to give it here, at least in
substance.[1]

i. 1–4. Introduction.

A. i. 5–ii. 27. First presentation of the two tests of fellow
ship with God (ethical and Christological theses) expressed
negatively. First exposure of the two "lies." No reference to
the mutual relations of the two theses.

I. i. 5–ii. 17. Walking in light the true sign of fellowship
with God (ethical thesis). Refutation of the first "lie."

    1. i. 5–ii. 6. The thesis itself put forward in two parallel
       statements.

        a. i. 5–10 (vv. 8–10 being subordinate to the main
           thought, to guard against possible misunder-
           standing).

        b. ii. 1–6. (1*b* and 2 being similarly subordinate). The
           chief differences between *a* and *b* consist in the
           terms used, Fellowship with God, Knowledge of
           God, Being in God; and Walking in Light,

---

[1] In one part an attempt at a different analysis has been substituted
(iii. 11–24) where I find myself unable to follow that of Häring.

Keeping the Commandments, Not-sinning, Keeping the Word.

2. ii. 7–17. The thesis, and the warning which it suggests, put forward on the grounds of the reader's circumstances and experience. The old command is ever new, because the full revelation of God is working in them. Further definition of walking in light and keeping the command as love of the brethren, as opposed to love of the world.

Subsections :

> *a.* ii. 7–11. General explanation. Love of the brethren.
>
> *b.* ii. 12–17. Individual application. Warning against love of the world.

II. ii. 18–27. Faith in Jesus as Christ the test of fellowship with God (Christological thesis). Refutation of the second " lie."

> 1. ii. 18. Appearance of Antichrists a sign of the last hour.
> 2. ii. 19–21. Their relation to the community.
> 3. ii. 22–25. Content and significance of their false teaching.
> 4. ii. 26–27. Repeated assurance that the readers are in possession of the truth.

B. ii. 28–iv. 6. Second presentation of the two theses, separately, but with special emphasis (cf. iii. 22–24) on their connection.

I. ii. 28–iii. 24. Doing of Righteousness (which in essence is identical with love of the brethren) the sign by which we may know that we are born of God. Warning suggested by this truth.

> 1. ii. 28–iii. 6. The thesis and the warning that we must recognize its truth, considered in connection with the duty of self-purification which is laid upon us by the gift of sonship and the hope of its consummation. Earnest warning (1) that there are more " Anomians " than is supposed, (2) that knowledge of God and sin are incompatible.

Subsections :

> *a.* ii. 28–iii. 3.
>
> *b.* iii. 4–6.

> 2. iii. 7–18. Explanation of the thesis, with earnest warning against deceivers.
>
> > *a.* iii. 7–10. Negatively. He who sins is of the Devil.
> >
> > *b.* iii. 10–17. By more particular definition of sin as failure to love the brethren, and of love as the opposite of this.
> >
> > > iii. 11, 12. [The nature and motives of love and hate.
> > >
> > > iii. 13–16. The attitude of the world. Love and life.

d

Hatred and death. The example of Christ, the revelation of love.

iii. 17, 18. The lesser proof of love and its absence.

3. iii. 19–22. This is the test by which we may know if we are of the truth, and so still the accusations of our heart. Confidence in God and the hearing of prayer.

iii. 23, 24. Transition to the second thesis. The command summed up in the two duties of belief and love. Obedience issues in fellowship. The test by which the reality of the fellowship may be proved. The gift of the Spirit.]

II. iv. 1–6. The Christological thesis. The Spirit which is of God confesses Jesus Christ come in flesh.

1. iv. 1–3. Content of the confession.

2. iv. 4–6. Attitude of the Church and the world.

C. iv. 7–v. 12. Third presentation of the theses. Both are shown to be connected. The reasons why they cannot be separated are given. Love the proof of fellowship with God, because God is Love. This love of God shown in the sending of His Son, as faith conceives it. Intentional intermingling of the two leading thoughts in two sections.

I. First explanation of the two ideas as now combined. Love based on faith in the revelation of love the proof of knowing God and being born of God.

1. iv. 7–12. Love based on the revelation of love.

    a. 7–10.

    b. 11, 12.

2. iv. 13–16. Faith in this revelation of love in Jesus through the Spirit.

3. iv. 17–21. This love based on faith in its relation to Judgment (17–18), recapitulation (19–21).

II. Second explanation of the connected thoughts. Faith as the base of love.

1. v. 1*a.* Faith the proof of being born of God.

2. v. 1*b*–4. As the ground of love of the brethren, love of God the sign of love of the brethren.

3. v. 5–12. Faith, in its assurance, the witness that Jesus is the Christ.

    v. 13–21. Conclusion.

The divisions adopted by Mr. R. Law in his study of the First Epistle (*The Tests of Life*: Edinburgh, T. & T. Clark, 1909) have many points of agreement with Häring's scheme. He finds in the Epistle a threefold application of three tests by which the readers may satisfy themselves of their being "begotten of God."

First Cycle, i. 5–ii. 28. The Christian life as fellowship with God, conditioned and tested by walking in the light.

Walking in the light tested by—

    a. Righteousness, i. 6–ii. 6.

    b. Love, ii. 7–17.

    c. Belief, ii. 18–28.

Second Cycle, ii. 29–iv. 6. The Christian life as that of Divine Sonship, approved by the same tests.

Divine Sonship tested by—

    a. Righteousness, ii. 29–iii. 10*a.*

    b. Love, iii. 10*b*–24*a.*

    c. Belief, iii. 24*b*–iv. 6.

Third Cycle, iv. 7–v. 21. Closer correlation of Righteousness, Love, and Belief.

    Section I. iv. 7–v. 3*a.* Love.

        a. The genesis of love, iv. 7–12.

        b. The synthesis of belief and love, iv. 13–16.

        c. The effect, motives, and manifestations of love, iv. 17–v. 3*a.*

    Section II. v. 3*b*–21. Belief.

        a. The power, content, basis, and issue of Christian belief, v. 3*a*–12.

        b. The certainties of Christian belief, v. 13–21.

The substantial agreement of this analysis with that of Häring is remarkable, as Mr. Law explains in an appended note that Häring's article was unknown to him at the time when he wrote the chapter which contains his analysis. It fails, however, to separate off the "Epilogue," and is hardly so helpful as Häring's scheme in tracing the (probable) sequence of thought. In parts it becomes rather an enumeration of subjects than an analysis. It also obscures the writer's insistence that the showing of love, in the sphere where circumstances made it possible, *i.e.* to the brethren, is the first and most obvious expression of the righteousness which is obedience to God's command, and which belief in Jesus as the Christ inspires.

An interesting correspondence between Dr. Westcott and Dr. Hort about the Divisions of the First Epistle has been published by the Rev. A. Westcott in the *Expositor* (iii. 481 ff., 1907). It contains several schemes, of which the most interesting is Dr. Hort's Second Scheme of Divisions (p. 486) and his remarks upon it (p. 485 f.). The scheme is as follows:

    i. 1–4. Introduction.

    i. 5–ii. 17. God and the true light: goodness, not indifference.

    ii. 18–iii. 24. Sonship to God, and hence likeness to His Son, and of *abiding* in Him.

iv. 1–v. 17. Faith resting on knowledge of the truth the
mark of the Divine Spirit, not indifference.

v. 18–21. Conclusion. The Christian knowledge: the
true and the false.

One paragraph of his appended remarks is so suggestive that
it must be quoted in full. "The base of all, the first and the
last, is the Christian knowledge, 'That which we have seen and
heard' (οἴδαμεν). This is the necessary condition of Faith (III.),
which is the necessary condition of Love (II.), which is the
necessary condition of obedience (I.). After the Prologue we
begin with this last simplest region, and feel our way downwards,
naturally taking with us the results already obtained. Obedience
is associated with light and the Father; Love, with abiding and
the Anointed Son; Faith, with truth and the Spirit." It would
be difficult to find in the whole literature of the Johannine
Epistles a more helpful clue in tracing the underlying connections
of the "aphoristic meditations" contained in this Epistle.
Mr. Law does not say whether this correspondence was known
to him when he framed his scheme. If not, his underlying
agreement with the suggestions of this paragraph, though not
with the actual scheme proposed, is highly significant. But
his threefold presentation of a twofold idea brings out more
clearly the writer's meaning and purpose. Belief and practice,
faith and works, and the connection between the two, is his real
subject. The showing of love is the most obvious example of
the doing of righteousness (= obedience).

It is interesting also to notice that Dr. Westcott was anxious
to transfer the passage iv. 1–6 from the third to the second
section (cf. Häring), to which Dr. Hort replied, " As far as I can
see, the symmetry of the Epistle cannot be restored if iv. 1–6
is thrown back." This is probably true if (p. 485) "the three
great divisions themselves have a ternary structure." Dr.
Westcott also pleads for the "retention of the Epilogue (v. 13–
21) instead of the connection of 13–17 with what precedes.
On both these points the arrangement preferred by Dr. Westcott
and Dr. Häring seems the better.

§ 5. THE FALSE TEACHERS.

The exact nature of the false teaching which is denounced in
these Epistles has been much disputed, and is still a matter of
controversy. The opponents have been held to be Jews, or
Judaizing Christians, or Gnostics, Judaizing or heathen, or some
particular sect of Gnostics, Basilides, Saturninus, Valentinus or
Cerinthus. Some have supposed the chief error denounced to
be Docetism, others Antinomianism. A majority of interpreters

still perhaps regard Cerinthianism, or teaching similar in character and tendency, as the main object of the writer's denunciation. This view has, however, been seriously challenged in late years by several writers, among whom Wurm and Clemen deserve special consideration. Though they differ in their solution of the problem, they both maintain that the common view is untenable, especially in the light of 1 Jn. ii. 23, which they regard as limiting the doctrinal differences between the writer and his opponents to questions of Christology; and as demonstrating that with regard to the doctrine of the Father, their views must have been identical, or at least divided by no serious difference of opinion. This would, of course, exclude Cerinthianism, as defined by Irenaeus, *Adv. Haer.* I. xxvi. 1, where the Creator of the world is described as *uirtus quaedam ualde separata et distans ab ea principalitate quae est super universa et ignorans eum qui est super omnia Deum.* Wurm finds in this verse convincing support for his view of the purely Jewish character of the opponent's teaching. Clemen draws from it and the preceding verse the conclusion that the writer sees the most serious error of his opponents in their denial that the historical Jesus is the Christ in the Johannine sense of that term, *i.e.* the pre-existent Son of God, who alone can reveal the Father to men. But they both agree that the position of Cerinthus is excluded. They certainly have done good service in drawing attention to the importance of the bearing of 1 Jn. ii. 23 on the subject, even if further consideration may suggest that the conclusion which they have drawn is not inevitable.

One or Many?

Before examining in greater detail the character of the views held by the false teachers, it may be well to consider whether the writer has in view the opinions of one party only in all the sections in which he denounces false teaching, or whether he is combating different enemies in different passages. The unity of the false teaching is assumed by Wurm and by Clemen, and is accepted by perhaps the majority of writers on the subject. In one sense this is probably true. The writer does not attack the Christological opinions of two or more definite parties in chs. ii., iv., and v. respectively, nor does he denounce the Christology of one party and the ethical shortcomings of another. The views which the writer's statements justify us in attributing to his opponents are not necessarily inconsistent. They might all have been held by the same party. But they do not form a complete system. They might have been held in conjunction with other opinions of the most diverse characters. The work of recon-

struction is always fascinating. But we have to remember how
few of the necessary bricks are supplied to us, and how large
a proportion of the building material we have to fashion for
ourselves. We are bound, therefore, to consider carefully any
hints which the writer himself gives us as to whether he has one
or many opponents to meet, and whether he regards them as
confined within one fold.

The expressions which he uses certainly suggest variety.
He tells us that the popular expectation is being fulfilled, though
not exactly in the way in which people were looking for it. The
saying, "Antichrist cometh," is finding its fulfilment in the
many Antichrists who have come to be (ii. 18). This hardly
suggests one leader and many likeminded followers, even if the
various sections have all separated themselves off from the true
body (ἐξ ἡμῶν ἐξῆλθαν). The readers are reminded that every
lie (πᾶν ψεῦδος) shows the characteristic of being derived from
some source other than the truth. The Antichrist is characterized by his denial that Jesus is the Christ. But every one
that denies Him to be the pre-existent Son of God is cut off from
all true knowledge of the Father (ii. 23). This statement is
made with reference to those who lead astray (περὶ τῶν πλανώντων
ὑμᾶς). The same variety of error may be traced in ch. iv. The
readers are warned not to give credence to every spiritual
utterance. The many spirits must be tested, because many
false prophets have gone out into the world (iv. 1). Every
spirit which denies Jesus is "not of God." This denial is the
mark of Antichrist, who is already working in the world in the
doings of his many subordinates. It is only in the fifth chapter
that the writer seems to deal more exclusively with one particular
form of error, the denial that Jesus who is the Son of God
(οὗτος) came by blood as well as by water, *i.e.* that both His
sufferings and His death were essential parts of His Messianic
work of salvation. This passage should not be allowed to
outweigh the impression left by the earlier chapters, that varieties
of false teaching are in the writer's mind in most of what he has
to say. And even in the fifth chapter most of the expressions
used leave the same impression. Throughout he tries to fortify
his readers by calling to their remembrance a few fundamental
truths which will safeguard them from the attacks of all the
varied dangers which threaten their faith, even if by way of
illustration he refers more particularly to one attack which they
had lately victoriously repelled. Truth is one, error is manifold,
is the burden of his message throughout. And error which is
manifold threatens in more forms than one.

Thus, if we may consider first the passages in which doctrinal
errors are denounced apart from those which deal with moral

dangers, the general impression left by these passages and by many individual expressions which occur in them, leads to the conclusion that the Epistle is directed against various forms of teaching. The writer sums up the different tendencies in them which seem to him most dangerous, and most characteristic of the times. He sets out clearly the corresponding truths which in his opinion will prove to be their safest antidote. At the same time his writing may have been occasioned by one special type of false teaching, or one special incident in the history of his Church in connection with it.

With this general caution in view it will be well to consider next how far various types of teaching are possibly reflected in the Epistle.

(a) *Judaism.*

If one single enemy is in view, it cannot, of course, be the Jews who have never accepted Christianity. Those of whom the writer is thinking first are men who "have gone out from us." The phrases used, in spite of the words "they were not of us," point to a definite secession of men who called themselves Christians and were recognized as such. They cannot refer to a sharper division between Jews and Christians who had hitherto been on more friendly terms. But this obvious fact does not necessarily exclude all reference in the Epistle to non-Christian Jews. The writer's object is clear. It is to keep his readers in the right path, which some of their former companions have been persuaded to leave. He must protect those who remain from all the dangers which threaten most seriously. And his insistence on the confession that Jesus is the Messiah makes it probable, if not certain, that the Jewish controversy was prominent among the dangers which threatened most loudly. The Jewish War and the destruction of Jerusalem must, of course, have affected most profoundly the relations of Judaism to Christianity. And the effect must have become manifest very soon after the taking of the Holy City. It not only embittered the hatred between Jews and Christians, which was often acute enough before, but it placed Jewish Christians who had not broken with their national hopes and aspirations in an almost desperate position. They had still perhaps hoped against hope for the recognition of Jesus as the Messiah by the majority of their nation. All such hopes had now been dashed to the ground. The Lord had not returned to save His people and nation, as they had hoped even to the last. And Christians had not been slow to point to the fate of Jerusalem as God's punishment on the nation for their rejection of the Christ. Jewish Christians could no longer expect anything but the bitterest hatred from the members of their own nation with whom they had hoped for reunion. Their Lord had delayed His promised return. And many were ready to ask in scorn, "Where is the promise of His coming?" It is hardly surprising if their Jewish brethren succeeded in persuading some at least among them that they had been mistaken in supposing that Jesus of Nazareth was the Messiah of their nation. And if some openly cast in their lot with their own nation, others who still remained faithful may have been sorely tempted to accept the view that Jesus was indeed a prophet, sent by God and endowed by Him with higher powers, but not the Deliverer of the nation, and not the unique Son of God, with whom the writer and his fellow Christians identified Him. Such a danger threatened primarily, of course, only Jewish Christians, but it affected the whole body. For it was an essential part of the Christian creed as they apprehended it that salvation is of the Jews. The Jewish controversy was prominent throughout the first half of the second century. It may have reached its height about the time of Barcochba's rebellion. But it must have entered upon an acute stage within a few years of the Fall of Jerusalem. It must have been a serious danger at any period to which it is possible to assign the date of our Epistle.

In this connection it is natural to take into account the evidence of the Fourth Gospel. It is hardly necessary to restate at any great length the obvious fact that the needs of the Jewish controversy are a dominant factor in the Evangelist's choice of subject-matter and method of presentation. His hostility to his own nation, or rather to those who in his opinion falsely represented it and had proved unfaithful to its true vocation, is one of the most prominent characteristics of his work. In the Epistle it is far less prominent, but it is difficult to discover any real difference in the situations which the Gospel and the Epistle presuppose in this respect.

On the other hand, it is unsafe to deduce the Jewish character of the false teaching denounced from the words of ch. ii. 22 f., πᾶς ὁ ἀρνούμενος τὸν υἱὸν οὐδὲ τὸν πατέρα ἔχει κ.τ.λ., as Wurm has done. He draws the following conclusions from the passage. (1) The false teachers themselves are not conscious of holding any views of God different from those of the faithful. (2) There was, in fact, no such difference in their teaching except such as was involved in the denial of the Son, the Revealer of the Father. The last statement is rather vague. It would admit of considerable differences of view as to the nature of the Father. And the first statement does not necessarily follow from the verses which are supposed to establish it. It is true, as Wurm and Clemen have pointed out, that the author states the fact

that the false teachers "have not the Father" as a consequence
of their Christology. He could hardly have written the words
unless these teachers actually claimed to "have the Father."
But it does not follow that they claimed the possession in the
same sense as orthodox Christians claimed it. And the whole
passage loses in point unless there actually were real differences
of view. The words can no doubt be interpreted of Jews whose
conception of God was not materially different from that of
Christians. But they are equally applicable, and they have far
more point, if the writer has in view types of Gnostic thought, in
which a claim was made to superior knowledge of the unknown
Father imparted to a few spiritual natures, and unattainable by
the average Christian. Of such teaching the views attributed to
Cerinthus by Irenaeus may, at any rate, serve as an illustration,
*Post baptismum descendisse in eum ab ea principalitate quae est
super omnia Christum figura columbae, et tunc annunciasse
incognitum patrem.* We compare the Greek of Epiphanius,
ἀποκαλύψαι αὐτῷ καὶ δι' αὐτοῦ τοῖς μετ' αὐτοῦ τοῦ ἄγνωστον πατέρα.
Writers like Clemen and Wurm have assumed, perhaps too
readily, that one possible interpretation of the passage is the
only possible explanation.

(b) *Gnosticism.*

The connection of the Epistle with Gnostic ideas is quite
apparent. There is, of course, no more necessity to interpret the
phrase ὁ λέγων ὅτι ἔγνωκα αὐτόν as presupposing any definite form
of Gnosticism unknown before the second century, than there is
to do so in the case of the Pauline ἡ γνῶσις φυσιοῖ, or εἴ τις
ἀγαπᾷ τὸν θεὸν οὗτος ἔγνωσται ὑπ' αὐτοῦ. Though σπέρμα may be
the *terminus technicus* of Gnosis, our author's doctrine of γεννηθῆναι ἐκ θεοῦ will explain its use in iii. 9, however we may
interpret the meaning of σπέρμα in the phrase (σπέρμα αὐτοῦ ἐν
αὐτῷ μένει). A reference to the system of Basilides is far from
being the only possible explanation (Pfleid. ii. 414). But
Gnostic ideas are clearly a serious menace to the readers. The
essence of the writer's ἀγγελία is that God is light, and the
following reiteration of this in negative form may well be aimed
at the view that the Father of all is unknowable, or that what
can be known of Him is revealed exclusively to a few (σκοτία ἐν
αὐτῷ οὐκ ἔστιν οὐδεμία, cf. οἴδατε πάντες), unless, indeed, σκοτία
must be taken in an ethical sense, as in what follows (there can
be no fellowship with God, who is all light, for those who fail to
obey His ἐντολαί). The condemnation of those who say that
they "have not sin" points in the same direction. The use of
the first person plural shows that the danger is regarded as

imminent, if not actually present among the members of the community. The intellectual claims of the "illuminati" are met by insistence on the duty of love, and the obligations which it involves. And the confession demanded of "Jesus Christ come in the flesh" is the writer's protest against the Gnostic doctrine of the impossibility of any real and complete union between the spiritual seed and that which is flesh (cf. Jn. i. 14). The writer's own sympathy with many Gnostic ideas is well known. Perhaps his greatest service, not only to his own generation but to all times, is his power "of absorbing into Christianity the great spiritual tendencies of his age," thus "disarming their possible antagonism for his own age" and perpetuating their influence in subsequent ages.

(c) *Docetism.*

The connection of this Epistle and 2 Jn. with Docetism has been recognized from early times. Cf. Polycarp, vii., πᾶς γὰρ ὃς ἂν μὴ ὁμολογῇ Ἰησοῦν Χριστὸν ἐν σαρκὶ ἐληλυθέναι ἀντίχριστός ἐστιν: Tertullian, *De carne Christi*, xxiv.; Dion. Alex. *ap.* Eus. *H. E.* vii. 25. 19, ταῦτα γὰρ (1 Jn. i. 2, 3) προανακρούεται, διατεινό- μενος, ὡς ἐν τοῖς ἑξῆς ἐδήλωσεν, πρὸς τοὺς οὐκ ἐν σαρκὶ φάσκοντας ἐληλυθέναι τὸν κύριον. And the same view has found favour down to the present time. It is to be found in the *Religions- geschichtliche Volksbücher.* Cf. Schmiedel, *EBOJ*, p 29, "Concerning Jesus these opponents of the writer taught that He is not the Christ (ii. 22). Here, too, we recognize again the assertion of the Gnostics, that Jesus is only the man with whom the Christ who came down from heaven was united for a time, and only in some loose kind of connection" (*nur lose*; cf. *DVE*, p. 116, *nur aüsserlich*). This is seen more clearly in iv. 2 (*DVE*). They denied that Jesus Christ came in flesh; an expression directed equally against the other view of the Gnostics, that "He had a body only in appearance." Cf. *Encycl. Bibl., s.v.* John, son of Zebedee, 57, "More precisely the false teachers disclose themselves to be Docetics." It is, how- ever, unfortunate that the term "Docetism" has both a wider and a narrower signification. It can be used in a more popular sense to characterize all teaching which denied the reality of the Incarnation, and therefore the reality and completeness of the Lord's humanity. It may also be used more precisely of teaching which assigned to the Lord a merely phantasmal body, maintain- ing that He had a human body, of flesh and blood, only in appearance. The expressions used by Polycarp do not neces- sarily go beyond the wider and more popular usage. They contain no certain reference to Docetism in the stricter sense

of the term. And the language of the Johannine Epistles does
not necessarily presuppose the more precise Docetism. A
comparison of the language of Ignatius makes this quite clear.
Cf. Ign. *ad Smyrn.* ii. καὶ ἀληθῶς ἔπαθεν, ὡς καὶ ἀληθῶς ἀνέστησεν
ἑαυτόν. οὐχ ὥσπερ ἄπιστοί τινες λέγουσιν τὸ δοκεῖν αὐτὸν πεπονθέναι, αὐτοὶ τὸ δοκεῖν ὄντες, καὶ καθὼς φρονοῦσιν καὶ συμβήσεται
αὐτοῖς, οὖσιν ἀσωμάτοις καὶ δαιμονικοῖς: *ad Trall.* x, εἰ δὲ . . .
λέγουσιν τὸ δοκεῖν πεπονθέναι αὐτόν, αὐτοὶ ὄντες τὸ δοκεῖν, ἐγὼ τί
δέδεμαι; The watchword "Jesus Christ come in flesh" held good
against both these forms of teaching, and the former naturally
led to the latter. All Gnostic insistence on the incompatibility
of flesh and spirit led in the same direction. But there is
nothing in our Epistles which proves the existence of the
stricter Docetism to which the letters of Ignatius bear witness.
The false teachers are still apparently concerned with the earlier
stage of the problem, the relation between the real man Jesus of
Nazareth and the higher power with which He was brought into
temporary connection.

(d) *Cerinthianism.*

We have seen, if the suggested interpretation of the Christological passages is in the main correct, that the author is trying
to strengthen his readers' defences against dangers which threaten
from more than one quarter. As the Epistle proceeds, however,
one particular danger becomes more prominent, and the passage
in ch. v. contains clearer reference to one definite form of error
than is probably to be found in the earlier chapters. Since the
days when Polycarp told the story of John, the disciple of the
Lord, and Cerinthus in the Baths of Ephesus, the view has been
commonly held that the Johannine Epistles, if not the Gospel
as well (cf. Jerome, *In Joann.*), were directed, at any rate in
part, again the heresy of Cerinthus. This view has been
seriously challenged by many writers. The grounds on which
Wurm and Clemen have declared against it have been already
considered. If the statements of ii. 23 f. do not exclude the
teaching of Cerinthus about the unknown Father, and the
creation of the world (*non a primo Deo factum esse mundum
docuit sed a uirtute quadam ualde separata ab ea principalitate
quae est super universa et ignorante eum qui est super omnia
Deum*), the more definite references of ch. v. (especially οὐκ
ἐν τῷ ὕδατι μόνον ἀλλ' ἐν τῷ ὕδατι καὶ ἐν τῷ αἵματι) are certainly
more easily explained in connection with the teaching of
Cerinthus, as recorded by Irenaeus (*et post baptismum descendisse
in eum ab ea principalitate quae est super omnia Christum figura
columbae, et tunc annunciasse incognitum patrem, et uirtutes per-*

fecisse in fine autem revolasse iterum Christum de Iesu, et Iesum passum esse et resurrexisse, Christum autem impassibilem perseverasse, existentem spiritalem), than by any other known system. The writer is denouncing the view that the passion was no essential part of the Messianic work of salvation. While they admitted that His baptism by John was a real mark of His Messianic career, a means by which He was fitted to carry out His work for men, the opponents refused to see a similar mark in the Crucifixion. He came by water but not by blood. This corresponds admirably with what Irenaeus tells of Cerinthus, and the reference to Cerinthianism is strongly maintained by Zahn (*Einleitung*, sec. 70), and also by writers of a different school, as Knopf (*Nachapostol. Zeit.* p. 328 ff.). So far as concerns the type of teaching which is referred to, there can be little doubt that it is the most probable view. But as the exact tenets of Cerinthus are a matter of dispute, it may be well to consider the accounts of it which we possess in greater detail.

Our chief authorities for the views of Cerinthus are Irenaeus and Hippolytus. As usual the contents of Hippolytus' *Syntagma* must be deduced, and in part conjectured, from the writings of Epiphanius, Philaster, and pseudo-Tertullian. The *Refutatio* of (?) Hippolytus gives us hardly anything beyond material for reconstructing the original Greek of Irenaeus (Hipp. *Philos.* vii. 33). And as usual the Epiphanian account affords an interesting field for conjecture, where his statements cannot be checked by the other two writers who used the *Syntagma*, and are not derived from Irenaeus.

The *Syntagma* of Hippolytus must have contained at least the following information: (1) Cerinthus was the successor of Carpocrates. (2) His teaching resembled that of his predecessor as regards (*a*) The person of Christ. He was the son of Joseph and Mary. Philaster, *Cerinthus successit huius errori et similitudini uanitatis docens de generatione Saluatoris*; ps.-Tert. *Similia docens, Christum ex semine Ioseph natum proponit, hominem illum tantummodo sine diuinitate contendens*; Epiph. τὰ ἴσα τῷ προειρημένῳ εἰς τὸν Χριστὸν συκοφαντήσας ἐξηγεῖται καὶ οὗτος ἐκ Μαρίας καὶ ἐκ σπέρματος Ἰωσὴφ τὸν Χριστὸν γεγενῆσθαι. (*b*) The creation of the world. The world was made by angels. Cf. Phil. *deque creatura angelorum*; ps.-Tert. *nam et ipse mundum institutum esse ab angelis* (which Hilgenfeld has rightly restored for *illis*); Epiph. καὶ τὸν κόσμον ὁμοίως ὑπὸ ἀγγέλων γεγενῆσθαι.

His teaching differed from that of Carpocrates in its more sympathetic attitude towards Judaism. Cf. Phil. *in nullo discordans ab illo eo nisi quia ex parte solum legi consentit quod a Deo data sit*, which Lipsius rightly restores in Greek, ἀλλ᾽ ἢ ἐν τούτῳ μόνον ἐν τῷ ὁμολογεῖν ἀπὸ μέρους τὸν νόμον, ὅτι ἀπὸ θεοῦ δίδοται. Epiph. ἐν τῷ προσέχειν τῷ Ἰουδαισμῷ ἀπὸ μέρους. The *Syntagma* would seem also to have stated that Cerinthus regarded the God of the Jews as an angel, and probably as one of the κοσμοποιοὶ ἄγγελοι, by one of whom the Law was given to Israel. Cf. ps.-Tert. *ipsam quoque legem ab angelis datam perhibens, Iudaeorum Deum non Dominum sed angelum promens*; Epiph. φάσκει δὲ οὗτος τὸν νόμον καὶ τοὺς προφήτας ὑπὸ ἀγγέλων δεδόσθαι, καὶ τὸν δεδωκότα νόμον ἕνα εἶναι τῶν ἀγγέλων τῶν τὸν κόσμον πεποιηκότων, in the light of which we must interpret the sentence of Philaster, unintelligible as it stands, *et ipsum Deum Iudaeorum eum esse aestimat qui legem dedit filiis Israel.*

From this point onwards there is nothing more to be gathered from pseud.-Tertullian. Philaster adds a number of further details which emphasize the Judaizing character of Cerinthus' teaching and views. He tells us that he insisted on circumcision (cf. Epiph. ch. v. περιετμήθη ὁ Ἰησοῦς περιτμήθητι καὶ αὐτός), and on the keeping of the Sabbath; and that he taught that Christ had not yet risen from the dead, but would rise hereafter (*Christum nondum surrexisse a mortuis sed resurrecturum annuntiat*"; cf. Epiph. ch. vi. Χριστὸν πεπονθέναι καὶ ἐσταυρῶσθαι, μήπω δὲ ἐγηγέρθαι, μέλλειν δὲ ἀνίστασθαι ὅταν ἡ καθόλου γένηται νεκρῶν ἀνάστασις); that he rejected the authority of S. Paul (cf. Epiph. ch. v. τὸν Παῦλον ἀθετοῦσι); that he paid honour to the traitor Judas; that he acknowledged the Gospel according to S. Matthew only (cf. Epiph. ch. v. χρῶνται γὰρ τῷ κατὰ Ματθαῖον εὐαγγέλιον ἀπὸ μέρους), rejecting the other three Gospels and the Acts; that he blasphemes the blessed Martyrs; and that he was the mover of the sedition against the Apostles, insisting on the circumcision of all converts; and that the Apostolic decree was promulgated against the movement instigated by him (cf. Epiph. ch. iii, who also adds to his crimes the opposition to S. Paul on his last visit to Jerusalem). The agreements between Epiphanius and Philaster are sufficiently marked to justify the view that Hippolytus in his *Syntagma* assigned some such Judaizing position to Cerinthus, though the attribution of many of the same tenets to "Ebion," by Hippolytus and by Irenaeus, raises doubts as to the accuracy of the details. The *Syntagma* is in substantial agreement with Irenaeus as to Cerinthus' views about the person of Christ and the creation of the world by an inferior power. The Judaizing views attributed to him are not inconsistent with anything in Irenaeus' account. The only statement that really conflicts with his account is that concerning the resurrection of Christ. But we have found nothing so far to connect the teaching about the Baptism and Passion, given by Irenaeus, which offers the most striking resem-

blances to that denounced in ch. v. of the Epistle, with the
earlier Hippolytean treatise. Lipsius however, (p 118), finds
reasons for doing so in that part of the Epiphanian account
which is derived mainly from Irenaeus (i. 21, cf. Hipp. *Philos.*
vii. 33). When all the definitely Irenaean matter is taken away,
the remainder may be of the nature of explanatory additions
made by Epiphanius himself; and this view is maintained by
Hilgenfeld (*Ketzergeschichte des Urchristenthums*, p. 413). But
Lipsius thinks that it must be derived from another source.
For the sake of clearness it will be best to give the passage in
full.

Epiphanius.

οὐκ ἀπὸ τῆς πρώτης καὶ ἄνωθεν δυνάμεως τὸν κόσμον γεγενῆσθαι,
ἄνωθεν δὲ ἐκ τοῦ ἄνω θεοῦ μετὰ τὸ ἀδρυνθῆναι τὸν Ἰησοῦν τὸν ἐκ
σπέρματος Ἰωσὴφ καὶ Μαρίας γεγεννημένον κατεληλυθέναι τὸν
Χριστὸν εἰς αὐτόν, τουτέστι τὸ πνεῦμα τὸ ἅγιον, ἐν εἴδει περιστερᾶς
ἐν τῷ Ἰορδάνῃ καὶ ἀποκαλύψαι αὐτῷ καὶ δι' αὐτοῦ τοῖς μετ' αὐτοῦ τὸν
ἄγνωστον πατέρα, καὶ διὰ τοῦτο ἐπειδὴ ἦλθεν ἡ δύναμις εἰς αὐτὸν
ἄνωθεν δυνάμεις ἐπιτετελεκέναι, καὶ αὐτοῦ πεπονθότος τὸ ἐλθὸν
ἄνωθεν ἀναπτῆναι ἀπὸ τοῦ Ἰησοῦ ἄνω, πεπονθότα δὲ τὸν Ἰησοῦν καὶ
πάλιν ἐγηγερμένον, Χριστὸν δὲ τὸν ἄνωθεν ἐλθόντα εἰς αὐτὸν ἀπαθῆ
ἀναπτάντα, ὅπερ ἐστὶ τὸ κατελθὸν ἐν εἴδει περιστερᾶς, καὶ οὐ τὸν
Ἰησοῦν εἶναι τὸν Χριστόν.

Irenaeus (cf. Hipp. vii. 33).

οὐχ ὑπὸ τοῦ πρώτου θεοῦ γεγονέναι τὸν κόσμον, ἀλλ' ὑπὸ δυνάμεως
τινὸς κεχωρισμένης καὶ ἀπεχούσης τῆς ὑπὲρ τὰ ὅλα ἐξουσίας
(? αὐθεντίας, *principalitate*) καὶ ἀγνοούσης τὸν ὑπὲρ πάντα θεόν, τὸν δὲ
Ἰησοῦν ὑπέθετο μὴ ἐκ παρθένου γεγενῆσθαι (*impossibile enim hoc ei
uisum est*) γεγονέναι δὲ αὐτὸν ἐξ Ἰωσὴφ καὶ Μαρίας υἱὸν ὁμοίως τοῖς
λοιποῖς ἅπασιν ἀνθρώποις καὶ δικαιότερον γεγονέναι [καὶ φρονιμώτερον]
καὶ σοφώτερον, καὶ μετὰ τὸ βάπτισμα κατελθεῖν εἰς αὐτὸν τὸν ἀπὸ τῆς
ὑπὲρ τὰ ὅλα αὐθεντίας, τὸν Χριστὸν ἐν εἴδει περιστερᾶς καὶ τότε κηρύξαι
τὸν ἄγνωστον πατέρα, καὶ δυνάμεις ἐπιτελέσαι, πρὸς δὲ τῷ τέλει
ἀποστῆναι τὸν Χριστὸν ἀπὸ τοῦ Ἰησοῦ, καὶ τὸν Ἰησοῦν πεπονθέναι
καὶ ἐγηγέρθαι, τὸν δὲ Χριστὸν ἀπαθῆ διαμεμενηκέναι πνευματικὸν
ὑπάρχοντα.

Apart from particular expressions, some of which find
parallels in his account of Carpocrates (cf. *Haer.* xxvii. 2, τῆς
ἄνω δυνάμεως, ἀπεστάλθαι ὑπὸ τοῦ αὐτοῦ πατρὸς εἰς τὴν αὐτοῦ ψυχὴν
δυνάμεις), the non-Irenaean matter in Epiphanius is confined to
the identification of the Christ who descended on Jesus with
the Holy Spirit, the mention of the Jordan, the phrase τὸ ἐλθὸν
ἄνωθεν (ὁ ἄνωθεν ἐλθών), and the denial that Jesus is the Christ.

There is nothing here that Epiphanius could not have added by way of explanation and amplification. At the same time there is no obvious reason for the mention of the Spirit, unless Epiphanius is combining two accounts, one of which spoke of Christ and the other of the Holy Spirit as the power who descended on Jesus. It is noticeable that in Lipsius' attempted reconstruction of the *Syntagma* (μετὰ δὲ ἀδρυνθῆναι τὸν Χριστὸν ἐληλυθέναι εἰς αὐτὸν τὸ πνεῦμα τὸ ἅγιον ἐν εἴδει περιστερᾶς καὶ ἀποκαλύψαι αὐτῷ καὶ δι᾽ αὐτοῦ τοῖς μετ᾽ αὐτὸν τὸν ἄνω θεόν, τὸν δὲ Χριστὸν ἐπειδὴ ἦλθεν εἰς αὐτὸν ἄνωθεν δύναμις δυνάμεις ἐπιτετελεκέναι καὶ αὐτοῦ πεπονθότος τὸ κατελθὸν ἀναπτῆναι ἄνω) most of the matter and much of the language is to be found in Irenaeus. But on the whole it seems probable that the Hippolytean account did contain a statement that a higher power (? the Holy Spirit) came upon Jesus (? the Christ) and left Him before the Passion. And if the original teaching of Cerinthus was that the Spirit descended on Jesus at the Baptism, there is a special significance in the language of the Epistle, τὸ πνεῦμα ἐστὶ τὸ μαρτυροῦν. The place of the Spirit, the writer would say, was to bear witness, not to perform the higher function which some had attributed to Him. We may perhaps compare the language of the Prologue to the Gospel, where the overestimation of the Baptist, whom possibly some had identified with the Messiah, and almost certainly many had extolled at the expense of Jesus of Nazareth, is similarly set aside (οὐκ ἦν ἐκεῖνος τὸ φῶς ἀλλ᾽ ἵνα μαρτυρήσῃ περὶ τοῦ φωτός). And if this was the original teaching of Cerinthus, it would not be inconsistent with the stress laid on the denial that Jesus is the Christ. Even if he admitted that the descent of the Spirit at the Baptism raised Him to the Messianic office (more probably he would regard it as setting Him apart for a prophet), he certainly would not allow the identification of Jesus from his birth with the Christ, in the Johannine sense of the term, the pre-existent Son of God.

We may then safely conclude that though other forms of false teaching are dealt with in the Epistles, the writer has specially in view the teaching of some opponent whose views were, at any rate, very similar to those of Cerinthus, so far as we can now determine them. He seems to have combined those Gnostic and Judaizing tendencies which the writer regarded as most dangerous. And the particular views which we have good grounds for attributing to him, whether they defined the relation of Jesus to the Christ, or that of the Spirit to Christ (*i.e.* Jesus), offer the most satisfactory explanation of the language of the fifth chapter of the First Epistle.

Ethical Errors.

It is, of course, clear that the writer of these Epistles is combating errors of life and conduct as well as of doctrine. And it is almost a matter of certainty that he has in view the same opponents in what he says on both subjects. He could hardly have laid such stress on the necessary connection between true belief and right practice, if the errors of conduct which he denounces were conspicuously absent from the lives of those whose teaching he condemns. This has been clearly stated by Wurm, though he goes too far in maintaining that the praise which the writer bestows on his readers excludes the possibility that his warnings against certain practical errors could have special reference to them. It was clearly one of the chief dangers of the situation, as the writer viewed it, that those who had "gone out" had left many sympathizers behind, and many more who hardly knew how to make up their minds. There are, however, no grounds for supposing that in those passages which deal with moral shortcomings the writer has an altogether different party of opponents in view. As in the case of the Christological errors, he is content to point out the chief tendencies in which he foresees most danger. Again, his words have a wider reference than the one particular body of opponents, but he writes with the memory fresh in his mind of the recent withdrawal of a particular party from his Church, and their withdrawal was most probably the occasion of the First Epistle.

There is no evidence that this party had condoned, or been guilty of, the grosser sins of the flesh. That is not the most natural interpretation of the passage on which such a view has generally been based (ii. 16). By ἐπιθυμία τῆς σαρκός the writer seems to mean all desires which come to the natural man as yet untouched by the influence of the Spirit of God. The Johannine usage of the word σάρξ suggests this wider reference, by which the expressions used are not restricted to the fleshly sins.

But though the Epistle offers no traces of Antinomianism, it is clear that the opponents claimed that knowlege of God, fellowship with God, and love for God are compatible with disregard of at least some of the requirements of the Christian code. The words ὁ λέγων ὅτι ἔγνωκα αὐτὸν καὶ τὰς ἐντολὰς αὐτοῦ μὴ τηρῶν ψεύστης ἐστίν are certainly directed against the false teachers, even if the writer is not thinking of them in i. 6, 8, 10. And in the following verse (ii. 5) the emphasis on ἀληθῶς (ἐν τούτῳ ἡ ἀγάπη τοῦ θεοῦ τετελείωται) suggests the same thought. They must have claimed to know God as ordinary Christians could not know Him, without recognizing the obligation of complete obedience to the whole of His commands, or of living a life in conscious imitation of the life of the Master (ὀφείλει καθὼς ἐκεῖνος περιεπάτησεν καὶ αὐτὸς οὕτως περιπατεῖν). The following section (ii. 7 ff.) on the "new command," however the "old" and the "new" are to be interpreted, shows that their special failure was a want of recognition in everyday life of the primary Christian duty, love of the brethren. The full significance of the passage is perhaps most apparent if we assume that the writer claims that the command to love the brethren is contained implicitly in the moral requirements of the Old Testament, recognized by himself and his opponents alike as having authority, but that it was placed in a wholly new light in the teaching and example of the Christ, who said ἐντολὴν καινὴν δίδωμι ὑμῖν ἵνα ἀγαπᾶτε ἀλλήλους καθὼς ἠγάπησα ὑμᾶς (Jn. xiii. 34); and that he makes the claim in opposition to a denial on the part of the false teachers that this was part of the requirements of God. They must have been unwilling to recognize that the ordinary and less enlightened members of the community had any real claims upon them. They may have preferred to stand well with the more intelligent Jews and heathen in whose midst they lived (μὴ ἀγαπᾶτε τὸν κόσμον), cf. ii. 15, 16.

The writer returns to the subject in ch. iii., to which ii. 29 leads up. As Weiss has pointed out, iii. 4 would be a feeble argument against Antinomianism. To meet that he must have exchanged his subject and predicate. But the passage is significant nevertheless. It most naturally suggests that the opponents condemned "lawlessness," but failed to see that all sin is lawless, being disobedience to the Divine law, which has been made known to men in various ways. The duty of obedience to certain definite precepts they recognized, but not the sinfulness of all falling short of the ideal of human life realized in the life of the Son of Man on earth. Again all becomes clear if we may suppose that their conduct was regulated by the moral precepts of the Old Testament rather than by the more exacting requirements of the "λόγος αὐτοῦ" which had now been put before men. In ver. 7 the words μηδεὶς πλανάτω ὑμᾶς may contain a more definite allusion to particular opponents. The doing of righteousness constitutes the only claim to be righteous, and again "He" has set the standard of doing (καθὼς ἐκεῖνος ἔστιν δίκαιος). The indifference of action as compared with other supposed qualifications, such as, for instance, descent from Abraham, or the possession of the "pneumatic" seed, is clearly part of the opponents' creed. They must have claimed to be δίκαιοι without admitting the necessity of "doing the works."

Thus on the practical as well as on the theoretical side we

e

seem to trace the same mixture of Jewish and Gnostic ideas which must have formed the most pressing dangers to the moral and spiritual life of a Christian community towards the end of the first century or at the beginning of the second, or perhaps even later. Such matters really afford very little material for accurate dating. No account has been taken of the Chiliastic views attributed to Cerinthus by Caius of Rome and others. If the attribution is correct, they are not inconsistent with his Judaizing position. The implied suggestions of immorality are not supported by any tangible evidence. In all other respects the teaching attributed to Cerinthus by the more trustworthy heresiologists affords a typical example of the errors which are condemned in the Johannine Epistles.

§ 6. LITERARY HISTORY.

In tracing the history of books and documents it is important to emphasize the difference between echoes, influences, direct use and direct quotation, with or without indication of authorship. Professor Bacon has rightly called attention to this in his recent work on the Johannine Problem. The distinction has always been recognized by competent scholars in dealing with the Books of the New Testament, though they have held very different opinions as to what may be reasonably concluded from the facts of usage. The undoubted attribution of the Epistles to John by name is not found in extant works till the last quarter of the second century. The use of them can, however, be traced at a much earlier date. The following list of "echoes and influences" of the Epistles which have been found in the writings of the second century and early decades of the third, are not all equally certain, but at least deserve consideration.

Clem. Rom. xlix. 5. ἐν τῇ ἀγάπῃ ἐτελειώθησαν πάντες οἱ ἐκλεκτοὶ τοῦ θεοῦ.

Clem. l. 3. ἀλλ' οἱ ἐν ἀγάπῃ τελειωθέντες.

I iv. 18. ὁ δὲ φοβούμενος οὐ τετελείωται ἐν τῇ ἀγάπῃ.

The verbal similarity is interesting, but the meaning is different at least in the first passage. The 49th chapter has clearer reminiscences of 1 Co. xiii. The opening sentence, ὁ ἔχων ἀγάπην ἐν Χριστῷ ποιησάτω τὰ τοῦ Χριστοῦ παραγγέλματα, suggests more clearly the teaching of the Johannine Epistles. But no weight can be attached to this coincidence of language.

Polycarp, ad Phil. c. vii. πᾶς γὰρ ὃς ἂν μὴ ὁμολογῇ Ἰησοῦν Χριστὸν ἐν σαρκὶ ἐληλυθέναι, ἀντίχριστός ἐστιν.

I iv. 2. πᾶν πνεῦμα ὃ ὁμολογεῖ Ἰησοῦν Χριστὸν ἐν σαρκὶ ἐληλυθότα ἐκ τοῦ θεοῦ ἐστίν, καὶ πᾶν πνεῦμα ὁ μὴ καὶ ὃς ἂν μὴ ὁμολογῇ τὸ μαρτύριον τοῦ σταυροῦ ἐκ τοῦ διαβόλου ἐστίν.

ὁμολογεῖ τὸν Ἰησοῦν ἐκ τοῦ θεοῦ οὐκ ἔστιν· καὶ τοῦτό ἐστιν τὸ τοῦ ἀντίχριστου, ὃ ἀκηκόατε ὅτι ἔρχεται.

I iii. 8. ὁ ποιῶν τὴν ἁμαρτίαν ἐκ τοῦ διαβόλου ἐστίν.

I ii. 18. καθὼς ἠκούσατε ὅτι ἀντίχριστος ἔρχεται καὶ νῦν ἀντίχριστοι πολλοὶ γεγόνασιν.

I ii. 22. Τίς ἐστιν ὁ ψεύστης εἰ μὴ ὁ ἀρνούμενος ὅτι Ἰησοῦς οὐκ ἔστιν ὁ Χριστός; οὗτός ἐστιν ὁ ἀντίχριστος, ὁ ἀρνούμενος τὸν πατέρα καὶ τὸν υἱόν.

II 7. πολλοὶ πλάνοι ἐξῆλθαν εἰς τὸν κόσμον, οἱ μὴ ὁμολογοῦντες Ἰησοῦν Χριστὸν ἐρχόμενον ἐν σαρκί· οὗτός ἐστιν ὁ πλάνος καὶ ὁ ἀντίχριστος.

The importance of this passage justifies a full presentation of the evidence. The connection between the passage in Polycarp and 1 Jn. iv. 2, or 2 Jn. 7, is obvious. No one who has read the Johannine Epistles and the Epistle of Polycarp can doubt on which side lies the probability of originality. And the way in which Polycarp seems to use the language and thoughts of the Johannine Epistles is closely parallel to his use throughout his Epistle of the language and contents of other books of the New Testament. The obvious connection of the first sentence with the language of S. John's Epistles makes it natural to see in the second, which contains the Johannine phrase ἐκ τοῦ διαβόλου ἐστίν, an echo of the teaching of the First Epistle of S. John on the Passion as being, equally with the Baptism, characteristic of the Lord's Messianic work (οὗτός ἐστιν ὁ ἐλθὼν δι' ὕδατος καὶ αἵματος). If so, the case for the connection with the First Epistle is strengthened. The sentences in Polycarp give the reason for his appeal to the Philippians to serve the Lord with all fear and reverence, as the Lord Himself commanded, and the Apostles who preached His Gospel to them, and the Prophets who predicted His coming, "abstaining from offences and from false brethren, and from those who bear the name of the Lord in hypocrisy, who lead foolish men astray" (οἵτινες ἀποπλανῶσι κενοὺς ἀνθρώπους, cf. 1 Jn. ii. 26, ταῦτα ἔγραψα ὑμῖν περὶ τῶν πλανώντων ὑμᾶς). The context recalls the situation of the Second Epistle (2 Jn. 10 f.), the language and thought are more closely connected with the First. The passage may be said to *prove* the acquaintance of Polycarp with the teaching contained in the Epistles, or with the man who taught it. It establishes a very high degree of probability that he was acquainted with the actual Epistles. In view of it there would have to be very strong reasons to justify us in placing the Johannine Epistles later than the Epistle of Polycarp. And it must be remembered that his Epistle, if genuine, must be dated *immediately* after the martyrdom of Ignatius (see Polycarp, *ad Phil.* c. xiii.).

Papias (Eus. *H. E.* iii. 39. 3). (ἔχαιρον) . . . τοῖς τὰς παρὰ τοῦ κυρίου τῇ πίστει δεδομένας (*sc.* ἐντολάς) καὶ ἀπ᾽ αὐτῆς παραγινομένας τῆς ἀληθείας.
Eus. iii. 39. 17. κέχρηται δ᾽ ὁ αὐτὸς μαρτυρίαις ἀπὸ τῆς Ἰωάννου προτέρας ἐπιστολῆς.

III 12. Δημητρίῳ μεμαρτύρηται ὑπὸ πάντων καὶ ὑπὸ αὐτῆς τῆς ἀληθείας.

The use of the phrase αὐτὴ ἡ ἀλήθεια by the "Presbyter" and by Papias may, of course, be an accidental coincidence, but it is not without significance in the light of Eusebius' statement, which we have not the slightest reason for discrediting. The First Epistle, if not the two smaller letters, must have been known and valued during the first quarter of the second century. The evidence does not amount to actual proof, as it is, of course, impossible to distinguish between personal acquaintance with the author and his teaching, and knowledge of the actual text of the Epistles. The evidence does not exclude the possibility of such teaching being embodied in Epistles at a later date. But there can be little doubt as to which hypothesis is the simpler and the more natural.

Didache, c. x. μνήσθητι Κύριε, τῆς ἐκκλησίας σου τοῦ ῥύσασθαι αὐτὴν ἀπὸ παντὸς πονηροῦ καὶ τελειῶσαι αὐτὴν ἐν τῇ ἀγάπῃ σου.

I iv. 18. οὐ τετελείωται ἐν τῇ ἀγάπῃ.

τελειῶσαι ἐν τῇ ἀγάπῃ may be a reminiscence of the language, as it certainly recalls the thought, of the Epistle.

Hermas, *M.* iii. 1. ὅτι ὁ Κύριος ἀληθινὸς ἐν παντὶ ῥήματι, καὶ οὐδὲν παρ᾽ αὐτῷ ψεῦδος.

I ii. 27. τὸ αὐτοῦ χρίσμα—ἀληθές ἐστιν καὶ οὐκ ἔστιν ψεῦδος.

The coincidence of language may possibly suggest a connection between the two passages, but it certainly does not prove it.

Ep. to Diognetus, xi. 14. οὗτος (cf. § 3, οὗ χάριν ἀπέστειλε Λόγον) ὁ ἀπ᾽ ἀρχῆς ὁ καινὸς φανεὶς καὶ παλαιὸς εὑρεθείς.

I i. 1. ὃ ἦν ἀπ᾽ ἀρχῆς.

x. 2. ὁ γὰρ θεὸς τοὺς ἀνθρώπους ἠγάπησε . . . πρὸς οὓς ἀπέστειλε τὸν υἱὸν αὐτοῦ τὸν μονογενῆ.

I iv. 9. ἐν τούτῳ ἐφανερώθη ἡ ἀγάπη τοῦ θεοῦ ἐν ἡμῖν, ὅτι τὸν υἱὸν αὐτοῦ τὸν μονογενῆ ἀπέσταλκεν ὁ θεὸς εἰς τὸν κόσμον (cf. Jn. iii. 16, 17).

3. ἐπιγνοὺς δὲ τίνος οἴει πληρωθήσεσθαι χαρᾶς ἢ πῶς ἀγαπήσεις τὸν οὕτως προαγαπήσαντά σε ;

I iv. 19. ἡμεῖς ἀγαπῶμεν, ὅτι αὐτὸς πρῶτος ἠγάπησεν ἡμᾶς.
I i. 4. ἵνα ἡ χαρὰ ἡμῶν ᾖ πεπληρωμένη.

The echoes of Johannine thought are obvious, and on the whole the similarity is greater with the Epistle than with the Gospel.

Ep. Lugd. et Vienn. (Eus. v. i. 10). Ἔχων δὲ τὸν παράκλητον ἐν ἑαυτῷ, τὸ πνεῦμα τοῦ Ζαχαρίου, ὃ διὰ τοῦ πληρώματος τῆς ἀγάπης ἐνεδείξατο, εὐδοκήσας ὑπὲρ τῆς τῶν ἀδελφῶν ἀπολογίας καὶ τὴν ἑαυτοῦ θεῖναι ψυχήν. ἦν γὰρ καὶ ἔστιν γνήσιος Χριστοῦ μαθητής, ἀκολουθῶν τῷ ἀρνίῳ ὅπου ἂν ὑπάγῃ.

I iii. 16. Ἐν τούτῳ ἐγνώκαμεν τὴν ἀγάπην, ὅτι ἐκεῖνος ὑπὲρ ἡμῶν τὴν ψυχὴν αὐτοῦ ἔθηκεν· καὶ ἡμεῖς ὀφείλομεν ὑπὲρ τῶν ἀδελφῶν τὰς ψυχὰς θεῖναι.

The connection with Johannine thought and expression is quite unmistakable. The true following of the Lamb, as shown in the readiness of Veltius Epagathus to lay down (? stake) his life for the brethren, is almost certainly a reminiscence of the First Epistle.

Irenaeus, III. xvi. 5. "Quemadmodum Ioannes Domini discipulus confirmat dicens Haec autem (Jn. xx. 31). . . . Propter quod et in epistola sua sic testificatus est nobis Filioli, nouissima hora est (1 Jn. ii. 18, 19, 21—in the form Cognoscite ergo quoniam omne mendacium extraneum est et non est de ueritate—22 to Antichristus)."

8. "Quos et Dominus nobis cauere praedixit et discipulus eius Ioannes in praedicta epistola fugere eos praecepit dicens Multi seductores exierunt in hunc mundum (2 Jn. 7, 8 to operati estis). Et rursus in Epistola ait Multi pseudo-prophetae exierunt de saeculo (1 Jn. iv. 1–3 to omnis Spiritus qui soluit Iesum non est ex Deo sed de Antichristo est). Haec autem similia sunt illi quod in euangelio dictum est, quoniam Uerbum caro factum est et habitauit in nobis. Propter quod rursus in Epistola clamat, Omnis qui credit quia Iesus est Christus, ex Deo natus est, unum et eundem sciens Iesum Christum," etc.

We have now come to the age of definite quotation by name. Irenaeus' use of the Epistles in this passage, the only one in which he makes definite quotations, is interesting. It reminds us of the differences of custom in quotation by the writers of the last quarter of the second century, and perhaps of the difference between what was customary in definitely theological treatises as opposed to letters, or apologetic writings. We should, for instance, be in a better position to determine Justin's exact use of N.T. writings if his *Syntagma* against Heresies had been preserved. The quotation is also interesting if considered in connection with other evidence of this period and that which succeeded it, as suggesting that, in some places, at any rate, the

first two Epistles of S. John were known and used before the
third gained as wide a circulation.

Clem. Alex. *Str.* ii. 15. 66. Φαίνεται δὲ καὶ Ἰωάννης ἐν τῇ
μείζονι ἐπιστολῇ τὰς διαφορὰς τῶν ἁμαρτιῶν ἐκδιδάσκων ἐν τούτοις·
Ἐάν τις ἴδῃ τὸν ἀδελφὸν αὐτοῦ ἁμαρτάνοντα ἁμαρτίαν μὴ πρὸς
θάνατον, αἰτήσει, καὶ δώσει αὐτῷ ζωήν, τοῖς ἁμαρτάνουσι μὴ πρὸς
θάνατον· εἶπεν· Ἔστι γὰρ ἁμαρτία πρὸς θάνατον· οὐ περὶ ἐκείνης
λέγω, ἵνα ἐρωτήσῃ τις. πᾶσα ἀδικία ἁμαρτία ἐστί, καὶ ἔστιν ἁμαρτία
μὴ πρὸς θάνατον (1 Jn. v. 16 f.).

Ib. Str. iii. 4. 32. καί· Ἐὰν εἴπωμεν, φησὶν ὁ Ἰωάννης ἐν τῇ
ἐπιστολῇ, ὅτι κοινωνίαν ἔχομεν μετ' αὐτοῦ, τουτέστι μετὰ τοῦ θεοῦ,
καὶ ἐν τῷ σκότει περιπατῶμεν, ψευδόμεθα καὶ οὐ ποιοῦμεν τὴν
ἀλήθειαν· ἐὰν δὲ ἐν τῷ φωτὶ περιπατῶμεν ὡς αὐτὸς ἐν τῷ φωτί,
κοινωνίαν ἔχομεν μετ' αὐτοῦ καὶ τὸ αἷμα Ἰησοῦ τοῦ υἱοῦ αὐτοῦ
καθαρίζει ἡμᾶς ἀπὸ τῆς ἁμαρτίας (1 Jn. i. 6 f.).

Ib. Str. iii. 5. 42. καὶ πᾶς ὁ ἔχων τὴν ἐλπίδα ταύτην ἐπὶ τῷ
κυρίῳ ἁγνίζει, φησίν, ἑαυτὸν καθὼς ἐκεῖνος ἁγνός ἐστιν.

Ib. 44. Ὁ λέγων, ἔγνωκα τὸν κύριον, καὶ τὰς ἐντολὰς αὐτοῦ μὴ
τηρῶν ψεύστης ἐστίν, καὶ ἐν τούτῳ ἡ ἀλήθεια οὐκ ἔστιν, Ἰωάννης
λέγει.

Ib. Str. iii. 6. 45. πρῶτον μὲν τὸ τοῦ ἀποστόλου Ἰωάννου.
Καὶ νῦν ἀντίχριστοι πολλοὶ γεγόνασιν, ὅθεν ἐγνώκαμεν ὅτι ἐσχάτη
ὥρα ἐστίν. ἐξ ἡμῶν ἐξῆλθον, ἀλλ' οὐκ ἦσαν ἐξ ἡμῶν· εἰ γὰρ ἦσαν ἐξ
ἡμῶν, μεμενήκεισαν ἂν μεθ' ἡμῶν.

Ib. Quis div. salv. 37. 6. θείως γε καὶ ἐπιπνόως ὁ Ἰωάννης· Ὁ
μὴ φιλῶν, φησί, τὸν ἀδελφὸν ἀνθρωποκτόνος ἐστί (1 Jn. iii. 15),
σπέρμα τοῦ Καίν, θρέμμα τοῦ διαβόλου.

Ib. Str. iv. 16. 100. Τεκνία μὴ ἀγαπῶμεν λόγῳ μηδὲ γλώσσῃ
<φησὶν> Ἰωάννης τελείους εἶναι διδάσκων, ἀλλ' ἐν ἔργῳ καὶ ἀληθείᾳ.
ἐν τούτῳ γνωσόμεθα ὅτι ἐκ τῆς ἀληθείας ἐσμέν (1 Jn. iii. 18 f.)· εἰ
δὲ ἀγάπη ὁ θεός (1 Jn. iv. 16) ἀγάπη καὶ ἡ θεοσέβεια· Φόβος οὐκ
ἔστιν ἐν τῇ ἀγάπῃ, ἀλλ' ἡ τελεία ἀγάπη ἔξω βάλλει τὸν φόβον
(1 Jn. iv. 18)· αὕτη ἐστὶν ἡ ἀγάπη τοῦ θεοῦ, ἵνα τὰς ἐντολὰς αὐτοῦ
τηρῶμεν (1 Jn. v. 3).

Ib. Str. v. 1. 13. Ἀγάπη δὲ ὁ θεός· ὁ τοῖς ἀγαπῶσι γνωστός
(1 Jn. iv. 16).

Ib. Str. iv. 18. 113. Ἀγάπη τοίνυν καὶ ὁ θεὸς εἴρηται, ἀγαθὸς
ὢν (1 Jn. iv. 16).

Ib. Quis div. salv. 38. Ἀγάπη καλύπτει πλῆθος ἁμαρτιῶν· ἡ
τελεία ἀγάπη ἐκβάλλει τὸν φόβον· (1 Jn. iv. 18) οὐ περπερεύεται
κ.τ.λ.

Clement makes full use of the First Epistle, and recognizes
at least *two*. The question whether he commented on all three
Epistles, or on two only, in his *Adumbrationes*, is discussed
subsequently.

Muratorian Fragment.

"Quid ergo mirum si Ioannes tam constanter singula etiam in epistulis suis proferat, dicens in semetipsum 'quae uidimus oculis nostris et auribus audiuimus et manus nostrae palpauerunt, haec scripsimus uobis.' Sic enim non solum uisorem se et[1] auditorem, sed et scriptorem omnium mirabilium domini per ordinem profitetur.

"Epistola sane Judae et superscriptae[2] Iohannis duae in catholica habentur et Sapientia ab amicis Salomonis in honorem ipsius scripta."

The text is taken from Dr. Zahn's *Grundriss d. Geschichte d. NT. Kanons*, p. 78. It is not necessary here to go over again the controversy raised by the different interpretations of these two passages in the *Muratorianum* which have been maintained by competent scholars. There can be no doubt that the (Greek) author of the document regarded the Epistles as the work of John the Apostle. But there is nothing to suggest that the Church for which he speaks (? Rome) accepted as Scripture more than *two* Johannine Epistles. Students can only feel astonishment at such statements as that of Dr. Gregory (*Canon and Text of the New Testament*, p. 132), "The way in which these two small Epistles of John are named seems odd," which assumes a reference to the two shorter letters in the second paragraph quoted, without further discussion. This will be more fully discussed later on in connection with the other evidence for the circulation of only two Johannine Epistles.

Origen, *In Joann.* v. 3 (*ex* Euseb. *H. E.* vi. 25), Τί δεῖ περὶ τοῦ ἀναπεσόντος ἐπὶ τὸ στῆθος λέγειν τοῦ Ἰησοῦ, Ἰωάννου, ὃς εὐαγγέλιον ἓν καταλέλοιπεν, ὁμολογῶν δύνασθαι τοσαῦτα ποιήσειν, ἃ οὐδὲ ὁ κόσμος χωρῆσαι ἐδύνατο; ἔγραψε δὲ καὶ τὴν Ἀποκάλυψιν, κελευσθεὶς σιωπῆσαι καὶ μὴ γράψαι τὰς τῶν ἑπτὰ βροντῶν φωνάς, [καταλέλοιπε] καὶ ἐπιστολὴν πάνυ ὀλίγων στίχων, ἔστω δὲ καὶ δευτέραν καὶ τρίτην, ἐπεὶ οὐ πάντες φασὶ γνησίους εἶναι ταύτας· πλὴν οὐκ εἰσὶ στίχων ἀμφότεραι ἑκατόν.

Origen makes very full use of the First Epistle. There are no quotations or "echoes" of the smaller Epistles. At least none are recorded in Lommatzsch's indices, or in the volumes at present published in the Berlin *Corpus*. We do not know the original Greek of the passage in the VIIth Homily on Joshua (§ 1) which Rufinus translated, "Addit nihilominus adhuc et Ioannes tuba canere per epistolas" (Lomm. xi. 63).

Tertullian's use of the First Epistle is full. He frequently

---

[1] Sed et MS (acc. to Zahn the et is a later addition).
[2] Su erscrictio Iohannes duas (? ἐπιγεγραμμέναι).

quotes it by name.   It is unnecessary to quote the passages here
in full.   Their evidence has been used in the Appendix on the
Latin text of the Epistle.   His use of the Second Epistle is
doubtful, and there is no trace of the Third in his writings.

The evidence which has been quoted above shows that the
date of the Johannine Epistles cannot reasonably be placed
later than the first decade of the second century.   The first
Epistle was known and valued by the generation of Papias and
Polycarp, and it was not only towards the close of their lives
that they became acquainted with it.   So far as their origin is
concerned, it is difficult to separate the two shorter Epistles from
the First.   They bear on their face marks of genuineness which
can hardly be seriously questioned.   They deal practically with
questions, about the limits within which hospitality should be
shown to travelling teachers, which are known to have been
matters of controversy in the first half of the second century,
and which probably often called for solution some considerable
time before that.   It is almost inconceivable that any one should
have written them "to do honour" to some "great light" of
earlier times, or to the Apostle himself, as the Asiatic Presbyter,
of whom Tertullian tells us, tried to do honour to S. Paul by
writing the Acta Pauli, or as the "friends" of Solomon, perhaps
Philo himself, in the view of the author of the Muratorian
Fragment, thought to honour the Jewish king.   No one would
have created for the glorification of an Apostle, or even a
Presbyter, the very dubious situation of disputed authority which
the Third Epistle reveals.   Even if his object had been rather
to gain Apostolic or early authority for particular methods of
treating strangers, he could hardly have done his work so badly
as such a theory would imply.   The reasons for preferring at a
later date the view which attributes the authorship to an Elder
as opposed to the "Apostolic" author of the First Epistle, are
obvious.   It is almost impossible to find any serious reason to
explain their survival except the authority and reputation of
their real author, whoever he may have been.   They go with the
First Epistle ; and in view of their contents, their preservation,
and the traditions attached to them, we are fully justified in
attributing their authorship to the Elder, who doubtless "lived
on till the time of Trajan," and whose authority and reputation
in the province of Asia stood so high throughout the second
century.

The history of the reception of the three Epistles into the
Canon of the New Testament is more difficult to trace.   There
is no doubt that the First Epistle was generally accepted before
the close of the second century.   The only certain exception is

the Canon of Edessa, where we know from the Doctrine of
Addai that as late as the fourth century (? fifth) the statement
that no books should be accepted as Scripture, to be read in
church, except the Gospel (*i.e.* the Diatessaron), the Acts, and
the Epistles of Paul, was retained without comment in the
legendary account of the origins of Christianity in that quarter.
The same Canon is found in the Syrian Canon (? *c.* 400 A.D.),
found in Cod. Syr. 20 (saec. ix.) of the convent of S. Catharine
on Mt. Sinai[1] (A. S. Lewis, London, 1894).   The chief evidence
for the acceptance of only one Epistle is as follows.   (1)
Eusebius' knowledge of the use and acceptance of the Epistles in
early times led him to place only the First Epistle among the
ὁμολογούμενα, the two smaller Epistles being placed among
the ἀντιλεγόμενα, γνώριμα τοῖς πολλοῖς, with the added caution,
" whether they be by the Evangelist, or by another of the same
name."[2]   (2) The statement by Origen, quoted above, that the
authorship of the two smaller Epistles is disputed, and the fact
that he does not seem to have quoted them, which in his case is
perhaps significant.   (3) The Canon of the Peshitta, in which
only three Catholic Epistles find a place, a Canon which is
frequently found in the East.   But the acceptance of the " seven-
letter" Canon must be dealt with later on.   (4) The protest of
the scribe of the Cheltenham list (Mommsen's Canon? 360 A.D.),
or of his predecessor, who has added after the mention of the
three Johannine Epistles the words "una sola," as after that of
the two Petrine Epistles.[3]   On the other hand, we have earlier
evidence of the use of 2 John as authoritative in Africa.   (5) In
the attribution of the two smaller Epistles to the " Elder," in
the Roman list of 382 (cf. *JTS*, 1900, i. 554–560), where the
influence of Jerome is clearly to be seen, " Iohannis apostoli
epistula una alterius Iohannis presbyteri epistulae duae."

The evidence for the acceptance of the first two Epistles
without the third is less clear, and not very easy to interpret.
But it is sufficiently definite and widespread to deserve serious
consideration.   (1) We have seen how Irenaeus confuses the two
Epistles.   There is no trace of the use of the Third Epistle in
his writings.   (2) We have evidence of the use of the first two
Epistles in Africa in Cyprian's time.   He himself frequently
quotes the First Epistle, and the quotation of 2 Jn. 10, 11 by
Aurelius a Chullabi (*Sententiae Episcoporum*, 81, p. 459, ed.
Hartel) vindicates for it a place in the African, at least in the
Carthaginian, Bible of that period.   Again we find no trace of
the Third Epistle.   (3) The usage of Gaul and Africa is sup-

[1] All three Epistles are, of course, absent from the Canon of Marcion.
[2] Euseb. *H. E.* iii. 25.
[3] Epistulae Iohannis III ūr CCCL una sola (Zahn, *Grundriss*, p. 81).

ported by that of Rome. There can be little doubt as to what is the natural interpretation of the language used by the author of the Muratorian Fragment. When he is dealing with the Gospels, and feels himself obliged to defend the Fourth Gospel against attacks which clearly had been made on it, probably by Caius, he quotes the Epistle in support of his view that the Fourth Gospel was the work of an eye-witness of the ministry, to prove that the author plainly declares himself not only a witness, but also a hearer and recorder of all the wonders of the Lord in order. When he comes to that in the Epistles, he makes the plain statement that in his Church two Epistles of John are received. There is nothing to suggest that he excludes the First, which he has already quoted elsewhere, or that he is dealing now only with doubtful books. Dr. Zahn's argument[1] on this point would seem to prove too much, for it involves the consequence that the only books which the Roman Church at that time treated as undoubted Scripture were those contained in the restricted Canon of Edessa, Gospel(s), Acts, Pauline Epistles. (4) The fact that the Latin epitome by Cassiodorus, and Clement's *Adumbrationes* on the Catholic Epistles, contain notes on the first two Epistles of S. John only, is significant. The evidence of Eusebius, who states that Clement commented on all the (seven) Catholic Epistles, as well as on Barnabas and the Petrine Apocalypse, which is supported by Photius, must be set against this. But the suspicion is at least well grounded that the general statement of Eusebius may be loose. On the other hand, no stress can be laid on Clement's use (see above, p. lvi) of the phrase ἐν τῇ μείζονι ἐπιστολῇ. It is equally compatible with his recognition of three Epistles or of two. And later writers who undoubtedly accepted all seven Catholic Epistles frequently quote the First Epistles of Peter and John as "the Epistle" of those writers.

It is difficult to estimate the exact bearing of this evidence; but in view of its distribution, and the definite character of some of it, we can hardly neglect it. It is quite natural that, even where it was fully accepted, the Third Epistle should have left hardly any trace of its existence. There is scarcely a phrase in it, not found in the other Epistles, which we should expect to find quoted. But such as it is, the evidence points to a period when only two Johannine Epistles were generally accepted in the West, and perhaps at Alexandria, a Church which is frequently found in agreement with the West rather than the East, in matters connected with the Canon as well as in matters of greater importance. The Second Epistle would seem to have come into circulation more rapidly than the Third. The evidence does

[1] *Geschichte des NT. Kanons*, pp. 213–220.

not, at any rate, justify the usual treatment of the two shorter
letters as a pair of inseparable twins. With the possible exception of one phrase (ἀπ᾽ αὐτῆς τῆς ἀληθείας) in Papias' quotation,
or summary, of the words of the Presbyter, we find no certain
trace of language of the Third Epistle till the time of Augustine
and Jerome. It was known to Origen, whose influence on
Eusebius is perhaps most clearly seen in his treatment of the
books which form the first section of his "Antilegomena." It is
possible that his predecessor Clement treated it as Scripture.
But it seems to have been very little used. It is quoted by
Augustine and Jerome, and formed part of the Bible out of
which Augustine selected his "Speculum," which must, of course,
be clearly distinguished from the *Liber de Divinis Scripturis*,
generally known as 'm,' in which there is no quotation from the
Third Epistle. The text found in the Speculum is, of course,
Vulgate, whether that text goes back to S. Augustine himself, as
Professor Burkitt supposes (*JTS* xi. 263 ff., 1910), or is due to
subsequent alteration. Sabatier's attempt to reproduce fragments
of an old Latin translation of the Third Epistle from the
quotations in Augustine and Jerome, shows that it probably
existed in an old Latin pre-Vulgate text,—a fact which is placed
beyond doubt by the fragment contained in the Latin of Codex
Bezae.

The history of the smaller Epistles is closely connected with
that of the substitution of the seven-letter Canon of Catholic
Epistles for the three-letter Canon of the East, and of which a
short sketch must now be given.

In the East the Epistle of James, which Origen certainly
treated as Scripture in some sense, though not without recording
the doubts which were felt about it, was soon added to the
generally recognized Epistles, 1 Peter and 1 John. These three
letters form the Canon of Catholic Epistles in the Peshitta.
And this three-letter Canon is found in all the provinces which
were under the influence of Antioch. Chrysostom, who was
moved from Antioch to Constantinople in 398, knows and uses
no other Catholic Epistles. The same Canon is found in the
Cappadocian Fathers, Basil, Gregory of Nazianzum, and Gregory
of Nyssa in the last quarter of the fourth century. According
to Lietzmann,[1] the same can be proved to have been the usage
of Methodius of Olympus about 300 A.D. During the fourth
century the process of replacing this shorter Canon by the fuller
seven-letter Canon was begun and in most places carried through.
It is fully recognized by Eusebius in several places, and his
formal list, in which the five Epistles, James, Jude, 2, 3 John,

---

[1] "Wie wurden die Bücher des Neuen Testaments heilige Schrift?"
(*Lebens Fragen*, ed. Weinel), Tübingen, 1907.

2 Peter are separated off from the rest of the Antilegomena, suggests that it is the Canon which he himself preferred. In this he was no doubt influenced by the statements of Origen about these letters. In 367, Athanasius put it forward in his thirty-ninth Festal Letter as the official list of Egypt. It is, however, found still earlier in Cyril of Jerusalem (340). The fact that the letters always are found in the same order, wherever this Canon is used in the East, suggests that here its adoption was a matter of definite policy, due probably to the necessity for uniformity felt by the Nicenes in their struggle with the influence of the Court. The varying orders found in the West point to a more natural and gradual process of adoption. It may be noticed that Gregory of Nazianzum names all seven Epistles in his list of the Canon, but his own practice seems to have been to quote only those found in the shorter Canon. Both the three- and the seven-letter Canons are mentioned in the list of Amphilochius of Iconium in Lycaonia. In the Island of Cyprus, Epiphanius is a supporter of the seven-letter Canon. On the other hand, Theodoret of Cyrus (430–450) apparently uses in his writings only the three letters. In the Syriac Bible the seven Epistles appear first in the recension of Philoxenus of Mabug (500).

Enough has been said of the history of the reception of the Johannine letters in the West. The acceptance of the Athanasian Canon, which contained the three letters of S. John, and its final supremacy in the West, were due to the influence of Augustine and Jerome. As we see from the Canon Mommsenianus, it did not pass without protest.

Thus the literary history of the letters shows that the assignment of an early date to the two shorter letters, especially to the Third, depends on the internal evidence of their character and content rather than on external attestation. Their final acceptance was undoubtedly due to the belief of the men of the fourth century, and in part of the third, in their Apostolic origin. During the earlier period of their obscurity they would hardly have been preserved but for the respect felt for their author. Internal evidence is practically decisive against the hypothesis of forgery. The question of their authorship is part of the wider problem, which still awaits a satisfactory solution, of the authorship and date of the "Ephesian Canonical Writings" and of the personality of the Ephesian "Elder."

§ 7. THE TEXT.

The following list gives most of the older and more important manuscripts and authorities for the text of the Epistles :

B.   δ1. Codex Vaticanus. Rome. Vat. Gr. 1209 (iv.).

א.   δ2. Codex Sinaiticus. Petersburg (iv.).

C.   δ3. Codex Ephraimi. Paris. Bibl. Nat. 9 (v.); 1 Jn. i. 1 τους—(2) εωρα[κομεν], iv. 2 εστιν—(3 Jn. 2) ψυχη.

A.   δ4. Codex Alexandrinus. London. Brit. Mus. Royal Libr. I. D. v.–viii. (v.).

Ψ.   δ6. Athos. Lawra 172 (β52) (viii.–ix.).

13 (= 33 ᵍᵒˢᵖ.).   δ48. Paris. Bibl. Nat. Gr. 14 (ix.–x.).

48 (= 105 ᵍᵒˢᵖ.).   δ257. Oxford. Bodl. Misc. Gr. 136 (A.D. 1391).

P.   α3. Petersburg. Bibl. Roy. 225 (ix.). Palimpsest. 1 Jn. iii. 20–v. 1 του.

389.   α74. Patmos. Ιωαννου 16 (x.).

25.   α103. London. Brit. Mus. Harley 5537 (A.D. 1087). 1 Jn. v. 14–2 Jn. 5 missing.

61.   α162. London. Brit. Mus. Add. 20003, and Kairo βιβλ. πατριαρχ 351 (A.D. 1044).

Apl. 261.   α7. Sinai 273 (ix.).

S.   α2. Athos. Lawra 88 (α88) (viii.–ix.).

L.   α5. Rome. Angel. 39 (ol. A. 2. 15) (ix.).

384.   α54. Chalki. Εμπορ. Σχολη 26 (x.).

9.   α189. Cambridge Univ. Libr. Kk. vi. 4 (xi.–xiⁱ.). See Westcott, p. 91, who gives a list of the interesting readings contained in this MS. It is not included in von Soden's list of the manuscripts of which he used collations for the text of the Catholic Epistles.

Old Latin Version.

h. *Fleury Palimpsest*, ed. S. Berger, Paris, 1889, and Buchanan, *Old Latin Biblical Texts*, Oxford (v.). 1 Jn. i. 8–iii. 20.

q. Ziegler, *Itala Fragmente*. Marburg, 1876. 1 Jn. iii. 8–v. 21.

m. *Liber de divinis Scripturis sive Speculum*, ed. Weihrich. Vienna Corpus xii., 1887. The following verses are quoted: 1 Jn. i. 2, 3, 8, 9, ii. 9, 10, 21, 23, iii. 7–10, 16–18, iv. 1, 9, 15, 18, v. 1, 6–8, 10, 20, 21; 2 Jn. 7, 10, 11.

Augustine's *Tractatus*. 1 Jn. i. 1–v. 12.

Egyptian Versions.

Sahidic.   Balestri, *Sacrorum Bibliorum Frag. Copto-Sahid. Mus. Borgiani*. Vol. iii. (continuation of Ciasca). 1904. 1 Jn. i. 2–v. 15; 2 Jn. 5–13; 3 Jn.

Woide, *Appendix ad editionem N.T. Graeci.* Oxford, 1799. 1 Jn. i. 1–v. 21 ; 2 Jn. ; 3 Jn.

Delaporte, *Revue Bibl. internat.* Nouvelle Serie ii., 1905. 1 Jn. i. 1–iii. 7, iii. 9–21, iii. 24–iv. 20. Gives by far the most interesting form of the Sahidic text.

Bohairic. Horner, *The Coptic Version of the N.T. in the Northern Dialect.* Vol. 4. Oxford, 1905.

Armenian Version.

Armenian Bible, ed. Zohrab. Venice.

These Epistles do not offer many problems of special difficulty or interest so far as the determination of the true text is concerned. A comparison of the texts published by Westcott and Hort with Nestle's text, shows how few instances there are in which serious doubt exists. The chief interest of the textual problems which they present lies in the history of the glosses which have been inserted into their text, and a few paraphrases which have been substituted for the true texts. The most famous of these glosses, the addition of the " Heavenly Witnesses," does not stand by itself. The tendency to gloss is most marked in Latin authorities, but it can be traced in the Egyptian and other versions, and cursive Greek manuscripts offer a few instances of its presence in Greek. An attempt has been made to collect the evidence for the Old Latin text of the Epistle in an Appendix. The critical notes which have been added to each verse are based on Tischendorf's eighth edition, supplemented where possible from later sources of information. For the Egyptian Versions (Bohairic and Sahidic), fresh collations have been made, and also for the Armenian. Tischendorf's information has been reproduced, as it stands in his edition, where it appears to be correct. Corrections and additions are given under the symbols **boh, sah, arm.** The heavier type should make it possible to see at a glance the extent to which Tischendorf's information has been supplemented or modified.

The attempt has also been made to extract from von Soden's *Die Schriften des Neuen Testaments,* 1. ii. C, the variants in the text of these Epistles which are to be found in Greek MSS, quoted by him, but which are not contained in Tischendorf's critical apparatus. The number of instances in which it has been necessary to add a note of interrogation may form some indication of the difficulty of using von Soden's book for this purpose. It is much to be hoped that the stores of interesting information as to the readings of Greek MSS, especially min-

uscules, which are contained in his great work, may be published
in some form which would render them available for general
use. In the citation of these readings von Soden's system of
notation has been reproduced, so that the new material is easily
distinguishable. At the end of each *group* of MSS quoted, the
number which the *first* MS in the group bears in Gregory's list
has been added in brackets. In the case of δ MSS (*i.e.* those
which contain the Gospels as well as the Acts and Catholic
Epistles, etc.), Gregory's Gospel number has been given. It may
be noticed that several of the readings of δ6 (Ψ) are of considerable interest. As the Latin text has been dealt with in an
appendix, no attempt has been made to revise Tischendorf's
presentation of its evidence.

It may be worth while to give some account of von Soden's
assignment of variants to his different groups.

For the *I–H–K* text he claims the following readings :

1 Jn. i. 4. ημεις (υμιν, C K a ϛ).

ii. 19. εξ ημων ησαν (ησαν εξ ημων).

iii. 2. om. δε (after οιδαμεν) (habet K L a ϛ).

iii. 14. om. τον αδελφον (after ο μη αγαπων) (habet
C K a ϛ).

iv. 12. τετελειωμενη εστιν εν ημιν (τετ. εν ημιν εστιν).

v. 10. εαυτω (αυτω).

v. 20. και οιδαμεν, A a (οιδαμεν δε : om. και).

2 Jn. 5. καινην γραφων σοι (γραφων σοι καινην).

The following cases he regards as uncertain :

1 Jn. ii. 10. εν αυτω ουκ εστιν (ουκ εστιν εν αυτω, W^{mg}).

iii. 23. εντολην] + ημιν (om. K L a ϛ).

2 Jn. 12. υμων (ημων, W^{mg}).
πεπληρωμενη η.

3 Jn. 9. εγραψα] + τι (om. τι, K L a ϛ : αν, 13 a).

H. Uncertain :

1 Jn. iii. 5. om. ημων after αμαρτιας (habet ημων, ℵ C a ϛ).

iii. 7. (?) παιδια, W^{mg} (τεκνια).

iii. 19. την καρδιαν (τας καρδιας).

2 Jn. 9. προαγων (παραβαινων).

"Sonderlesarten" :

1 Jn. ii. 18. om. ο before αντιχριστος (habet ο, A K L a ϛ).

I. Variants due to reminiscences of other passages :

1 Jn. i. 4. υμων, W^{mg} 1 (ημων). Cf. Jn. xv. 11.

---

1 *i.e.* the margin of Westcott and Hort's edition.

1 Jn. i. 5. ~αυτη εστιν. Cf. Jn. i. 19.
    επαγγελια (αγγελια). Cf. ii. 25.

  ii. 27. μενετω (μενει). Cf. ver. 24.

  ii. 28. εχωμεν (σχωμεν). Cf. iii. 21, iv. **17.**

  iii. 11. επαγγελια (αγγελια). Cf. ii. 25.

  iii. 15. αυτω, (εαυτω, W^mg). Cf. ver. 9.

  v. 20. αληθινον) + θεον. Cf. Jn. xvii. 3.
    η ζωη η. Cf. i. **2,** ii. 25 ; Jn. xiv. 6.

Doubtful cases of a similar kind :

1 Jn. i. 5. απαγγελλομεν (αναγγ-). Cf. ver. **2.**

  i. 8. ~εν υμιν ουκ εστιν. Cf. ver. 5.

  i. 9. αμαρτιας] + ημων. Cf. ver. 9, iii. **5.**

  ii. 12. υμων (υμιν). Cf. Mt. vi. 15.

  ii. 24. ~πατρι . . . υιω. Cf. ver. 22.

  iii. 10. δικαιοσυνην] pr. την. Cf. ver. **7** ; Mt. **v. 6,**
    vi. 1, 33.

  iii. 18. om. εν. Cf. context.

  iii. 23. τω υιω . . . Χω̄ (τω ονοματι του υιου . . . Χῡ)
    Cf. Jn. iii. 36, ix. 35.

  iv. 19. πρωτον (πρωτος).

  iv. 16. om. μενει (2°). Cf. iii. 24 ([μενει], W).

  iv. 19. αγαπωμεν) + τον θῡ. Cf. ver. 20.

  v. 6. ~αιματι . . . υδατι. Cf. Jn. xix. 34.

  v. 10. υιω (θεω). Cf. ver. 10^a.

3 Jn. 7. ονοματος] + αυτου. Cf. 1 Jn. ii. **12** ; Ro. i. **5.**
    παρα (απο). Cf. 2 Jn. 4.

Doubtful cases of other kinds :

1 Jn. i. 9. καθαρισει (-ση).

  ii. 6. om. ουτως.
    ~ουτως και αυτος.

  iv. 3. om. εκ.

  v. 16. ινα) + τις. Cf. Jn. ii. **25.**

  v. 21. εαυτους (εαυτα).

2 Jn. 3. υμων (ημων).
    απο (παρα).

"Sonderlesarten" :

1 Jn. i. 3. om. δε.

  ii. 8. ημιν (υμιν).

  ii. 26. πλανοντων.

  ii. 29. ιδητε (ειδητε).
    γεγενηται.

  iii. 17. θεωρει (-ρη).

1 Jn. iii. 19. πεισωμεν.
　　iv. 20. μισει (-ση).
2 Jn. 6. om. ινα, 2⁰.
　　11. om. αυτω.
　　12. ηβουληθην.
3 Jn. 4. ταυτης (τουτων).
　　8. γενωμεθα (γιν-).
　　9. εγραψα) + αν.
　　10. om. εκ.
　　11. ο, 2⁰) + δε.

K. Uncertain:
1 Jn. iii. 15. αυτω (εαυτω, Wᵐᵍ).
　　iii. 17. θεωρει (-ρη).
　　v. 20. γινωσκωμεν.
*K*ʳ. 1 Jn. iii. 1. om. και εσμεν.
　　iii. 18. om. εν.
　　iii. 19. πεισωμεν.
　　iv. 16. om. μενει (2⁰).
　　iv. 20. μισει.
　　v. 4. ημων.
　　v. 10. εαυτω.
　　v. 11. ∼ο θεος ημιν.
　　v. 20. γινωσκομεν.
　　v. 21. εαυτους.
3 Jn. 8. γενωμεθα.
　　10. om. εκ.
"Sonderlesarten" *K*ʳ :
1 Jn. ii. 24. ∼πατρι . . . υιω.
　　iii. 24. om. και (3⁰).
2 Jn. 5. εχομεν.
　　9. ο (2⁰)] + δε.
*K*ᶜ. 2 Jn. 8. απολεσητε . . . ειργασασθε . . . απολαβητε
(1 Jn. iii. 15. αυτω.
　　iii. 17. θεωρει. Cf. 1.)
1 Jn. iii. 10. δικαιοσυνην] for την.
　　iii. 18. om. εν.
　　iv. 16. om. μενει (2⁰).
K. "Sonderlesarten" :
1 Jn. i. 3. om. και (2⁰).
　　i. 7. Iῡ] + Xῡ.
　　ii. 4. om. οτι.
　　ii. 7. αδελφοι (αγαπητοι).
　　　　ηκουσατε) + απ αρχης.

f

1 Jn. ii. 13. γραφω (εγραψα).
     ii. 24. υμεις) + ουν.
     ii. 27. εν υμιν μενει.
          αυτο (αυτου).
          μενειτε (μενετε).
     ii. 28. οταν (εαν).
     ii. 29. om. και (W^{mg}).
     iii. 1. υμας (ημας).
     iii. 13. om. και.
          αδελφοι) + μου.
     iii. 16. τιθεναι (θειναι).
     iii. 18. τεκνια] + μοι.
     iii. 19. γινωσκομεν (γνωσομεθα).
     iii. 21. καρδια] + ημων.
     iii. 22. παρ (απ).
     iv. 3. om. τον.
          Ιησουν] + Χν.
              + Χν εν σαρκι εληλυθοτα.
     iv. 19. αγαπωμεν) + αυτον.
     iv. 20. πως (ου).
     v. 2. τηρωμεν (ποιωμεν).
     v. 4. υμων.
     v. 5. om. δε.
     v. 6. om. και πνευματος.
     v. 9. ην (οτι).
     v. 13. ~αιωνιον εχετε.
          εχετε) + και ινα πιστευητε.
          ~τοις πιστευουσιν—θεου ante ινα
     v. 15. παρ (απ).
2 Jn. 3. Ιησου] pr. κ̄ν̄.
     6. ~εστιν η εντολη.
     7. εισηλθον (εξηλθον).
     9. διδαχη (2°)] + του Χ̄ῡ.
     12. ελθειν (γενεσθαι).
3 Jn. 4. om. τη.
     7. εθνων (εθνικων).
     8. απολαμβανειν (υπ-).
     12. οιδατε (οιδας).
     13. γραφειν (γραψαι).
          om. σοι.
          γραψαι (γραφειν).

"Sonderlesarten" of unknown origin :

　1 Jn. ii. 23. εχει ⌢ εχει (*i.e.* om. ο 2°—εχει 2°).
　　　iii.　1. om. και εσμεν.
　　2 Jn.　6. om. ινα (1°).
　1 Jn. iv.　2. γινωσκεται.
　　2 Jn. 11. ο γαρ λεγων.
　　2 Jn.　8. απολεσωμεν . . . ειργασαμεθα . . . απολαβωμεν.
　　3 Jn.　5. εις τους (τουτο).

Where it seemed necessary for the sake of clearness, the other
variant or variants have been added in brackets.　The readings
adopted by Westcott and Hort and by Nestle have been
underlined.　If the agreement of these two authorities may be
taken as affording a rough standard of what is probably the true
text, it will be seen at once that the variants which von Soden
claims for the I–H–K text, if we neglect differences in the order
of words, are with one exception (και οιδαμεν for οιδαμεν δε)
those which have been accepted as part of the true text by the
best critics.　The same is, however, true of most of the small
class of readings which he attributes, mostly with some expression
of doubt, to the "H" text.　Indeed, by the test of intrinsic
probability, these readings stand as high as those claimed for
the I–H–K text.　It is difficult to believe, for instance, that
προάγων (2 Jn. 9) is not the true text, softened down by later
influences to παραβαίνων.　It is also difficult to suppose that the
occurrence of the word in Mk. x. 32 (Jesus "going before" His
disciples on the way to Jerusalem) had any influence on the
Johannine text here.　But von Soden's treatment of the "H"
text may perhaps throw valuable light on the readings where the
other authorities for the "H" text part company with δ1–2 (B ℵ),
a subject which needs further investigation.　It is also interesting
to notice how seldom the readings assigned to "I" or "K"
have been accepted as original.　The inclusion of the *omission*
of και πνευματος (1 Jn. v. 6) among the "Sonderlesarten" of K is
interesting.　Does this imply that the true text of the passage
ran ο ελθων δι υδατος και αιματος και πνευματος, and that the words
και πνευματος were removed in the "K" recension because of the
absence of corresponding words in the second half of the verse?
On the whole, it would seem that we must wait for the publication of von Soden's Greek text before we can make much use
of the information contained in his section on the text of the
Catholic Epistles, except in so far as it supplies us with information about new readings not known before, or at least not
recorded in the *apparatus criticus* of the ordinary editions.

　　It may, however, be worth while to append a list of the MSS
which he assigns to his three Recensions, and which have been

fully examined for the purposes of his great work. The symbols used by Tischendorf and Gregory are given below the von Soden numbers.

1. H Recension.

$\delta 1$ $\delta 2$ $\delta 3$ $\delta 4$ $\delta 6$ $\delta 48$ -257[1] 3 74   103 162
B $\aleph$ C A Ψ 33 (13AK) 33   P 389 25   61.

2. I Recension.

I^{a}. 70 -101 7 -264 200–382 $\delta 505$ 252
    505 40   Apl. 261   233   83   231   69 (31AK)   391

   $-\delta 459$ $\delta 203$ $-\delta 300$ -552
    489 (195AK)   808 (265AK)   218 (65AK)   217

   $\delta 454$ 170 175 192 502 397 -205 -106
    794 (262AK) 303 319 318 116 96   51   179

   -164 -261 184 158 $\delta 157$ $-\delta 507$
    —   142 —   395 547 (202AK) 241 (104AK)

   56   64   65   1100 -55 $\delta 254$ (? a254) -110
   316 328 317 310 236   26   332

   $-\delta 457$ $-\delta 500$ $\delta 156$ 256 361
    209 (95AK)   205 (93AK)   226 (108AK)   24   248

   113 110
   235 332.

I^{b}. (a) 62   365 396 472 398 $\delta 206$ 253
       498 214 —   312 69   242 (105AK) 2.

    (β) 78 -157 469 $\delta 370$
       —   29   215 1149 (288AK).

I^{c}. (a) 208 370 116 551
       307 353 —   216.

    (β) 364 -486 114 -174 506
       137 —   335 252 60.

3. K Recension.

   2   5   54   186 $\delta 255$ 394 500
   S   L   384 223 58 (35AK)   —   45.

K^{c}. 186 $\delta 255$
    223 57 (35AK).

K^{r}. (used for 1 Jn. v. only).
   358 462 $\delta 463$
   38   169 656 (213AK).

[1] In accordance with von Soden's usage, when a number is given without a preceding letter it belongs to the a group (Acts and Catholic Epistles, etc.).

§ 8. COMMENTARIES, ETC.

The following list of Commentaries, Articles, and Books has been compiled more especially with reference to what has been used in the preparation of this edition. The fullest bibliographies are to be found in Holtzmann (*Hand-Kommentar*) and Luthardt (*Strack-Zöckler*).

Ancient Greek—
  Clement of Alexandria, only extant in Cassiodorus' Latin Summary of the Adumbrationes on Jn. i. ii. (Clement, *al.*, ed. Stählin, iii. p. 209, 1909).
  Oecumenius.
  Theophylact.
  Catena, ed. Cramer.

Latin—
  Augustine, *Tractatus x. in Epistolam Ioannis ad Parthos* (Migne, iii. 1. P.L. 34).
  Bede.

Modern—
  Wettstein.
  Bengel.
  Lücke, 1820–1856.
    Translation, *Commentary on the Epp. of S. John.* Thomas Clark, 1837.
  Huther (in Meyer, 1855–1880).
    Translation, *Critical and Exegetical Handbook to the General Epp. of James and 1 John.* T. & T. Clark, 1882.
  F. D. Maurice, *The Epistles of S. John.* Macmillan & Co., 1857.
  Ebrard, "Die Briefe Johannis," Königsberg, 1859 in (*Olshausen's Biblischer Commentar*).
  Ewald, *Die Johanneischen Schriften.* Göttingen, 1861.
  Haupt, *1 John.* 1869.
    Translation, *The First Epistle of S. John.* (Clark's Foreign Theological Library, 1879.)
  Rothe, *Der Erste Johannis Brief praktisch erklärt.* 1878. A most valuable Commentary.
  Westcott, *The Epistles of S. John.* Macmillan, 1883–1892.
  Plummer (*Cambridge Greek Testament for Schools and Colleges*). 1884–1886.
    Pulpit Commentary. 1889.
  Lias (*Cambridge Bible for Schools*). 1887.
  B. Weiss (Meyer. 6th edition, 1899). In the preparation of the notes of the present book the 5th edition (1888) was used.
  Luthardt (*Strack-Zöckler Kurzgef. Kommentar*, iv.). 1895.

Poggel, *II, III John.* 1896.
W. Karl, *Johanneische Studien,* i., *der 1ᵉʳ Johannesbrief.*
   1898.
Belser. 1906.
Baumgarten (J. Weiss, *Die Schriften des NT.* ii. 3, pp.
   315–352). 1907.
Holtzmann (*Hand-Commentar zum NT.* iv.). 1908
   ("besorgt von W. Bauer").
D. Smith (*Expositor's Greek Testament,* v.). 1910.
Windisch (*Lietzmann's Handbuch zum NT.* iv. 2). 1911.

Monographs and Articles:
   Hilgenfeld, *Das Evangelium und die Briefe Johannis*
      nach ihrem Lehrbegriff dargestellt. 1849.
   Holtzmann, *Das Problem des 1 Johannesbr. in seinem*
      Verhältniss zum Evang. Jahrbuch für Protestant.
      Theologie. 1881, 1882.
   Häring (Theodor), "Gedankengang u. Grundgedanke des
      1 Joh." (*Theolog. Abhandlungen Carl von Weizsäcker*
      gewidmet). Freiburg in B. 1882.
   Harnack, *Ueber den III Joh. Texte u. Untersuchungen,* xv.
      3, 1897.
   Stevens, *The Johannine Theology.* New York, 1894.
   Wilamowitz, *Hermes,* 1898, p. 531 ff.
   Weisinger, *Studien u. Kritiken,* 1899, p. 575 ff.
   J. R. Harris, *Expositor,* 1901, p. 194 ff.
   Wohlenberg, *Neue Kirchliche Zeitschrift.* 1902.
   Gibbins, *Expositor,* 1902, p. 228 ff.
   Wurm, *Die Irrlehrer im 1ᵗᵉⁿ Johannes Brief.* 1903.
   Chapman, *Journal of Theological Studies,* 1904, pp. 357 ff.,
      517 ff.
   Bartlet, *JTS,* 1905, p. 204 ff. (in answer to Chapman).
   Clemen, *Zeitschrift für NT. Wissenschaft* (Preuschen),
      1905, p. 278.
   Salmond, article in Hastings' *Bible Dictionary.*
   P. W. Schmiedel, articles in *Encyclopædia Biblica,* also
      Religionsgeschichtliche Volksbücher: Das 4 Evangelium
      gegenüber den 3 ersten. Evangelium, Briefe, u.
      Offenbarung des Joh. nach ihrer Entstehung u. Bedeu-
      tung. 1906.
   Expositor, June 1907. Correspondence between Drs.
      Westcott and Hort. The Divisions of the First
      Ep. of S. John.
   Law, *Tests of Life* (Lectures on 1 Jn.). T. & T. Clark,
      1909.
   Findlay, *Fellowship in the Life Eternal.* Hodder, 1909.

General :
Wellhausen, *Erweiterungen u. Anderungen im 4ten Evangelium.*
Spitta, *Das 4 Evangelium.* 1910.
Pfleiderer, *Das Urchristentum.* Berlin, 1902.
Translation. *Primitive Christianity.* Montgomery, London, 1906.
Knopf, *Nachapostolische Zeitalter*, p. 328 ff., 1905.
Zahn, *Einleitung in das NT.* First edition, 1897.
Translation (from the 2nd edition), 1909 : T. & T. Clark.
Jülicher, *Einleitung.*
Translation. *An Introduction to the New Testament.*
J. P. Ward. London, 1904.

§ 9. The Second and Third Epistles. Authorship.

The Second and Third Epistles of S. John naturally form a pair. They are almost exactly of the same length. Their length is probably determined by the size of an ordinary papyrus sheet (Zahn, *Einl.* ii. 581. Rendel Harris).

It is hardly necessary to discuss the question of their common authorship. The similarity between them is too close to admit of any explanation except common authorship or conscious imitation. It would tax the ingenuity of the most skilful separator to determine which is the original and which the copy. They probably do not deal with the same situation, though many writers have found a reference to the Second Epistle in the Third (ἔγραψά τι τῇ ἐκκλησίᾳ). But the similarity of their style and the parallelism of their structure point clearly, not only to common authorship, but to nearness of date.

The following phrases show the close similarity of their general structure :

B′	Γ′
ὁ πρεσβύτερος.	ὁ πρεσβύτερος.
οὓς ἐγὼ ἀγαπῶ ἐν ἀληθείᾳ.	ὃν ἐγὼ ἀγαπῶ ἐν ἀληθείᾳ.
ἐχάρην λίαν ὅτι εὕρηκα ἐκ τῶν τέκνων σου περιπατοῦντας ἐν ἀληθείᾳ.	ἐχάρην γὰρ λίαν . . . μαρτυρούντων σου τῇ ἀληθείᾳ καθὼς σὺ ἐν ἀληθείᾳ περιπατεῖς.
	ἵνα ἀκούω τὰ ἐμὰ τέκνα ἐν τῇ ἀληθείᾳ περιπατοῦντα.
πολλὰ ἔχων ὑμῖν γράφειν.	πολλὰ εἶχον γράψαι σοι.
οὐκ ἐβουλήθην διὰ χάρτου καὶ μέλανος.	ἀλλ᾽ οὐ θέλω διὰ μέλανος καὶ καλάμου σοι γράφειν.
ἀλλὰ ἐλπίζω γενέσθαι πρὸς ὑμᾶς.	ἐλπίζω δὲ εὐθέως σε ἰδεῖν.
καὶ στόμα πρὸς στόμα λαλῆσαι.	καὶ στόμα πρὸς στόμα λαλήσομεν.
ἀσπάζεταί σε τὰ τέκνα τῆς ἀδελφῆς σου.	ἀσπάζονταί σε οἱ φίλοι.

It may be a question how much of this should be referred to epistolary convention, and how much should be regarded as the *sondergut* of the writer. But the close resemblance, coupled with complete independence in the parts where circumstances and subject-matter naturally lead to diversity, can hardly be explained on any other theory except that the two letters are by the same hand.

A more serious question is raised when the two letters are compared with the First Epistle. Here there is a certain amount of evidence, both external and internal, which is not conclusive of difference of authorship, but at least needs serious consideration.

They have many phrases which recall, or are identical with, those of the First Epistle. We may notice the following:

μένων ἐν τῇ διδαχῇ, 2 Jn. 9.	ὁ μένων ἐν τῇ ἀγάπῃ, 1 Jn. iv. 16.
τὴν ἀλήθειαν τὴν μένουσαν ἐν ἡμῖν, 2 Jn. 2.	ὁ λογὸς τοῦ θεοῦ ἐν ὑμῖν μένει, 1 Jn. ii. 14.
περιπατοῦντας ἐν ἀληθείᾳ, 2 Jn. 4 ; cf. 3 Jn. 3.	ἐν τῷ φωτὶ περιπατῶμεν, 1 Jn. i. 7.
περιπατῶμεν κατὰ τὰς ἐντολάς, 2 Jn. 6.	
ὁ κακοποιῶν οὐχ ἑώρακεν τὸν θεόν, 3 Jn. 11.	καθὼς ἐκεῖνος περιεπάτησεν 1 Jn. ii. 6.
	τὸν θεὸν ὃν οὐχ ἑώρακεν, 1 Jn. iv. 20.
	πᾶς ὁ ἁμαρτάνων οὐχ ἑώρακεν αὐτόν, 1 Jn. iii. 6.
ὁ ἀγαθοποιῶν ἐκ τοῦ θεοῦ ἐστίν.	ἐκ τοῦ θεοῦ ἐστέ, 1 Jn. iv. 4.
ἡ μαρτυρία ἡμῶν ἀληθής ἐστιν, 3 Jn. 12 (cf. Jn. xxi. 24).	ἀληθές ἐστιν καὶ οὐκ ἔστιν ψεῦδος, 1 Jn. ii. 27.
ἀλήθεια thrice in each Epistle.	once in 1 Jn.
ἡ ἀλήθεια twice in 2 Jn., thrice (four times) in 3 Jn.	eight times in 1 Jn.
οὗτος καὶ τὸν πατέρα καὶ τὸν υἱὸν ἔχει, 2 Jn. 9.	πᾶς ὁ ἀρνούμενος τὸν υἱὸν οὐδὲ τὸν πατέρα ἔχει.
θεὸν οὐκ ἔχει, 2 Jn. 9.	ὁ ὁμολογῶν τὸν υἱὸν καὶ τὸν πατέρα ἔχει, 1 Jn. ii. 23.
(ἐντολὴν) ἣν εἴχομεν ἀπ' ἀρχῆς, 2 Jn. 5.	ἐντολὴν παλαιὰν ἣν εἴχετε ἀπ' ἀρχῆς, 1 Jn. ii. 7.
καθὼς ἠκούσατε ἀπ' ἀρχῆς, 2 Jn. 6.	ἣν ἠκούσατε ἀπ' ἀρχῆς, 1 Jn. iii. 11.
οἱ μὴ ὁμολογοῦντες Ἰησοῦν Χριστὸν ἐρχόμενον ἐν σαρκί.	ὃ ὁμολογεῖ Ἰησοῦν Χριστὸν ἐν σαρκὶ ἐληλυθότα, 1 Jn. iv. 2.
οὗτός ἐστιν . . . ὁ ἀντίχριστος, 2 Jn. 7.	οὗτός ἐστιν ὁ ἀντίχριστος, ὁ ἀρνούμενος τὸν πατέρα καὶ τὸν υἱόν, 1 Jn. ii. 22.
ἡ μαρτυρία ἡμῶν ἀληθής ἐστι, 3 Jn. 12.	εἰ τὴν μαρτυρίαν τῶν ἀνθρώπων λαμβάνομεν, 1 Jn. v. 9.
οὐχ ὡς ἐντολὴν γράφων σοι καινήν, 2 Jn. 5.	οὐκ ἐντολὴν καινὴν γράφω ὑμῖν, 1 Jn. ii. 7.
ἐλπίζω γενέσθαι πρὸς ὑμᾶς . . . ἵνα ἡ χαρὰ ἡμῶν πεπληρωμένη ᾖ, 2 Jn. 12.	ταῦτα γράφομεν ἡμεῖς ἵνα ἡ χαρὰ ἡμῶν ᾖ πεπληρωμένη, 1 Jn. i. 4.
αὕτη ἐστὶν ἡ ἀγάπη, ἵνα περιπατῶμεν . . . 2 Jn. 6.	αὕτη ἐστὶν ἡ ἐντολὴ αὐτοῦ ἵνα πιστεύωμεν, 1 Jn. iii. 23.
οὔτε ἐπιδέχεται . . . καὶ κωλύει, 3 Jn. 10.	Cf. οὔτε . . . ἔχεις καὶ . . . ἐστιν, Jn. iv. 11.

We may also notice the thoroughly Johannine method of emphasizing an idea by parallel clauses, one positive and the other negative. Cf. 2 Jn. 9 ; 3 Jn. 11.

A careful comparison of these instances of words, phrases, and constructions which are common to the two smaller Epistles and the larger Epistle establishes beyond the possibility of doubt the intimate connection between the two.   A knowledge of the First Epistle, or of its contents, seems almost necessarily presupposed in some passages of the smaller Epistles.   Cf. especially 2 Jn. 9, 3 Jn. 11.   2 Jn. 12 need not contain an actual reference to 1 Jn. i. 4, but it gains in point if it is written in view of what is said there about the "fulfilment of joy."   In the one case it is the written, in the other the spoken, word that is lacking to assure the fulness of joy which comes of fellowship.   And it is interesting to notice the similarity of the results obtained by a comparison of 2 and 3 John with 1 John to those which appear when we compare the Gospel and the First Epistle.   The connection is indisputable.   We are compelled to choose between common authorship and conscious imitation.   And the freedom with which the same and similar tools are handled points clearly to the former as the more probable alternative.

The internal evidence of different authorship on which Pfleiderer depends is not conclusive.   He notices (1) the anonymous and general character of the First Epistle, as compared with the address of the Second to a particular Church, and the Third to an individual, named Caius, and the use of the title "The Presbyter" by the author in both.   (2) The common identification of this "Presbyter" with John the Presbyter is supported by no valid reasons.   There must have been many other "Presbyters," and those addressed would know who was meant, though it was not the famous "Presbyter" of Papias. We really know nothing of Papias' Presbyter except that he "handed down" a Chiliastic saying attributed to the Lord. Such an one was not likely to have busied himself with Gnostic theology and anti-Gnostic polemic.   In his case the term "Elder" is used in the natural sense of the term; in these Epistles it is a title of office, used by one who claims respect for his official position, who dictates to the faithful as to the company they are to keep, gives letters of commendation to wandering preachers, and is offended at their being neglected. (3) The anti-Gnostic polemic of 2 John is the same as that of Polycarp, *ad Phil.* vii. 1, pure docetism, as found in Ignatius, and not the milder and later separation between Jesus and Christ.

Of these reasons some are pure assumptions, and others are fully accounted for by the (possible) differences of circumstance. There is nothing in the Epistles which necessitates an official use of the term "Elder," though one who is aged may be in a position to speak and act with authority.   The authority which

the author claims is far greater than ever attached to the office
of "Presbyter."

The question of whether "pure Docetism" is earlier than
"dualistic separation" of the kind attributed to Cerinthus is an
open one. But where is the justification for differentiating
between the Second and the First Epistles in this respect? The
language of the Second is hardly intelligible without reference to
the First. It may certainly be interpreted in the same sense.

The reasons brought forward by Jülicher (*Einleitung*, p. 218)
are not more convincing. The expressions ἐχάρην λίαν, βλέπετε
ἑαυτούς (cf. 1 Jn. v. 21, φυλάξατε ἑαυτά), μισθὸν πλήρη ἀπολαμβάνειν, συνεργοὶ γινώμεθα, ἀγαθοποιεῖν, do not prove much. The
use of the singular only of Antichrist is equally unconvincing,
especially in view of 1 Jn. ii. 22. The difference between ἐληλυθότα and ἐρχόμενον is at least less striking than the resemblance of
the rest of the passages. The apparent contradiction between
3 Jn. 11, ὁ κακοποιῶν οὐχ ἑώρακεν τὸν θεόν, and Jn. i. 18, 1 Jn.
iv. 12, could easily be paralleled by similar "contradictions" in
the Gospel (cf. also Jn. xiv. 9).

Both writers also lay stress on the external evidence. That
the two smaller Epistles found their way into the Canon apart
from the First is partly true. There is, however, considerable
evidence for the acceptance of *two* Johannine Epistles, *i.e.* 1, 2 Jn.,
before the three were generally recognized. And the private
character of the smaller Epistles, as well as their relative un-
importance, are quite enough to account for their more gradual
acceptance, even if they were written by the author of the First.
Pfleiderer's statement, that the Second and Third Epistles are
described in the Muratorian Fragment as written in John's
name to do honour to him, rests on a very doubtful interpretation
of the passage in which two Johannine Epistles, almost certainly
the First and Second, are mentioned, after which comes the
sentence dealing with the Wisdom of Solomon.

Schwartz[1] regards the two Epistles as, "in contrast to the First,
genuine letters of a real Elder," whose name, however, cannot have
been John, or it would not have been necessary "to cut away his
real name, in order to bring these interesting documents into the
Canon." This is an excellent reason for supposing that the name
John never stood in these Epistles. It does not help us to
determine the probability or improbability of the view that the
letters were written by one John, who described himself as "the
Elder" without adding his name.

The impossibility of a Chiliast such as Papias' "John the
Elder" having any part in the composition of the Johannine
literature is emphasized by many writers, especially by Pfleiderer

[1] *Ueber den Tod der Söhne Zebedai*, p. 47.

and Réville ("ce presbytre Jean en qui le millénaire Papias
saluait un de ses maîtres," *Le Quatrième Évangile*, p. 50). All we
know of him, if in this case we may trust Irenaeus more than
many writers are usually willing to do, is that Papias recorded
on his authority the famous Chiliastic saying about the fruitfulness of the Messianic kingdom.   In what sense he interpreted
it we do not know.   If the Presbyter to whom Papias owes his
account of S. Mark is the same, as would seem most probable,
he was certainly capable of sound judgment and careful appreciation.   And one phrase which occurs in the Third Epistle recalls,
or is recalled by, the words of Papias' preface (ἀπ᾽ αὐτῆς τῆς ἀληθείας).   It is somewhat hasty to assume that the "Presbyter
venerated by the Chiliastic and stupid Papias" (Réville, p. 316)
was incapable of anything "spiritual."   He handed down a
'Chiliastic" saying, or one which was perhaps too grossly
'Chiliastic" in its literal meaning to have been taken literally,
even by the Elder who handed it down.   His views were
probably Millenarian.   It would be difficult to find any one
"venerated" at the end of the first or beginning of the second
century who did not in some sense share the ordinary Chiliastic
expectation of most Christians.   But as to how "gross," or how
"stupid," his views were we really know nothing.   Even Papias
may have been better than Eusebius thought him.   In any case
we have but slender evidence to justify the transference of all his
"stupidities" to the Elder John whose traditions he has preserved.
The position of authority, not claimed so much as used and acted
upon, by the author of these two Epistles, is such as perhaps
could only belong to a representative of the older generation.
Whether it would be natural for John the Apostle to describe
himself as "the Elder" is at least open to question.   There can be
no doubt of the naturalness of the title if used by such an one as
John the Elder, the disciple of the Lord.

We have every reason to believe that an "Elder" held a
predominant position in Asia Minor about the close of the first
century.   There are valid reasons for calling him John.   His
relation to John the son of Zebedee is a mystery which, at present
at least, we have not enough evidence to enable us to solve.
Harnack's conjecture, based on the most natural interpretation
of the fragment of Papias' preface which Eusebius has preserved,
that he was a pupil of John the Apostle, and in some sense a
disciple of the Lord, is perhaps the hypothesis which leaves
fewest difficulties unsolved.   That he is the author of the two
smaller Epistles is the view which seems to be best supported by
external tradition and by internal probability.   The arguments in
favour of different authorship for Gospel, First Epistle, and the
two shorter Epistles are not negligible, but they are not con-

clusive. The theory which attributes to him some share at least
in the *writing* of Gospel and First Epistle is the most probable
conjecture that we can at present make. To what extent he is
answerable for the matter of either is a difficult problem, perhaps
insoluble in the present state of our knowledge. Most of the
difficulties which every historical inquirer must feel to stand in
the way of attributing the Gospel (in its present form) and the
Epistle (they are less in this case than in that of the Gospel) to
the son of Zebedee are modified, though they are not removed, by
the hypothesis that a disciple is responsible for the final redaction
of his master's teaching. The longer and the more carefully the
Johannine literature is studied, the more clearly one point seems
to stand out. The most obviously "genuine" of the writings are
the two shorter Epistles, and they are the least original. To
believe that an author, or authors, capable of producing the
Gospel, or even the First Epistle, modelled their style and
teaching on the two smaller Epistles, is a strain upon credulity
which is *almost* past bearing. Are we not moving along lines of
greater probability if we venture to suppose that a leader who
had spent his life in teaching the contents of the Gospel, at last
wrote it down that those whom he had taught, and others, "might
believe, and believing might have life in His name"; that after
some years he felt that the message of the Gospel had not produced the effect on their lives and creed which he had expected,
and that he therefore made the appeal of the First Epistle, ὃ
ἠκούσατε ἀπʼ ἀρχῆς μενέτω, bidding them make use of what they
already knew, and assuring them that in it they would find the
help they needed to face the circumstances in which they now
found themselves placed? The differences between the two
writings may well be due to the needs of a simpler and more
popular appeal. It is the circumstances of the hearers and their
capacity to understand which determine his message, rather
than any very clear change in his own position or opinions. At
the same time or at a later period he may have had to deal with
the special circumstances of a particular Church or particular
individuals, and again the special circumstances of his hearers
and their intellectual and spiritual capacity have determined the
form and the substance of his appeal. The term "Catholic" is
a misleading one. It has perhaps misled the critical even more
than the conservative interpreters of these Epistles. It is
impossible to understand these letters if they are regarded as
having been originally composed as a message to the whole
Church, or for all time. The writer knows those whom he
addresses. He writes with full knowledge of their immediate
circumstances and of their spiritual powers. If we are to
interpret his words, we must consider, not so much what he could

have said himself, as the circumstances which tied him down to saying that which his readers could understand. It is possible that advancing years may have modified his views, and even weakened his powers. But the special circumstances which called for his intervention, and perhaps the νωθρότης of his hearers, offer a far more probable explanation of the difference which we cannot but feel between the spiritual heights of the Gospel and the common-place advice of the shorter Epistles. He who proclaimed ὁ λόγος σάρξ ἐγένετο may still have believed it, though he finds himself compelled to write μὴ μιμοῦ τὸ κακὸν ἀλλὰ τὸ ἀγαθόν, and to make appeals to his personal authority in the case of those to whom his deeper thoughts were as a sealed book.

§ 10. THE SECOND EPISTLE.

The chief object of this letter is to give the Church or the family to whom it is addressed, clear advice and instruction about the reception of Christians from other Churches. The duty of hospitality was recognized and enforced. We may compare He. xiii. 2.

It was a necessary part of the duty of each Church, or of some leading members in it, during the whole of the period when the union of the various members of the Christian body was being secured by the work of "Apostles, Prophets, Evangelists, Teachers," who went about from place to place, while the resident officers were expected to submit to the authority of the higher *rank*. In the opinion of the Elder, who clearly claims to exert his authority over all the Churches in the sphere in which he lives, there was danger of the abuse of hospitality. False teachers are taking advantage of the opportunity to disseminate their errors. So he lays down the two practical tests which may form guiding principles in offering hospitality to strangers. They are the same points which are insisted upon in the First Epistle. Those who carry out the Gospel in their lives, who "walk in love," and who recognize fully the reality and the permanence of the Incarnation, who "confess Jesus Christ coming in the flesh," are to be received. The Progressives who do not abide in the "teaching of the Christ" must be refused. Even to give them greeting is to participate in their evil works. Incidentally the Elder takes the occasion thus offered to encourage those who are faithful, who are "walking in truth," and to urge on them once more the duty of "walking in love" as well as of remaining true to the teaching which they had heard "from the beginning." He reserves what he has to say at greater length, till he has the opportunity of seeing and conversing with them, on the visit which he hopes soon to be able to pay them.

The situation recalls that of the Didache, where the same difficulty of how the "Prophets" are to be received is seriously felt and discussed at length. There the danger is rather of those who make a regular custom of demanding maintenance as Prophets who come in the name of the Lord, and so of living in idleness at the expense of others. In the Epistle the dissemination of false teaching is the chief danger to be guarded against. It would be rash to describe the situation found in the Didache as a later development than that which is suggested in this letter. At the same time the similarity of the circumstances does not necessitate the assignment of both writings to exactly the same date. Development was at different rates in different places. From what we know of the history of the Asiatic Churches, we might naturally expect stages to be reached there at an earlier date than in some other regions. The evidence, therefore, of this resemblance to the Didache should be used with caution in determining the date of the Epistle. In itself the parallel is clear and interesting. We may also compare the praise bestowed on the Smyrnaeans by Ignatius for their hospitable reception of Philo and Agathopus (Ign. *Sm.* 10), or Polycarp's thanks to the Philippians for their kindness to the prisoners (Pol. *ad Phil.* 1).

The well-known controversy about the destination of this Epistle shows no signs of a final settlement. The view that it was addressed to an individual lady and not to a Church has of late been most vigorously supported by Rendel Harris (*Expositor*, 1901). Advocates of this view have found her name either in Electa or in Kyria, which is not unknown as the name of a woman (cf. Lücke, p. 444).

The names of Mary and Martha have also been suggested, the former because of the incident recorded in Jn. xix. 27, the latter for a supposed play on the name (Martha-domina-Kyria). It is hardly necessary to discuss seriously these conjectures of Knauer and Volkmar. The name Electa is almost certainly excluded by ver. 13, and by the improbability of two sisters bearing the same name. If the letter is addressed to an individual, the name is clearly not given. The use of Κυρία is very wide. It may be a purely formal title of courtesy. It is certainly used frequently by near relations, whether as a token of affection, or mark of courtesy real or assumed. In spite of Rendel Harris' ingenious suggestions, the use of the word by relations, even if the Editors of Papyri are frequently right in translating it "My dear," does not go very far towards establishing the view that we have in this Epistle a "love-letter." The

formal use of κυρία is undoubtedly well established, and the
character of the Epistle can only be determined by more
general considerations.   If we examine the whole contents of
the letter we can hardly escape the conclusion that a Church
and not an individual is addressed.   The language of ver. 1,
"Whom I love in truth, and not I only, but all who know the
truth," is at least more natural if it is addressed to a community.
It is clear from ver. 4 that the writer can only praise the conduct
of some of the "children," while the address in ver. 1 is general,
"and her children."   If it is necessary to assume that the word
τέκνα has a narrower meaning in ver. 1 than in ver. 4, the difficulty,
such as it is, is about the same whether the reference is to a
single family or to a whole Church.   Jülicher's argument (*Einleitung*, p. 216) does not gain much by the inclusion of this
point.   We cannot say more than that the references to the
whole family in ver. 1, and to a part of it in ver. 4, are rather more
natural if the "family" be a Church.   On the other hand, the
change between singular and plural (4, 5, 13 as compared with
6, 8, 10, 12) certainly favours the view that a Church is addressed.   Interesting parallels of a similar change between
singular and plural have been noticed in the Book of Baruch.
And, as Jülicher truly says, the general contents of the letter are
"anything rather than private in character."

§ 11. THE THIRD EPISTLE.

The general outline of the circumstances which led to the
writing of this Epistle may be traced with some certainty,
though there are many details which cannot be so certainly
determined.

There can be no doubt that it is addressed to an individual,
and not to a Church: though nothing is known for certain
about the Caius to whom it is sent; and his identification with
any of the other bearers of that name who are mentioned in
the New Testament, or known to early tradition, is extremely
precarious.

The object of the letter is to claim the good services of
Caius on behalf of some travelling Missionaries who are about
to visit Caius' Church, and who are either members of the
Church over which the Elder presides, or have recently visited
it.   It would seem that the Missionaries had previously visited
the Church of Caius, and had been hospitably received by him.
On their return to (?) Ephesus they had borne public witness
at a meeting of the Church to the kindness which they had
received at his hands.   On the ground of this the Elder confidently appeals to Caius to repeat his former kindness, when

the occasion arrives, on their next visit to his Church. He claims on their behalf hospitality and help. They should be "sent forward" in a manner worthy of the Master whom they served. And they had a right to claim support, for they had maintained the Pauline custom in their work among heathen, of receiving nothing from those to whom they preached (cf. Ac. xx. 35 ; 1 Th. ii. 9 ; 2 Th. iii. 8). All Christians (ver. 8) were bound to support and help forward such work to the best of their power. To do so was to work for the Truth, or rather to make themselves fellow-workers with Truth itself.

The Elder had previously written to the Church of which Caius and Diotrephes were members. But Diotrephes, whose ambition was known to the Elder, and who had succeeded in gaining an ascendency over the Church, or at any rate over the majority of its influential members, had managed either to suppress the letter, or to persuade the Church to ignore its contents. He not only refused himself to receive those who came with the Elder's commendation, but made it his policy to try to drive out of the Church those who were anxious to take the opposite course, if he could not succeed in preventing their efforts by simpler methods (ver. 10). It was time for the Elder to intervene. He has to remind Caius and those who will listen to his admonitions that there are such things as right and wrong. Their choice will show whether they are Christians in anything more than name. To do the right is the sign of the birth from God, and of the enjoyment of the Vision of God.

It would seem that Diotrephes had found his opportunity in the suspicion in which Demetrius was held by the Church. He is clearly one who possessed the esteem of the Elder, and who had been recommended to Caius' Church by him. His relation to that Church and to the travelling Missionaries is not equally certain, and different views have been held on this point. Some have regarded him as one of the Missionaries, or as their leader, to whom the Elder had borne witness in a previous letter of commendation. Others have thought, from the separate mention of him and of the travellers, that he had nothing to do with them, but was a member of the Church to which the letter is addressed. Such a view is quite possible. Without accepting the over-ingenious conjecture of Dom Chapman, that the Elder had already mentally designated him Bishop of the Church, it is certainly natural to suppose, with Wilamowitz, that one of the main objects of the letter is to serve as a letter of com-mendation for Demetrius, and that he at least travelled with the Missionaries on the journey which forms the occasion of the Epistle, whether he was actually one of their company or not. It would, of course, be fairly easy to form a good many hypotheses which would all suit the few facts of the situation known to us. It is better to confine ourselves to the simplest and most natural. And that would seem to be that Demetrius was one of the band of Missionaries whom the Church of Caius and Diotrephes had special reasons to mistrust. It seems to need all the authority, official or personal, which the Elder possessed, and all his personal influence with a faithful friend, to ensure a hospitable reception for one who has, in his opinion unjustly, fallen under suspicion.

If it is idle to identify the recipient of the letter with any other Caius known to the New Testament, it is even less profitable to attempt the identification of Demetrius. Dom Chapman's suggestion, that he is the Demas of 2 Ti. iv. 10 (Δημᾶς γάρ με ἐγκατέλιπεν ἀγαπήσας τὸν νῦν αἰῶνα καὶ ἐπορεύθη εἰς Θεσσαλονίκην), has little in its favour save its necessity to complete a fabric of conjecture of which the ingenuity is far more apparent than its probability. Prof. Bartlet's suggestion, that Demetrius the silversmith (of Ac. xix. 24) is more likely, may be placed slightly higher in the scale of probability. But the game of guessing is misleading in attempts to reconstruct the unknown circumstances under which the Epistle was written. It is more reasonable to confine our attention to what may be legitimately deduced from the actual references of the Epistle.

A further question is raised by ver. 9. Are we to identify the letter to which reference is there made with the Second Epistle? In favour of this have been urged (1) the close connection of the two Epistles in tradition; (2) the probability that 2 Jn. is addressed to a Church; (3) the close connection between the two Epistles in thought and language. Of these arguments the first is of doubtful value. The connection is hardly so close as is often supposed, the evidence for a period of acceptance of two Johannine Epistles (i.e. 1, 2 Jn.) without the third is really considerable. The others deserve serious consideration, and in reference to (3) we must certainly remember that the object of both letters is to a large extent the same, the determination of the rules which should guide Churches in the matter of receiving and offering hospitality to travelling Teachers. In some ways the negative rules of 2 Jn. form a natural supplement to the more positive suggestions of the Third Epistle. But, on the other hand, serious difficulties are raised by (1) the absence of any mention in 3 Jn. of the False Teachers, and (2) the absence in 2 Jn. of any reference to Diotrephes, or to the high-handed proceedings of an official or prominent member of the Church. Of these reasons, which are urged by Harnack, the first is the most important. The high-handed action of any prominent member might naturally succeed rather than precede the

g

reception of the letter which contained the Elder's instructions.
He also urges that 2 Jn. presupposes an altogether different
state of feeling and opinion in the Church to which it is
addressed as compared with what we may naturally conclude
from the Third Epistle.   The attitude of the two Churches to
strangers is quite different.   Perhaps a more convincing reason
is found in the fact that the Second Epistle does not contain
the matter which we should expect to find in the "suppressed"
letter to which the Elder refers in 3 Jn.   It must have dealt
with the question (or questions) of the reception of Demetrius
and the travelling Missionaries; at least it is natural to suppose
that 3 Jn. is written to secure through the good services of a
private friend what the Elder had demanded in a more public
way.   It is, of course, possible that the reception of his requirements in 2 Jn. had been such that he now hesitated to make
public the different requests which he writes to Caius.   But the
former supposition is the more natural.   We should probably
therefore add this instance to the many indications in the
Epistles of the N.T. of a wider correspondence than has been
preserved in the Canon.

§ 12. HISTORICAL BACKGROUND OF THE TWO EPISTLES.

Within the last few years a number of ingenious, if highly
conjectural, reconstructions have been attempted of the circumstances which called out the two Epistles, with more or less complete identifications of the persons named, and of the Churches
addressed.   Detailed criticism of many points suggested by
these schemes is perhaps better reserved for the notes on the
text.   But some general account of one or two of them may be
attempted.

The most ingenious, and possibly the least convincing, is
that which Dom Chapman contributed in his articles in the
Journal of Theological Studies (1904, pp. 357 ff., 517 ff.).   Seeing
rightly that the language in which Demetrius is commended by
the Elder clearly implies that he had for some reason or other
fallen under suspicion, he puts forward the bold conjecture
that Demetrius is the Demas of 2 Ti. iv. 10 who forsook S.
Paul when danger became acute (contrast Col. iv. 14), "having
loved this present world."   Dom Chapman reminds us that the
Second Epistle to Timothy found him at Ephesus, and suggests
that the Asiatic Churches were inclined to take a harsh view of
the conduct of Demas.   In the recipient of this Epistle he sees
the Caius of Corinth, whose hospitality is praised in Ro. xvi. 23
("mine host and of the whole Church"); and following the early
tradition recorded by Origen (on Ro. x. 41), that this Caius

became the first Bishop of Thessalonica, he suggests that Demas, who was perhaps a Macedonian, when he left Rome had travelled to Thessalonica, which he may have left when the reception of 2 Timothy made his position there untenable. At a later date he wished to return, and when he presented himself with a commendatory letter from the Elder he was well received by Caius, but the "pratings" of Diotrephes persuaded the Church to refuse him hospitality. He now has to pass through Thessalonica on his way westwards, and bears a second letter from the Elder to secure a more friendly reception. It is perhaps sufficient here to suggest that imaginary reconstructions of this kind do very little to help forward the study of history. A series of propositions, none of which are in themselves either impossible or specially probable, when combined into a single hypothesis fail to form a satisfactory basis for exegesis. And the question naturally arises, have we sufficient ground for assuming that the Elder would claim such a position of authority in respect of the Churches of *Macedonia* as is implied in the words and threatened action of the Third Epistle?

His suggestions with regard to the Second Epistle are even more hazardous. The description of the Church as loved by *all* who know the truth, and as having heard the commandment *from the beginning*, is specially applicable to Antioch or Rome. The "elect sister" is naturally the Church of Ephesus. He connects ἐκλεκτός, a word foreign to the Johannine vocabulary, with the emphatic reference in 1 P. v. 13, ἡ ἐν Βαβυλῶνι συνεκλεκτή, and suggests that the phrase "walking in truth, as we received commandment for the faith," should be interpreted in the light of Jn. x. 17, 18, where the "Father's command" is connected with the laying down of life. The community to whom these words are addressed must have proved their faithfulness by martyrdom. So we are led to the conclusion that it is the Church of Rome which is addressed. The False Teachers have lost their footing in Asia Minor, the First Epistle has closed the doors of Asiatic Churches to them. So they are making attempts elsewhere, and the warning is issued to the Church of the metropolis. Such is the hypothesis in general outline. It is supported by many ingenious suggestions as to details. But the interpretation of ver. 4 in connection with Jn. x. 17 is too doubtful to serve as a foundation.

Professor Bartlet (*JTS*, 1905) has pointed out several of the difficulties presented by the text of the Epistles, if it is translated correctly, to these ingenious conjectures, while he rightly welcomes the correct appreciation of the significance of the terms in which Demetrius is commended. His suggestion that

Demetrius the silversmith may be meant, is at least as probable as Dom Chapman's conjecture. And his further suggestion that Thyatira is more probably the Church of Caius and Demetrius has at least the merit of looking in the right quarter, within the natural sphere of the Elder's influence and authority.

Dr. Rendel Harris has made no attempt at so complete a restoration of the background of these Epistles. The instances which he quotes of κυρία used in the correspondence of near relatives are interesting. He has hardly succeeded in *proving* that even in such cases it is used as a term of affection, rather than of courtesy, or (?) mock courtesy. And even if this point were proved, it would not go far towards proving that in this particular Epistle it is so used. Its official and ceremonious use is in any case far more frequent. By itself it hardly establishes the personal and affectionate character of the letter, or justifies the description of it as a "love-letter." The question of "lady" or "Church" must be determined by the general character of the letter. He has also noticed an interesting parallel to the language of 2 Jn. 8, in Ru. ii. 12, which should form a welcome addition to our Biblical marginal references, and to the many indications that the author of the Johannine Epistles was well acquainted with the Scriptures of the Old Testament. But it would be safer *not* to deduce from the occurrence of ἐργασία and μισθὸς πλήρης in one verse in Ruth the suggestion that the recipient of this letter was elderly, a heathen Christian, and probably a widow !

In this connection we should perhaps mention the conjecture of Thoma,[1] that Pergamos should be regarded as the Church with which the Second Epistle deals, on the ground, according to the *Apostolical Constitutions* (vii. 46), that Caius was ordained bishop of that Church by John. The list of "Bishops" mentioned in *Ap. Con.* vii. 46 is worth quoting : James the brother of the Lord, Symeon, ὁ τοῦ Κλεόπα, Jude the brother of James, Zacchaeus, Cornelius, Theophilus, Euodius, Ignatius, Annianus, Avilius, Linus, Clement, Timothy, John, "by me John," Ariston, Strataias, Ariston, Gaius (Mycenae), Demetrius (Philadelphia), Dionysius, Marathones (?), Archippus, Philemon, Onesimus, Crescens, Aquila, Nicetas, Crispus. It might perhaps afford interesting evidence as to the contents of the Canon. But its predominantly Biblical character hardly inspires confidence.

Of a very different character to these curiosities of exegesis

---

[1] Thoma, *Genesis des Johannes Evangeliums*, p. 791. Thoma does not lay much stress on the point, "Dies wäre Pergamus, wenn die Sage der apost. Constitutionen von dem dortigen Bisthum des Gaius einen Grund und Werth hat,"

is the important contribution of Harnack to the interpretation
of these Epistles (*Texte u. Untersuchungen*, xv. First Series).
Their chief importance lies in the information they afford with
regard to a certain stage of the development of Church life and
organization in the Asiatic province. The position of the Elder is
unique. He is widely known. It is unnecessary for him to add
his own name to the title which will serve to identify him. If
he lives in Ephesus, the members of other Churches are his
children (*3.* 4). He claims the right to lead them, and to know
no greater joy than to hear that they are walking in the paths
of truth. He claims his share in the work which has brought
the Churches to their present state (ἃ ἠργασάμεθα, *2.* 8). Assured
of being in the truth himself, he claims to judge whether others
are " walking " in it, and have witness borne to them by it (*3.* 2, 3 ;
2. 1–4 ; *3.* 12). He does not hesitate to place his own witness
by the side of the witness of the truth itself (*3.* 12). He uses
the plural of authority (*3.* 9, 10, 12 ; *2.* 8). As leader and
as judge he threatens in the confident assurance that his personal
intervention will put an end to what is wrong (*3.* 10). From a
distance he issues his commands to individuals and to Churches
alike. The sphere of his authority is apparently large. Within
it he administers praise or censure ; he assigns punishment or
reward without hesitation. He passes the most absolute judgments on prominent persons (*3.* 10, 12). He receives, through
members of other Churches who travel, or through Evangelists,
in full Church assembly (*3.* 6) or in other ways (*2.* 4), statements
about the teaching and behaviour of Churches and of leading
individuals (*3.* 3 ff., 12), and makes use of these reports in his
letters. We are reminded of S. Paul's dealings with his Churches,
and of his similar claims to authority and practical use of it.
We may be surprised that thirty years after the death of Paul
another should hold such a position in Asia. But this is no proof
that the work of Paul had fallen to pieces. The testimony of
Irenaeus and Polycarp proves the contrary. The position which
has been described might well be held by the " Elder " of whom
tradition knows, and whom Papias describes as a disciple of the
Lord. Such an one could maintain his claim to the position
of patriarchal monarchic authority which we find presupposed
in these Epistles.

Harnack next turns to the evidence of the relation of the
Elder to the travelling Missionaries and the Churches. The
Third Epistle is written to accredit some travelling Evangelists
to Caius ; the Second, to warn some Church or individual against
certain travelling false teachers. The custom to which these
facts point is neither new nor of very long standing (*3.* 7 ; cf.
2. 10, 11). The importance of such teachers is clearly seen if

we compare *3*. 8 with *2*. 11. The writer does not identify
himself with them, but he values them and their work highly
(*3*. 6, ἀξίως τοῦ θεοῦ). Their work is missionary, not among those
who are already brethren, from whom they ought to receive
support, as they obey the Lord's command. On their return to
the place whence they set out they appear before the assembly of
the Church and tell how they have prospered, and how they
have been received (*3*. 6). Thus the Elder uses them as a
means by which he can exercise control over his Churches.
But a reaction is making itself felt against this supervision.
Diotrephes regards the Elder and the travelling brethren as
forming one party. He tries, apparently with success, to set
his Church against them. He would withdraw it from this
supervision which the Elder claims to exercise. He will not
"receive" his messengers. And the majority of the Church
apparently lean to the side of Diotrephes, though the Elder
still has his friends (*3*. 15). The Elder cannot be sure that the
letter which he wrote will ever reach the Church. Yet he feels
sure of victory, if he comes in person. Here then we have to
notice the leading of a single man. We have reached the
beginnings of the monarchical Episcopate. We are in the heat
of the struggle of the old patriarchal provincial mission organization against the consolidation of the individual Churches,
as they threw off all outside influence and developed the
Episcopate. Diotrephes takes the lead in this movement.
The Elder mistrusts the new movement, and tries to keep it
under his control. He sees in it only the ambition of individuals. Yet he fights for a failing cause. He is obliged
to confess the dangers of false teaching being disseminated by
the travelling Missionaries. By addressing the Church as Κυρία
he practically recognizes its independence. Harnack's question,
"Would Paul have done so?" is suggestive.

Thus these two Epistles give us a valuable contribution to
the history of an obscure period. We get a glimpse into the
earlier stages of the development of the monarchical Episcopate.
The differences which we find in Ignatius fifteen or twenty years
later are noticeable. In his time monarchical Episcopacy is
established throughout Asia. Each Church is independent; it
receives from outside only brotherly advice. The danger arising
from heretical teachers who travel from place to place is still
felt acutely. But travelling "prophets and teachers" and
supervising "elders" have disappeared. The change which
these Epistles show us in the making is already made in this
region.

It seems almost impertinent to criticize this admirable summary of the position which forms the background of the two

Epistles.   Few would question the importance of its contribution
to the understanding of their contents.   It is, however, doubtful
whether it points to exactly the right moment in the development
of the organization of the Asiatic Churches.   And its weakest
part is the attitude which it represents the Elder as having
assumed with regard to the new movement.   It is clear that
the old system is breaking down.   The generation of those who
could claim and exercise the kind of authority, recognized and
accepted as valid but unofficial, which the " Elder " clearly
regards as his by right, and which he is confident he can still
maintain, is passing away.   Those who have a right to speak
and act in virtue of their connection with earlier days have
almost dissappeared.   And in his own case he can no longer
be sure of his authority, if it is exercised only from a distance.
The personal ambition of individual members of the Churches
is getting beyond his control.   In one case he cannot feel sure
that his letter will reach those for whom it was intended.   He is
doubtful as to the reception which will be given to those who
come with his own personal commendation.   He is evidently
afraid that false teaching, which he has succeeded in silencing
in his own Church, if we may use the evidence of the First
Epistle in this connection, will receive only too ready a welcome
in a neighbouring Church.   It is equally clear that an ambitious
member of a Church can count on a widespread feeling of dis-
content with the present informal arrangements and customs,
which he can utilize to further his own views and perhaps
interests.   But is this the struggle of the local Churches to free
themselves and set up a local Episcopate?   Or is the Episcopate
the means adopted to deal with the private ambitions of individual
members of Churches who have made themselves prominent,
and the danger which arose from the spread of various forms
of teaching, and of division and dissension in consequence?
And what was the attitude of the Elder to the new movement?
Is he struggling against it?   Or did he see in some such change
of organization a way of meeting the danger which the old system
could no longer control?   Will Caius or Diotrephes be the first
monarchical Bishop, of Pergamus or of Thyatira?

The passages which Harnack quotes to show the connection
of the Elder with the " Bishops " of Asia certainly do not point
to his having fought a losing battle against the new movement.
The tradition which these passages embody has doubtless been
modified in the light of later views about Episcopacy.   But
while this is almost certainly the case, it is going in the face of
such evidence as we possess to represent the Elder as opposed
to a movement with which he is always represented as being in
close connection.

The following passages may be quoted.   They prove quite
clearly the connection of the elders with the Episcopal movement in Asia so far as tradition is concerned.

> Mur. Fr. l. 10: "Cohortantibus condiscipulis et epis-
> copis suis."
>
> Victorinus Petau. *Schol. in Apoc.* xi. 1: "Conuenerunt ad
> illum de finitimis provinciis omnes episcopi."
>
> Jerome, *de Vir. Illus.* 9: "Scripsit euangelium, rogatus ab
> Asiae episcopis, aduersus Cerinthum."   Cf. Euseb. *H. E.*
> vi. 14 (Clement): προτραπέντα ὑπὸ τῶν γνωρίμων.
>
> Augustine, *Prologue to the Tractatus in Joann.* : "Compulsus
> ab Episcopis Asiae scripsit."
>
> Clem. Alex. *Quis Dives*, 42: ἀπῄει παρακαλούμενος καὶ ἐπὶ
> τὰ πλησιόχωρα τῶν ἐθνῶν, ὅπου μὲν ἐπισκόπους καταστήσων,
> ὅπου δὲ ὅλας ἐκκλησίας ἁρμόσων, ὅπου δὲ κλήρῳ ἕνα γέ τινα
> κληρώσων τῶν ὑπὸ τοῦ πνεύματος σημαινομένων.

Most of these passages are too late to give satisfactory
evidence; all of them except the last may be later paraphrases
of the προτραπέντα ὑπὸ τῶν γνωρίμων which is found in Clement,
but which he has received from tradition.   The passage from the
well-known story of the Robber which Clement tells in the *Quis
Dives* proves that at a comparatively early date the name of the
Elder was connected with the development of Church organization in Asia which resulted in the monarchical Episcopacy.   His
exact share in the process may not be determinable now.   But
the evidence of tradition which represents him as in thorough
sympathy with the movement is too strong to ignore, when it
is in no way contradicted by the evidence of the Johannine
Epistles in themselves.   The modification of Harnack's interpretation of the "background" which has been suggested above
is at least as natural as his, and it is in conformity with what may
be reasonably deduced from the earliest and most trustworthy
traditions about the Elder as they are to be found in Clement.
And on the whole it is better suited to the evidence of Ignatius,
and his attitude towards the monarchical Episcopate.

NOTES ON 1 JOHN.

— ⁑ —

1-4. Introduction.

1. ὁ ἦν ἀπ᾽ ἀρχῆς] What the writer has to announce about
the Word of Life, the revelation of life, is no new discovery.
The revelation began with creation. It was continued in the
history of the nations and the People, in the work of Prophets,
Psalmists, Legislators. It culminated in the earthly life and
teaching of Jesus of Nazareth. The mystery, which is as old
as creation, was gradually revealed, till it was completely manifested in Jesus the Christ, the Son of God. The words περὶ
τοῦ λόγου τῆς ζωῆς necessitate some such interpretation of the
phrase. It cannot refer to the eternal, pre-existent nature of
the personal Word, though in the writer's conception this is
no doubt included. The whole message of God's revelation,
as it has been gradually unfolded, is the object of the writer's
ἀγγελία. The mystery which he takes his part in "revealing"
is concerned with the eternal reality underlying the phenomena
apparent to sense-perception and needed to explain them. What
he has to say is one stage in its unveiling; his words are part of
a process of teaching which began when "God said, Let there
be light." Cf. Rothe, p. 18; part of his note may be quoted or
paraphrased. "The thought of an original being, which has its
object in itself, is indeed the most abstract thought to which
human consciousness can reach; but yet it lies close to hand,
and no one can dispense with it who examines attentively
himself and his surroundings. That which falls under the
cognizance of sense-perception shows itself to the careful observer
to be untrue. But every intelligent man must feel the desire to
find somewhere an existence which has not come into being,
but which *is* from eternity, and to be able to rest on this. This
the Apostle has found. He cries triumphantly to his readers
that he knows of a Being, transcending all that is transitory, the
ground of what is temporal and finite. Such a reality can only
be found in so far as it is revealed under material forms and
enters into the world of matter. In Christ the writer claims to
have found this eternal reality, which transcends the limits of

I

the sensible and material. What he has seen in Jesus and heard from Him is to himself indubitable evidence of the truth of his claim." This passage, which is really a paraphrase in more modern terms of thought of the Johannine conception of ζωή, does not, of course, explain by strict grammatical exegesis the meaning of the opening phrases of this Epistle, but it is an admirable expression of ideas which may reasonably be connected with them, and as such it deserves full consideration.

ἀρχῆς] Anarthrous. Cf. Jn. i. 1, vi. 64, xvi. 4 ; Gn. i. 1. That which is regarded by us as "beginning." The anarthrous use of the word makes it denote "character, according to man's apprehension," rather than a definite fact or point of time. The parallels in Genesis and the Prologue of the Gospel exclude the possibility of a reference *merely* to the beginning of the Christian dispensation. For the writer's use of ἀρχή, cf. note on ii. 7.

ὃ ἀκηκόαμεν] The author justifies his claim to be able to announce "that which was from the beginning" on the fact that a revelation of it has been made under the conditions of time and space, so that it has become intelligible to finite understanding. The perfect has its full force. A revelation has been made in terms which men can understand, and the results are abiding. What the writer and his contemporaries have heard and seen remains with them, so that they can make it known to others who have not themselves had the same privileges.

The "hearing" may perhaps include the whole revelation, of the nature of God and His relation to the world, from the beginning. But if it is not confined to the earthly life of Jesus Christ, that is what the writer has prominently in view.

ἑωράκαμεν τοῖς ὀφθαλμοῖς] The revelation has been made through nature and through man. All the human powers of perception are necessary to grasp its fulness, and can be used for that purpose. The τοῖς ὀφθαλμοῖς emphasizes the personal experience of the writer, and those whom he associates with himself by the use of the first person plural. The terms used in this preface can only be interpreted *naturally* as a claim on the writer's part to have been an actual eye-witness of the earthly life of Jesus Christ. It is not *impossible* to suppose that the writer uses them metaphorically of a spiritual vision, the completeness of which can best be described under the metaphors of sense-perception. Such an interpretation, however, is forced and unnatural in the extreme. Clemen's confession (*ZNTW* vi. 281, 1905), that he can suggest no really satisfactory explanation of the words αἱ χεῖρες ἡμῶν ἐψηλάφησαν on these lines, is significant. Nothing but absolute necessity could justify their reference to "spiritual" perception. If on other grounds it is impossible to suppose that this Epistle, or other writings which cannot easily be separated from it, could have been written by an eye-witness of the life of Christ on earth, we should, of course, be compelled to accept this forced interpretation of the words; unless we admitted that the writer has put forward a false claim. But it is well to recognize that such a course is of the nature of a desperate expedient. Such a claim might naturally be met with the ironical words of Philo (*de Decalogo,* p. 195), ὦ οὗτος, ἃ μήτ᾽ εἶδες μήτ᾽ ἤκουσας, ὡς ἰδών, ὡς ἀκούσας, ὡς παρηκολουθηκὼς ἅπασιν, ἀφικόμενός μοι μαρτύρησον, which Windisch (*Handbuch zum NT.* iv. 2, p. 105) quotes to illustrate the phraseology of this passage. There can be no doubt as to what is the natural interpretation of the writer's words. These considerations hold good also against Karl's idea of ecstatic vision (*Johanneische Studien,* p. 3). The hypothesis that the writer when using the first personal plural identifies himself (?) and his readers with the Christian body, *some* of whom had actually seen the "Lord," is open to less objection, but is not really satisfactory. This use of the plural is quite natural in the passage which has sometimes been quoted from Irenaeus (v. i. 1), "*per auditum nostrum uocem eius percipientes.*" Irenaeus is emphasizing the fact that the Incarnation was the only means of teaching men the truth about God. In the Introduction to Book V. he has reminded his readers that the Church tradition goes back to Christ Himself. And Christ alone could teach men, in that as God He knows the things of God, and as man He can explain them intelligently to His fellow-men. Here the writer is contrasting his position with that of his readers. He will hand on to them what *he and his fellows* have seen and heard, that they too, though they have not seen, may believe and share his joy. See Briggs, *The Messiah of the Apostles,* p. 464; Findlay, *Fellowship in the Life Eternal,* pp. 87–89.

The passages quoted from Tacitus, *Agricola,* c. 45 (*Mox nostrae duxere Heluidium in carcerem manus*), and Augustine, *Ep.* 88. 8 (*nostri oculi ab armatis uestris calce et aceto extinguuntur*), are not quite parallel. Tacitus, a member of the Senate, but absent from Rome at the time of the incident to which he refers, can naturally, addressing the public in a highly rhetorical passage, identify himself with the disreputable action of the body to which he belongs. Augustine, speaking as a Catholic, and addressing Donatists, can with equal propriety say, "We suffer persecution at your hands." But here the writer, speaking as a Christian to Christians, is emphasizing what he and others with whom he identifies himself, have to give to the Christians to whom he writes. "What we have seen and heard *we* tell *you,* that *ye* may share our joy." The "we" are clearly distinguished from the whole body of Christians.

ὃ ἐθεασάμεθα] The "message" has so far been viewed in its permanent results. It has been "heard" and "seen" so that those who first received it have it as an abiding possession which they can impart to others. Now the facts of its reception are presented in such a way (by the use of the aorist) as to emphasize their character. The different tenses are used with reference to the same object under different aspects. Emphasis is first laid on the results, then on the method. The aorist presents its object as a complete fact, or series of facts regarded as one whole, having a definite character. The witness is not only abiding, it is also satisfactory in kind. It rests on complete and intelligent use of adequate opportunities. There is no reason for restricting the object of the two aorists to the disciples' experiences after the Resurrection. Such a distinction must have been more clearly marked if the writer intended his readers to grasp it. The special reference of ψηλαφᾶν to Lk. xxiv. 39 (ἴδετε τὰς χεῖράς μου καὶ τοὺς πόδας μου . . . ψηλαφήσατέ με καὶ ἴδετε), or to the incident recorded in Jn. xx. 26–29, where the word is not used, appears to be very doubtful. It is simpler to suppose that the same object is described in different ways, corresponding to the natural distinction in meaning between the perfect and aorist. But see Westcott, and comp. Ign. *Smyr.* iii. Cf. also Tert. *Adv. Prax.* xv., *de An.* xvii., *de Pat.* iii.

ἐθεασάμεθα] If βλέπειν is to "look," and ὁρᾶν to "see," θεᾶσθαι is to "behold," intelligently, so as to grasp the meaning and significance of that which comes within our vision. Cf. Mt. vi. 1 ; [Mk.] xvi. 14 ; Lk. vii. 24 ; Jn. i. 14, 38, iv. 35, xi. 45 ; Acts i. 11 ; Ro. xv. 24 ; 1 Jn. iv. 12, 14. In the LXX the word occurs only eight times, and in the later books ; cf. 2 Ch. xxii. 6, and especially 2 Mac. iii. 36 ἅπερ ἦν ὑπ' ὄψιν τεθεαμένος. The word nearly always suggests careful and deliberate vision which interprets, rightly or wrongly, its object. The witnesses have not only seen and remembered. Their "seeing" was of such a character as to enable them to appreciate rightly the significance of what they saw.

καὶ αἱ χεῖρες ἡμῶν ἐψηλάφησαν] Cf. Lk. xxiv. 39, already quoted, and the note on ἑωράκαμεν. The Lord's command in Luke, and the incident recorded by the writer in his Gospel, illustrate the meaning of the words. But their reference is wider than to any definite events between the Resurrection and the Ascension.

ψηλαφᾶν is to *grope* or *feel after* in order to find, like a blind man or one in the dark ; hence to *handle, touch.* The idea

of searching sometimes disappears altogether. It may also be
used in the sense of "examine closely." Cf. Polyb. viii. 18. 4
(quoted by L. and S.), πᾶσαν ἐπινοίαν: Gn. xxvii. 12, μήποτε
ψηλαφήσῃ με ὁ πατήρ μου (of Isaac): Dt. xxviii. 29, ἔσῃ ψηλαφῶν
μεσημβρίας: Is. lix. 10, ψηλαφήσουσιν ὡς τυφλοὶ τοῖχον: Ps. cxiii.
15, χεῖρας ἔχουσι καὶ οὐ ψηλαφήσουσι: Job xx. 10 (A), αἱ δὲ χεῖρες
αὐτοῦ ψηλαφήσουσιν ὀδύνας. Here it naturally suggests all the
evidence available for sense-perception other than hearing and
sight. Possibly it emphasizes the reality of that with which
they had been brought into contact, in opposition to the
Docetism which may have characterized the views of the writer's
opponents. It certainly marks the intimate character of their
personal intercourse with the Lord. Their opportunities
included all that was necessary to make their witness ἀληθινή
as well as ἀληθής, satisfactory in kind as well as accurate so far
as it went. They were competent witnesses who spoke the truth.
Cf. Jn. xix. 35.

περὶ τοῦ λόγου τῆς ζωῆς] Dr. Westcott's phrase "the revelation of life" probably gives most accurately the meaning of the
words: the whole message which reveals, or which gives life.
Compare Jn. vi. 68, ῥήματα ζωῆς αἰωνίου, and Jn. iii. 34, τὰ
ῥήματα τοῦ θεοῦ. The exact meaning of the genitive is doubtful.
As a rule, when (ὁ) λόγος is followed by a genitive, not of a
person, the genitive expresses the contents of the message. Cf.
Mt. xiii. 19 (τῆς βασιλείας), Ac. xiii. 26 (τῆς σωτηρίας ταύτης),
xiv. 3, xx. 32 (τῆς χάριτος αὐτοῦ), xv. 7 (τοῦ εὐαγγελίου); 1 Co. i.
18 (ὁ τοῦ σταυροῦ); 2 Co. v. 19 (τὸν λόγον τῆς καταλλαγῆς); Eph.
i. 13 (τῆς ἀληθείας); Ph. ii. 16 (λόγον ζωῆς ἐπέχοντες); Col. i. 5
(τῆς ἀληθείας τοῦ εὐαγγελίου); 1 Th. ii. 13 (λόγον ἀκοῆς); 2 Ti. ii.
15 (τῆς ἀληθείας); He. vi. 1 (τῆς ἀρχῆς τοῦ Χριστοῦ); Apoc. i. 3
(τοὺς λόγους τῆς προφητείας). On the other hand, where (τῆς)
ζωῆς is added to a noun as a qualifying genitive it generally,
though not always, denotes "life-giving," or some cognate idea.
Cf. Jn. v. 29 (ἀνάστασιν), vi. 35 (ὁ ἄρτος), 48, 68 (ῥήματα, cf. 63),
viii. 12 (τὸ φῶς); Ac. ii. 28 (ὁδούς, = Ps. xvi. 11), iii. 15 (τὸν
ἀρχηγόν), v. 20 (τὰ ῥήματα); Ro. v. 18 (δικαίωσιν), vi. 4 (καινότητι);
Ph. ii. 16 (λόγον), iv. 3 (βίβλῳ); 2 Ti. i. 1 (ἐπαγγελίαν), Ja. i.
12 (τὸν στέφανον); 1 P. iii. 7 (χάριτος); Apoc. ii. 7 (τοῦ ξύλου),
10 (τὸν στέφανον), iii. 5 (τῆς βίβλου), xi. 11 (πνεῦμα), xvi. 3
(ψυχή), xvii. 8 (τὸ βιβλίον), xx. 12, 15, xxi. 27, xxi. 6 (τοῦ ὕδατος),
xxii. 1 (ὕδατος), 2 (ξύλον), 14, 19 (τὸ ξύλον), 17 (ὕδωρ). But the
two meanings are not mutually exclusive. The message which
announces life gives life (cf. Jn. v. 39).

περί] What the writer has to announce concerns the word of
life. He does not claim to handle the whole message. He has
something to tell about it. On the bearing of this preparation

as the meaning of the whole verse, see the note on ὁ ἦν ἀπ' ἀρχῆς.

2. For the use of parenthesis to emphasize or explain a specially important word, cf. Jn. xix. 35. In this parenthesis the emphatic word is ἐφανερώθη, which is repeated at the end of the verse. The writer and his circle could bear their witness about the word of life, because the life had been *manifested*, to men and under conditions which made it possible for men to apprehend its nature. The reference is in quite general terms. ἡ ζωή is never used to express the being of the (personal) Logos, or pre-existent Christ.

According to Weiss, φανεροῦν never denotes the becoming visible of that which was before invisible, but the making clear of what was hitherto unknown (he compares Jn. ii. 11, iii. 21, vii. 4, ix. 3, xvii. 6). But the distinction is hard to maintain in view of the Johannine usage of verbs of sight to include the understanding of that which falls under the ocular vision (cf. Jn. iii. 3). φανεροῦν may be used of all processes of making known, whether intellectual or sensible.

ἀπαγγέλλομεν] It is doubtful whether a distinction can be maintained between ἀπαγγέλλειν, "to repeat with reference to the source from which the message comes," and ἀναγγέλλειν, "to report with reference to the persons addressed" (ver. 5). See ver. 3, ἀπαγγέλλομεν καὶ ὑμῖν ἵνα καὶ ὑμεῖς κ.τ.λ.

τὴν ζωὴν τὴν αἰώνιον] For the double article, cf. ii. 25, and ver. 3, ἡ κοινωνία ἡ ἡμετέρα : Jn. x. 11, ὁ ποιμὴν ὁ καλός. The idea is first put forward generally, and then more particularly defined.

It is strange to find it stated (Weiss, *Comm.* p. 28) that αἰώνιος is always used in the N.T. in the sense of endless duration, or even that ζωὴ αἰώνιος denotes in S. John (as in S. Paul) "our everlasting further life (*ewiges weiterleben*) after the death of the body" (Karl, p. 6). It would be truer to say that it *never* has the sense of endless duration. On the other hand, it does not denote what is supra-temporal. It can only mean "belonging to the age" of which the writer is speaking or thinking, and so comes to mean possessed of the characteristics of that age. If the "age to come" is supra-temporal, then αἰώνιος denotes that the subject which it qualifies has this characteristic.

"Spiritual" probably suggests its meaning most clearly in popular language. The words which it is used in the N.T. to qualify are : πῦρ, ζωή, κόλασις, κρίσις, ἁμάρτημα (Mk. iii. 29, *v.l.* κρίσεως), σκηναί, χρόνοι, θεός, βάρος, δόξης, οἰκία, ὄλεθρος, παράκλησις, κράτος, δόξα, ἐλπίς, σωτηρία, κρίμα, λύτρωσις, πνεῦμα, κληρονομία, διαθήκη, βασιλεία, εὐαγγέλιον. Of the 71 instances of its use in the N.T., 44 are passages in which it qualifies ζωή.

Its meaning is best considered in the light of this fact. It is
noticeaole that in the Johannine Gospel and Epistles, where it
occurs 23 times, it is never used in any other connection.

ἥτις] The life manifested in Christ, to which His personal
disciples could bear witness on the strength of what they had
seen and heard, is eternal, *inasmuch* as it is in union with the
Father that it attains to its true realization. The distinction
between ὅς and ὅστις, which disappears altogether in late Greek,
can still, as a rule, be traced in the New Testament, where in all
probability ὅστις is never a mere substitute for the relative. It
either suggests a reason for what has been stated before, as here,
or it introduces the designation of a class to which the antecedent belongs. (Cf. Mt. vii. 26, xiii. 52.)

πρός] Cf. Jn. i. 2, ἦν πρὸς τὸν θεόν, and Dr. Westcott's note on
the differences of meaning between πρός and other prepositions
denoting relations. Expressed in simpler language, the particular
force of πρός would seem to be that it suggests a relation
realized in active communion and intercourse. Cf. Mk. vi. 3,
οὐκ εἰσὶν αἱ ἀδελφαὶ αὐτοῦ ὧδε πρὸς ἡμᾶς; ix. 19. The true life of
the Son was realized in union and communion with the Father.
By means of the Incarnation it was manifested to men.

3. ὃ ἑωράκαμεν καὶ ἀκηκόαμεν] Resumption. The announcement rests on eye- and ear-witness. The difference in order, if
it is not purely a matter of rhythm, may perhaps throw more
emphasis on the earthly life of the Incarnate Logos, in which
what was seen naturally takes precedence of what was heard,
as contrasted with the wider description of revelation in ver. 1,
where hearing must come before seeing. The treatment of
minute differences in this Epistle, and in the Johannine writings
generally, is a difficult question. There can be no doubt that
very often they are either deliberate, and intended to convey
some slight change of meaning, or the outcome of the exact
train of thought which has led to the particular expression.

καὶ ὑμῖν] To find in these words a proof that the writer is
addressing a circle of readers different from those among whom
he began his Apostolic work, and therefore a special appropri-
ateness in their use by one who had changed the sphere of his
activity from Palestine to Asia Minor, is forced. (Cf. Zahn,
Einleitung in das NT. p. 566, "früher an anderen Orten . . .
jetzt im Kreise der Gemeinden, an welche der 1 Jo. gerichtet
ist"; trans. iii. p. 358.) Such a thought could not have been
conveyed to his readers by so obscure a hint. It is always
dangerous to read into the words of this Epistle the things which
any particular theory of its authorship make it desirable to find
there. On the other hand, the words do not "show the readers
of this Epistle to be those who are the hearers of all his

Apostolic preaching" (Weiss, p. 30). Their more probable significance is suggested by the following καὶ ὑμεῖς. What the eye-witnesses have heard and seen they announce to others as well, in order that *they too* may share the fellowship which Apostles and disciples have so long enjoyed.

κοινωνίαν ἔχητε] The exact phrase is found only in this Epistle in the N.T. The writer is rather fond of the use of ἔχειν with a substantive to intensify the meaning of a verb. Cf. his use of it with ἁμαρτίαν, χρείαν, παρρησίαν, ἐλπίδα, ζωήν, κόλασιν. As contrasted with the simple verb, which merely expresses the fact, it may perhaps suggest the sense "to have and enjoy." Κοινωνεῖν is always used of active participation, where the result depends on the co-operation of the receiver as well as on the action of the giver. Cf. Philo, *Leg. ad Caium*, § 4 (quoted by Grimm), τίς οὖν κοινωνία πρὸς Ἀπόλλωνα τῷ μηδὲν οἰκεῖον ἐπιτηδευκότι; 1 Co. x. 16, οὐχὶ κοινωνία τοῦ σώματος τοῦ Χριστοῦ ἐστίν; It does not properly denote a merely passive sharing, as μετοχή can express, though the words are sometimes used interchangeably; cf. 2 Co. vi. 14, τίς γὰρ μετοχὴ δικαιοσύνῃ καὶ ἀνομίᾳ ἢ τίς κοινωνία φωτὶ πρὸς σκότος; see T. S. Evans in the *Speaker's Comm.* on 1 Co. x. 16.

καὶ . . . δέ] Cf. Jn. vi. 51, καὶ ὁ ἄρτος δέ: 3 Jn. 12, καὶ ἡμεῖς δὲ μαρτυροῦμεν. It may be considered doubtful whether "the καί emphasizes, while the δέ serves as connecting particle." The use of καὶ . . . δέ would seem rather to develop and intensify a thought or idea. See Ellicott on 1 Ti. iii. 10. "Fellowship, I say; and remember that the fellowship of which we speak, and which we enjoy, is no less than fellowship with God and His Son." Comp. Jn. xvii. 11, 20–23.

μετὰ τοῦ πατρὸς κ.τ.λ.] Fellowship with God became possible when Christ revealed Him to men as the Father, with whom His children could enter into communication. Such fellowship, *i.e.* that which is possible between parent and child, is only realized in and through Jesus Christ, the man whom God sent to make Him known. The title Ἰησοῦς Χριστός always emphasizes both ideas, of the historical life and human nature of Jesus of Nazareth, and of the Divine commission of God's Messiah. And the use of the title "Son" (μετὰ τοῦ υἱοῦ αὐτοῦ) emphasizes His capacity to make God known. The writer can conceive of no adequate knowledge of God which can be apprehended by man except in so far as it is revealed in a real human life, by one who is an only-begotten Son of God. Only a Son can reveal the Father. Only an only-begotten Son, who, so to speak, sums up in Himself all the qualities of His Father, which are completely reproduced in one heir, and not distributed among many children, is in a position to make such a revelation complete. The burden of the writer's message is summed up in the last verse of the Prologue to the Gospel, "God hath no *man* seen at any time; God only begotten (or the only-begotten Son), who is in the bosom of the Father, He hath declared Him."

4. ταῦτα] The reference is most probably to the contents of the Epistle, "already present to the writer's mind." There are many instances in which it is a matter of dispute whether the writer, in using οὗτος, αὕτη, ταῦτα, τοῦτο, ἐν τούτῳ, ἐκ τούτου, διὰ τοῦτο, etc., intends to refer to what has preceded or what follows. Both usages are found in the Epistle, but the reference forward would seem to be his prevailing custom. Sixteen instances may be noted where the reference is to what follows (preceded by καί, i. 4, ii. 3, iii. 23, 24; without καί, ii. 6, iii. 1, 8, 10, 16, iv. 2, 9, 13, 17, v. 4, 11, 14) as against seven where the reference to what preceded is at least probable (without καί, ii. 22, 26, iv. 6, v. 6, 13, 20; preceded by καί, iv. 3). Here the reference is probably to what follows. The ταῦτα are not identical with the message described in ver. 3, nor are they contrasted with it. They are the part of it, or the things to be said in explanation of it, which it is expedient that the author should communicate in writing. *Scriptio valde confirmat* (Bengel).

γράφομεν ἡμεῖς] Both words are emphatic. The αὐτόπται have always borne their witness by preaching or teaching. Now there is much that the survivors, or survivor, must write down. In this context ἡμεῖς must mean "we who have seen and heard," whether the seeing and hearing are to be interpreted literally or metaphorically. And the literal interpretation is undoubtedly the most natural. The word contains no claim to Apostolical authority, unless, indeed, none but Apostles could rightly claim to be witnesses of what has been described in vv. 1-3. And it does not justify the view that at the time of writing many still survived who had seen the Lord. The conditions are satisfied if even one survivor only is speaking in the name of those of whom he is the last representative, especially if he is addressing Christians among whom the later survivors had spent their last years. It points quite naturally to the "Johannine" circle at Ephesus, but it does no more than point. It offers no proof. The plur. γράφομεν does not occur again in the Johannine Epistles.

ἵνα . . . ᾖ πεπληρωμένη] For the resolved tense, cf. Jn. xvi. 24. And for the sense, cf. Jn. xv. 11, xvii. 13, iv. 36, iii. 29. The writer's joy is increased the more his readers can realize the fellowship of which he has spoken, and to promote which is the object of his letter.

ἡμῶν] It is very difficult to decide between the readings ἡμῶν and ὑμῶν. The former is supported by better MSS, and the latter may possibly be affected by assimilation to Jn. xvi. 24. On the other hand, ἡμεῖς is almost certainly the true text just before, and the reading ὑμῶν offers a pointed contrast, " we who have seen must write, that you who have not seen may enter into full joy." And it is a contrast which would not appeal to scribes. Perhaps, however, the ἡμῶν suits best the thought of the writer. He would not dissociate himself, and other teachers, from the common joy felt by all when his readers attain "fellowship." In the spiritual harvest, sower and reaper rejoice together.

2. εωρακαμεν] pr. ο B³ 40 : + και ακηκοαμπεν 40 | την ζωην] om. K | την αιωνιον] om. boh-cod.

3. ακηκοαμεν] και εωρακαμεν ℵ harl. | και 1°] om. boh-cod.

απαγγελλομεν] pr. και ℵ kˢᶜʳ am. arm-codd. Thphyl. : καταγγελλομεν Γᵇ ²⁵³ᶠᶠ (Greg. 2).

και υμιν ℵ A B C P 7. 13. 40. 68. 180 harl. syrˢᶜʰ etᵖ sah. arm. aeth. Did. Aug.] om. και K L al. pler. cat. vg. arm-codd. cop. syrᵖ ᵗˣᵗ Dionys. Oec. Aug.

και υμεις] om. και sah. syrˢᶜʰ.

και η κοινωνια δε] om. και boh-txt.: om. δε C* P 13. 27. 29. 69. 81. 180 aˢᶜʳ* vg. sah. arm. (uid.) syrᵖ.

αυτου] om. sah.

4. γραφομεν] scripsimus, am. harl. : γραφω K⁴⁵³ (62) arm-codd. boh-codd.

ημεις ℵ A* B P 13 harl.* sah.] υμιν Aᶜᵒʳʳ al. fere. om. cat. vg. syrᵘᵗʳ cop. arm. aeth. Thphyl. Oec.

ημων ℵ B L 31. 39. 40. 42. 57. 76. 78. 95. 98. 99. 100. 101. 105. 114. 177. 190. 1ˡᵉᶜᵗ 13ˡᵉᶜᵗ 14ˡᵉᵉᵗ 3ᵖᵉ al⁸ ˢᶜʳ am. fu. harl. tol. sah. syrˢᶜʰ arᵉ Thphylᶜᵒᵐ Oecᶜᵒᵐ] υμων A C K P al. plu. vgᶜˡᵉ demid. cop. syrᵖ arm. aeth. Thphylᵗˣᵗ Oecᵗˣᵗ.

πεπληρωμενη] + εν ημιν C*.

ινα] ut gaudeatis et vg. (om. gaudeatis et am.).

A. i. 5–ii. 27. First description of the two signs of fellowship with God, expressed negatively. First refutation of the twofold " lie." The " ethical " and " christological " theses presented one after the other, without any definition of their mutual relations.

I. i. 5–ii. 17. *Walking in light the true sign of fellowship with God* (ethical thesis). Refutation of the one " lie."

1. i. 5–ii. 6. The thesis maintained in two parallel statements.

(*a*) i. 5–10. The nature of God and the consequent relation of man to God.

i. 5–10. Having stated that his object in writing is to enable his readers to enter into fellowship, and that the mutual fellowship of Christians leads onwards to that higher fellowship with God in Christ on which indeed it is based, the writer proceeds to deduce from the nature of God the conditions under which fellowship with Him is possible. He does so by setting aside three false pleas often urged by those who claim such fellowship, the denial of the bearing of moral conduct on spiritual communion, of the responsibility for sinful action, of the actual fact

of having sinned. With regard to the first two he states by way
of contrast the provision made by God for overcoming the
hindrances which would seem to prevent the possibility of
fellowship with God, in the case of those who by their conduct
or their confession refuse to shelter themselves behind such
false pleas. The verses which follow contain a similar contrast,
expanded into a different form in order to meet a difficulty
which might be suggested by what has been said in this
passage.

5. The nature of God. God is light, and therefore only those
whose conduct can be described as "walking in light," can enjoy
fellowship with such a Being.

In form the opening of the Epistle is closely parallel to that
of the Gospel. This verse corresponds to Jn. i. 19, and it is
introduced in exactly the same way (καὶ αὕτη ἐστὶν ἡ μαρτυρία).
There also the idea of "witness" is taken up from the middle
verses of the Prologue, just as ἀγγελία here takes up the
ἀπαγγέλλομεν of vv. 2, 3.

καί] The connection with what immediately precedes is not
obvious. According to Dr. Westcott it must be found in the
idea of fellowship. "Fellowship must repose upon mutual
knowledge" (p. 14). If we are to have fellowship with God
and with the brethren, we must know what God is and what we
are. False views on either subject must prove a fatal barrier
to true fellowship. But see the preceding note. It would
seem to be simpler to find the connection further back in the
idea of the "announcement." He makes his announcement,
contained in the letter he finds it necessary to write (ver. 4), with
a special purpose which he has now stated. And the burden
of the announcement is this, that God is light, and men must
walk in light if they would enjoy His fellowship.

ἀγγελία] The simplest form of the word is chosen, as the
writer wishes to describe its twofold aspect as a message *from*
God *to* those whom he addresses, in the following words. It
is an ἀπαγγελία from God Himself, ἣν ἀκηκόαμεν ἀπ᾽ αὐτοῦ.
It is also an ἀναγγελία meant for those to whom he writes
(καὶ ἀναγγέλλομεν ὑμῖν). The word may also suggest that the
message contains a conception of God which men could not
have formed for themselves without His help. It is a "revelation and not a discovery," it is the message which has come from
God to be delivered to men.

φῶς ἐστίν] Anarthrous to express quality. God's nature is
best described as "light." τὸ φῶς would have suggested light
in some particular relation, cf. Jn. i. 5–9. φῶς describes His
nature as He is, the description being true so far as it goes,
though not complete. The primary idea suggested by the word

in this context is "*illumination*." It is of the nature of light
that it is and makes visible. God's nature is such that He must
make Himself known, and that knowledge reveals everything
else in its true nature. That this thought is present here is
suggested by the following section (ii. 3 ff.). That God can be
"known," and by those to whom the author is writing, is one of
the leading ideas on which he lays special stress. But in view
of the use of the metaphor of light and darkness in the Bible
generally, and especially in S. John, and of the immediate
context in this Epistle, it is impossible to exclude the ethical
meaning from the signification of the word here. The context
shows that this is the idea which he is most anxious to emphasize. The word must suggest the notes of Holiness and
Purity as essential to God's nature. The conditions of fellowship on which he insists are closely akin to the Levitical " Be
ye holy, for I am holy, saith the Lord." The full meaning,
however, of what is contained in words is not limited to the
sense in which they were probably used and understood by the
writer and his first readers. Jesus' revelation of God as
" Father" goes far beyond what was understood of it by the
men of His own generation. For the more permanent meaning
of the sentence, and the further ideas which it may be regarded
as connoting, see Dr. Westcott's note (p. 16 f.); Findlay, p. 102.

καὶ σκοτία κ.τ.λ.] This is not a mere repetition of the
sentence in negative form, in accordance with the writer's love
of double expression by parallel clauses, positive and negative.
And it probably does not merely emphasize the "perfect realization in God of the idea of light." It emphasizes rather the
completeness of revelation. God is not the ἄρρητος σιγή, or
βυθός, of the more developed Gnostic systems, or the " unknowable" God of the Gnostic thought which preceded those
systems. Though complete knowledge of God is impossible,
He can be truly "known" here and now, under the conditions
and limitations of human life. His nature is "light," which
communicates itself to men, made in His image, till they are
transformed into His likeness. From the ethical side, the
words also emphasize the conditions of fellowship. Walking
in darkness *must* exclude from the fellowship of Him "in whom
is no darkness at all." Conduct is not the matter of indifference
that in some of the teaching of the time it was made out to be.
With the order of ideas here, λόγος, ζωή, φῶς, σκοτία (vv. 2, 5),
comp. the same sequence in the Prologue to the Gospel
(1, 2, 4, 5).

καὶ 1°] om. boh-codd.
εστιν αυτη א B C K L P 31. 40. 69. 105. 137 a^ser c^ser al. fere.^60 syr^p txt
Thphyl. Oec.] αυτη εστιν A 13 al. uix. mu. cat. arm. vg. syr^sch et p mg.

η αγγελια א^c A B K L al. fere.⁷⁰ Cat. Did. Thphyl^{comm} Oec^{comm} vg.
syr^{sch} arm. aeth.] η επαγγελια C P 13. 31. 40. 69. 70. 73. 137 a^{scr} al. uix^{mu}
sah. cop.(?) syr^p Thphyl^{txt} Oec^{txt}: $\frac{\gamma\alpha\pi\eta\ \tau\eta s\ \epsilon}{\eta\ \alpha\pi\alpha\gamma\gamma\epsilon\lambda\iota\alpha s}$ א* (sic). An obvious
assimilation to a commoner word by careless scribes.

απ] παρ *I*^{a 264} (233) *O*⁴⁶ (154).

και 20] om. boh-txt.

αναγγελλομεν] απαγγελλομεν 18. 40. 69. 98. 100. 137. 180. 57^{lect} a^{scr}.

εν αυτω ουκ εστιν א A C K L P al. pler. cat. vg. arm. syr^p Or. Did.
Aug.] ουκ εστιν εν αυτω B 13. 31 aeth. boh. (uid.) Or. Caes.

6–10. The relation of man to God as determined by the fact that God is light.

6. This revelation of God is not made to satisfy speculative curiosity. It bears directly on practical life. If truly apprehended, it puts aside three false pleas often put forward by men to excuse their "love of darkness."

The first of these pleas is the "indifference of moral conduct to spiritual communion." Fellowship with God is impossible where men "walk in darkness." The light transforms those who receive it. Those who continue to practise the works of darkness cannot be in fellowship with the light. To assert the opposite is to state what is contrary to the facts as we know them (ψευδόμεθα). Now that the revelation of God as light has been made by Jesus Christ, such language is a deliberate lie. And the actual conduct of those who make such a statement belies the claim they put forward to have fellowship with God. Their actions are not an expression in life of the moral ideal revealed by Jesus Christ. They "do not the truth."

ἐὰν εἴπωμεν] The form of the sentence introduces a not impossible, perhaps a not unlikely, contingency. And the use of the first person plural, where the writer is thinking of his τεκνία, with whom he is in spiritual fellowship, and with whom he identifies himself as "compassed with infirmity" and not free from the dangers to which he knows them to be exposed, is an indication that the influence of his opponents had made itself felt both in thought and practice among those who were in the main still faithful to the "truth" as he conceived it. Throughout the Epistle he writes under a pressing sense of danger. He is not wasting his weapons on purely hypothetical situations, of the realization of which he felt no serious apprehension.

μετ' αὐτοῦ] the Father. The expression must have the same reference as the ἐν αὐτῷ of the preceding verse.

ἐν τῷ σκότει περιπατῶμεν] Cf. ii. 11, (ὁ μισῶν) ἐν τῇ σκοτίᾳ περιπατεῖ: Jn. viii. 12, περιπατήσῃ ἐν τῇ σκοτίᾳ: cf. Jn. xi. 9, 10. The metaphor used by the Lord in the Gospel has already become part of the natural religious language of Christian

The use of περιπατεῖν of conduct (cf. the Hebrew הלך) is

common in S Paul and S. John. In the Synoptic Gospels it is found only in Mk. vii. 5, περιπατοῦσιν . . . κατὰ τὴν παράδοσιν. Cf. Ac. xxi. 21, τοῖς ἔθεσιν περιπατεῖν. For the LXX usage, cf. Pr. viii. 20, ἐν ὁδοῖς δικαιοσύνης περιπατῶ : Ec. xi. 9, περιπάτει ἐν ὁδοῖς καρδίας σου ἄμωμος : and for the use of "walk" in connection with φῶς, Is. ii. 5, δεῦτε πορευθῶμεν τῷ φωτὶ κυρίου.

For the false views combated in this verse we may compare Clem. Al. *Str.* iii. 4. 30, τοιαῦτα καὶ οἱ ἀπὸ Προδίκου ψευδωνύμως Γνωστικοὺς σφᾶς αὐτοὺς ἀναγορεύοντες δογματίζουσιν υἱοὺς μὲν φύσει τοῦ πρώτου θεοῦ λέγοντες αὐτούς, καταχρώμενοι δὲ τῇ εὐγενείᾳ καὶ τῇ ἐλευθερίᾳ ζῶσιν ὡς βούλονται· βούλονται δὲ φιληδόνως· and 5. 40, ἀδιαφόρως ζῆν διδάσκουσιν : and later, πᾶς βίος ἀκίνδυνος ἐκλεκτῷ. Iren. I. vi. 2, τὸ πνευματικὸν θέλουσιν οἱ αὐτοὶ εἶναι ἀδύνατον φθορὰν καταδέξασθαι, κἂν ὁποίαις συγκαταγένωνται πράξεσιν.

σκότει] The distinction can hardly be maintained in this Epistle between σκότος, "the concrete thing called darkness," and σκοτία, "its abstract quality" (cf. ii. 11); or, as Dr. Westcott defines it, "darkness absolutely, opposed to light," and "darkness realized as a state." The form σκότος occurs only here and in Jn. iii. 19 in the Johannine writings.

οὐ ποιοῦμεν τὴν ἀλήθειαν] Cf. Jn. iii. 21, ὁ δὲ ποιῶν τὴν ἀλήθειαν ἔρχεται πρὸς τὸ φῶς, ἵνα φανερωθῇ αὐτοῦ τὰ ἔργα ὅτι ἐν θεῷ ἐστιν εἰργασμένα, where the thoughts of this verse find expression in a positive form. Compare also Neh. ix. 33, ὅτι ἀλήθειαν ἐποίησας : and for the opposite expression, Apoc. xxi. 27, ὁ ποιῶν βδέλυγμα καὶ ψεῦδος : xxii. 15, ὁ φιλῶν καὶ ποιῶν ψεῦδος. To "do the truth," or to "do a lie," are natural expressions in the Johannine system of thought in which ἀλήθεια has a far wider signification than that with which its modern connotation familarizes us. The Johannine usage corresponds with the meaning of the Hebrew אמת, which denotes *reliability, faithfulness,* and therefore, when it refers to what is spoken, *truth.* We may compare the phrases עשֹׂה חסד ואמת, Gn. xxiv. 49, xlvii. 29; Jos. ii. 14 ; 2 S. xv. 20 ; and הלך באמת, 1 K. ii. 4, iii. 6 ; 2 K. xx. 3 ; Is. xxxviii. 3. The "truth" has no exclusive reference to the sphere of the intellect. It expresses that which is highest, most completely in conformity with the nature and will of God, in any sphere of being. In relation to man it has to do with his whole nature, moral and spiritual as well as intellectual. "Speaking" the truth is only one part of "doing" the truth, and not the most important. To "do the truth" is to give expression to the highest of which he is capable in every sphere of his being. It relates to action, and conduct and feeling, as well as to word and thought.

εαν] +γαρ A.
τω σκοτει] τα σκοτια H⁸⁶ (Ψ).

7. "Walking in the light," *i.e.* the conscious and sustained endeavour to live a life in conformity with the revelation of God, who is "light," especially as that revelation has been made finally and completely in Jesus Christ, is the necessary condition of fellowship. Where this condition is fulfilled, fellowship is real. To claim it is no lie. Comp. "The righteous . . . will live in goodness and righteousness, and will walk in eternal light" (Book of Enoch xcii. 4).

αὐτός ἐστιν] The contrast is significant. Men "walk" in light, God "is" in it. Findlay, pp. 100–102.

μετ' ἀλλήλων] The strict antithesis to ver. 6, "if we claim fellowship with God, while our conduct does not correspond to the claim, we lie," would naturally be, "if we walk in light we can claim fellowship with God." This has led to the alteration of ἀλλήλων in some texts, αὐτοῦ or *cum Deo* being substituted for it. These readings are clearly attempts at simplification. The writer follows his usual custom. Instead of contenting himself with an exact antithesis, he carries the thought a step further. Fellowship among Christians "shows the reality of that larger spiritual life which is life in God" (Wstct.). It is based on fellowship with God, and it is the active realization of that fellowship. As Christians enter into fuller fellowship with each other, the more fully they come to live the life "in God" into which they have been born again. μετ' ἀλλήλων cannot mean "we with God, and God with us" (Aug. Ew. etc.), nor can it *mean* that we share with each other the Divine indwelling (Karl), though mutual fellowship is the first step in the path which leads to that.

καί] And where the endeavour to "walk in light" is carried out (it depends on the exercise of man's will whether or not the endeavour is made), the removal of sin, which hinders fellowship with God, is possible in consequence of what the Son of God has gained for men by His human life, the power of which has been set free by death so as to become available for all men.

τὸ αἷμα κ.τ.λ.] As Westcott has pointed out, the significance of "blood" in Jewish thought is most clearly expressed in Lv. xvii. 11. The blood "atones" through the life which is said to be "in" the blood. The power of Christ's life, freely rendered to God, throughout His life and in His death, and set free by death for wider service than was possible under the limitations of a human life in Palestine at a definite date, is effective for the gradual (καθαρίζει) removal of sin in those who attempt to realize their union with God in Him. The use of καθαρίζει determines the sense to be the *removal* of sin rather than the cancelling of guilt. As ritual cleanness was the condition of approach to God under the Jewish sacrificial system, so the "blood" of Christ cleans men's consciences for God's service and fellowship. See Briggs, *The Messiah of the Apostles*, p. 469.

καθαρίζει] In the Synoptists the word is used especially of cleansing from leprosy (see also its use in Mt. xxiii. 26, τὸ ἐντός: Lk. xi. 39, τὸ ἔξωθεν). In the Fourth Gospel it does not occur, but the adjective καθαρός is found in the Discourses of the Upper Room (xiii. 10, 11, xv. 3). In Acts it is used in the sense of "pronouncing clean" (x. 15, xi. 9), and also (xv. 9) with τὰς καρδίας: cf. 2 Co. vii. 1; Eph. v. 26; Tit. ii. 14; He. ix. 14, 22, 23, x. 2; Test. Rub. iv. 8. In the LXX it is found as the equivalent of טהר and הקה in the senses (1) to cleanse, (2) to pronounce clean. The present tense may point to the νίψασθαι, of which even ὁ λελουμένος has frequent need in his walk through a soiling world (Jn. xiii. 10). "Docet hic locus gratuitam peccatorum veniam non semel tantum nobis dari, sed perpetuo in ecclesia residere" (Calvin).

Ἰησοῦ τοῦ υἱοῦ αὐτοῦ] Cf. iv. 15, v. 5; He. iv. 14 (ἀρχιερέα μέγαν . . . Ἰησοῦν τὸν υἱὸν τοῦ θεοῦ). As man He gained the power to help men. As Son of God His help is effective.

πάσης ἁμαρτίας] Sin in all its forms and manifestations; Mt. xii. 31. Cf. Ja. i. 2, πᾶσα χαρά: Eph. i. 8, πᾶσα σοφία: and for the singular, 1 Jn. iii. 4, 8, 9. The writer is apparently thinking of sin as an active power, showing itself in many forms, rather than of specific acts of sin. Weiss' interpretation "all sins," *i.e.* not only of the pre-Christian period of a man's life, but also those committed in the course of Christian life, would require the plural. But in general sense it is correct, and rightly throws the emphasis on πάσης, sin in whatsoever form it may manifest itself. Karl's limitation of the meaning to sins committed before men became Christians ("d. h. von der vor dem Christentum begangenen"), is not justified by the words used by the writer. And the reason suggested, that "post-Christian" sins require also intercession (*Johannische Studien*, pp. 18, 82), is a curious instance of the perversion of an excellent principle, that of interpreting the Epistle by the help of the Epistle itself.

δε] om. 29. 66** harl.* boh-txt. | εστιν] *ambulat,* boh-txt.
μετ αλληλων א Aᶜᵒʳʳ B C K L P etc.] μετ αυτου A* ᵘⁱᵈ tol. Clem. Tert. Did. : *cum Deo,* harl.
του υιου αυτου ιυ χυ H²⁵⁷ (33) Iᵃ ¹⁹² (318).
ιησου א B C P 29. 69** aˢᶜʳ fu. syrˢᶜʰ ᵉᵗ ᵖ ᵗˣᵗ sah. boh-txt. arm. aethʳᵒ Clem. Fulg.] +Χριστου A K L al. pler. cat. vg. boh-codd. syrᵖ c* aethᵖᵖ Tert. Aug. Bed.
του υιου αυτου] om. aeth. Aug. (semel) Iᶜ ¹⁷⁴.
καθαριξει] καθαρισει 5. 106. 13ˡᵉᶜᵗ 14ˡᵉᶜᵗ al.² ˢᶜʳ : καθαριει 6. 7. 29. 66** Aug. (*bis*) : *purgabit,* sah. cop.

8. The second false plea denies the abiding power of sin as a principle in one who has committed sins. To those who hold such a view, sin ceases to be of any importance. It is merely a passing incident which leaves behind it no lasting consequences. The plea rests on self-deception. It can only be maintained by those who shut their eyes to the teaching of experience, in themselves or in others. And they lead themselves astray. The consequences must be fatal unless men acknowledge their mistake and retrace their steps.

ἐὰν εἴπωμεν] For the general idea, cf. Pr. xx. 9, τίς παρρησιάσεται καθαρὸς εἶναι ἀπὸ ἁμαρτιῶν, and xxviii. 13, ὁ ἐπικαλύπτων ἀσέβειαν ἑαυτοῦ οὐκ εὐοδωθήσεται.

ἁμαρτίαν οὐκ ἔχομεν] Cf. πίστιν ἔχειν, to have faith, as an active principle working in us and forming our character. To "have sin" is not merely a synonym for to commit sins. This is necessitated by the contrast demanded by ver. 10 between ἁμαρτίαν οὐκ ἔχομεν and οὐχ ἡμαρτήκαμεν. "Sin" is the principle of which sinful acts are the several manifestations. So long as a Christian commits sins, sin is an active power working in him ; and its power still remains after the forgiveness of sins which he received at his baptism. To deny this is to refuse to accept the teaching of experience.

In the N.T. the use of the phrase ἁμαρτίαν ἔχειν is confined to this Epistle and the Fourth Gospel (ix. 41, xv. 22, 24, xix. 11). The meaning of the phrase in the Gospel has been raised as an objection to the interpretation given above. It is maintained that in the Gospel it has a quite definite sense, and that it "specifically denotes the guiltiness of the sin" (Law, *The Tests of Life*, p. 130); and it is suggested that the meaning here must be, "If we say that we have no guilt, no responsibility for the actions, wrong in themselves, which we have committed." It is probably true that as compared with the simple verb the phrase accentuates the ideas of guilt and responsibility. And in the passages in the Gospel where the phrase occurs these ideas are prominent. But they are contained in the Hebrew conception of sin, emphatically developed in the teaching of the N.T., rather than in the one expression as opposed to the other. He who has committed sin is responsible for his action, just as much as he who "has sin" and who feels, or should feel, in himself the presence of a power which manifests itself in his sinful acts. And though the idea of guilt is prominent in the use of the phrase in the Gospel, especially in xv. 22, where the antithesis, "Now they have no excuse for their sin," must be noticed, it does not exhaust the meaning of the phrase as used there. Cf. ix. 41, εἰ τυφλοὶ ἦτε οὐκ ἂν εἴχετε ἁμαρτίαν. If they had been as ignorant, and conscious of their ignorance,

2

as the man whom they had condemned, they might have learned, and whatever "sin" they had would have lost its power. But their refusal to see the truth when it was presented to them, and their insistence that they knew, in spite of this, gave their sin an abiding power over them. Henceforth it could prevent any possibility of their seeing the truth. And the same idea is present in ch. xv. The rejection of Christ's words by His opponents had given sin a power over them, which it could never have had but for their missing the opportunity of better things. As it was, they not only had "sin" as an active power established in them and working its will, but they had no excuse to offer for its presence there (πρόφασιν οὐκ ἔχουσιν περὶ τῆς ἁμαρτίας αὐτῶν, which cannot mean "they have no excuse for their guilt," and which is not merely antithetical but adds a further point). This meaning is especially clear in ver. 24. The "sin" which had got its hold, in consequence of their rejecting Him in spite of what He had done among them, had conceived and brought forth hate (νῦν δὲ καὶ ἑωράκασιν καὶ μεμισήκασιν is the contrast to ἁμαρτίαν οὐκ εἴχοσαν). And the phrase may possibly be used with something of the same meaning in xix. 11, ὁ παραδιδοὺς . . . μείζονα ἁμαρτίαν ἔχει, though in this case the simpler meaning "the greater guilt" is more plausible. But even here the thought may be of the power which sin acquires over him who admits it. Sin could now work with more fatal power in the High Priest, who knew the relative power of God and of the Roman governor, and who incited him to his crime against justice, than in Pilate, who in spite of his greater power was more ignorant than the Jew. Even if the phrase meant no more in the Gospel than the denotation of the "guiltiness of the agent," it would not necessarily bear exactly the same meaning in the Epistle. The writer likes to put new meaning into the phrases he repeats. But probably, though the exact *nuance* may be different in the two writings, the fundamental idea expressed is the same. It is the special characteristic of the writer that he loves to use his phrases, of which his store is but scanty, with slightly different shades of meaning.

ἑαυτοὺς πλανῶμεν] The phrase, as contrasted with the simple πλανώμεθα, emphasizes the agent's responsibility for the mistake. The evidence is there; only wilful blindness refuses to accept it. We have no excuse for the sin which we "have," in spite of our denial of the fact. See Findlay, p. 106.

πλανᾶν always suggests the idea of leading astray from the right path (cf. ii. 26, iii. 7 ; Jn. vii. 12 ; Apoc. ii. 20, xii. 9, etc.). The mistake must have fatal consequences until we lead ourselves back into the way of truth.

καὶ ἡ ἀλήθεια κ.τ.λ.] The statement that we have not sin, shows that those who make it have not "truth" working in them as an inner and effective principle. For the meaning of "truth," cf. note on ver. 6. It is more than the sense of truth, uprightness and honesty of self-examination and self-knowledge (cf. Rothe, *ad loc.*). It can be regarded both objectively and subjectively, either as something that can be done (ver. 6), an external standard in accordance with which actions must be shaped, or as an inner principle, working from within and moulding a man's inner life.

ουκ εστιν ℵ B L al. pler. sah. syr^p aeth. Tert. Oec.] post ημιν A C K P 5. 13. 31*. 65. 69. 137. 180 a^{scr} al.$^{2\,scr}$ cat. m^{75} vg. syr^p arm. Thphyl. Cyp. Lcif. Aug. Probably an accidental alteration, possibly due to Latin influence, and, at any rate, naturally maintained in Latin authorities.

9. The existence of sin, even in those who have entered the Christian community, is a patent fact. But it does not make impossible that fellowship with God which sin interrupts. In those who acknowledge the fact, God has provided for its forgiveness and removal.

πιστὸς καὶ δίκαιος] Not "faithful *because* He is just," and justice in His relation to men includes the necessity of His fulfilling the promises which He has made. The two adjectives are co-ordinate. God's faithfulness is shown in the fulfilment of His promises. He is just, in that, in spite of men's failures to fulfil their obligations, He remains true to the covenant which He made with them; and this includes forgiveness on certain conditions. It is probable that throughout the Bible this idea of faithfulness to His covenant in spite of man's unfaithfulness, is the primary signification of δικαιοσύνη θεοῦ. Cf. He. x. 23, πιστὸς ὁ ἐπαγγειλάμενος, and Ro. iii. 25, εἰς ἔνδειξιν τῆς δικαιοσύνης αὐτοῦ διὰ τὴν πάρεσιν τῶν προγεγονότων ἁμαρτημάτων ἐν τῇ ἀνοχῇ τοῦ θεοῦ.

ἵνα] Defines the sphere in which the faithfulness and the justice are shown. In view of the usage of the writer, and the frequency of the definitive ἵνα in papyrus documents, it is difficult to maintain the "telic" force of ἵνα throughout the N.T. It may be worth while to collect (roughly) the passages in the Johannine books where the "telic" force has given way to the definitive: Jn. i. 27, ἄξιος ἵνα λύσω: ii. 25, οὐ χρείαν εἶχεν ἵνα τις μαρτυρήσῃ: iv. 47, ἠρώτα ἵνα καταβῇ: v. 7, ἄνθρωπον οὐκ ἔχω ... ἵνα βάλῃ: vi. 29, τοῦτό ἐστι τὸ ἔργον ἵνα πιστεύητε: 39, τοῦτο ἐστὶν τὸ θέλημα ... ἵνα ... μὴ ἀπολέσω: cf. 40; viii. 56, ἠγαλλιάσατο ἵνα ἴδῃ: ix. 22, συνετέθειντο ... ἵνα ἐάν τις αὐτὸν ὁμολογήσῃ Χριστὸν ἀποσυνάγωγος γένηται: xi. 50, συμφέρει ... ἵνα ἀποθάνῃ: 57, δεδώκεισαν ... ἐντολὰς ἵνα ἐάν τις γνῷ ... μηνύσῃ:

xii. 23, ἐλήλυθεν ἡ ὥρα ἵνα δοξασθῇ: xiii. 1, ἦλθεν αὐτοῦ ἡ ὥρα
ἵνα μεταβῇ: 2, βεβληκότος εἰς τὴν καρδίαν ἵνα παραδοῖ: 29, λέγει
αὐτῷ . . . ἵνα δῷ: 34, ἐντολὴν καινὴν δίδωμι ἵνα ἀγαπᾶτε: xv. 12,
αὕτη ἐστὶν ἡ ἐντολὴ . . . ἵνα ἀγαπᾶτε: 13, μείζονα ταύτης . . .
ἵνα . . . τὴν ψυχὴν . . . θῇ: xvi. 2, ἔρχεται ὥρα ἵνα πᾶς ὁ
ἀποκτείνας ὑμᾶς δόξῃ: 7, συμφέρει . . . ἵνα . . . ἀπέλθω: 30, οὐ
χρείαν ἔχεις ἵνα . . . ἐρωτᾷ: 32, ἔρχεται ὥρα καὶ ἐλήλυθεν ἵνα
σκορπισθῆτε: xvii. 3, αὕτη ἐστὶν ἡ αἰώνιος ζωὴ ἵνα γινώσκωσιν:
15, ἐρωτῶ ἵνα ἄρῃς: 24, θέλω ἵνα . . . ὦσιν: xviii. 39, ἔστι δὲ
συνήθεια . . . ἵνα . . . ἀπολύσω: xix. 31, ἠρώτησαν . . . ἵνα
κατεαγῶσιν: 38, ἠρώτησεν . . . ἵνα ἄρῃ.   1 Jn. ii. 27, οὐ χρείαν
ἔχετε ἵνα τις διδάσκῃ: iii. 1, ποταπὴν ἀγάπην δέδωκεν . . . ἵνα
κληθῶμεν: 11, αὕτη ἐστὶν ἡ ἀγγελία . . . ἵνα ἀγαπῶμεν: 23, αὕτη
ἐστὶν ἡ ἐντολὴ αὐτοῦ ἵνα πιστεύσωμεν: iv. 17, ἐν τούτῳ τετελείωται
. . . ἵνα παρρησίαν ἔχωμεν: 21, ταύτην τὴν ἐντολὴν ἔχομεν . . .
ἵνα . . . ἀγαπᾷ: v. 3, αὕτη ἐστὶν ἡ ἀγάπη . . . ἵνα . . . τηρῶμεν:
16, οὐ . . . λέγω ἵνα ἐρωτήσῃ.   2 Jn. 6, αὕτη ἐστὶν ἡ ἀγάπη, ἵνα
περιπατῶμεν, αὕτη ἡ ἐντολή ἐστιν . . . ἵνα περιπατῆτε.   3 Jn. 4,
μειζοτέραν τούτων οὐκ ἔχω χαράν, ἵνα ἀκούω.   Apoc. vi. 11, ἐρρέθη
αὐτοῖς ἵνα ἀναπαύσωνται: xiii. 12, ποιεῖ . . . ἵνα προσκυνήσουσιν:
13, ποιεῖ σημεῖα μεγάλα, ἵνα πῦρ ποιῇ . . . καταβαίνειν: 15,
ποιήσῃ [ἵνα] . . . ἀποκτανθῶσιν: 16, ποιεῖ πάντας . . . ἵνα δῶσιν
αὐτοῖς [καὶ] ἵνα μή τις δύνηται ἀγοράσαι: xix. 8, ἐδόθη αὐτῇ ἵνα
περιβάληται.   Though a few of them might possibly be interpreted differently, there is abundant evidence to establish the
usage.

ἀφῇ] The determination of the meaning of this word from
the sense of "send away" is tempting but unsound.   Those
who can remember the light which was thrown, at least for
themselves, on the whole subject of forgiveness, by F. D.
Maurice's insistence on the view that ἀφιέναι means to "send
away," and not to let off a penalty or to cancel a debt, will
always be grateful for what he said on the subject.   But though
right in substance, it must be confessed that linguistically his
interpretation cannot be defended.   The application of the word
to "sin" is almost certainly suggested by the metaphor of the
remission or cancelling of debts.   At the same time it must be
remembered that, as in the case of most metaphorical expressions
which are used to emphasize some particular point of similarity,
in respect of which comparison is possible, it is confusing to
transfer all the associations of the metaphor to the new subject
which it is used to illustrate.   As applied to "sins" it suggests
the cancelling of the outstanding debt, the removal of that
barrier to intercourse between man and God which is set up by
sin.   And the transaction must be real and not imaginary.   God
cannot treat it as non-existent, unless it has been actually or

potentially removed or destroyed. ἀφιέναι is used in the N.T. in the sense of "remission" in the following passages: with ὀφείλημα or ὀφειλή, Mt. vi. 12, xviii. 32: with παράπτωμα, Mt. vi. 14, 15; Mk. xi. 26: with ἁμαρτία or ἁμάρτημα, Mt. ix. 2, 5, 6, xii. 31; Mk. ii. 5, 7, 9, 10, iii. 28, iv. 12; Lk. v. 20, 21, 23, 24, vii. 47–49, xi. 4, cf. xvii. 3, 4; Jn. xx. 23; Ja. v. 15; 1 Jn. ii. 12: with τὸ δάνιον, Mt. xviii. 27; without a direct object (or subject), Mt. xii. 32, xviii. 21, 35; Lk. xxiii. 34, also in Mk. xi. 25, Lk. xii. 10; with ἡ ἐπίνοια τῆς καρδίας, Ac. viii. 22; with ἀνομία, Ro. iv. 7 (= Ps. xxxii. 1). The use of κρατεῖν in Jn. xx. 23 must be interpreted in the light of this usage of ἀφιέναι. It stands by itself in the N.T.

καθαρίσῃ . . . ἀδικίας] Cf. Jer. xl. 8, καὶ καθαριῶ αὐτοὺς ἀπὸ πασῶν τῶν ἀδικιῶν αὐτῶν ὧν ἡμάρτοσάν μοι. In ἀφιέναι the *metaphor* is borrowed from the cancelling of debt, but the idea which the metaphor is used to illustrate is ethical. There is therefore no need to equate the meaning of καθαρίζειν to that of ἀφιέναι. It should certainly be interpreted in an ethical sense.

πάσης ἀδικίας] Cf. πάσης ἁμαρτίας. Injustice in whatever form it may manifest itself. ἀδικία denotes injustice, failure to maintain right relations with other men or with God. If God is faithful to forgive sins according to His promise, He is also "just," not only to fulfil the terms of His covenant, but also to provide for the cleansing or removal of those injustices of which men have been guilty in their relations with God or with other men.

ἐαν]+ δε *I*ᵃ ⁵⁵¹ (216).
ημιν] om. **arm-codd.** sah.
αμαρτιας (2°) A B C K L P al. pler. m tol. vgᵐᵍ Cyp. Hier. Aug. Thphyl. Oec.]+ημων א C 5. 26. 68. 69. 98 aˢᶜʳ jˢᶜʳ vg. syrᵘᵗʳ sah. **boh-txt.** arm. aeth. Dam. Aug. Hier. : *ea* **boh-cod.** : +πασας *I*ᵃ ¹⁴⁰² (219).
ημας] om. C | αδικιας] pr. αμαρτιας καὶ *O*⁴⁶ (154).

10. The third false plea is the denial of the fact of having committed sin. Though a man may allow the abiding power of sin as a principle in those who have sinned, or the existence of sin in Christians after forgiveness, he may yet deny that he has himself sinned. To do so is to deny the truth of God's revelation. Apart from actual statements in Scripture (cf. Ps. xiii. (xiv.) 3, lii. (liii.) 2), the whole plan of God's dealings with men is based on the assumption that all have sinned. To deny the fact in our own case is to make Him a liar, since it is implied in His whole message to us. His word can have no place in the development of our being.

ἡμαρτήκαμεν] have committed no **act** of sin, **of** which the consequences remain.

ψεύστην] Cf. Jn. viii. 44, 55; 1 Jn. ii. 4, 22, iv. 20. And for the exact phrase, 1 Jn. v. 10.

ὁ λόγος] Like the truth, the word can be viewed objectively or subjectively, an external message or an inward force effective and active in men. There is, of course, no reference to the personal Logos, though the word implies a more personal relationship than ἀλήθεια. It suggests the speaker. Cf. Jn. viii. 37, ὁ λόγος ὁ ἐμὸς οὐ χωρεῖ ἐν ὑμῖν: He. iv. 12; Ja. i. 21; 1 Jn. ii. 14.

ουκ εστιν] post ημιν 69. 137 a^{scr} arm. syr^p arm. Thphyl.
ημιν]+ *habitans*, **arm.-osc.**

(*b*) ii. 1–6. Further statement of the conditions of fellowship. Knowledge and obedience.

1, 2. The remedy for sin (in the case of those who acknowledge that they have sinned, in contrast with i. 10).

3–5a. Obedience the sign of knowledge.

5b, 6. Imitation the sign of union.

1. The recognition of the universality of sin, from which even Christians are not actually free, might lead to a misconception of its true character. Men might easily pass too lenient judgments on its heinousness, and ignore the responsibility of those who give way to its promptings. If it is impossible for any one, even the Christian, to escape sin, why condemn with such uncompromising severity failures for which men cannot reasonably be held responsible? Why strive so earnestly against what is inevitable? The writer hastens to warn his readers against such conclusions. Sin is wholly antagonistic to the Christian ideal; his whole object in trying to set out that ideal more clearly is to prevent sin, not to condone it. His aim in writing is to bring about "sinlessness" (ἵνα μὴ ἁμάρτητε). And the Christian scheme includes means by which such an aim may be gradually realized. Whenever any one gives way to any act of sin, such as must interrupt the intercourse and fellowship between men and God, which it is the great aim of Christ's work to establish, the means exist by which this fellowship may be restored. Christians have an "advocate" with the Father (πρός: cf. i. 2), who is able and willing to plead their cause, to present their case truly and completely, to transact their business, to speak for them, if non-legal phrases convey the meaning more clearly. And His mediation is addressed to one who is Father of both Advocate and suppliants, as eager as they can be that the fellowship should be restored, on the only terms on which such fellowship *can* be restored, the removal of the sin which has interrupted it.

τεκνία μου] The "Elder," who is perhaps the representative of a generation which has almost passed away, naturally thinks of the younger generation to whom he is speaking as his "children."

And when he wishes to emphasize the importance of the thought which he has to teach, he naturally falls into the language of affectionate endearment. Whether he is thinking of them as his "sons in the faith," who owe their conversion to Christianity to his ministry, is uncertain. We do not know the historical circumstances of the case with sufficient accuracy to determine.

ταῦτα] must refer to the contents of the whole Epistle, already present to the mind of the writer, rather than to the preceding chapter or any part of it, though to some extent the main teaching of the Epistle has been already declared in outline.

ἵνα μὴ ἁμάρτητε] The aorist suggests definite acts of sin rather than the habitual state, which is incompatible with the position of Christians who are in truth what their name implies. Those who are bathed need not save to wash their feet; cf. Jn. xiii. 10.

καὶ ἐάν] The sentence introduced by these words is not contrasted with the preceding, but added to it "as a continuous piece of one message." The writer's object is to produce " sinlessness." And this is not a fruitless aspiration after an ideal which cannot possibly be realized, for the means of dealing with the sin which he desires to combat are at hand.

παράκλητος] Most of the information which is of real importance in determining the meaning and usage of this word in the Johannine writings (it is not found elsewhere in the N.T.) is to be found in the notes of Wettstein and Westcott. The article on the word in Hastings' *Dictionary of the Bible* (iii. 665) gives a very clear summary of the evidence; cf. also Jülicher's shorter statement in the *Encyclopaedia Biblica* (iii. 3567).

The passages where it occurs in the N.T. are Jn. xiv. 16, 26, xv. 26, xvi. 7; 1 Jn. ii. 1. The meaning "advocate" is clearly needed in the Epistle, it is possible in xv. 26, and probable in xvi. 7. In xiv. 16, 26 it must have the wider and less technical meaning of one called in to help.

As regards the use of the verb παρακαλεῖν, it has the sense of *comfort* in the LXX (cf. Gn. xxxvii. 35, where it is used with reference to Jacob) and in the N.T. (cf. Mt. v. 4, ὅτι αὐτοὶ παρακληθήσονται, where the influence of Is. lxi. 2, παρακαλέσαι πάντας τοὺς πενθοῦντας, is clear). The use of παράκλησις in the sense of *comfort* is also well established (cf. 2 Co. i. 3, 4, διὰ τῆς παρακλήσεως ἧς παρακαλούμεθα). But its original meaning was to *send for, summon to one's aid*, corresponding to the Latin *aduocare*. The following passages are often quoted: Xen. *Anab.* i. 6. 5, Κλέαρχον παρεκάλεσε σύμβουλον, ὃς . . . ἐδόκει τροτιμηθῆναι μάλιστα τῶν Ἑλλήνων: Aesch. *Ctes.* 200, τί δεῖ σε Δημοσθένην παρακαλεῖν; ὅταν παρακαλῆς κακουργὸν ἄνθρωπον καὶ τεχνίτην λόγων κλέπτεις τὴν ἀκρόασιν. With this corresponds the classical use of the word παράκλητος. It is used as an adjective; cf. Dion. Cass. xlvi. 20, τὴν ἀγορὰν . . . δούλων παρακλήτων πληρώσας, but more often absolutely; cf. Demosthenes, *de Falsa Legatione*, 341, αἱ τῶν παρακλήτων αὗται δεήσεις καὶ σπουδαὶ τῶν ἰδίων πλεονεξιῶν εἵνεκα γίγνονται. Diogenes Laertius, iv. 7, *Bion*. πρὸς τὸν ἀδολέσχην λιπαροῦντα αὐτῷ συλλαβέσθαι· τὸ ἱκανόν σοι ποιήσω, ἐὰν παρακλήτους πέμψῃς καὶ μὴ αὐτὸς ἐλθῇς. The meaning of the word is thus clearly wider than that of "advocate" in English. Though it is used specially in connection with the law courts, it denotes any friend called upon to give help, either by pleading or giving evidence, or in virtue of his position and power. Its Latin equivalent is "aduocatus," rather than "patronus," which corresponds more in meaning to our "advocate." The distinction is clearly defined by Asconius Pedianus, in a note on Cicero, *in Q. Caecilium*, "Qui defendit alterum in iudicio, aut *patronus* dicitur, si orator est, aut *aduocatus* si aut ius suggerit, aut praesentiam suam commodat amico."

The form of the word is passive (cf. κλητός, ἐκλεκτός, ἀγαπητός, etc.). It must mean one who is called to the side of the suppliant, not one who comforts or consoles, or exhorts. The meaning "comforter" or "consoler" can attach to the word only in so far as that expresses the good office which he who is called in performs for the friend who claims his help.

The usage of the Septuagint corresponds. In Zec. i. 13, παρακλητικός is used to translate the Hebrew נִחֻמִים, ῥήματα καλὰ καὶ λόγους παρακλητικούς. In Job xvi. 2, מְנַחֵם is translated by παρακλήτωρ (παρακλήτορες κακῶν πάντες). But it should be noticed that two of the later versions (Aquila, Theodotion) render it by παράκλητοι. Symmachos has παρηγοροῦντες, an indication that in later Greek the meaning of παράκλησις was beginning to influence that of παράκλητος.

Philo's usage corresponds with the classical. The Paraclete is the advocate or intercessor; cf. *de Josepho*, c. 40, ἀμνηστίαν ἁπάντων παρέχω τῶν εἰς ἐμὲ πεπραγμένων· μηδενὸς ἑτέρου δεῖσθε παρακλήτου: *de Vita Moysis*, iii. 14, the High Priest is said rightly to bear the symbol of the Logos (τὸ λογεῖον is the LXX expression for the breast-plate), ἀναγκαῖον γὰρ ἦν τὸν ἱερώμενον τῷ τοῦ κόσμου πατρὶ παρακλήτῳ χρῆσθαι τελειοτάτῳ τὴν ἀρετὴν υἱῷ πρός τε ἀμνηστείαν ἁμαρτημάτων καὶ χορηγίαν ἀφθονωτάτων ἀγαθῶν, where the parallel to the Johannine thought is clearly marked, whether the Cosmos or the Logos is to be regarded as the "son perfect in virtue" who is used as Paraclete. In another passage usually quoted, *de Opificio Mundi*, c. 6, οὐδενὶ δὲ παρακλήτῳ· τίς γὰρ ἦν ἕτερος, μόνῳ δὲ ἑαυτῷ χρησάμενος ὁ θεὸς ἔγνω δεῖν εὐεργετεῖν . . . τὴν . . . φύσιν, Jülicher may be right in saying that the only feasible meaning is something like "instructor," "adviser," so far as concerns the duty which the Paraclete is needed to perform; but the point of the sentence is that God confers His benefits on nature *Himself*, without using the help or services of another. Cf. also *In Flaccum*, §§ 3, 4.

The word occurs as a loan-word in the Targum and Talmudic literature, in the sense of helper, intercessor, advocate. It is used in the Targum on Job xvi. 20 and xxxiii. 23 as a paraphrase of מליץ taken in the sense of "interpreter." The latter passage is especially interesting, as showing the late Jewish view of the need of angelic agency to "redeem a man from going to the pit."

In the Talmud, פרקליט is used for "advocate," in opposition to קטיגור (κατήγορος; cf. Apoc. xii. 10, ὁ κατήγωρ). "He who performs one precept has gotten to himself one paraclete, and he who commits one transgression has gotten to himself one accuser" (*Pirke Aboth*, iv. 15; Taylor, p. 69). "Whosoever is summoned before the court for capital punishment is saved only by powerful paracletes; such paracletes man has in repentance and good works; and if there are nine hundred and ninety-nine accusers, and only one to plead for his exoneration, he is saved" (*Shab.* 32*a*). The sin-offering is like the paraclete before God; it intercedes for man, and is followed by another offering, a thank-offering for the pardon obtained (Sifra, Megora iii. 3). These and other passages are quoted in the *Jewish Encyclopaedia*, *s.v.* (ix. 515). The same usage is found in early Christian literature, where the use of the word is independent of the Johannine use of the term; cf. 9, 2 Clement. vi. 9, τίς ἡμῶν παράκλητος ἔσται ἐὰν μὴ εὑρεθῶμεν ἔργα ἔχοντες ὅσια καὶ δίκαια; Barnabas, c. xx. καταπονοῦντες τὸν θλιβόμενον, πλουσίων παράκλητοι, πενήτων ἄνομοι κριταί.

The connection of the word with the ordinary meaning of παράκλησις is found in Rufinus' translation of the *De Principiis*; cf. ii. 7. 3, "Paracletus uero quod dicitur Spiritus sanctus, a consolatione dicitur. Paraclesis enim Latine consolatio appellatur." He goes on to suggest that the word may have a different meaning when applied to the Holy Spirit and to Christ. "Videtur enim de Saluatore Paracletus dici deprecator. Utrumque enim significat in Graeco Paracletus, et deprecatorem et consolatorem."

Origen seems to have understood the word in the sense of "intercessor." Cf. *Comm. in Joann.* i. 38, τὴν περὶ ἡμῶν πρὸς τὸν πατέρα προστασίαν αὐτοῦ δηλοῖ παρακαλοῦντος ὑπὲρ τῆς ἀνθρώπων φύσεως καὶ ἱλασκομένου, ὡς ὁ παράκλητος καὶ ἱλασμός.

In Chrysostom it has the sense of "comforter," *Hom. in Jo.* 75, ἐπειδὴ γὰρ οὐδέπω αὐτὸν ἐγνωκότας εἰκὸς ἦν σφόδρα ἐπιζητεῖν τὴν συνουσίαν ἐκείνην, τὰ ῥήματα, τὴν κατὰ σάρκα αὐτοῦ παρουσίαν, καὶ μηδεμίαν δέχεσθαι παραμυθίαν ἀπόντος· τί φησιν; ἐρωτήσω τὸν πατέρα καὶ ἄλλον παράκλητον δώσει ὑμῖν· τουτέστιν· ἄλλον ὡς ἐμέ.

In Cyril of Jerusalem the sense is not limited to that of "comforting"; cf. *Catechesis*, xvi. 20, Παράκλητος δὲ καλεῖται, διὰ τὸ παρακαλεῖν καὶ παραμυθεῖσθαι καὶ συναντιλαμβάνεσθαι τῆς ἀσθενείας ἡμῶν: Ro. viii. 26 being quoted in support, with the explanation of ὑπερεντυγχάνει "δῆλον δὲ ὅτι πρὸς τὸν θεόν."

The evidence of the old Latin Version is similar. In the Epistle "aduocatus" is used, in the Gospel either "aduocatus" or "paraclitus." This is not seriously affected by the evidence adduced by Rönsch (*Itala ü. Vulgata*, p. 348), that "aduocare" acquired the meaning of "to comfort" (cf. Tertullian, *adv. Marc.* iv. 14, where the παρακαλέσαι τοὺς πενθοῦντας of Is. lxi. 2 is translated "*aduocare* languentes." "Advocare" is a natural translation of παρακαλεῖν (cf. Tert. *Pudicit.* 13; Iren. III. ix. 3, v. xv. 1, and the Vulgate of Is. xl. 2, quoted by Rönsch), and owes any connection with the idea of "comforting" that it may have to that fact. Augustine's "Paracletus, id est Consolator," throws no light on the meaning and usage of the Greek word. The other versions do not throw much light on the subject. In Syriac, Arabic, Aethiopic, and Bohairic it is transliterated, and in the Sahidic also in the Gospel, while it has "he that prayeth for us" in the Epistle. The Vulgate has "Paracletus" in the Gospel and "Aduocatus" in the Epistle. This, no doubt, influenced the modern versions. Wycliffe renders "Comforter" in the Gospel and "Advocate" in the Epistle; and Luther also has "Tröster" in the Gospel and "Fürsprecher" in the Epistle.

Thus the evidence of early use supports the evidence of the form of the word, which is naturally passive. Its meaning must be "one called to the side of" him who claims the services of the called. The help it describes is generally assistance of some sort or other in connection with the courts of law; but it has a wider signification also,—the help of any one who "lends his presence" to his friend. Any kind of help, of advocacy, intercession, or mediation may be suggested by the context in which it is used. In itself it denotes merely "one called in to help." In the Epistle the idea of one who pleads the Christian's cause before God is clearly indicated, and "advocate" is the most satisfactory translation. This sense suits some of the passages in which it is used in the Gospel; in the others it suggests one who can be summoned to give the help that is needed in a wider sense. There is no authority for the sense of "Comforter," either in the sense of "strengthener" or "consoler," which has been so generally connected with it in consequence of the influence of Wycliffe and Luther, except Patristic interpretations of its meaning in S. John.

The suggestion of Zimmern (*Vater, Sohn, u. Fürsprecher in der babylonischen Gottesvorstellung*), that its use in Christian and Jewish thought may be connected with the Babylonian myth of the intervention of Nusku (the Fire God), who "acts as the advocate of men at the instance of Ea and Marduk," has not been favourably received. So far as concerns the Johannine use of the term Paraclete, far simpler explanations are to be found in its use in Philo and Rabbinic Judaism. In reality it hardly needs explanation. It was probably a common word, and the obvious one to use. Moulton and Milligan (*Expositor*, vol. x., 1910) quote the illustrations of its use, one from "a very illiterate letter" of the second century A.D. where it has been restored (BU 601¹²), καὶ τὸν ἀραβῶνα τοῦ Σαραπίωνος παρακλος (*l.* παράκλητος) δέδωκα αὐτῷ, where they suggest that it may mean "on being summoned," and an instance of the use of ἀπαράκλητος, OGIS 248²⁵ (175–161 B.C.), ἀπαρακλήτους.

Deissmann (*Licht von Osten*, p. 243, n. 1) lays stress on the use of the word in Aramaic as a proof of its frequency in vulgar Greek. Its use in the Targums and Talmudic Literature is important. The extent of the author's acquaintance with Rabbinic thought is at last beginning to be recognized.

ἔχομεν] Augustine's comment is worth quoting, "Maluit se ponere in numero peccatorum ut haberet aduocatum Christum, quam ponere se pro Christo aduocatum et inueniri inter damnandos superbos." As frequently the writer identifies himself with the rest of the Christian Body. They actually possess and have experience of the means, which are *potentially* available for the whole world. And the need is felt by the whole Church, not because any of them might, but whenever any one does fall. The lapse of one is a matter which concerns the whole body (ἐάν τις . . . ἔχομεν).

Ἰησοῦν Χριστὸν δίκαιον] As true man (Ἰησοῦν), He can state the case for men with absolute knowledge and real sympathy. As God's anointed messenger to men (Χριστόν), He is naturally fitted for the task and acceptable to Him before whom He pleads. As δίκαιος He can enter the Presence from which all sin excludes. He needs no advocate for Himself. Comp. Book of Enoch xxxviii. 2, liii. 6, where the Messiah is called "the Righteous One."

αμαρτητε] αμαρτανητε 14*. 69. 137 aˢᶜʳ Cyr. Dam.
και] om. **boh-codd.**
εαν τις αμαρτη] *si peccetis*, **arm-codd.**
πατερα] θεον arm. Eus. Did. : *deum patrem*, Tert. Cels. ad Vigil.
Ιησουν Χριστον] post δικαιον Iᵃ ¹⁹² (318).
Χριστον] om. Iᵇ ¹⁶¹* (173) : + *Dominum nostrum et* **boh-cod.**
δικαιον] for και Iᵇ ¹⁵⁷ (29) : om. Iᵇ ⁶² (498) : *suffragatorem* Cyp-cod.

2. αὐτός κ.τ.λ.] " Himself is a propitiation for our sins." His advocacy is valid, because He can Himself bear witness that the only condition on which fellowship between God and man can be restored has actually been fulfilled, *i.e.* the removal of the sin by which the intercourse was interrupted. He is not only the High Priest, duly qualified to offer the necessary propitiation, but also the propitiation which He offers. The writer's meaning is most safely determined by reference to Old Testament theories of sacrifice, or rather of propitiation. In spite of the absence of direct quotations, there can be no doubt that the author of this Epistle is greatly indebted to the Old Testament. If the hand is the hand of a Hellene, it expresses the thought of a Jew. His mind is steeped in the thoughts of the Old Testament. Though he has lived among Greeks and learned to express himself simply in their language, and to some extent has made himself acquainted with Hellenic thought, he is really as much a stranger and a sojourner among them as his fathers were. He may have some acquaintance with Gnostic theories of redemption, which Greek thought had been borrowing from the East from at least the beginning of the century before Christ, his own thoughts on the subject are the outcome of his knowledge of the Scriptures. His views on propitiation therefore, as on all other subjects, must be considered in the light of the Old Testament.

The object of propitation in Jewish thought, as shown in their Scriptures, is not God, as in Greek thought, but man, who has estranged himself from God, or the sins which have intervened between him and his God. They must be "covered" before right relations can be restored between the Deity and His worshippers. This is the dominant thought in the sacrificial system of the priestly code. It is the natural outcome of the sufferings of the nation before and during the Exile which had deepened their sense of sin, and of Jehovah's estrangement from His people. The joyous sacrificial feast which the Deity shares with His worshippers consequently gives place, in national thought and feeling, to the ritual of the day of Atonement and the whole system of sin-, trespass-, and guilt-offering. Both ideas, the sacrificial feast which forms the ground of closer union between God and men, and the propitiatory offering by means of which interrupted relations can be restored, have, of course, their counterpart in Christian thought and teaching. But it is the latter which dominates the writer's thought here, in an age in which failure and disappointment are fast clouding the clearer vision of God. The dominant idea which is common both to the Old Testament type and the Christian counterpart is that of the absolute holiness of God, who dwells in the light to which no man can approach, till he has put away the sin which cannot enter the presence of God. So far as the means are concerned, the ceremonial has given way to the spiritual. The work of the Christ, who in His life and death freely and voluntarily offered Himself in complete surrender to the will of God and the work of righteousness, has made possible the removal of the sin which keeps men from God. So far as they attach themselves to Him their sins are covered, for the possibility of their final removal is assured.

αυτος] om. **boh-cod.**

ιλασμος] post εστιν A 68. 180 vg. syr^sch Eus. Or. Cypr. Hil. Aug.

δε των ημετερων] I^b 396 (–) I^c 116.

δε] om. I^c 364 (137) K δ359.

μονον] μονων B 1. 21. 33. 37. 66*. 80*. 101* al. pauc. sah. **boh-codd.** (ui d.) Or.

3. The author has stated that his object in writing is to produce sinlessness, and that if sin intervenes to interrupt the fellowship between man and God, there is a remedy (vv. 1, 2). He now proceeds to point out the signs of Christian life, as realized in knowledge of God and union with God. They are to be found in obedience and in Christ-like conduct. Knowledge of God includes, of course, much more than obedience to His commands, but its genuineness and reality can be thus tested. The writer can conceive of no real knowledge of God which does not issue in obedience, wherever the Divine will has been revealed in definite precepts.

In the Johannine system, "knowledge" is never a purely intellectual process.[1] It is acquired by the exercise of all the faculties of intellect, heart, and will. Fellowship and acquaintance are its cognate ideas. It is developed in the growing experience of intercourse. This conception, which dominates the whole Old Testament idea of "knowing God" and of God "knowing" men (cf. Am. iii. 2), is similarly developed in S. Paul's "knowing God, or rather being known of Him" (Gal. iv. 9). The stress laid in the Johannine writings on the true knowledge of God is certainly connected with the necessity which the author felt of combating certain stages of Gnostic thought. But to see in the language of this and other similar verses of this Epistle any necessary reference to the particular stage of second-century Gnosticism which immediately preceded the more definite systems of Marcion and Valentinus, is precarious. We know too little about the development of Gnostic ideas before Basilides to say *either* that the stage of Gnosticism implied in the Fourth Gospel had or had not been reached by the year

[1] " Dei cognitio res est efficax. Neque enim nuda imaginatione cognoscitur Deus, sed quum se intus cordibus nostris per Spiritum patefacit " (Calvin).

100 A.D. or before that date, *or* that a considerable number of years must have passed before the Church could have demanded so definite a break with opinions of this kind as is suggested in the Second and Third Epistles (cf. Schmiedel, *Evangelium, Briefe und Offenbarung Johannis*, pp. 38, 19).

ἐν τούτῳ] points forward, as usually. Cf. note on i. 4.

γινώσκομεν, ἐγνώκαμεν] The tenses are significant. We learn to perceive more and more clearly that our knowledge is genuine through its abiding results in a growing willingness to obey.

τὰς ἐντολὰς αὐτοῦ τηρῶμεν] The phrase τηρεῖν τὰς ἐντολὰς (τὸν λόγον) is characteristic of the Johannine books, including the Apocalypse. It occurs in the Gospel 12 times, in the First Epistle 6, and in the Apocalypse 6 (cf. also Apoc. i. 3, τὰ ἐν αὐτῷ γεγραμμένα). Elsewhere it is found only in Mt. xix. 17, εἰ δὲ θέλεις εἰς τὴν ζωὴν εἰσελθεῖν, τήρει τὰς ἐντολάς. Cf. Mk. vii. 9 (τὴν παράδοσιν); 1 Ti. vi. 14, τηρῆσαί σε τὴν ἐντολὴν ἄσπιλον. Cf. also Sifre, Deut. 48, quoted by Schlatter (*Sprache u. Heimat des 4ten Evangeliums*). "When a man keeps the ways of the law, should he sit still and not do them? Rather shouldest thou turn to do them." As opposed to φυλάσσειν (*custodire*), τηρεῖν (*obseruare*) denotes sympathetic obedience to the spirit of a command, rather than the rigid carrying out of its letter. We may contrast Mk. x. 20, ταῦτα πάντα ἐφυλαξάμην ἐκ νεότητός μου (= Lk. xviii. 21, ἐφύλαξα). As knowledge is not confined to the intellect, so obedience penetrates beyond the latter to the spirit. It may be noticed that the Vulgate has *obseruare* in this verse, *custodire* in ver. 4, and *seruare* in 5, facts which suggest that no Latin rendering was felt to be an exact equivalent, or completely satisfactory rendering, of the Greek word τηρεῖν. In the Gospel *seruare* is the regular rendering.

τὰς ἐντολάς] The various commands, or definite precepts, in which those parts of the whole θέλημα which are known to us have found expression.

καὶ] om. *I*ᵃ 397 fff (96).
γινωσκομεν] γινωσκωμεν A : *cognoscemus* boh-ed.
τηρωμεν] φυλαξωμεν אˣ : τηρησωμεν *H*ᵟᵟ (Φ).

4. The test is adequate, and may be applied with certainty; for there is no such thing as knowledge which does not issue in corresponding action. The man who claims to have knowledge of God which does not carry with it as its necessary consequence the attempt to carry out His will, thereby declares himself a liar. There is no room for self-deception. The falsehood, if not conscious and deliberate, is without excuse. For the converse thought, that the doing of the will leads to fuller knowledge, cf. Jn. vii. 17.

ὁ λέγων] The verse is closely parallel to i. 6, 8, 10. The form of expression is more individualized than the conditional sentences used there. It is the direct and definite statement of the writer conscious of the fact that he is dealing with a real danger, and probably with a statement that has been actually made, by men against whose influence he is trying to guard his τεκνία. If there is no reason to see in it an attack on any particular Gnostic teacher, it clearly deals with statements which they have heard, and to which they have shown themselves ready to listen.

ψεύστης ἐστίν] The falseness of the claim is the point which is emphasized. At the same time the form of expression chosen declares its inexcusableness. Contrast i. 8 (ἑαυτοὺς πλανῶμεν). As compared with the verb (i. 6, ψευδόμεθα), it may perhaps suggest that the statement is a revelation of the character of the man who makes it. "The whole character is false" (Westcott). He who claims knowledge without obedience "has" the sin which he has allowed to gain foothold. If light is seen and not followed, deterioration of character is the inevitable result.

καὶ . . . ἐστίν] The antithetical clause is not merely a repetition of the positive statement in a negative form. The "truth" is regarded by the writer as an active principle working in a man. It is not concerned with the intellect alone. It corresponds to the highest effort of man's whole nature. Cf. Jn. viii. 32.

ἐν τούτῳ] In such an one. In the Gospel and Epistles of S. John, when οὗτος refers back, it always denotes the subject or object, *as previously described*; cf. Jn. i. 2 (οὗτος, the Logos who is θεός), v. 38, τούτῳ ὑμεῖς οὐ πιστεύετε (one sent by God).

οτι ℵ A B 18. 25. 27. 33**. 65. 66**. 68. 69. 98. 101. 177. 180 a^scr d^scr j^scr 57^lect syr^ute Clem. Cyp. Lcif. Aug. Amb.] om. C K L P al. plu. cat. aeth^ute Clem. Oec.

και] om. και A P 13. 27. 29 | εντου τω] *in Eo* **boh-codd.** : om. ℵ 19. η] om. 21. 34. 56. 100. 192. o^scr Ψ.

αληθεια)+του θεου ℵ 8. 25 aeth. : +αυτου 19^a : +εν αυτω 19^b.

5. Again the thought is carried further in the statement of the opposite. The whole word is substituted for the definite precepts, and knowledge gives way to love. Perfect obedience gains the whole prize. For love is greater than knowledge.

ὃς δ' ἂν τηρῇ] The statement is made in its most general form. Contrast the preceding verse, and i. 6 ff. The difference shows that the writer has in view definite "Gnostic" claims. Knowledge is not the possession of a few "pneumatic" individuals. In contrast with the claim of such an one, whose conduct shows the falsity of his claim, is set the possibility of obtaining the higher prize, the perfection of love, open to all who are willing to obey. The "chance o' the prize of learning love" is not reserved to the few who think that they "know."

αὐτοῦ τὸν λόγον] The order of the words throws the emphasis on αὐτοῦ, which takes up the αὐτόν of the Gnostic's claim. The teaching of the God, whom he claims to know, is very different from the views expressed in his claim.

The λόγος is the sum of the ἐντολαί, or rather it is the whole of which they are the parts. Love is not made perfect in a series of acts of obedience to so many definite commands. It reaches its full growth only when God's whole plan is welcomed and absorbed. The ἐντολαί offer adequate tests of the truth or falsehood of any claim to know God. But something more is needed before Obedience can have her perfect work.

ἡ ἀγάπη τοῦ θεοῦ] The love of God has been interpreted in three ways, according as the genitive is regarded as subjective, objective, or qualitative; God's love for us, or our love for God, or the love which is characteristic of Him, which "answers to His nature" and which when "communicated to man is effective in him towards the brethren and towards God Himself." The second gives the simplest and most natural meaning to the words in their present context. The love for God of which man is capable is only fully realized in absolute obedience. At the same time we must remember that it is the teaching of the author that it is God's love for men which calls out the response of man's love for Him. "We love Him, *because* He first loved us." Comp. ii. 15, iii. 17, iv. 12, v. 3.

ἀληθῶς] The true state of the case as contrasted with the false plea set up by the man who claims to have knowledge without obedience. The emphatic position, however, of the word suggests that it may reasonably be regarded as one of the many signs which are to be found in this Epistle, that the writer feels strongly the need of encouraging his readers with the assurance of the reality of their Christian privileges. Certainty is within their grasp if they will use the means which have been placed at their disposal. Comp. Jn. viii. 31.

τηρη] τηρει K 13. 100. 142 c^scr 57^lect : τηρησει I^a δ453 (5).
τον] om. I^a δ203 (265).
αληθως] om. 27. 29. 66**.

5b, 6. Imitation the sign of Union.

The test of union with God is the imitation of His Son. This is not stated directly, as in the case of knowledge (ver. 3), but the claim to "abide in Him" is said to carry with it the moral obligation to "follow the blessed steps of His most holy life." See Findlay, p. 149.

ἐν αὐτῷ μένειν] This form of expression is peculiar to the

Johannine writings (Gospel and First Epistle). It is the equivalent, in his system of thought, of the Pauline ἐν Χριστῷ εἶναι, of which it was a very natural modification, if it is to be attributed to the author, and not to his Master. The longer the Lord delayed His coming, the more it came to be realized that union with Christ under the conditions of earthly existence must be an abiding rather than a short tarrying. The idea had taken its new shape before the "last hour" was thought to have struck. Bengel points out a climax: *cognitio* (ver. 3), *communio* (5), *constantia* (6).

ἐκεῖνος] For the use of ἐκεῖνος with reference to Christ, cf. 1 Jn. iii. 3, 5, 7, 16, iv. 17; Jn. vii. 11, xix. 21, ix. 12, 28, and perhaps also xix. 35 (Zahn, *Einleitung*, ii. 481; cf. Introd. p. iv).

περιπατεῖν] See note on i. 6. For its use in the Johannine writings, cf. Jn. viii. 12, xi. 9 f., xii. 35; 1 Jn. i. 6, 7, ii. 11; 2 Jn. 4, 6; 3 Jn. 3, 4.

εν τουτω] post θεου P 31 : om. H δ² (א) (?) (cf. Tisch. ver. 4) Iᶜ ¹¹⁶* (–).

γινωσκομεν] *cognoscemus,* boh-ed.

καθως . . . περιπατειν] *sic ambulare sicut* (+ *et* codd.) *ille ambulauit,* arm.

και . . . περιπατειν] om. L.

και αυτος] post ουτως Iᵃ ⁶⁵ (317) Iᶜ ¹⁷⁴ : om. sahᵈ.

ουτως א C K P al. pler. cat. cop. syrᵖ arm. Salv. Thphyl. Oec.] om. A B 3. 34. 65. 81. 180 dˢᶜʳ vg. sah. aeth. Clem. Or. Cyr. Cyp. Aug. The omission may possibly be due to the similarity of the preceding word, but the evidence against it is very strong.

2. ii. 7–17. Proof of the ethical thesis from the circumstances in which the readers find themselves, and from their previous experience. The old commandment is always new in the grow-ing light of God's revelation. "Walking in light" and "keeping the commandments" further defined as love of the brethren.

(*a*) **7–11.** General. Brotherly love.

(*b*) **12–17.** Individual. Warning against love of the world.

7–8. The Commandment, old and new.

It is hardly necessary to discuss the interpretations which regard the "old" and the "new" as different commandments, the old commandment being the injunction to "walk as He walked," and the new, the call to brotherly love. But assuming the identity of the old and the new, the commandment has been interpreted in three different ways. (1) With reference to i. 5 ff., to give proof of "walking in light" by the confession of sin and the avoiding of everything sinful. (2) With reference to the verses immediately preceding, to "walk as He walked." Of these the second is the most natural, but it is not necessary to find a reference to any actual words of the Epistle which have pre-ceded. The expressions which follow, "of which ye were in

3

possession from the beginning," "the word which ye heard,"
make such a reference improbable. (3) The expression ἐντολὴ
καινή recalls so vividly the language of the Gospel, and the connection with the duty of brotherly love insisted upon in vv.
9 and 10 is so clear, that we are almost compelled to interpret
the passage in accordance with Jn. xiii. 34, ἐντολὴν καινὴν δίδωμι
ὑμῖν ἵνα ἀγαπᾶτε ἀλλήλους, καθὼς ἠγάπησα ὑμᾶς, where the
"newness" is to be found in the new standard required, καθὼς
ἠγάπησα ὑμᾶς, rather than in the duty of mutual love, which was
recognized in the Jewish law. In meaning this interpretation
is practically identical with (2). "The idea of the imitation of
Christ is identical with the fulfilment of love" (Westcott). And
it gives the most natural meaning to the description of the
commandment as old, and yet new "in Him and in you." The
old commandment, "Thou shalt love thy neighbour," which was
already contained in the Mosaic law, if not also to be found in
the conscience of those who "having no law, are a law unto
themselves," received a new meaning and application in the
light of Christ's teaching and example, and in the lives of His
followers. And it had lately acquired a deeper meaning in contrast with the loveless intellectualism, which the writer clearly
regarded as one of the worst dangers in the teaching and
example of his opponents.

ἀγαπητοί] The first occurrence of the writer's favourite form
of address in these Epistles. Cf. iii. 2, 21, iv. 1, 7 ; 3 Jn. 1, 2,
5, 11. No conclusion can be drawn from its use as to the
meaning of the command. The reading of the received text
(ἀδελφοί) is found in the vocative only once in these Epistles.
Both words are suitable expressions to introduce an appeal to the
readers to show their brotherhood in Christ by active brotherly
love, whether the writer has primarily in view, as the objects of
the love which he inculcates, Christians as Christians, or men
as men. The attestation, however, is decisive in favour of
ἀγαπητοί. And, on the whole, it is not only more in accordance
with his style, but suits his appeal better. The ἀδελφοί may
have been suggested by the language of vv. 9, 10.

ἀπ᾽ ἀρχῆς] The meaning of this expression must, of course, be
determined from the context in each case. It is used eight
times in the First Epistle, and twice in the Second. In i. 1 it
recalls the use of ἐν ἀρχῇ in the first chapter of Genesis and in
the Prologue of the Gospel. Its use in iii. 8 (ἀπ᾽ ἀρχῆς ὁ διάβολος
ἁμαρτάνει) is similar. Twice in this present chapter (ii. 13, 14)
it occurs in the phrase, "Ye have known Him who is from the
beginning." The remaining instances in the two Epistles all
have reference to the "old" command. The repetition of the
words at the end of ver. 7 (ὃν ἠκούσατε [ἀπ᾽ ἀρχῆς]) in the

Received Text is almost certainly wrong. They have probably
been introduced from the similar phrase in ver. 24.

Where the phrase is used of the "old" command, it may
refer either to the early days of the Mosaic legislation, or to the
beginning of the education of each convert to whom the writer
is speaking, or to the beginning of his life as a Christian. A
reference to the teaching of Judaism on the subject of "love"
seems, on the whole, to satisfy the conditions best in each case.
But it is probably a mistake to attempt to define the meaning of
the phrase very rigidly. Long continuance is suggested rather
than a definite starting-point. It is not easy to determine
whether the writer is thinking of the beginning of the life of each
of his readers, or of their religious consciousness, or of their
Christian life. The point can be settled only by the more general
consideration of the character of the false teaching combated in
these Epistles. The real force of the expression is to heighten
the contrast of the "newer" teaching which placed knowledge
higher than love. The writer has in view the

> "Many Antichrists, who answered prompt
> 'Am I not Jaspar as thyself art John?
> Nay, young, whereas through age thou mayest forget?'"

He is confident that as against the "glozing of some new
shrewd tongue" that which was "from the beginning" will prove
to be "of new significance and fresh result."

ὁ λόγος ὃν ἠκούσατε] "The word which ye heard" must be
that which was told them by their teachers, whether Jewish or
Christian or both. The command to love one's neighbour was
common to both. ὁ λόγος more naturally suggests a whole
message rather than one definite command. But it may refer
to the new commandment of Jn. xiii. 34, regarded as a rule of
life rather than a single precept.

αγαπητοι ℵ A B C P al.[20] cat. vg. sah. cop. syr[utr] arm. Did. Thphyl.
Aug. Bed.] αδελφοι K L al. plur. aeth[utr] Oec. : om. j[scr] : αδελφοι μου
I[c] δ[299] (–).

ειχετε] εχετε 27. 29. 34. 42. 57[lect] 58[lect] a[scr] k[scr] : *habemus* **sah** :
habebamus **arm-ed.**

η 1[o]] pr. και I[a 7].

η κουσατε ℵ A B C P 5. 13. 27. 29. 39. 40. 65. 68. 81. 180 d[scr] j[scr] vg.
sah. cop. syr[utr] arm. aeth. Aug. Thphyl.]+απ αρχης K L al. longe plur.
cat. Oec.

8. The command, which is as old as the Law of Moses, even
if the writer did not regard it as implicitly contained in the story
of Cain and Abel (cf. iii. 11, 12, ἵνα ἀγαπῶμεν ἀλλήλους· οὐ
καθὼς Κάιν κ.τ.λ.) becomes new "in Him (*i.e.* Christ) and in you."
The ἐντολή, "Thou shalt love thy neighbour," received an
altogether new meaning and scope in the light of Christ's

teaching as to "Who my neighbour is," of His own example shown most clearly in His treatment of Tax-gatherers and Aliens, and of the carrying out of His example by His followers in the admission of Gentiles to the full privileges of Christianity on equal terms with the Jews. In Christ and in Christians the old command had gained "new significance and fresh result." The verse had, no doubt, a special significance in view of the recent victory gained over the false teaching, and its depreciation of the law of love, which characterized the conduct and the thought of its supporters. The author rightly saw in recent events how the Church had "rescued the law of love" from the darkness which threatened to overwhelm it. The true light was shining more brightly in consequence, and the darkness more quickly passing away. But though these recent events were the occasion, they do not exhaust the meaning of the words, which have a far wider reference. Wurm, who argues with great plausibility for the reference to the victory over the false teachers (see esp. p. 104), apparently confines the reference to that incident too narrowly. Though it affords a fairly adequate explanation of the words ἐν ὑμῖν, it is unsatisfactory as an explanation of ἐν αὐτῷ. The new significance of the law of love in Christ and in Christians had a far wider application. The light of the true knowledge of God was already shining and dispelling the darkness of exclusiveness by the light of love wheresoever the "darkness overtook it not."

πάλιν] The word clearly introduces another description of the same commandment, not another command. Cf. Jn. xvi. 28, πάλιν ἀφίημι τὸν κόσμον, where πάλιν cannot mean "a second time," and 1 Co. xii. 21, οὐ δύναται ὁ ὀφθαλμὸς εἰπεῖν τῇ χειρί . . . ἢ πάλιν ἡ κεφαλὴ τοῖς ποσίν. Cf. also Jn. xix. 37; Ro. xv. 10, 11, 12; 1 Co. iii. 20; (?) 2 Co. x. 7, xi. 16; He. i. 5, (?) 6, ii. 13, iv. 5, x. 30. The use of πάλιν in the N.T. to introduce another quotation in proof of the same point, or a further thought about the same subject, is fully established.

ὅ] The antecedent to the neuter relative is the clause ἐντολὴν καινὴν γράφω ὑμῖν. "It is a new commandment that I write unto you." The order lays the emphasis on ἐντολὴν καινήν. It is the "newness" of the old command which is said to be true in Him and in His followers.

ὅτι . . . φαίνει] The shining of the true light reveals the true character of that which the darkness hid or obscured. The force of the present tense in παράγεται and φαίνει is significant. They must be interpreted as presents. All is not yet clear and known, but the process has already begun. The darkness is passing away. Contrast "It has become bright as the sun upon earth, and the darkness is past" (Book of Enoch lviii 5)

There are many indications in the Epistle that the writer
regards the Parousia as imminent. Cf. especially ver. 18, ἐσχάτη
ὥρα ἐστίν. The present verse throws some light on the difficult
question of the relation between the teaching of the Gospel
and that of the Epistle on the subject of the Parousia. In
the Epistle the expectation is more clearly stated and more
obviously felt than in the Gospel, though in the earlier work the
idea of "the last day" not only receives definite expression,
but is something more than an obsolete conception, alien to
the author's real thoughts and sympathy, or a mere condescension to popular Christianity, fed on Apocalyptic expectation
and unable to bear a purely spiritual interpretation. A difference of emphasis is not necessarily a change of view. It is
doubtful if the two conceptions are really inconsistent. Their
inconsistency would not be felt by a writer of the particular
type of thought which characterizes the author. Their meeting
point lies in the idea of "manifestation," which is his characteristic expression for the Parousia, as also for the earthly life of
the Lord. For him the "Presence" is no sudden unveiling of
a man from heaven, who in the twinkling of an eye shall destroy
the old and set up the new. It is the consummation of a process
which is continuously going on. It is the final manifestation of
the things that are, and therefore the passing away of all that
is phenomenal. As eternal life "is" now and "shall be" hereafter, as judgment is a process already going on, because men
must show their true nature by their attitude to the Christ, while
its completion is a final act; so the Parousia is the complete
manifestation of that which is already at work. The time of
its completion is still thought of as "the last day," and "the
day of judgment." The true light is already shining, and the
darkness is passing away. But He who is coming will come.

καινην] om. *I*ᵃ ¹¹⁰⁰ (310) *K* δ¹⁶¹.
ο . . . αυτω] *in qua est ueritas*, boh. | εστιν] μενει *H* δ³ (C) *I*ᵃ ²⁰⁰ᶠ.
ο εστιν αληθες] om. *I*ᵃ ⁷⁰.
αληθες] post αυτω A.
εν υμιν] א B C K L al. longe plur. cat. vg. sah. boh-ed. syrˢᶜʰ etᵖ ᵗˣᵗ arm.
aeth. Thphyl. Oec. Aug. Bed.] εν ημιν A P 4. 7. 9. 22. 29. 31. 34. 47.
76* cˢᶜʳ tol. boh-cod. syrᵖ ᵐᵍ Hier. : om. εν *H* δ¹⁶² (269).
σκοτια] σκια A.

9. The true light was already shining and gaining ground.
The darkness was passing away. But it had not yet passed.
The perfect day had not yet dawned. All had not yet recognized
the light. And all who claimed to have done so could not
make good their claim. The true light, when once apprehended,
leads to very definite results. The claim to have recognized it,
if not borne out by their presence, is false. These results are

presented in sentences similar to vv. 4 and 6. The writer puts before his readers the cases of typical individuals, he that saith, he that loveth, he that hateth. The falsity of the claim is sharply stated. At the same time the form of expression (ἐν τῇ σκοτίᾳ ἐστὶν ἕως ἄρτι) would seem to suggest that there is more excuse for self-deception. The claimant is not called ψεύστης (v. 4). "It is always easy to mistake an intellectual knowledge for a spiritual knowledge of the Truth" (Westcott). To claim to have knowledge of God, actually realized in personal experience (γινώσκειν), without obeying his commands, is deliberate falsehood. To claim spiritual illumination without love may be due to the fact that we are deceiving ourselves. It may be the result of mistaken notions as to the function of the intellect. Those who put forward such a claim only show that their apprehension of the "light" is not at present so complete as they imagine.

The "light" is, of course, that which illumines the moral and spiritual spheres. Cf. Origen, *Comm. in Joann.* xiii. 23, φῶς οὖν ὀνομάζεται ὁ θεὸς ἀπὸ τοῦ σωματικοῦ φωτὸς μεταληφθεὶς εἰς ἀόρατον καὶ ἀσώματον φῶς, διὰ τὴν ἐν τῷ φωτίζειν νοητοὺς ὀφθαλμοὺς δύναμιν οὕτω λεγόμενος. In virtue of such "light" it is possible for men to go forward in moral duty and spiritual growth, just as the light of the sun makes it possible for them to walk on the earth's surface without stumbling or tripping up (cf. Jn. xi. 9 f.).

μισῶν] The writer naturally does not deal with the possibility of intermediate states between love and hatred. In so far as the attitude of any particular man towards his fellow-man is not love, it is hatred. In so far as it is not hatred, it is love. The statements are absolute. The writer is not now concerned with their applicability to the complex feelings of one man towards another in actual life, or how the feelings of love and hatred are mingled in them. It is his custom to make absolute statements, without any attempt to work out their bearing on actual individual cases. His work is that of the prophet, not of the casuist.

τὸν ἀδελφὸν αὐτοῦ] The full meaning of these verses can be realized only in the light of the revelation of the brotherhood of all men in Christ. In spite of the statements which are usually made to the contrary, we are hardly justified in saying that this universalism is beyond the writer's vision. The Christ of the Fourth Gospel is the Light of the World, but the command to love one another is given to those who have recognized His claims. In the Epistle, Christ is the Propitiation for the whole world. But this is potential rather than actual. The writer has to deal with present circumstances, and polemical aims undoubtedly colour the expression of his views. Prophet and

not casuist as he is, he is nevertheless too much in earnest to
lose sight of the practical. Vague generalities are not the instruments with which he works. A vapid philanthropy, or a pre-
tentious cosmopolitanism, which might neglect the more obvious
duties of love lying closer to hand, would find no favour with
him. The wider brotherhood might be a hope for the future, as
it is for us. But the idea of brotherhood was actually realized
among Christians, though in his own community it is clear that
much was still wanting in this respect. It is of this brotherhood
that he is primarily thinking. In his letters to individuals this
is even clearer than here (cf. 3 Jn. 5, 10). And the usage of
the word ἀδελφοί in the New Testament certainly favours this
view. At the same time, the wider view of the Sermon on the
Mount and the Parable of the Good Samaritan is in no way
contradicted by the more limited statements of this Epistle.
The language used here lends itself easily to a similar expansion.
The Lord had summarized the teaching of the Mosaic Law in
the words, "Thou shalt love thy neighbour and hate thine
enemy." The new light had revealed the brotherhood of all
men. In its light the term "brother" includes both classes,
neighbours and enemies, whom the Law had separated. He
who now hates his "brother" has not had his mental vision
cleared by the light. The writer's words can easily be made
to convey the wider truth. He certainly would not contradict
it. What he enforces is the first step towards its realization.
And he is always thinking of the next step which his readers
must take. Note the emphatic position of ἕως ἄρτι : the light is
shining and he is in darkness still.

Om. *totum comma* **sah**d.
εν 2°] pr. ψευστης εστιν και ℵ 15. 43. 98. 137 arm. aeth. Cypr.
σκοτια] σκια 100 (mg.).

10. The contrast is, as usual, stated in terms which carry it
a stage further, μένειν being substituted for εἶναι. It is possible
that a man might attain to the light. He cannot abide in it
without showing that love which the new light has revealed to
be the true attitude of Christian to Christian, and of man to
man. Cf. Jn. xii. 46, ἵνα πᾶς ὁ πιστεύων εἰς ἐμὲ ἐν τῇ σκοτίᾳ μὴ
μείνῃ : viii. 35, ὁ υἱὸς μένει εἰς τὸν αἰῶνα. The slave may learn
much, but he cannot abide in the house for ever.

σκάνδαλον . . . ἔστιν] The stumbling-block may be that which
a man puts either in his own way, or in that of his neighbour.
The word is not found elsewhere in the Johannine books,
except Apoc. ii. 14 (βαλεῖν σκάνδαλον ἐνώπιον τῶν υἱῶν Ἰσραήλ).
The verb is found in Jn. vi. 61, xvi. 1. The general usage of
the New Testament, and perhaps the use of the verb in the

Fourth Gospel, is in favour of the second interpretation. And
it gives a possible sense. He who loves his neighbour not only
abides in the light himself, but is also free from the guilt of
causing others to offend. But the general context almost
requires the other explanation. The effect of love and hate on
the man himself is the subject of the whole passage. The
sphere of his moral and spiritual progress or decline is regarded
as being within himself. The occasions of falling are within.
Cf. Hos. iv 17, ἔθηκεν ἑαυτῷ σκάνδαλα. This may be suggested
by what is probably the true form of the text, σκάνδαλον ἐν αὐτῷ
οὐκ ἔστιν, internal stumbling-block, causing offence within, there
is none. Possibly ἐν αὐτῷ may refer to ἐν τῷ φωτί, " In the
light there is nothing to cause stumbling." Cf., however, Jn. xi.
9, 10. For the phrase itself we may compare the Rabbinic
הַמֵּבִיא תְקָלָה לַחֲרֵיבוֹ quoted by Schlatter from Sifre, Num. v. 15.

εν αυτω B K L P al. pler. cat. vg. syr^p arm. Thphyl. Oec. Aug.] post
εστιν ℵ A C 5. 105 j^scr m syr^sch sah. Lcif.

11. The first part of this verse repeats verse 9. The
remainder emphasizes the dangers of the state described. The
man's mental, moral, and spiritual state must affect his conduct.
He "walks" in that in which he "is." He who walks about in
darkness can have no idea whither he is going. At every
moment he is in danger of falling. Hatred perverts a man's
whole action, and prevents conscious progress toward any
satisfactory goal. The darkness in which he has chosen to
abide ⟨μισῶν⟩ has deprived him of the use of those means which
he possesses of directing his course aright. It is an over-
fanciful interpretation which sees in the last words of the verse
any reference to the idea that darkness, or want of the opportunity of using them, actually destroys the organs of vision.
There is no reason to suppose that the writer had this physical
truth in view as he wrote. He may be thinking of Is. vi. 10;
comp. Ro. xi. 8-10 and the close parallel in Jn. xii. 35.

εστιν] μενει P.
τους οφθαλμους] post αυτου 2° 3. 42. 57. 95. 101.
αυτου 2°] om. ·K̄² δ¹⁶¹ (261).

12-17. Warning against love of the World. The appeal
based on the readers' position and attainments.

12-14. Grounds of the appeal.
15-17. Warning.
12. Before passing on to the more direct application of the
general principles which he has now stated in outline, the writer
reminds his readers of what their position is and what is involved
in it. He knows that they are harassed by doubts as to the

validity of their Christian position, so he hastens to assure them
of it, and to use his assurance as the ground of the appeal which
he is making. He writes to them the Epistle which is in course
of composition (γράφω), because they *are* already members of the
community of light. In virtue of what Christ is and has done,
the sin which separates them from God has been, *actually* in part,
potentially altogether, removed. The old, in their experience, and
the young, in their strength, have a power which stands them in
good stead. They *can* enjoy fellowship with God who is light,
and in the communion of that fellowship they can see clearly so
as to " walk " without stumbling, to avoid the false allurements
of the world, and the consequences which would follow their
acceptance of the false teaching of the many antichrists whose
presence shows that the last hour is come. And the reasons
which led him to write that part of his letter which has already
been penned (ἔγραψα; cf. 27, where the ταῦτα shows that the
reference is to the preceding verses) are similar. Those who
have learned by experience the truth of the Fatherhood of God
can confess the sins which their Father is faithful and just to
forgive, and as παιδία who need and can obtain fatherly discipline
and guidance they can go forward in the strength of love. Thus
their position as Christians is the ground of his appeal. Much
can be said to them which it would be impossible to address to
those outside. Most, in fact, of what he has to say is of the
nature of calling to remembrance that which they already know.
The true safeguard against their present dangers lies in their
realizing their Christian position, in carrying out in life the faith
and knowledge which they already possess, in rekindling the
enthusiasm of earlier days which has now grown cold. The
experience of age, and the vigour of youth and early manhood,
supply all that is needed to restore health in Christian thought
and life. The life of the society is safe if the two classes of
which it is composed will contribute of their treasure to the
common store, and use for themselves and for the community
the powers of which they are in actual possession.

γράφω] The present naturally refers to that which is in the
course of composition, the letter as a whole. The present tense
is used in i. 4, ii. 1, 13 (*bis*). In each case the reference may be
to the whole Epistle, though where ταῦτα is used it has suggested
to some the probability of a more limited reference. The
simplest explanation of the use of the aorist in ver. 14 (ἔγραψα) is
that the writer turns back in thought to that part of the letter
which he has already finished, the writing of which can now be
regarded as a simple complete act. Of the many explanations
which have been offered this would seem on the whole to be
the most natural, and least unsatisfactory. The suggestion that

the author wished to vary the monotony of six repetitions of the
same word need hardly be taken seriously.   He is afraid neither
of monotony nor of repetition, and the slight changes which he
introduces into his repetitions are seldom, if ever, devoid of
significance.   A reference to a former document, either the
Gospel, or a lost Epistle, is not probable.   The reasons given
for having written do not suit the Gospel, while they fit it
admirably with the present Epistle, and with that part of it
which has already taken shape.   The Gospel was undoubtedly
written for Christians rather than for those who were still " of the
world."   But its object was to instruct, to increase faith and
deepen spiritual life, by imparting wider knowledge and clearer
understanding of the real meaning of things already known.
The aim of the Epistle is to emphasize the important points of
what the readers have already grasped, and to persuade them
to use their knowledge to meet present dangers.   It was because
of the knowledge which all possessed, of the Christian experience
of the elder, and the strength and achievements in the Christian
warfare of the younger among his readers, that he could make
his appeal.   But for that, he could not have written what he had
written.   A reference to a former Epistle must almost necessarily
have been made clearer and more definite.   It is, of course, quite
possible that he had written to them before the present occasion.
That the Canon has preserved but a selection of the Apostolic
and sub-Apostolic correspondence is proved by the references
contained in the Pauline Epistles, and probably in 3 Jn. 9.
And if such a letter had been written, it might have been misunderstood and have required further explanation or justification
(cf. Karl, p. 32), as S. Paul found on two occasions during his
correspondence with the Corinthians.   But there is nothing in
the passage to suggest that this was the case.

It is still more difficult to suppose that the presents and the
aorists have exactly the same reference.   The use of the
" epistolary aorist " by which the author mentally transfers
himself to the position of the recipients of the letter, or " regards
his letter as ideally complete," is established.   But it does not
give us a satisfactory explanation of the change from present to
aorist.   Law's suggestion (*The Tests of Life*, p. 309), that after
writing as far as the end of ver. 13 " the author was interrupted
in his composition, and that, resuming his pen, he naturally
caught up his line of thought by repeating his last sentence," is
ingenious.   But again it must be noticed that there is nothing
to indicate that such a break actually took place.   Repetition
with slight changes not insignificant is a regular feature of the
author's style.

On the whole, the explanation to which preference has been

given above is the best solution of a difficult problem, unless we prefer to leave it in the class of problems insoluble without the fuller knowledge of the exact circumstances, which doubtless made the writer's meaning, and reasons for writing as he did, quite clear to those who read his words.

τεκνία] The use of the diminutive is confined in the New Testament to the Johannine writings, with the exception of one passage in S. Paul (Gal. iv. 19) where the reading is doubtful. It occurs only once in the Gospel. Its use is comparatively frequent in the Epistle (ii. 1. 12, 28, iii. 7, 18, iv. 4, v. 21). It is a natural word for the aged disciple, or Apostle, to use when addressing the members of a Church of whom many were no doubt his "sons in the Faith," and practically all must have belonged to a younger generation than himself. Differences of meaning must not always be pressed, but the word expresses community of nature, as contrasted with παιδία, which suggests the need of moral training and guidance (cf. 1 Co. xiv. 20, μὴ παιδία γίνεσθε ταῖς φρεσίν). Throughout the Epistle the word seems to be used as a term of affection for the whole society to which the author writes. The final warning of the Epistle (v. 21) against idols, literal or metaphorical, could hardly be addressed to the children as opposed to the grown-up members of the community.

The regular usage of the word in the Epistle has an important bearing on the next difficulty which these verses present, the question whether a double or triple division of the readers is intended. In the former case the clauses containing the vocatives τεκνία and παιδία are addressed to the whole community, which is then divided into the two classes of πατέρες and νεανίσκοι. This is now generally recognized as the most satisfactory interpretation. A triple division in which fathers are the middle term, could only be accepted as a last necessity. It might be possible, as Karl maintains, that the writer should first state the two extremes and then add the mean. But it is in the last degree improbable. Augustine's explanation, "Filioli, quia baptismo neonati sunt, patres, quia Christum patrem et antiquum dierum agnoscunt, adolescentes, quia fortes sunt et ualidi," fails to justify the relative position of the last two terms. And both terms, τεκνία and παιδία, have their significance as addressed to the whole body. All the children of the Kingdom share in the forgiveness of sins which Christ has won for them, and all are παιδία; for the teaching and exhortation, which he has found it necessary to impart to them, show that none of them has finished his Christian education. Not even the eldest of them is as yet τέλειος.

ὅ τι] The third difficulty of the passage is the meaning of

ὅτι. Does it introduce the contents of what is written, or the reasons for writing? Usage is probably in favour of the "causal" meaning. There is no certain instance in the Epistle of the use of ὅτι after γράφω in the "declarative" sense (cf. ver. 21). The "contents" are generally expressed by an objective accusation (ταῦτα, ἐντολὴν καινήν). But this is not decisive. It is a question which must be decided by the general meaning of the individual passage. In these verses the causal meaning certainly gives the better sense. Rothe, indeed, makes out a case for the declarative. "Here again (as in i. 5) John gives expression in another pregnant formula to that which he has to say to them. Shortly summarized it is this. He would have them know that in their case none of the necessary conditions for a complete Christianity are wanting, in all its real earnestness and joyful confidence. He adds further that this is not the first time that he has written this to them" (*Der erste Brief Johannis*, p. 61 f.). In other words, he has nothing new to tell them as Christians. He is merely reminding them of what they are. But surely the writer is doing more than this. He does not merely remind them of their Christian standing. He is trying to show them how their position as Christians enables them to meet the dangers to which they are exposed, and so to justify and enforce the appeal which he is making. It is *because* they are in fellowship with God and have real experience of the Fatherhood of God that he can appeal to them with confidence that his appeal will meet with a response.

ἀφέωνται] Cf. Lk. v. 20, 23, vii. 47, 48, and (probably) Jn. xx. 23. The present is used in Matthew and Mark.

διὰ τὸ ὄνομα αὐτοῦ] The "name" always stands for that which is implied by the name. In Jewish thought the name is never merely appellative. Because Christ is what He is, and has done what He has done, true relations between God and man have again become possible. If any definite name is intended, it is probably the name "Jesus Christ" (cf. ii. 1). The expression is not the mere equivalent of "because of His position as Paraclete and Propitiation." See Briggs, *The Messiah of the Apostles*, p. 475.

The origin of the phrase is probably to be found in the Old Testament doctrine that God continued His kindness to Israel, in spite of their rebelliousness, for His name's sake. Cf. especially Ezk. xx. 8, 9, "They rebelled—but I wrought for My name's sake"; xxxvi. 22, "I do not this for your sakes, O house of Israel, but for Mine holy name." It has, however, acquired a somewhat different meaning as used by the author. We may also compare the Rabbinic parallel, quoted by Schlatter, "The

wise say, For His name's sake He dealt with them (לְמַעַן שְׁמוֹ
עָשָׂה עִמָּהֶם, Mechilta, Ex. xiv. 15, 29*b*).

τεκνια] τεκνα 1. 10. 40 : παιδια 27. 29. 66**. 68. 103. 106 al.[10] sah. cat.
Sev.

　　υμιν] υμων L 31. 68. 99 a[scr] j[scr] k[scr] sah[d].

13. πατέρες] The word is more naturally taken as referring
to actual age than to length of Christian experience. "The
knowledge which comes of long experience is the characteristic
endowment of mature years." But the τὸν ἀπ' ἀρχῆς shows that
the writer is thinking of length of years as giving the opportunity
of maturity of Christian experience. And he writes in full view
of the circumstances. The full significance of the Person of
Jesus Christ was apprehended only very gradually either in the
society of His followers, or by its individual members. And in
the knowledge which had been thus slowly gained was to be
found the corrective of the false views which were leading men
astray (ver. 27). The knowledge of the fathers, as well as the
strength of the young men, was needed to meet the difficulties of
the time.

　　τὸν ἀπ' ἀρχῆς] The Word who was in the beginning with
God, of whose manifestation in human life the writer and his
contemporaries had been witnesses, and in whom the "fathers"
had come to believe with growing knowledge and fuller conviction as they gained experience, though they had not seen Him.
The phrase, "Him who is from the beginning," would have no
special significance here as applied to God. On the other hand,
the refusal, on the part of many among whom the writer lived, to
believe that the pre-existent Logos had become truly incarnate in
Jesus of Nazareth, and to go forward in that belief to closer
fellowship, seemed to him to be the most serious intellectual
danger which threatened the Church of his day.

　　νενικήκατε τὸν πονηρόν] "The characteristic of youth is
victory, the prize of strength." The conquest of evil, here represented as the result of an active struggle with a personal foe (τὸν
πονηρόν), is as characteristic of the earlier years of Christian
endeavour as is the fuller knowledge gained through experience
of its later years. The words have probably a primary reference
to the victory which had been gained in the assertion of the
truth, and which led to the withdrawal of the false teachers. But
they were meant to go beyond their original reference. If it was
"better age, exempt from strife should know," it was also "better
youth should strive toward making." And in both cases the
appeal is made on the ground of what has already been gained.
To the younger generation belonged the strength, already trained
and tested, which the experience of the elders could guide. And

both could rely on what had been acquired through past successes
in the special efforts which the present and the future demanded
from the whole Society.

εγνωκατε] εγνωκαμεν $I^{b\ 62\ 161}$ (498).
νενικηκατε] ενικησατε $I^{b\ 62\ 161}$ (498) K^2.
τον πονηρον] το πονηρον $\aleph$ 95.

14. For the moment the writer's thoughts turn back to what
he has already written.   In what he has already said he has
treated them as παιδία, still in need of discipline and guidance.
Their faith had not yet grown to maturity.   And this was true of
all alike, young and old, the thinkers as well as the soldiers of
the Society.   But it was in virtue of their Christian standing that
he could speak to them as he did.   In the Jewish Synagogue or
in the Christian Church they had all learned to know God as
their Father.   The elders among them had made real progress
in their realization of what the Christ really is.   The younger
and more active converts had gained the strength which comes
of victory over evil.   Perhaps they had rendered conspicuous
service in the recent crisis.   And their powers had matured in
the strife.   The message of the Gospel was a living force within
them, and permanently active.   It was abiding in them.   There
were flaws in the work which needed mending.   It had been
necessary to treat them, young and old alike, as not yet "grown
up."   The false pleas which many among them were only too ready
to listen to, if not to urge, must be sharply and clearly exposed.
Statements which they might well make, perhaps in some cases
had made, must be called quite definitely "lies."   He must not
shrink from plain language.   But he could never have ventured
to use the language which he had not hesitated to address to
them, had it not been for the great progress which they had
already made in the things of Christ.   Strength and experience
were really theirs.   Reproofs could be uttered and appeals made
with full confidence of success.   Their Christian faith was sound,
even though their hands might be slack, and their minds somewhat listless.   For them victory and knowledge were abiding
results, and not mere incidents in past history.

ἔγραψα] Cf. the notes on ver. 12.   The γράφω of the Received
Text is probably due to an attempt to get a series of three in the
right order of age, by correctors who failed to grasp the general
arrangement of these verses.

εγραψα 1° $\aleph$ A B C L P al.[35] cat. sah. cop. syr[utr] arm. aeth. Or.] γραφω
K al. sat. mul. arm[cdd aliq] Oec. fu. demid. harl. Aug.
εγραψα 2° . . . αρχης] om. vg-ed.
εγραψα 2°] scribo, vg-ed.
εγραψα 3°] scribo, vg-ed.
τον απ αρχης] το απ αρχης **B.**
του θεου] om. B sah.

15–17. Warning against love of the world.

The writer appeals to his readers, on the ground of their Christian standing, to avoid the love of the world. For him the world is the whole created system, considered as apart from God and opposed to God. But there is a tendency to narrow down its meaning either to humanity as estranged from God or regardless of God, or to all that is opposed to the Christian view. Such love for the present and finite, either as a whole or in its several parts, excludes the possibility of the higher love, of God and of men as brethren in Christ, which is the essential characteristic of "walking in light," and the observance of which sums up the whole of Christian duty in one command, at once old and new. The evil desires which assail men through the lower part of their nature in general, or through the sense of vision in particular, or through the external good which falls to their lot, if regarded and used as opportunities for display, have their origin not in the Father, but in the world which has broken loose from Him. And the world and the desires which it fosters are alike transitory. Only that which falls in with God's will, and carries forward His purpose, is of permanent value and lasting character.

15. ὁ κόσμος is not merely "an ethical conception" in the Johannine system, "mankind fallen away from God." Such an interpretation leaves no intelligible sense to the phrase τὰ ἐν τῷ κόσμῳ. It is the whole system, considered in itself, apart from its Maker, though in many cases the context shows that its meaning is narrowed down to "humanity." In the view of the writer, no doubt man is its most important part, the centre of the whole. But here it is used in its wider sense. The various interpretations which have been given of the phrase can be found in Huther and elsewhere. The majority of them are in reality paraphrases of particular instances of its use. As contrasted with ὁ κόσμος, τὰ ἐν τῷ κόσμῳ are the individual objects which excite admiration or love. In the next verse they are spoken of collectively. Comp. Ja. i. 27, iv. 4.

ουκ εστιν] post πατρος P Aug. : post αυτω 31.
του πατρος ℵ B K L P al. pler. cat. vg. sah. cop. syr^utr arm. Or. Dam. Thphyl. Oec. Aug.] του θεου A C 3. 13. 43. 65. 58^lect d^scr harl. aeth^utr : του θεου και πατρος 15. 18. 26. 36 **boh-cod.** (uid.).

16. The attempt to find in the terms of this verse a complete catalogue of sins, or even of "worldly" sins, is unsatisfactory. The three illustrations of "all that is in the world" are not meant to be exhaustive. The parallelism to the mediaeval uoluptas, auaritia, superbia is by no means exact. We may compare the sentence quoted by Wettstein from Stobaeus, φιληδονία μὲν ἐν ταῖς ἀπολαύσεσι ταῖς διὰ σώματος, πλεονεξία δὲ ἐν τῷ κερδαίνειν, φιλοδοξία δὲ ἐν τῷ καθυπερέχειν τῶν ἴσων τε καὶ ὁμοίων : but it is an illustration of the natural tendency to threefold division rather than an exact parallel. Still less successful is the attempt to find instances of the three classes in the Temptation of our Lord. The "desire of the simplest support of natural life" is hardly an ἐπιθυμία τῆς σαρκός. The first temptation turned on the wish, or the suggestion, to use super-natural powers to gratify a natural want. The "offer of the kingdoms of the civilized world" is not very closely connected with the "lust of the eyes." Nor again is the "call to claim an open manifestation of God's protecting power" an obvious instance of the use of gifts for personal ostentation. All such endeavours to find an ideal completeness in the *ad hoc* statements of a letter, written to particular people to meet their special needs, are misleading.

The opposition in this verse is not strictly accurate. "The things that are in the world" suggest objects, whether material or not, which call out desires or boasting rather than the feelings of desire or pride themselves. But it is quite in keeping with the author's style.

τῆς σαρκός] σάρξ denotes human nature as corrupted by sin. Cf. Gal. v 17 (ἡ γὰρ σὰρξ ἐπιθυμεῖ κατὰ τοῦ πνεύματος, τὸ δὲ πνεῦμα κατὰ τῆς σαρκός). The genitive is subjective, the desire which the flesh feels, in that which appeals to the man as gratifying the flesh. There is no need to narrow down the meaning any further to special forms of desire. There is really nothing in the Epistle to suggest that the grosser forms of immorality were either practised or condoned by the false teachers.

ἡ ἐπιθυμία τῶν ὀφθαλμῶν] The desire for all that appeals to the man as gratifying his sense of vision, a special form of the more general desire already described. Comp. πνεῦμα ὁράσεως, μεθ' ἧς γίνεται ἐπιθυμία (*Testament of Reuben* ii. 4).

ἀλαζονεία] Cf. Ja. iv. 16, νῦν δὲ καυχᾶσθε ἐν ταῖς ἀλαζονίαις ὑμῶν· πᾶσα καύχησις τοιαύτη πονηρά ἐστιν, and Dr. Mayor's note, who quotes Arist. *Eth. Nic.* iv. 7. 2, δοκεῖ ὁ ἀλάζων προσποιητικὸς τῶν ἐνδόξων εἶναι καὶ μὴ ὑπαρχόντων καὶ μειζόνων ἢ ὑπάρχει. Comp. *Testament of Dan* i. 6 ; *Joseph* xvii. 3.

The substantive is found in Ro. i. 30 ; 2 Ti. iii. 2. Love of display by means of external possessions would seem to be what is chiefly intended here. Βίος is always life in its external aspect, or the means of supporting life. Cf. iii. 17, ὃς ἂν ἔχῃ τὸν βίον τοῦ κόσμου : Lk. viii. 14, xv. 12.

ἐκ τοῦ πατρός] All such desires and feelings are not part of that endowment of humanity which has come from the Father. They are a perversion of man's true nature as God made him.

They have their origin in the finite order in so far as it has
become estranged from God.

τω] om. $I^{a\ 200f.}$ $δ457$ (83) $I^{b\ 365-398*}$.
η 1°] εστιν $I^{c\ 114}$ (335).
και 2°] om. $I^{a\ 382}$ (231) $Aπρ$ 1.
η 3°] om. $I^{a\ 264}$ (233).
ουκ εστιν] post πατρος $I^{a\ δ180}$ (1319).

17. All such objects of desire must in the end prove unsatisfactory, because of their transitory character.   Permanent value
attaches only to such things as correspond to God's plan for the
world and for men.   He that fulfils God's destiny for himself
"abideth for ever."   "In the mind of God, values are facts, and
indestructible facts.   Whatever has value in God's sight is safe
for evermore ; time and change cannot touch it."

> "All that is, at all,
> Lasts ever, past recall ;
> Earth changes, but thy soul and God stand sure :
> What entered into thee
> That was, is, and shall be."

αυτου] om. A 5. 13. 27. 29. 66** arm^{zoh} Or.
του θεου] αυτου $I^{a\ 367}$ (308) O^{36}.

εις τον αιωνα]+quomodo Deus manet in aeternum tol. Cyp. Lcif. Aug. :
+sicut et ipse manet in aeternum Cyp. Aug. : +quemadmodum ille qui est
in aeternum sah.   These glosses, which are not uncommon, especially in
Latin authorities, have a special interest in view of the textual phenonema
of ch. v.

II. ii. 18–27. Belief in Jesus as the Christ the sign of fellowship with God.   (Christological Thesis.)   The truth in contrast
with the second "lie."

> (1) Appearance of Antichrists the sign of the end (18).
> (2) Their relation to the Church (19–21).
> (3) Content and meaning of their false teachings (22–25).
> (4) Repeated assurance that the Readers are in possession
>   of the Truth (26, 27).

18–21. The writer passes by a natural transition from the
thought of the transitoriness of the world to that of its approaching
end.   The many forms of false teaching which have appeared are
embodiments of the spirit of Antichrist, and therefore are sure
signs of the nearness of the end.   The coming of Antichrist had
formed part of the Apostolic teaching which had been imparted
to them all.   His "coming" was a recognized sign of the im-
minence of the Parousia.

It is a matter of dispute whether the false teachers, or the
spirits of error who inspire them, are to be regarded as so
many precursors and heralds of Antichrist himself, in whom all
the various forces of hostility to Messiah are to be gathered up

4

for the one final conflict, or whether the many false teachers
are to be thought of as actual manifestations of Antichrist,
convincing proofs that the spirit of Antichrist is already present
in the world.   The form of the sentence, καθὼς ἠκούσατε . . . καὶ
νῦν is in favour of the latter explanation.   "You have always
been taught that Antichrist is to come.   The prophecy is now
being fulfilled in the many Antichrists who have made their
appearance."   Such an interpretation would be natural among
the Disciples of the Lord.   Had He not taught His Apostles to
see the fulfilment of what Malachi, and others, prophesied about
the Return of Elijah before the great and terrible Day of the
Lord in the coming of John Baptist?   And it is in complete
harmony with the author's way of thinking.   In the Johannine
teaching the present working of forces is not always clearly
distinguished or sharply separated from their final manifestation.
The author can speak of "having passed from death unto life,"
and still look forward to a "raising up at the last day" without
betraying any consciousness of the supposed inconsistency,
which a certain type of criticism has found in his method of
presentation.   He would probably have regarded with complete
indifference the question of whether the many antichristian
forces, of whose present working he was assured, were to find
their consummation in the person of a single opponent before
the final manifestation of his Lord and his God, or not.   There
is no reason to suppose that he could not have found room for
such a figure in his scheme of expectation.   His immediate
concern is with the relation of the many false teachers, who now
show forth the spirit of Antichrist, to the Christian community.
They had separated themselves off from the society of Christians,
and their action was to the writer clear proof that their connection
with that body could never have been more than superficial.
Those who had "gone out" could never have been really "of"
the community which they had not hesitated to leave, or in true
union and fellowship with the Christ.   It was necessary for the
health of the body that all such should be clearly seen to be no
true members of it.   Their true character needed to be disclosed.
And the readers could discover the truth for themselves if they
were willing to use and trust the powers of discernment
which they possessed.   In their baptism they had received the
anointing of the Holy One, even as the Kings and Priests of
the old Covenant were anointed with the oil which symbolized
the gift of God's Spirit.   What had then been granted to a few
was now extended to all.   They *all* possessed the gift of knowledge which enabled them to grasp the truth of what Christ had
revealed.   In what he wrote to them the author was not teaching
new truths.   He was recalling to their mind what they already

knew. And knowing the truth, they knew that no falsehood
could have anything to do with it.

(1) 18. The appearance of Antichrists the sign of the end.

παιδία] He still addresses them by the title which emphasizes
their need of instruction and guidance. Cf. ver. 14, and perhaps
iii. 7.

ἐσχάτη ὥρα] The absence of the article emphasizes the
character of the period. It suggests no idea of a series of periods
of stress which are to precede the several comings of Christ.
The conception of many partial "comings" has a very important
place in the elucidation of the permanent value of the New
Testament expectations of the Coming of the Christ, but it
is not to be found in those expectations themselves. The
Johannine teaching, whatever its origin may be, has taught us
to spiritualize the New Testament expression of the doctrine of
the last things. But the writer held firmly to the expectation
of a final manifestation of the Christ at "the last day," and he
seems to have expected it within the remaining years of his
own lifetime. When he uses the phrase "last hour" he clearly
means the short period, as he conceived it to be, which still
remained before the final manifestation of the last day. The
phrase is found here only in the New Testament. The expression ἡ ἐσχάτη ἡμέρα occurs in the Gospel (seven times),
and never without the article. Its use is confined to the
Gospel. Cf. Ac. ii. 17 (αἱ ἐσχ. ἡμ.); 2 Ti. iii. 1 (ἐσχ. ἡμέραι);
1 P. i. 5 (ἐν καιρῷ ἐσχάτῳ); Jude 18 (ἐν ἐσχάτῳ χρόνῳ). The use
of ὥρα in connection with the coming of Christ is frequent in
the Gospels, Mt. xxiv. 36 (= Mk. xiii. 32), xxiv. 42, 44, 50,
xxv. 13; Lk. xii. 40, 46. Cf. Ro. xiii. 11; Apoc. iii. 3.

The "last hour" is the last period of the interval between
the first and second coming of the Christ. Christian expectation
had inherited from Jewish apocalyptic the doctrine of a period of
extreme distress which was immediately to precede the coming
of Messiah, and in which the hostility of the World Powers was
to culminate in a single opponent. In the prevalence of so
many false views about the Person of Jesus, and His relation
to God, the writer sees the surest signs of their approach,
and probably the true fulfilment of the prediction of His
coming.

καθὼς ἠκούσατε] Cf. Mt. xxiv. 15, 24; Mk. xiii. 6; Ac. xx. 30,
and especially 2 Th. ii. 3. The subject formed part of the
general apostolic teaching. As in ver. 24, the aorist refers
to the time when they were instructed in the faith.

ἀντίχριστος] The preposition can denote either one who takes
the place of another (cf. ἀνθύπατος), or one who opposes (cf.
ἀντιστράτηγος, used of the opposing general, Thucyd. vii. 86, as

well as in later times for the Propraetor). The word may therefore mean one who, pretending to be the Christ, really opposes
Him and seeks to destroy His work. The word is found in the
N.T. only here and in ii. 22, iv. 3; 2 Jn. 7. But though the
word appears first in these Epistles, the idea is undoubtedly
taken over from Jewish Apocalyptic thought, to which it is also
probable that early Babylonian, or at least Semitic, nature-myths
had contributed. It is imposible to explain the references
to the subject which are found in the New Testament (Synoptic
Eschatological discourses, Pauline Epistles, especially 2 Th. ii.,
and Apocalypse) from the New Testament itself and the apocalyptic portions of Daniel and Zechariah. There must have
been some popular tradition, at once definite within certain
limits and varying according to the circumstances of the times,
from which the N.T. writers have drawn independently. The
late Christian writers, who may have derived the name from
the passages in these Epistles, have certainly drawn their material
from other sources besides the books of the N.T. The Johannine
Epistles contribute nothing but the first mention of the name.
The author refers to a popular tradition only to spiritualize it.
He makes no substantial addition to our knowledge of its
content (see additional note).

ἔρχεται] *sit uenturus* (vg.), cf. Mk. ix. 12, Ἡλείας μὲν ἐλθὼν
. . . ἀποκαθιστάνει. The present expresses the fact as the subject
of common teaching, rather than as about to be realized immediately. Cf. the use of ὁ ἐρχόμενος, Mt. xi. 3, xxi. 9; Mk.
xi. 9; Lk. vii. 19, 20, xiii. 35; Jn. i. 15, 27, vi. 14, xii. 13;
Ac. xix. 4; (?) 2 Co. xi. 4; He. x. 37.

γεγόνασιν] "have come to be," "have arisen." Their appearance was a natural outcome of the growth of Christianity. As
the truth of what Christ really was came to be more and more
clearly realized in the gradual growth of Christian life and experience, those who had been attracted to the movement by partial
views and external considerations, which had nothing to do with
its essential import, were necessarily driven into sharper antagonism. Growth necessitated the rejection of that which did not
contribute to true life. In the extent of such developments the
writer finds clear indication that the process is nearing completion
(ὅθεν γινώσκομεν).

ὅθεν γινώσκομεν ὅτι] It is the writer's favourite method of
exposition first to make his statement and then to state the
facts by which his readers can assure themselves of its truth.
When their first enthusiasm had died out, and delay had brought
disappointment, the question was often being asked, "How
can we know?" "From the fact just stated we come to
know."

παιδια] αδελφοι *I*ᵃ ¹⁷⁵ (319).
ωρα 1°] for τη C*.
και] om. k.
οτι ℵ B C K P al. pler. cat. vg. syrᵘᵗʳ aeth. Or. Epiph. Ir. Cypr.] om. A L
17. 96. 100. 142 aethʳᵒ.
αντιχριστος ℵ* B C 3. 5. 58ˡᵉᶜᵗ arm. Or. Epiph.] pr. ο ℵᶜ A K L al. pler.
cat. Thphyl. Oec. : αντιχρηστος *I*ᵃ ²⁰⁶ᶠ· ¹⁹²· ¹⁷³ (83).
γινωσκομεν] γινωσκωμεν A.

(2) **19. ἐξῆλθαν**] Cf. 3 Jn. 7. The word indicates (1) that originally they were members of the community, "they drew their
origin from us," (2) that they had now separated themselves
from the community. It suggests, if it does not compel us to
assume, that their "going forth" was their own act, and not
due to excommunication. But it is useless to attempt to reproduce by conjecture the exact historical circumstances, which
were too well known to both writer and readers to need further
elucidation. The false teachers had ceased to belong to the
community to which they had formerly attached themselves—
of the manner of their going forth, or of the exact causes which
led to it, we are ignorant.

ἀλλά] In spite of their external membership, they had never
been true members of the Body.

οὐκ ἦσαν ἐξ ἡμῶν] Their connection was purely external.
They did not share the inner life.

εἰ γάρ] Cf. iv. 20, v. 3 ; 2 Jn. 11 ; 3 Jn. 3, 7. As a rule, the
writer uses the more "objective" ὅτι to state the cause.

ἐξ ἡμῶν] The emphasis is now laid on the words ἐξ ἡμῶν.
They were not ours ; if ours they had been, they would have
remained with those to whom they (inwardly) belonged.

μεμενήκεισαν ἄν] The word μένειν, though it is here the
obvious word to use in any case, had a special significance for
the writer. "The slave abideth not in the house for ever. The
son abideth for ever." The test of true discipleship was to
"abide" in the truth, as made known by those who had seen
the Lord and been taught by Him. The writer cannot conceive
the possibility of those who had ever fully welcomed the truth
breaking their connection with the Christian society. External
membership was no proof of inward union. The severing of the
connection showed that such membership had never been anything but external.

μεθ' ἡμῶν] naturally expresses outward fellowship as distinguished from inward communion.

It was natural that the authors of theories of predestination
should find in this verse confirmation of their doctrine.

The writer follows his usual practice, which was also the
practice of his Master, of making absolute statements without
qualification. But the whole teaching and aim of his Epistle

shows that he recognized the danger, and therefore the possibility, of those who were truly "members of Christ" falling
away. "The subject here is neither a *donum perseverantiae*,
nor a distinction of the *Vocati* and *Electi*."

ἀλλ' ἵνα] For the elliptic use of ἵνα, cf. Jn. i. 8, xiii. 18;
Apoc. xiv. 13. The result is contemplated as part of the Divine
purpose. Some such phrase as τοῦτο γέγονεν must be supplied,
or the sense may be brought out by a paraphrase, "they had
to be made manifest" ("Sie *sollten* offenbar werden," Weiss).

οὐκ εἰσὶν πάντες ἐξ ἡμῶν] It is tempting to take the negative
as qualifying πάντες, in spite of the fact that the two words are
separated by the verb. In this case the meaning would be that
the incident, or incidents, to which the verse refers served a
wider purpose than the mere unmasking of the individuals concerned. It showed that external membership is no proof of
inward union. Their unmasking was necessary, for not all who
were external members of the Church really and inwardly belonged to it. But the usage of the New Testament in general,
and of the author in particular, is decisive against such an
interpretation of οὐ . . . πᾶς when the negative is separated
from the πᾶς. Cf. Mt. xxiv. 22; Mk. xiii. 20; Lk. i. 37; Ac. x. 14,
xi. 8; 1 Co. i. 29; Gal. ii. 16; Eph. iv. 29, v. 5; Jn. iii. 15, 16, vi. 39;
1 Jn. ii. 21; Apoc. vii. 1, 16, ix. 4, xviii. 22, xxi. 27, xxii. 3.
There is no parallel instance of οὐ . . . πάντες where the words
are separated. But the usage with the singular, and the influence
of Hebrew and Aramaic forms of expression on the style of the
writer, suggest that the plural should be understood as the
singular undoubtedly must be interpreted. And the meaning
thus obtained is supported by the context. The subject is, of
course, the "Antichrists," who have severed their connection
with the Christian Body. The interpretation given above suffers
from the extreme awkwardness of having to break the sentence
by taking ὅτι in a casual sense. "Their detection had to be
brought about; for all members are not true members, and the
fact must needs be made clear." It is still more awkward to
suppose (as Weiss) that the sentence is continued, "as if ἵνα
φανερωθῇ had preceded." It seems clear, therefore, that the
negative must qualify the verb, according to the usual construction of οὐ . . . πᾶς, and לֹא . . . כֹּל. And the meaning must
be, "they had to be made manifest; it was necessary to show
that none of them, however specious their pretensions, however
much they differed in character or in opinions, were truly
members of the Body." The extent of the apostasy, and the
variety of attack, had caused surprise and alarm. The writer
assures his "children" that it had its place and purpose in the
counsels of Him who saith, "A whole I planned." The author

finds comfort and assurance, for himself and for his readers, in
the thought that whatever happens is included in the one purpose of God, however much appearances may seem to indicate
the contrary. He has his own language in which to express
the Pauline τοῖς ἀγαπῶσιν τὸν θεὸν πάντα συνεργεῖ εἰς ἀγαθόν.

εξ ημων 3° B C 69. 137 aˢᶜʳ arm. syrˢᶜʰ etᵖ aeth. Amb. Optat.] post ησαν
א A K L P al. pler. cat. vg. Clem. Cyr. Epiph. Thphyl. Oec. Ir. Tert. Cypr.
Or. Did.

μεμενηκεισαν] μεμενηκεσαν Iᵃ ᵟ⁴⁵⁴ (262) Iᵇ ⁴⁷² Iᶜ ³⁶⁴ K⁵⁰⁰: μενενηκασιν
Iᵃ ²⁶⁴· ³⁹⁷ᶠᶠ· ¹¹⁰* (233) Iᵇ ᵟ³⁶⁸ Iᶜ ³⁵³· ¹⁷⁴·

φανερωθωσιν] φανερωθη 69 aˢᵉʳ syrˢᶜʰ etᵖ ᵐᵍ·
εισιν] ησαν Iᵃ ⁶⁴ (328) Iᶜ ¹⁷⁴ K⁴⁵³·
om. παντες 69 aˢᵉʳ syrᵘᵗʳ Ir. Eph.
ημων (?)] υμων Hᵟ⁶ (Ψ).

20. If the readers had trusted their own knowledge and
Christian experience it would have been unnecessary for the
writer to point out the antichristian tendency of the false
teachers who had "gone forth." The readers would have
detected it themselves. What he writes is an appeal to their
knowledge rather than an attempt to supply its deficiencies by
instruction. In virtue of the gift of the Holy Spirit which all
had received at baptism, they all had knowledge to deal with the
circumstances of the case. See Findlay, p. 223.

χρίσμα] The idea is suggested by the preceding ἀντίχριστοι.
They had the true unction of which the opponents claimed to
be in possession.

It is hardly correct to say that according to its form the word
χρίσμα must denote, not the act of anointing, but the anointing
oil (Salböl, Weiss). Words ending in -μα can certainly denote the
action of the verb, regarded as a whole rather than in process,
and in a sense corresponding to the use of the cognate accusative.
The use of the word in the O.T., where it occurs chiefly in
Exodus, points in the same way. Τὸ ἔλαιον τοῦ χρίσματος is the
usual translation of שֶׁמֶן הַמִּשְׁחָה. Cf. Ex. xxix. 7, λήψῃ τοῦ ἐλαίου
τοῦ χρίσματος: xxxv. 14, 19, xxxviii. 25 (A, χρίσεως B), xl. 7
(χρίσεως B), xl. 13, ὥστε εἶναι αὐτοῖς χρίσμα ἱερατίας εἰς τὸν
αἰῶνα (לְהְיֹת לָהֶם מָשְׁחָתָם לִכְהֻנַּת עוֹלָם); xxx. 25, ποιήσεις αὐτὸ
ἔλαιον χρίσμα ἅγιον (וְעָשִׂיתָ אֹתוֹ שֶׁמֶן מִשְׁחַת קֹדֶשׁ), ἔλαιον χρίσμα
ἅγιον ἔσται (שֶׁמֶן מִשְׁחַת קֹדֶשׁ יִהְיֶה). Thus χρίσμα denotes the
act of anointing rather than the oil which is used in the action.
It always translates מִשְׁחָה and not שֶׁמֶן.

Anointing was the characteristic ceremony of consecrating
to an office, and of furnishing the candidate with the power
necessary for its administration. It is used of *priests*, Ex.
xxix. 7, xl. 13 (15); Lv. vi. 22; Nu. xxxv. 25: of *kings*,
1 S. ix. 16, x. 1, xv. 1. xvi. 3, 12; 1 K. xix. 15, 16: of *prophets*,

1 K. xix. 16; Is. lxi. 1. Those who were so consecrated were regarded as thereby endued with the Holy Spirit, and with divine gifts. Cf. 1 S. xvi. 13, ἔχρισεν αὐτὸν . . . καὶ ἐφήλατο πνεῦμα Κυρίου ἐπὶ Δαυεὶδ ἀπὸ τῆς ἡμέρας ἐκείνης: Is. lxi. 1, πνεῦμα κυρίου ἐπ᾽ ἐμέ, οὗ εἵνεκεν (יַעַן) ἔχρισέν με. Under the new dispensation the special gift, which in old times was bestowed on the few, is the common possession of all. Cf. Joel ii. 28 (iii. 1); Ac. ii. And in virtue of the gift of the Holy Ghost *all* have knowledge. The true text emphasizes the universality o. the possession among Christians (οἴδατε πάντες), and not of the knowledge which it conveys (πάντα). The possession by all of them of the knowledge which enables them to discern, and not the extent of their knowledge, is the ground of the writer's appeal.

ἀπὸ τοῦ ἁγίου] The evidence is not decisive as to whether the writer meant these words to refer to the Father or to the Son, or, indeed, whether he was conscious of the necessity of sharply defining the distinction. All things which men receive from the Father, they have from the Son, in virtue of their connection with Him. The definition of personality which later ages found to be necessary was apparently not present to the consciousness of the writer. Sometimes he distinguishes Father and Son with absolute clearness. At other times he uses language which may be applied indifferently to either. The relation of the Son to the Father is not conceived in accordance with ideas of personality which belong to later ages.

Ὁ ἅγιος τοῦ Ἰσραήλ is frequently found as a title of God in the O.T. Cf. Ps. lxx. 22, lxxvii. 41; Is. i. 4, v. 16, xvii. 7, 8, xxx. 12, 15, xxxvii. 23, xli. 20: ὁ ἅγ. Ἰσ., xliii. 3, xlv. 11, xlix. 7, lv. 5. The absolute use of ὁ ἅγιος is rare, and confined to late books, Hab. iii. 3; Bar. iv. 22, v. 2 (A, τοῦ αἰωνίου B); Tob. xii. 12, 15 (κυρίου א).

The usage of the Apocalypse (iii. 7, ὁ ἅγιος ὁ ἀληθινός) favours the reference to God. On the other hand, in Mk. i. 24, Jn. vi. 69, ὁ ἅγιος τοῦ θεοῦ is used of Christ. And the teaching of the later discourses in S. John on the subject of the Mission of the Spirit by Christ, and in His name, makes the reference to Christ more probable. We may also compare Ac. iii. 14, τὸν ἅγιον καὶ δίκαιον. The evidence, therefore, though not conclusive, is on the whole in favour of referring the title to Christ, if a sharp distinction ought to be made.

By their chrism they were set apart for the service of the Holy One, and endued with the powers necessary for that service. It is immaterial whether the writer speaks of God or of Christ as the immediate source of their holiness.

καὶ οἴδατε πάντες] The reading of the Received Text is an obvious correction. It presents a smooth and easy text which

is in reality far less suitable to the context than the reading of
the older authorities. The emphasis is on "knowing." This is
brought out with greater force and clearness by the omission of
the object. Under the new covenant, knowledge is the common
possession of all. The chrism is no longer confined to kings
and priests. The gift of the Spirit, of which it is the symbol and
the "effective means," is for all Christians alike. Incidentally
also the difference between the old covenant and the new serves
to emphasize the more pressing difference between the claims of
a select few to have a monopoly of knowledge, and the Christian
view that the gifts of the Spirit are for all. Cf. Lk. xi. 13, πόσῳ
μᾶλλον ὁ πατὴρ ὁ ἐξ οὐρανοῦ δώσει πνεῦμα ἅγιον τοῖς αἰτοῦσιν αὐτόν;

κat 1°] sed vg.
χρισμα] χαρισμα Iᵃ ⁵⁰² (116).
και 2°] om. B sah.
παντες ℵ B P 9 arm. sah. Hesych.] παντα A C K L al. pler. vg. cop.
syr. aeth. Did. Thphyl. Oec.
(?) om. οιδατε, ~εχετε post και 2° K ⁵⁰⁰.

21. The writer's appeal to his readers to use their power of
discernment is based on their knowledge, not on their need of
instruction. But for such knowledge it would be useless to
make the appeal.

ἔγραψα] refers, as usual, to what has been already written,
and especially to what immediately precedes.

καὶ ὅτι πᾶν ψεῦδος κ.τ.λ.] This clause may be either subordinate
to the preceding one, depending on the verb οἴδατε, or co-ordinate
with it; (1) if ὅτι is demonstrative the meaning will be, "Because
you know the truth, and know that no lie is of the truth, and
therefore must reject the lie the moment its true character is
made manifest"; (2) if the ὅτι is causal, the sentence must mean,
"I have written what I have written because you have knowledge,
and because no lie has its source in the truth. Those who
know the truth are in a position to detect at once the true
character of that which is opposed to it." In the first case, they
need teaching that the thing is a lie, and they will at once reject
it. In the second, their knowledge of the truth enables them to
detect at once the character of its opposite. The latter gives the
fullest sense, and that which is most in harmony with the context.
If he can but awaken their knowledge, his task is done. They
possess the means, if they will only use them. The whole object
of the Epistle is to "stir up the gift that is in them."

πᾶν . . . οὐκ ἔστιν] For the construction, see the notes on
ver. 19. And for ἐκ, cf. vv. 16, 19 and Lk. xx. 5.

οτι 2°] om. Iᵇ ᵟ³⁶⁸ (266).
και] om. boh-ed.
παν] om. C.

(3) 22-25. Content and meaning of the false teaching, 22 ff.
Falsehood finds its consummation in the one lie, which denies
that Jesus of Nazareth is the Christ, *i.e.* not merely the Jewish
Messiah, but also the Christ according to the wider conception
of His office which finds its expression in the Fourth Gospel and
in this Epistle.   Such a denial is the very work of Antichrist, who,
setting himself up for Christ, destroys the work of the true Christ.
The denial of the Son carries with it the denial of the Father also.
The false teachers, whether Jews who claim to worship the same
God as the Christians after a true fashion, or "Gnostics" who
claim a superior and exclusive knowledge of the Father of all,
forfeit their claim by rejecting the revelation of Himself which He
has given in His Son Jesus Christ.   The confession of the Son,
in word and in life, affords the only true access to the Father.

22. τίς] Cf. v. 5, τίς ἐστιν ὁ νικῶν . . . εἰ μή; there is no other
exact parallel in the N.T.   The expression is forcible.   No one
else stands for falsehood so completely as he who denies that
Jesus is the Christ.

ὁ ψεύστης] The article is not merely generic, denoting the
individual who adequately represents the class.   It denotes *the*
liar, *par excellence*, in whom falsehood finds its most complete
expression.   Cf. Jn. iii. 10 (σὺ εἶ ὁ διδάσκαλος ;).

οὐκ ἔστιν] For the double negative, cf. Lk. xx. 27 (οἱ
ἀντιλέγοντες ἀνάστασιν μὴ εἶναι) ; He. xii. 19 (παρῃτήσαντο μὴ
προσθεῖναι).   We are hardly justified in seeing any special force
in the retention of "a redundant οὐ in a clause of indirect
discourse depending on a verb meaning to deny" (cf. Burton,
N. T. Moods and Tenses, p. 181, § 473).

Ἰησοῦς οὐκ ἔστιν ὁ Χριστός] The following clause shows that
ὁ Χριστός has come to mean much more than the Jewish
Messiah.   It includes a special relationship to God which was
not a necessary part of Jewish Messianic expectation.

It is not easy to determine how far there is any special
reference in the phrase, as used here, to the separation of Jesus
from the Christ, according to the Cerinthian, or Gnostic, distinction of the human Jesus from the higher being, or "aeon,"
according to later Gnostic terminology, who descended on Jesus
at the Baptism, and left Him before the Passion.   It may well
include such a reference, without its meaning being thereby
exhausted.   The "master-lie" is the denial of the true nature of
the Incarnate Christ, as the writer and his fellow-Christians had
come to know Him.   Cerinthianism may be included, but
Cerinthus is not ὁ ἀντίχριστος.   And there is no reason for
assuming that the many Antichrists, in whose appearance the
writer sees the fulfilment of the saying "Antichrist cometh," all
taught exactly the same doctrine.

οὗτος] The liar, who denies the truth of the Incarnation. Cf.
Jn. i. 2, 7, vi. 46, vii. 18, xv. 5 ; 1 Jn. v. 6. 20 ; 2 Jn. 7, 9. The
reference of οὗτος in this writer is always to the subject, *as
previously described.*

ὁ ἀντίχριστος] The writer spiritualizes, if he does not altogether depersonalize, the popular conception. The spirit of
Antichrist finds its fullest expression in the denial of Father and
Son. The writer is not specially interested in the literal fulfilment of the legend. He would probably have met curious
questions on the subject with the answer, ἐν τούτῳ ὁ λόγος ἐστὶν
ἀληθινὸς ὅτι Ἀντίχριστος ἔρχεται. πολλοὶ πλάνοι γεγόνασιν, οἱ μὴ
ὁμολογοῦντες Ἰησοῦν Χριστὸν ἐν σαρκὶ ἐληλυθότα, or words to the
same effect.

ὁ ἀρνούμενος κ.τ.λ.] Cf. Introduction, p. xlii. Recent writers
like Wurm (*Die Irrlehrer Bibl. St.* viii.) and Clemen (in
ZNTW vi. 3, 1905, p. 271 ff.) are right in insisting on the
importance of this and the following clause in determining the
character of the false teaching combated in these Epistles. But
the clauses do not compel the conclusion that the false teachers
agreed with the writer in their doctrine of God, and differed only
in their Christology. The writer sees in their Christological
views the starting-point of their errors, and he points out that
these views involve wholly false conceptions of God, and debar
those who hold them from any true intercourse or conscious
communion with the Father. He certainly draws from their
Christology the conclusion that they "have not the Father."
But these words would apply to any teachers who claimed to have
special and unique knowledge of the Father, not only to those
whose views on the subject agreed with the views of the writer.
There is nothing in the words to exclude a reference to Cerinthus,
or similar teaching, although he held the Creator of the World to
be "uirtus quaedam ualde separata et distans ab ea principalitate
quae est super universa, et ignorans eum qui est super omnia
Deum " (Iren. i. xxvi. 1). It is therefore quite possible that a
polemic against Cerinthus is included, even if we regard Irenaeus,
rather than the reconstructed *Syntagma* of Hippolytus, as giving
the truer account of Cerinthus' teaching.

The words would have special force if one of the most
prominent of the false teachers had put forward the view that
the giver of the Law, or the God of the Jews, was only one of
the ἄγγελοι κοσμοποιοί, and not the supreme God. Such an one
certainly denied not only the Son, but the Father as revealed by
the Son.

But the writer is not concerned with the details of a system.
He is dealing with the general tendency of certain types of
teaching. And his argument is that since all true knowledge of

God comes through the revelation of Him made by Jesus Christ, before and by means of the Incarnation, those who reject this revelation in its fulness can have no conscious communion (ἔχειν) with the Father whom He revealed, whatever superior knowledge of God, as the Father of all, they may claim to possess.

τις] + γαρ I^c 258 (56).
ει μη] om. I^c 114 (335).
Ιησους] pr. ο I^b 253 (2).
αντιχρηστος I^a 382. 173 (231).
τον πατερα] το πνευμα I^a δ454 (262).
υιον] + αρνειται H^δ6 (Ψ).

23. ἔχει] "As one who enjoys the certain possession of a living friend." Cf. 2 Jn. 9.[1]

ὁ ὁμολογῶν] For the stress laid on ἀρνεῖσθαι and ὁμολογεῖν, cf. Jn. i. 20, ix. 22, xii. 42.

ο I^1] om. I^a 397 fff. (96) I^c 364 : + ουν K.
πας] om. I^b 472 (312).
ο ομολογων . . . εχει 2°] om. K L al. plur. Oec.

24. ὑμεῖς] For the construction, cf. Jn. vi. 39, viii. 45, x. 29, xvii. 2, 24. The ὑμεῖς is placed in emphatic contrast with the Antichrists whose true position has been made manifest. The readers only need to make sympathetic use of what they already possess. The truth which had always been theirs must be given full scope to abide and grow, and it will supply the answer to all new difficulties as they arise. It will enable them intuitively to reject all that is not on the line of true development.

ἀπ' ἀρχῆς] Probably refers to the beginning of their life as Christians. It may, however, include what many of them had heard in the Jewish synagogue. The true message "began" with the beginning of the revelation contained in the Jewish scriptures.

ἐὰν ἐν ὑμῖν κ.τ.λ.] The form of the sentence is characteristically Johannine. By repetition, stress is laid on the importance of the teaching. It is an indication of the value set upon his words by the authoritative teacher, who knows the vital import of his message for those to whom he delivers it in their present circumstances. And the changed position of ἀπ' ἀρχῆς

---

[1] Some editors connect this with ver. 22, putting a full stop at ὁ ἀντίχριστος and a colon at τὸν υἱόν. thus : "This is the Antichrist. He that denieth the Father (denieth) the Son also : every one that denieth the Son hath not the Father either." But the ellipse of the verb would leave us with a very awkward sentence. It should be noted, however, that the maker of the Bohairic Version understood the words in a similar sense. "This is Antichrist, because he that denieth the Father denieth also the Son." The same interpretation is necessitated by the reading of Ψ (see von Soden, *Die Schriften des NT.* p. 1860).

emphasizes the approved character of the message. It reaches back to the very beginning.

καὶ ὑμεῖς κ.τ.λ.] The apprehension of the truth leads to real communion with God through His Son. As truth is appropriated their fellowship with the Divine grows and becomes more real. It is obvious that to the writer μένειν means something more than "standing still." It is the "abiding" of the son who grows up in the house.

υμεις 1° א A B C P 13. 27. 29. 66**. 68. 69. 76. 81. 14^lect 57^lect a^scr vg. syr^p arm. Cyr.]+ουν K L al. pler. cat. Thphyl. Oec. Aug. It was natural that the frequent use of ουν in the Gospel should cause its occasional insertion by later scribes in the Epistle.

απαρχης 1°] om. *I*^c 208 (307).

εν (? 1°)] for και *I*^a 397t. 205 261 (96) *O*^46.

ηκουσατε] ακηκοατε א (et 2°): ηκουσαμεν *I*^b 62 (498).

εαν 1°] pr. και *I*^c 551 (216): +δε *K* δ459 (195).

om. εν 2° א*.

μεινη] μενη K 95. 105.

απ αρχης 2°] post ηκουσατε 2° א (ακηκοατε) vg. harl. sah. cop. syr^sch.

εν 3° . . . πατρι] εν τω πατρι και εν τω υιω א 4. 5. 38. 68. 80. 98. 104 c^scr h^scr syr^sch aeth. sah^d.

om. εν 4° B vg. boh-cod. Aug. | πατρι] πνευματι *I*^a δ505 (31).

25. αὕτη] has been interpreted as referring either backward, to the abiding in the Son and in the Father; or forward, to the eternal life. In favour of the former it has been urged that the Gospels contain no definite promise by Christ of eternal life which would justify the latter interpretation. But there are many passages in the Fourth Gospel which clearly imply such a promise. And the reference forward is in accordance with the writer's style. Cf. i. 5, etc. In either case the meaning is much the same, whether the promise is of eternal life, or of abiding communion with the Father and the Son. In the writer's view, eternal life "consists in union with God by that knowledge which is sympathy" (Westcott). Cf. Jn. xvii. 3.

αὐτός] Christ. Cf. iii. 3, and other passages.

αυτος] om. **boh-codd. sah.**

ημιν] υμιν B 31* am. fu.

αιωνιαν B.

(4) **26, 27**. Repeated assurance of the readers' knowledge of the Truth.

26. ταῦτα] What has been said about the false teachers, and how the danger can be detected and met (18–25). The reference to the whole section is far more natural than to the exhortation to "abide" only (ver. 24 f., cf. Weiss). The words are not aimless. They serve to close the subject, and in connection with what follows to account for the brevity of his treatment of it. The writer has only to call to their remembrance the essential features of their own faith, and the grave issues raised by the antichristian teaching. The chrism which they have received will enable them to do the rest for themselves. They are in possession of all that is necessary for self-defence, if they use the power which has been given to them.

ἔγραψα] Cf. ver. 14. The clearness of the reference here points to the most probable meaning of that verse. There is no need to suppose (with Karl) that there is a reference to a former Epistle, which had been misunderstood, through the readers applying to the whole Church what had been said with reference only to the guilty members, who had now "gone forth."

πλανώντων] The danger is present and real, but the use of the present tense does not determine the extent to which the opponent's efforts had met with success. Cf. Rev. xii. 9.

ταυτα]+ δε ℵ syr^{sch}.
πλανουντων A.
περι . . . υμας] *ne quis uos seducat* arm.; *de eo qui uos seducit* boh-cod.

27. καὶ ὑμεῖς] For the nominative absolute, cf. ver. 24. The position of ὑμεῖς is significant. The readers must meet the attempts to lead them astray by efforts on their own part. Warning and exhortation are of no avail without their active response.

τὸ χρίσμα ὃ ἐλάβετε] Cf. Jn. xiv. 26, xvi. 13.

ἀπ' αὐτοῦ] From Christ, who is thought of as the source of the anointing, according to His promise to His disciples (Jn. xiv.). Throughout this passage, with the probable exception of ver. 29, αὐτός seems to refer to Christ. This is the customary usage of the Epistle, except where the context determines otherwise.

χρείαν ἔχετε] Cf. Jn. ii. 25, xvi. 30; and with the infinitive, Jn. xiii. 10.

ἵνα] One of the many instances of the purely definitive use of ἵνα. Attempts to find in it any *telic* force produce altogether forced interpretations.

The gift of the Spirit which they received when they were baptized into Christ's name was an abiding gift (cf. Jn. i. 33). Its teaching is universal, it covers the whole ground where instruction is needed, and it is true. It is not the lie which the Antichrists have made of it. And though there was need of growth and development, all that was necessary and true was already contained implicitly in the teaching which they had received at the beginning. What they were taught at the first gave the standard by which all later developments must be measured. Their rule of life and thought, in accordance with

which they "abide" in Christ, is the true teaching of the Spirit,
which they received from the first days of their conversion.
They must abide "as He taught them." The earliest teaching
had not been superseded by a higher and altogether different
message, as the Gnostics would have it. They needed no
further teaching. What they had received covered the necessary
ground. It was true. It had not been superseded by deeper
truths.

If this is the writer's meaning, the second part of this verse
(ἀλλ᾽ ὡς . . . αὐτοῦ) forms only one sentence : μένετε ἐν αὐτῷ ὡς . . .
διδάσκει, καὶ ἀληθές ἐστιν . . ., καὶ καθὼς ἐδίδαξεν. The method
of their abiding is characterized in three ways. They dwell
in Christ, (i.) in accordance with the teaching which they have
received, (ii.) which is sufficient, and true, (iii.) and permanent,
never having been altered or superseded (διδάσκει περὶ πάντων,
ἀληθές, καθὼς ἐδίδαξεν), though they are, or ought to be, continually learning more of its meaning.

It is, however, possible to divide the sentence and make καὶ
ἀληθές, etc., the apodosis to ὡς τὸ αὐτοῦ κ.τ.λ. "*As* the unction
teaches all that you need to know, *so* it is true and no lie. And
as He taught you from the beginning, you abide in Him (or
possibly you abide in the teaching which was taught you from
the beginning). You have not to learn a new and better
Christianity."

But the introduction of an apodosis by καί is not in the
writer's style, and the result is a very weak climax. "The
teaching you have received is not only comprehensive, it is true
and not false." On the other hand, if καθώς is taken as resumptive, we get a natural sequence, which is quite suitable to the
context and the writer's general thought. The unction which
they received gives a teaching which is comprehensive, true,
homogeneous. The later lessons grow out of the earlier, which
need not be unlearned. To abide in Christ is to live by the
lessons which were first learned, the import of which has grown
with the growth of their experience and spiritual intelligence.
Some Latin texts make ἐν αὐτῷ = ἐν τῷ χρίσματι: ver. 28 shows
that it must mean "in Christ."

ἀλλ᾽ ὡς] The reading ἀλλά is obviously a correction to
simplify a difficult sentence.

μένετε] may be either indicative or imperative. The preceding μένει strongly supports the former alternative. Cf. ver. 29 ;
Jn. v. 39, xii. 19, xiv. 1, xv. 18, 27, where we have a similar
doubt.

ψεῦδος] not ψευδές, which falls short of it, in much the same
way as in English "the statement is false," would differ from
"the whole thing is a lie."

χρισμα 1°] χαρισμα B 10**.

απ] παρ $I^{a\ 200f}$ (83) $I^{c\ 114}$ Aθ.

μενει א A B C P 5. 13. 31. 68 d^{scr}* vg. sah. cop. aeth. Ath. Did. Cyr. Thphyl. Aug.] post υμιν K L al. pler. cat. syr^{p} Oec. : μενετω P 6. 7. 8. 13. 27. 29. 31. 66**. 68. 69. 81. 137 a^{scr} d^{scr} vg. syr^{p} Thphyl. Aug. : *maneat* (s. *manebit*) *in uobis* arm.

διδασκη] διδασκει C K L 13. 31**. 100. 101. 106 al.^{4 scr} : pr. *scribat uobis aut* boh. : διδαξη H^{δ6} (Ψ) $I^{a\ 200}$ (-ει) δ355 K^{500}.

υμας (? 1°) ημας και ημεις υμιν $I^{a\ 258}$ (56).

αλλ ως] αλλα B 25 aeth. Aug. Hier.

αυτου 2°] αυτο A K L al. longe. pl. cop. Thphyl. Oec. Hier.

χρισμα 2°] χρισματα $I^{a\ 382.\ 173.\ 1402}$ (231) : χαρισμα 10** : πνευμα א* 25. 81 cop. aeth. Cyr. : +ο ελαβετε απ αυτου $I^{a\ δ180}$ (1319).

υμας 2°] ημας H^{257} (33) $I^{a\ 70.\ 175}$.

αληθες] αληθης א.

εστιν ? 1°] $I^{c\ 250}$ (56).

ψευδος] ψευδες C (uid.) P : +*in eo* sah. : *mendax* boh.

και καθως] om. και A sah. Aug.

εδιδαξεν] εδιδαξαμεν H^{162} (61).

υμας 3°] ημας $I^{a\ 175}$ (319) $I^{a\ 258}$.

μενετε] μενειτε K L al. longe. plur. cat. Thphyl. Oec. : μεινατε $I^{a\ 2001}$ (83).

αυτω]+τω θεω $I^{c\ 258}$ (56).

? ? υμας∽υμας $I^{a\ 200f.}$ (83) etc.

28, 29. These verses are transitional, and it is doubtful whether they should be attached to the preceding or the following section. The "aphoristic meditations" of this Epistle do not always lend themselves to sharp division.

28. The need of constancy, and its reward. Confidence in the presence of the Judge.

28. καὶ νῦν] can hardly be taken as temporal, the exhortation to abide being specially needed in view of the nearness of the Parousia, which is expected in the immediate future, at the end of the last hour, which has already struck. The general use of the phrase seems to be to introduce a statement, especially a prayer, exhortation, or command, which is regarded as the necessary deduction from the requirements of present circumstances. "Since the case is so," "such being the case," would perhaps bring out the meaning most clearly by paraphrase. Cf. Jn. xvii. 5 ; Ac. iii. 17, vii. 34 (= Ex. iii. 10), xiii. 11, xx. 22, 25, xxii. 16, xxvi. 6 ; 2 Jn. 5. Contrast Jn. xi. 22. Cf. also Ac. v. 38, xvi. 37.

τεκνία] The term of affection, which appeals to their common (spiritual) nature, is used to enforce the exhortation. Cf. vv. I, 12 ; Jn. xiii. 33 ; Gal. iv. 19 ; 1 Jn. iii. 7, 18, v. 21.

✗ **μένετε ἐν αὐτῷ]** The words are resumptive of ver. 27. What is there stated as a fact (*indic.*) the writer now repeats as an exhortation. He would have them continue in that which they have. And their greatest possession is their personal fellowship with their Master. The strength of the Society lies in the personal relationship of the members to the Head.

The use of φανερωθῇ, and of παρουσία in the next clause, make it almost certain that the reference of ἐν αὐτῷ is to Christ, in spite of the difficulties raised by the next verse.

ἵνα κ.τ.λ.] The nearness of the day affords a new motive for the effort to which they are urged. The nearer the Parousia of their Lord the greater the need of constancy. As soon as the last hour has run its course, the Master will appear, and will look for workmen who need not to be ashamed.

ἐὰν φανερωθῇ] The ὅταν of the *Receptus* introduces a thought alien to the context. It would suggest an uncertainty as to the date of the Coming which is excluded by what has preceded. The signs of the time are clear. Events have shown that it is the "last hour." The form of conditional used (ἐάν, *c. subj.*) introduces a pure possibility, without any hint as to the degree of its probability. If that happens which, as circumstances have shown, may befall them now at any moment, they must be in a position not to be ashamed, when the object of their longing expectation is there.

φανερωθῇ] φανεροῦσθαι and φανεροῦν are used of all the manifestations of the Lord, in the flesh, after the Resurrection, at the Second Coming. Cf. (*a*) Jn. i. 31, ii. 11, vii. 4; 1 P. i. 20; 1 Jn. i. 2, iii. 5; (*b*) [Mk.] xvi. 12, 14; Jn. xxi. 1, 14; 1 Jn. iii. 2, 8; (*c*) Col. iii. 4; 1 Ti. iii. 16 (cf. 2 Ti. i. 10); 1 P. v. 4. The verb is used of the "manifestation" of the works of God (Jn. ix. 3), and Christ is said to have "manifested" His name. It is never used directly of God in the N.T. Whether tle "manifestation" is to the eye of the body or of the mind has to be determined by the context. The word would seem generally to carry the suggestion that the appearance is not only seen but understood, or capable of being understood, in its true significance.

The writer would hardly speak of the Second Coming of Christ as a manifestation of the Father, though doubtless he expected that through it men would learn much about God not known before (cf. Weiss).

παρρησίαν σχῶμεν] It was natural that the rather abrupt σχῶμεν should have been altered to the more usual ἔχωμεν (cf. 1 Jn. iii. 21, iv. 17, v. 14; Eph. iii. 12; He. x. 19, and contrast He. iii. 6). But the charge involves a slight loss of force. It is the fact of possession, not its continuance, that the writer would naturally emphasize.

παρρησία is used especially of freedom or boldness of speech, in accordance with its etymological meaning. But it has acquired the more general meaning of confidence, as here. Cf. Lightfoot's note on Col. ii. 15. It is a favourite word of the writer's, who is responsible for 13 out of the 31 instances of its

5

use in the N.T. In some of these passages the idea of
"publicity" is suggested, but in probably every instance that of
"boldness" or "confidence" is really most prominent. For its
use in the LXX, cf. Lv. xxvi. 13 ; Job xxvii. 10 ; Pr. i. 20, xiii. 5 ;
3 Mac. vii. 12 ; for the corresponding verb, cf. Job xxii. 26 ; Ps.
xi. 6, xciii. 1. As a rule it occurs in renderings which paraphrase
the Hebrew, but in Lv. xxvi. 13 it is used to translate קוֹמְמִיּוּת,
uprightness. "I made you to go upright," *i.e.*, as free men, is
translated, or rather paraphrased, ἤγαγον ὑμᾶς μετὰ παρρησίας.
The passages which best illustrate its use here are Job xxvii. 10,
μὴ ἔχει τινὰ παρρησίαν ἔναντι αὐτοῦ; and Job xxii. 26, εἶτα
παρρησιασθήσῃ ἐναντίον Κυρίου. Cf. also Test. Rub. iv. 2, ἄχρι
τελευτῆς τοῦ πατρός μου οὐκ εἶχον παρρησίαν ἀτενίσαι εἰς τὸ
πρόσωπον αὐτοῦ.

καὶ μὴ αἰσχυνθῶμεν κ.τ.λ.] Cf. Pr. xiii. 5, ἀσεβὴς δὲ αἰσχύνεται
καὶ οὐχ ἕξει παρρησίαν. The idea would seem to be that of with-
drawing ashamed from His presence, shrinking back from a
✗ sense of guilt. In this case the word is used as a middle rather
than a passive. Cf. 1 P. iv. 16, εἰ δὲ ὡς Χριστιανός, μὴ αἰσχυνέσθω. For the phrase, cf. Sap. Sir. xxi. 22 f. πρὸς μωροῦ ταχὺς
εἰς οἰκίαν, ἄνθρωπος δὲ πολύπειρος αἰσχυνθήσεται ἀπὸ προσώπου.
ἄφρων ἀπὸ θύρας παρακόπτει εἰς οἰκίαν, ἀνὴρ δὲ πεπαιδευμένος ἔξω
στήσεται. Cf. προσέχετε ἀπό and φυλάσσεσθε ἀπό.

He who "abides in Him" will have no cause to shrink away
abashed from the Presence of the Judge, but may await His
verdict with confidence as an ἐργάτης ἀνεπαίσχυντος (2 Ti. ii. 15).

ἐν τῇ παρουσίᾳ] Here only in the Johannine writings. In the
N.T. the use of the word with reference to the Second Coming
is confined to Mt. xxiv., the earlier Pauline Epistles (1, 2 Co.,
1, 2 Th.), James and 2 Peter.

Very interesting light has been thrown on the Christian use
of παρουσία by the discoveries of papyrus documents and other
sources of common Greek. Cf. Deissmann, *Licht von Osten*,
p. 268 ff. As he points out, the use of the word is best interpreted by the cry, "See thy King cometh unto thee." From
the Ptolemaic period to the second century A.D. there is
abundant evidence that in the East the word was the usual
expression for the visit of a King or Emperor. In Egypt, special
funds were raised by taxation to meet the expenses of such visits.
In Greece a new era was reckoned from the visit of Hadrian.
The earliest mention is rightly interpreted by Wilcken (*Griech-
ische Ostraka*, i. p. 274 ff.), ἄλλου (*sc.* στεφάνου) παρουσίας ιβ' to
refer to the collection made to provide a crown to be presented
on the occasion of the visit ; and in the Tebtunis Papyri (48. 9 ff.)
there is an interesting description of the efforts made by the
village elders in connection with the expected visit of Ptolemy II.

(B.C. 113), καὶ προσεδρευόντων διά τε νυκτὸς καὶ ἡμέρας μέχρι τοῦ τὸ προκειμένον ἐκπληρῶσαι καὶ τὴν ἐπιγεγραμμένην πρὸς τὴν τοῦ βασιλέως παρουσίαν ἀγορὰν π. . . . . The same usage is found in Asia; cf. Dittenberger, *Sylloge*, 226. 85 f. τήν τε παρουσίαν ἐμφανισάντων τοῦ βασιλέως (3rd cent. B.C.). The word is also used of the appearance of the god Asclepios in his temple (Dittenberger, *Sylloge*, 803. 34, τάν τε παρουσίαν τὰν αὐτοῦ παρενεφάνιξε ὁ Ἀσκλάπιος. In Latin, *Adventus* was used in the same way. Cf. the coins struck to commemorate Nero's visit to Corinth, *Adventus Aug. Cor.* Altars were also erected to commemorate visits of members of the Imperial family, as in Cos, in memory of the visit of C. Caesar (A.D. 4). The word was naturally used by Christians of the advent of their King, whether they thought of the Coming as a first visit, the earthly life having been merely a condescension in which He appeared in humility and not as Messiah, or as a second visit. Ἐπιφάνια seems to have been similarly used of the visits of the Emperor. Many of the words and titles which Christians loved to use of their Lord had a special significance as protests against the blasphemy of the popular Emperor Worship.

τεκνια]+μου K. h. 22. 37. 40. 56 b^scr l^scr sah. cop. syr^sch aeth. : τεκνα H³ (P).

μενετε] μενειτε H^162 (61).

εαν אABCP 5. 13. 26. 27. 29. 36 d^scr sah. cop. arm.] οταν KL al. pler. cat. syr^utr Thphyl. Oec. : οτε I^a 397 fff (96).

σχωμεν א^cABCP 15. 26. 27. 40. 66**. 68 d^scr Thphyl.] εχωμεν א* KL al. pler. cat. Oec. : *habeatis* boh-ed.

παρρησιαν]+προς αυτον I^c 258 (56).

αισχυνθωμεν] *confundamini* boh.

απ αυτον] post αυτου 2° א : om. arm-codd.

απ] παρ 69. 137 a^scr : επ H^δ6 (Ψ).

29. Doing righteousness, the sure sign of the new birth.

29. In thought this verse is closely connected with the preceding. The ground of the appeal to "abide in Him" was ✗ their expectation of the speedy return of their Lord in glory, and their desire to be able to meet Him with confidence and joy, and not to have to shrink away abashed from His presence. This naturally raises the thought of the conditions which would make such a meeting possible. Those only who are His own can look forward with unclouded confidence, and His own are those who share His qualities, especially those which characterize the Judge, righteousness and justice. The doing of justice is the sure sign, and the only sign, that they are "born of Him." And so the meditation passes over to the next subject on which the writer wishes to dwell, the being born of God.

ἐὰν εἰδῆτε] The intuitive knowledge of what God, or Christ, is, makes it possible for those who possess it to learn by the

experience of life (γινώσκειν) what are the true signs of being
"born of Him." To act in accordance with those qualities
which correspond to His nature is the only certain sign of true
fellowship with God, which is the result of the Divine begetting.

✗ ἐάν] A protasis introduced by ἐάν, c. subj., does not necessarily
present the fact as uncertain. If the condition is fulfilled, the
results follow. No hint is given as to the probability of fulfilment.

✗ δίκαιός ἐστιν] It is very difficult to determine whether the
subject of this word is God or Christ. On the one hand, a
change of reference between vv. 28 and 29 would be very
awkward, if not impossible ; and it is really certain that ἐν αὐτῷ,
ἀπ' αὐτοῦ, and αὐτοῦ in ver. 28 must refer to Christ. No other
explanation of ἐὰν φανερωθῇ and παρουσία is natural, or even
possible. And these considerations almost compel us to refer
δίκαιος to Christ. On the other hand, a change of reference in
the verse itself is still more difficult, at any rate at first sight ;
and Johannine usage is almost decisive in favour of referring ἐξ
αὐτοῦ γεγέννηται to God. To be "born of God" is a favourite
phrase of the writer's (cf. Jn. i. 13), especially in this Epistle
(iii. 9, iv. 7, v. 1, 4, 18), whereas he never uses the expression
"to be born of Christ." He does, however, speak of being born
of the Spirit ; and the language of the Prologue to the Gospel,
ἔδωκεν αὐτοῖς ἐξουσίαν τέκνα θεοῦ γενέσθαι (Jn. i. 12), the subject
of ἔδωκεν being the Logos, suggests a sense in which being
"born of God" might also be regarded as being "born of
Christ," who is always thought of as being and giving the life of
God which comes to men.

It is more satisfactory to avoid any solution of the difficulty
which might seem to presuppose a confusion of thought between
God and Christ in the mind of the writer. Our inability to
determine his exact meaning was probably not shared either by
the writer or his readers, whose minds were full of the truth that
Christ is God revealed to man.

✗ If, therefore, a change of reference is impossible, the whole
verse is best referred, as in Bede, to Christ. The conception
"born of Christ" is not antagonistic to the Johannine lines of
thought, though the expression is not found elsewhere. We
must, however, remember that abrupt changes of subject were
natural to Hebrew thought and expression which are almost
impossible in Western language. Their occurrence in the O.T.
is too frequent to need illustration. And it is quite possible that
the expression ἐξ αὐτοῦ γεγεννῆσθαι may have become stereotyped
for the writer and his circle, who would immediately interpret it as
meaning "born of God." To a mind steeped as the writer's was
in the thoughts of God and Christ, αὐτός and ἐκεῖνος had perhaps

become almost proper names; the context or the special phrase used would make it perfectly clear to the writer, and to his readers as well, what was meant.

πᾶς . . . γεγέννηται] The doing of righteousness is the sign of the birth from God and its effect,—an effect which nothing else can produce, and so a certain sign. The more logical order would have been, "He that is born of God doeth righteousness."

ειδητε ℵ B C al. mu. vg. **arm.** Aug. syr^{utr} sah.] ιδητε A K L P al. pler. cat. cop. aeth.: οιδατε I^{b δ507} (104) I^{a δ157} I^{c 551}.

om. και B K L al. pler. cat. am. harl. tol. cop. syr^p arm. aeth. Thphyl. Oec. Aug. Amb.

την] om. I^{b 365, 472} (214) I^{c 364}.

γεγεννηται] γεγενηται P 31. 69*. 177* a^{scr} al. mult. syr. : +και υπ αυτου οραται ο δε ποιων την αμαρτιαν ουκετι οραται υπ αυτου I^{c 325} (2).

ADDITIONAL NOTE.

Though the name Antichrist occurs first in this Epistle in extant literature, the Epistle itself throws no light on its meaning. The conception cannot be explained from the N.T., or even from the Bible alone. The researches of Bousset and others have demonstrated the existence of a more or less definite Antichrist legend, independent of the N.T., and common to Jewish and Christian apocalyptic expectation, of which use is made in several N.T. writings. The legend cannot be explained on historical lines; it received modifications from time to time in consequence of definite historical events, and the experiences of Jews and Christians at different periods. But it always had an independent existence. Historical events modified the expectations for the future which find expression in its terms, but they did not create it. Its origin is probably to be traced to the wide-spread myth of a primeval monster, consisting of, or inhabiting, the waters and the darkness, which was subdued by the God of creation, but not destroyed, and which would again raise its power against the God of heaven in a final conflict before the end of all things. This tradition, especially in its Babylonian form of the cleaving of Tiâmat, the Sea-monster, by Marduk the son of Ea, who divided its carcase into two and formed the sea and the heavens, was well known among the Hebrews, and has left its traces in several passages of the O.T. It may be quoted as given by Gunkel from the cuneiform inscriptions (*Schöpfung und Chaos*, p. 21). "In the beginning, before heaven and earth were named, when as yet the 'Urvater' Apsû, and the 'Urmutter' Tiâmat, mingled their waters, when none of the gods had been created, no name named, no fate determined, then first the gods came into being. They were named Luḥmu and Laḥamu, Asnar and Kisar, and last Anu. (The next sentences are destroyed, but to judge from what follows they must have contained the account of the origin of the gods of the Upper World and of the Deep.)   Then the myth relates how Tiâmat, the mother of the gods, together with all the Powers of the Deep, rebelled against the Upper Gods.   The only extant part of this is a conversation between Apsû and Tiâmat, describing their plan against the gods.   Apparently the origin of light was described in connection with this rebellion.

Next follows the description of the war between Tiâmat and the gods.   On the one side Ansar appears as leader.   Anu, Ea, and his son Marduk are also mentioned.   Luḥmu and Laḥamu appear in the background.   On the other side is Tiâmat, who has gained over some of the "gods" to her side.   She created eleven fearful monsters, and placed the god Kingu as leader over them, whom she took for her husband, and laid on his breast the "amulet."   Against this host Ansar sent forth first Anu, then Ea ; but Anu withdrew, and Ea was frightened and turned back.   Finally, he betook himself to Marduk, Ea's son, one of the youngest of the gods.   Marduk declares that he is prepared to go forth against Apsû and Tiâmat, but he will only consent to be the avenger of the gods if they in full assembly ratify his authority as equal with their own.   The assembly is called, and the destiny of Marduk is determined.   His power shall be without equal, and his dominion shall be universal.   His word shall have the magic power of calling things into being and causing them to disappear.   And as a sign of this a cloak is placed in their midst, which at Marduk's word disappears and appears again.   The story next tells of Marduk's arming.   His weapons are bow and quiver, a sickle-shaped sword, and a weapon which he receives from the gods as a present, apparently the thunderbolt, represented as a trident.   He has also a net, the present of Anu, and all the winds accompany him as confederates.   Armed for the fight, he goes forth on his chariot drawn by terrible animals.

As he approaches Kingu, and the gods, his helpers, who accompany him, Marduk challenges Tiâmat to the combat, "Come hither, I and thou will fight."   When they fought the wise among the gods caught Tiâmat in the net.   Through her opened jaws he sent the hurricane, and filled her belly with fearful winds.   Then with the crescent sword he cut through her body.   He cast her corpse away and stood upon it.   Then Marduk overcame the gods, her helpers ; he broke their weapons, and cast them into the net.   So, too, he made fast the eleven creatures.   Kingu met the same fate.   Marduk tore from him the "amulet," and placed it on his own breast.   Then he turned to Tiâmat again.   He split her head, and caused the north wind

to carry her blood to hidden places. The gods, his fathers, offer
presents to the victor.

Then was the Lord appeased. He divided the body of
Tiâmat into two parts. Of the one part he made the vault
of heaven, and placed before it bars and watchers, that the waters
should not stream forth. He placed the vault of heaven over
against the primeval ocean, and built the heavens as a palace,
corresponding to the primeval ocean, conceived of as a palace.
Then Marduk created the stars, the sun and the moon, and the
other planets ; he placed the stars of the zodiac, and determined
the course of the stars and the twelve months. The following
tablets are lost ; there is extant only a small fragment which deals
with the creation of animals, in which these classes of land
animals are distinguished, cattle, wild animals, and reptiles. The
myth closes with a hymn in honour of Marduk, to whom are
given names which celebrate his power as Lord of all, "as sheep
may he tend the gods, all of them."

There are many traces of this or similar myths to be found
in the O.T., though the number of them may have been
exaggerated by Gunkel. The most important are perhaps
Is. li. 9 f. ; Ps. lxxxix. 10 ff. ; Job xxvi. 12 f., ix. 13 ; Is. xxx. 7
(especially if the pointing הַפְּשֶׁבֶת be adopted); Ps. xl. 5,
lxxiv. 12–19 ; Is. xxvii. 1 ; Job xl. 25, xli. 26 ; Ezk. xxix.
3–6a, xxxii. 2–8. These passages suggest that such myths were
popular in Israel, and used by prophets and other writers to
illustrate and emphasize their warnings and teaching. The points
of similarity between the Hebrew and Babylonian myths on
which Gunkel lays stress are the following (p. 112 ff.). Originally the "all" was water. The primeval ocean was personified
as a fearful monster. The Babylonian Tiâmat corresponds to
the Hebrew תהום, which is always used anarthrously as a proper
name. The common Hebrew name for the monster Rahab
may have its parallel in Babylonian myth, but this is not proved.
Both myths represent the monster as a dragon, and with many
heads. Other similar beings are mentioned, the "helpers" of
the dragon, among whom one is prominent. In Babylonian
myths, Kingu is associated with Tiâmat ; in Hebrew we find
Rahab and Tannin, Leviathan and Tannin, Leviathan and
Behemoth, Rahab and Naḥas Bariah. In Henoch (ch. lx.),
Behemoth and Leviathan are represented as male and female, as
are Kingu and Tiâmat in the Babylonian story.

These powers of the deep are in the Babylonian legend
opposed to the gods of the Upper World, among whom Marduk
is predominant. Even in the Hebrew story the appearance of
other gods seems occasionally to be referred to (Job xli. 25,
xxxviii. 7 ; Ps. lxxxix. 7).

The monsters rebel against the Upper Gods, and claim the sovereignty of the World for themselves. In the Hebrew story the special trait of the opponents of Jahve is their overruling and rebellious pride.

Before Marduk's victory, other gods had attempted the fight. There is perhaps a similar reference in Job xli. 11, 25.

Then Marduk appears. His arming is described. He comes on a chariot with horses, armed with sword and net, or with the terrible weapons of the thunder god.

Before the fight there are shrieks of abuse or reproach. In the fight itself the victory is gained by wisdom rather than by strength. The "net" has its part to play. The helpers of the monster are overthrown, they bow beneath him. In the Babylonian story he "puts them to shame"; cf. Ps. lxxxix. 10; Job ix. 13.

The corpse of the monster is not buried. This is several times referred to in Hebrew. Out of it the God makes the world. In some forms of the Hebrew story the fruitfulness of land that before was waste is derived from the blood and the flesh of the dragon (Gunkel, p. 111). The Babylonian myth relates that Tiâmat was divided in twain—into the upper and lower waters. In Ps. lxxiv. 13 we hear of the dividing of the sea, paralleled with the breaking of the heads of the dragons, and in Job xxvi. 13 of the bars of heaven (LXX, κλεῖθρα οὐρανοῦ δεδοίκασιν αὐτόν). At any rate, in both stories the victory over the monster is followed by the creation of the world.

Whatever exact parallels may be drawn between the Babylonian myths and allusions to similar stories which may be found, or reasonably supposed to exist, in passages in the O.T., there can be little doubt that Hebrew mythology knew of some such fight between the God of their race and the primeval monster of the deep. One particular form in which the myth seems to have been known is of special interest in connection with the legend of Antichrist. In at least one version the Dragon or monster was represented as not destroyed, but overcome. According to Is. xxx. 7, it is "brought to rest."[1] When God captured him, he "spake soft words," and became His servant for ever (Job xli. 3, 4). God "played" with him (Job xli. 5; Ps. civ. 26). He lay at the bottom of the deep, but he must obey God (Am. ix. 3). He could still be dangerous, so God set watchers over him (Job vii. 12). He is put to sleep, but he still could be "waked" (Job iii. 8, xli. 10). Bars were placed to prevent his breaking forth (? Job xxvi. 13 LXX).

Thus the starting-point of the legend is probably to be found in the stories of the combat between God and the primeval

[1] If Gunkel is right in pointing הם שֶׁבֶת as a passive participle.

monster, which was overcome and bound, but not killed ; and which should once more break forth and rebel against God, to be overthrown in a final victory before the end of all things. But it took more definite shape in forms which reflected the experiences of the people at the hands of their enemies. Many of the passages which speak of the quelling of the sea describe also the subduing of the peoples who set themselves against God. In consequence of the sufferings of the people at the hands of their enemies, the doctrine was developed that Israel was indeed the chosen of God, but that for their sins they had been given over to the heathen powers ; and this led to the expectation of a great final struggle with the World-Powers before the perfecting of the kingdom. This is clearly seen in Ezk. (xxxviii. 2, xxxix. 1, 6) in the prophecy of Gog, the prince of Magog, and the gathering of the Northern nations, regarded as types of the World-Power from which the final outburst against the people of the Lord should come. Zec. xii.–xiv. describes the final oppression of the people by the hostile powers. All nations are gathered against Jerusalem (xiv. 2), and the Lord appears on the Mount of Olives to save His people.

The attempt of Antiochus iv. (Epiphanes—God manifest in human form) of Syria to suppress Judaism and to Hellenize the nation, naturally led to further development of the idea. The World-Power is no longer an instrument for punishment in Jahve's hands, but His opponent, who goes forth to destroy the centre of His kingdom. Whether the βδέλυγμα τῆς ἐρημώσεως of Daniel is to be interpreted as the "smoke of the heathen sacrifice in the Temple, ascending from the altar erected there to Zeus in Dec. 168" or not, the author of the book certainly describes the past and present history of God's kingdom in relation to the World-Powers in the light of the events of that period, and points forward to a speedy rescue, and the completion of God's work for His people.

The World-Power is presented first (ch. ii.) as a colossal image of gold, silver, brass, and iron, which is finally shattered by the stone broken off from the mountains without human intervention, and later under the imagery of the four beasts coming up from the sea. The opposition of the world—as presented in the four successive empires, the Chaldaean, Median, Persian, and Greek— is to culminate in the "horn" on the fourth beast's head, with "eyes like the eyes of a man, and a mouth speaking great things,"—a clear reference to Antiochus Epiphanes. If the book was written at a time when the Maccabean successes had already driven out the idolatrous Zeus-worship from the Temple, the writer might easily expect a great victory and extension of the power of the opponent before the Divine intervention, when the judgment begins, the World-Power is overthrown, and dominion given to the "Saints," *i.e.* the members of the Jewish Church preserved through the great tribulation and cleansed by it. In Dn. vii. 13 we read that one like unto a son of man was brought before the Ancient of days, and dominion was given unto him, and a kingdom, that all people should serve him. As the idea of a personal Messiah became more prominent, the expectation of a single personal opponent was developed. But on this point (of a personal Messiah) Jewish apocalyptic varied frequently during the next two centuries.

In Nu. xxiv. 17 the "Star" which shall come forth out of Jacob . . . and break down all the sons of tumult must be noticed, and the Septuagint translation of ver. 7 is significant:

$$\text{ἐξελεύσεται ἄνθρωπος ἐκ τοῦ σπέρματος αὐτοῦ,}$$
$$\text{καὶ κυριεύσει ἐθνῶν πολλῶν·}$$
$$\text{καὶ ὑψωθήσεται ἡ Γὼγ βασιλεία (εαυτου Α F),}$$
$$\text{καὶ αὐξηθήσεται ἡ βασιλεία αὐτοῦ.}$$

α′ σ′ θ′ have ὑπὲρ Γώγ, which is still clearer. The Hebrew מאגג was read as מגוג. The Septuagint translation seems to have been coloured by the expectations of Messiah and Antichrist.

The Third Book of the Sibyllines (iii. 652), which is generally attributed to the Maccabean period, speaks of the advent of a King who shall make war to cease:

$$\text{καὶ τότ' ἀπ' ἠελίοιο θεὸς πέμψει βασιλῆα,}$$
$$\text{ὃς πᾶσαν γαῖαν παύσει πολέμοιο κακοῖο,}$$
$$\text{οὓς μὲν ἄρα κτείνας, οἷς δ' ὅρκια πιστὰ τελέσσας.}$$

But the storm is to burst from many points, and is directed against God's people and house, not against the Messiah. And there is no single opponent. Gog and Magog are the names of lands:

Cf. 319,   αἰαῖ σοί, χώρα Γὼγ ἠδὲ Μαγὼγ μέσον οὖσα
Αἰθιόπων ποταμῶν.

According to Sieffert, Palestinian pre-Christian literature has no personal anti-Messiah.

In the Book of Enoch xc. 16 it is predicted that other parts of the Macedonian Empire, under the leadership of Greeks, will gather themselves together against the people. "All the eagles and vultures and ravens and kites assembled together and brought with them all the sheep of the field (apostate Jews), and they all came together and helped each other to break that horn of the ram. 19. And I saw till a great sword was given to the sheep, and the sheep proceeded against all the beasts of the field to slay them; and all the beasts and the birds of heaven fled before their face"; but in xc. 56 ff. the appearance of Messiah is first described *after* the close of the wars. Cf. 37, "And I saw that a white bull was born, with large horns; and all the beasts of the field and all the birds of the air feared him, and made petition to him all the time."

In the Psalms of Solomon (B.C. 90), Messiah Himself destroys the foes by the word of His mouth.

Cf. xvii. 27, ὀλοθρεῦσαι ἔθνη παράνομα ἐν λόγῳ στόματος αὐτοῦ (cf. **Is.** xi. 4), and generally the whole passage 23–36.

In the Fourth Book of Ezra, chs. xii., xiii., to which a Flavian date is assigned, and in which the fourth beast of Daniel is clearly identified with Rome, the heathen peoples are over-come by the Messiah, who comes out of the sea. Cf. xiii. 5, "Lo, there was gathered together a multitude of men, out of number, from the four winds of heaven, to make war against the man that came out of the sea."

In the Apocalypse of Baruch (xl. 1, 2), statements in this passage are taken over to describe the destruction of the last godless king. "The last leader of that time will be left alive, when the multitude of his hosts will be put to the sword and be bound; and they will take him up to Mt. Sion, and My Messiah will convict him of all his impieties, and will gather and set before him all the works of his hosts. And afterwards he will put him to death."

Thus in the Jewish literature which is unaffected by Christian modifications the development of the idea of Antichrist cannot be very clearly traced; but the idea is to be found there, gaining or losing ground in accordance with the perpetually shifting character of Messianic expectations.

It is easier to trace the development of the subject in Christian literature. The idea of the growth of self-seeking till it culminates in self-deification finds its natural sphere in Christian thought. And speculations about the spread of opposition to God and His Messiah are stripped of their national and political clothing and spiritualized. In the eschatological discourses of the Synoptic Gospels it is difficult to distinguish between original saying and subsequent interpolation and comment, even if we reject the view that they have their origin in a Jewish Apocalypse the contents of which have been put into the mouth of Jesus. But they are at least good evidence of eschatological views held by Christians at a comparatively early date. In Mt. xxiv. ff. there is no doctrine of a personal Antichrist. The βδέλυγμα ἐρημώσεως of Daniel, whatever be the exact mean-ing assigned to it by the speaker or by later interpretation, is connected with the approaching tribulations of the last days and the national sufferings of the Jews. The Son of Man, a title which seems to be definitely Messianic, at least in the Similitudes of Enoch, is represented as about to come on the clouds of heaven (cf. Dn. vii.). But the hostile peoples are still conceived of as God's instruments to punish. The "kingdom," however, is separated from the national fate of Israel. The "Son of man" is opposed, not as in Daniel by world-rulers who destroy the Jewish theocracy, but by false prophets and false Messiahs (Mt. xxiv. 5). Popular "Messianism" is rejected by Jesus in the history of the Temptation (iv. 1 ff.) and in the rebuke to Peter (xvi. 23). He condemns the selfish aspirations of national zealots (cf. Jn. vi. 15, x. 8, v. 43), though He can train the enthusiasm of such men to the better work of heralding the kingdom (Mt. x. 4).

These views were taken up into the Apostolic preaching, and form the basis of what S. Paul taught at Thessalonica. He combines them with several traits clearly borrowed from Jewish popular expectation. The doctrine of one single opponent, in whom all that is antichristian culminates, is clearly seen in his conception of the Man of Sin. Whether the Second Epistle to the Thessalonians is genuine in its present form or not, there can be little doubt that the picture drawn in the 2nd chapter is mainly Pauline. Its exact agreement with the circumstances of his time is remarkable : or, at any rate, a perfectly natural interpretation of all that is said there can be found if it is explained on these lines. The coming of Christ cannot be till the apostasy is fully developed, and the opposition to the Christ is consummated in the appearance of the Man of Sin, the Son of perdition, who opposes and exalts himself against all that is called God, and is worshipped, and sets up his throne in God's Temple. Apparently this "Man of Sin" is to be an apostate Jew. The mystery of lawlessness, which is already working, is clearly the Jewish opposition to the work of Christianity, of which S. Paul had been the victim in every place where he had proclaimed the Christ since his conversion, and which had been specially virulent at Thessalonica (Ac. xvii. 5 ; cf. 1 Th. ii. 15, 16). Throughout his career, S. Paul found in Jewish opposition the worst hindrance to the spread of the Gospel. It would reach its climax in the appearance of Antichrist. At present its working was restrained by the power of the Roman Empire (τὸ κατέχον), concentrated as it was in the person of a single ruler (ὁ κατέχων). Till a far later period of his life, he always found support and protection in the authorities of the Empire of which he was a citizen. It was an essential part of his conception of the last things that "So long as Rome lasts, lasts the World." This much is certain, whether or not we choose to see in ὁ κατέχων an allusion to the name of Claudius (*qui claudit*). But he was conscious of the weakness as well as the strength of the Roman position. And he expected its downfall, and the overthrow of all authority and law, during the time of stress which was to precede the "unveiling" of the Christ. The freaks of Caligula had brought this home to all thinking men. And in his picture of the Man of Sin, S. Paul borrows traits from the episode of Caligula's attempt to set up his statue, in the guise of Zeus, in the Jewish Temple. Thus the opposition of Judaism, which had lost its opportunity when it crucified the Messiah, is the main factor in the war against the Christ. But heathen opposition had to be encountered as well, and in particular it had proved a serious obstacle at Thessalonica (1 Th. ii. 14) ; and this will account for any heathen traits in the picture of the opponent.

It may be worth noticing in this connection that the thought of *Jewish* opposition and unbelief may help to explain a difficult section of the Second Epistle to the Corinthians (vi. 14–vii. 1). If S. Paul is there thinking first of the evil effect of *Jewish* companionship, though heathen contamination is not altogether excluded (ver. 16), the want of connection between the passage and the sections which precede and follow is less pronounced. And in later Jewish literature Beliar is the name for Antichrist, whether he is conceived of as apostate Jew (Ascension of Isaiah) or Roman Emperor (Sibylline Oracles, iii. 63, ἐκ δὲ σεβαστηνῶν ἥξει Βελίαρ μετόπισθεν, unless, indeed, the passage indicates a *Samaritan* origin of Antichrist). It is at least probable that when S. Paul wrote this section of 2 Corinthians, he still thought of Antichrist as the person in whom Jewish opposition to the faith should find its consummation.

But, however this may be, it is at least clear that the passage about the Man of Sin in 2 Thess. is most naturally interpreted, if we suppose that S. Paul is developing a popular legend in the light of Christ's teaching about the last things, his own experiences at the hands of his countrymen, the episodes of the desecration of the Temple by Antiochus and the attempt of Caligula to set up his statue within its precincts. Recent experiences and historical incidents have added new traits to a well-known popular conception. And both the legend and the events are needed to explain the picture.

The use of the Antichrist legend is equally clear in the Apocalypse. Gunkel has clearly shown the impossibility of interpreting the 12th chapter on purely historical lines. And many of the details recall most vividly the legend of the Sea monster, which shall once more raise war against the Lord's anointed. It is very probable that a Jewish Apocalypse which itself borrowed traits from older mythological traditions to describe the birth of Messiah, born in heaven, caught up to the throne of God and hidden in the wilderness till the appointed time, has been incorporated by the seer, and adapted to the circumstances of Christ and the Church, the borrowed details in many cases being quite unsuitable to their new application, in order to comfort his readers with the thought that their sufferings are really but a stage in the working out of God's purpose for their final triumph. That which is woe for the earth, is matter of rejoicing in heaven, when the Dragon is cast down, and the first stage in the process of his destruction is accomplished. The hostility of the Dragon to the Messiah, the consequent war between Michael and the Dragon and their respective hosts, the identification of the Dragon with the old serpent, the Devil and Satan, the deceiver of the whole world, and the Water cast out as a river to destroy the Woman, are all reminiscences of popular myths of which traces have been found throughout the O.T. and elsewhere in the New.

In ch. xiii. 1 the beast coming up out of the *sea* points the same way, though here the adaptation of the myth to the circumstances of Roman history are clear, whether the solution of the riddle of xiii. 18 is to be found in the older guess of נרון קסר, and the sufferings of the Neronic persecution, or Deissmann's suggestion of Καισαρ θεος and the Emperor-worship of the time of Domitian, is preferred.

Perhaps the clearest use of the Antichrist legend is to be found in xiii. 11, where the "two horns like unto a lamb" of the beast that came up out of the earth, emphasize his attempt to deceive by pretending to be the Messiah.

The 17th chapter, which offers the clearest indications of the identification of the beast with Rome, now regarded by Christians as the great enemy, and no longer the restraining and protecting power which S. Paul found in the Empire, shows how the mythical figure gains new attributes in consequence of new experiences, but does not throw much light on the older myth. But the gathering together of the nations, Gog and Magog, for the war in xx. 7, 8, recalls the earlier feature of the legend.

In the Epistles of S. John there is no real use of the legend itself at all. They contribute nothing but the name to our knowledge of it. The writer refers to a popular legend which had formed the basis of Apostolic teaching, as in earlier times the prophets and psalmists had made use of similar mythological ideas to enforce the lessons which they had to teach. But the process of spiritualization is complete. The writer finds in the false teaching which is growing apace the fulfilment of the popular expectation of the coming of the great antagonist who is to lead the last and final opposition of the powers of the world to the

kingdom of the Christ. Whether this opposition **is** soon to
culminate in the work of a single opponent he leaves uncertain.
It is not a matter which interests him. The mystery of lawlessness is already working in those who are inspired by the
spirits who do not confess Jesus Christ come in flesh. In this
the "word" *Antichrist cometh* is fulfilled. The writer's business
is with the reality to which the legend points; with the legend
itself he has but little to do.

It is unnecessary here to trace the further developments of
the Antichrist legend in later Jewish and Christian expectation.
They show a more or less definite, but continually shifting,
popular tradition which took its start in the old myth of the
Sea-monster overcome, but only confined and not destroyed, by
the power of God, which should once more break its bonds,
and make a last attack on the powers of light before the final
establishment of the Messianic kingdom.

B. ii. 28–iv. 6.

Second presentation of the two theses, ethical and Christological, the two being discussed separately, but with express
reference to their connection.

I. ii. 28–iii. 24.

The doing of righteousness, especially genuine brotherly
love, the true sign of the Birth from God. Corresponding
exhortation.

1. ii. 28–iii. 6.

The thesis, and the exhortation to recognize this truth,
shown by the obligation, involved in the gift of Divine kinship
and the hope of its completion, of self-purification. The wide
prevalence of antinomianism. The incompatibility of knowledge
of God and yielding to sin.

(*a*) ii. 28–iii. 3.
(*b*) iii. 4–6.

ii. 28–iii. 3.

The gift of Divine kinship carries with it the obligation to
self-purification.

1. This verse is closely connected with the preceding. It is
a meditation on the last words of that verse, ἐξ αὐτοῦ γεγέννηται.
The writer is trying to restore the waning enthusiasm of his
readers, and to recall them to their first love. He therefore
reminds them of their high privilege and position. God has
given them proof of His love. He has bestowed on them
the rank and title of His children, sharers in His nature. And
it is no mere title. It corresponds to real facts, if they will
but realize them, and respond to them. And these facts are
the cause of the hostile attitude of the world. Those who do

not know God have no sympathy with those who share H's nature.

An interesting parallel to this passage is found in *Pirqe Aboth*, iii. 22 (ed. Taylor, 1897), "Beloved are Israel that they are called children of God ; greater love (was it that it) was made known to them that they are called children of God, as it is said, Ye are the children of the Lord your God" (Dt. xiv. 1). We may also compare and contrast (cf. Windisch, *ad loc.*) Philo, *de confusione ling.* 146 f. (Cohn, ii. p. 257) καὶ γὰρ εἰ μήπω ἱκανοὶ θεοῦ παῖδες νομίζεσθαι γεγόναμεν, ἀλλά τοι τῆς ἀειδοῦς εἰκόνος αὐτοῦ, λόγου τοῦ ἱερωτάτου. The emphasis on the direct relation of Christians to God is characteristic of the Epistle, though the writer conceives of this relationship as realized in and through Christ.

ἴδετε ποταπήν] Cf. Gal. vi. 11, ἴδετε πηλίκοις ὑμῖν γράμμασιν ἔγραψα : and for the combination with ποταπός, Mk. xiii. 1, ἴδε ποταποὶ λίθοι. In the N.T. ποταπός generally suggests surprise, and very often something of an admirable character (*qualem*, Latt. verss.). Cf. Mt. viii. 27 ; Lk. i. 29, vii. 39. 2 P. iii. 11 (ποταποὺς δεῖ ὑπάρχειν ὑμᾶς ἐν ἁγίαις ἀναστροφαῖς;). The Latt. verss. never use *cujas*, ποταπός having lost its reference to *place*.

ἀγάπην] Love, not token of love. "The Divine love is, as it were, infused into them, so that it is their own, and becomes in them the source of a divine life."

δέδωκεν] is better supported than the aorist, and is intrinsically superior. The results of what they have received are permanent and abiding. Nowhere else in N.T. does ἀγάπην διδόναι occur.

ὁ πατήρ] suggested by the following τέκνα θεοῦ. Cf. Rev. xxi. 7.

ἵνα τέκνα θεοῦ κληθῶμεν] Another instance of the definitive ἵνα. It is difficult to find any "full telic" force here. God did not give His love to men in order that they might be called sons. The greatness of His love to them was manifested in this, that He allowed Himself to be called their Father. Cf. ver. 11, αὕτη ἐστὶν ἡ ἀγγελία, . . . ἵνα ἀγαπῶμεν. According to the general usage of this Epistle and the Fourth Gospel, τέκνα θεοῦ emphasizes the community of nature as distinguished from the dignity of heirship. The "being called" includes the "being," but it is not synonymous with it. It lays special stress on the dignity of the Christian title and position.

καὶ ἐσμέν] An awkward parenthesis, which scribes naturally dropped, as in the *Receptus*, or adapted to the sentence, as in the Latin Versions, *et simus*. But it is in the author's style. Cf. the true text of Jn. i. 15, κέκραγεν λέγων—οὗτος ἦν ὁ εἰπών— Ὁ ὀπίσω μου ἐρχόμενος, and also Apoc. i. 6 ; 2 Jn. 2. And it also adds force to the sentence. "It is no mere empty title. It is a realized fact, though some are in danger of forgetting it." Justin seems to have known this verse; *Dial. c. Try.* 123 (353 B), οὕτως καὶ ἡμεῖς ἀπὸ τοῦ γεννήσαντος ἡμᾶς εἰς θεὸν Χριστοῦ,—καὶ θεοῦ τέκνα ἀληθινὰ καλούμεθα καὶ ἐσμέν, οἱ τὰς ἐντολὰς τοῦ Χριστοῦ φυλάσσοντες.

διὰ τοῦτο] Because they knew not God. As usual, the reference of τοῦτο is to what follows. They do not recognize us, because they did not know God. Those who failed to know God (οὐκ ἔγνω) in creation, in history, in the revelation made by Jesus Christ, naturally fail to know those who are of like nature.

αγαπην] post πατηρ H δ⁶ (Ψ).
δεδωκεν ℵ B C K L P al. longe plu. Thphyl. Oec.] εδωκεν A L 13. 27 cˢᶜʳ dˢᶜʳ.
ημιν] υμιν B K* 22. 31*. 80. 100 : post πατηρ H²⁵⁷ (33).
τεκνα θεου κληθωμεν] κληθητε τεκνα θῦ Iᵃ δ³⁸² (?).
και εσμεν] και εστιν H¹⁶² (61) Iᵃ ³⁹⁷ᶠ. ²⁰⁵. ¹⁰⁶. ²⁶¹ (96) : om. K L al. plu. armᶻᵒʰ.
ημας] υμας ℵ* K L P al.⁴⁰ arm-codd. Thphyl. Oec.
εγνω] εγνωκατε P 192 : εγνωτε 100 al. pauc.
αυτον]+ο κοσμος Iᶜ ¹⁷⁴ (252).

2. The thought of τέκνα θεοῦ is expanded in connection with the thought of the Parousia. Here and now they have attained to the position of "children of God." Their present dignity is as nothing compared with the glory which shall be revealed. The exact conditions of their future state have not yet been made clear. What has already become matter of common knowledge is that, the more fully Christ is revealed, the closer will be their likeness to Him. What they have seen of Christ incarnate has raised them to the position of God's children. If He is fully made manifest, those who see Him as He is "will be consummated in the divine likeness to which it was the divine purpose that they should attain" (Westcott). Cf. Gn. i. 26. All is not yet made manifest, but they have so learned the Christ that they know that it is "God's task to make the heavenly period Perfect the earthen."

ἀγαπητοί] Cf. iii. 21, iv. 11, and contrast ii. 7, iv. 1, 7. The word is used here, not to introduce a new section, but to call attention to a further meditation on what has preceded. The writer uses the term which reminds his readers of their and his common share in the gift which God has given.

νῦν τέκνα θεοῦ ἐσμέν] Cf. καὶ ἐσμέν of the preceding verse. What they have at present justifies their full confidence for the future, which will bring the complete unfolding of that which is even now present, though its manifestation is hindered by the circumstances in which they are placed.

6

οὔπω ἐφανερώθη] For οὔπω with the aorist, where the writer is not looking back on a time separated by an interval from that of writing or speaking, cf. Mk. xi. 2 (οὐδεὶς οὔπω ἐκάθισεν); 1 Co. viii. 2 (εἴ τις δοκεῖ . . . οὔπω ἔγνω); He. xii. 4 (οὔπω μέχρις αἵματος ἀντικατέστητε); Apoc. xvii. 10 (ὁ ἄλλος οὔπω ἦλθεν), 12 (βασίλειαν οὔπω ἔλαβον). The statement denies that there has ever yet been a moment at which it could be said ἐφανερώθη, where the aorist would be either timeless, or expressive of what has just happened. There is no necessary reference to any occasion "on which the revelation might have been expected," such as the manifestation of the Risen Lord (Westcott).

οἴδαμεν] We know enough to justify confidence even if no complete revelation has as yet been made. Great as are our privileges now, how far greater then! Nothing short of being like God in Christ. Contrast γινώσκομεν (ii. 3, 18, iii. 24, etc.): here no *progress* in knowledge is suggested: we are *aware* of the future likeness.

ἐὰν φανερωθῇ] May mean either (1) *if it shall be revealed*, i.e. our future condition (τί ἐσόμεθα), or (2) "if He shall be revealed," *i.e.* Christ. The first is the more natural interpretation so far as grammar is concerned. It connects the words naturally with the preceding οὔπω ἐφανερώθη. And it gives an adequate meaning to the words. "If our future glory is revealed, it will be found to be not less than likeness to God, the open vision of whose glory shall transform us." In favour of (2) is the use of φανερωθῇ of Christ in ver. 28 of the preceding chapter, and the general sense of the passage. Throughout the passage the writer's thoughts are turned to the revelation of Christ in His glory at His Parousia. If He be manifested in His true glory, the vision will change us to His likeness. Cf. 2 Co. iii. 18, τὴν δόξαν Κυρίου κατοπτριζόμενοι τὴν αὐτὴν εἰκόνα μεταμορφούμεθα ἀπὸ δόξης εἰς δόξαν: Col. iii. 4, ὅταν ὁ Χριστὸς φανερωθῇ . . . τότε καὶ ὑμεῖς σὺν αὐτῷ φανερωθήσεσθε ἐν δόξῃ. And if the use of φανεροῦσθαι in ii. 28 partly suggests this interpretation, in spite of the intervening οὔπω ἐφανερώθη, where the τί ἐσόμεθα determines the meaning of the verb, it must also be remembered that the language of soliloquy and meditation has to some extent its own rules. To one pondering over the future glory of the Son of God, in the light of the present revelation of the Risen Lord, which suggests so much more than it actually reveals, the words ἐὰν φανερωθῇ could probably have but one meaning. To us it would have been clearer if the subject had been definitely expressed. It does not follow that the same is true of the writer, or of those for whose sakes he is giving written form to his meditations. Very possibly they had often heard him meditate on the theme ἐὰν φανερωθῇ. He uses the word φανεροῦσθαι eighteen times, and in twelve Christ is the subject, though most of them refer to His manifestation in the flesh.

ὅμοιοι] Contrast Ph. ii. 6, τὸ εἶναι ἴσα θεῷ. And for the thought, cf. Plato, *Theaetetus*, 176 B, φυγὴ δὲ ὁμοίωσις τῷ θεῷ κατὰ τὸ δυνατόν: Greg. Thaum. *Paneg. in Origenem*, c. 12, τό γε πάντων τέλος οὐχ ἕτερόν τι οἶμαι ἢ καθαρῷ τῷ νῷ ἐξομοιωθέντα προσελθεῖν τῷ θεῷ καὶ μένειν ἐν αὐτῷ. Apoc. xxii. 4, καὶ ὄψονται τὸ πρόσωπον αὐτοῦ. *Similes, quia beati,* says Bede.

ὅτι] "Because we shall see Him as He is." What men saw of Jesus of Nazareth, when He manifested His glory under the limitations of human life, raised them to the position of τέκνα θεοῦ, in the case of all who received Him (Jn. i. 13). How much greater transforming power shall there be in the vision of Him as He is, no longer veiled by the conditions of earthly life !

It is possible to take ὅτι κ.τ.λ. as giving the proof of the *knowledge* (οἴδαμεν). We know that we shall be like Him, for we know that we shall see Him; and only the pure in heart shall *see* God. He is visible only to those who share His nature. Like is perceived by like alone. But if the writer had meant this he surely would have expressed himself differently. He often leaves not a little for his readers to supply. But he demands from them the use of spiritual insight rather than of mental acuteness. Weiss' explanation is too ingenious for its context.

τεκνα] post θεου P 31.
τι] οτι *I*ᵃ²⁷⁰ (54) Λ⁵⁵⁹ (415).
οιδαμεν]+δε K L al. pler. cat. syrˢᶜʰ cap. sahᵈ aeth. Or. Dam. Thphyl.
οτι (? 2°)] pr. και *I*ᵃ³⁹⁷ᶠ·²⁰⁵·¹⁰⁶·²⁰¹ (96) : και *I*ᵃ¹⁵⁸ (395).
οψομεθα] οψωμεθα 31 al.²ˢᶜʳ : *uidemus*, bohᵉᵈ.

3. The possession of such a hope is the strongest incentive to absolute purity. The hope is not really grasped except by those whose striving towards this goal is eager and constant. The hope is not stated to be the necessary condition of the purity, but the purity is the necessary result of the hope. It is not denied that other causes may produce a similar result. But where such a hope really exists the striving after purity must follow. The Christian hope is incompatible with moral indifference. No one, not even the "Gnostic," is raised by it above the moral obligations. And the purity aimed at is absolute. The standard is nothing less than the perfected human life of the glorified Christ.

πᾶς] The use of πᾶς in this Epistle and in the Gospel is instructive. It generally sets aside the claims of some party or other who claimed special privileges or exemptions for themselves.

ὁ ἔχων . . . ἐπ᾽ αὐτῷ] The form of expression emphasizes the thought of hope possessed and enjoyed as a sure possession (ἔχειν ἐλπίδα being stronger than the simple verb), and which rests on the Christ, and is therefore surely and securely grounded. Contrast Ac. xxiv. 15, ἐλπίδα ἔχων εἰς τὸν θεόν, *reaching as far as* (Westcott). Cf. 1 Ti. iv. 10, v. 5. See Introduction, p. iv; also 1 Ti. vi. 17; 1 P. i. 13, 21. ἐπ᾽ αὐτῷ must, of course, refer to Christ.

ἁγνίζει] Cf. Ex. xix. 10 f. ; Nu. viii. 21 ; Jos. iii. 5 ; 1 Es. vii. 10, and also Jn. xi. 55. Those who appeared before God at the Jewish feasts were required first to purify themselves from all Levitical and ceremonial uncleanness. The hope of appearing before the presence of God, and of seeing Christ as He is, necessarily inspires its possessors with the desire of putting away every defilement which clouds the vision of God, even as the human nature of the Christ, made perfect through the discipline and suffering of earthly life, has even now been exalted to the unveiled presence of the Father.

καθώς] He has attained, and those who hope to attain likewise will naturally spare no effort to follow the same path. But καθώς suggests a pattern, rather than introduces a motive.

ἐκεῖνος] For the change of pronoun, cf. Jn. v. 39, and perhaps xix. 35. Throughout the Epistle ἐκεῖνος used absolutely refers to Christ. Cf. ii. 6 (note).

ἁγνός] For the difference between ἁγνός and καθαρός, see Westcott's note. Καθαρός seems to state the objective fact, ἁγνός emphasizes the subjective feeling. The Vulg. commonly has *castus* for ἁγνός, but here has *sanctus*.

την ελπιδα] *fidem*, sah[d].
ταυτην] om. *I*[a 70. 367] (505).
επ αυτω] επ αυτον 2. 25. 30.
post εαυτον boh-sah. (*in eo*) : εν αυτω 31.
εαυτον] αυτον 31* o[scr].

4. πᾶς] Cf. ver. 3 (note). In contrast with those who seek to cleanse themselves from all defilement, are set those who continue to do the sin which defiles and separates from God. There is no special class of *illuminati*, superior to the obligation to keep the moral law. The test of progress is obedience. Those who fail to do the will of God, to work out the best of which their nature is capable, are breaking the law of God, which is the law of their being. All sin is law-breaking ; all falling short of the highest possible is disobedience to God's law for men, the law of self-realization after the pattern of the Christ. He that fails to do righteousness breaks the law.

τὴν ἀνομίαν] ἀνομία here is, of course, not the antinomianism of the "Gnostic." The condemnation of that would have required the converse of the statement here made, "All ἀνομία is sin." But the writer is undoubtedly thinking of the claim made by the superior "Gnostic," that he is at liberty to follow the leading of his own desires, without being under any obligation to the moral law, which is only binding on the ignorant and the inferior. The sins of which the writer is thinking are failures to fulfil the law of love, rather than grosser sins of the flesh, which are hardly, perhaps never, referred to in this Epistle. But whatever form they take, sinful acts are not matters of indifference. In the case of all men, even the most intelligent, they are transgressions of a valid law. He who stoops to them shows himself thereby to be no true τέκνον θεοῦ.

καὶ ἡ ἁμαρτία κ.τ.λ.] The καί adds a clause which carries the thought a step further. Not only is "doing sin" a violation of law, but sin in its very nature is a transgression of the law of God. It is the self-assertion of the finite against the eternal will of Him who has the right to claim absolute obedience.

την 1°] om. 31.
η 2°] pr. και ℵ* : (?) om. I^a 200 (83).
εστιν] + δε H δ2* (ℵ).

5. καὶ οἴδατε κ.τ.λ.] Not only does he who commits sin break a Divine law, but he stultifies the whole purpose of the Incarnation. Christ was manifested to men in His earthly life in order to take away sin, to destroy and remove it. And being sinless Himself, it was in His power to do so. To these two great incentives to self-cleansing, the purpose of the Incarnation, and the power of the Incarnate Christ, the writer can appeal as to part of the normal Christian consciousness, whether he includes himself (οἴδαμεν) or speaks only of his readers (οἴδατε).

ἐκεῖνος] Cf. ver. 3. The writer apparently sees no difficulty in using ἐκεῖνος and αὐτός in the same verse with reference to the same subject: though, of course, the case where ἐκεῖνος stands first is not strictly parallel to those in which it follows the use of αὐτός, as in ver. 3.

ἐφανερώθη] The word is used more frequently, as here, by the writer with reference to Christ's first coming, or manifestation, in the flesh. Cf. 1 Ti. iii. 16 ; 1 P. i. 20.

ἄρῃ] Take away, i.e. destroy. The Hebrew נשא is used in both senses of taking away and bearing. But it is differently translated into Greek in the two cases. Αἴρειν expresses the former, φέρειν the latter. Cf. Is. liii. 11, τὰς ἁμαρτίας αὐτῶν αὐτὸς ἀνοίσει.

τὰς ἁμαρτίας] whether used absolutely, or with the addition of ἡμῶν, denotes the many acts in which the sin of humanity is expressed. The concrete expression is more forcible than the absolute (τὴν ἁμαρτίαν).

ἁμαρτία ἐν αὐτῷ οὐκ ἔστιν] cf. Jn. vii. 18, ἀδικία ἐν αὐτῷ οὐκ ἔστιν. The statement is made of the whole human life of the Christ (ἔστιν), and is not confined to the earthly part of it. In virtue of His sinlessness He can accomplish the purpose of the Incarnation; and the thought also suggests the means by which it can be accomplished, a thought which is further developed in the next verse. Cf. Augustine, "In quo non est peccatum ipse uenit auferre peccatum. Nam si esset in illo peccatum, auferendum est illi, non ipse auferret."

> οιδατε A B C K L al. pler. vg. boh-codd. syr. aeth. Tert. Aug.]
> οιδαμεν ℵ 40. 98 tol. sah. arm. boh-ed. Fulg.
>
> τας αμαρτιας A B P 5. 13. 27. 66**. 81 am. fu. demid. harl. tol. cop. syr. aeth. Tert. Aug. Fulg.]+ημων ℵ C K L al. pler. cat. vg. sah. syr. Ath. Thphyl. Oec.
>
> εν αυτω] post εστιν ℵ sah. cop. aeth.

6. In so far as union with the Sinless is realized, sin ceases to be. The doing of sin shows that the Christ has never been fully seen or known. The statements are made absolutely, after the writer's wont. They must, of course, be interpreted in the light of i. 8 ff., where the writer makes it clear that he does not mean that those who have realized their union with Christ have actually attained as yet to a state of complete sinlessness. Where sin is, the vision of the Christ has not yet been made perfect. There is nothing to show that the writer is describing the *general* character of the Christian, which remains unchanged by separate sinful acts, inasmuch as they are foreign to it and do not affect it as a whole. The statement is made absolutely without reference to the modifications necessary when it is applied to the individual case.

ἐν αὐτῷ μένειν] As contrasted with εἶναι, μένειν perhaps suggests in this context the necessity of human effort.

οὐχ ἁμαρτάνει] Augustine has supplied the necessary modification, "In quantum in ipso manet, in tantum non peccat," a sentence which Bede has incorporated in his Commentary (cf. Westcott's note).

ἑώρακεν . . ἔγνωκεν] The vision and the knowledge have their abiding results. ὁρᾶν is used by the writer of spiritual vision. It cannot be restricted here (as by Weiss) to those who had actually seen the Lord in the flesh, ἔγνωκεν being added to meet the case of later disciples. Cf. Bede, "Visionem dicit et cognitionem fidei, qua iusti etiam in hac uita deum uidere delectantur, donec ad ipsam speciem apertae visionis eius in futuro preueniant, de qua supra dicitur, Quoniam uidebimus eum sicuti est," a passage which is also based on Augustine's

comment, "est illuminatio per fidem, est illuminatio per speciem."
If the two words are to be distinguished here, ὁρᾶν lays stress
on the object, which appears and is grasped by the mental vision,
γινώσκειν on the subsequent subjective apprehension of what is
grasped in the vision, or it is unfolded gradually in experience.

πας 2°] pr. και 38. 67 (mg.). 95. 96**. 97 (mg.) h^scr vg. syr. aeth. arm.
Or. Thphyl. Aug. (senel): pr. διο I^c 258 (56).
εγνωκεν] εγνω I^b 365. 472 (214) I^c 208. 116 (307) K^δ359 (479).

2. iii. 7–18. Elucidation of the thesis (ethical), and earnest
warning against those who would lead them astray.

(*a*) **7–10.** Further meditation on the Divine Birth. The
opposite statement. He that sinneth is of the Devil.

(*b*) **10–17.** Clearer definition of sin as failure to love the
brethren, and of its opposite, love.

7. The views of the false teachers were plausible, and there
was imminent danger of some of the faithful being seduced.
But the facts were clear. He, and he only, who shows the
fruits of righteousness in what he does, is righteous. Righteousness is always known by its fruits. There are no heights of
knowledge, or superior kinds of nature, for which action is a
matter of indifference.

τεκνία] If this is the true reading, the appeal is again made
to their common (spiritual) nature. There is some authority for
the reading παιδία, which would be equally suitable. The danger
would have been less imminent, if they had used their own powers,
and shown themselves less dependent on the moral guidance of
others.

μηδεὶς πλανάτω] Cf. ii. 26. They must yield to the seduc-
tions of no one, however prominent his position or plausible
his arguments. It is, of course, possible that the writer is
thinking of some particular opponent.

ὁ ποιῶν] Cf. i. 6, iii. 4, etc. If the character is true, the
whole life will be an expression of it, even as the whole of
Christ's life was a continuous expression of the character and
person in whom God could be well pleased.

ἐκεῖνος] Cf. vv. 3, 4 (notes). Righteousness was fully realized
in Him who set the Christian standard. No lower ideal would
prove a sufficient incentive to holiness, *i.e.* the highest self-
realization of which the nature of man is capable, who was
created in order to grow into the likeness of God.

τεκνια ℵ B K L al. pler. cat. Thphyl. Oec. m vg. syr. Tert. Aug.] παιδια
A C P 5. 13. 27. 29 arm. (uid.) cop. syr^p mg Lcif.: +μου 15. 26. 36. 68
cat. sah. syr^sch aeth.
μηδεις] μη τις A.
ποιων δικαιοσυνην (? ? cf. v. Soden, p. 1856)] δικαιος ων H^δ86 (Ψ).
δικαιος (? 2°)] om. H^δ48 (33).
την 2°⁻ om. ℵ*.

8. ὁ ποιῶν τὴν ἁμαρτίαν] The contrast to 7*b*. He whose whole course of action is the expression of "sin," belongs to the Devil, from whom the life which animates him is derived, as the higher life which issues in righteousness proclaims its possessor a τέκνον θεοῦ.

ἐκ τοῦ διαβόλου ἐστίν] Cf. Bede, "Non carnis originem ducendo ex diabolo sicut Manichaeus impurissime de cunctis credit hominibus : sed imitationem uel suggestionem peccandi sumendo ab illo, quomodo et nos filii Abrahae sumus facti, imitando fidem Abrahae," a suggestive note, though it ignores the nearer illustrations of the context.

ἀπ' ἀρχῆς] The meaning of ἀπ' ἀρχῆς has been variously interpreted. It has generally been understood either of (1) the beginning of "sinning," *i.e.* the Fall of Adam, or events which preceded the first sin of man ; or (2) the beginning of the existence of the Devil. His first act was one of sin. The uncertainty of both these interpretations has led Rothe and others to give the phrase a logical rather than a temporal meaning. "Satan sins, the author would say, '*par principe,*' for the sake of sinning. Other sinners sin for the sake of another. In contrast to him all human sin is derived." Whether the actual phrase can bear such an interpretation or not, the point of view of the readers has surely been overlooked. The writer must have intended a meaning which the words could suggest to them. The phrase must therefore be interpreted in accordance with Jn. viii. 44, i. 1 ; Gn. i. 1, etc. The attempt to assign a definite date, so to speak, is a mistake. "The earliest times spoken of in Genesis" would perhaps be the nearest popular paraphrase. "From the first" would give its meaning with fair accuracy. It denotes the earliest events which have any bearing on the point at issue. From the very first, long before the first actual sin of any man, "the devil sinneth," and the course begun from the first has been continued ever since. All human sin, therefore, has its origin in what is external to the man who sins. It comes from an external source. It is not self-originated or part of man's nature. As Westcott has said elsewhere, "There is no view of human nature so inexpressibly sad as that which leaves out the Fall." As also F. D. Maurice has said, "There has been no period of the existence of human beings in which they have not been liable to the assaults of this Tempter."

There is nothing in the passage to suggest that the writer held a "dualistic" view of the origin of evil, considering the Devil "an originally evil being" ; but it is manifest that he believed in a personal Tempter. Cf. Jn. viii. 44.

εἰς τοῦτο ἐφανερώθη κ.τ.λ.] All such action is in direct opposition to the purpose of the Incarnation of the Son of God, who

was manifested in the flesh in order to destroy the works of the
Devil, *i.e.* the sins which he has introduced into the lives of men.

λύσῃ] "destroy." The word generally includes the suggestion of destroying, undoing or dissolving, that which forms the
bond of cohesion. Cf. Jn. ii. 19, v. 18, vii. 23 (the Lord
"dissolved" the Jewish sabbatical tradition by applying to the
question the higher principle of the duty of restoring man to his
true self). Windisch aptly quotes the λογίον of the Egyptian
Gospel, ἦλθον καταλῦσαι τὰ ἔργα τῆς θηλείας.

o 1°] +δε A 25. 68 kˢᶜʳ tol. boh-ed. arm. aeth. Lcif.
λυσῃ] λυσει B 100 : λυθη P.

9. He who is begotten of God must be in character like God
who begat him. Sin, which is of the Devil, finds no place in
him.

ὁ γεγεννημένος] Compare and contrast Jn. i. 13, ἐκ θεοῦ
ἐγεννήθησαν. Here the writer emphasizes not only the initial
act, or the single act, but its permanent results.

ἁμαρτίαν οὐ ποιεῖ] Anarthrous and therefore qualitative. He
does not do that which is sinful in character. But the absence
of the article should not be pressed.

ὅτι σπέρμα] The seed which produces the new life in him
(cf. Jn. i. 13), as a permanent and abiding factor.[1] The interpretation which equates σπέρμα with the Word of God ("semen
dei, id est uerbum dei," Bede, from Augustine, who adds, "unde
dicit Apostolus, Per Euangelium ego uos genui, 1 Co. iv. 15)
receives some support from 1 P. i. 23; Ja. i. 18, but is hardly
in accordance with the Johannine teaching, in which the Spirit
is the author of the new birth (cf. Jn. iii.). Wohlenberg in an
interesting paper has pleaded for the interpretation which
identifies σπέρμα θεοῦ with God's children collectively (cf. Jn.
viii. 33, σπέρμα 'Αβραάμ). It has the advantage of referring αὐτοῦ
and ἐν αὐτῷ to the same person (God's children abide in Him),
but it makes the following clause, οὐ δύναται . . . γεγέννηται, very
difficult both in grammar and sense. As Law has pointed out,
the last clause must then have run ("and they cannot sin, because
they abide in Him"). Still less can be said for Karl's interpretation of the words as referring to Christ. Cf., however,
Justin, *Apol.* i. 32, where we perhaps have an echo of this.[2]

οὐ δύναται κ.τ.λ.] The fact that he has been begotten of God
excludes the possibility of his committing sin as an expression of
his true character, though actual sins may, and do, occur, in so
far as he fails from weakness to realize his true character. Cf.

[1] Cf. Philo, *De Ebriet.* 30 (Cohn, ii. p. 176), τὰ τοῦ θεοῦ σπέρματα.
[2] οἱ πιστεύοντες αὐτῷ ἄνθρωποι ἐν οἷς οἰκεῖ τὸ παρὰ τοῦ θεοῦ σπέρμα, ὁ
λόγος.

Jn. viii. 33, 39. Every τέκνον must reproduce the works of his father. In so far as any man is a τέκνον θεοῦ he "cannot" do the works of the Devil. The writer speaks, however, here as elsewhere, in the absolute language of the prophet rather than with the circumspection of the casuist. On the N.T. doctrine of Birth from God, see Windisch, p. 118.

πας] pr. διο αγαπητοι I^{c 258} (56).
γεγεννημενος] γεγενημενος K 99. 100. 177* j^{scr} o^{scr} al. pauc.
του (? 1°)] om. H^{δ48} (33) I^{a 106} (179).
αμαρτιαν ου ποιει] *non peccat* sah. boh.
σπερμα] pr. το I^{c 551} (216) O⁴⁶ (154).
αυτου] *dei* sah^d: om. I^{a 382} (231).
αμαρτανειν] αμαρτιαν ποιησαι I^{a 158} (395).
οτι] οστις I^{a 264} (233).

10. ἐν τούτῳ] This may possibly refer to what has preceded, the not-doing or the doing of sin, which are the distinguishing characteristics of the classes into which the writer divides mankind. But it is more probable, and more in accordance with the writer's usual custom, that the reference is to what follows, the achievement of, or the failure to achieve, righteousness and love (cf. ii. 3). For the construction, cf. the note on i. 4.

φανερά] The writer is striving to give his readers a distinguishing test which can be easily applied. It is, of course, to the judgment of men, not the judgment of God, that the two clues become manifest.

τέκνα τοῦ διαβόλου] cf. Acts xiii. 10, υἱὲ διαβόλου, and Jn. viii. The teaching of this section of the Epistle can hardly be understood without reference to the 8th chapter of the Gospel, with which it is intimately connected.

πᾶς] There are no exceptions on the ground of superior knowledge or "pneumatic" nature; cf. notes on vv. 3, 4.

καὶ ὁ μὴ ἀγαπῶν] The doing of righteousness might be too vague and general a test. The writer therefore narrows it down to one special form of righteousness which is in fact the basis of the whole, and in the exercise of which the false teachers had apparently shown themselves particularly lacking. Cf. Ro. xiii. 9, εἴ τις ἑτέρα ἐντολή, ἐν τῷ λόγῳ τούτῳ ἀνακεφαλαιοῦται, ἐν τῷ· ἀγαπήσεις τὸν πλησίον σου ὡς σεαυτόν.

τὸν ἀδελφὸν αὐτοῦ] The writer is obviously thinking of members of the Christian Society, not thereby excluding the wider duty on which the Sermon on the Mount and the Parables insist. The object of the Epistle is to suggest practical tests. They must be practical and such as are easily applied. No statement is made to the effect that he who confines his love to his Christian brethren has completely fulfilled the law of Christ. The writer has a special object in what he says, and he writes in view of the failure in this respect of showing love to fellow-Christians, which was conspicuous in the case of the false teachers, in spite of their claims to intellectual and spiritual superiority. There is nothing inconsistent with the teaching of the Christ in laying special stress on the first stage in obeying it. The experience of a lifetime, and especially of his later years, would seem to have taught the writer the necessity of charity *beginning* at home.

εν τουτω] εκ τουτου $I^{a\ 200f}$ (83).

πας] pr. και C* uid aeth.

ποιων δικαιοσυνην ℵ A B C K L P al. omn^uid cat. harl. tol. **arm.** cop. syr. aeth. Did. Thphyl. Oec.] ων δικαιος m vg. (am. fu. demid.) sah. syr. Or. Cyp. Lcif. Aug. : δικαιος ων H δ6 (Ψ). An interesting "Western" variant, which can hardly claim to be original. The context requires the practical test of "doing."

δικαιοσυνην ℵ B L al. plu. Dam.] pr. την A C K P h al. fere.²⁰ Dam.

ο 2°] om. $I^{a\ 382}$ (231).

αυτου]+ ουκ αγαπα τον θν $I^{a\ 70}$ (505).

11. The original message of the Gospel, nay, the whole history of God's revelation of Himself to men from the earliest times, is summed up in the command to exercise mutual love. He therefore who does not love his brother shows thereby that he cannot be ἐκ τοῦ θεοῦ.

αὕτη ... ἵνα] The αὕτη, which refers to what follows, excludes the possibility of any "telic" force being retained by ἵνα here; cf. Jn. xvii. 3, and the close parallels in Jn. xiii. 34, xv. 12; 1 Jn. iii. 23, iv. 21, v. 16. See also 1 Jn. v. 3; 2 Jn. 5, 6; cf. note on i. 9. The declarative, or definitive, use of ἵνα to introduce the contents of a command, or the like, is fully established for S. John.

ἀγγελία] The message of the Gospel, of which the law of love is the basis. The reading ἐπαγγελία does not suit the context, and it is obviously due to the careless substitution of a commoner word. Except in this passage, ἀγγελία is found only once in the N.T. (1 Jn. i. 5). On the other hand, ἐπαγγελία occurs 51 times, but only once in the Johannine writings (1 Jn. ii. 25).

ἦν ἠκούσατε ἀπ' ἀρχῆς] The law of love was an essential part of the earliest presentation of the Gospel. It formed part of the earliest teaching which the readers had received. The contents, however, of ver. 12 suggest that in the words ἀπ' ἀρχῆς the writer's thought goes back to still earlier times. The earliest stories of the beginnings of the race bear witness to the fatal consequences of disobedience to the law of love.

αγγελια A B K L al. plu. cat. Thphyl. Oec^com vg. Aug.] επαγγελια ℵ C P 27. 29. 40. 66**. 69. 99 a^scr n^scr al. mu. harl. syr. sah^wb cop. arm. aeth. Did. Cyr. Oec^txt Lcif. : *uerbum* sah^d.

ινα αγαπωμεν] *ut diligatis* boh-ed. arm^usc: ινα αγαπατε $I^{a\ 113}$ (235).

12. The story of Cain is the typical example of the "want" of brotherly love. The form of the reference here is conditioned by what the writer has to say about the hatred which Christians must expect from the world. Men's deeds are the natural outcome of their charcater and inclinations. Evil deeds are the expression of a character which takes pleasure in what is evil. Righteousness must always provoke the hostile feeling of those whose delight is in evil. And feelings must sooner or later express themselves in action.

οὐ καθώς] Cf. 2 Co. viii. 5, καὶ οὐ καθὼς ἠλπίσαμεν ἀλλὰ ἑαυτοὺς ἔδωκαν: Jn. xiv. 27, οὐ καθὼς ὁ κόσμος δίδωσιν, and especially Jn. vi. 58, οὗτός ἐστιν ὁ ἄρτος ὁ ἐξ οὐρανοῦ καταβάς, οὐ καθὼς ἔφαγον οἱ πατέρες καὶ ἀπέθανον, where the construction is irregular, as here. The comparison is incomplete in form. It may be paraphrased "the feelings of Christians for each other must not be like, rather they must be the exact opposite of, those of Cain, whose hatred of righteousness led him to the violent murder of his brother." Schlatter aptly quotes in illustration (p. 149), בְּאֵיזֶה אָח. לֹא בְּקֵין לְהֶבֶל קֵין הָרַג אֶת־הֶבֶל, Pes. Kah. 16. 126a.

ἐκ τοῦ πονηροῦ ἦν] Every man must draw his life and power from one source or the other. His deeds show to whom he belongs and has attached himself. The writer never denies the individual freedom of choice. He only traces things back to what he believes to be their ultimate spiritual sources.

ἔσφαξεν] The verb always includes the idea of violence. In the N.T. σφάζειν is found only here and in the Apocalypse. Cf. Apoc. vi. 4, ἵνα ἀλλήλους σφάξουσιν: 9, τὰς ψυχὰς τῶν ἐσφαγμένων διὰ τὸν λόγον τοῦ θεοῦ: xviii. 24, πάντων τῶν ἐσφαγμένων ἐπὶ τῆς γῆς. It is also used of the Lamb, and of the "head" of the beast (xiii. 3). In the LXX its most frequent use is sacrificial (cf. Gn. xxii. 10, of Isaac; Ex. xxix. 11; Lv. i. 5; Nu. xi. 22, etc.); but see also Jg. xii. 6 (A), σφάζουσιν αὐτοὺς ἐπὶ τὰς διαβάσεις τοῦ Ἰορδάνου: 1 K. xv. 33, ἔσφαξε Σαμουὴλ τὸν Ἀγὰγ ἐνώπιον Κυρίου: 1 Mac. i. 2, καὶ ἔσφαξε βασιλεῖς, etc.

χάριν τίνος] The violent deed was only the last expression of that antipathy which righteousness always calls out in those who make evil the guiding principle of their life. This view, that the cause of the murder of Abel is to be found in the character of Cain as manifested in his actions, is hardly in accord with the narrative of Genesis (iv. 8 ff.), but it is quite in keeping with the suggestions read into that narrative by the adherents of the allegorical method of exegesis. We may compare Philo's treatment of the subject, who finds indications of Cain's φιλαυτία in the fact that he only offered his sacrifice "after several days," and not at once, with the readiness which should distinguish the

service of God ; and that he offered of the fruits, not of the first-
fruits.   Cf. also He. xi. 4, where the stress is laid on the character
of the sacrifices offered ($\pi\lambda\epsilon\acute{\iota}ο\nu\alpha$ $\theta\upsilon\sigma\acute{\iota}\alpha\nu$), rather than on the
general character of all the actions of the two men.

του (? 1°) om. I^a 397^{ffff} (96) | τον] pr. *Abal*, **sah**^{d}.
om. και . . . αυτου aeth.
τινος χαριν I^a^{55} (236).
ου] pr. *et* **sah**^{d}.
αδελφου αυτου] αβελ I^a^{264} (233).
δικαια] *bona* arm.

13-16. The ground of the world's hatred of those who love,
and the glory of love, which gives life, in Christ.

13-15. Those who can interpret aright the true meaning of
the story of Cain and Abel will feel no surprise at the attitude
of the world towards Christians.   It only expresses the hostility
which that which is good must always call out in that which is
evil.   Our love for the brethren assures us that we have already
passed out of the state of hatred and death, and now abide in
that of life.   For life is love.   He who does not love is still in
the state of death.   Every one who does not love his brother is
a murderer, in the eyes of all to whom the true issues of things
are manifest, even though he has so far stayed his hand from
violence.   And your common consciousness as men tells you
that no murderer can have the higher life in him as a permanent
and abiding principle of action.

13. μὴ θαυμάζετε] cf. Jn. iii. 7 (μὴ θαυμάσῃς), where the aorist
emphasizes the immediate feeling aroused by a particular thought,
or action, rather than the more permanent feeling called out
by what is continuous.   Cf. also Jn. v. 28, where the form of
sentence refers to the continuous feeling, not to the momentary
surprise, which the fact that the hour was coming, when all the
dead should hear the voice of the Son of God, might occasion.
The construction with the present imperative is the usual construction in the Johannine writings, the aorist subjunctive being
only used in the passage quoted above.   Here it is significant.
The hatred of the world was an abiding attitude, always liable
to provoke unchristian retaliation, and always a temptation to the
more "intelligent" to neglect their duty to their weaker brethren.

μη A B C^{corr} K L al. pler. vg. sah. cop. syr. Lcif. Did. Thphyl. Oec.]
pr. και ℵ C* P 15. 18. 29. 36. 66**. 98. 191 cat.* syr. am. aeth.
αδελφοι ℵ A B C D al. mu. cat. vg. arm. Lcif. Did.]+μου K L al.
longe. plu. syr. sah. cop. aeth. (ημων) Thphyl. Oec.
υμας] ημας **sah**. I^a^{1402} (219) O^{46} (154).

14. ἡμεῖς οἴδαμεν] The appeal is to the Christian consciousness, shared by writers and readers alike.   Their experience as
Christians has taught them that conscious life is dormant till

it is called out in active love and fellowship. Cf. Augustine (*Tract.* v. 10), "Nemo interroget hominem ; redeat unusquisque ad cordem suum : si ibi inuenerit charitatem fraternam, securus sit quia transiit a morte ad uitam."

ὁ μὴ ἀγαπῶν] The statement is put in its most general form. The state in which love has not been called out into conscious activity is a state of death. Life is the chance of learning how love not only "might be," but "is."

The addition of τὸν ἀδελφόν in the *Receptus* is natural in the light of the preceding clause and of ver. 16. But it narrows down the writer's meaning unnecessarily. In his more absolute statements he shows himself fully aware that the duty of love is absolute, and has a wider application than the Christian Society, even as the Christ is the propitation for the whole world, though in a practical Epistle he lays most stress on what is first practicable.

τους αδελφους]+ημων ℵ 68. 58^lect syr. **sah.**

ο μη αγαπων ℵ A B 13. 27. 29. vg. sah^db arm. Did. Lcif. Aug.]+τον αδελφον C K L P al. pler. sah^w cop. syr. Thphyl. Oec. Cassiod. (+αυτου P al.^10 sah^w cop. syr. aeth.) : τους αδελφους 15.

ο]+δε I^a 256 (24).

15. πᾶς ὁ μισῶν κ.τ.λ.] Cf. Aug. (*Tract.* v. 10). "Non movet manus ad occidendum hominem, homicida iam tenetur a Domino ; uiuit ille, et iste iam interfector iudicatur." Hatred is the moving cause, whether or not the occasion for its final display has presented itself and been used. Cf. Mt. v. 23, 24.

ἀνθρωποκτόνος] Cf. Jn. viii. 44, the only other instance of its use in the N.T. It is, of course, used here in its literal sense of actual murderer, not of the murderer of the soul.

οἴδατε] It is axiomatic. Their natural consciousness as men will tell them that the higher life cannot be communicated as a permanent possession to such an one. The writer does not avoid the use of irony when it suits his purpose.

μένουσαν] Cf. Jn. i. 32, 33, v. 38, vi. 27 ; 1 Jn. ii. 14, 24 ; 2 Jn. 2. The word suggests that eternal life is both "a continuous power and a communicated life." Wohlenberg's attempt to connect the word μένουσαν with the following verse (Μένουσαν ἐν τούτῳ ἐγνώκαμεν τὴν ἀγάπην) is ingenious rather than convincing. Though it is not absolutely necessary to the sense, its position is justified by the μένει of ver. 14, and it serves to heighten the impossibility of the rejected hypothesis.

πᾶς . . . οὐ] The usual "Hebraistic" expression, or at least the form of expression which a Jew writing Greek would naturally adopt. Cf. 1 Jn. ii. 19, 21, etc. ; and see Moulton's note, *Grammar of New Testament Greek*, vol. i. p. 245 f. Such phrases as χωρὶς πάσης ὑπερθέσεως show that "vernacular usage" only needed to be extended "under the encouragement of a similar idiom in Hebrew." But so far as the evidence goes it would seem that there has been "extension" in the Semitic direction. The construction is not found in the Gospel.

αυτου] εαυτου B.
οιδατε] οιδαμεν *l*ᶜ ¹¹⁴ (335) sah^wb boh. : pr. ουκ *l*ᵃ δ⁵⁰⁵ (69).
πας 2°]+ο *l*ᵇ δ³⁷⁰ (1149).
εν αυτω B K al. plu. Thphyl. Oec.] εν εαυτω ℵ A L C P al.³⁰.
αιωνιον] om. *l*ᶜ ¹¹⁶. ¹¹⁴ (–).
μενουσαν] om. sah^d.

16–18. Description of true love, and exhortation to its practice. The essence of love was manifested once for all, finally and completely, when the Christ gave His life for men. We know what true love really is in the light of that example. And we cannot but recognize our obligation to follow it, if need be even to the last sacrifice, for our brethren. There is, however, a simple test by which we can know at once whether we are at least on the road which leads to the possession of true love. He who is unwilling to give of his external possessions, where need is obvious and well known to him, has not even begun to cherish true love for God in his soul. True love proves itself in action. It cannot stop short at expressions of which the tongue is the instrument. It must show by actual deeds that the words in which it is professed correspond to real feelings of the heart.

16. ἐν τούτῳ] The reference is to what follows, according to the writer's usual custom, especially when a clause with ὅτι follows.

τὴν ἀγάπην] Absolute. There is no need to supply a genitive, τοῦ Χριστοῦ or τοῦ θεοῦ. The true nature of love was manifested in such a way that men could learn to realize it, with abiding effects on their character and life (ἐγνώκαμεν).

ἐκεῖνος] He : neither writer nor readers feel the need for further definition by the addition of a name. Cf. the notes on vv. 3, 4.

ἐκεῖνος ὑπὲρ ἡμῶν] He for us : the Christ, the Son of God, for such as we are. The contrast is heightened by the order of the words. There are no depths of sacrifice to which true love will not stoop.

τὴν ψυχὴν αὐτοῦ ἔθηκεν] Neither of the O.T. phrases, which are usually quoted, שׂים נפשׁ בכפו and השׂים נפשׁ אשׁם (Is. liii. 10), afford a sufficiently close parallel to suggest an interpretation. The additions, of בכפו in the one case, and אשׁם in the other, determine the exact sense of שׂים. The Rabbinic phrases quoted by Schlatter (on Jn. x. 11) all have נתן. The usage of the Fourth Gospel is a safer guide. Cf. Jn. x. 11, 15, 17, 18, xiii. 37–38, xv. 13, and also xiii. 4, τίθησι τὰ ἱμάτια. The latter passage suggests the idea of laying aside, as a garment is put off, which agrees well with the use of the phrase in Jn. x. 18. The usage of τιθέναι in Jn. ii. 10, τὸν καλὸν οἶνον τίθησιν, can hardly help us to determine its meaning here. The phrase does not occur again in the Johannine Books. The Latin translation "*dat*" in Jn. x. 11 is, of course, derived from the Western variant δίδωσιν (א D). Elsewhere the Vulgate uses *ponere*. Spitta's suggestions (*ZNTW* x. [1909] p. 78), that the phrase is used rightly in vv. 11, 15, in the sense of risking or staking his life for the sheep, and taken up in a different sense (of giving, or laying down) in the later interpolation of vv. 17, 18, is worthy of consideration, but it has perhaps been influenced by the Hebrew phrase, where the meaning, as has been pointed out, is determined by the added בכפו. If the distinction is to be maintained, the present verse agrees with the "later" passage.

καὶ ἡμεῖς κ.τ.λ.] It is not clear whether this clause is added to the first clause, ἐκεῖνος . . . ἔθηκεν, and governed by ὅτι, or is to be regarded as a consequence of the example set by the Christ. The obligation, which all good men recognize, to sacrifice their lives, if need be, for others, may be part of the means whereby we learn what true love is. Such a κοινὴ ἐννοία of good men throws the clearest light on the nature of love. But the obligation, as felt by "us," may also be regarded as the consequence of what Christ has done. When once the perfect example has been set, the duty of all disciples to follow it is clear. Grammatically the first is preferable. But the use of καί in this Epistle is wide. The writer always thinks as a Hebrew, and this is reflected in his forms of expression. The second interpretation is therefore grammatically admissible. And it has the advantage of far greater simplicity and directness. The emphatic ἡμεῖς, moreover, is in favour of it.

εγνωκαμεν] εγνωμεν *I*c 551 (216) : γινωσκομεν *I*c 114 (335).

την αγαπην]+του θεου 52 vg. (am. demid. harl.) **arm**-codd. **boh**-codd. : +*ipsius* m tol. Vig. : +*eius*, Ambrst.

την ψυχην αυτου εθηκεν υπερ ημων *I*a 200f (83).

ημων] υμων *I*a 175. 502 (319) *I*b 398. 78. δ507. δ368 (69).

υπερ των αδελφων] post ψυχας *I*a δ457 (209) *I*b δ507 (241) *I*c 551 (216) *K* δ200 (922).

εθηκεν] τεθεικεν 4. 31. 40 : τεθηκεν *I*a 264. δ505 (233) : ponit ante την φυχ. αυτου 31*.

υπερ] περι P.

των αδελφων] αλληλων **boh.** *I*c 114 (335) : +ημων *I*a 101. 7 (40).

θειναι א A B C P 5. 15. 26. 27. 29. 68] τιθεναι K L al. pler. Thphyl. Oec.

17. The practical test. Wider obligations may be acknowledged with all readiness in theory, where a more homely test reveals the extent of a man's failure. The writer is always enforcing the truth that philanthropy begins at home. Cf. Philo,

De Post. Cain, 86 (Cohn, ii. 18), τί γὰρ ὄφελος λέγειν μὲν τὰ βέλ
τιστα, διανοεῖσθαι δὲ καὶ πράττειν τὰ αἴσχιστα; σοφιστῶν οὗτος ὁ
τρόπος.

τὸν βίον τοῦ κόσμου] Well paraphrased in Augustine's version,
facultates mundi. Βίος always denotes life in its *external* aspects.
Cf. ii. 16, ἡ ἀλαζονία τοῦ βίου: Mk. xii. 44 (= Lk. xxi. 4);
I Ti. ii. 2 ; 2 Ti. ii. 4 ; and for the verb, I P. iv. 2, τὸν ἐπίλοιπον
ἐν σαρκὶ βιῶσαι χρόνον. Cf. also Ac. xxvi. 4, τὴν . . . βίωσίν μου
ἐκ νεότητος. Consequently, βίος is rare in the N.T., while ζωή
occurs more than a hundred times.

θεωρῇ] Behold : not merely cast a passing glance, but see,
long enough to appreciate and understand the circumstances of
the case. Cf. Jn. xx. 6 ; Ac. iv. 13 ; Apoc. xi. 11 f.

χρείαν ἔχοντα] Cf. ii. 27 ; and for the use of the phrase
absolutely, Mk. ii. 25 ; Ac. ii. 45, iv. 35 ; Eph. iv. 28.

κλείσῃ] Cf. Ps. lxxvi. (lxxvii.) 10, ἢ συνέξει τοὺς οἰκτειρμοὺς
αὐτοῦ ἐν τῇ ὀργῇ αὐτοῦ; cf. also Dt. xv. 7, ἐὰν γένηται ἐν σοὶ
ἐνδεής . . . οὐκ ἀποστέρξεις τὴν καρδίαν σου. The word perhaps
suggests that a barrier has to be raised against the natural
human feelings which the contemplation of such a case calls out.

τὰ σπλάγχνα] Cf. Pr. xii. 10, τὰ δὲ σπλάγχνα τῶν ἀσεβῶν
ἀνελεήμονα. The word is not found in the earlier parts of the
Septuagint, and only in this passage is it used to translate רחֲמִים,
which in the Psalms is paraphrased by οἰκτιρμοί (Ps. xxiv.
(xxv.) 6, and in Isaiah (xlvii. 6) by ἔλεος. See Lightfoot's note
on Ph. i. 8. The classical distinction between σπλάγχνα and
ἔντερα (not in N.T.) is not to be found in Hebrew forms of
expression.

τοῦ θεοῦ] The context determines that the genitive must be
objective. Cf. v. 3.

εχη] εχει τις *I*ᶜ ²⁵⁸ (56).
θεωρη] θεωρει K L 29. 40 al^plus **20**.
αυτου (? 1º)] om. *I*ᵃ ⁷.
κλεισῃ] κλεισει L 13 al.
απ αυτου] om. *I*ᵇ δ¹⁸⁰ (1319).
εν] επ *I*ᵃ ⁷⁰ (505) *I*ᵇ ²⁵³ᶠ (2) *K*⁴⁵³ δ⁴⁰¹ (62).

18. τεκνία] The appeal is made, as usual, on the ground of
the common spiritual nature which they all share.

ἐν ἔργῳ καὶ ἀληθείᾳ] The phrase is contrasted with λόγῳ and
γλώσσῃ. Practical love corresponds to inward truth. Much
protestation is a mere exercise of the tongue.

τεκνια א A B C P al¹⁵ cat. m am. syr. arm. Clem. Dam. Aug.]+μου
K L al. longe. plur. vg. (fu. demid. etc.) syr. sah. cop. aeth. Thphyl. Oec.
αγαπωμεν] αγαπατε H δ⁶ (Ψ).
λογω] pr. εν H δ⁶ (Ψ) *I*ᵃ ¹⁰¹· ²⁶⁴· ⁶⁵ (40) : pr. τω *I*ᵃ ¹⁷⁵· ⁵⁰² (319).
μηδε] και א syr. aeth.

τη γλωσση A B C K L al. plu. Dam. Thphyl.] om. τη ℵ P al. sat. mu.
cat. arm. Clem. Oec.

εν] om. K al. permu. cat. Dam. Oec.

αληθεια] + *quia sumus ex ueritate* sah[d].

19 f. The consciousness that their love for God is true and
active, assures men of their fellowship with God, that they are
"of the truth." The choice of phrase is determined by the
language of ver. 18. Practically it is equivalent to εἶναι ἐκ τοῦ
θεοῦ. And the consciousness of this fellowship brings assurance,
in spite of what the conscience has to tell of thoughts and
deeds which mar its realization. Even before God, in whose
presence no falsehood can stand, the Christian can "still" his
heart: for the all-knowing God is greater than the accusing
conscience. Knowing all, He knows that the love is true, and
is the determining element of the character, notwithstanding the
many failures which interrupt its complete realization. His
knowledge is absolute. He can see the whole, and He has
accepted the love which is real and active as sufficient ground
for admitting the man to His fellowship. Cf. Jn. xxi. 17, πάντα
σὺ οἶδας, σὺ γινώσκεις ὅτι φιλῶ σε. The accusations of conscience
are stilled in the presence of omniscient holiness, which is perfect
love.

At first sight the omniscience of God may seem a strange
ground for the confidence of men, who are conscious of sins
that interrupt their fellowship with God. "If as natural men we
shrink from allowing our neighbours to see into our heart, much
more are we terrified at the thought that the holy God penetrates
to the depth of our hearts" (Rothe). But in the case of
Christians, who are conscious of the relationship to God in which
they stand, it is otherwise. Their security lies in the fact that
this relationship has been established by one who knows all the
circumstances of the case. There is no fear of alteration in the
light of fuller knowledge.

But how can such confidence be said to be derived from the
practice of love, in the sphere in which it is first possible, *i.e.* in
love of the brethren? The answer is that in such activities they
have learned to know of a love, other than that based on physical
kinship, which is not merely the "cloak of self-seeking"; and the
more clearly its true character is recognized, the more clearly it
is seen that such love is of the very Being of God. So the all-
knowing "were the all-loving too." The surest ground of our
confidence is the knowledge that "our help standeth in the *name*
of the Lord," who is love.

Thus the general meaning of these verses is fairly plain.
They have always been recognized as touching the very heart of
the Christian faith. The exact interpretation, however, of each

clause is a matter of considerable difficulty. The meaning of
πείσομεν is disputed, as also of the first and second ὅτι. The
difficulties caused by the sequence of two clauses introduced by
ὅτι have led to the removal of the second ὅτι from some texts.

(1) If πείσομεν is taken in its usual sense of "persuade,"
(a) the fact of which we "persuade our heart" may be left
unstated, to be gathered from the context. If so, we must
supply "that we are of the truth" from the preceding verse.
This is grammatically unobjectionable, and gives an adequate
sense. Even though our heart (conscience) convicts us of sins
which separate us from God, we can nevertheless persuade
ourselves that we are really of the truth, because God is greater
than our hearts, in knowledge and in love, and has recognized
our position, in spite of, or perhaps we should say in consequence
of, the fact that He knows all, and so is qualified to judge.
(β) The fact may be found in the second clause, "that God is
greater than our heart." Against this the objection is hardly
valid that the fact is too obvious to be disputed. The question
is not of the objective truth of the fact, but of our subjective
apprehension of it, under circumstances which make its realization peculiarly difficult (ἐὰν καταγινώσκῃ κ.τ.λ.). On the other
hand, Dr. Westcott's objection would seem to hold good, that
"the consciousness of a sincere love of the brethren does not
furnish the basis of the conviction of the sovereign greatness of
God." (γ) If the first suggestion (a) is felt to be unsatisfactory,
there is some authority for the absolute use of πείθειν in the
sense of "*still*," assure, appease, tranquillize. Cf. Mt. xxviii. 14,
καὶ ἐὰν ἀκουσθῇ τοῦτο ἐπὶ τοῦ ἡγεμόνος, ἡμεῖς πείσομεν καὶ ὑμᾶς
ἀμερίμνους ποιήσομεν (where, however, the reference may be to
the contents of ver. 13, the asserted theft of the body by the
disciples); 2 Mac. iv. 45, ἐπηγγείλατο χρήματα . . . πρὸς τὸ πεῖσαι
τὸν βασιλέα. We can appease our heart, can still the qualms of
conscience, with the knowledge that God who knows all has
admitted us to His fellowship and love, a fact of which we are
assured by the active love for others which His love has kindled
in our hearts. This is perhaps the simplest interpretation,
though as an explanation of πείσομεν it is less natural than (a).

(2) The exact meaning of ὅτι in each clause and their mutual
relations are of less moment. The meanings "that" or "because" have to some extent come under consideration in connection with πείθειν. But the relation of the first clause to the
second is doubtful. (a) The second ὅτι may be regarded as
resumptive, either in the sense of "that," or "because." The
resumptive is more natural in the former than in the latter case.
It is possible in either case. But the use of the resumptive ὅτι
after so short a clause is not really natural, and is not in accord

with the style of the writer. (β) The first ὅτι may be relative,
"Whereinsoever our heart condemns us," the second ὅτι being
taken in the sense of either "that" or "because." This interpretation relieves the sentence of an awkward and unnecessary
resumptive particle, and it may be paralleled by instances of the
use of ὅ τι ἄν in the Gospel, which are not indeed identical, but
are sufficiently similar to justify its adoption here. Cf. Jn. ii. 5,
xiv. 13, xv. 16. If we take into consideration the author's habit
of throwing forward for the sake of emphasis a word or words
which stand outside the general construction of his sentence,
we may feel justified in assuming that he has here made use of an
accusatival clause (of respect) in rather loose connection with
the rest of the verse. For the use of ὅ τι ἄν (ἐάν), cf. Mk. vi.
23 ; Lk. x. 35.

In what has been said, it has, of course, been assumed that
the omniscience of God is alleged as a ground for confidence
not for fear (if our own heart condemn us, the judgment of
omniscient justice must be far more severe). The opposite view
has been stoutly maintained by Wohlenberg in the series of
articles referred to above (*Neue Kirkliche Zeitschrift*, 1902,
p. 636 ff.), and also by Findlay (*Expositor*, November, 1905).
Cf. also the comment of the Catena (Cramer, viii. 128), ἐάν,
φησίν, ἁμάρτωμεν οὐ λανθάνομεν, οὐδὲ διαφευξόμεθα· εἰ γὰρ ἁμαρ-
τάνοντες τὴν καρδίαν ἑαυτῶν λαθεῖν (? ins. οὐ) δυνάμεθα, ἀλλὰ
νυττόμεθα ὑπὸ τοῦ συνειδότος, πόσῳ μᾶλλον τὸν θεὸν πράττοντές τι
τῶν φαύλων (? μὴ) δυνηθῶμεν λαθεῖν;

It makes the connection between vv. 19 and 20 almost impossible to explain. It can only be done by interposing a
thought which is left altogether without expression in the passage.
"We shall assure our heart—and we shall have great need to do
so ; for if *our* conscience condemn us, how much more severe
must necessarily be the verdict of the omniscient God!" If this
is what the writer meant, he has severely taxed the powers of
his readers to follow his argument. And the aim of the whole
passage is surely to give assurance, and not to strike terror into
their hearts. There is nothing in the passage to indicate that
vv. 20 and 21 are intended to meet the circumstances of two
different classes of people, the self-confident and the self-
distrustful.

In the explanation given of this passage it has been assumed
that ἐν τούτῳ refers back to the previous verse, which is contrary
to the common usage of the writer, though perhaps not unparal-
leled. It is, however, possible to find the test of knowledge,
and consequent assurance, in the sentence ὅτι μείζων—πάντα.
The thought of God's power and omniscience may give us
assurance that we are "of the truth." We have been accepted

52027

by one who knows all the circumstances.   In view of the
writer's usage there is much to be said for this interpretation.
The general meaning of the passage is not affected by it.
Windisch is inclined to regard the passage as corrupt, and
suggests that we should read οὐ πείσομεν, and cut out the clause
ὅτι ἐάν . . . καρδία as an interpolation based on ver. 21.   Thus
amended, the passage would certainly contain a warning to the
self-confident, against which no exception could be taken.   But
the best criticism on the suggestion is his own next sentence,
"Das beste ist freilich man bleibt bei der Konstatierung: der
Text is verderbt."   The writer knows how to use the irony of
the commonplace, but he did not use it here.

εν τουτω A B 40 d^scr al^5 vg. cop. syr. Clem.] pr. *et* **sah. boh**-cod. : om.
ℵ C K L P al. longe. plu. cat. syr. aeth. Dam. Thphyl. Oec. Aug. : αλλ εκ
τουτου 69 a^scr.

γνωσομεθα ℵ A B C P 6. 7. 15. 18. 22. 27. 29. 33. 36. 40. 66**. 68. 69.
137 a^scr j^scr cat. sah. cop. arm. Clem. Dam.] γινωσκομεν K L al. pler. vg.
syr. Thphyl. Oec. Aug.

εσμεν] εστι *I*^a 158 (395).

πεισομεν] πεισωμεν 5. 27. 29. 69 a^scr al. fere.^10 Thphyl.

την καρδιαν] A* B 66** sah. **boh**. syr. aeth. Aug.] τας καρδιας ℵ A^2
C K L P al. fere. omn. cat. vg. arm. syr. Thphyl. Oec.

εαν] αν A al. pauc.

καταγινωσκη ημων] post καρδια *I*^b 469 (215).

καταγινωσκη] καταγινωσκει L 13. 100. 106. 107*. al^5.

οτι 2° ℵ B C K L al. plu. cat. syr.] om. A 13. 33. 34. 63 d^scr (vg.
sah^bw cop. arm. aeth. Oec. Aug. non exprimunt).

μειζων] μειζον K.

εστιν] om. *I*^a 252-δ459 55 (391) *I*^b 209f (386).

θεος] κυριος C.

ημων 2°] om. **arm**-ed.

παντα] pr. τα *I*^a 261. 106. 216 (142).

21 ff.   If our conscience acquits us, the result is a feeling of
joyful confidence in the sight of God, and the consciousness
that our prayers are answered, because of our obedience and
willing service.

ἀγαπητοί] Cf. ii. **7**, iii. **2**, one of the writer's favourite forms
of address, and frequent in this second part of the Epistle, in
which the main topic is love (iv. **1, 7, 11**).

ἐὰν κ.τ.λ.] The clause is most naturally interpreted in its
widest sense, regarded neither as an antithesis to ver. 20 nor as
a continuation of it.   It includes all cases in which the verdict
of the conscience is favourable, both those in which there has
been no condemnation, and those in which assurance has been
gained in spite of the condemnation of the heart, from the
thought of the greatness and omniscience of God.

ἡ καρδία μὴ καταγινώσκῃ] Contrast the order of ver. 20.   The
stress is here laid on the faculty which passes judgment.   The
writer follows his usual custom of stating a principle absolutely,

without considering the modifications which become necessary when it is applied to the individual case.   In so far as the conscience passes a verdict of acquittal, the results stated necessarily follow.   And the statement is made in the most absolute form, "if the heart do not condemn," though ἡμῶν has naturally been supplied in many texts, after καρδία and again after καταγινώσκῃ. The reading of B (ἔχει for ἔχομεν), which makes the heart the subject of the apodosis as well as of the protasis, is interesting. The form of ver. 20, however, makes it improbable that this is the original text.

παρρησίαν] Cf. ver. 14 and note.   Boldness and confidence are the ideas which the word generally suggests, while here that of freedom of intercourse in "speaking with God" in prayer is prominent.   The phrase denotes, of course, the boldness and freedom from restraint with which the children can approach their Father always, rather than the clear conscience and confidence with which they can await the verdict of the Judge on the Last Day.

αγαπητοι] αδελφοι ℵ.

εαν] αν A.

η καρδια A B 13. 27. 30. 66**. 113 fu. Or. Dam. Aug.]+ημων ℵ C K L al. pler. cat. vg. (am. demid. harl. tol.) arm. syr. sah. cop. aeth. Or. Dam. Thphyl. Oec. cat. Cyp. Did.

μη] om. I^a 397 (96) I^b δ^206* (242).

καταγινωσκη B C 68. Or.] καταγινωσκει A L 13. 100. 106 al.^3 scr al. aliq. Dam. :+ημων ℵ A K L al. pler. cat. vg. sah. cop. syr. arm. aeth. Or. Dam. Did.

εχομεν] εχωνεν 13 al. pauc. Dam. : εχει B 29.

22.   The second result of the favourable verdict.   All requests are granted which can be put forward in the freedom of intercourse which has been described.   For the conditions which make it possible are obedience to the Divine commands, and willing and active serving in doing whatever is known to be according to His will.   Every true prayer is the expression of the desire to obey and to do the will in those matters with which the request is concerned.   We may compare the noble Jewish saying, "Do His Will as if it were thine, that He may do thy will as if it were His."

The two clauses express the two duties of obedience and willing service.   True obedience to the Will of God must become spontaneous before it is made perfect.

τὰ ἀρεστά] The particular things which are pleasing in His sight, in the circumstances with reference to which the prayer is offered.   Cf. Jn. viii. 29, οὐκ ἀφῆκέν με μόνον, ὅτι ἐγὼ τὰ ἀρεστὰ αὐτῷ ποιῶ πάντοτε, the only other instance of the use of τὰ ἀρεστά in the New Testament (ἀρεστόν, Ac. xii. 3, vi. 2).   Cf. the Pauline εὐάρεστος, Eph. v. 10, δοκιμάζοντες τί ἐστιν εὐάρεστοι τῷ κυρίῳ: Col. iii. 20, τοῦτο γὰρ εὐάρεστόν ἐστιν ἐν κυρίῳ. Cf. He. xiii. 21, ποιῶν ἐν ἡμῖν τὸ εὐάρεστον ἐνώπιον αὐτοῦ διὰ Ἰησοῦ Χριστοῦ.

For the general teaching of this verse on the subject of prayer, cf. Mk. xi. 24, διὰ τοῦτο λέγω ὑμῖν, πάντα ὅσα προσεύχεσθε καὶ αἰτεῖσθε, πιστεύετε ὅτι ἐλάβετε, καὶ ἔσται ὑμῖν: Jn. xiv. 12, 13, xvi. 23, ix. 31. The most interesting parallel is to be found in Job xxii. 23–27, of which the present verse may contain reminiscences, as Holtzmann suggests; cf. especially ver. 26 f. εἶτα παρρησιασθήσῃ ἐναντίον Κυρίου, ἀναβλέψας εἰς τὸν οὐρανὸν ἱλαρῶς. εὐξαμένου δέ σου πρὸς αὐτὸν εἰσακούσεταί σου, δώσει δέ σοι ἀποδοῦναι τὰς εὐχάς.

o εαν] οτι αν K⁵⁰⁰ (45).
εαν] αν B 31. 42. 105 aˢᶜʳ Dam.
αιτωμεν A B C K L al. omnᵘⁱᵈ] αιτωμεθα ℵ Or. : αιτησομεν Jᵃ¹⁷³· ᵟ⁴⁵⁴ (156).
λαμβανομεν] accipiemus vg. boh. arm-codd. sah. syr. Cyp. Lcif.
απ] ℵ A B C 5. 13. 27. 29. 33. 34. 68. 69. 137 aˢᶜʳ 8ᵖᵉ Dam.] παρ K L al. pler. cat. Or. Dam. Thphyl. Oec.
τηρουμεν B C L al. plu. Dam.] τηρωμεν ℵ A K 40. 98 al.⁴.

23, 24. Transition to the other command (of right belief), the fulfilment of which is also a sign that our religious standing is right. These two verses are clearly transitional, and serve to emphasize what is essential in the matter of obedience to His commands, and so to lead the way to the second statement of the Christological thesis, the necessity of a true confession and right belief. The commandments are summed up in the One Command, of belief and love. The following of the Christ, shown most clearly and characteristically in active love of men, is the essential condition of fellowship. And this fellowship is mutual. We abide in Him. He abides in us. The human side and the Divine are both essential parts of the Christian standing. Real fellowship issues in obedience. He who abides in Him keeps His commandments, not as a series of literal precepts, but as a life-giving principle (τηρεῖν, as contrasted with φυλάσσειν). And we are assured of the reality of the fellowship by the presence of the Spirit which He has given us. In these transitional verses three new points are introduced: (1) The mention of πιστεύειν, here for the first time used in the Epistle. (2) The emphasis on the Divine side of the fellowship, αὐτὸς ἐν ἡμῖν. (3) The mention of the Spirit.

(1) The introduction of the idea of "believing" is as abrupt here as it is in the partly parallel passage in the Gospel, vi. 29, τοῦτό ἐστι τὸ ἔργον τοῦ θεοῦ ἵνα πιστεύητε εἰς ὃν ἀπέστειλεν ἐκεῖνος, where the *emphasis* is on personal trust and devotion (πιστεύειν εἰς), rather than on conviction as to the truth of certain facts about the object of πιστεύειν (πιστ. c. dat.). The reason of this

difference of stress is clear.   Thus far in the Epistle, emphasis has
been laid on the necessity of obedience to the commands of the
Christ, especially to the law of love.   The following of the Christ
has been shown to be the necessary expression of Christian life,
without which it is a "lie" to claim that the life is that of a
Christian.   But He must be followed because of what He *is*.
Conviction, therefore, as to what He is must necessarily precede
obedience to what He commands.   No other peasant of Galilee
has the right to command the allegiance of men.   The writer is
anxious to remind his readers of this, since the preceding
meditations, which deal rather with practical issues, might tend
to obscure its importance.

(2) The transitional verses, which helped to introduce the
section of the Epistle here brought to its close, emphasized the
human side of the fellowship of Christians with God (ii. 28, μένετε
ἐν αὐτῷ).   But the Divine side is essential, and on this the writer
proceeds to lay stress in the following chapter.   In the second
part of ver. 24 this is made clear, γινώσκομεν ὅτι μένει ἐν ἡμῖν.
"Fellowship with God, and consciousness of it, rest upon the
acknowledgment and appropriation of a divine act and of the
divine nature of love" (Haupt).

(3) Christians are conscious that God "abides in them"
because they are conscious of the presence of the Spirit which
God has given them.   The repetition of this statement in iv. 13
shows that the words must be taken in this sense here.   The
thought is developed in the next section of the Epistle.   God
has really given His Spirit to men, though all spiritual influences
to which men feel themselves to be subject are not the work of
God's Spirit.   Men must distinguish between the true and the
false.

23. αὕτη] points forward according to the writer's usual
custom.   Cf. note on i. 5.

ἵνα πιστεύσωμεν] The ἵνα is definitive, as elsewhere in the
Epistles and Gospel where it is preceded by αὕτη.   The aorist
is probably the true text.   As contrasted with the present πιστ-
εύωμεν, which was not unnaturally substituted for it, it lays stress,
not on the initial act of faith (this is only *one* of the uses of the
aorist, and not the most frequent), but on the whole process
conceived as an unity.   The conviction is regarded as one fact,
not as a continuous process continuously exercising its influence
on men.   The aorist emphasizes the single fact, without in any
way suggesting the length of time occupied in its manifestation.
It can quite naturally sum up the action, or actions, of a period
or of a lifetime, which it regards as "one act at once."

τῷ ὀνόματι] The construction (*c. dat.*) expresses conviction of
the truth of a statement rather than devotion to a person (εἰς

c. acc.). The expression, therefore, denotes conviction that Christ really is that which His name implies Him to be. It would, of course, be a serious misstatement of the facts to state that this is all, or the chief part, of what the writer means by πιστεύειν. Cf. Scott, *The Fourth Gospel*, p. 267, "It is evident, even to a superficial reader, that the 'believing' so constantly insisted on by John is something much narrower and poorer than the Pauline 'faith.' It implies not so much an inward disposition of trust and obedience, as the acceptance of a given dogma. To 'believe' is to grant the hypothesis that Jesus was indeed the Christ, the Son of God,"—a very misleading statement, somewhat modified, however, by the succeeding paragraphs. But by using this particular construction (*c. dat.*) the writer does in certain cases emphasize this particular meaning. When he defines the "work of God" in Jn. vi. 29, he is careful to use a different expression (ἵνα πιστεύητε εἰς ὃν ἀπέστειλεν).

τοῦ υἱοῦ αὐτοῦ Ἰησοῦ Χριστοῦ] "A compressed creed," the complete revelation of the Father, the man who lived on earth a true human life, the promised Messiah who fulfilled the expectations of Jews and of all men. Cf. Jn. xx. 31. It is only in living out the commands of such an one that men can realize the fulness of their nature.

καὶ ἀγαπῶμεν] All His commands are summed up in the one command to love, obedience to which must begin with those closest to hand.

καθὼς ἔδωκεν] The new command was to love according to a new standard, καθὼς ἠγάπησα ὑμᾶς, Jn. xiii. 34. The references to the discourses of the Upper Chamber are very obvious throughout these verses.

πιστευσωμεν B K L al. pler. cat. Oec.] πιστευωμεν ℵ A C al.²⁵ fere. (-σομεν 99. 100) Thphyl.

τω . . . Χριστου ℵ B C K L al. pler. vg. etc.] τω ον. αυτου ιυ χω A 43 (uid.) : τω υιω αυτου ιυ χω 3. 13. 15. 18. 26. 37. 67. 81 dˢᶜʳ al. pauc. aeth. τω ονοματι] εις το ονομα 5. 58ˡᵉᶜᵗ.

ιησου] pr. του κυ Iᵃ ⁶⁵ (317).

εδωκεν] post εντολην Iᵃ ⁷⁰ᶠ (505) Iᵇ ⁴⁷² (312).

εντολην] post ημιν Iᵃ ¹⁷⁰· ²⁵⁴ (303) Iᵇ δ²⁰⁶ (242) Iᶜ ¹⁷⁴ (252).

ημιν ℵ A B C al. mu. cat. vg. etc. Thphyl. Oec-cod. Lcif.] om. K L h al. fere.⁶⁰ Oec. ed.

24. καὶ ὁ τηρῶν κ.τ.λ.] Cf. Jn. xiv. 10, etc., and the latter part of xvii. The chief point in dispute in this verse is the reference of the pronouns. At first sight the reference to Christ's command in ver. 23 would suggest that in this verse αὐτοῦ, etc., must be referred to Christ. But in ver. 22 the ἐντολαί are spoken of as God's commands, and the αὐτοῦ of ver. 23 must refer to God (τοῦ υἱοῦ αὐτοῦ). It is therefore more natural to interpret them in the same way in this verse. Cf. iv. 13, where the reference must be to God. It is true that in the Last Discourses μένειν is generally connected with Christ, but cf. xvii. 21, ἵνα αὐτοὶ ἐν ἡμῖν ὦσιν. It is in Christ that fellowship with God is realized.

τηρεῖν] Cf. the note on ii. 4.

αὐτὸς ἐν αὐτῷ] See the note above (2). The divine side of the relation is brought out in ch. iv.

ἐν τούτῳ] Either (1) ἐν τῷ τηρεῖν τὰς ἐντολὰς αὐτοῦ, in the fact of our obedience to His commands we realize His fellowship with us, or (2) ἐκ τοῦ πνεύματος, the gift of the Spirit, of which we are conscious, assures us of the fact of fellowship. The repetition of the verse, in a slightly altered form, in iv. 13 makes it almost necessary to interpret the phrase thus.

οὗ] An ordinary instance of attraction. The genitive is not partitive. With the partitive genitive S. John commonly has ἐκ : 2 Jn. 4 ; Jn. i. 24, vii. 40, etc.

ἔδωκεν] emphasizes the fact. In iv. 13 the permanent effects of the gift are brought into prominence.

και 3° א° A B C K L al. pler. vg. syr. cop. rell.] om. א* 18. 38. 80. 95**. 137 c^scr al. ² scr sah. Aug.

εν τουτω] εκ τουτου I^c 114 (335).

εν ημιν μενει I^a δ^180 (1319) I^c 551 (216).

ημιν 2° A B C L al. pler. cat. fu. Bas.] post εδωκεν א K 22. 25. 31. 34. 38. 42. 57. 68. 69. 80. 137 a^scr al^plus 10 vg. (am. demid. harl. tol.) sah. cap. syr. arm. Ath. Cyr. Thphyl. Oec. Aug.

II. iv. 1–6. The Christological thesis. The Spirit which is of God recognizes Jesus as the Christ come in flesh.

1. iv. 1–3. Content of the Confession.

iv. 1–3. In accordance with his usual custom, the writer finds a transition to a new section in the repetition of the last prominent idea. The gift of the Spirit ensures to them knowledge. But all spiritual activities of the time could not be traced back to the Spirit of God as their source. The suggestions of every spirit could not be accepted as true. As at Corinth in the days of S. Paul, spiritual phenomena must be tested. And the reader's experience supplied them with a test by which they could know whether the spirits were of God or not. The surest criterion was the confession of the Incarnation, or rather of the Incarnate Christ. Those who saw in Jesus of Nazareth as He appeared on earth in fleshly form the complete revelation of the Father, were of God. Those who refused to confess Jesus were not of God. Such a refusal was the peculiar characteristic of Antichrist, whose coming they had been taught to expect, and whose working they could already perceive.

1. ἀγαπητοί] Cf. ii. 7, etc. The writer appeals to the common bond of love which unites them all, in order to call

out their best efforts for the common good.　This address now becomes frequent (1, 7, 11), the main topic being love.

μὴ παντὶ πνεύματι πιστεύετε] Cf. Didache, xi. 8, οὐ πᾶς δὲ ὁ λαλῶν ἐν πνεύματι προφήτης ἐστίν, ἀλλ' ἐὰν ἔχῃ τοὺς τρόπους Κυρίου. ἀπὸ οὖν τῶν τρόπων γνωσθήσεται ὁ ψευδοπροφήτης καὶ ὁ προφήτης. All spirit-inspired utterances are not to be accepted as necessarily true. Πιστεύειν with the dative always means to accept as true, to believe in the truth of statements made by any one. Cf. Jn. viii. 31, πρὸς τοὺς πεπιστευκότας αὐτῷ 'Ιουδαίους.

ἀλλὰ δοκιμάζετε] Cf. 1 Co. xii. 10, ἄλλῳ δὲ διακρίσεις πνευμάτων, where the "discerning of spirits" is one of the recognized kinds of χαρίσματα. In the earlier generations the spiritual phenomena which accompanied the growth of Christianity were a cause of grave anxiety to all Christian leaders. It needed a special grace to distinguish between the true and the false. They might be delusions or impostures; if real, they might be evil. Cf. 1 Th. v. 19–21, τὸ πνεῦμα μὴ σβέννυτε· προφητείας μὴ ἐξουθενεῖτε· πάντα δὲ δοκιμάζετε. It would generally have been far easier to say, with the ἰδιώτης of Corinth, μαίνεσθε. The difficulty, which culminated in Montanism, is of periodic recurrence. But the writer reminds his hearers that the grace of discernment was part of the Christian endowment, if Christians were willing to use the χάρισμα which they possessed. Compare the passage quoted above from the Didache; and, for the danger of yielding to the opposite temptation, compare the preceding sentences (xi. 7), καὶ πάντα προφήτην λαλοῦντα ἐν πνεύματι οὐ πειράσετε οὐδὲ διακρινεῖτε· πᾶσα γὰρ ἁμαρτία ἀφεθήσεται, αὕτη δὲ ἡ ἁμαρτία οὐκ ἀφεθήσεται. Compare also xii. 1, πᾶς δὲ ὁ ἐρχόμενος ἐν ὀνόματι Κυρίου δεχθήτω· ἔπειτα δὲ δοκιμάσαντες αὐτὸν γνώσεσθε· σύνεσιν γὰρ ἕξετε δεξιὰν καὶ ἀριστεράν. The plurals here cannot refer to an individual official.

ὅτι πολλοὶ κ.τ.λ.] The clause explains the necessity for the testing. The spirit of evil has sent forth his messengers into the world, and their activity is well known.

ψευδοπροφῆται] Cf. Mt. vii. 15, προσέχετε ἀπὸ τῶν ψευδοπροφητῶν. Did. xi. 6.

ἐξεληλύθασιν] Contrast the tense of ii. 19, where the definite fact of their separation from the Body of the Faithful is stated. Here the thought is of their sending forth by the Spirit who inspires them, and of the effect of their mission in the world. Here ὁ κόσμος is used in its natural sense of the world of men, and is not specially contrasted with the Christian Body.

πιστεύετε] πιστευητε 31 al.² scr.
τα πνευματα] pr. παντα K: παν πνα H δ⁶ (Ψ).
του] om. Iª δ²⁵⁴.
εστιν] εισιν Iᵇ δ⁵⁰⁷ (241).

2. 'ν τούτῳ] refers to what follows, according to the customary usage of this Epistle.

γινώσκετε] The word may be taken either as imperative or indicative. At first sight the use of the imperative in ver. 1 would seem conclusive as to the interpretation of this verse. But an appeal to his readers' knowledge and experience is more in accordance with the writer's method. The aim of the whole Epistle is to remind them of what they already possess, and to base on it an appeal to them to make use of that which they have. In the Christian faith, as it has been taught to them from the beginning, they have adequate provision against the dangers to which they now find themselves exposed. All that is needed is that they should use what they already possess. They must trust the powers with which the Christ has endowed them. Cf. ii. 29. Nowhere in the Epistle does the imperative follow ἐν τούτῳ: ii. 3, 5, iii. 16, 19, 24, iv. 13, v. 2.

The reading γινώσκεται, which has passed into the Vulgate (*cognoscitur*), is an obvious corruption, the interchange of αι and ε being perhaps the commonest itacism in Greek manuscripts. The direct appeal to his readers is far more congruous with the author's style, and suits the context better.

τὸ πνεῦμα τοῦ θεοῦ] Here only in the Johannine books. Cf. ver. 13, ἐκ τοῦ πνεύματος αὐτοῦ. The vacillation between singular and plural, and the various genitives connected with πνεῦμα, may perhaps serve as indications that the doctrine of the Spirit is not yet clearly defined in precise terms.

ὁμολογεῖ] The verb is used in the Johannine books with the following constructions: (1) absolutely, cf. Jn. i. 20, xii. 42 ; (2) with ὅτι, cf. 1 Jn. iv. 15 ; (3) with the single accusative, cf. 1 Jn. i. 9 (τὰς ἁμαρτίας), ii. 23 (τὸν υἱόν), iv. 3 ('Ιησοῦν) ; (4) with the double accusative, cf. Jn. ix. 22, ἐάν τις αὐτὸν ὁμολογήσῃ Χριστόν. The construction of 2 Jn. 7, οἱ μὴ ὁμολογοῦντες 'Ιησοῦν Χριστὸν ἐρχόμενον ἐν σαρκί, is parallel to this verse, and equally obscure. Three constructions are possible here. (1) 'Ιησοῦν Χριστόν may be the object and ἐληλυθότα ἐν σαρκί the predicate. The confession of Jesus Christ as one who has come in the flesh is the test proposed. We may perhaps compare S. Paul's test in 1 Co. xii. 3, οὐδεὶς δύναται εἰπεῖν Κύριος 'Ιησοῦς εἰ μὴ ἐν πνεύματι ἁγίῳ. In favour of this construction is the natural connection which it gives of 'Ιησοῦν Χριστόν, which can hardly be separated unless the context clearly suggests their separation. (2) The form of ver. 3, according to the true text, is in favour of regarding 'Ιησοῦν as object and the rest of the words as predicate. The error which the writer condemns seems to have been the rejection of the identity of the historical man Jesus with the pre-existent Christ, truly incarnate in His manhood, in favour of the view that some higher power, as the Aeon Christ, descended upon the man Jesus at the Baptism, and left him before the Passion. There is nothing in the Epistle which compels us to suppose that the author is combating pure Docetism, though, of course, such teaching would be excluded by the phrases used in these verses, in whatever way they are interpreted. The construction of Jn. ix. 22 may perhaps be urged as supporting this interpretation. And it probably emphasizes most clearly the view on which the writer wishes to lay stress. It is the denial of Jesus as the incarnate Christ which he regards as the source of all error, as the true text of ver. 3 (μὴ ὁμολογεῖ Ἰησοῦν) shows. But so far as grammar and syntax are concerned this separation of Ἰησοῦν from Χριστόν, without anything in the context to necessitate it, or even to suggest it, is difficult. (3) The simplest construction is, therefore, that in which the whole phrase is regarded as connected. The confession needed is of one who is Jesus Christ incarnate, a man who lived on earth a true human life under the normal conditions of humanity, and who is also the pre-existent Christ who manifested God's glory in this form. And the true text of ver. 3 favours this construction, if it is not regarded as too awkward.

But whichever construction be adopted, the confession demanded is not of the truth of certain propositions about a certain person, but the confession of a Person, of whom certain propositions are true, who is possessed of the nature and qualities which they define. It is a confession not of the fact of the Incarnation, but of the Incarnate Christ.

ἐν σαρκὶ ἐληλυθότα] The phrase describes the method rather than the fact. The revelation of God was made to men by the Son of God appearing in human form and living a human life. It was given in a form which made it comprehensible to men, and its effects were abiding (ἐληλυθότα). Its whole validity depended on the Revealer being true man, who could speak to men as one of themselves. The guarantee for its completeness and its intelligibility was destroyed if the Revealer and the man were not one and the same. And the confession involved allegiance to the Person of the Revealer; without that men could not make the revelation their own. *Non sonando, sed amando* (Bede).

The reading ἐληλυθέναι which is found in some important authorities is a natural correction of a difficult and somewhat awkward phrase. When Polycarp uses the passage he not unnaturally substitutes the infinitive for the participle. (Polycarp, *ad Philipp*. vi. 3 f., ἀπεχόμενοι τῶν σκανδάλων καὶ τῶν ψευδαδέλφων καὶ τῶν ἐν ὑποκρίσει φερόντων τὸ ὄνομα τοῦ κυρίου,

οἵτινες ἀποπλανῶσι κενοὺς ἀνθρώπους. Πᾶς γὰρ ὃς ἂν μὴ ὁμολογῇ
Ἰησοῦν Χριστὸν ἐν σαρκὶ ἐληλυθέναι, ἀντίχριστός ἐστιν). But it
misses the point. True confession is allegiance to a Person and
not acceptance of a doctrinal statement. Only the spirits which
inspire men to make such a confession are " of God."

τουτω] + ουν *I*c 258 (56).

γινωσκετε ℵc A B C L al. sat. mu. sah. syrp aethutr Ir. Lcif.] γινωσκεται K al. fere.50 vg. syrsch Cyr. Thphyl. Did. Aug. : γινωσκομεν ℵ* 9. 14*.
69 ascr arm. *cognoscemus* boh-ed. : *cognoscetis* boh-codd.

θεου 1°] + *et spiritum erroris* sah.

ο 1°—πνευμα 2°] om. *I*a δ457-119 (209).

Ιησουν Χριστον] Χριτον Ιησουν C arm-codd.

εληλυθοτα ℵ A C K L etc.] εληλυθεναι B 99. Cf. Polycarp (? ver. 3)
Thdrt. vg. Ir. Cyp. Or. Lcif. Did.

3. The simple accusative τὸν Ἰησοῦν is undoubtedly the true
text. The variants Ἰησοῦν Χριστόν, κύριον, ἐληλυθότα ἐν σαρκί
are natural attempts to expand an abrupt phrase from the preceding verse. The interesting variant λύει which is presupposed
in several Patristic passages must be discussed separately. It is
not the only instance of an explanatory gloss which has influenced
the text of this Epistle.

The shorter text emphasizes clearly the personal character of
the confession (see the notes on the preceding verse). And it
lays the right stress on the danger which threatened the readers
of listening to those who undervalued the importance of the
human life and personality of Jesus of Nazareth.

τοῦτο] The denial of Jesus.

τὸ τοῦ ἀντιχρίστου] Either the Spirit which comes from Antichrist, or more probably the special characteristic of Antichrist.
The work of Antichrist was already being done in the world.

ὃ ἀκηκόατε] Cf. ii. 18, ἠκούσατε ὅτι Ἀντίχριστος ἔρχεται. The
" coming " of Antichrist formed part of common Jewish expectation and Christian teaching. The readers had been taught what
to expect, and ought to find no difficulty in detecting its
beginnings among them.

ἤδη] Cf. Jn. iv. 35, ὅτι λευκαί εἰσιν πρὸς θερισμὸν ἤδη, and ix.
27, εἶπον ὑμῖν ἤδη. With these three exceptions, of which iv. 35
is doubtful, the Johannine use of ἤδη is to qualify the words
which follow.

πνευμα (? 1°)] om. *H*257 (33) *I*a 70. 65. 172 (505) | ο (? 1°) + αν *I*a 70 (505) |
μη] om. *I*b δ152 (491).

ο μη ομολογει] λυει vg. (*soluit*) Ir. Or. Aug. Fulg. cdd. uet. op Socr.
Cf. Lcif. Tert.

τον ιησουν A B h 13. 27. 29. 69 ascr cddduet ap. Socrat. Cyr. Thdt. vg.
fu. harl. tol. syrutr boh-ed. arm-cod. aeth. Ir. Or. Lcif. Did.] ιησουν
κυριον ℵ: τον ιησουν χριστον L al. plu. boh-codd. cat. Oec. : τον χ͞ρ ι͞ν
*I*a 192. δ254. δ454 (318) *I*c 364-208. δ299 (137): ιησουν χριστον K al. plus30 Polyc.

Thyphl. am. demid. sah. **arm**-ed. Aug. Tert. : + εν σαρκι εληλυθοτα א K L al. pler. cat. syr^utr arm. Thphyl. Oec. Tert. (*uenisse*) Cyp. : + εν σαρκι εληλυθεναι H ^δ48 (33) *Aπρι* (*K*) Polyc.

    τον] κυ̅ /^c 487 (−).

    εκ] om. K L k^scr al. plus^10 cat.

    τουτο − ο 2°] *hic est Antichristus quem* **sah**. **boh**. **arm**.

    το] om. *I*^a δ203ff. 254 (205) *K* δ364 (51) | τον 2°] om. *I*^a 264 (233).

    ο 2°] ο τι א 5. 6. 39. 100 : ου *H* δ6 (Ψ).

    ακηκοατε] ακηκοαμεν *H* δ2 (א) *I*^a δ453-173 (5).

The evidence for the reading λύει = *soluit* in this verse is mainly Latin ; before von der Goltz's discovery, described below, it was almost exclusively so. The statements of Clement, Origen, and Socrates are most naturally explained as proving the existence of such a reading in Greek. Taking the evidence roughly in chronological order, we must notice first that of Irenaeus, though it is unfortunately only preserved in a Latin dress. In iii. 16. 8 (Massuet, 207), Irenaeus is denouncing the Gnostics who distinguish between Jesus, the Christ, the Only-begotten, the Saviour. He accuses them of making many Gods, and Fathers many, and of dividing up the Son of God. The Lord warns us to beware of such, and John, His disciple, in his afore-mentioned Epistle says, "Multi seductores exierunt in hunc mundum qui non confitentur Iesum Christum in carne uenisse. Hic est seductor et Antichristus. Videte eos, ne perdatis quod operati estis (2 Jn. 7, 8). Et rursus in epistola ait : Multi pseudoprophetae exierunt de saeculo. In hoc cognoscite spiritum Dei. Omnis spiritus qui confitetur Iesum Christum in carne uenisse, ex Deo est. Et omnis spiritus qui soluit Iesum, non est ex Deo, sed de Antichristo est." The actual reading, "qui soluit Iesum," may be due to the Latin translator ; but it must be noticed that it suits the preceding words of Irenaeus, *comminuens autem et per multa diuidens Filium Dei*, so much better than the common reading μὴ ὁμολογεῖ (*non confitetur*), that it is more natural to suppose that Irenaeus had in his Greek text either λύει or some equivalent phrase, unless his translator has very freely paraphrased the whole passage to bring it into agreement with the text of the Epistle with which he was acquainted. (See, however, Westcott, p. 157.)

The evidence of Clement of Alexandria was also available only through Latin sources. The Latin summary of his *Hypotyposes* has no equivalent for this passage ; but in the summary of the Second Epistle we find, "Adstruit in hac epistola perfectionem fidei extra caritatem non esse, et ut nemo diuidat Iesum Christum, sed unum credat Iesum Christum uenisse in carne," words which do not go far towards proving that Clement knew of the reading λύει in Greek, but

when taken in connection with two passages in Origen suggest
the possibility that the reading was known at Alexandria in
Clement's time.

In the Latin version of Origen's Commentary on S. Matthew,
§ 65, the reading "soluit Jesum" is found. The passage is an
explanation of the parable, Mt. xxiv. 14. The man who went on
a journey being naturally identified with the Lord, Origen raises
the difficulty, " How can He be said to go on a journey who
promised that where two or three are gathered together in His
name, He will be in their midst?" He finds a solution of the
difficulty which he has raised in the distinction between the
Lord's divine and human natures. "Secundum hanc divinitatis
suae naturam non peregrinatur, sed peregrinatur secundum
dispensationem corporis quod suscepit." He adds other
instances of statements which must be referred to His human
nature, and then adds, "Haec autem dicentes non soluimus
suscepti corporis hominem, cum sit scriptum apud Joannem
' Omnis spiritus qui soluit Iesum non est ex Deo' sed unicuique
substantiae proprietatem seruamus." The whole argument is so
thoroughly in Origen's style, that we should hestitate to attribute
the quotation of the verse in this form to the Translator, though
we cannot be certain that Origen read λύει in his Greek text.
The passage has been quoted frequently, but it is curious that
another passage in the part of his *Commentary on S. Matthew*
which is extant in Greek has been generally overlooked. I had
noted the passage several years ago, but have seen no reference
to it earlier than Dr. Zahn's *Introduction*. In xvi. 8, Origen is
commenting on the words δοῦναι τὴν ψυχὴν αὐτοῦ λύτρον ἀντὶ
πολλῶν. He notices that the ψυχή is given as the λύτρον, not the
πνεῦμα nor the σῶμα. He adds the caution that in saying this he
has no wish to disparage the ψυχή of Jesus, but wishes only to
insist on the exact statement made. And he adds, Πλὴν σήμερον
οὐ λύω τὸν Ἰησοῦν ἀπὸ τοῦ Χριστοῦ, ἀλλὰ πολλῷ πλέον οἶδα ἐν
εἶναι Ἰησοῦν τὸν Χριστόν. The passage may only be an echo of
such expressions as are found, *e.g.*, in Irenaeus III. xii. 7, "Qui
autem Iesum separant a Christo." But a comparison of these
two passages in the same Commentary certainly leave the
impression that the reading λύει was known to Origen. The
matter is determined if the Scholion is correct which is found in
the Athos MS, containing information about Origen's text which
von der Goltz has described in *Texte und Untersuchungen*, N. F.
ii. 4. The Scholion, which is quoted on p. 48 of von der Goltz's
work, is as follows: ὃ λύει τὸν Ἰησοῦν. Οὕτως ὁ Εἰρηναῖος ἐν τῷ
τρίτῳ κατὰ τὰς αἱρέσεις λόγῳ καὶ Ὠριγενὴς ἐν τῷ η΄ τόμῳ τῶν εἰς
τὸν πρὸς Ρωμαίους ἐξηγητικῶν καὶ Κλήμης ὁ Στρωματεὺς ἐν τῷ περὶ
τοῦ πάσχα λόγῳ. Von der Goltz points out that the 8th Book of

Origen's Commentary would seem to have contained his exposition of Ro. v. 17–vi. 16, and in Rufinus' translation (v. 8 ; Lomm. p. 386) 1 Jn. iv. 2 is quoted, so that it is not unlikely that in the original Greek the quotation included the third verse with the reading λύει. Thus, if we may trust the evidence of the Scholion, and there are no good grounds for not doing so, in the three instances where extant Latin evidence suggested that the reading was known to Greek writers, we have now definite evidence that it was found in their Greek text.

The only other Greek evidence for the reading is the well-known passage of Socrates about Nestorius (*H. E.* vii. 32), αὐτίκα γοῦν ἠγνόησεν ὅτι ἐν τῇ καθολικῇ Ἰωάννου γέγραπτο ἐν τοῖς παλαίοις ἀντιγράφοις ὅτι πᾶν πνεῦμα ὃ λύει τὸν Ἰησοῦν ἀπὸ τοῦ θεοῦ οὐκ ἔστι. ταύτην γὰρ τὴν διάνοιαν ἐκ τῶν παλαιῶν ἀντιγράφων περιεῖλον οἱ χωρίζειν ἀπὸ τοῦ τῆς οἰκονομίας ἀνθρώπου βουλόμενοι τὴν θεότητα· διὸ καὶ οἱ παλαιοὶ ἑρμηνεῖς αὐτὸ τοῦτο ἐπεσημήναντο, ὥς τινες εἶεν ῥαδιουργήσαντες τὴν ἐπιστολήν, λύειν ἀπὸ τοῦ θεοῦ τὸν ἄνθρωπον θέλοντες. Again this language may be "satisfied by the supposition that he was acquainted with the Latin reading and some Latin commentary" (Westcott, p. 157). But this can hardly be called the most natural interpretation of his words.

The evidence of Tertullian and Augustine points to the early existence of the phrase in connection with the passages in the Johannine Epistles, though it is not always certain whether this passage or the similar words in the Second Epistle are referred to. The most important passage is *adv. Marc.* v. 16, "Johannes dicit processisse in mundum praecursores Antichristi spiritus, negantes Christum in carne uenisse et soluentes Iesum." Augustine in a somewhat different manner appears to comment on both readings. After explaining the words "qui non confitetur Iesum Christum in carne uenisse" by the suggestion that the denial is to be found in the want of love which divides the Church, he continues, "adeo ut noueritis quia ad facta retulit et omnis spiritus, ait, qui soluit Iesum." Later on he has "soluis Iesum et negas in carne uenisse." The natural explanation of his treatment of the passage is that in his text the words "qui soluit Jesum, non est ex Deo" (the addition of "in carne uenisse" after "Iesum" in Migne must be an error) followed the clause "qui non confitetur Iesum Christum in carne uenisse." There are other instances of supplementary glosses in Augustine's text of this Epistle. The quotation in the *Testimonia* of Cyprian (ii. 8), "Omnis spiritus qui confitetur Iesum Christum in carne uenisse, de Deo est, qui autem negat in carne uenisse, de Deo non est, sed est de Antichristi spiritu," shows that the reading "soluit" was not found in the earliest form of the old Latin text, in spite of its presence in all Latin MSS except Codex Frisianus.

8

On the whole, then, the Latin evidence points to the probability
that this reading crept into the Latin texts at an early date,
being first introduced as an explanatory gloss, which subsequently displaced the reading it was inserted to explain.
The history of its appearance in Greek authorities is still obscure,
but may perhaps be explained in the same way.

And the internal evidence points in the same direction. It
is far easier to explain ὃ λύει as an attempt to emphasize the
bearing of the verse on the heretical views of the "Separators,"
than *vice versa*. As Wurm has acutely observed, the reading ὃ
μὴ ὁμολογεῖ, etc., could only have been introduced as an explanatory gloss on ὃ λύει at a time when the meaning of this
phrase had been forgotten. But it is certainly found during the
period when the reading "qui soluit" could cause no difficulty
and was perfectly well understood. Neither reading can be
later than Irenaeus, and at that date there could have been no
motive for the alteration of λύει if it had been the original
reading. On the other hand, the correction of μὴ ὁμολογεῖ into
λύει would give special point to the passage as a condemnation
of a particular form of heresy, which at that time had to be
combated.

2. **iv. 4–6.** Attitude of the Church and the world towards
this confession.

4–6. If they are true to themselves the readers have nothing
to fear from the activities of the Antichristian spirits at work in
the world. In virtue of the new birth, which as Christians they
have experienced, they have gained the victory over the false
prophets, and the fruits of the victory are theirs, unless they
deliberately forfeit them. The victory was not gained in their
own strength. It was God who fought for them and in them.
And God is greater than the devil who rules in the world. The
false prophets are essentially "of the world." All that dominates
their life and action comes from it. Their teaching is derived
from its wisdom, not from the revelation which God has given
in His Son. And so their message is welcomed by those who
belong to the world. For like associates with like. The writer
and his fellow-teachers are conscious that they derive their true
life from God. And those who are of God, and therefore live
their lives in learning to know Him better, in the gradual
assimilation of the revelation of Himself which God is making
in His Son, receive the message. It is only rejected by those
who are not of God, and so are not learning to know Him.
Thus from the character of those who welcome their respective
messages we learn to recognize and distinguish the spirit of
truth and the spirit of falsehood.

4. ὑμεῖς] The readers, whom he has instructed in the Faith, and whom he naturally addresses as his "little children," using the privileges of age and position when he wishes to speak emphatically, in words either of warning or of exhortation. Cf. ii. 1, 12, 28, iii. 7, 18, v. 21. The emphatic pronoun separates the readers from the false teachers.

ἐκ τοῦ θεοῦ ἐστέ] Cf. Jn. viii. 23, xvii. 14, 16 ; 1 Jn. iii. 19, v. 19, ii. 19. By the phrase εἶναι ἐκ the writer seems to denote more than merely "belonging to." It suggests primarily spiritual dependence. A man is said to be "of God," "of the Devil," who draws all his inspiration, all that dominates and regulates his thought and action, from the sources out of which he is said to be. Εἶναι ἐκ τοῦ θεοῦ denotes especially the state of those who have experienced the spiritual regeneration which is the true note of the Christian, and who are true to their experience. Εἶναι ἐκ τοῦ κόσμου is the state of those who still, whether nominally Christian or not, draw their guidance from human society, considered as an ordered whole, apart from God.

νενικήκατε] by remaining true to the Christianity which they had been taught ἀπ᾽ ἀρχῆς, rather than by the expulsion of the false prophets (αὐτούς) from the community.

ὅτι] There was no cause for boasting of their victory. It was God who worked in them, as the Devil worked and ruled in the world. *Noli te extollere. Vide quis in te vicit* (Aug.).

υμεις] pr. και *I*ᵃ ⁷⁰ (505) : pr. οτι *I*ᵇ ⁴⁷². ¹⁶¹ (312) | εκ] *filii* sahᵈ.
εστε] *nati estis* sahʷ | τεκνια] τεκνα 31 cˢᶜʳ al. pauc. : om. boh-sah.
νενικηκατε] ενικησατε *I*ᶜ ¹¹⁴ (335) | υμιν] ημιν *I*ᵃ ⁷⁵ (394) | ο 2°] om.
*I*ᵃ ³⁸². δ²⁵⁴ (231) | εν τω κοσμω] εκ του κοσμου *I*ᵃ 397ᶠᶠᶠᶠ (96) *I* ᵇ ⁶²-δ¹⁶¹ (767).

5. ἐκ τοῦ κόσμου εἰσίν] See the notes on ver. 4. The false teaching drew its strength from the wider knowledge of the world, rejecting or failing to appreciate the essential truth of the revelation made in Jesus Christ incarnate.

ἐκ τοῦ κόσμου λαλοῦσιν] Their teaching corresponds to their sphere. And it is welcomed by the like-minded.

ἀκούει] Cf. Oecumenius, τῷ γὰρ ὁμοίῳ τὸ ὅμοιον προστρέχει. There was apparently need of encouragement in view of the success which the false teachers had secured. Cf. again Oecumenius, εἰκὸς γάρ τινας τούτων καὶ ἀσχάλλειν ὁρῶντας ἐκείνους μὲν τοῖς πολλοῖς περισπουδάστους, ἑαυτοὺς δὲ καταφρονουμένους.

δια τουτο] pr. και 69 aˢᶜʳ : και 68. 103 Did.
λαλουσιν] om. *I*ᵇ ⁶² (498).
ακουει αυτον (?) ο κοσμος *I*ᵃ ⁶⁵ (317).

6. ἡμεῖς] The contrast with ὑμεῖς (ver. 5) suggests that the teachers and not the whole body of Christians are meant. They know whence they draw the inspiration of their life and work. And they will be recognized by those who have begun to live the eternal life which consists in knowing God and His messenger (cf. Jn. xvii. 3).

ὁ γινώσκων τὸν θεόν] The phrase is used as practically equivalent to εἶναι ἐκ τοῦ θεοῦ, but it emphasizes one particular point in the continual progress made by those who "are of God," viz. the knowledge of Him which comes from experience of life in fellowship with Him.

ὃς οὐκ ἔστιν κ.τ.λ.] They cannot know or welcome the truth, because the principles which guide their thoughts are not derived from the truth.

ἐκ τούτου] Cf. Jn. vi. 66, xix. 12, in neither of which verses is the meaning exclusively temporal. The phrase is not used again in the Epistle, or in the Johannine writings, with γινώσκειν. As compared with ἐν τούτῳ it may perhaps suggest a criterion which is less obvious, and which lies further away from that which it may be used to test. The character of their confession offers an immediate test of the spirits. It requires a longer process of intelligent observation to determine the character of the reception with which the message meets. The "test" here is the fact that the one message is welcomed by those who are of God and know God, the other only by those who are of the world. Cf. Jn. xv. 19.

γινώσκομεν] The preceding ἡμεῖς and ἡμῶν make it natural to refer this to the teachers, and grammatically this is no doubt the more correct interpretation. But when the writer is meditating, rather than pursuing a course of logically developed thought, his meditation is apt to pass out into wider spheres, and it is more than probable that he now includes in the first person plural the whole body of those whom he is addressing, as well as the teachers, with whom he began by associating himself.

τὸ πνεῦμα τῆς ἀληθείας κ.τ.λ.] The Spirit of God, of which the essential characteristic is truth, and the spirit of the Devil, or of Antichrist, which is characterized by falsehood, the active falsehood which leads men astray (πλάνης).

ο] pr. και Iᶜ ²⁵⁸* (56).
ος . . . ημων 2° ℵ B K al. pler. vg. etc.] om. A L a 3. 142. 177*
ος] pr. και Iᶜ ³⁶⁴ (137).
εκ τουτου] εν τουτω A vg. sah. cop.
πνα (? 1°, 2°)] πρα Iᵃ ²⁰⁵⁻²⁶¹ (51).

C. iv. 7–v. 12.

Third presentation of the ethical and Christological theses. They are not only shown to be connected (as in *B*), but the proof of their inseparability is given. Love is the basis of our knowledge of fellowship with God, because God is love. And this love of God is manifested in the sending of His Son, as faith comprehends it. So the two main thoughts of the Epistle, Faith in Jesus Christ and Love of the Brethren, are intertwined in this passage, which may be divided into two sections.

I. iv. 7–21. First meditation on the two thoughts now combined. Love based on faith in the revelation of Love which has been given, the test of our knowledge of God and of our birth from God.

II. v. 1–12. Faith as the ground of love.

I. 1. iv. 7–12. Love based on the Revelation of Love.

(a) 7–10. The writer grounds an appeal to his "beloved" hearers for mutual love on the true nature of love as manifested in the Incarnation. True love is not merely a quality of nature, and on that analogy included in our conception of the Deity. It has its origin in God. Human love is a reflection of something in the Divine nature itself. Its presence in men shows that they have experienced the new birth from God and share in that higher life which consists in gradually becoming acquainted with God. Where love is absent there has not been even the beginning of the knowledge of God, for love is the very nature and being of God. And God's love has been manifested in us. God sent His only-begotten Son, in whom His whole nature is reproduced, who alone can fully reveal it to men, into the world of men with a special purpose. That purpose was to enable men to share the higher spiritual life which He imparts (ἵνα ζήσωμεν δι' αὐτοῦ). The nature of true love is manifested in those who have begun to share that life. True love is something which gives itself, neither in return for what has been given nor in order to get as much again: even as God gave His Son, not as a reward for the love which men had showed to Him, but as a boon to those who had only manifested their hostility to Him, in order to remove the obstacles which intervened between God and men.

7. ἀγαπητοί] One of the writer's favourite words. It occurs ten times in the Epistles, though not in the Gospel. It is his usual method of address when he wishes to appeal to the better thoughts and feelings of his readers, or, to use S. Paul's phrase, to "open the eyes of their hearts." It emphasizes the natural grounds of appeal for mutual love, which can most readily be called out among those who are loved or lovable.

ἡ ἀγάπη ἐκ τοῦ θεοῦ ἐστίν] The whole of the Biblical revelation of God emphasizes the fact that man is made in the image of God, not God in the image of man, however much our conceptions of God are necessarily conditioned by human limitations. It suggests that whatever is best in man is the reflection, under the limitations of finite human existence, of something in the nature of God. The true nature of love cannot be appreciated unless it is recognized that its origin must be sought beyond human nature. We may compare the doctrine of " Fatherhood" insisted upon in Eph. iii. 15.

πᾶς ὁ ἀγαπῶν] It is generally recognized that love is here presented, not as the cause of the new birth from God or of the knowledge of God, but as their effect. The presence of love is the test by which the reality of their presence in any man may be known. The discussion of the question whether the writer intends to present the relation of the being born of God to the knowledge of God as one of cause and effect, or of effect and cause, is perhaps idle. He who loves shows thereby that he has experienced the new birth from God which is the beginning of Christian life, and that its effects are permanent and abiding. He also shows that he has entered upon that life which consists in the gradual acquiring of the knowledge of God. Whether this process of acquiring knowledge begins before, and leads to, the new birth, or only begins after that has been experienced and is its consequence, is not stated. The question was probably not present to the writer's mind.

η αγαπη] post εστιν *I*ᵃ ¹⁷⁵ (319).
του (? *I*º)] om. *I*ᶜ ¹¹⁶ (–).
ο αγαπων]+τον θεον A : +*fratrem* demid. tol. Fulg. : +*fratrem suum.* Did. : cf. *omnes qui diligunt se inuicem* sahᵈ.
και ¹º—(8) εστιν] om. syrᵖ.
γεγεννηται] γεγενηται 99. 177*. 180 jˢᶜʳ lˢᶜʳ Dam.

8. The negative counterpart of ver. 7, the statement being made, as usual, with a slight difference.

οὐκ ἔγνω] He shows by his want of love that the process of knowledge never even began in him.

ὅτι ὁ θεὸς ἀγάπη ἐστίν] Love is not merely an attribute of God, it is His very Nature and Being ; or rather, the word expresses the highest conception which we can form of that Nature. Holtzmann's note is worth quoting. " Even the false gnosis realized that God is light and spirit. But when here and in ver. 16 love is put forward as the truest presentation of God, this is the highest expression of the conception of God. It passes entirely beyond the limitations of natural religion. It does not come within the category of Substance, but only those of Power and Activity. It opens the way for an altogether new presentation of religion based on the facts of moral life."

⌐ ¹º—θεον] post εστιν syrˢᶜʰ : om. ℵ* 192 dˢᶜʳ arm-cdd. aeth. : ο μη αγαπων ουκ εγνωκεν ℵᶜ.
ο ¹º] pr. οτι *I*ᶜ ¹⁷⁴ (252) : +δε *I*ᶜ ²⁵⁸ (56).
ουκ εγνω] om. εγνωκεν ℵᶜ 31 : ου γινωσκει A 3. 5. 13 al.⁴ arm. Or. cf. Lcif. Did. Fulg. : *non cognoscit* sah.

9. ἐν τούτῳ] The true nature of God's love has now been shown, in a way which men can understand and appreciate, in the fact and the purpose of the Incarnation. God gave His best, that men might be enabled to live the life of God.

ἐν ἡμῖν] Not "among us," still less "to us." If the writer had meant "God's love to us," he would doubtless have used the Greek words which would convey that meaning, ἡ ἀγάπη τοῦ θεοῦ (ἡ) εἰς ἡμᾶς. The preposition has its full force. God sent His Son that men might live. The manifestation of His love is made *in* those who have entered upon the life which He sent His Son to give.

τὸν μονογενῆ] The idea presented by μονογενής in the Johannine books would seem to be that of the one and only Son who completely reproduces the nature and character of His Father, which is concentrated in one, and is not, so to speak, divided up among many brethren. It emphasizes the completeness of the revelation of God which He is able to give, as well as the uniqueness of the gift.

ἵνα ζήσωμεν] Cf. the note on ἐν ἡμῖν. The love was manifested in a definite act with a definite object.

εν 1°] pr. και οτι *I*ᵃ 200f. 254. 502 (83) *I*ᵇ 78-157 (-): pr. και *I*ᶜ 114 (335).
του θεου] *eius* arm-codd.
εν ημιν] om. *I*ᵇ 253-559 (2).
απεσταλκεν] απεστειλεν K 29. 38. 42. 57 al. plus¹² Ath.
ο θεος] om. 15. 18. 25. 98. 100 al.⁵ arm. aeth. Aug.
ζησωμεν] ζωμεν א*.

10. True love is selfless. It is not a mere response. It gives itself. The sending of God's Son was not the answer of God to something in man. It was the outcome of the very Nature of God. Cf. Odes of Solomon, iii. 3, 4, "I should not have known how to love the Lord, if He had not loved me. For who is able to distinguish love, except the one that is loved?"

ἱλασμόν] Cf. ii. 2. God could not give Himself while men's sins formed a barrier between them and Him. True love must sweep away the hindrances to the fulfilment of the law of its being. While Vulg. has *propitiatio*, Aug. has *litator*, and Lucif. *expiator*, emphasizing the fact that that which reconciles is a person.

η αγαπη] + του θεου א sah. cop.
ηγαπησαμεν] ηγαπηκαμεν B | ηγαπησεν] pr. πρωτος K δ364 (51).
αυτος] εκεινος A : pr. Deus sahʷ.
απεστειλεν] απεσταλκεν א.
περι] υπερ *I*ᵃ 200 (83) : om. *I*ᶜ 174 (252).

(*b*) **11, 12.** Love of the Brethren the test of Fellowship.
In the light of such a manifestation of God's love there can

be no question about the obligation to mutual love among those who have experienced it. True knowledge always finds expression in action. The true nature of God cannot be made visible to the eye. His presence cannot be seen. But it is known in its results. Where love is, there we know that God abides in men. His abiding in men is the most complete expression of His love.

11. ἀγαπητοί] Cf. ver. 7. The loving address is here used for the sixth and last time.

οὕτως] Cf. Jn. iii. 16, of which this verse seems to be an echo. Οὕτως defines the way in which God manifested the true nature of love, by giving His Son.

καὶ ἡμεῖς] The writer and his readers, or more generally the Christian Family, those who have experienced and appropriated the revelation of love. Those who have learned the true character of love are under the strongest obligation to carry out, in such spheres as they can, the lesson which they have learned. The proper result of divine birth is divine activity.

ο θεος] post ημας *I*[b] 253f. 559. δ152. δ260 (2).
οφειλομεν και ημεις *I*[a] δ453-173 (5).

12. θεὸν κ.τ.λ.] Cf. Jn. i. 18, where the order of the first two words is the same. The absence of the article throws the emphasis on the nature and character of God. As He is in His true nature He cannot be made visible to the eyes of men, so that they can grasp the meaning of what they see (θεᾶσθαι, contrast the ἑώρακεν of the Gospel, which merely states the fact).

ἐὰν κ.τ.λ.] What cannot be seen can be known by its fruits. Mutual love is a sign of the indwelling of God in men. "Through our love for each other (as Christians) we build the Temple, in which God can dwell in and among us" (Rothe). His love for men receives its most perfect expression in His giving Himself to men, and entering into fellowship with them.

αὐτοῦ] There is the usual division of opinion as to whether the genitive is subjective or objective, or whether the two meanings are to be combined, the love which comes from God and which He causes to exist in men. The context on the whole favours the view that it should be taken as subjective. God's love to men is realized most fully in His condescending to abide in men. Cf. ver. 9, ἐφανερώθη ἡ ἀγάπη τοῦ θεοῦ ἐν ἡμῖν.

12. θεον] pr. αδελφοι *I*[a] 170 (303).
τετελειωμενη] pr. τετελειωται και 13 : post ημιν A 5. 13. 31. 68. 69 a[scr] vg. Thphyl. : *perfecta erit* sah[d].
εν ημιν] post εστιν K L al. pler. cat. sah. cop. syr[utr] arm. aeth. Oec. Aug.

13–16a. Proofs of Fellowship. The gift of the Spirit. The witness of those who actually saw the manifestation of love in the Life of Jesus. By means of the Spirit, of which He has

given us, we are conscious that fellowship between Him and
us really exists. Furthermore, the great proof of His love, the
sending of His Son as Saviour of the world, rests on certain
witness. We who lived with Him on earth, and have seen and
understood the meaning of what we saw, can bear true witness.
All who accept the fact that Jesus of Nazareth, who lived on
earth as a man among men, is the Son of God, and who mould
their lives in accordance with this confession, are in true fellowship with God. And we who saw Him have learned to know
and to believe the love which God has for us, and shows in us.

13. The writer passes from the facts to Christian consciousness of the facts. We are assured that fellowship between God
and us really exists, because He has given us of His Spirit, and the
effects of His gifts are permanent. Cf. iii. 24, where the same
conclusion is reached. For the use of the preposition, cf. Mt.
xxv. 28, δότε ἡμῖν ἐκ τοῦ ἐλαίου ὑμῶν. For the general arrangement of the matter, cf. 1 Jn. ii. 5, 6.

μενομεν] + και ημεις 13.
αυτος] + est s. manet sah. boh. : + (?) ο θεος I^a 158 (395).
πῦς] πρs O^46 (154).
δεδωκεν ℵ B K L al. plur. cat. Ath. Cyr.] εδωκεν 13. 27. 29 c^scr Ath.
Bas. Cyr.

14. Beside the internal witness of the Spirit, there is also the
external witness of those who saw the great proof of God's love.
Their vision was complete, and lasting in its results. The
testimony, therefore, which they bear is sure.

ἡμεῖς] The word must here refer to the actual eye-witnesses
of the life of Jesus on earth. The exaggeration of the view
which finds "the αὐτόπται of the Province"[1] in each use of the
first person plural of the pronoun in the Epistle, should not be
allowed to obscure the natural meaning of certain expressions
which it contains; cf. 1 Jn. i. 1. The verb looks back to
ver. 12: "God Himself no one has ever yet beheld; but we
have beheld His Son.

σωτῆρα] Cf. Jn. iv. 42, οὗτός ἐστιν ἀληθῶς ὁ σωτὴρ τοῦ κόσμου.
The purpose of the mission was to restore the fellowship which
had been gradually forfeited.

τεθεαμεθα ℵ B K L al. longe. pler. cat. Thphyl. Oec.] εθεασαμεθα A 27.
29. 33. 34. 66**. 68. 98 al. aliq. Cyr.
μαρτυρουμεν] testati sumus sah.
απεσταλκεν] απεστειλεν I^a 396fff (96) I^b 78-157 (–) O^46 (154).
υιον] + αυτου I^c 364. 259 (137).

15. ὁμολογήσῃ] Cf. iv. 2 and notes. The confession is stated
variously; cf. iv. 2; 2 Jn. 7, and the various confessions in the
Gospel. The essential point seems to be the identity of Jesus,

[1] Cf. Holtzmann on 3 Jn. 9.

the man who lived on earth a human life, with the Son of God, who as only-begotten Son of His Father could reveal the Father to men.   In the thought of the writer no other conditions could assure the validity of the revelation and the possibility of its comprehension by man.   He who " confesses " this, *i.e.* makes this belief the guiding principle of his life and action, is assured of the truth of his fellowship with God.   Thus the work of the original witnesses is continued in the " confession " of those who " have not seen and yet have believed."   Such a confession is as sure a test of Divine fellowship as " mutual love."   As it cannot be true unless it issues in such mutual love, it is difficult to distinguish the two.   The writer probably puts it forward rather for its value as an objective sign to others, than for its power of giving assurance to him who makes it.   In the Christian community there is external as well as internal assurance to be found by those who look for it.

16a. καὶ ἡμεῖς ἐγνώκαμεν καὶ πεπιστεύκαμεν] If, as seems probable, the first person plural still refers to the writer and other teachers who, like him, had seen the Lord on earth, he is thinking of his early experiences in Galilee or Jerusalem, when growing acquaintance passed into assured faith, which had never since been lost.   Contrast the order in the confession of S. Peter, Jn. vi. 69.   The growth of knowledge and the growth of faith act and react on each other.

ἐν ἡμῖν] The love which God has for men is manifested in those who respond to it, in whom it issues in higher life.   But perhaps it is safer to regard the preposition as a trace of the influence of Aramaic forms of expression on the writer's style.

ομολογηση] ομολογη A 5 | ιησους] κ̅σ̅ *I*ᵃ ¹⁰¹ (40) : χ̅σ̅ κ̅σ̅ *I*ᵃ ³⁸² (231) : +χριστος B m. **arm**-codd.   Cf. Tert.
αυτος] ουτος *I*ᵃ ᵟ⁴⁵⁷⁻¹¹⁰ (209) : +*est* s. *manet* **boh. sah.**
πεπιστευκαμεν και εγνωκαμεν **arm.** | πεπιστευκαμεν] πιστευομεν A 13 am. tol. cop.
την αγαπην]+*Dei* am.* arm.
εχει] εσχεν H ᵟ⁶ (Ψ).
εν ημιν] μεθ ημων *I*ᵃ ³⁹⁷ᶠᶠᶠᶠ. ᵟ¹⁵⁷ (96).

16b–21. Love and Faith in relation to Judgment.   The nature of true love.

Since God is love, he who abides in love abides in God and God in him.   Thus the test of love can give full assurance with regard to the reality of our fellowship with God.   It is a logical deduction from the very nature of God.   Love has been made perfect in us when, and only when, we can look forward with entire confidence to the great day of God's judgment, knowing that as the exalted Christ abides in the Father's love, so we abide in it so far as that is possible under the conditions of our present existence. Where full confidence is not yet possible, love is not yet made perfect, for fear and dread have no place in true love. It drives them out completely from the sphere of its activity. For fear has in itself something of the nature of punishment, and he who experiences it has not yet been made perfect in love. How then can we say that we have love? Because our love, in whatever degree we possess it as yet, has its origin in something that is above and beyond us. It has its origin in God. It is called out in response to the love which God has for us. But our claim to love can be put to an obvious test. Love is active, and must, if it is real, go forth to those who need it. If any one claims to love God and does not show love to his brethren, his claim is not only false, but reveals a falseness of character. Love will show itself wherever an object of love is to be found. He who will not take even the first step can never reach the goal. If the sight of his brother does not call out his love, the fact shows that he cannot have love enough to reach as far as God. And for us the matter is determined, once for all, by the Master's command. He has said, "The first commandment is, Thou shalt love the Lord thy God. And the second is this, Thou shalt love thy neighbour as thyself."

16b. ὁ θεὸς κ.τ.λ.] Cf. ver. 8, where love is shown to be the necessary condition of knowledge of God. Here it is presented as the necessary condition of fellowship.

ὁ μένων κ.τ.λ.] Cf. ver. 12, where the writer emphasizes the fact that God's love for men is shown most completely in His willingness to "abide" in us. Here the emphasis is laid on the mutual character of the intercourse, ἐν τῷ θεῷ μένει καὶ ὁ θεὸς ἐν αὐτῷ, and especially on the human side. By abiding in love, the Christian realizes the divine fellowship.

καὶ 4°—μενει 2°] om. Syr^sch | ο 4°] om. *H*^δ2 (א)—μενει 2° א B K L al. fere.^50 sah. cop. syr^p arm. Cyp. Aug.] om. A al. sat. mul. cat. vg. aeth. Thphyl. Oec. Cyp.

17. ἐν τούτῳ κ.τ.λ.] Two interpretations of this verse are possible, according as the words refer to what precedes or to what follows. Ἐν τούτῳ may recapitulate the clause ἐν τῷ θεῷ μένει καὶ ὁ θεὸς ἐν αὐτῷ. Love finds its consummation in the realization of this mutual fellowship. But it would be truer to say that love is made perfect, not in fellowship generally, but in perfect fellowship; and this is hardly expressed by the words. And in the general usage of the author ἐν τούτῳ refers to what follows, whenever the sentence contains a clause which allows of such a reference. Such clauses are either added without connecting particle, or are introduced by ὅτι, ἐάν, or ὅταν. There is no certain instance of the construction ἐν τούτῳ ἵνα.

But Jn. xv. 8 should probably be interpreted in this way (ἐν τούτῳ ἐδοξάσθη ὁ πατήρ μου, ἵνα καρπὸν πολὺν φέρητε). And the writer's use of the purely definitive ἵνα is so well established that such a construction causes no difficulty. If ἐν τούτῳ refers to the clause introduced by ἵνα the meaning will be that love is made perfect in full confidence, It has been perfectly realized only by those who can look forward with sure confidence to the judgment of the Great Day. Such confidence is the sign of perfect love. The thought is developed further in ver. 18. Cf. also ii. 28.

παρρησίαν] See the note on ii. 28.

μεθ' ἡμῶν] As contrasted with ἐν ἡμῖν (‭‬א) it is possible that the phrase may emphasize the co-operation of men in the realization of fellowship, "In fulfilling this issue, God works with man" (Westcott, who compares Ac. xv. 4). But it is at least equally possible that the usage of the Hebrew preposition עם may have influenced the choice of preposition.

ὅτι κ.τ.λ.] The ground of the assurance. Those who have attained to fellowship share, in some degree, the character of the Christ, as He is in His exalted state, in perfect fellowship with the Father. Cf. Jn. xvii. 23, ἐγὼ ἐν αὐτοῖς καὶ σὺ ἐν ἐμοί· ἵνα ὦσιν τετελειωμένοι εἰς ἕν. Those who are like their Judge, can await with confidence the result of His decrees. The fellowship is limited by the conditions of earthly life (ἐν τῷ κόσμῳ τούτῳ). Οὗτος "emphasizes the idea of transitoriness." But so far as it goes the fellowship is real.

ἐκεῖνος] is generally used in this Epistle of the exalted Christ; cf. ii. 6, iii. 3, 5, 7, 16.

ἐν τῇ ἡμέρᾳ τῆς κρίσεως] Cf. ii. 28, ἐὰν φανερωθῇ. However much the writer may seek to spiritualize the ordinary Christian, or even the Synoptic, eschatology, he has not eliminated from the sphere of his theological thought the idea of a final "day" of judgment, when the processes which are already at work shall reach their final issue and manifestation. The attempts which have been made to draw a distinction in this respect between the Gospel and the Epistle cannot be said to have been successful.

η αγαπη] +του θεου 96 al^pauc vg^cle tol. sah^bw : eius arm.
μεθ ημω"] + εν ημιν ‭‬א.
εχωμεν] εχομεν ‭‬א K al.⁵: σχωμεν I^b 78 (–).
τη] om. I^a δ454 (794).
ημερα] αγαπη ‭‬א.
οτι . . . εσμεν] ut . . . simus sah^bw (non liquet sah^d).
κρισεως] + προς τον ενανθρωπησαντα I^c 208-116. 356 (307).
εκεινος] κακεινος 13 al.².
εστιν] ην εν τω κοσμω αμωμος και καθαρος ουτως I^c 116. 356 (–).
εσμεν] εσομεθα ‭‬א.

18. Fear, which is essentially self-centred, has no place in love, which in its perfection involves complete self-surrender.

The two cannot exist side by side. The presence of fear is a sign that love is not yet perfect. "Love cannot be mingled with fear" (Seneca, *Ep. Mor.* xlvii. 18).

κόλασιν ἔχει] not only "includes the punishment which it anticipates," but is in itself of the nature of punishment. Till love is supreme, it is a necessary chastisement, a part of the divine discipline, which has its salutary office. κόλασις is used in the New Testament only here and in Mt. xxv. 46, cf. 2 Mac. iv. 38. (Contrast the use of τιμωρία, "requital.") The expression must mean here more than "suffers punishment," as in Hermas, *S.* ix. 18. 1, ὁ μὴ γινώσκων θεὸν καὶ πονηρευόμενος ἔχει κόλασίν τινα τῆς πονηρίας αὐτοῦ.

ἔξω βάλλει] Cf. Mt. v. 13, xiii. 48; Jn. vi. 37, ix. 34, xii. 31, xv. 6. Love must altogether banish fear from the enclosure in which her work is done.

ὁ δὲ φοβούμενος κ.τ.λ.] Till fear has been "cast outside," love has not been made perfect. Cf. Philo, *quod Deus sit immut.* 69 (Cohn, ii. 72), τοῖς μὲν οὖν μήτε μέρος μήτε πάθος ἄνθρωπου περὶ τὸ ὂν νομίζουσιν, ἀλλὰ θεοπρεπῶς αὐτὸ δι᾽ αὐτὸ μόνον τιμῶσι τὸ ἀγαπᾶν οἰκειότατον, φοβεῖσθαι δὲ τοῖς ἑτέροις, quoted by Windisch.

εν τη] η *I*ᶜ ¹¹⁴ (335): om. τη *I*ᵇ ²⁵³ (2).
φοβος (? 2°)] φοβούμενος *I*ᵃ δ¹⁵⁷ (547) *I*ᶜ ¹⁷⁴ (252).

19. ἡμεῖς] We Christians, as in ver. 17. The point has been much disputed whether the verb (ἀγαπῶμεν) is to be interpreted as an exhortation (conjunctive) or as a statement of fact (indicative). The attempt to construe it as a conjunctive has led to various modifications of the text, the introduction of a connecting particle οὖν, never found in the true text of this Epistle (cf., however, 3 Jn. 8), or the insertion of an object for the verb (τὸν θεόν, αὐτόν, *inuicem*). And both modifications would be natural if the clause is to be taken as hortatory. But a further meditation on the nature of love as manifested in us is more suitable to the context, and it gives a deeper meaning to the words. Our love is not self-originated. It has a divine origin. It is called out in response to what God has given. Thus interpreted, the words offer a far more powerful incentive to the exercise of love than a mere exhortation, and they have their natural place in the writer's thoughts. God is love; by the path of love we can enter into His fellowship (16): in our case love is made perfect in proportion as it casts out fear and establishes full confidence (17, 18). And it rests on something greater and stronger than our own powers. It is the response of our nature to the love which God Himself has shown. Such love which He has called out in us must find an object. If it fails to find out the nearer object, it will never reach the further (19, 20). And besides this, there is the Lord's express command (21).

αὐτός] The variant ὁ θεός is probably a true explanation. But αὐτός is not only better attested, it is more in harmony with the writer's style.

πρῶτος] Cf. Jn. i. 42.

ημεις ℵ B K L al. longe. plur. cat. sah. cop. syrᵖ arm. Thphyl. Oec. Aug.] + ουν A 5. 8. 13. 31. 98. 101. 105. 106**. 107. 177** gˢᶜʳ kˢᶜʳ al. pauc. vg. syrˢᶜʰ.

αγαπωμεν A B 5. 27. 29. 66** fu. aeth. **boh**-codd. Aug. Pelag. Bed.] *scimus* **sah**. : + τον θεον ℵ 13. 33. 34. 68. 69. 91. 137 aˢᶜʳ cˢᶜʳ dˢᶜʳ vg. demid. harl. tol. sur. **boh**-ed. arm. Leo : + αυτον K L al. longe. plur. cat. Thphyl. Oec. Aug. : + *inuicem* am. Leo.

αυτος ℵ B K L al. pler. cat. harl. sah. cop. syr. arm. aeth. Thphyl. Oec Aug.] ο θεος A 5. 8. 13. 14*. 33. 34. 81. vg. Pelag.

πρωτος] πρωτον 5. 8. 25. 40. 69. aˢᶜʳ.

ηγαπησεν] ηγαπηκεν 13.

20. ἐάν τις εἴπῃ] Cf. i. 6, ἐὰν εἴπωμεν, and the more definite ὁ λέγων (ii. 4). The false claim is mentioned quite generally. At the same time, it is not improbable that the false teachers, who claimed to possess a superior knowledge of the true God, may also have laid claim to a superior love of the Father, who was "good," and not merely "just," as the God of the Old Testament. And the emphasis laid throughout the Epistle on the duty of mutual love makes it clear that their "superior" love had been more or less conspicuous in its failure to begin at home, or to master the import of the Lord's verdict, ἐφ᾽ ὅσον οὐκ ἐποιήσατε ἑνὶ τούτων τῶν ἐλαχίστων, οὐδὲ ἐμοὶ ἐποιήσατε.

μισῇ] Cf. ii. 9.

ψεύστης ἐστίν] He not only states what is false (ψεύδεται), but reveals by his false claim a real falseness of character, if the difference between two possible forms of expression is to be pressed.

ὁ γὰρ κ.τ.λ.] Love must express itself in action. He who refuses to make use of the obvious opportunities, which his position in this world affords him, cannot entertain the highest love.

ὃν ἑώρακεν] Cf. Oec. ἐφελκυστικὸν γὰρ ὅρασις πρὸς ἀγάπην, and the saying of Philo, *de Decalogo*, § 23 (Cohn, iv. 296), ἀμήχανον δὲ εὐσεβεῖσθαι τὸν ἀόρατον ὑπὸ τῶν εἰς τοὺς ἐμφανεῖς καὶ ἐγγὺς ὄντας ἀσεβούντων.

οὐ δύναται] The reading of ℵ B, etc., is perhaps more impressive and more in agreement with the writer's love of absolute statement than the variant which Westcott condemns as "the rhetorical phrase of the common text" (πῶς δύναται). At the same time the latter reading suggests a new point. The man who rejects the obvious method of giving expression to love in

the case of those whom he has seen, has no way left by which
he can attempt the harder task of reaching out to that which is
invisible.

> οτι] om. ℵ Aug. (*bis*).
> αγαπω] post θεον 1° *I*ᵃ ⁷⁰ (505) : αγαπα *I*ᶜ ⁵⁵¹ (216) : ηγαπηκεν *H* δ⁴⁸ (33).
> μιση] μισει K h al.²⁵ cat. Dam. Thphyl.
> γαρ] om. *I*ᵃ ¹⁵⁸ (395) *I*ᵇ ¹⁵⁷ (29).
> ου δυναται] ℵ B 27. 29. 66**. 68. 69 aˢᶜʳ sah. syr. Lcif.] πως δυναται
> A K L al. pler. cat. vg. syr. cop. arm. aeth. Dam. Thphyl. Oec. Cyp. Aug.
> αγαπαν] αγαπησαι 13 al.².

21. The duty of love not only follows necessarily from what
God has done for us, it rests on His direct commandment.

ἀπ᾽ αὐτοῦ] naturally refers to God, as the variant in the
Vulgate interprets it, though here as elsewhere, in the language
of meditation, when the writer is of Semitic origin, a change of
person is by no means impossible.

The most direct statement of the command is Mk. xii. 29 ff.,
where the Lord quotes the command of Dt. vi. 4, 5. The writer
no doubt knew the Marcan passage, even if he had not himself
heard the saying which it records, when it was originally spoken.
Cf. also Jn. xiii. 34.

> εχομεν] *accepimus* **sah.** **boh**-codd.
> απ αυτου] απο του θεου A vg. am. demid. harl. **tol.**
> om. θεον . . . τον 2° B* A* (uid.).
> om. και 2° 13. 34.
> αυτου (? 2°)] εαυτου *I*ᶜ ¹¹⁴ (335).

II. v. 1–12. Second presentation of the two main thoughts
closely combined together. Faith the ground of love.

1. **v. 1a.** Faith the sign of the Birth from God (cf. ii. 29,
iv. 7, Love).

2. **v. 1b-4.** The love of God which is the true ground of
love of the brethren, is the sign of love of the brethren
(contrast iv. 20).

3. **v. 5–12.** Faith, in its full assurance, the witness to Jesus
as being the Christ.

1. **v. 1a.** Faith the sign of the Birth from God.

1 ff. The writer has shown that love has its origin in the
nature of God, and is not merely an affection of human nature.
He has also reminded his readers how their love for God, the
reflex of His love for us, can be tested. The truth of our claim
to love God is shown in our attitude towards the brethren. He
now proceeds to show why this is so, and how we can be sure of
the sincerity of our love for others. The love of a child for its
father and for its brother or sister are facts of nature. Every one
who loves the father who begat him naturally loves the other
children whom his father has begotten. The facts of the

spiritual birth are analogous. What is true of the human family is also true of the Divine Society. If we love the Father who hath "begotten us again," and the reality of that love is shown in our active obedience (ποιῶμεν) to His commands, we may be assured that our love to His other (spiritual) children is real and sincere. Every one that believeth that Jesus is the Christ shows by that belief, as it manifests itself in word and deed as well as in intellectual conviction, that he has experienced the new birth. Those who are "born of God" must love all His children, as surely as it is natural that any child should love his father's other children.

1. πᾶς ὁ πιστεύων κ.τ.λ.] Cf. Jn. i. 12 f. ὅσοι δὲ ἔλαβον αὐτόν, ἔδωκεν αὐτοῖς ἐξουσίαν τέκνα θεοῦ γενέσθαι, τοῖς πιστεύουσιν εἰς τὸ ὄνομα αὐτοῦ . . . οἳ . . . ἐκ θεοῦ ἐγεννήθησαν. Where true faith in Jesus as God's appointed messenger to men is present, there the new birth has taken place. The writer does not state whether faith is the cause or the result of the new birth. The point is not present to his thoughts, and his argument does not require its elucidation. What he wishes to emphasize is the fact that they go together. Where true faith is the new birth is a reality, and has abiding and permanent consequences. The believer has been born of God. But incidentally the tenses "make it clear that the Divine Begetting is the antecedent, not the consequent of the believing." "Christian belief, which is essentially the spiritual recognition of spiritual truth, is a function of the Divine Life as imparted to men" (Law).

ὁ πιστεύων] Πιστεύειν ὅτι expresses belief in the truth of a statement or thesis. The phrase used in the passage quoted above from the Gospel (πιστεύειν εἰς τὸ ὄνομα) suggests complete and voluntary submission to the guidance of a Person, as possessed of the character which his name implies. But though the writer is careful to distinguish the two, he would have been unable to conceive of any true faith stopping short at intellectual conviction of the abstract truth of a statement like that which follows in the clause introduced by ὅτι, which had no effect on the shaping of a man's conduct. He would have regarded the belief that Jesus is the Christ as inseparable from faith in Jesus *as* Christ. Neither belief nor knowledge are for him purely intellectual processes.

Ἰησοῦς ἐστὶν ὁ Χριστός] The exact form of this confession of faith is conditioned by the antichrists' denial (cf. ii. 22, ὁ ἀρνού-μενος ὅτι Ἰησοῦς οὐκ ἐστὶν ὁ Χριστός). It lays stress on the identity of the man Jesus with the Christ who became incarnate in Him, as opposed to the theories, then prevalent, of the descent of a higher power on Jesus at the Baptism, which left Him before the Crucifixion.

καὶ πᾶς ὁ ἀγαπῶν κ.τ.λ.] The child's love for its parent naturally carries with it love for brothers and sisters. The step in the argument, "Every one that is born of God loveth God," is passed over as too obvious to require statement. We are again reminded that we have to deal with the language of meditation.

αγαπα B 7. 13. 33. 62 om. demid. tol. sah. Hil. Aug.]+καὶ ℵ A K L P al. pler. cat. vg. harl. syr. arm. aeth. boh. Cyr. Thdt. Thphyl. Oec. Hil. Aug. Bed.

ὁ χριστος εστιν *J* b δ260f (440).

γεγενηται *J* a δ505*. δ459*. 552*. 256. 1402 (69).

τον 2°] το ℵ 31.

2. As usual a test is added by which the sincerity of the love may be determined. Ἐν τούτῳ points forward. This is clearly the established usage of ἐν τούτῳ in the Epistle, but difficulty has been felt in thus explaining it here, because the clause to which it points forward is introduced by ὅταν, instead of the usual constructions, ἐάν, ὅτι, or a disconnected sentence. But the difficulty is not serious, and it is probable that ἐν τούτῳ should be interpreted as usual. Whenever our love to God is clear, and issues in active obedience to His will, we know by this that our love for His children is real. Weiss' explanation, which makes ἐν τούτῳ refer back to the statement immediately preceding (πᾶς ὁ ἀγαπῶν κ.τ.λ.), is perhaps at first sight easier. "When, or as soon as, we love God, we love also the children of God, in accordance with the law that love for him who begets has as its necessary consequence love for those whom he has begotten" (p. 150). Thus the duty of loving the brethren is deduced from the natural law of affection, as well as being directly commanded by God. But the other interpretation is more in accordance with the writer's wish to emphasize the Divine origin of love. There is certainly no need to reduce the verse to the merest repetition of what has been already said, by the transposition of the objects "Hereby we know that we love God, when we love the children of God," as Grotius and others have suggested.

τὰ τέκνα τοῦ θεοῦ] The use of this phrase instead of "the brethren" is significant. True love, which has its origin in God, is called out by that in its object which is akin to the Divine. Every one who has been born of God must love all those who have been similarly ennobled. Love of God bears witness to, and has witness borne to itself by, love of the godlike.

τα τεκνα του θεου] *filium Dei* arm. boh-codd. : *Dominum* aeth. | οταν] *si* boh.

οταν . . . αγαπωμεν] εν τω αγαπαν τον θεον 13. 191. 57lect.

ποιωμεν B 27. 29. 64. 69. 106. 15lect ascr dscr gscr vg. sah. cop. syr. arm. aeth. Thphyl. Lcif. Aug.] ποιουμεν 5. 17. 33. 34 : τηρωμεν ℵ K L P al. pler. cat. tol. cav. Oec. : τηρουμεν 31* al.2.

om. ποιωμεν—(3) αυτου 1° A 3. 42. 66** 100. 101.

The reading τηρῶμεν is clearly a correction to the more usual phrase which occurs in ver. 3.   In itself the reading of B, etc., is more forcible.   It emphasizes the active character of the obedience which testifies to the love felt for God and therefore for the brethren.

3. The first clause justifies the addition of the last clause of ver. 2, καὶ τὰς ἐντολὰς αὐτοῦ ποιῶμεν.   Obedience to His commands is the necessary outcome of love to God.   There is no such thing as true love of God which does not issue in obedience.

αὕτη . . . ἵνα] Cf. Jn. xvii. 3.   The definitive ἵνα generally introduces an ideal not yet actually attained.   This is perhaps the only class of ideas whose contents it is used to define.

τηρῶμεν] Contrast ver. 2 (ποιῶμεν).   Actual "doing" is the test of love.   But love includes more of obedience than the actual carrying out of definite commands.   It accepts them as the expression of an underlying principle, which is capable of moulding the whole character, and which must be kept alive and given scope to work.

βαρεῖαι] Cf. Mt. xxiii. 4, δεσμεύουσιν δὲ φορτία βαρέα : Lk. xi. 46, φορτίζετε τοὺς ἀνθρώπους φορτία δυσβάστακτα : and contrast Mt. xi. 30, τὸ φορτίον μου ἐλαφρόν ἐστιν.   The word cannot here mean "difficult to fulfil."   It suggests the idea of a heavy and oppressive burden.   The commands may be in themselves difficult to carry out, and yet not burdensome, if the Christian is possessed of adequate power to fulfil them, in virtue of his Christian standing and love : *dilige et quod vis fac* (Augustine). Windisch regards vv. 3 and 4 as intended to show the possibility of fulfilling the Divine commands, and of realizing the Divine ideal for men.   (1) On the side of God, He does not demand what is too hard for men.   Cf. Philo, *de spec. leg.* i. 299, p. 257, αἰτεῖται . . . ὢ διάνοια, παρὰ σοῦ ὁ θεὸς οὐδὲν βαρὺ καὶ ποικίλον ἢ δύσεργον, ἀλλὰ ἁπλοῦν πανὺ καὶ ῥάδιον.   ταῦτα δ᾽ ἐστὶν ἀγαπᾶν αὐτὸν ὡς εὐεργέτην, εἰ δὲ μή, φοβεῖσθαι γοῦν ὡς ἄρχοντα καὶ κύριον . . . καὶ τῶν ἐντολῶν αὐτοῦ περιέχεσθαι καὶ τὰ δίκαια τιμᾶν.   (2) On man's side, the necessary power has been given to him.   But this interpretation ignores the form of the sentence (ὅτι πᾶν κ.τ.λ.).

γαρ] om. *H*⁸⁶ (Ψ) *K*² (S) sah^w boh-codd.

4. And this power each Christian has, in virtue of the new birth from God.   The statement is made in its most abstract form (πᾶν τὸ γεγεννημένον) which emphasizes the power of the new birth rather than its possession by each individual (πᾶς ὁ γεγεννημένος).   Every one who is born of God has within himself a power strong enough to overcome the resistance of all the powers of the world, which hinder him from loving God.

καὶ αὕτη κ.τ.λ.] For the form of expression, cf. i. 5 ; Jn. i. 19.

Our faith, the faith that Jesus of Nazareth is the Messiah, the
Son of God, accepted not as an intellectual conviction but as a
rule of life, overcame in our case the powers of the world, which
fight for a different principle of life. The aorist (νικήσασα)
naturally points to a definite act, or fact. The writer must be
thinking either of the conversion of each member of the community, "the moment when he ἐπίστευσεν," or else of some
well-known event in the history of the Church or Churches
addressed. The most natural reference is to the definite with-
drawing of the false teachers from the fellowship of the Church.
There is no obvious reference to the victory of Christ over the
world (cf. Jn. xvi. 33, ἐγὼ νενίκηκα τὸν κόσμον) which His followers
share in virtue of their faith, *i.e.* in so far as they unite themselves
with Him.

πας ο γεγεννημενος *I*[a 173] (156).

ημων ℵ A B K P al. pler. cat. vg. etc.] υμων L 3. 42. 57. 98. 105. 191
al. fere.[20] aeth.

5. τίς ἐστιν] Cf. ii. 22, τίς ἐστιν ὁ ψεύστης εἰ μὴ κ.τ.λ. The
appeal is to practical experience. He who has realized what
Jesus of Nazareth really was, and he alone, has in himself the
power which overcomes the forces of the world which draw men
away from God; cf. 1 Co. xv. 57.

ὁ υἱὸς τοῦ θεοῦ] Cf. verse 1, ὁ χριστός. The fuller p' rase
brings out the meaning more clearly, though the writer probably means much the same by both titles. He varies his
phrase to leave no doubt about his meaning. The πρῶτον
ψεῦδος of the false teachers was the denial, not that Jesus was
the Messiah of the Jews, but that He was the complete revelation of the Father, the assertion that the higher Power that was
in Him was only temporarily connected with Him during a
part of His earthly life.

τις εστιν A L al. pler. vg. sah. Oec.] pr. *et* **arm.** : + δε ℵ (B) K P 13. 29.
66**. 68. 69 a[scr] al. fere.[15] cat. cav. demid. tol. cop. syr. arm. Did. Cyr.
Thphyl. (τις δε εστιν B cav. demid. tol. Did.).

ο πιστευων] ο πιστευσας P.

ιησους + *Christus* **arm-codd. boh-codd.**

εστιν] om. *I*[a 1402] (219).

ο υιος] pr. ο χριστος 13. 56 : ο χς *I*[c 258] (56).

6–9. He, the pre-existent Son of God, was sent from heaven
by God to do His will. He came to earth to fulfil His Mission.
In His fulfilment of it, two events are prominent: the Baptism
by which He was consecrated to His Messianic work, and the
Passion by which He completed His work of atonement and
propitiation. His coming was not in the water of John's
Baptism alone, it was realized even more fully in the Blood

which He shed upon the Cross. "He that came" is the title which best characterizes His work. The function of the Spirit was different. It was to bear witness. He was the witness-bearer. And He was fitted for His office, for truth is of the essence of His being. He is the truth. And the witness may be trusted, for it is threefold. The witness-bearers are three : the Spirit, whose very nature qualifies Him for the office; the water of John's Baptism, after which He was declared to be the Son of God ; and the blood shed upon the Cross, where testimony was again given to the fact that He is the Son of God, for His death was not like that of other men. Thus the three witnesses all tend to the same point. They establish the one truth that Jesus is the Christ, the Son of God.

6. Of the many interpretations of this passage which have been suggested, only three deserve serious consideration: (1) A reference to the two Christian Sacraments of Baptism and the Eucharist naturally suggested itself to many interpreters of the Epistle, especially in view of the 4th and 6th chapters of the Gospel. But it is open to more than one fatal objection. If ὕδωρ can be satisfactorily explained of Baptism, αἷμα is never found in the New Testament as a designation of the Eucharist. And, secondly, the form of the sentence, ὁ ἐλθὼν δι' ὕδατος καὶ αἵματος, almost necessitates a reference to definite historical facts in the life of Christ on earth which could be regarded as peculiarly characteristic of the Mission which He "came" to fulfil. If the writer had intended to refer to the Christian Sacraments, he must have said ὁ ἐρχόμενος. It is hardly necessary to point out that any interpretations which refer one of the expressions to a rite instituted by Christ, and the other to something which happened to Him (as, *e.g.*, the Christian rite of baptism, and the atoning death on the Cross), are even less satisfactory. See *Cambridge Greek Testament.*

(2) The reference to the incident recorded in Jn. xix. 34 was also natural, considering the stress laid upon it by the author of the Gospel, and the exact language in which he records the result of the piercing of the Lord's side by the soldier's lance, ἐξῆλθεν αἷμα καὶ ὕδωρ. This incident gives a definite fact which would justify the use of the aorist (ὁ ἐλθών). And the difference in order (αἷμα καὶ ὕδωρ) offers no real difficulty. It is easily explicable as a consequence of the writer's desire to throw special emphasis on the αἷμα, which he develops further in the next clause, οὐκ ἐν τῷ ὕδατι μόνον ἀλλ' ἐν τῷ ὕδατι καὶ τῷ αἵματι. But it is difficult to see how this incident could be regarded as characterizing the Lord's Mission as a whole. No doubt the incident, as the writer had seen it or heard the account of it from a trustworthy and competent witness, had made a deep

impression upon him. It had suggested to him the significance of "blood" and "water" as symbolizing two characteristic aspects of the Lord's work, cleansing and life-giving. But the incident itself could hardly be thought of as the means whereby He accomplished His work. As an explanation of the actual words used, ὁ ἐλθὼν δι᾽ ὕδατος καὶ αἵματος, it fails to satisfy the requirements of the case.

(3) We are thus thrown back on the explanation of Tertullian, Theophylact, and many modern commentators, who see in the words a reference to the Baptism of Jesus by John the Baptist, in which at the beginning of His ministry He was consecrated to His Messianic work and received the gift of the Spirit descending upon Him and *abiding* on Him, and the Death on the Cross by which His work was consummated. The terms used refer definitely to the historical manifestation of the Son of God, and compel us to look for definite and characteristic events in that history by means of which it could be said that His mission was accomplished, His "coming" effected. The two great events at the beginning and the end of the ministry satisfactorily fulfil these conditions. At the Baptism He was specially consecrated for His public work, and endowed with the Spirit which enabled Him to carry it out. And His work was not finished before Calvary. The Death on the Cross was its consummation, not a mere incident in the life of an ordinary man, after the Higher Power had left Him, which had temporarily united itself with His human personality for the purposes of His mission of teaching.

The middle clause of the verse distinguishes two facts, and lays emphasis on the latter. The repetition of both preposition and article brings this out clearly. The statement is as precise as grammar can make it. And the whole statement, including what is said about the function of the Spirit as witness-bearer, is no doubt conditioned by the special form of erroneous teaching which had made so precise a statement necessary.

Though Tertullian apparently adheres to this interpretation, his mention of it shows the early connection of this passage with the incident at the Crucifixion, recorded in Jn. xix. 34. Cf. Tert. *de Baptismo*, 16, "Uenerat enim per aquam et sanguinem, sicut Ioannes scripsit, ut aqua tingueretur, sanguine glorificaretur, proinde nos facere aqua uocatos, sanguine electos. Hos duos baptismos de uulnere perfossi lateris emisit, quatenus qui in sanguinem eius crederent, aqua lauarentur, qui aqua lauissent, etiam sanguinem potarent."

The combination of the historical and sacramental explanation is well illustrated by Bede, " Qui uenit per aquam et sanguinem, aquam uidelicet lauacri et sanguinem suae passionis: non

solum baptizari propter nostram ablutionem dignatus est, ut
nobis baptismi sacramentum consecraret ac traderet, uerum
etiam sanguinem suum dedit pro nobis, sua nos passione
redimens, cuius sacramentis semper refecti nutriremur ad
salutem." Considering his usual dependence upon Augustine,
this may be taken as probably giving that writer's comment on
the passage, especially if we compare his comment on the passage
in the Gospel (*Tract.* cxx. 2), "*Aperuit*, ut illic quodammodo
uitae ostium panderetur, unde Sacramenta Ecclesiae manauerunt,
sine quibus ad uitam quae uera uita est non intratur. Ille sanguis
in remissionem fusus est peccatorum : aqua illa salutare temperat
poculum ; haec et lauacrum praestat et potum."

The passage was naturally allegorized by the Alexandrian
School ; cf. Clement, " Iste est qui uenit per aquam et sanguinem "
et iterum "quia tres sunt qui testificantur, Spiritus, quod est
uita, et aqua quod est regeneratio ac fides, et sanguis, quod est
cognitio," where the interpretation illustrates the absence of
historical sense which usually characterizes the Allegorists.   It
would, of course, be possible to interpret the passage of the
whole of the life of Jesus on earth, in which the Son of God was
manifested in flesh, ὕδωρ and αἷμα being used as symbols of two
different aspects of the work which He accomplished during that
life, as, *e.g.*, cleansing and life-giving, according to the recognized Biblical usage of the terms.   But if this had been intended
the context must have made it plain that this was the meaning
which the writer wished to convey.   His readers could hardly
have deduced it from the passage as it stands.

οὗτος] Jesus, who is both Christ and Son of God.   For this
use of οὗτος to emphasize the character of the subject as
previously described, see Jn. i. 2, 7, iii. 2 (xxi. 24) ; 1 Jn. ii. 22,
cf. 2 Jn. 7.   He who came *was* both Christ and Son of God.
The incarnation of the Son of God in human nature was not a
merely temporary connection during part only of the earthly life
of Jesus of Nazareth.

ὁ ἐλθών] The article is significant.   He is one whose office
or work is rightly characterized by the description given.   And
the aorist naturally refers to definite historical facts, or to the
whole life regarded as one fact.   It is hardly safe to find in
the expression ὁ ἐλθών a distinct reference to the (?) Messianic
title ὁ ἐρχόμενος, and so discover in the phrase a special indication of the office and work of Messiah.   The idea emphasized
in this and similar expressions would seem to be generally the
course of action taken in obedience to the command of God.
The "coming" of the Son corresponds to the "sending" of
the Father.   It expresses the fulfilment of the Mission which
He was sent to accomplish.   As that Mission was Messianic

in character, Messianic ideas may often be suggested by the phrase, but they are secondary. "He who accomplished the Mission entrusted to Him by God" seems to be the meaning of the word.

δι' ὕδατος καὶ αἵματος] The difficulty of the phrase is reflected in the attempts to modify the text. Cf. the critical note. The phrase should express means by which the "coming" was accomplished, or elements by which it was characterized. Cf. 2 Co. v. 7, διὰ πίστεως περιπατεῖν. The tense of ἐλθών excludes any primary reference to the Christian sacraments, even if ὕδωρ and αἷμα could be used to indicate them (see note at the beginning of the verse). As has been pointed out, the order of the words is not in itself decisive against such a reference or against a reference to the incident recorded in Jn. xix. 34 (ἐξῆλθεν αἷμα καὶ ὕδωρ). The real objection to the latter view is the difficulty of seeing how that incident could be regarded as characteristic means by which the "coming" was accomplished. It may well have suggested to the writer the peculiar significance of two aspects of the coming, but can hardly be regarded as an event by means of which the coming was fulfilled. On the other hand, the Baptism and the Crucifixion were both important factors in the carrying out of the Mission which He came to fulfil, and in this light they stand out more prominently than any other two recorded events of the Ministry.

οὐκ ἐν τῷ ὕδατι μόνον] The writer evidently feels that further precision is necessary to make his meaning clear and unmistakable. It is clear that he has to deal with a form of teaching which denied the reality, or at least the supreme importance, of the coming ἐν τῷ αἵματι. The use of the article is natural, where the reference is to what has been mentioned before. The repetition of both article and preposition certainly suggests that two different events are referred to, a point which the earlier phrase δι' ὕδατος καὶ αἵματος left doubtful.

The difference in meaning between the two prepositions used is not very clear. The events may be regarded as instruments by which the Mission was accomplished; or, on the other hand, water and blood, or rather the realities which they symbolize, may be thought of as spheres in which the work, or purpose, of the Mission was characteristically realized. But the influence of Semitic forms of expression may have gone far towards obliterating any difference in meaning between the two forms of expression. Cf. Lv. xvi. 3 (ἐν μόσχῳ); 1 Co. iv. 21 (ἐν ῥάβδῳ . . . ἢ ἐν ἀγάπῃ); He. ix. 12 (διὰ τοῦ ἰδίου αἵματος εἰσῆλθεν), 25 (εἰσέρχεται . . . ἐν αἵματι ἀλλοτρίῳ).

καὶ τὸ πνεῦμα κ.τ.λ.] Τὸ μαρτυροῦν expresses the characteristic office of τὸ πνεῦμα, as ὁ ἐλθών does of οὗτος. It is not merely equivalent to μαρτυροῦν. Christ was the fulfiller of the Divine plan. Cf. He. x. 7 (Ps. xl. 8), τότε εἶπον· ἰδοὺ ἥκω, ἐν κεφαλίδι βιβλίου γέγραπται περὶ ἐμοῦ τοῦ ποιῆσαι, ὁ θεός, τὸ θέλημά σου. The special function of the Spirit is to bear witness to what the Christ was and came to do. It is not improbable that in the false teaching which is here combated, a totally different function had been assigned to the Spirit (cf. Introduction, p. xlix). We may, perhaps, see a parallel instance in the description of the proper function of the Baptist contained in the Prologue of the Gospel, (οὐκ ἦν ἐκεῖνος τὸ φῶς) ἀλλ᾽ ἵνα μαρτυρήσῃ περὶ τοῦ φωτός. To the Baptist also some had assigned a different and a higher function. Perhaps, however, the sequence of thought in the passage as a whole may be brought out more clearly by a simpler interpretation, which does not exclude a secondary reference to the ideas which have been suggested. "He" came both by water and by blood. Both bore witness to the char- acter of His Mission. But there was other witness, and more important. The Spirit is *the* witness-bearer. And so the witness is threefold. It fulfils the requirements of legally valid attestation. If we recognize the proper place and function of the Spirit, we gain assurance which cannot be shaken.

The present tense excludes the need of any definite historical reference in the case of the Spirit, as, for instance, the Voice at the Baptism, or the Voice which spake from heaven shortly before the Passion (Jn. xii. 28).

The best explanation of the author's meaning is to be found in the account of the function of the Paraclete in Jn. xv. 26, τὸ πνεῦμα τῆς ἀληθείας, ὃ παρὰ τοῦ πατρὸς ἐκπορεύεται, ἐκεῖνος μαρτυρήσει περὶ ἐμοῦ. Cf. also Jn. xiv. 26, xvi. 8–10, 13–15.

ὅτι] Either declarative or causal. The former gives a possible meaning. The Spirit "carries with it immediately the conscious- ness of its truth and reality," is in itself the best witness to its own nature, which is truth. But this is alien to the context. The emphasis is on the function of witnessing. This function the Spirit can perform perfectly, because the Spirit is the truth. The very nature of the Spirit is truth. Cf. Jn. xv. 26. By its very nature it is not only capable of bearing true witness, but it is also constrained to do so. It cannot deny itself.

ελθων] pr. υς του θυ *I*ᶜ ²⁵⁸ (56).

και αιματος B K L al. plu. vg. (am. fu. demid. harl.) syrˢᶜʰ Cyr. Thphyl. Oec. Tert.]: pr. και πνευματος 5. 68. 83 arm. aeth. : και πνευ- ματος 54. 103. 104 Cyr. Ambr. : om. *I*ᵃ ¹⁵⁸ (56) *I*ᵇ ⁶²⁻¹⁶¹. ⁴⁷² (498) *I*ᶜ δ²⁹⁹ (–) : +και πνευματος 6. 7. 13. 15. 18. 25. 29. 30. 33. 34. 36. 39. 66** . 69. 80. 98. 101. 137 (+αγιου 33. 34. 39) aˢᶜʳ al. pauc. cav. tol. sah. cop. syrᵖ Cyr.

αιματος] pr. δι *I*ᵃ ¹⁸⁴ (–) *K*⁵⁰⁰ (45).

ιησους χριστος ℵ A B L al. plu. arm. Cyr. Thphyl. Oec. : χριστοι

ιησους Κ Ρ h 15. 22. 33. 34. 36. 39. 56. 100. 192 cat. **arm-codd.** sah.
Ambr. : ιησους ο χριστος minusc. uix. multi. syr^p Thphyl^comn Oec^comr.

μονον] μονω Β.

εν τω υδατι . . . αιματι] εν τω αιματι . . . υδατι Ρ 31*. 83 arm. : εν τω
υδατι . . . πνευματι Α 21. 41 Cyr. : εν τω αιματι . . . πνευματι 66**. 80 :
+et spiritu cav. tol. aeth.

τω 2°] om. H^δ6 (Ψ).

εν 3° Α Β L Ρ 4. 5. 13. 17. 18. 21. 33. 40. 41. 66**. 80. 83. 118 j^scr
k^scr cat. Cyr.] om. ℵ Κ al. plu. vg. **boh-cod.** Cyr. Thphyl. Oec.

τω 3°] om. H^162. 103 (61).

και το] οτι I^a 397fff (96).

το πνευμα 2°] χριστος 34 vg. arm^usc : om. το H^δ6 (Ψ) I^a 158 (395).

7. ὅτι τρεῖς κ.τ.λ.] The witness to the fact that Jesus is the
Christ, the Son of God, is trustworthy. It fulfils the conditions
of legally valid witness, as laid down in Dt. xix. 15, οὐκ ἐμμενεῖ
μάρτυς εἷς μαρτυρῆσαι κατὰ ἀνθρώπου κατὰ πᾶσαν ἀδικίαν καὶ κατὰ
πᾶν ἁμάρτημα καὶ κατὰ πᾶσαν ἁμαρτίαν ἣν ἂν ἁμάρτῃ· ἐπὶ στόματος
δυὸ μαρτύρων καὶ ἐπὶ στόματος τριῶν μαρτύρων στήσεται πᾶν ῥῆμα.
Cf. Dt. xvii. 6 ; Mt. xviii. 16 ; 2 Co. xiii. 1 ; Jn. viii. 17. It is obvious that the same interpretation must be given to πνεῦμα, ὕδωρ,
and αἷμα here as in the preceding verse. The Christ "came"
by water and by blood, and the Spirit bore witness to Him and
to His Mission. The witness of the Spirit is supported by the
witness of the water and the blood. The means by which He
accomplished His Mission are subsidiary witnesses to its character. And the witnesses agree. The Spirit, and the opening
and closing scenes of the Ministry as interpreted by the Spirit,
bear similar witness to the Christ.

εἰς τὸ ἕν εἰσιν] Are for the one thing, tend in the same
direction, exist for the same object. They all work towards the
same result, the establishing of the truth that Jesus is the Christ,
the Son of God.

εισιν] om. I^b 157 (29).
μαρτυρουντες] μαρτυρουσιν H^δ6 (Ψ) I^c 114f (335).
και 1°] om. I^b δ602ffff (522).
και 3°] om. H^δ6 (Ψ).
και το υδωρ post αιμα **arm-codd.**
το 4°] om. I^a 70 (505).

8. εἰ τὴν μαρτυρίαν κ.τ.λ.] Cf. Jn. v. 36. If we accept the
testimony of men when it satisfies the conditions of evidence
required by the law, much more are we bound to accept the
witness which we possess in this case, for it is witness borne by
God Himself. Cf. also Jn. viii. 18, καὶ μαρτυρεῖ περὶ ἐμοῦ ὁ πέμψας
με πατήρ, and x. 25, τὰ ἔργα ἃ ἐγὼ ποιῶ ἐν τῷ ὀνόματι τοῦ πατρός
μου ταῦτα μαρτυρεῖ περὶ ἐμοῦ. Neither here nor in iv. 11 does
the εἰ indicate any doubt : it is known to every one that we do
accept such testimony.

ὅτι αὕτη κ.τ.λ.] Such witness is greater, and therefore more

worthy of our acceptance, because it is Divine witness, and
deals with a subject on which God, and God alone, is fully
competent to speak.   It concerns His Son.   God has borne
witness concerning His Son.   In this case the Divine witness
alone is ἀληθινή in the full sense of the term, though other kinds
of witness may be true so far as they go.

ὅτι μεμαρτύρηκεν] The reading ὅτι is undoubtedly right.   If
the reading ἦν, of the *Textus Receptus*, be adopted, the αὕτη
must refer back to the witness already described, *i.e.* that borne
by the three witnesses, the Spirit, the water, and the blood, or by
the one witness, the Spirit, who interprets the evidence of the
historical facts.   The witness meant must be the witness borne
to the truth that Jesus is the Christ.   If ὅτι is accepted, it may
be taken in three ways : (1) Causal.   In this case αὕτη must
refer to what has preceded, the witness already described.   Such
is the witness, Divine and legally valid, for God really *has borne
witness* to His Son.   By laying the stress on the verb μεμαρτύρηκεν it is perhaps possible to make sense of the passage in
this way.   But such an interpretation is very harsh, and not in
conformity with the author's style.

(2) ὅ τι.   This is the witness, *i.e.* that which He has borne
concerning His Son.   This use of ὅ τι in the Johannine writings
is not certainly established, though perhaps we should compare
Jn. viii. 25, τὴν ἀρχὴν ὅ τι καὶ λαλῶ ὑμῖν.   In the present context
it would be intolerably harsh.

(3) It is far more natural and in accordance with the author's
style (cf. Jn. iii. 19, αὕτη δέ ἐστιν ἡ κρίσις ὅτι τὸ φῶς ἐλήλυθεν
κ.τ.λ.) to regard the ὅτι as declarative.   The value of the
witness consists in this, that He has given it concerning His
Son.   There can be no more trustworthy witness, so far as
competence to speak is concerned, than that which a father
bears to his own son.   The essence of the witness is that it is
the testimony of *God* to *His Son*.   In the Gospel, μαρτυρεῖν
περί is very frequent (i. 7, 8, 15, ii. 25, v. 31, 32, etc.), elsewhere
very rare.

των ανθρωπων] του θεου ℵ* | του θεου (? 1°)] των αιων Iᵇ δ⁶⁰² (522) | om.
οτι I° K arm. | η μαρτυρια 2°] post θεου 2° Iᵃ | οτι 2° ℵ A B 5. 6. 13. 27. 29.
34. 66** vg. sah. cop. arm-codd. Cyr. Aug.] ην K L P al. pler. cat. arm-
codd. Thphyl. Oec. : qui arm-ed. | περι τον υιον αυτου] *de filio suo Iesu
Christo* arm-codd.: +*quem misit saluatorem super terram.   Et filius
testimonium perhibuit in terra scripturas perficiens ; et nos testimonium
perhibemus, quoniam uidimus eum, et annunciamus uobis ut credatis et
ideo* tol.

10. He who trusts himself to the guidance of t'ie Son has in
his own experience the witness which God bore to Him, it has
become part of himself.   He who does not accept the witness

as true has not only missed the truth, but has made God a liar ; for he has set aside as false the witness which God has borne concerning His own Son.

ἐν αὐτῷ] in himself, as is made clear in the paraphrase of א (ἑαυτῷ). The passage must describe the "testimonium spiritus internum."

ὁ μὴ πιστεύων] The subjective negative is rightly used. It lays emphasis on the character rather than the fact of non-belief. A general class is described by its significant characteristic. But in N.T. οὐ with the participle is rare, in the Johannine writings only Jn. x. 12. See J. H. Moulton, *Gr. of N.T. Grk.* i. p. 231.

τῷ θεῷ] This construction (*c. dat.*) expresses, as usually, acceptance of the statement rather than surrender to the person. The variants τῷ υἱῷ, Jesu Christo, miss the point of the verse.

ψεύστην] Cf. i. 10. There is no room for ignorance or misconception. To reject the witness is to deny the truthfulness of God. He has spoken and acted deliberately, and with absolute clearness. The testimony has been borne. The things were not done in a corner. The witness must therefore either be accepted or rejected. It cannot be ignored or explained away.

πεποίηκεν] The tense suggests a definite choice of which the effects abide. The rejection has been made, and its effects are inevitable. The aorist (οὐκ ἐπίστευσεν, A, etc.) is not so forcible.

οὐ πεπίστευκεν] The negative emphasizes the actual fact rather than its character (contrast ὁ μὴ πιστεύων). The choice has been made, and its consequences are manifest.

οὐ πεπίστευκεν εἰς τὴν μαρτυρίαν] The nearest parallel to this expression is Jn. ii. 23 (πολλοὶ ἐπίστευσαν εἰς τὸ ὄνομα αὐτοῦ, *i.e.* believed on Jesus as Messiah, as being that which His name implied, and were ready to follow Him as Messiah, till they discovered how different His conception of the Messianic office was from theirs). It seems to denote devotion to a person possessed of those qualities which the witness borne to him announces, or at least to the idea which is expressed in that witness.

ἣν μεμαρτύρηκεν κ.τ.λ.] The phrases of ver. 9 are repeated for emphasis ; each point is dwelt upon. The witness has been borne, once for all ; it cannot be ignored or set aside. It has been borne by God Himself, in a case where His word alone can be final, as it concerns His own Son. In the writer's view there can be no excuse for refusing to accept evidence which is so clear and satisfactory. Cf. Rothe, "If God did not will that men should believe on Jesus, He led men into a terrible temptation. So if we would keep our conception of God pure, we must ascribe this intention to Him in His ordering of the world. We generally put forward prominently whatever tells against Faith, but leave on one side what speaks for it. We ought first to answer satisfactorily the question, how it could be possible that this Faith should so widely permeate humanity before we investigate the force of our doubts, and then we should rest assured that Christianity is *non sine numine*"; a striking comment, even if it can hardly be said to be called out by the exact expressions of the text.

om. totum comma *I*ᵃ ³⁹⁷ᶠᶠᶠᶠ (96) | του θεου] om. **arm-cod.** | την μαρ-τυριαν ℵ B K L P al. longe. plur. cat. sah. syr. arm. Cyr. Thphyl. Oec. Aug.]+του θεου A al. plus¹² vg. cop. aeth. :+*eius* m. | αυτω A B K L P al. fere.⁵⁴ cat. Thphyl.] εαυτω ℵ al. muᵘⁱᵈ Cyr. Oec. | μη]om. *I*ᵃ ¹⁷⁵ (319) | τω θεω ℵ B K L al. longe. plur. cat. **boh-codd.** syr. Cyr. Thphyl. Oec. Aug. Vig.]τω υιω A 5. 27. 29. 66** al. plus¹² vg. syr. : τω υιω του θῦ 56 sah. arm. **boh-ed.** *filio eius* aeth. : Iesu Christo m : om. am.* | αυτον] *deum* m sah. | ου πεπιστευκεν ℵ B K L P etc.] ουκ επιστευκεν ℵ : ουκ επιστευσεν A 5. 33. 34 dˢᶜʳ | εις 2°—ην] *Deo qui* **arm-cod.** | εμαρτυρηκεν ℵ | om. ο θεος 4 dˢᶜʳ jˢᶜʳ vg. codd. aeth. Cyr. Aug. Vig.

11. At last the witness, some of the essential characteristics of which have been already described, is actually defined. So far the writer has only taught his readers that it is Divine witness, borne by a father to his son, and that those who believe on the son have it in themselves, as a possession which experience has made part of themselves. Now he definitely states in what it consists. God bore witness to His Son when He gave life to men,—that higher spiritual life which they can realize and make their own only in so far as they unite themselves to Jesus, the Christ, the Son of God.

αὕτη . . . ὅτι] Cf. Jn. iii. 19 (αὕτη δέ ἐστιν ἡ κρίσις, ὅτι τὸ φῶς ἐλήλυθεν κ.τ.λ.); 1 Jn. v. 14, αὕτη ἐστὶν ἡ παρρησία . . . ὅτι ἐάν τι αἰτώμεθα . . . ἀκούει ἡμῶν. The constructions with ἵνα, and with the nominative, are rather common in S. John.

The witness which God bore consisted in the fact that He gave life to men, by sending His Son that men might have life in Him. Cf. Jn. x. 10, ἐγὼ ἦλθον ἵνα ζωὴν ἔχωσιν καὶ περισσὸν ἔχωσιν. The sending of the Son on a mission, truly character-ized by the Water of the Baptism and the Blood shed on the Cross, and of which the object was to implant a new life in men, was the witness borne by God to the nature and character of Jesus of Nazareth.

ζωὴν αἰώνιον] The anarthrous phrase emphasizes character or quality. The gift was something which is best described as "spiritual life."

ἔδωκεν] The tense emphasizes the fact, apart from its conse-quences. The reference is to the historic fact of the mission of Him who came by Water and by Blood.

ἡμῖν] We Christians.   The gift of life is a witness only where
it has been received.

καὶ αὕτη ἡ ζωὴ κ.τ.λ.] This clause is part of the "witness,"
not an additional statement made about the life.   The witness
is the gift of a life which is *in* the Son.

εδωκεν] δεδωκεν 69. 99 aˢᶜʳ lˢᶜʳ | ο θεος B 31. 3⁸. 137 hˢᶜʳ syrᵖ]
post ημιν ℵ A K L P al. pler. cat. vg. syr. arm. | αυτη]+εστιν A | om.
εστιν A 100.

12. This verse explains more fully the last clause of the
preceding verse.   It is probably of the nature of an appeal to
the reader's experience.   Those who lived with Christ on earth
found that they gained from Him a new power which transformed their life into a new and higher life.   And the later
generations had similar experience by which to judge, though
they had not actually companied with Him during His life on
earth.

ὁ μὴ ἔχων κ.τ.λ.] In the negative statement there are two
slight changes which have their significance: (1) The addition
of τοῦ θεοῦ to τὸν υἱόν.   God is the source of life.   The Son of
God alone can give it to men.   He that cannot gain it from that
source cannot find it.   (2) The position of τὴν ζωήν, which is
placed before the verb, and thus becomes more emphatic.
Whatever else the man may have in the way of higher endow-
ments, spiritual life is not within his grasp.   In the positive
statement the emphasis was laid on the actual possession (ἔχει
τὴν ζωήν).   We have here another close parallel with the Gospel
(see Jn. iii. 36).

ὁ μὴ ἔχων] The negative (μή) generalizes the statement.   A
class of men is described who are distinguished by this
characteristic.

τον υιον 1°]+του θεου 8. 25. 34. 69 aˢᶜʳ boh-codd. | την ζωην 1°]
τον υιον 31: ζωην αιωνιον Iᵃ ᵟ⁴⁵⁹ (489):+αυτου O⁴⁶ (154) Iᶜ ³⁶⁴ (137) | om.
του θεου vg. (am. demid.) arm-codd. Aug. Tert. | την ζωην 2°] post
εχει 2° Iᵇ ᵟ³⁷⁰ (1149):+αυτου O⁴⁶ Iᶜ ³⁶⁴.

13-17. I have written thus about belief in Jesus as the Son
of God, and the witness of the Spirit, and the witness of God,
which consists in the life which He gave to men through Jesus
Christ, in order that you might feel assurance as to the possession
of true life, you who believe in Jesus who is the Son of God.
Such confidence is realized in prayer, in knowing by experience
that, whenever we ask anything of God according to His will, He
hears our prayer.   And if we are thus conscious that God has
heard, we already possess, in anticipation, the thing we asked
for.   The Almighty Sovereign has said, "Let it be," there is no
further doubt about the matter, even though actual possession

may be delayed for long years. This is more clearly seen in intercession for the brethren. If any man see his fellow-Christian sinning, so long as his sinning is not such as leads inevitably to final separation from Christ and the life which God gives in Him, he will naturally intercede for him, and will gain life for him, even if it be long delayed, in the case of all whose sin is not unto death. There is sin which must lead, if persisted in, to final exclusion from life. I do not say that this comes within the sphere of Christian intercession. But in any case there is full scope for intercession. For all unrighteousness is sin, and there is such a thing as sin which does not necessarily lead to final exclusion from life.

ταῦτα ἔγραψα] Cf. ii. 26, where the reference is clearly to the preceding section about the False Teachers. Cf. also ii. 14, which the triple ἔγραψα probably refers to that part of the Epistle which had already been written. The present verse does not really present an exact parallel to the conclusion of the Gospel (Jn. xx. 31) which immediately precedes the appendix (ch. xxi.). Even if the reference is to the whole Gospel and not to the σημεῖα recorded in ch. xx., that reference is determined by the preceding words (ἃ οὐκ ἔστιν γεγραμμένα ἐν τῷ βιβλίῳ τούτῳ). Here it would seem most natural to refer the words to the preceding section of the Epistle (v. 1–12), in which the writer has put forward his view of Faith in Jesus, the Christ, the Son of God, as the necessary condition of the realization of that spiritual life which God has given to men through Jesus Christ, and which again is the real witness of God to the nature and character of His Son. The following explanation of ὑμῖν as those who believe in the *name* of the Son of God, makes the reference to the whole of this section almost certain.

ὑμῖν κ.τ.λ.] For the separation of the explanatory clause (τοῖς πιστεύουσιν κ.τ.λ.), cf. ver. 16, δώσει αὐτῷ ζωήν, τοῖς ἁμαρτάνουσιν μὴ πρὸς θάνατον, where the change in number creates a still greater strangeness of expression, and Jn. i. 12, ἔδωκεν αὐτοῖς ἐξουσίαν τέκνα θεοῦ γενέσθαι, τοῖς πιστεύουσιν εἰς τὸ ὄνομα αὐτοῦ.

This separation of τοῖς πιστεύουσιν κ.τ.λ. from ὑμῖν has led to several attempts to improve the text: (1) The clause τοῖς πιστεύουσιν . . . θεοῦ has been added immediately after ὑμῖν in the *Receptus*. (2) This clause has been retained in its proper place; but for τοῖς πιστεύουσιν has been substituted (a) the nominative, οἱ πιστεύοντες, or (b) a second final clause, καὶ ἵνα πιστεύητε. The nominative (2a) is found with and without the insertion of a clause, τοῖς πιστεύουσιν, etc., immediately after ὑμῖν. Thus, on the assumption that the reading of B (ὑμῖν ἵνα εἰδῆτε ὅτι ζωὴν ἔχετε αἰώνιον τοῖς πιστεύουσιν κ.τ.λ.) is original, the genesis of the other variants can be easily explained. The parallels quoted

above show that it presents a text completely in harmony with
the writer's style.

ἵνα εἰδῆτε] Cf. ii. 1, ἵνα μὴ ἁμάρτητε, and iii. 24, ἐν τούτῳ
γινώσκομεν. There are many signs in the Epistle of the writer's
consciousness that his readers' loss of their first enthusiasm and
zeal for the Christian faith had led to their feeling uncertain
about their position. They lacked "assurance."

εἰδῆτε] The knowledge which they need must be intuitive.
If they realize who and what the Christ is, and the relation in
which they stand to Him, they will at once "perceive and know"
that they are in possession of life.

πιστεύουσιν εἰς τὸ ὄνομα] Cf. ver. 10 and Jn. ii. 23. The
phrase must imply devotion to a person possessed of the qualities
which his name denotes. It is unlikely that πιστεύειν is used
with the two constructions (c. dat., εἰς c. acc.) in the same passage
in exactly the same sense. Here the full force of the construction with εἰς is needed to bring out the sense. The knowledge follows as a matter of course where the self-surrender is
complete.

ταυτα] pr. και Γ^{c 258} (56) | εγραψα] post υμιν H^{δ6} (Ψ) | υμιν ℵ A B h 5.
6. 13^{uid} 29. 66**. 81. 142. 162 vg. sah. cop. syr. arm. aeth. Cassiod.]+τοις
πιστευουσιν εις το ονομα του υιου του θεου K L P al. pler. cat. Thphy!.
Oec. :+τοις πιστευουσιν 126 | εχετε A B al. sat. mu. cat. vg. syr^p Cassiod.]
habemus arm-codd. : post αιωνιον ℵ K L P al. plus⁵⁰ Thphyl. Oec. | τοις
πιστευουσιν ℵ* B syr.] οι πιστευοντες ℵ^c A 5. 6. 13. 29, 66**. 81. 142. 162.
vg. cop. aeth. : και ινα πιστευητε K L P h al. pler. cat. arm. Thphyl. Occ.
(πιστευσητε h 37. 57 : om. και 57 arm-codd.).

14. καὶ αὕτη] The object of the preceding section was to
produce assurance in the readers that they were in possession of
the new life. This assurance is now described as παρρησία,
boldness or confidence, with perhaps special reference to the
original meaning of the word, absolute freedom of speech. It is
said to consist in the fact that God hears them whenever they
ask anything according to His will, *i.e.* it is realized in true
prayer, which always brings with it the consciousness that it is
heard. This is the fourth mention of the Christian's confidence;
we have it twice in relation to the Judgment (ii. 28, iv. 17), and
twice in relation to prayer (iii. 21 and here).

ἣν ἔχομεν πρὸς αὐτόν] which we have and enjoy in realized
fellowship with God. In describing relations, πρός generally
denotes that which "goes out towards," a relation realized in
active intercourse and fellowship. Cf. Jn. i. 1, 2; Mk. vi. 3 (οὐκ
εἰσὶν . . . ὧδε πρὸς ἡμᾶς; living our life).

ὅτι] One of the common constructions used by the writer to
introduce the description of that to which αὕτη, or ἐν τούτῳ, or
some such expression refers. Our παρρησία with God is based

on the fact that He hears whatsoever we ask κατὰ τὸ θέλημα αὐτοῦ.

ἐάν τι κ.τ.λ.] The necessary condition of the hearing ; subject to this condition, that it is not in opposition to the Divine will, the hearing is assured whatever the petition may be.

αἰτώμεθα] The more subjective form of expression is chosen. But it is doubtful whether any definite and clear difference in meaning between the middle and the active can be pressed. Cf. Mt. xx. 20, 22 (αἰτοῦσα . . . αἰτεῖσθε); Jn. xvi. 24, 26 (οὐκ ἠτήσατε . . . αἰτεῖτε . . . ἐν τῷ ὀνόματί μου αἰτήσεσθε).

κατὰ τὸ θέλημα αὐτοῦ] Cf. Jn. xiv. 13, ὅ τι ἂν αἰτήσητε ἐν τῷ ὀνόματί μου τοῦτο ποιήσω.

ἀκούει ἡμῶν] Cf. Jn. ix. 31, οἴδαμεν ὅτι ὁ θεὸς ἁμαρτωλῶν οὐκ ἀκούει, ἀλλ᾽ ἐάν τις θεοσεβὴς ᾖ . . . τούτου ἀκούει: Jn. xi. 41 f. ; Ps. xvi. (xvii.) 6. The word naturally includes the idea of hearing favourably.

εχωμεν A al. pauc. | οτι εαν τι ℵ B K L P al. pler. sah. syr. arm.] οτι ο εαν 13 arm.(uid.) sah. boh. : οτι αν A : οτι εαν 31*. 68. 191. 58^lect | αιτωμεθα] αιτωμεν Iᵃ δ⁶⁰² (522) θελημα] ονομα A aeth. | αυτου] του θῡ Iᵃ ⁵⁵ (236) Iᵇ ²⁰⁹f. (386).

15. ἐὰν οἴδαμεν] For the indicative after ἐάν, cf. 1 Th. iii. 8, ἐὰν στήκετε, and J. H. Moulton's Grammar of N.T. Greek, p. 168, where among others the following instances from papyri are quoted, ἐὰν δεῖ, ἐὰν οἶδεν, ἐὰν δ᾽ εἰσίν, ἐὰν φαίνεται.

Our consciousness that we are heard in whatsoever we ask, the necessary condition not being repeated, brings with it a consciousness of possession. In the certainty of anticipation there is a kind of possession of that which has been granted, though our actual entering upon possession may be indefinitely delayed. God has heard the petition : the things asked for, for which we have asked not without effect (ἠτήκαμεν), are in a sense already ours. This is perhaps the most natural explanation of the verse.

But it is possible that the writer, while meditating after his wont on the subject of prayer, is trying to find expression for a view of prayer which gives a more literal meaning to the words ἔχομεν τὰ αἰτήματα. In the preceding verse he has laid stress on the fact that what he has to say applies only to such prayers as are offered κατὰ τὸ θέλημα αὐτοῦ. This excludes any prayer which is the expression of the supplicant's own wish on any subject, except in so far as it is identical with the will of God on that subject. He may therefore have thought of true prayer as including only requests for knowledge of, and acquiescence in, the will of God in the matter with which the prayer is concerned, rather than as a statement of the supplicant's wish,

accompanied by a readiness to give it up, if it is in opposition
to God's will. In the case of such prayers the supplicant can
enter into immediate and conscious possession of the thing asked
for, whether the answer to his own formulated or felt wish be yes
or no. The statement may be literally true οἴδαμεν ὅτι τὰ
αἰτήματα ἔχομεν. Cf. Mk. xi. 24.

αἰτήματα] Here only in the Johannine writings. Cf. Lk.
xxiii. 24, ἐπέκρινεν γενέσθαι τὸ αἴτημα αὐτῶν : Ph. iv. 6, τὰ αἰτήματα
ὑμῶν γνωριζέσθω πρὸς τὸν θεόν.

ἠτήκαμεν] The voice and tense emphasize the objective fact
and its results.

ἀπ᾽ αὐτοῦ] The Received Text has altered this into the
commoner παρ᾽ αὐτοῦ. Cf., however, 1 Jn. i. 5, ii. 20, 27, iv. 21 ;
3 Jn 7. In the Gospel παρά is the commoner usage in similar
contexts. Thus the reading of ℵ B is truer to the style of the
Epistle, while the usage of the Gospel has apparently influenced
the later text.

om. και . . . ημων ℵ* A 19*. 96* | οιδαμεν 1°] ιδωμεν ℵᶜ | om. εαν 1°
vg. Did. | o] οτι Iᵃ δ457-110. δ463 (209) | εαν 2°] αν A B K al. sat. mu. Oec. |
αιτωμεθα] αιτησωμεθα Iᵃ δ353 (999?) | εχωμεν H δ2*. δ6 (ℵ) Iᵃ 7. 70. δ353
| αιτηματα]+ημων Iᵃ 175 (319) sah | ητησαμεν Iᵃ 200f. 64 (83) Aᵖρ 20 (36)
Iᵇ 78ff (—) (ητηκαμεν expl. sahᵇ) | απ ℵ B 5. 13 al.⁵] παρ A K L P al.
pler. cat. | απ αυτου] a *Domino* sah.

16, 17. Intercession naturally finds its most obvious sphere
in the new society itself. The writer therefore goes on to state
its possibilities and its limitations. If any member of the body
sees that his brother is committing sin, so long as it be not of
such a character as must inevitably lead to final separation from
the life of God, it goes without saying that he will exercise his
power of intercession for him. And such is the power of intercession that he will be able to gain for him life, in every case
where the sin is of the character described. There *is* such a
thing as sin unto death, which tends to final separation from
God, and which if persisted in must inevitably lead to that
result. It is not clear that in such a case appeal can be made
to the Common Father on behalf of a fellow-Christian. For
such an one it may be that prayer can only be offered as for one
who has forfeited his Christian privileges. But all injustice,
every failure to maintain in our action right relations with God
or with man, is sin. There is sin which is not of the fatal and
final character described above. So there is plenty of scope
left for the exercise of brotherly intercession.

ἁμαρτάνοντα ἁμαρτίαν] cf. Lv. v. 6, περὶ τῆς ἁμαρτίας αὐτοῦ ἧς
ἥμαρτεν : Ezk. xviii. 24, ἐν ταῖς ἁμαρτίαις αὐτοῦ αἷς ἥμαρτεν. The
accusative is added here because of the qualifying clause which
succeeds (μὴ πρὸς θάνατον). It does not strengthen the verb.

The present participle, "sinning a sin" (RV.), perhaps indicates seeing the sinner ἐπαυτοφώρῳ.

ἐάν τις ἴδῃ] The subjunctive with ἐάν simply states the possibility.

μὴ πρὸς θάνατον] The μή is naturally used after ἐάν; it can hardly be pressed to make the judgment subjective, that of the τις.

αἰτήσει] The future is used either for the imperative, or because it is assumed as a matter of course that the brother will intercede for the brother.

δώσει] The subject of the verb may be either God, or the man who intercedes. The abrupt change of subject which the former view would require is perhaps decisive against it. And in virtue of his intercession and its power the Christian may be said to "give" life. Cf. Ja. v. 15, ἡ εὐχὴ τῆς πίστεως σώσει τὸν κάμνοντα, and (ver. 20) σώσει ψυχὴν αὐτοῦ ἐκ θανάτου.

τοῖς ἁμαρτάνουσιν] For the construction, cf. ver. 13.

ἔστιν ἁμαρτία πρὸς θάνατον] The phrase is probably suggested by the Old Testament conception of sins רמה ביד (Nu. xv. 30, cf. 31 וְהַנֶּפֶשׁ אֲשֶׁר תַּעֲשֶׂה בְּיָד רָמָה . . . וְנִכְרְתָה הַנֶּפֶשׁ הַהוּא מִקֶּרֶב עַמָּהּ). Deliberate and wilful transgression as opposed to sins committed unwittingly, were punished by the cutting off of the sinner "from among his people." We may also compare Nu. xviii. 22, where it is said that after the setting apart of the Levites for the service of the Tabernacle, any of the people who came near to the Tabernacle of the Congregation would be guilty of sin and die, וְלֹא־יִקְרְבוּ עוֹד בְּנֵי יִשְׂרָאֵל אֶל־אֹהֶל מוֹעֵד לָשֵׂאת חֵטְא לָמוּת, which is translated in the LXX, καὶ οὐ προσελεύσονται ἔτι οἱ υἱοὶ Ἰσραὴλ εἰς τὴν σκηνὴν τοῦ μαρτυρίου λαβεῖν ἁμαρτίαν θανατηφόρον, with which may be compared the Targum (Onk.) לְקַבָּלָא חוֹבָה לִמְמָת. It is probable that in Rabbinic thought the words למות חטא were taken closely together, though this is against the meaning and pointing of the Hebrew text. There may therefore be a direct connection between the verse and the words in Nu. xviii. 22. Cf. the note on ver. 17.

The form of expression would seem to indicate that the author is not thinking of one particular sin, definite though un-named. "There is such a thing as sin which leads to death." Such a *state* of sin may find expression in different acts. In the author's view any sin which involves a deliberate rejection of the claims of the Christ may be described as "unto death." If *persisted* in it must lead to final separation from the Divine life. Πρὸς θάνατον must, of course, denote a tendency in the direction of death, and not an attained result. The whole phrase thus suggests a "kind of sinning" (if the phrase may be allowed) rather than any definite act of sin, which leads inevitably in a certain direction. Its only possible issue, if it is persisted in, must be spiritual death. Deliberate rejection of Christ and His claims was probably most prominent in the writer's thought. It is, of course, possible that in connection with what he has said in the earlier part of this chapter about the witness of the Spirit, he may have had in view the saying of the Lord recorded in Mk. iii. 29 (Mt. xii. 32 ; Lk. xii. 10). But nothing in this passage offers any clear proof of such a connection.

οὐ περὶ ἐκείνης κ.τ.λ.] The writer does not forbid such intercession. He merely abstains from commanding it. Such cases lay outside the normal sphere of Christian intercession. They must be left to God alone. If the meaning often attributed to ἐρωτᾶν as distinguished from αἰτεῖν, "the request which is based upon fellowship, upon a likeness of position," is to be pressed, the words contain their own justification. Prayer of "brother for brother, as such, addressed to the Common Father," is out of the question where brotherhood has been practically renounced. But this interpretation, which emphasizes not that which the petitioner has in common with him to whom he makes his request, but rather with those on whose behalf he prays, is very doubtful. And the distinction itself between αἰτεῖν, the seeking of the inferior from the superior, and ἐρωτᾶν, which is said to imply a certain equality or familiarity between the parties (see Trench, *Synonyms*, § xl.), is far from being certainly established. The distinction drawn by Dr. Ezra Abbott between αἰτεῖν, "to ask for something to be given (not done), the emphasis being on the thing asked," and ἐρωτᾶν, "to request a person to do (rarely give) something, the emphasis being thus on the person requested," is perhaps more naturally applicable here. We may hesitate to entreat God to act on behalf of one who has practically renounced his allegiance. But the difference in meaning and usage between αἰτεῖν and ἐρωτᾶν is not very clear. And the evidence of the papyri, while it shows clearly that ἐρωτᾶν was the natural word to use in invitations, and to that extent supports the former of the two distinctions which have been maintained, does not help much in settling the question.

ιδη] ειδη 13 vg. Hil. Aug. : οιδεν *I*ᵃ ¹⁷⁵ (319) | αμαρτανοντα] αμαρτη-σαντα *I*ᵇ ⁸³⁶⁸ (823) | μη ¹⁰] την *I*ᵃ ⁵⁵² (217) | αιτησει και δωσει] αιτησις και δωσις ℵ* : *petat* (*petet* fu. : *petit* am. harl.) *et dabitur* vg. Cf. Tert. sah. cop. : *petat pro eo et dabit . . . deus* tol. | δωσει] *dabunt* boh | ζωην]+ *eternam* boh-codd. | τοις αμαρτανουσιν μη προς θανατον] τοις μη αμαρτανουσιν αμαρτιαν μη προς θανατον A : *peccanti non ad uitum* vg. : *sed non his qui usque ad mortem peccant* tol. | αιτησει]+τον θν *I*ᵃ ²⁵⁰ᶠ (133) | αυτω] post ζωην *I*ᵃ ⁵⁰² (116) *I*ᵇ ³⁹⁶ᶠ (?? om. αυτω) ³⁶⁵⁻³⁹⁸ *I*ᶜ ²⁰⁸. ¹¹⁶ (307) τοις . . . θανατον 2°] τω μη προς θανατον αμαρτανοντι *I*ᶜ ³⁶⁴ (137) | αμαρτια] pr. η

*I*ᵃ ¹⁷³ (15ᶜ) | ου περι] υπερ *I*ᶜ ³⁶⁴ (137) | ου] pr. και 13. 57ˡᵉᶜᵗ 58ˡᵉᶜᵗ | ερωτηση] ερωτησει Κ*: ερωτησης Νᵒ arm. : pr. τις 15. 26. 36. 43. 98. 101 dˢᶜʳ vg. syr. Clem. Or. Tert.

17. πᾶσα ἀδικία] Unrighteousness is one manifestation of sin, just as lawlessness is another. The most natural interpretation of the verse is that which sees in it a statement of the wide scope which exists for the exercise of Christian intercession, in spite of certain necessary limitations of its sphere. Windisch suggests that the difficulty might be removed by placing ver. 17 before 16c (ἔστιν ἁμαρτία πρὸς θάνατον).

καί ἐστιν ἁμαρτία οὐ πρὸς θάνατον] The fact is stated objectively (οὐ). The distinction bet.veen sins "unto death" and "not unto death" is illustrated by Schöttgen from Rabbinic writers. His first quotation, however, from Yoma 50. 1, is not convincing (חטאת שמתו בעליה למיתה חטאת ציבור היא ולא למיתה), as חטאת seems to refer to the animal offered or set apart as a sin-offering (see Goldschmid). The expression in Sota 48. 1, שׁ בו עצון מיתה, offers a more satisfactory parallel.

παντα [? πασα] pr. αρα *I*ᵃ ⁰⁴⁵⁴· ¹⁷⁵ (794) | αδικια] post αμαρτια 1ᵒ *H* ⁸⁶ (Ψ): *in iustitia* arm-ed. | om. ου 13. 67**. vg. sah. syr. arm. aeth. Tert.

18. οἴδαμεν] Cf. iii. 2, 14. The knowledge is intuitive. That which is stated follows immediately from the very nature of God, and of the life which He has given to men.

πᾶς ὁ γεγεννημένος κ.τ.λ.] Cf. iii. 9. The perfect expresses the abiding results of the "begetting." In so far as they are realized they exclude the possibility of sin. Following his usual custom, the writer states the truth absolutely, without stating the modifications which become necessary as it is applied to individual cases in actual experience. The preceding section as well as the early part of the Epistle sufficiently shows that he recognized the actual fact of sin in Christians.

ὁ γεννηθεὶς ἐκ τοῦ θεοῦ] If the reading ἑαυτόν be adopted, the meaning must be that he who has once for all experienced the new birth keeps himself from the evil in virtue of the power which the new birth places within his reach. In the first clause of the verse the permanent consequences of the initial act are emphasized; here the stress is laid on the act itself. The fact of the new birth enables him to keep himself free from the attacks of the evil one. This sense is not badly expressed in the paraphrase of the Vulgate, "sed generatio Dei conservat eum," a rendering which may have been influenced by the similar passage in iii. 9, πᾶς ὁ γεγεννημένος ἐκ τοῦ θεοῦ ἁμαρτίαν οὐ ποιεῖ, ὅτι σπέρμα αὐτοῦ ἐν αὐτῷ μένει. It is found in Greek (ἡ γέννησις) in two cursives.

The reading, however, of B and the original hand of A (αὐτόν) has strong claims to be regarded as original. It is difficult to see why ἑαυτόν should ever have been altered into αὐτόν, which is apparently far more difficult, unless, indeed, the change was due to accidental carelessness at a very early stage in the transmission of the text. And the evidence of the Latin, supported as it now is by two Greek cursives, is of considerable importance in favour of this reading (*generatio Dei conseruat eum* vg., cf. *natiuitas Dei custodit illum* Chromatius).

If αὐτόν is original, it can hardly be explained, as Weiss suggests, by referring the phrase ὁ γεννηθεὶς ἐκ τοῦ θεοῦ "directly to the fact of the begetting from God, which keeps him who has experienced it." This would be a very strained expedient. It is still more unnatural to refer αὐτόν to God, as Karl does (*Der aus Gott gezeugte hält ihn (seine Gebote)*. Τηρεῖ αὐτόν cannot mean "observes His commandments." With an accusative of the person τηρεῖν always has the sense in the N.T. of watching or guarding, in a friendly or hostile spirit. It would be far better to read αὐτόν (cf. Jn. ii. 24, οὐκ ἐπίστευεν αὐτόν).

But no explanation of the change from the perfect to the aorist participle is altogether satisfactory, if both are referred to the same person, *i.e.* the man who has experienced the new birth. The interpretation, therefore, which refers ὁ γεννηθεὶς ἐκ τοῦ θεοῦ to Christ deserves serious consideration. It is true that the expression γεννηθῆναι ἐκ τοῦ θεοῦ is not used elsewhere in the Johannine writings of Christ, unless the Western variant in Jn. i. 13, ὃς . . . ἐκ θεοῦ ἐγεννήθη, for which there is interesting Patristic evidence in the second century, is to be regarded as original. We may also compare Jn. xviii. 37, ἐγὼ εἰς τοῦτο γεγέννημαι καὶ εἰς τοῦτο ἐλήλυθα εἰς τὸν κόσμον, and the language of the Messianic Psalm, ἐγὼ σήμερον γεγέννηκά σε, which has some claim to represent the true text in Lk. iii. 22. Thus interpreted the passage has a fairly close parallel in Jn. xvii. 15, ἵνα τηρήσῃς αὐτοὺς ἐκ τοῦ πονηροῦ, and ver. 12, ἐγὼ ἐτήρουν αὐτοὺς ἐν τῷ ὀνόματί σου ᾧ δέδωκάς μοι καὶ ἐφύλαξα καὶ οὐδεὶς ἐξ αὐτῶν ἀπώλετο. Cf. Apoc. iii. 10, κἀγώ σε τηρήσω ἐκ τῆς ὥρας τοῦ πειρασμοῦ.

It may be noticed that τηρεῖν is never used in the Johannine writings with the accusative of the reflex pronoun, or in the N.T. with such an accusative absolutely. Cf. 2 Co. xi. 9, ἀβαρῆ ἐμαυτὸν ἐτήρησα: I Ti. v. 22, σεαυτὸν ἁγνὸν τήρει: Ja. i. 27, ἄσπιλον ἑαυτὸν τηρεῖν: Jude 21, ἑαυτοὺς ἐν ἀγάπῃ θεοῦ τηρήσατε. An interesting article in support of the reference to Christ was contributed by Wohlenberg to the *Neue Kirchliche Zeitung* in 1902 (p. 233 ff.).

ἅπτεται] The word probably suggests the idea of laying hold of in order to harm. Cf. Gn. xxvi 11; Jos. ix. 25 (19); Jer. iv.

10; 4 Mac. x. 4; Ps. civ. (cv.) 15.   Schlatter quotes from Siphre
to Nu. vi. 26, אֵין הַשָּׂטָן נוֹגֵעַ בְּהֶם.

οιδαμεν] οιδα *I*ᵃ ³⁹⁷ (96) : + δε *I*ᵇ ³⁷⁰ (353) | γεγενημενος 99 jˢᶜʳ | ο γεννηθεις
εκ] η γεννησις *I*ᶜ ¹¹⁴· ¹¹⁶ (335) : *generatio* vg. | γεννηθεις] γεγεννημενος
*I*ᵃ ⁷ᵗ· *I*ᶜ ¹⁷⁴ (252) | τηρει] μαρτυρει | *I*ᵇ δ⁶⁰² (522) | αυτον A* B 105 vg.]
εαυτον **ℵ** Aᶜᵒⁿ K L P al. pler. cat. Or. Eph. Thphyl. Oec.

19. οἴδαμεν] Cf. the notes on ver. 18.   What has been stated
generally (πᾶς ὁ γεγεννημένος κ.τ.λ.) is now applied to the readers
themselves, with whom the writer identifies himself (οἴδαμεν).

Εἶναι ἐκ τοῦ θεοῦ denotes, as elsewhere in the Johannine
writings, the state which is the consequence of the γεννηθῆναι ἐκ
τοῦ θεοῦ.   Cf. Jn. viii. 47; 1 Jn. iv. 4–6.

καί] The clause is probably to be regarded as added independently, and not as subordinate to the ὅτι.

ὁ κόσμος ὅλος] The world as a whole, in its entirety, if the
expression is to be distinguished from ὅλου τοῦ κόσμου (ii. 2), "the
whole world."

ἐν τῷ πονηρῷ] The preceding ὁ πονηρός determines that
this is masculine and not neuter, as Rothe suggests.   For
the construction, cf. Soph. *O. C.* 247, ἐν ὑμῖν ὡς θεῷ κείμεθα
τλάμονες.   Christians are conscious, immediately and intuitively,
of the difference between the power which dominates their
life and that which controls absolutely the life, intellectual and
moral, of the world, *i.e.* of the world of men so far as they
remain estranged from God.

οιδαμεν] + δε 104 cˢᶜʳ boh-ed. | ολος] om. boh-cod. | εν] επι 31.

20. ἥκει] Cf. Jn. viii. 42, ἐξῆλθον καὶ ἥκω.   The Christ, the
Son of God, has fulfilled His mission.   He has done the work
which is characterized by His name, and the effects of it are
with us still.

διάνοιαν] Cf. Eph. iv. 18, ἐσκοτισμένοι τῇ διανοίᾳ (in Eph. i.
18, quoted by Holtzmann, the true text has καρδίας not διανοίας),
1 P. i. 13, τὰς ὀσφύας τῆς διανοίας ὑμῶν: Pr. ii. 10, ἔλθῃ ἡ σοφία
εἰς τὴν διάνοιαν.   The word is not found elsewhere in the Johannine writings.   The faculty of knowing, or discerning, seems to
be what it expresses.   It is worth noting that γνῶσις also is
absent from the Johannine writings, and νοῦς occurs only twice
(Rev. xiii. 18, xvii. 9).

ἵνα γινώσκομεν] The indicative, or at least the short o, is
well supported here, as in Jn. xvii. 3; ἵνα γινώσκουσι receives
considerable support (A D G L Y Δ Λ 33), and in that case the
form can hardly be regarded as a "corrupt pronunciation" of
the subjunctive.   For ἵνα with the future indicative, cf. Mk. xv. 20,
ἵνα σταυρώσουσιν (*v.l.*): Lk. xiv. 10, ἵνα . . . ἐρεῖ σοι: xx. 10, ἵνα

. . . δώσουσιν αὐτῷ: Jn. vii. 3, ἵνα καὶ οἱ μαθηταί σου θεωρήσουσιν:
xvii. 2, ἵνα . . . δώσει (v.l.) αὐτοῖς: Ac. v. 15, ἵνα . . . ἐπισκιάσει
(v.l.): xxi. 24, ἵνα ξυρήσονται: 1 Co. ix. 18, ἵνα . . . θήσω: (?) ix.
21, ἵνα κερδανῶ: xiii. 3, ἵνα καυθήσομαι (v.l.): Gal. ii. 4, ἵνα ἡμᾶς
καταδουλώσουσιν: 1 P. iii. 1, ἵνα . . . ἄνευ λόγου κερδηθήσονται:
Apoc. iii. 9, ἵνα ἥξουσιν καὶ προσκυνήσουσιν: vi. 4, ἵνα ἀλλήλους
σφάξουσιν: vi. 11, ἵνα ἀναπαύσονται (v.l.): viii. 3, ἵνα δώσει: ix. 5, ἵνα
βασανισθήσονται: xiii. 12, ἵνα προσκυνήσουσιν: xiv. 13, ἵνα ἀναπαή-
σονται: xxii. 14, ἵνα ἔσται: ix. 4, ἵνα μὴ ἀδικήσουσι: ix. 20, ἵνα μὴ
προσκυνήσουσιν.   For its use with the present indicative the evidence is less clear, as in most cases there are variant readings. Cf.
(besides Jn. xvii. 3) Jn. iv. 15, ἵνα . . . μηδὲ διέρχομαι (v.l.): v. 20,
ἵνα ὑμεῖς θαυμάζετε (v.l.): Gal. iv. 17, ἵνα αὐτοὺς ζηλοῦτε: Tit. ii.
4, ἵνα σωφρονίζουσι (v.l.): Apoc. xii. 6, ἵνα ἐκεῖ τρέφουσιν αὐτήν
(v.l.): Gal. vi. 12, ἵνα μὴ διώκονται (v.l.): Apoc. xiii. 17, ἵνα μή τις
δύναται (v.l.); in 2 P. i. 10 the reading is found in some MSS,
σπουδάσατε ἵνα διὰ τῶν καλῶν ὑμῶν ἔργων βεβαίαν ὑμῶν τὴν κλῆσιν
καὶ ἐκλογὴν ποιεῖσθε.   The same uncertainty is found in sub-
Apostolic writers.   Preuschen quotes Barn. vi. 5 ; Ign. *Eph.* iv. 2 ;
Tr. viii. 2 (*Handwörterbuch*, p. 530). On the whole, the evidence
seems to point to traces of the occasional use of a vulgarism
subsequently corrected.   There is much to be said for Professor
Deissmann's view, that the Fourth Gospel is "ein echtes Volks-
buch" (*Beiträge zur Weiterentwicklung der Religion*, p. 131).

ἵνα κ.τ.λ.] The clause is dependent on διάνοιαν, which it
explains, not on δέδωκεν.

τὸν ἀληθινόν] *i.e.* God, the One who alone completely corresponds to His "Name," in whom the idea is completely
realized. The attempt to make God the subject of δέδωκεν,
notwithstanding the preceding ἥκει, and to interpret τὸν ἀληθινόν
of Christ, hardly needs serious refutation, in spite of the support
which it receives from Bengel.

The God who "fulfils the highest conception" of Godhead
can only be known through the faculty of discernment given to
men by His own Son, by means of His historic appearance on
earth. The writer is already mentally contrasting the true with
the false conceptions of God against which he warns his readers
in the last verse of the Epistle.

καὶ ἐσμὲν ἐν τῷ ἀληθινῷ] ἀληθινός must have the same
reference here as in the preceding clause. It can only refer to
God.   The nearest parallel to the language of this verse is to be
found in Jn. xvii. 3, ἵνα γινώσκουσίν σε τὸν μόνον ἀληθινὸν θεὸν καὶ
ὃν ἀπέστειλας Ἰησοῦν Χριστόν: 22 f. ἵνα ὦσιν ἓν καθὼς ἡμεῖς ἕν.
ἐγὼ ἐν αὐτοῖς καὶ σὺ ἐν ἐμοί, ἵνα ὦσιν τετελειωμένοι εἰς ἕν.   There
is really no difficulty in supposing that a writer who makes use
of the phrase ἔχειν τὸν πατέρα should use the words εἶναι ἐν τῷ

ἀληθινῷ with reference to God. This interpretation is supported by the following clause. To interpret the words ἐν τῷ υἱῷ αὐτοῦ Ἰησοῦ Χριστῷ as being in apposition to ἐν τῷ ἀληθινῷ, appended in order to leave no doubt as to the change of reference in τῷ ἀληθινῷ, is far less natural than to find in these words (ἐν τῷ υἱῷ κ.τ.λ.) a description of the method in which union with God is realized. The Thebaic (Sahidic) version has "in the Life" for ἐν τῷ ἀληθινῷ: with which should be compared the reading of some MSS of the Bohairic (see the critical note).

ἐν τῷ υἱῷ αὐτοῦ Ἰ. Χ.] The difficulty of regarding these words as being in apposition to ἐν τῷ ἀληθινῷ, added so as to make it clear who is meant by that phrase, has been already stated so far as it affects the meaning of ὁ ἀληθινός in this verse. The grammatical difficulty of such an explanation is also very great. Αὐτοῦ naturally refers to the immediately preceding τῷ ἀληθινῷ. To pass over the natural antecedent and make it refer to τὸν ἀληθινόν, which is not even the subject of the principal sentence, is extremely harsh.

Interpreted naturally, the words supply a needed explanation. It is in virtue of their relation to Christ, and their fellowship with Him, that Christians realize their fellowship with God. Cf. 1 Jn. i. 3, καὶ ἡ κοινωνία δὲ ἡ ἡμετέρα μετὰ τοῦ πατρὸς καὶ μετὰ τοῦ υἱοῦ αὐτοῦ Ἰησοῦ Χριστοῦ. If the Christ of S. John says (vi. 44), οὐδεὶς δύναται ἐλθεῖν πρός με ἐὰν μὴ ὁ πατὴρ ὁ πέμψας με ἑλκύσῃ αὐτόν, He also says (xiv. 6), οὐδεὶς ἔρχεται πρὸς τὸν πατέρα εἰ μὴ δι' ἐμοῦ.

οὗτός ἐστιν ὁ ἀληθινὸς θεός] If τῷ ἀληθινῷ be taken as referring to Christ, these words must also refer to Him. And in earlier times they were usually so interpreted. But it is hardly true to say that this interpretation is logically an absolute necessity (Weiss). It might, no doubt, be mere tautology to say of the ἀληθινός that He is ὁ ἀληθινὸς θεός. But οὗτος in the Gospel and Epistles is not used merely to avoid the repetition of a name. It seems often to refer to the previous subject, *as previously described.* Here God has been described as truly made known in Jesus Christ. The God who completely fulfils the highest conception of Godhead is the God who has been revealed in Jesus Christ, as contrasted with all false conceptions of God, against which the readers are warned in the next verse. For this use of οὗτος, cf. Jn. i. 2, οὗτος ἦν ἐν ἀρχῇ πρὸς τὸν θεόν, the Logos who can be described as θεός; i. 7, οὗτος ἦλθεν εἰς μαρτυρίαν, the *man sent* contrasted with the Divine Logos; i 33, οὗτός ἐστιν ὁ βαπτίζων, He on whom the Spirit descended *and remained*; iii. 2, οὗτος ἦλθεν πρὸς αὐτόν, the ruler of the Jews; iv. 47, the βασιλικός whose son was sick; 1 Jn ii. 22, οὗτός ἐστιν ὁ ἀντίχριστος, he who denies that Jesus is the Christ; v. 6, οὗτός

ἐστιν ὁ ἐλθών, Jesus the Son of God; 2 Jn. 7 οὗτός ἐστιν ὁ
πλάνος καὶ ὁ ἀντίχριστος, the representative of the class of
deceivers who deny "Jesus Christ coming in flesh."

καὶ ζωὴ αἰώνιος] This addition has often been held to render
the reference of οὗτος to Christ necessary, it being regarded as
not accidental that in the Gospel it is only of Christ that it is said
that He is life (xi. 25, xiv. 6). But the language of Jn. v. 26,
ὁ πατὴρ ἔχει ζωὴν ἐν ἑαυτῷ, justifies the expression here used if it
refers to God. He is in the Johannine writings represented as
the true source of spiritual life, which He has imparted to men
in His Son. The writer would remind his readers that in spite
of the claims to higher knowledge put forward by some, it
remains true that he who hath not the Son hath not the Father.
The God whom Jesus Christ revealed is the true source of
life.

Holtzmann aptly quotes 2 Jn. 7 as proof that in the Johannine
writings οὗτος may refer to the subject of the preceding sentence
rather than to the name which has immediately preceded
(πολλοὶ πλάνοι . . . οἱ μὴ ὁμολογοῦντις Ἰ. Χ. ἐρχόμενον ἐν σαρκί.
οὗτός ἐστιν ὁ πλάνος καὶ ὁ ἀντίχριστος). The reference is naturally
to the subject uppermost in the writer's thoughts, and the
contents of the preceding verses introduced by the triple
οἴδαμεν make this plain: πᾶς ὁ γεγεννημένος ἐκ τοῦ θεοῦ . . . ἐκ
τοῦ θεοῦ ἐσμέν . . . ἵνα γινώσκομεν τὸν ἀληθινόν . . . καὶ ἐσμὲν
ἐν τῷ ἀληθινῷ. It is God—the true One—of whom we have
been begotten—of whom we are—whom Jesus Christ came to
make known—so that men could enter into fellowship with Him.

οιδαμεν δε ℵ B K al. sat. mu. cop. Thphyl. Oec.] και οιδαμεν A al.[20]
cat. m[7] vg. sah. syr. arm. Did. Cyr. : οιδαμεν L P al.[9] aeth. Cyr. Did. : om.
δε I[c 470] (229) | ηκει]+et carnem induit nostri causa et passus est et
resurrexit a mortuis; adsumpsit nos m[7] tol. Cf. Hil. quod filius dei uenit
et concarnatus est propter vos et passus est, et resurgens de mortuis
assumsit nos et dedit nobis intellectum optimum ut etc. | ο υιος] ο λογος
Did. | δεδωκεν] εδωκεν A 5. 13. 69*. 104 a[scr] c[scr] al. aliq. Did. Cyr.
| γινωσκομεν ℵ A B* L P 98. 99. 101. 180 c[scr] g[scr*] Cyr.] γιωσκωμεν B[s] K
al. pler. Did. Bas. Cyr. Thphyl. Oec. | τον αληθινον ℵ[c] B K L al. plur.] το
αληθινον ℵ* sah. Vig. Facund. : eum qui uerus est m[7]. Cf. syr. arm.
Cyr. Hil. Faustin. Fulg.]+θεον A 5. 6. 7. 8. 13. 17. 27. 40. 66**. 69. 80.
81. 98[mg] 99. 106 a[scr] d[scr] al. fere.[15] vg. boh-ed. arm[usc] aeth. Ath. Did.
Bas. Cyr. Aug. Pelag. | και εσμεν] και ωμεν 34 : et simus m[7] vg. Hil. |
εν τω αληθινω] in uita sah. : in uita et haec uita erat boh-codd. : om.
boh-ed. : in uerbo m[7] | om. εν τω 2° 33. 34. 45. 56. 162 a[scr*] vg. m[7] Did.
Bas. Cyr. | ιησου χριστω ℵ B K L P al. pler. cat. m[8] demid. tol. syr. sah.
cop. arm. aeth. Ath. Did. Hil. Aug. Pelag.] om. A 162 vg. am. fu. harl. | θεος
om. m[8] am. Hil. Vig. | ζωη αιωνιος] ζωην αιωνιον παρεχων H[86] (Ψ) : ζωη
ℵ A B 13. 34. 57. 66**. 105. 126. 180 al.[10] Did. Ath. Bas. Cyr. Euthal.]
ζωη η K a[scr] al. mu. Ath. Cyr. : η ζωη η L P 5. 31. 38. 40. 68. 69. 105.
137. 191 al.[15] cat. Ath. Cyr. Thphyl. | αιωνιος]+et resurrectio nostra m[8]
Hil. Faustin. Vig. (+in ipso Faustin.).

21. τεκνία] The writer's favourite form of address to introduce an appeal.

φυλάξατε ἑαυτά] If the use of the active with the reflexive can be regarded as "emphasizing the duty of personal effort," it is significant. The danger is great. It needs all the effort which they can make to guard against it. With the peremptory aorist imperative, cf. ἐξάρατε (1 Co. v. 13), and ἐκτινάξατε (Mk. vi. 11).

ἀπὸ τῶν εἰδώλων] All the false images of God which men have made for themselves instead of accepting the true revelation of Him given in His Son. The expression embraces all false conceptions of God. It is not exhausted by the particular conceptions of the (Gnostic) false teachers against whose views the Epistle is directed. And it is not probable that the writer intends only actual objects of pagan worship, as Zahn suggests, finding in the verse an indication of the character of the readers to whom the Epistle is addressed (cf. also Windisch, *ad loc.*). If any limited reference is necessary, it must be found in the untrue mental images fashioned by the false teachers.

φυλαξασθαι *H* δ48 (33) | εαυτα ℵ* B L h 23. 29. 31 cscr 58lect al. fere.[15]] ταυτα *H* δ6 (Ψ): εαυτους ℵc A K P al. pler. cat. Thphyl. Oec. | των] pr. παντων *H* δ6 (Ψ) | ειδωλων ℵ A B 1. 13. 27. 29. 34. 65. 66**. 68 dscr am. demid. tol. sah. boh. syr. arm. aeth.]+αμην K L P al. pler. vg. fu. harl.

SEPARATE NOTE.

The Text of 1 Jn. v. 7, 8.

μαρτυρουντες]+ εν τω ουρανω ο πατηρ ο λογος και το αγιον πνευμα και ουτοι τρεις εν εισι και τρεις εισιν οι μαρτυρουντες εν τη γη ϛ′. It is not necessary now to prove at any great length the spuriousness of this interesting but unfortunate gloss. Its style and want of conformity to the context would be sufficient to condemn it, even if it had considerable support from trustworthy authorities for the text. Without it the passage runs clearly. The threefold witness is first given, which satisfies the requirements of the law; and after the witness which is legally valid among men, is given the "greater witness" of God, which is precisely defined in ver. 9, though the exact meaning of the words is doubtful. The "heavenly witnesses" destroy the natural sequence of the passage. And the personal use of ὁ λόγος is wholly alien to the style of the Epistle, and also of the Gospel, where it is confined to the Prologue. In the earliest form in which the words appear in Greek, the absence of articles and copulae, where Greek would require their presence, betrays at once their derivation from Latin.

It is enough to recapitulate the well-known and often stated facts that the words are not found (as part of the Johannine text) (1) in any Greek manuscript with the exception of two very late MSS, obviously modified by the text of the Latin Vulgate, and in the margin of a third, the marginal note being in a seventeenth century hand; (2) in any independent Greek writer; (3) in any Latin writer earlier than Priscillian; (4) in any ancient version except in the Latin, where it is absent from the older forms of the old Latin as found in Tertullian, Cyprian, and Augustine; from the Vulgate as issued by Jerome, according to the testimony of the Codices Amiatinus and Fuldensis; and from Alcuin's revision (Codex Vallicellianus). And even when it first appears in the Vulgate, in the "Theodulfian" recension, the earthly witnesses are placed before the heavenly.

The history of the gloss has been well told by Wettstein, Tischendorf, and Westcott, from whose work the accounts in most commentaries are obviously derived. New light has been thrown on the subject in the interesting monograph of Künstle, *Das comma Joanneum auf seine Herkunft untersucht*, 1905), and some interesting suggestions as to the origin of the celebrated "Codex Britannicus," on the authority of which Erasmus in fulfilment of his rash promise introduced the clause into the text of his Third Edition, by Dr. Rendel Harris in his *History of the Leicester Codex*.

The history of the gloss itself naturally begins much earlier than the history of its introduction into the actual text of the Epistle.

The passage in Tertullian (*adv. Praxeam*, c. 25), which has often been quoted as containing an allusion to the verse, is really proof that he knew no such reading in the Epistle: "ita connexus patris in filio et filii in paraclito tres efficit cohaerentes, alterum ex altero, qui tres unum sunt, non unus, quomodo dictum est Ego et pater unum sumus, ad substantiae unitatem, non ad numeri singularitatem."

Unfortunately there is no direct quotation of the passage in Cyprian: though the citation and interpretation of 1 Jn. v. 6–8 in the pseudo-Cyprianic tract, *de rebaptismate*, c. 15, witnesses to the early Latin text, which has no trace of the heavenly witnesses. "Et spiritus est qui testimonium perhibet, quia spiritus est ueritas: quia tres testimonium perhibent, spiritus et aqua et sanguis, et isti tres (in)[1] unum sunt."

The well-known passage in Cyprian, *de Catholicae ecclesiae unitate*, c. 6, shows how easily the language of 1 Jn. v. 8 was interpreted of the Three Persons of the Trinity: "dicit Dominus Ego et pater unum sumus et iterum de Patre et Filio et Spiritu

---

[1] See von Soden, *Das Lat. N. T. in Afrika*, p. 280.

sancto scriptum est Et tres unum sunt." In favour of this, which is the natural interpretation of Cyprian's words, is the reference to him in Facundus, *pro defensione trium capit.* i. 3, who, after giving the same interpretation of the Spirit and the water and the blood, adds, "Quod tamen Ioannis apostoli testimonium b. Cyprianus, Carthaginiensis antistes et martyr, in epistola siue libro quem de unitate sanctae ecclesiae scripsit, de patre et filio et spiritu sancto dictum intelligit."

Augustine's interesting interpretation (*Contra Maximinum,* ii. 22) of 1 Jn. v. 8, which he quotes in the form "Tres sunt testes, spiritus et aqua et sanguis et tres unum sunt," shows that this interpretation was traditional in his time, so that he can assume that the writer of the Epistle intended the "unum" to refer to the three persons symbolized by the Spirit, water, and blood, and not to the symbols, which are different in substance. Incidentally it shows also, of course, that the heavenly witnesses formed no part of his text.

It may be worth while to quote from Berger's *Histoire de la Vulgate* the evidence from the passage which he has there collected.

Leon Palimpsest (vii.) :

> *et sps est testi*[1]
> monium *quia sps est ueritas* [8] *quoniam*
> tres sunt, qui t*estimonium dant in terra*
> sps et *aqua et sanguis* [7] *et tres sunt*
> qui tes*timonium dicunt in caelo pa*
> ter *et uerbum et sps scs et hi tres unum*
> sunt *in xpo ihu* [9] *si testimonium hominum*
> accip . . .

Compl.[1] (Madrid Univ. Lib. 31) ix. "Quia tres sunt qui testimonium dant in terris, aqua sanguis et caro (mg. uel spiritus) et tria hec unum sunt et tria sunt qui testimonium dicunt in celo Pater Verbum et Spiritus et hec tria unum sunt in Christo Jhesu."

Leg.[1] (Cathedral of Leon, 6) x. "Quia tres sunt qui testimonium dant in terra Spiritus et aqua et sanguis et tria haec unum sunt et tria sunt sunt qui testimonium dicunt in caelo Pater Verbum et Spiritus et hii tres unum sunt in Christo Ihesu."

Group of Toletanus, viii. (Madrid B.N.). Cauensis viii.–ix. (Rom. formerly Cloister of La Cana, Salerno). Leg.[2]**. Gothicus Legionensis, A.D. 960 (S. Isidio. Leon). Osc. Bible of Huesca xii. (Madrid Archaeol. Mus. 485). Compl.[2,3] x.–xii. Codices 32–34, Madrid Univ. Libr. B.N. Paris, 321. xiii. dem. Cod. Demidorianus xiii.

---

[1] The words and letters in italics are conjecturally supplied by the Editor, being illegible in the MS.

"Quia [1] tres sunt qui testimonium dant [2] in terra Spiritus et [3] aqua et sanguis et hi [4] tres unum sunt in Christo Ihesu.[5] Et [6] tres sunt [7] qui testimonium dicunt [8] in caelo Pater uerbum et [9] Spiritus [10] et hii tres unum sunt.

[1] quoniam, cpl.[3]   [2] dicunt, tol.   [3] om. osc. cpl.[3] 321 dem.
[4] om. dem.   [5] om. dem.   [6] om. tol. cpl.[2] quia, 321**.
[7] om. et tres sunt, cpl.[3]   [8] dant, cpl.[2] 321, dem.   [9] om. 321*.
[10] +sanctus, osc. cpl.[2, 3] 321.

Berne University Lib. A. 9, Saec. xi. (Vienne au Dauphiné): "Quoniam tres sunt qui testimonium dant [1] spiritus aqua et sanguis et tres unum sunt." [2]

[1] +in terra *sec. man.*   [2] +et tres sunt qui testimonium dicunt in caelo Pater et Filius et Spiritus Sanctus et hii tres unum sunt *sec. man.*

Paris B.N. 4 and 4[2]. ix. and x. (given by Chapter of Puy to Colbert in 1681) addition in nearly contemporary hand to 1 Jn. v. 7: "Quoniam tres sunt qui testimonium dant in caelo Pater Verbum et Spiritus et tres unum sunt: et tres sunt qui testimonium dant in terra sanguis aqua et caro. Si testimonium," etc.

Paris B.N. 2328, viii. ix. Codex Lemouicensis: "Quia tres sunt qui testimonium dicunt in terra spiritus aqua et sanguis et hi tres unum sunt: et tres sunt qui testimonium perhibent Verbum et spiritus et tres unum sunt in Christo Ihesu."

B.N. 315, xii.–xiii.: "Quoniam tres sunt qui testimonium dant in terra caro aqua et sanguis: et tres sunt qui testimonium dant in terra Pater Verbum et S.S. et hi tres unum sunt."

B.N. 13174, ix. (fin.): "Quoniam tres sunt qui testimonium dant spiritus aqua et sanguis et tres unum sunt."

A second hand, almost contemporary, adds: "Quoniam tres sunt qui testimonium dant in terra Spiritus aqua et sanguis et tres unum sunt et tres sunt qui testimonium dicunt in caelo Pater Verbum et Spiritus sanctum et hi tres unum [sunt]."

This (M. Berger adds) is substantially the text of the first hand of Bible of Theodulf.

B.N. 11532 (Lothaire II. A.D. 855–86), from Corbie: "Quoniam tres sunt qui testimonium dant [1] spiritus aqua et sanguis et tres unum sunt et tres sunt qui . . .[2] testificantur[3] Pater verbum et spiritus et tres unum sunt."

[1] +in terra *sec. man.*   [2] de caelo p. m. sup. ras.   [3] testimonium dicunt in caelo *sec. man.*

Vienna Bibl. Imp. 1190, ix. (inc.). First hand gives ver. 8 without interpolation. In a second nearly contemporary hand is added, "Quoniam tres sunt qui testimonium perhibent in terra aqua sanguis et caro et tres in nobis sunt et tres sunt qui testimonium perhibent in caelo Pater Verbum et spiritus et hi tres unum sunt."

With this may be compared the reading found in Bibl. Mazarine 7 : " Quoniam tres sunt qui testimonium dant in caelo Pater Verbum et Spiritus et tres sunt qui testimonium dant in terra caro sanguis et aqua et hi tres in nobis unum sunt."

With these must be compared the quotation in the treatise "Contra Varimadum" attributed by Chifflet in his edition of 1664 to Vigilius of Thapsus, and claimed by Künstle for the Spaniard Idacius Clarus (cf. Künstle, p. 16 ; Herzog-Hauck, 20. 642, *s.v.* Vigilius von Thapsus), which is almost identical with the reading of the second hand of the Vienna MS.

S. Gall. 907.   In the hand of "Winitharius."   viii. : " Quia tres sunt qui testimonium dant spiritus et aqua et sanguis et tres unum sunt : sicut in celo tres sunt Pater Verbum et Spiritus et tres unum sunt."

S. Gall. 83.   Part of the MSS of Hartmut (841–872) : "Quia tres sunt qui testimonium dant spiritus et aqua et sanguis et tres unum sunt : sicut in caelo tres sunt Pater Verbum et Spiritus et tres unum sunt."

Genève I. (x.–xi.), given to the Chapter of S. Peter by the Bishop Frederic (1031–1073).   Representing an Italian text (Berger, 140 ff.) : " Quia tres sunt qui testimonium dant spiritus et aqua et sanguis et tres unum sunt : et tres testimonium perhibent in caelo Pater Verbum et Spiritus et tres unum sunt."

Theodulfian recension (B.N. 9380) ix. : " Quia tres sunt qui testimonium dant in terra spiritus aqua et sanguis et tres unum sunt et tres sunt qui testimonium dicunt in celo Pater et Filius et Spiritus sanctus et hi tres unum sunt."

The earliest certain instance of the gloss being quoted as part of the actual text of the Epistle is in the *Liber Apologeticus* (? A.D. 380) of Priscillian (ed. Schepps. Vienna Corpus xviii., 1889) : "Sicut Ioannes ait : Tria sunt quae testimonium dicunt in terra : aqua caro et sanguis ; et haec tria in unum sunt.   et tria sunt quae testimonium dicunt in caelo : pater, uerbum et spiritus ; et haec tria unum sunt in Christo Iesu."   With this must be compared the readings of the Leon Palimpsest, Compl.[1], Leg.[1], all of which agree, if Berger has rightly restored the text of the Palimpsest, in connecting the words *in Christo Iesu* with the heavenly witnesses, placed, of course, *after* the earthly witnesses. The two latter MSS give some support to the peculiarities of Priscillian's text, the use of the neuter (*tria*) and the substitution of *caro* for *spiritus*.

The evidence of the *Expositio Fidei*, published by Caspari from the Ambrosian MS (i. 101 sup.) which contained the Muratorian fragment, is also important : "Sicut euangelista testatur quia scriptum est, 'Tres sunt qui dicunt testimonium in caelo pater

uerbum et spiritus': et haec tria unum sunt in Christo Iesu.
Non tamen dixit 'Unus est in Christo Iesu.'"

The close agreement of this with Priscillian's quotation is
evident. Unfortunately, the value of its evidence is difficult to
determine. Caspari, its editor, regards the creed as African, of
the fifth or sixth century. Dom Morin would attribute it to
Isaac the Jew and the times of Damasus (372). Künstle regards
it as clearly anti-Priscillianist and Spanish. If Dom Morin is
right, its early date gives it a special importance. But the view
that Priscillian is attacked in it is a satisfactory explanation of that
part of it which is concerned with the *Comma Joanneum.*

It may, however, be doubted whether later authorities do not
preserve an earlier form of the interpolation. The date of the so-
called Speculum is uncertain. Probably it is not later than the
first half of the fifth century. Künstle brings forward some
indications of its connection with Spain and the orthodox
opponents of Priscillian. The form in which it quotes our
passage is of considerable interest. It occurs in c. ii., of which
the heading is *De distinctione personarum patris et filii et spiritus
sancti,* and runs as follows : [1] "Quoniam (quia C) tres sunt qui
testimonium dicunt in terra, spiritus aqua et sanguis : et hii tres
unum sunt in Christo Iesu, et tres sunt qui testimonium dicunt
in caelo, pater, uerbum et spiritus : et hii tres unum sunt."

The agreement of this with the group of MSS quoted above
from Berger is at once evident. Their common source cannot be
of recent date. And intrinsically their reading has the appearance of being, if not original, at least earlier than the Priscillian
form. The words *in Christo Iesu* are far more natural in
connection with the earthly witnesses than at the end of the
second clause.[2] The form of text found in the Leon palimpsest,
where there is no clause "et hii tres unum sunt" after the earthly
witnesses, suggests how the connection of the phrases "hi tres
unum sunt in Christo Iesu," if originally referring to the earthly
witnesses, might have become attached to the second verse
(heavenly witnesses) by the mechanical process of the insertion
of a marginal gloss, originally containing an interpretation, after

---

[1] *De divinis Scripturis suie Speculum,* ed. Weihrich, Vienna Corpus xii.

[2] There is possibly support for the addition "in Christo Iesu" to the
clause about the unity of the earthly witnesses in the Latin translation of
Clement of Alexandria's *Adumbrationes* on the Epistle. "Quia tres sunt qui
testificantur Spiritus, quod est uita, et aqua, quod est regeneratio ac fides, et
sanguis, quod est cognitio, 'et his tres unum sunt.' *In Saluatore* quippe istae
sunt virtutes salutiferae, et uita ipsa in ipso filio eius exsistit." Even if this is
so, we are uncertain how much to refer to Clement and how much to his
abbreviator. Cf. Cassiodorus, *Complexiones in Ioannis Epist. ad Parthos* :
"Cui rei testificantur in terra tria mysteria aqua sanguis et spiritus, quae in
passione domini leguntur impleti ; in caelo autem pater et filius et Spiritus
sanctus ; et hi tres unus est deus."

the word *sanguis*. The form in which Priscillian quotes the verses suited admirably his peculiar view as to the distinction of persons in the Trinity.[1] If the *Speculum* is anti-Priscillianist, it is far more probable that the common use of the clause about the heavenly witnesses as part of the text of S. John's Epistle is to be explained by the supposition that it had already found its way into some copies of the Epistles at an earlier date, than that Priscillian is first responsible for its insertion, while his opponents accepted his text and used it against him by means of a different interpretation, and, perhaps, a slight alteration.

This point has been well discussed by M. Babut in his *Priscillien et le Priscillianisme* (Bibliothèque de l'École des hautes études, Sciences historiques et philologiques, 169, Paris, 1909), Appendix, iv. 3, p. 267 ff. He points out the great difficulties which met Künstle's suggestion that the insertion of the comma into the text of the Epistle is due to Priscillian himself: (1) His opponents never accuse him of having falsified the text of a Canonical Book. (2) To quote his own interpolation in his *Apology* would have been an inconceivable act of audacity. (3) Such a falsification could hardly have been accepted by all Catholic theologians, and, as Künstle has shown, the reading was universally accepted in the ninth century. (4) The verse is found in several orthodox works of the fifth century. Its acceptance must therefore have been almost immediate by Priscillian's enemies. It is far more probable that both Priscillian and his opponents found the gloss in the text of their Bibles.

The confession of faith presented by the Catholic bishops of Africa to the vandal king Hunnerich in 484 (Victor Vitensis, *Historia Persecutionis*, ed. Petschenig, Vienna Corpus, vii. 46 ff.), is proof of the presence of the insertion in the Johannine text towards the end of the fifth century: "Et ut adhuc luce clarius unius diuinitatis esse cum patre et filio spiritum sanctum doceamus, Ioannis euangelistae testimonio comprobatur; ait namque: Tres sunt qui testimonium perhibent (dant *cod*) in caelo pater uerbum et spiritus sanctus et hi tres unum sunt."

Unfortunately the whole passage is not quoted, and therefore the quotation throws litttle light on the history of the gloss. Künstle, again, claims a Spanish source for the whole confession. Whether he is justified in doing so or not must be left to the specialist to determine. The quotation has *not* the variant *dicunt*, supposed by Berger to be Spanish (p. 163).

It is certain that the gloss was accepted by Fulgentius of

---

[1] M. Babut rejects Künstle's statement that Priscillian *denied* the distinction as too absolute. He adds, "mais il est vrai qu'il les distingue mal et qu'il tend, en plusieurs textes, à les fondre en une seule. On a raison de parler de *panchristisme*" (p. 273).

Ruspe († 533). Though the treatise *De fide Catholica adv. Pintam* is not recognized as his work, the quotations in his *Responsio contra Arianos* and *De Trinitate* determine the matter.[1] Here, also, it is only the gloss which is quoted. We do not know the relation in which it stood to the rest of the passage in his text of the Epistle. It may be worth while to add the exact text, which differs in the two quotations. The variants in brackets are from the *De Trinitate*.

"Tres sunt qui testimonium perhibent (dicunt) in caelo pater uerbum et spiritus: et (hi) tres unum sunt." For *perhibent*, cf. Cod. Lemonicensis, Vienna B.I. 1190, Geneva. 1.

The evidence for the African use of the passage which has been supposed to be derived from Vigilius of Thapsus (490) is too uncertain to afford much help.

The quotation in the First Book *de Trinitate* (Migne, *P. L.* lxii. 243), which is not by Vigilius, has an interesting text.

"Tres sunt qui testimonium dicunt in caelo pater uerbum et Spiritus et in Christo Iesu unum sunt."

The form of text contains Spanish affinities even if Künstle is not right in claiming a Spanish origin for the twelve books *de Trinitate*.

The quotation in the treatise *c. Varimadum* (c. 5, Migne, *P. L.* lxii. 359) is still more interesting:

"Tres sunt qui testimonium perhibent in terra aqua sanguis et caro et tres in nobis sunt. Et tres sunt qui testimonium perhibent in caelo pater verbum et Spiritus et ii tres unum sunt." Cf. Vienna B.I. 1190, Bibl. Mazarine. Here, again, the connection with Spanish types of text is far more certain than any possible connection with Africa or Vigilius.

The pseudo-Hieronymian prologue to the Catholic Epistles, which is found in the Codex Fuldensis (546), though that MS does not contain ver. 7 in its text of the Epistle, affords additional evidence of the prevalence of the gloss in the sixth and probably in the fifth century.

"Non ita est ordo apud Graecos qui integre sapiunt . . . illo praecipue loco, ubi de unitate trinitatis in prima Iohannis epistula positum legimus, in qua ab infidelibus translatoribus multum erratum esse fidei ueritate comperimus, trium tantummodo uocabula, hoc est aquae sanguinis et spiritus in ipsa sua editione ponentes, et patris uerbique ac spiritus testimonium omittentes, in quo maxime et fides catholica roboratur et patris et filii et spiritus sancti una diuinitatis substantia comprobatur."

Künstle would again find a Spanish origin for this prologue, attributing it to Peregrinus, the orthodox sponsor of Priscillianist writings; but on what grounds he does not say.

[1] See, however, Westcott, p. 194, who refers to *C. Fabian.* fragm.

11

The evidence of Ziegler's Freisingen fragment, now in the Staatsbibliothek at Munich, must be considered next. The passage runs as follows:

QM TR es sunt qui testificantur

IN TERRA · SPs ET AQUA ET SAnguis et tres sunt qui tes

TIFICANTUR IN CAELO PaTER Et uerbum et sps scs et hi

TRES UNUM SUNT · SI TEST . . .

(The legible letters are given in capitals.)

If Ziegler is right in his identification of the text of this fragment with that of Fulgentius of Ruspe, we have again important evidence of the existence of the gloss in Africa at an early date. This is, however, already attested for the sixth century, and the fragment cannot be earlier than that. If the text of the quotation which has been given above for Fulgentius is correct, there are differences between his text and that of this fragment, at any rate in this passage. And M. Berger has pointed out the similarity between the text of the Leon Palimpsest and the Freisingen fragment in these verses (*Histoire*, p. 9). The closeness of similarity between the two texts is seen in the note which gives a comparison of their readings where the two can be tested. It will be seen that their agreement in readings *certainly* attested by both is very close indeed, and it is possible that a more accurate restoration of the illegible parts would reveal even closer resemblance.[1] This agreement includes, in the

[1] Leon Palimpsest.	Ziegler.
1 Jn. iv. 3–6.	
in carne uenisse	om. (*reading* qui non confitetur IHM)
hic	hoc
quod	quem
4. eum	eos
is	his
saeculo	+est
audit nos	nos audit
ex hoc	hinc.
v. 3–11, 12–16.	
5. *est*	+autem
quoniam	quia
6. *aquam et spm*	om. *et spm* (no room)
8. te*stimonium dant*	*testificantur* (suits better)
7. te*stimonium dicunt*	*test*ificantur
sunt *in xpo ihu*	om. in x. i. (certain)
9. *quo*niam	*quia*
10. filio 2°	in do

small space under consideration, the readings hoc (*hic*) est illius
Antichristi (iv. 3), the priority of the earthly witnesses, as we
should naturally expect in such early texts, the absence of the
clause affirming the unity of the earthly witnesses.   They differ in
their translations of μαρτυρεῖν (unless, indeed, testificari should be
supplied in the doubtful places of the Leon Palimpsest), and
probably, with regard to the addition in Christo Iesu after unum
sunt in ver. 8, which cannot be certainly claimed for the
African text, unless the *Speculum* can be definitely connected
with Africa.   It would certainly be rash to assume an early
African form of the text from which these words were absent as
opposed to the early Spanish form which undoubtedly had
them, and probably in this place.   It is always possible that
their absence from later texts may have affected the manuscript
transmission of the text of early quotations.   We are again
brought to the conclusion that the relation between early African
and Spanish texts needs further investigation.

The gloss was certainly known as part of the text of the
Epistle in Africa in the fifth century.   Its acceptance as part
of the text cannot be proved in any country except Spain in
the fourth century.   There it was undoubtedly used by Priscillian
(? 380).   The influence of his work and writings on the Latin
text of the Bible, which passed over into orthodox circles through
Peregrinus and others, is an undoubted fact.   It is through the
Theodulfian Recension of the Vulgate that the gloss first gained
anything like wide acceptance.   A large proportion of the
earlier evidence for the gloss can be very plausibly traced to
Spanish influences.   Thus the importance of the name of
Priscillian in the history of the insertion is fully established.   But
Künstle has not proved his point that Priscillian was the first
who introduced the words into the text of S. John's Epistle, or
even that this first took place in Spain.   At least it may be said
that the evidence of Spanish manuscripts, of the form in which
the gloss is found in Priscillian, and of its use by his opponents,
suggest the probability that Priscillian was not responsible for its
first introduction.   But these reasons are not conclusive.   In one
point Priscillian has preserved the true reading against (?) all
Latin authorities, reading, with regard to the earthly witnesses,
in unum sunt.   It is a possible explanation of the textual facts
that the words *in Christo Iesu* were first connected with the
passage by Priscillian, either as part of the text or as an explanation.   In the place which he assigns to them they support
his "*Panchristismus*" admirably.   Their first connection with

13. aeternam habetis	habetis aeternam
14. *quodcunque*	quidquid
15. *scimus*	siscim^us.

the earthly witnesses *may* be due to their removal by Peregrinus or some orthodox opponent of Priscillian to a place where they did not give such clear support to Priscillian's views.

At present we cannot say more than that the insertion was certainly known in Africa in the fifth century. The connection between the Spanish and African texts still requires investigation. Though its acceptance as part of the text of the Epistle cannot be proved for any locality except Spain in the fourth century, it does not necessarily follow that it is of Spanish origin.

In view of the clear evidence that Priscillian in 380 knew, or made the words part of his text, it is difficult to maintain an African origin for the gloss, which did *not* form part of the text of Augustine, who died A.D. 430. On this point Jülicher's interesting review of Künstle's work (Göttingen : Anzeigen, 1905, pp. 930–935) perhaps hardly does justice to the strength of Künstle's position, though it rightly calls attention to some inaccuracies in his quotations and defects in his methods of presenting the evidence. Ziegler's theory of the African origin of the gloss is now faced by great, if not insuperable, difficulties. But the subject needs further investigation by competent Latin scholars.

There is no trace of the presence of the gloss in any Oriental version or in Greek writers, except under the influence of the Vulgate.

The following note in Zohrab's edition of the Armenian Bible is of sufficient interest to deserve quotation in full. I am indebted for the translation to my friend and colleague Mr. N. McLean, Tutor and Lecturer of Christ's College, Cambridge. The note has been somewhat curtailed by paraphrase.

"Oscan here as in many other places altered the Armenian text from the Latin, adding, 'Who witnesses that Christ is the Truth. For there are three who witness in heaven, the Father, the Word, and the Holy Spirit, and the three are one : and there are three who witness on earth, Spirit, Water, and Blood, and the three are one. If of men,' etc. But of eighteen of our MSS, old and new, and two Catholic interpreters in addition, one only from the new, written in A.D. 1656, ten years before the edition of Oscan, thus puts the text 'That the Spirit is truth. There are the three who testify in heaven, the Father, the Word, and the Holy Spirit, and these three are one. And there are three who testify on earth, the Spirit, the Water, and the Blood. If of men,' etc. And although there was also another more ancient copy which contained a similar text, nevertheless it plainly appeared that the first writing had been erased, and the longer text adjusted to its space by another writer. All our MSS, whether of the whole Scriptures or of missals, as well as numerous Greek older copies, have only the text which we have been compelled to edit (*i.e.* the true text without the gloss)."

The close parallel to the history of the insertion of the gloss in the Greek text is of some interest.

According to Westcott, it first appears in Greek in a Greek version of the Acts of the Lateran Council in 1215. Its first appearance in a Greek MS of the N.T., the Graeco-Latin Vatican MS *Ottobon.* 162 (xv.), betrays the use of the Vulgate, ὅτι τρεῖς εἰσὶν οἱ μαρτυροῦντες ἀπὸ τοῦ οὐρανοῦ πατὴρ λόγος καὶ πνεῦμα καὶ οἱ τρεῖς εἰς τὸ ἕν εἰσι· καὶ τρεῖς εἰσὶν οἱ μαρτυροῦντες ἐπὶ τῆς γῆς τὸ πνεῦμα τὸ ὕδωρ καὶ τὸ αἷμα. The *Codex Britannicus* (Dublin, Montfort 34, saec. xvi.) is even more slavish (ἐν τῷ οὐρανῷ, οὗτοι οἱ τρεῖς, πνεῦμα ὕδωρ καὶ αἷμα). Erasmus fulfilled his promise to the letter in his third edition. He follows the MS that had been "provided" exactly, except that he inserts καί before ὕδωρ, and does not remove the clause καὶ οἱ τρεῖς εἰς τὸ ἕν εἰσιν, which rightly had a place in his earlier editions.

The history of the Montfort Codex, which Dr. Dobbin pronounced to be "a transcript with arbitrary and fanciful variations" of the Oxford MS *Lincoln* 39, has been further investigated by Dr. Rendel Harris in his "Leicester Codex," 1889. Both MSS were at one time in the possession of the same owner, Chark. His reasons for suggesting that the MS was actually forged by a Franciscan of the name of Roy (or Froy), perhaps at the instigation of Henry Standish, provincial master of the order in England, will be found on pp. 46–53 of the "Leicester Codex." They are plausible, even if they do not compel assent. He has at least proved that the MS was in the hands of Franciscans at a date very near to that of its actual production.

Before the appearance of Erasmus's third edition in 1522 the gloss had already been printed in Greek in the Complutensian Polyglott in 1514. The text is obviously derived, if not taken immediately from the Vulgate, though the supply of the necessary articles and copulas to make the sentences Greek has partially concealed its close dependence upon the Latin.

NOTES ON 2 JOHN.

1–3. Introduction and salutation.

1. ὁ πρεσβύτερος] The use of πρεσβύτερος as a more or less official title in Asia Minor, the Islands, and Egypt has been discussed by Deissmann, *Bibel Studien*, 153 ff., *NBS* 60 ff. Cf. also H. Hauschildt, in Preuschen's *ZNTW*, 1903, p. 235 ff., and Deissmann, *Licht vom Osten*, p. 25. Its use in Egypt as a title, and in connection with the Temples, as well as in other connections, is well established at an early date. The evidence of Papias and Irenaeus points to a prevalent Christian usage of the word, especially in Asia, to denote those who had companied with Apostles, and had perhaps been placed in office by them ; who could, at any rate, bear trustworthy witness as to what Apostles taught. It is natural to suppose that throughout the fragment of his Introduction, which Eusebius quotes, Papias uses the expression πρεσβύτερος in the same sense. The elders are the men from whom he has himself well learnt and well remembered the illustrative matter for which he finds a place in his book beside his interpretations of the Lord's words, or whose statements as to what the Apostles said he had learnt by inquiry whenever he met those who had companied with them. This interpretation is supported by the comments of Eusebius on the passage (*H. E.* iii. 39. 7), τοὺς τῶν ἀποστόλων λόγους παρὰ τῶν αὐτοῖς παρηκολουθηκότων ὁμολογεῖ παρειληφέναι, *i.e.* he learnt from elders who had companied with Apostles the words of the Apostles, obtaining his information either directly from the elders themselves, or indirectly from those who had companied with the elders. Irenaeus uses similar language, *adv. Haer.* v. xxxiii. 3, "Quemadmodum presbyteri meminerunt qui Iohannem discipulum Domini uiderunt audisse se ab eo quemadmodum de temporibus illis docebat Dominus et dicebat ": iii. xxxvi. 1, ὡς οἱ πρεσβύτεροι λέγουσιν Τότε καὶ οἱ μὲν καταξιωθέντες τῆς ἐν οὐρανῷ διατριβῆς ἐκεῖσε χωρήσουσιν. Any individual member of such a class might naturally be styled ὁ πρεσβύτερος, as Papias speaks of ὁ πρεσβύτερος Ἰωάννης, or ὁ πρεσβύτερος, and Eusebius (*H. E.* iii. 39. 14) of τοῦ πρεσβυτέρου Ἰωάννου παραδόσεις. The absolute use of the phrase in Papias (καὶ τοῦθ᾽ ὁ πρεσβύτερος ἔλεγε) and in 2 and 3 John makes it the distinctive title of some member of the circle to whom the words are addressed, or at least of one who is well known to them. The circle is in all three cases Asiatic. It is natural to suppose that Papias is referring to the John whom he elsewhere describes as John the Elder. And it is equally natural to see in the author of these two Epistles, who so describes himself, the Elder John whom Papias so carefully distinguishes from the Apostle. The usage of the word is most naturally explained if he is the last survivor of the group, though the possibility of other solutions is by no means excluded.

ἐκλεκτῇ κυρίᾳ] The interpretation of these words has been discussed generally in the Introduction. Those who have seen in this designation the name of an individual have explained it differently according as the first, or the second, or both words are regarded as proper names, or both are treated as descriptive adjectives, the actual name not being given. (i.) The view that Electa is a proper name is first found in Clement of Alexandria, "Scripta est ad Babyloniam quandam Electam nomine." It is uncertain whether "Babyloniam" is due to some confusion with the First Epistle of S. Peter on the part of either Clement or his excerptor and translator, or whether it is a conclusion drawn from the title Πρὸς Πάρθους by which the First Epistle was known (cf. the title of Augustine's Tractates). This view has been supported in recent years by Dr. J. Rendel Harris, who in an article in the *Expositor* (1901) to which reference has been made in the Introduction, collected several instances of the use of κύριος and κυρία by near relatives in letters contained in the Oxyrhynchus, and Fayum Papyri. Cf. Oxyrh. Pap. ii. 300 (p. 301), Ἰνδικὴ Θαεισοῦτι τῇ κυρίᾳ χαίρειν. He might have noticed a similar use of δέσποινα in one of the letters which he quotes (ἀσπάζομαι τὴν γλυκυτάτην μου θυγατέρα Μακκαρίαν καὶ τὴν δεσποίνην μου μητέραν ὑμῶν καὶ ὅλους τοὺς ἡμῶν κατ᾽ ὄνομα: cf. in the same letter, written by a father to his son, κἂν ὥς, δεσποτά μοι, ἀντίγραψον μοι ἐν τάχει). His view that κύριος, κυρία are thus proved to have been used as titles of affection, has been justly criticized by Professor Ramsay in a subsequent article in the same periodical, who sees in it more naturally a title of courtesy. Perhaps it would be better to regard its use as rather playful, or not to be taken too seriously. But the evidence adduced in any case does not go far towards proving that 2 John is addressed to an individual. The usage of individual address would necessarily be followed by a writer who wishes to personify a community to whom he writes. And the language of ver. 15

(τῆς ἀδελφῆς σου τῆς ἐκλεκτῆς) is almost fatal to the supposition that Electa is here used as a proper name.

(ii.) If the name is given at all it must be found in Kyria and not in Electa. Kyria as a proper name is found occasionally, and even in Asia Minor. Lücke quotes (p. 444) *Corp. Inscr. Gruter.* p. 1127, n. xi. Φένιππος καὶ ἡ γυνὴ αὐτοῦ Κυρία, and other instances. According to Holtzmann it is a common name for women, but he does not cite instances. Cf. Zahn, *Introd.* vol. iii., Eng. tr. p. 383, who refers to Sterrett, *The Wolfe Expedition*, pp. 138, 389. But on grammatical grounds this explanation is improbable. We should certainly expect the article with ἐκλεκτῇ. Cf. 3 Jn. 1, Γαίῳ τῷ ἀγαπητῷ : Ro. xvi. 13, Ῥοῦφον τὸν ἐκλεκτὸν ἐν κυρίῳ : Philem. Φιλήμονι τῷ ἀγαπητῷ : Oxyrh. Pap. 117, Χαιρέας Διονυσίῳ τῷ κυρίῳ ἀδελφῷ : 119, Θέων Θέωνι τῷ πατρὶ χαίρειν. These passages illustrate the grammatical difficulty of assuming that Κυρία is a proper name. The anarthrous ἐκλεκτῇ makes it very improbable.

(iii.) The language of ver. 13, ἀσπάζεταί σε τὰ τέκνα τῆς ἀδελφῆς σου τῆς ἐκλεκτῆς, makes it very unlikely that *both* words are to be regarded as proper names.

(iv.) The view, however, that an individual is addressed, has often been held by those who think that her name has not been recorded. As stated in the Introduction, the name of Mary the Mother of the Lord, and of Martha, have been suggested. The former suggestion was natural, if not inevitable, at an earlier date, in view of Jn. xix. 27 and the supposed residence of the Blessed Virgin in Asia, when the general historical setting of the Epistle was less carefully considered or understood than in recent times. A supposed play on the meaning of Martha was equally attractive to an earlier generation. No serious arguments can be brought forward in favour of either conjecture. If the theory of individual address is maintained, it is certainly better to assume that the name is not given. The combination of terms is a natural expression of Christian courtesy.

But the general character of the Epistle is almost decisive against the view that it is addressed to an individual. The subjects with which it deals are such as affect a community rather than an individual or a family, though much of its contents might be regarded as advice needed by the leading member of a Church on whom the duty mainly fell of entertaining the strangers who visited it. We must also notice (1) that the language of vv. 1–3, "Whom I and all who know the truth love because of the truth that abideth in us," suits a community far better than an individual. This is also true of the language of the salutation in ver. 13 which has been already quoted. (2) The interchange of singular and plural points to the same conclusion, εὕρηκα ἐκ τῶν τέκνων σου (ver. 4), ἐρωτῶ σε (ver. 5), βλέπετε ἑαυτούς (ver. 8), εἴ τις ἔρχεται πρὸς ὑμᾶς (ver. 10), ὑμῖν (ver. 12), ἀσπάζεταί σε (ver. 13).   Mr. Gibbins in an interesting paper in the *Expositor* (series 6, 1902, p. 232) has drawn attention to the similar changes between singular and plural which are found in Is. liv., lv. and Bar. iv., v., where the City and her inhabitants are addressed under the image of a woman and her children.   These parallels show clearly how natural was the transference of the prophetic language with regard to Jerusalem and its inhabitants to a Christian Church and its members. (3) The language of ver. 5, ἐρωτῶ σε, κυρία, οὐχ ὡς ἐντολὴν γράφων σοι καινήν, ἀλλὰ ἣν εἴχαμεν ἀπ᾿ ἀρχῆς, ἵνα ἀγαπῶμεν ἀλλήλους, with its clear reference to the Lord's "new commandment" given to His disciples, suggests a Church and not an individual. (4) The substance of what is said in vv. 6, 8, 10, 12 is clearly not addressed to children.   The "children" of the "Elect Lady" must certainly have reached the age of manhood.   (5) The nearest parallel in the N.T. is to be found in 1 P. v. 13, ἡ ἐν Βαβυλῶνι συνεκλεκτή, though we may hesitate to assume with Dom Chapman (*JTS*, 1904, pp. 357 ff., 517 ff.) that the reference in both cases is the same, the Church of Rome being addressed. We may perhaps also compare the language in which the Seer addresses the same Churches in the Apocalypse (i.–iii.).

The reference to the whole Church is already suggested by Clement, "significat autem electionem ecclesiae sanctae." Cf. also Jerome, *Ep.* 123. 12, *Ad Ageruchiam,* "Una ecclesia parens omnium Christianorum . . . praue haeretici in plures ecclesias lacerant . . . *Una est columba mea, perfecta mea, una est matris suae, electa genetrici suae* (Cant. vi. 8).   Ad quam scribit idem Iohannes epistolam, *Senior Electae dominae et filiis eius,*" where the reference to the Church is clear, though he apparently regards Electa as a proper name.

The reference to a *local* Church is found in the Scholiast, ἐκλεκτὴν κυρίαν λέγει τὴν ἐν τινὶ τόπῳ ἐκκλησίαν.   This explanation has been adopted by most modern commentators.

καὶ τοῖς τέκνοις αὐτῆς] Cf. Bar. iv. 30–32, θάρσει, Ἰερουσαλήμ, παρακαλέσει σε ὁ ὀνομάσας σε.   δείλαιοι οἱ σε κακώσαντες καὶ ἐπιχαρέντες τῇ σῇ πτώσει· δείλαιαι αἱ πόλεις αἷς ἐδούλευσαν τὰ τέκνα σου, δειλαία ἡ δεξαμένη τοὺς υἱούς σου.   v. 5, ἴδε σου συνηγμένα τὰ τέκνα ἀπὸ ἡλίου δυσμῶν . . . . χαίροντας τῇ τοῦ θεοῦ μνείᾳ. Gal. iv. 25, δουλεύει μετὰ τῶν τέκνων αὐτῆς.   The use of τέκνα, which emphasizes the idea of community of nature of those who have experienced the new spiritual birth, as contrasted with the Pauline υἱός, which often lays stress on the dignity of heirship, is characteristic of the author.   But it is not always safe to press the distinction.   The more general term, which includes

the whole family, would in many cases naturally be preferred
to υἱός, which, strictly speaking, applies only to sons.

οὓς ἐγὼ ἀγαπῶ] Cf. Gal. iv. 19, τέκνα (*v.l.* τεκνία) μου, οὓς
πάλιν ὠδίνω. Arguments, in favour of the view that a Church
is addressed, which are based on the use of the *masculine* relative are very precarious. In any case it would be the natural
construction κατὰ σύνεσιν. For the use of ἐγώ, cf. 3 Jn. 1. It
may be characteristic of the writer's style. But the emphatic
language of the rest of the verse suggests that the author is
thinking of those who do not love, and love "in truth."

ἐν ἀληθείᾳ] Cf. 3 Jn. 1, where the word is again anarthrous.
The phrase is not "merely adverbial," a periphrasis for "truly."
It suggests a love which is exercised in the highest sphere, which
corresponds to the truest conception of love. Cf. περιπατεῖν
ἐν ἀληθείᾳ, conduct in which everything is regulated by "truth."

καὶ οὐκ ἐγὼ κ.τ.λ.] The unsuitability of this language, if addressed to the members of a single family, has already been
pointed out. As addressed to members of a Church in which
the Elder can confidently reckon on faithful support, while he
is fully conscious of the existence of divisions and of strenuous
opposition to himself and his teaching, they offer no difficulty
and have their special significance.

τὴν ἀλήθειαν] Cf. 1 Jn. i. 6 (note). The truth, as revealed
by the Christ, and gradually unfolded by the Spirit, who is
"Truth." It covers all spheres of life, and is not confined to
the sphere of the intellect alone.

ο πρεσβυτερος] η συμπρεσβυτερος 93 : *Iohannes senior* tol. Cassiod. |
εκλεκτη] pr. τη 73 | Κυρια] pr. τη 31 | αυτης] αυτοις *I*ᵃ 65 (317) | ους] οις *I*ᵇ 62.
161 (498) | εν αληθεια αγαπω *I*ᵃ 158 (395) | και ουκ εγω ℵ B K P al. pler. vg.
sah. cop. syrᵖ arm. aeth.] ουκ εγω δε A 73 syrᵇᵒᵈˡ Thphyl. : + δε L | και 3°]
om. *I*ᵃ 170 (303) | εγνωκοτες] αγαπωντες *I*ᵃ δ157 (547).

2. διὰ τὴν ἀλήθειαν] The possession of the "truth" as an
abiding force which dominates the whole life calls out the love
of all who share the possession.

ἐν ἡμῖν] The author includes the Church to whom he is
writing, or at least its faithful members, in the numbers of those
who "know the truth."

καὶ μεθ' ἡμῶν ἔσται] An expression of sure confidence rather
than of a wish. The truth must always "abide" in the Society,
though individual members may fall away. For the parenthetical
construction, cf. 1 Jn. iii. 1, ἵνα τέκνα θεοῦ κληθῶμεν, καὶ ἐσμέν.

δια την αληθειαν] om. 27. 29. 66**. 106* fu. syrᵖ txt | μενουσαν B K
L P etc.] ενοικουσαν A : ουσαν 13. 65 dˢᶜʳ : om. 66** | ημιν] υμιν 22. 68.
100. 104 cˢᶜʳ jˢᶜʳ | και . . . αιωνα] *quia et uobiscum erit et nos in aeternum
uobiscum eritis* arm. | ημων] υμων 22. 68. 100. 104 aˢᶜʳ cˢᶜʳ jˢᶜʳ al. | εσται
εστιν 31 syrᵇᵒᵈˡ ᵉᵗ ᵖ : εστω *I*ᵃ 200f (83).

3. ἔσται μεθ᾽ ἡμῶν] The taking up of the language of the preceding verse is thoroughly in accord with the writer's habit.
Compare the repetition of ἀλήθεια in the preceding verse. The
wish expressed in ordinary salutations here "passes into assurance." Perhaps in view of their circumstances the need of
assurance was specially felt by writer and recipients as well.

χάρις, ἔλεος, εἰρήνη] This exact form of salutation is found
elsewhere in the Epistles to Timothy. It is a natural expansion
of the commoner χάρις καὶ εἰρήνη which in some sense combines the Greek and Hebrew forms of salutation; and it fits
in well with the general tone of later Epistles. Neither ἔλεος
nor the cognate verb occurs elsewhere in the Johannine writings.
Cf. Jude 2, ἔλεος ὑμῖν καὶ εἰρήνη καὶ ἀγάπη πληθυνθείη: Polycarp,
ad Phil. ἔλεος ὑμῖν καὶ εἰρήνη, and the Letter of the Smyrnaeans,
ἔλεος καὶ εἰρήνη καὶ ἀγάπη . . . πληθυνθείη.

παρὰ Ἰησοῦ κ.τ.λ.] The whole phrase brings into prominence
the views on which the author throughout lays most stress—the
Fatherhood of God, as revealed by one who being His Son *can*
reveal the Father, and who as man (Ἰησοῦ) can make Him
known to *men.* Cf. Jn. xx. 31, ἵνα πιστεύητε ὅτι Ἰησοῦς ἐστιν ὁ
Χριστὸς ὁ υἱὸς τοῦ θεοῦ. The words used contain implicitly the
author's creed.

ἐν ἀληθείᾳ καὶ ἀγάπῃ] The two vital elements of the Christian
Faith, the possession of the highest knowledge and its expression in action. They are the keynotes of the Epistle.

εσται μεθ ημων] om. A | εσται]+δε 15. 36 | ημων ℵ B L P al. sat. mu.
cat. am. sah. boh-ed. syrbodl aeth. Thphylcom Oeccom] υμων K al. plu.
vg. (et. fu. demid. harl. tol.) arm. boh-codd. (εστ. μεθ υμ. post αγαπη
arm. boh.) syrp. An obvious correction to the more usual 2nd pers. of
salutations | χαρις] χαρα *I*b 260 (440): + υμων και *I*c 116. 486. 356 (−) | ειρηνην]
pr. και *I*a 200f (83) | παρα ℵc A B L P al. pler.] απο ℵ* 11. 18. 19. 32. 40.
57. 68. 98. 105. 126 cscr. A natural correction to the more common.
usage of salutations; cf. Ro., 1, 2 Co. Gal. Eph. Ph. Col., 2 Th., 1, 2,
Ti. Philem. Apoc. Clement. Polycarp has παρά | (θεου . . . και 1°) om. sah.
| θεου (? ver. 3)] om. *I*a δ254 (?) *I*c 486 (−) | πατρος (? 1°)] pr. και *I*a 256 (24) |
παρα 2°] om. ℵ* 99 fscr am. | ιησου χριστου] pr. κυ ℵ K L P al. pler. cat.
tol. cop. syr. arm. Thphyl. Oec.: χυ υ H257 (33) *I*a δ203ff. 192 (808) | του 1°]
om. H δ6 (Ψ) *I*c 114 (335) | του 2°] pr. αυτου ℵ* | αγαπη και αληθεια *I*c 506 (60)
| και αγαπη] αγαπητη H δ6 (Ψ) | αγαπη] pr. εν *I*a δ203 (808): ερανη *I*b 365
(214).

4–11. "Counsel and warning."

4. ἐχάρην λίαν] Cf. 3 Jn. 3; Lk. xxiii. 8. We may compare
also St. Paul's use of εὐχαριστεῖν in the opening verses of *eight*
of his Epistles. It is part of the usual order of epistolary
composition to strike first the note of praise or thankfulness.
The aorist is probably not epistolary, the contrast of νῦν in
ver. 5 makes it almost certain that it refers to past time.

εὕρηκα] The connection of this word with ἐχάρην shows that

we have here one of the instances, of which there are several in
the N.T., which prove that in certain words the perfect is in this
period beginning to lose its special force, though the process
has not yet gone so far as is often maintained.   Cf. Burton,
N.T. Moods and Tenses, p. 44, who regards the usage as confined
in the N.T. to a few forms, ἔσχηκα, εἴληφα, ἑώρακα, εἴρηκα,
γέγονα.   To distinguish in this verse between the initial moment
(ἐχάρην) and the ground of it which still continues is precarious.

A comparison of 3 Jn. 3 suggests that the information
which caused his joy came to the Elder through travelling
brethren who, perhaps from time to time (cf. περιπατοῦντας),
brought him news of the sister Church.   There is no suggestion
of an earlier visit of his own to the Church to which he is now
writing.   In that case he would probably have used the aorist.

ἐκ τῶν τέκνων σου] He cannot praise the whole Church
without distinction.   All the members of the community had
not remained faithful to the "truth."   If "many" had not
themselves gone out into the world as deceivers (ver. 7), many
had listened to the seductive teaching of such deceivers.   It
seems probable that even the majority had been led astray.

περιπατοῦντας ἐν ἀληθείᾳ] Cf. ver. 1, and 3 Jn. 4.   The
"truth" corresponds to perfection in every sphere of being.

καθὼς ἐντολὴν ἐλάβομεν παρὰ τοῦ πατρός] Cf. Jn. x. 17 f. διὰ
τοῦτό με ὁ πατὴρ ἀγαπᾷ ὅτι ἐγὼ τίθημι τὴν ψυχήν μου, ἵνα πάλιν
λάβω αὐτήν.   οὐδεὶς ἦρεν αὐτὴν ἀπ’ ἐμοῦ, ἀλλ’ ἐγὼ τίθημι αὐτὴν ἀπ’
ἐμαυτοῦ.   ἐξουσίαν ἔχω θεῖναι αὐτήν, καὶ ἐξουσίαν ἔχω πάλιν λαβεῖν
αὐτήν.   ταύτην τὴν ἐντολὴν ἔλαβον παρὰ τοῦ πατρός μου.   Cf. Jn. xii.
49 ; 1 Jn. iii. 23.   The phrase ἐντολὴν λαβεῖν is used elsewhere
in the N.T. ; cf. Ac. xvii. 15 ; Col. iv. 10.   Dom Chapman's
ingenious suggestion, that the meaning of this verse should be
determined by the passage quoted from Jn. x., breaks down, as
Prof. Bartlet has shown, on a point of grammar.   The present
participle (περιπατοῦντας) could not be used in such a sense.
Men could hardly be said to continue in the exercise of the
"remarkable virtue" of martyrdom.   The command referred
to here must be either the "new commandment" to love as
Christ loved (cf. 1 Jn. iv. 21), which perhaps suits ver. 5 best,
or the commandment to faith and love ; cf. 1 Jn. iii. 23, καὶ αὕτη
ἐστὶν ἡ ἐντολὴ αὐτοῦ, ἵνα πιστεύσωμεν τῷ ὀνόματι τοῦ υἱοῦ αὐτοῦ
Ἰησοῦ Χριστοῦ καὶ ἀγαπῶμεν ἀλλήλους, καθὼς ἔδωκεν ἐντολὴν ἡμῖν.
On the whole the latter suits the whole context better.

λιαν] om. *I*ᵇ δ²⁶⁰ (440) : + μεγαλως *I*ᵃ ⁶⁵ (317) | ευρηκα] ευρον *I*ᵃ δ²⁵⁴*
(?) *K*³⁰⁶ (119) | σου] μου *I*ᵃ ⁷⁰ (505) | περιπατουντας] post. αληθεια *O*⁴⁶ (154) :
περιπατουντα 40. 67. 69. 101. 180 1ˢᶜʳ | καθως εντολην] *secundum mandatum*
quod arm. | καθως]+και *I*ᵃ ⁷⁰ (505) | ελαβομεν] ελαβον ℵ 13. 28.   An
accidental error (? from Jn. x. 18) | παρα] απο A 73 | του] om. B.

5. νῦν] The adverb is temporal. Cf. ver. 4, ἐχάρην.

ἐρωτῶ σε Κυρία] If ἐρωτᾶν has the special force of suggesting some sort of equality of position between the two parties concerned ("in the exercise of the full privilege of Christian fellowship," Wsct.), the emphasis is laid on the words οὐχ ὡς ἐντολήν. The Elder who has the right to command merely grounds a personal request, as between equals, on the old command laid on both alike by the Master. If, however, the special meaning of ἐρωτᾶν is to be found in the emphasis which it lays on the person addressed, as opposed to the thing asked (αἰτεῖν), then Κυρία is the emphatic word. He can ask in full confidence of the "Elect Lady" that which is no new command, pleading for the fulfilment of the old commandment laid on her and on all by the Lord. But ἐρωτᾶν was the *natural* word to use. Cf. Oxyrh. Pap. ii. 292, ἠρώτησα δὲ καὶ Ἑρμίαν τὸν ἀδελφὸν διὰ γραπτοῦ ἀνηγεῖσθαί σοι περὶ τούτου.

εἴχαμεν] The writer includes himself and all Christians among the recipients of the command. There is no need to limit his application of the first person plural to those who originally heard the command given.

ἵνα ἀγαπῶμεν ἀλληλούς] These words should probably be taken, not as dependent on ἐρωτῶ, but as defining the ἐντολή. The instances of the purely definitive ἵνα have been collected before.

ερωτω] ερωτωμεν /ᵃ ¹⁰¹· ⁷ᵗ· ⁶⁵ (40) **boh-cod.** | γραφων σοι καινην Β Κ L P al. pler. cat. sah. Thphyl. Oec.] καινην γραφων σοι ℵ A 5. 13. 31. 68 dˢᶜʳ vg. cop. Lcif. | γραφων] γραφω 64. 65. 66. 106 dˢᶜʳ* al. uix. mu. arm. aeth | καινην] inc. **sah**ᵇ | αλλα]+εντολην ℵ : +εντολην παλαιαν syrᵖ | ειχαμεν ℵ A] ειχομεν Β Κ L P al. pler. : εχομεν 31. 38. 68 aˢᶜʳ al. fere.²⁰ | ινα] pr. αλλ /ᵃ δ²⁵⁴ (?).

6. αὕτη ἐστίν . . . ἵνα] Cf. 1 Jn. v. 3, iii. 23. In the first Epistle the love which is said to consist in the "keeping" of His commandments is more clearly defined as the love of God. Here it is left undefined. The immediate context (ἵνα ἀγαπῶμεν ἀλλήλους) suggests that the writer is thinking especially of Christian brotherly love. The highest expression of this love is found in obedience to all the commands (however variously expressed) which God has enjoined in regulation of the relations between brethren. The clearest expression of love is obedience to the will of God, so far as He has revealed His will in definite precepts. It is quite in the writer's style to make the more absolute statement, even if he is thinking particularly of a special application.

αὕτη ἡ ἐντολή ἐστιν] The order of the words, if this is the true text, lays stress on ἡ ἐντολή. This is the one command in which all precepts are summed up.

καθὼς ἠκούσατε] If the reading ἵνα καθώς is correct, the ἵνα which precedes ἐν αὐτῇ must be resumptive. Cf. 1 Jn. iii. 20, according to a possible interpretation of that verse. The omission of ἵνα certainly appears to be an attempt at simplification. In either case the clause must be taken with what follows, and regarded as thrown forward for the sake of emphasis.

ἵνα . . . περιπατῆτε] In order to avoid the appearance of tautology most commentators interpret ἐν αὐτῇ as referring to ἀγάπη, the main subject of the verse. It would be tempting to refer it to the subject of the sentence ἀληθεία (ver. 4). The *one* command is that we should walk in truth as we have heard it from the beginning. This would suit the following verse. But the more natural reference is to the command. Cf. the Vulgate rendering *in eo* (sc. *mandato*). If this is possible, the emphasis must be on περιπατεῖν and καθὼς ἠκούσατε. The command which sums up all the precepts, which men show their love in obeying, is the command to active obedience to God's will as it has been revealed from the beginning of the Christian life, to "abide" in what they have always known, and to let it regulate their whole conduct and life.

και . . . αγαπη] om. aeth. | αυτου] του θῡ I[a 70] (505) | αυτη 2°] pr. *et* arm. boh-ed. | η εντολη] post εστιν ℵ (+αυτου) L P al. pler. ug[cle] et. demid. harl. tol. sah. cop. arm. Lcif. Thphyl. Oec. | καθως . . . περιπατητε] *ut incedamus in hoc quod audiuistis antiquitus* aeth. | καθως B L P al. pler. syr[bodl et p] Lcif. Thphyl. Oec] pr. ινα ℵ A K 13. 31. 73. al. mu. cat. vg. sah. cop. arm. | ινα 2°] om. K 13 al. mu. cat. vg. sah. boh. (uid.) arm. | εν αυτη] om. I[a 175] (319) | περιπατητε] περιπατειτε L 13 al. aliq. Thphyl. : περιπατησητε ℵ : *incedamus* arm-codd. boh-ed.

7. ὅτι] gives the reason for the preceding ἵνα ἐν αὐτῇ περιπατῆτε. If this refers to love, the reason given must be either (1) that the *presence* of such false teachers as are here described is likely to prove destructive to the exercise of mutual love among Christians, or (2) that their *teaching*, in denying the reality of the Incarnation, cuts away the whole foundation of Christian love as called out by the great act of love in which God expressed His love for the world. But both these interpretations are forced, and the contents of this verse point to a different interpretation of ver. 6, that, namely, which throws the emphasis on the word περιπατῶμεν. The command to mutual love grounded on true faith must be obeyed so as to find expression in action and conduct (περιπατεῖν). Otherwise the forces which make against obedience will be too strong. Many have joined the world, and their power to lead astray is great.

πλάνοι] Cf. 1 Jn. ii. 26, τῶν πλανώντων ὑμᾶς, and the accusation brought against the Lord by some of the crowd in Jn. vii. 12, πλανᾷ τὸν ὄχλον: cf. also Justin Martyr's λαοπλάνον. The substantive does not occur in the Johannine writings except in this verse.   The verb is fairly common in the Apocalypse.

ἐξῆλθαν] Cf. 1 Jn. iv. 1, πολλοὶ ψευδοπροφῆται ἐξεληλύθασιν εἰς τὸν κόσμον.   The verb probably does not refer to the excommunication or withdrawal of the false teachers (contrast 1 Jn. ii. 19, ἐξ ἡμῶν ἐξῆλθαν).   It suggests the idea that these deceivers have received their mission from the Evil One, in whose power "the whole world lieth."

οἱ μὴ ὁμολογοῦντες] The subjective negative is naturally used when a class is described and characterized.   They are distinguished by their refusal to confess the truth of the Incarnation.

Ἰησοῦν Χριστὸν ἐρχόμενον ἐν σαρκί] Cf. 1 Jn. iv. 2 ff., esp. ὁ ὁμολογεῖ Ἰησοῦν Χριστὸν ἐν σαρκὶ ἐληλυθότα, of which the present passage is almost certainly a reminiscence; cf. the notes on the earlier passage.   The chief difference is in the tense of the participle.   By the use of ἐρχόμενον instead of ἐληλυθότα the confession is taken out of all connection with time and made timeless.   In the First Epistle stress was laid on the historical fact and its permanent consequences.   Here the writer regards it as a continuous fact.   The Incarnation is not only an event in history.   It is an abiding truth.   It is the writer's view that humanity has been taken up into the Deity.   The union is permanent and abiding.   His view as to the exact difference in the relation of the Logos to the world and to mankind, which was brought about by the Incarnation, is not so clear.   All creation was "life in Him."   Before the Incarnation "He came to His own."   But it is clear that he regarded it as a completely new revelation of what human nature was capable of becoming, and as establishing the possibility for all future time of a more real union between God and man.   The Incarnation was more than a mere incident, and more than a temporary and partial connection between the Logos and human nature.   It was the permanent guarantee of the possibility of fellowship, and the chief means by which it is brought about.[1]

οὗτος κ.τ.λ.] Cf. 1 Jn. ii. 22 and 18.   The coming of Antichrist is fulfilled in the sum-total of all the evil tendencies in the work and influence of those who refuse to confess "Jesus Christ come in flesh."

ὁ πλάνος] The deceiver, *par excellence*, known as Antichrist in popular expectation.   As in the First Epistle, the writer uses the term as the convenient expression of the evil tendencies of his time.   He thus spiritualizes the popular idea, but he nowhere throws any light on the general character or the details of the

---

[1] There is, however, much to be said for the simpler explanation of ἐρχόμενον, which refers it to the future manifestation of the Parousia.   Cf. Barnabas vi. 9, ἐλπίσατε ἐπὶ τὸν ἐν σαρκὶ μέλλοντα φανεροῦσθαι ὑμῖν Ἰησοῦν.

popular legend. The use of the plural in some Latin and Syriac authorities, supported by one or two cursives, bears witness to the difficulties felt by those who did not easily understand the drift of his language.

εξηλθον (-θαν A) א A B al. plus¹⁵ cat. vg. (et. am. fu. demid. harl. Bed. m⁸ tol. *prodierunt,* Lcif. *progressi sunt*) sah. syrᵇᵒᵈˡᵉᵗᵖ arm. Ir. Ps. Chr.] εισηλθον K L P al. pler. Thphyl. Oec. Clearly a correction caused by the εις which follows. The form found in A is probably original | οι μη ομολογουντες] ο μη ομολογων *I*ᵃ ²⁰⁰ᶠ (83) | ερχομενον] om. *I*ᵃ ⁵⁵* (236) *I*ᵇ ²⁰⁹ᶠ (386) | σαρκι]+ει τις ουκ ομολογει *I*ν̄ Χ̄ν̄ ερχομενονεν σαρκι *I*ᵇ ³⁹⁶⁻³⁹⁸ (‒) *K*ᵇˡ δ³⁵⁹ (17) | ουτος . . . αντιχριστος] *hii fallaces et antechristi sunt* m⁸ : *isti sunt fallaces et antichristi* Lcif. : *hi sunt seductores et antichristi* syrᵖ ᵐᵍ : ουτοι εισιν οι πλανοι και οι αντιχριστοι *I*ᵃ ⁷⁰· ⁷ (505) *I*ᶜ ²⁵⁸ (56).

8. βλέπετε ἑαυτούς] Cf. Mk. xiii. 9, βλέπετε ὑμεῖς ἑαυτούς : 1 Co. xvi. 10, βλέπετε ἵνα ἀφόβως γένηται πρὸς ὑμᾶς : and for the form of expression, 1 Jn. v. 21, φυλάξατε ἑαυτά. "The use of the active with the reflexive pronoun . . . emphasizes the duty of personal effort."

ἵνα μὴ ἀπολέσητε κ.τ.λ.] The reading of B, etc., ἀπολέσητε —ἠργασάμεθα—ἀπολάβητε, is almost certainly the true text. The other variants are easily explained as attempts to reduce this reading to uniformity, by using either the first or the second person throughout.

ἠργασάμεθα] Cf. Jn. vi. 27, 28, ἐργάζεσθε . . . τὴν βρῶσιν τὴν μένουσαν : and for the thought of the reward, Jn. iv. 36, ἤδη ὁ θερίζων μισθὸν λαμβάνει καὶ συνάγει καρπὸν εἰς ζωὴν αἰώνιον, ἵνα ὁ σπείρων ὁμοῦ χαίρῃ καὶ ὁ θερίζων. Perhaps these passages offer a more probable source for the ideas of this verse than the quotation from Ru. ii. 12, ἀποτίσαι Κύριος τὴν ἐργασίαν σου· γένοιτο ὁ μισθός σου πλήρης παρὰ Κυρίου θεοῦ Ἰσραήλ, πρὸς ὃν ἦλθες πεποιθέναι ὑπὸ τὰς πτέρυγας αὐτοῦ, out of which Dr. Rendel Harris has elaborated his ingenious suggestion that the Lady to whom the Epistle is addressed was "a proselyte, a Gentile Christian, and a widow." Holtzmann's criticism of this suggestion as "allzu scharfsinnig" is not unmerited. It may be of interest to notice that the reference to Ru. ii. 12 is to be found in Wettstein, who has provided or anticipated far more of the best illustrative parallels than the acknowledgments of his work in later Commentaries would lead us to suppose. Wettstein also quotes the Targum, "retribuat tibi Deus retributionem bonam operum tuorum in hoc seculo et erit merces tua perfecta in seculo futuro a Deo Israelis," and also Xen. *Cyr. Exp.* vii. ἧκες ἂν πλήρη φέρων τὸν μισθόν.

For ἀπολαμβάνειν, cf. Ro. i. 27, ἀντιμισθίαν ἣν ἔδει . . . ἀπολαμβάνοντες: Oxyrh. Pap. ii. 298 (p. 299), ἐὰν δέ τι ἄλλο προσοφειληται . . . εὐθέως ἀπολήμψῃ.

εαυτους ℵ A B P Dam. etc.] *αυτους* K L Dam. Ir. Lcif. | *απολεσητε*,
απολαβητε ℵ (*απολησθε* ℵ*) A B 5. 13 40. 66**. 68. 73. 137 d^{scr} f^{scr} j^{scr}
al. fere.[15] cat. vg. sah. cop. syr^{utr} arm. aeth. Ir. Lcif. Ps.-Chr. Isid. Dam.
Thphyl^{com} Oec^{com}] *απολεσωμεν, απολαβωμεν* K L P 31 al. plu. Thphyl^{txt}
Oec^{txt} | *ειργασαμεθα* B (*ηργ-*) K L P 31 al. plu. sah. syr^{p mg} Thphyl^{txt}
Oec^{txt}] *ειργασασθε* ℵ A 5. 13. 40. 66**. 68. 73. 137 d f j^{scr} cat. vg. cop.
syr^{bodl et p txt} arm. aeth. Ir. Lcif. Ps.-Chr. Isid. Dam. Thphyl^{com} Oec^{com} :
ειργασαμεθα καλα K^{186} δ^{364} (223) | *πληρη*] *πληρης* L Dam. (? cf. Jn. i. 14).
According to Tischendorf's note it would seem that what is probably the
true text is supported by B sah. syr^{p mg} only. See note above.

9. ὁ προάγων καὶ μὴ μένων ἐν τῇ διδαχῇ] The phrase should
be taken as a whole. The sarcastic reference of *προάγων* to the
claims of false teachers to the possession of a higher knowledge
and more progressive intelligence was naturally misunderstood.
The *παραβαίνων* of the *Receptus* was the inevitable result.
What was not understood had to be corrected into an intelligible
commonplace. If this were the true text, we should have to
supply as object *τὴν διδαχήν* from the following ἐν τῇ διδαχῇ. But
the originality of *προάγων* is obvious. For the use of *προάγειν*,
Windisch quotes Sir. xx. 27, ὁ σοφὸς ἐν λόγοις προάξει ἑαυτόν.

The non-repetition of the article before μὴ μένων is significant. All "progress" is not condemned, but only such progress
as does not fulfil the added condition of "abiding in the teaching."

ἐν τῇ διδαχῇ τοῦ Χριστοῦ] There is nothing in the context or
the usage of the N.T. to suggest that τοῦ Χριστοῦ should be regarded as an objective genitive, the writer meaning by the phrase
"the apostolical teaching about Christ." Such an interpretation
would seem to be the outcome of preconceived notions of what
the author *ought* to have meant rather than of what his words
indicate. Cf. Jn. xviii. 19, ἠρώτησαν αὐτὸν . . . περὶ τῆς διδαχῆς
αὐτοῦ: Jn. vii. 16, ἡ ἐμὴ διδαχὴ οὐκ ἔστιν ἐμὴ ἀλλὰ τοῦ πέμψαντός
με . . . γνώσεται περὶ τῆς διδαχῆς, where there is the same transition to the absolute use of the word which is found in this
verse. Cf. also Mt. vii. 28; Mk. iv. 2; Lk. iv. 32; Ac. ii. 42;
Apoc. ii. 14 (τὴν διδαχὴν Βαλαάμ), ii. 15 (τῶν Νικολαιτῶν). The
"teaching" no doubt includes the continuation of Christ's work
by His Apostles, but it begins in the work of Christ Himself.
In the view of the writer all true teaching is but the application
of "ὁ λόγος ὁ ἐμός" He did not regard Paul or any other
Apostle as the inventor of most of what was characteristic of the
Christian Faith as he knew it.

θεὸν οὐκ ἔχει] Cf. 1 Jn. ii. 22 f., a passage of which this verse
is probably a summary. It is hardly intelligible except in the
light of that passage, or of teaching similar to that which it contains. The true revelation of God was given in Jesus Christ.
He who rejects the truth about Christ cannot enjoy the fellowship with God which Christ has made possible for men.

12

οὗτος καὶ κ.τ.λ.] Cf. 1 Jn. ii. 23 ff. and notes. As was pointed out in the Introduction and also in the notes on that passage, the words can refer equally well to Gnostic claims to a superior knowledge of the Father, and to Jewish opponents who shared with their Christian antagonists the belief in the God of Israel.

τας (? πας)] om. *I*ᵃ ¹¹⁰⁰ (310) | ο προαγων ℵ A B 98ᵐᵍ am. fu. harl. sah. **boh.** aeth.] ο παραβαινων K L P al. pler. cat. syrᵇᵒᵈˡ ᵉᵗ ᵖ (*qui transgreditur*) arm. Eph. Thphyl. Oec. : *qui recedit* vgᶜˡᵉ demid. tol. Lcif. Didˡᵃᵗ | μενων εν τη ιᵒ] εμμενων τη 31 | διδαχη ιᵒ] αγαπη 13 | του—διδαχη 2ᵒ] om. *I*ᵇ ³⁶⁵*. ³⁵⁶*. δ²⁶⁰ᶠ (214) *I*ᶜ ³⁵³. ¹⁷⁴. ⁵⁰⁵ (58) | του χριστου]του θῡ *I*ᵃ ⁵⁵ (236) *I*ᵇ ³⁷⁰ (1149): om. *I*ᵇ ¹⁵⁷ (29) | εχει] *nouit* **arm.** | μενων εν τη 2ᵒ] εμμενων τη 100 | μενων (? 2ᵒ)] παραμενων *I*ᵇ δ²⁶⁰ (440) | εν 2ᵒ] om. *H* δ⁶ (Ψ) | διδαχη 2ᵒ ℵ A B 13. 27. 29. 66**. 68 vg. sah. syrᵖ ᵗˣᵗ arm. Didˡᵃᵗ Fulg.]+*eius* syrᵇᵒᵈˡ ᵉᵗ ᵖ Lcif. : +του χριστου K L P al. pler. cat. **boh.**-ed. aeth. Thphyl. Oec. : (?)+του θῡ *I*ᵃ δ⁴⁵⁹ (125) | και τον πατερα και τον υιον] ℵ B K L P al. pler. cat. vgᶜˡᵉ sah. cop. syrᵇᵒᵈˡ ᵉᵗ ᵖ aeth. Lcif. Did.] και τον ῡν και τον π̄ρα A 13. 31 (om. τον 2ᵒ). 68 am. fu. demid. harl. tol. **arm.** Fulg. | και τον υιον] post εχει *I*ᵃ ⁷ (?) *I*ᶜ ²⁰⁸⁻¹¹⁶ (307) | εχει 2ᵒ] pr. ουκ *I*ᵇ δ²⁶⁰ (440).

10. εἴ τις ἔρχεται κ.τ.λ.] Cf. Didache xi. 1, 2, ὃς ἂν οὖν ἐλθὼν διδάξῃ ὑμᾶς ταῦτα πάντα τὰ προειρημένα δέξασθε αὐτόν· ἐὰν δὲ αὐτὸς ὁ διδάσκων στραφεὶς διδάσκῃ ἄλλην διδαχὴν εἰς τὸ καταλῦσαι, μὴ αὐτοῦ ἀκούσητε. There is nothing in the Epistle itself to indicate that this verse "at last discloses the special purpose of the whole Epistle." Its purpose is clearly to encourage those to whom it is addressed to continue in the active exercise of the faith and love which they had learned from Christ and His Apostles, even to the point of refusing hospitality to those who claimed to come in Christ's name, but who, in the writer's opinion, were destroying the work of Christ by their teaching.

The form of the conditional sentence used presents the case as more than a mere possibility, rather as something not unlikely to happen.

ἔρχεται πρὸς ὑμᾶς] The usage of ἔρχεσθαι in the Johannine Epistles is confined to the "coming" of Christ, or Antichrist, or of the brethren visiting another Church (3 Jn. 3), or of the Elder paying a formal visit (3 Jn. 10, ἐὰν ἔλθω). It is dangerous to read a special sense into common words. But clearly the accompanying condition, καὶ ταύτην τὴν διδαχὴν οὐ φέρει, limits the reference to those who claim to come as Christians, and to have a "teaching" to communicate to the members of the Church. The context excludes the idea that the writer is thinking of "casual visits of strangers." Those to whom he would refuse recognition claim to be received as brethren by fellow-Christians. In his view their conduct has made that impossible.

μὴ λαμβάνετε εἰς οἰκίαν] For the use of the verb, cf. Jn. i. 12, ὅσοι δὲ ἔλαβον αὐτόν· vi. 21, λαβεῖν αὐτὸν εἰς τὸ πλοῖον: xiii. 20, ὁ λαμβάνων ἄν τινα πέμψω ἐμὲ λαμβάνει.

χαίρειν . . . μὴ λέγετε] Elsewhere in the N.T. χαίρειν is only used in the greeting at the beginning of Epistles (Ac. xv. 23, xxiii. 26; Ja. i. 1). These passages throw no light on the question whether the welcome at meeting or the farewell greeting is meant. There is really nothing in the usage of the word or in the context to decide the question. We may perhaps compare Lk. x. 5, εἰς ἣν δ᾽ ἂν εἰσέλθητε οἰκίαν πρῶτον λέγετε· Εἰρήνη τῷ οἴκῳ τούτῳ. In the LXX the use of χαίρειν in this sense is confined to the letters contained in the Books of the Maccabees.

ει τις ερχεται] οτι εισερχεται I^c ^{506} (60) | ταυτην] post διδαχην 31 | αυτω] pr. εν I^c ^{114} (335).

11. This verse gives the grounds on which the injunctions of the preceding verse are based. The welcome and greeting contemplated are clearly such as express approval of the character and work of those who claim such reception.

κοινωνεῖ] always expresses a participation realized in active intercourse. It never denotes a mere passing sharing. Cf. 1 Ti. v. 22; 1 P. iv. 13.

τοῖς πονηροῖς] The form of expression is chosen which lays greatest stress on the adjective. Cf. 1 Jn. ii. 7, 8, i. 2, 3; Jn. x. 11.

ο (?)] om. I^{a} ^{1402} (219) K^2 (S) | λεγων] post γαρ K L P al. pler. cat. Ir. Thphyl. Oec. | αυτω] om. K al.^{25} Oec. | πονηροις]+ecce praedixi nobis ne in diem Domini condemnemini m^{63} :+ecce praedixi nobis ut in diem Domini nostri Jesu Christi non confundamini vg^{six}. Such additions are not uncommon in the text of the *Speculum*.

12, 13. Conclusion.

12. ὑμῖν] The position of the pronoun is perhaps emphatic. The writer of these Epistles is clearly well acquainted with the circumstances of those whom he addresses.

οὐκ ἐβουλήθην] One of the more certain instances in the N.T. of the epistolary aorist.

χάρτου καὶ μέλανος] Cf. the similar phrase in 3 Jn. 13, μέλανος καὶ καλάμου, and 2 Co. iii. 3, οὐ μέλανι ἀλλὰ πνεύματι. The material denoted is, of course, papyrus, the usual material for correspondence and for the cheaper kinds of books. Contrast 2 Ti. iv. 13, μάλιστα τὰς μεμβράνας. Cf. Jer xliii. (xxxvi.) 23, ἐξέλιπεν πᾶς ὁ χάρτης εἰς τὸ πῦρ.

γενέσθαι] If there is any difference of meaning between this word and the more usual ἐλθεῖν into which it has been altered in the *Textus Receptus*, γενέσθαι seems rather to mean to "pay a visit" (cf. 1 Co. ii. 3, xvi. 10, ἵνα ἀφόβως γένηται πρὸς ὑμᾶς). The intercourse which the coming makes possible is emphasized rather than the actual fact of coming. But cf. Tebtunis Pap. ii. 298 (p. 421), ἅμα τῷ λαβεῖν σε ταῦτά μου τὰ γράμματα γενοῦ πρὸς μέ, and also Jn. vi. 21 (ἐγένετο ἐπὶ τῆς γῆς), 25, πότε ὧδε γέγονας;

στόμα πρὸς στόμα] Cf. 3 Jn. 14, and 1 Cor. xiii. 12, πρόσωπον πρὸς πρόσωπον: Nu. xii. 8, στόμα κατὰ στόμα (פֶּה אֶל פֶּה).

ἵνα ἡ χαρὰ κ.τ.λ.] Cf. 1 Jn. i. 4; 3 Jn. 4. The object of the proposed visit is the same as that which the writer had in view in writing the First Epistle. It is generally to be noticed that the closest parallels in the Johannine writings are given some slightly different turn in different circumstances, which suggests that in both cases the writer is *using* his own favourite expressions rather than copying those of another.

εχων אᶜ A² B K L P al. pler. cat. vg. etc.] εχω א* A* 27. 29. 61. 64. 180 oˢᶜʳ: ειχον Kⁿˡ (17) arm. | υμιν] post γραφειν 99 al.³ ˢᶜʳ | γραφειν] γραψαι A 17. 73 gˢᶜʳ | ουκ] pr. *sed* arm. | μελανος και χαρτου sah. | αλλα ελπιζω א B K L P al. longe. plur. sah. syrᵇᵒᵈˡ ᵉᵗ ᴾ Thphyl. Oec.] ελπιζω γαρ A 5. 13. 27. 29. 66**. 73 dˢᶜʳ al.¹⁰ cat. vg. cop. arm. aeth. : ελπιζων 68 | γενεσθαι א A B 5. 6. 7. 13. 27. 33. 65. 66**. 68. 137. 180 dˢᶜʳ vg. syrᴾ Thphyl. Oecᶜᵒᵐ (παραγενεσθαι)] ελθειν K L P al. longe. plur. cat. tol. sah. syrᵇᵒᵈˡ arm. aeth. Oecᵗˣᵗ: *uidere* boh-ed. | λαλησαι] λαλησομεν *I*ᵇ ³⁹⁶ (-) | ημων א K L P al. pler. cat. syrᵇᵒᵈˡ ᵉᵗ ᴾ arm. Thphyl. Oec.] υμων A B 5. 13. 27. 29. 65. 66**. 68. 69. 73. 101. 104 cˢᶜʳ al.⁸ vg. cop. aeth. : *meum* sah. : om. 21. 37. 56. Nestle retains ημων in his Greek text, but it is probably a correction into conformity with the common reading in the First Epistle | πεπληρωμενη η א (ην א*) B vg. (et. fu. demid. harl. tol.) Thphyl.] η πεπληρωμενη A K L P al. omnᵘⁱᵈ cat. am. Oec.

13. The natural explanation of σέ and τὰ τέκνα is undoubtedly that which identifies the mother with her children, the Church, with the individual members of which it is composed. There is no difficulty in inventing hypotheses to account in other ways for the change between the singular and plural (cf. especially the ὑμᾶς of the preceding verse), and the absence of any greeting from the "elect sister" herself. But is it worth while in view of the fact that so much simpler an explanation lies ready to hand? Cf. Windisch, "Die Grüsse (nicht der Neffen und Nichten, sondern) der Glaubensgewissen am Orte des Schreibers."

τῆς ἐκλεκτῆς] Cf. ver. 1. The word does not occur elsewhere in the Johannine writings except in the Apocalypse (xvii. 14, οἱ μετ᾽ αὐτοῦ κλητοὶ καὶ ἐκλεκτοὶ καὶ πιστοί). But the writer's use of it is perfectly natural in the light of Jn. xv. 16, 19, ἀλλ᾽ ἐγὼ ἐξελεξάμην ὑμᾶς, and other passages in the Fourth Gospel and also in the Synoptists. Cf. 1 P. v. 13; Ro. xvi. 13.

ασπαζεται σε] *saluta* syrᴾ ᵗˣᵗ aeth. | της αδελφης] *matris* boh-cod. | της εκλεκτης] της εκκλησιας 15. 26 fu. : om. 73 : της εν εφεσω 114 : + η χαρις μεθ υμων 68. 69. 103 (μετα σου) syrᵇᵒᵈˡ ᵉᵗ ᴾ arm. : +*gratia et caritas uobiscum* aeth. : +αμην K L al. pler. cat. fu. syrᵇᵒᵈˡ ᵉᵗ ᴾ aethᴾᴾ Thphyl. Oec.

NOTES ON 3 JOHN.

---

1. ὁ πρεσβύτερος] Cf. 2 Jn. 1 note.

Γαΐω] Three persons of this name are mentioned in the N.T.
(1) Gaius the Macedonian, who is mentioned together with
Aristarchus in connection with the tumult in the theatre at
Ephesus (Ac. xix. 29). They are described as Macedonians,
fellow travellers of S. Paul. (2) Gaius of Derbe, one of S. Paul's
companions on his last journey to Jerusalem. (3) Gaius of
Corinth. Cf. Ro. xvi. 23, Γαΐος ὁ ξένος μου καὶ ὅλης τῆς
ἐκκλησίας: 1 Co. i. 14, Κρίσπον καὶ Γάιον, whom S. Paul
mentions as the only Corinthians, besides the household of
Stephanas, whom he had baptized himself. Of this Gaius,
Origen says that according to tradition he was the first Bishop
of Thessalonica. Cf. Origen, *Comm. in Ro.* x. 41, "*Fertur sane
traditione maiorum quod hic Gaius primus episcopus fuerit
Thessalonicensis ecclesiae.*" Dom Chapman's ingenious attempt
to connect the Epistle with Thessalonica on this ground is not
convincing (see Introd.). Coenen (*ZWTh.*, 1872, p. 264 ff.) has
attempted to show that Gaius of Corinth is intended in the
"fictitious" address of this Epistle, on the ground of the
similarity of the conditions prevailing here and at Corinth, as
testified by the Pauline Epistles. The similarities are of too
general a character either to compel identification or even to
make it probable. Coenen's interpretation of ὁ ἐρχόμενος (2 Co.
xi. 4) as a "pillar apostle whom S. Paul's opponents threatened to
invite to Corinth to overthrow his authority," is certainly not
helped by the statement in our Epistle of the Elder's intention
of paying a visit to the Church of Gaius. But perhaps it is not
necessary now to spend time in dealing with the theory that the
two smaller Johannine Epistles owe their origin to the desire of
the "great unknown" to gain credence for the view that his
more important forgeries (the Gospel and First Epistle) were
really the work of the son of Zebedee. As Windisch says, "III.
(*i.e.* 3 Jn.) für Fiktion zu erklären, widerspricht allen gesunden

Sinnen." The statement in *Const. Apostol.* vii. 46, that Gaius
was the first Bishop of Pergamus, is of too slight historical value
to guide our conjectures as to the recipient of this Epistle (*vid.*
Introd.). Bartlet's suggestion of Thyatira does not claim more
than relative probability. But all such attempts at identification
of the Church or the individual addressed are mere speculation.
Where our knowledge is inadequate the building up of hypothesis
is of the nature of pastime rather than of serious work. Truer
scholarship is seen in Harnack's less interesting judgment,
"Gaius, to whom (the Epistle) is addressed, receives no title of
honour. That he occupied a prominent position in his Church
is clear from what follows." In Commentaries, if not in peri-
odicals, the rule should be remembered that "there is a time to
keep silence."

τῷ ἀγαπητῷ] A favourite word of the writer of these Epistles,
in which it occurs ten times, though it is not found in the
Gospel. For its use in salutations, cf. Ro. i. 7, xvi. 5, 8, 9, 12 ;
Col. iv. 9, 14 ; 2 Ti. i. 2 ; Philem. 1.

ὃν . . . ἀληθείᾳ] Cf. 2 Jn. 1 (notes).

εγω] om. **boh-cod.**

2. περὶ πάντων] must be taken with εὐοδοῦσθαι. The writer
prays for the prosperity of Gaius in all respects, and especially
in the matter of health. There is no need to alter περὶ πάντων
into the conventional πρὸ πάντων of epistolary introductions.
The converse change would be far more likely to have taken
place.

εὐοδοῦσθαι] Bartlet's ingenious conjecture that the other name
of Gaius may have been Euodias, is again outside the sphere of
commentary. The word is part of the common and conventional
language of Epistles. For its use in the N.T., compare Ro. i. 10 ;
1 Co. xvi. 2. Cf. also Hermas, *Sim.* vi. 3, 5.

ὑγιαίνειν] The word may *possibly* suggest that Gaius' health
had caused his friends anxiety; but it certainly does not
necessarily do so. Its use in letters is conventional. Cf.
Oxyrh. Pap. ii. 293 (p. 293), Διονύσιος Διδύμῃ τῇ ἀδελφῇ
πλεῖστα χαίρειν καὶ διὰ παντὸ[ς] ὑγιαίνειν, and ii. 292 (p. 292),
πρὸ δὲ πάντων ὑγιαίνειν σε εὔχομαι ἀβασκάντως τὰ ἄριστα πράσσων.

καθὼς . . . ψυχή] Cf. Philo, *Quis rer. div. heres*, p. 514 (Wend-
land, iii. p. 65). Philo is commenting on "μετ᾽ εἰρήνης τραφείς"
(Gn. xv. 15). Πότε οὖν τοῦτο συμβήσεται; ὅταν εὐοδῇ μὲν τὰ ἐκτὸς
πρὸς εὐπορίαν καὶ εὐδοξίαν, εὐοδῇ δὲ τὰ σώματος πρὸς ὑγίειάν τε
καὶ ἰσχύν, εὐοδῇ δὲ τὰ ψυχῆς πρὸς ἀπόλαυσιν ἀρετῶν. The reference is to be found in Wettstein.

και ὑγιαινειν] om. **boh-codd.** | καθως]+και *I*ᶜ 364 (137).

3. ἐχάρην] Cf. 2 Jn. 4; Ph. iv. 10.

ἐρχομένων . . . καὶ μαρτυρούντων] The tense almost precludes the reference of the words to a single occasion, and their evidence should not be so interpreted in attempts to discover the historical setting of the Epistles. They suggest rather the means by which the Elder kept himself in touch with the Churches for whose welfare he regarded himself as responsible, and over which he exercised his supervision.

σου τῇ ἀληθείᾳ] As always in the Johannine writings, "truth" covers every sphere of life, moral, intellectual, spiritual. Those who visited Ephesus had from time to time borne witness that Gaius' whole life corresponded to the highest standard of life and conduct.

περιπατεῖς] Cf. note on 1 Jn. i. 6.

εχαρην γαρ A B C K L P al. pler. **boh-codd.** syr^bodl et p Thphyl. Oec.] om. γαρ א 4. 5. 6. 13. 25. 65. 100 d^scr vg. **boh-ed.** sah. arm. aeth. | σου] σοι *I*^a 64 (328) **sah.** (uid.) | τη αληθεια] την αληθειαν *I*^a 158. 1100 (395) : *caritati* **boh-cod.** | συ] pr. και 22. 56. 80. 98 **arm-codd.** (uid.) : om. A 37.

4. μειζοτέραν] Cf. ἐλαχιστοτέρῳ, Eph. iii. 8; Deissmann, *Bibel Studien*, p. 142, who quotes Pap. Lond. 130, μεγιστότατος.

τούτων] explained by the clause introduced by ἵνα. The plural is used instead of the singular, as the writer is thinking of more than one occasion on which he had experienced the joy of which he speaks. If this explanation of the plural is correct there is no need to correct the text by supplying ἤ before ἵνα, as Wilamowitz suggests (Hermes, 1898, p. 531). In his interesting note on the Epistle he does not offer any explanation of τούτων. Cf. Jn. xv. 13, μείζονα ταύτης ἀγάπην οὐδεὶς ἔχει, ἵνα τις τὴν ψυχὴν αὐτοῦ θῇ. The ἤ is actually found in one Greek cursive.

χαράν] The variant χάριν is probably due to a scribe, who substituted a commoner phrase. Cf. 2 Cor. i. 15. For χαρά, cf. 1 Jn. i. 4; 2 Jn 12; Philem. 7.

τὰ ἐμὰ τέκνα] Those over whom he exercises his fatherly supervision, whether actually his "children in the faith" or not. The bearing of this phrase on the meaning of τέκνα in the Second Epistle should not be overlooked.

μειζοτεραν] μειζοτερον *I*^b 78-157 (–) : μειζονα 137 | τουτων ουκ εχω] post χαραν *H*^257 (33) *I*^a 505. 192 (69) *O*^46 (154) | τουτων] ταυτης 27. 29. 31. 40. 66**. 68. 69. 73 d^scr al. fere.^10 sah. **boh-ed.** syr^bodl Dam. | ουκ εχω] post χαραν C 31. 68 aeth. | ουκ] om. *I*^c 364 (137) | εχων B* | χαραν א A C K L P al. pler. cat. tol. **arm. sah.**] χαριν B 7. 35 vg. cop. | ινα] pr. η 69 vg. (*maiorem horum . . . quam ut*) vid. sup. | ακουσω *I*^a 216 δ355 (301) | τεκνα] σπλαγχνα *I*^c 114 (335).

5. ἀγαπητέ] Cf. vv. 1, 2.

πιστὸν ποιεῖς] either (1) "thou doest a faithful thing," an action corresponding to the faith that is in thee, which is the

natural meaning of the word, if we consider the general usage of
the writer, though there is no exact parallel; or (2) "thou
makest sure whatsoever thou mayest do," thou doest that which
shall not "fail of its true issue," shall receive its due reward.
Cf. Xen. (quoted by Wettstein) ἂν μὲν δέῃ ταῦτα ποιεῖν πιστά,
ὁμήρους δοτέον.

ὃ ἐὰν ἐργάσῃ] The judgment is expressed absolutely, the
present tense being used. The ὃ ἐὰν ἐργάσῃ covers both the
past action, to which the recipients of Gaius' hospitality have
borne public witness before the Ephesian Church, and the future
benefits, which the Elder feels confident that Gaius will confer at
his request.

καὶ τοῦτο ξένους] For καὶ τοῦτο, cf. 1 Co. vi. 6, ἀδελφὸς μετὰ
ἀδελφοῦ κρίνεται, καὶ τοῦτο ἐπὶ ἀπίστων: Ph. i. 28, ἔνδειξις . . .
ὑμῶν δὲ σωτηρίας, καὶ τοῦτο ἀπὸ θεοῦ: Eph. ii. 8, τῇ γὰρ χάριτι
ἐστὲ σεσωσμένοι διὰ πίστεως· καὶ τοῦτο οὐκ ἐξ ὑμῶν. Its use in
Ro. xiii. 11 is rather different.

The recognition of the duty of φιλοξενία among Christians is
fully testified, 1 Ti. v. 10; Ro. xii. 13; He. xiii. 2; 1 P. iv. 9,
as also the special duties of the leaders in this respect, 1 Ti.
iii. 2; Tit. i. 8. Cf. also Herm. *Sim.* ix. 27, ἐκ δὲ τοῦ ὄρους τοῦ
δεκάτου, οὗ ἦσαν δένδρα σκεπάζοντα πρόβατά τινα, οἱ πιστεύσαντες
τοιοῦτοί εἰσιν· ἐπίσκοποι φιλόξενοι, οἵτινες ἡδέως εἰς τοὺς οἴκους
ἑαυτῶν πάντοτε ὑπεδέξαντο τοὺς δούλους τοῦ θεοῦ ἄτερ ὑποκρίσεως
. . . οὗτοι οὖν πάντες σκεπασθήσονται ὑπὸ τοῦ κυρίου διαπαντός.
Justin, *Apol.* i. 67, αὐτὸς (*sc.* ὁ προεστὼς) ἐπικουρεῖ . . . καὶ τοὺς
παρεπιδήμοις οὖσι ξένοις.

πιστον] pr. *uenim et* boh-cod.: πιστως *I*ᵃ 175 (319) | εργαση אּ B
C K L P al. omnᵘⁱᵈ cat. etc.] εργαξη A | τους] om. *H* δⁱ (Ψ) | και τουτο
א A B C 17. 27. 29. 33. 66**. 68. 81. 97. 126ᵐᵍ vg. syrᵇᵒᵈˡ ᵉᵗ ᵖ sah. cop. arm.
aeth.] και ταυτα *I*ᵃ 200ᶠ (83): και εις τους K L P al. pler. dˢᶜʳ (om. τους) cat.
Thphyl. Oec.

6. οἳ ἐμαρτύρησαν κ.τ.λ.] The ἀγάπη to which they bore
witness was clearly manifested in the hospitable reception of
those who were strangers to him, some of whom must subsequently have visited Ephesus. It is natural to interpret this
verse as referring to one of the occasions mentioned in ver. 3, or
more than one if the witness is to be regarded as a single fact,
though including a series of acts.

ἐνώπιον ἐκκλησίας] The absence of the article is significant.
The anarthrous phrase denotes a meeting of the Church at
which the witness was borne. Cf. 1 Co. xiv. 19, 35, ἐν ἐκκλησίᾳ:
Jn. xviii. 20, ἐν συναγωγῇ καὶ ἐν τῷ ἱερῷ: also vi. 59.

καλῶς ποιήσεις προπέμψας] The reading ποιήσας προπέμψεις is
probably a correction. καλῶς ποιήσεις is a common phrase in
letters, and no special stress should be laid on it. It is a con-

ventional expression. In many papyrus letters the double future occurs. Many letter writers would have written καλῶς ποιήσεις προπέμψεις. But the textual evidence does not justify our attributing such a solecism to the author. For the phrase, cf. Tebtunis Pap. i. 56, p. 167, καλῶς οὖν ποιήσῃς εὐχαριστῆναι πρῶτον μὲν τοῖς θεοῖς δεύτερον δὲ σῶσαι ψυχὰς πολλάς : 57, p. 168, καλῶς οὖν ποιήσεις ἀπολύσας αὐτούς : Oxyrh. Pap. ii. 294 (p. 294), εὖ οὖν ποιήσις γράψας μοι ἀντιφώνησιν : 297 (p. 298), καλῶς ποιήσεις γράψεις διὰ πιττακίων : 299 (p. 300), καλῶς ποιήσεις πέμψεις μοι αὐτάς : 300 (p. 301), καλῶς ποιήσεις ἀντιφωνήσασά μοι ὅτι ἐκομίσου : i. 116 (p. 182), καλῶς οὖν ποιήσαντες δότε παράμμωνι. It is so common that a schoolboy uses it sarcastically, ii. 119, καλῶς ἐποίησες οὐκ ἀπένηχές με μετὲ σοῦ εἰς πόλιν. Cf. also ps.-Aristias, 39, καλῶς οὖν ποιήσεις καὶ τῆς ἡμετέρας σπουδῆς ἀξίως ἐπιλεξάμενος ἄνδρας κ.τ.λ. : 46, καλῶς οὖν ποιήσεις . . . προστάξας.

προπέμψας] Cf. Tit. iii. 13, σπουδαίως πρόπεμψον ἵνα μηδὲν αὐτοῖς λείπῃ. It is also found in Acts and the earlier Pauline Epistles (Ro. ; 1, 2 Co.).

ἀξίως τοῦ θεοῦ] Cf. 1 Th. ii. 12, εἰς τὸ περιπατεῖν ὑμᾶς ἀξίως τοῦ θεοῦ τοῦ καλοῦντος ὑμᾶς κ.τ.λ. The adverb is also found with the following genitives : τῶν ἁγίων (Ro. xvi. 2), τῆς κλήσεως (Eph. iv. 1), τοῦ εὐαγγελίου τοῦ Χριστοῦ (Ph. i. 27), τοῦ κυρίου (Col. i. 10).

οἱ] ο K | σου] σοι *I*ᵃ ⁶⁴ (328): om. *I*ᵇ ⁸³⁰⁹ (35) | την αγαπην *H*¹⁶² (61) *I*ᶜ ³⁶⁴ (137) | εκκλησιας] pr. της *I*ᵃ ²⁰⁰· ¹⁷⁵· ¹⁰¹ (83) *O*⁴⁶ (154): *ecclesiarum eorum* boh-ed. | ους] ου B* | ποιησεις προπεμψας ℵ A B K L P etc. (ποιεις 7. 18. 27. 29. 68 demid. tol. al.) am. fu. tol. demid. boh-sah.] ποιησας προπεμψεις C vg. (*benefaciens deduces*) arm. (*deducis*) | αξιως] αξιους *I*ᵃ ⁷⁰· ¹⁷⁵ (505) | του θεου] τω θω *I*ᵃ ⁷⁰ᶠ (505) *O*⁴⁶ (154): om. *I*ᵃ ⁵⁵ (236).

7. ὑπὲρ γὰρ τοῦ ὀνόματος] gives the reason why they deserve such help. For the phrase, cf. Ac. v. 41, χαίροντες . . . ὅτι κατηξιώθησαν ὑπὲρ τοῦ ὀνόματος ἀτιμασθῆναι. We may also compare Ro. i. 5, ὑπὲρ τοῦ ὀνόματος αὐτοῦ. Dom Chapman's interpretation of the phrase as hinting at "withdrawal from the scene of persecution," or even banishment, at a time when the mere fact of being a Christian was enough to procure condemnation (cf. 1 P. iv. 14, εἰ ὀνειδίζεσθε ἐν ὀνόματι Χριστοῦ : 15, μὴ ὡς φονεύς . . . εἰ δὲ ὡς Χριστιανός, μὴ αἰσχυνέσθω) is wholly unnatural. As Bartlet has pointed out, it might be possible if the phrase used were διὰ τὸ ὄνομα.

The absolute use of τὸ ὄνομα, which is found in the passage quoted from Acts (cf. also Ph. ii. 9), is also to be found in Ignatius (*ad Eph.* iii. εἰ γὰρ καὶ δέδεμαι ἐν τῷ ὀνόματι : vii. εἰώθασιν γάρ τινες δόλῳ πονηρῷ τὸ ὄνομα περιφέρειν ἄλλα τινὰ πράσσοντες ἀνάξια θεοῦ : *ad Philad.* x. δοξάσαι τὸ ὄνομα). The "name" is clearly that of Christ. The fact that their having gone out on behalf of the name is put forward as the reason why they deserve hospitality, certainly does not carry with it the necessity of regarding the "name" as that of "brother." Missionaries no doubt proclaimed the brotherhood of believers, but their first duty was to proclaim the name of Christ.

ἐξῆλθαν] probably from Ephesus, though Dr. Westcott's more cautious statement, "from some Church well known to the Apostle and Gaius," is alone completely justified by the facts known to us from the Epistle and by the language used.

μηδὲν λαμβάνοντες] The form of the sentence (μηδέν) states more than the bare fact. It was their custom, a custom which emphasized the character of their work, to carry out the spirit of the Commission to the Twelve (Mt. x. 8, δωρεὰν ἐλάβετε, δωρεὰν δότε), and the tradition established by Paul (cf. 2 Co. xii. 14, ἑτοίμως ἔχω ἐλθεῖν πρὸς ὑμᾶς, καὶ οὐ καταναρκήσω οὐ γὰρ ζητῶ τὰ ὑμῶν ἀλλ᾽ ὑμᾶς: 1 Th. ii. 9, νυκτὸς καὶ ἡμέρας ἐργαζόμενοι πρὸς τὸ μὴ ἐπιβαρῆσαί τινα ὑμῶν ἐκηρύξαμεν εἰς ὑμᾶς τὸ εὐαγγέλιον τοῦ θεοῦ. They carried out as their rule of mission work the Pauline custom of refusing support from those amongst whom they were working as Missionaries. They had therefore a special claim on the hospitality and help of the Churches in places through which they had to pass. There is an interesting parallel to the sentence in the Didache xi. 6, ἐξερχόμενος δὲ ὁ ἀπόστολος μηδὲν λαμβανέτω εἰ μὴ ἄρτον, ἕως οὗ αὐλισθῇ, ἐὰν δὲ ἀργύριον αἰτῇ ψευδο-προφήτης ἐστίν. It is hardly necessary to deal at length with the interpretation which connects ἐξῆλθαν with ἀπὸ τῶν ἐθνικῶν, and bases their claim to help on the fact that they had been expelled from their home because of their faith, "eiecti erant propter religionem ab extraneis, nihilque secum apportauerunt" (Carpzov quoted by Poggel).

ἀπὸ τῶν ἐθνικῶν] For λαμβάνειν with ἀπό, cf. Mt. xvii. 25, ἀπὸ τίνων λαμβάνουσιν τέλη; and for the contrast between Christians and ἐθνικοί, cf. Mt. v. 47, ἐὰν ἀσπάσησθε τοὺς ἀδελφοὺς ὑμῶν μόνον, τί περισσὸν ποιεῖτε; οὐχὶ καὶ οἱ ἐθνικοὶ τὸ αὐτὸ ποιοῦσιν;

του ονοματος ℵ A B C K L P al. plu. cat. am. fu. sah. cop. syrᵖ txt arm-ed. Thphyl. Oec. Bed.]+αυτου minusc. mu. vg. demid. syrᵇᵒᵈˡ et ᵖ arm-cod. aeth. | λαμβανοντες] λαβοντες lᵇ ¹⁵⁷ (29) | απο] παρα 5. 13. 29. 118 dˢᶜʳ al.⁵ | εθνικων ℵ A B C al.¹² fu. tol. (gentilibus) boh-ed.] εθνων K L P al. longe. plu. boh-codd. : gentibus vg. am. demid. sah.

8. ἡμεῖς οὖν] In view of their policy of refusing support from the heathen to whom they minister, we Christians are under a special obligation to do what we can to forward their work.

ὀφείλομεν] Cf. 1 Jn. ii. 6, iii. 16, iv. 11, and Jn. xiii. 14.

ὑπολαμβάνειν] The ἀπολαμβάνειν of the *Textus Receptus* must be merely a scribe's error; the word is always used in the sense of receiving or getting, or getting back what is due (cf.

2 Jn. 8, μισθὸν πλήρη ἀπολάβητε). ὑπολαμβάνειν occurs elsewhere in the N.T. only in the Lucan writings, in the various
senses of *answer*, *suppose*, *receive* (νεφέλη ὑπέλαβεν αὐτὸν ἀπὸ τῶν
ὀφθαλμῶν, Ac. i. 9). The usage of the LXX is similar. But in
other Greek it is often used in the sense of *receiving* with
hospitality, and especially of *supporting*. Cf. Strabo, p. 653, οἱ
εὔποροι τοὺς ἐνδεεῖς ὑπολαμβάνουσιν. It suggests support as well
as welcome.

τοὺς τοιούτους] Cf. 1 Co. xvi. 16, ἵνα καὶ ὑμεῖς ὑποτάσσησθε
τοῖς τοιούτοις καὶ παντὶ τῷ συνεργοῦντι, and ver. 18, ἐπιγινώσκετε
οὖν τοὺς τοιούτους. All who act on such principles have a claim
on our help and support.

συνεργοὶ γιν. τῇ ἀληθείᾳ] The word may mean either (1)
become fellow-workers with them in the cause of the truth, or
(2) become fellow-workers with the Truth. In support of (1) are
quoted 2 Co. viii. 23, κοινωνὸς ἐμὸς καὶ εἰς ὑμᾶς συνεργός: Col.
iv. 11, οὗτοι μόνοι συνεργοὶ εἰς τὴν βασιλείαν τοῦ θεοῦ. There is
no other example of συνεργός with the dative in the N.T., the
usual construction being with the genitive, either of the person
or the work, or with a preposition. But the dative with συνεργεῖν
is not uncommon. Cf. Ja. ii. 22, ἡ πίστις συνήργει τοῖς ἔργοις
αὐτοῦ. Cf. also 1 Es. vii. 2, συνεργοῦντες τοῖς πρεσβυτέροις τῶν Ἰ. :
1 Mac. xii. 1, ὁ καιρὸς αὐτῷ συνεργεῖ. In view of this usage, and
the writer's use of ἀλήθεια, which he often almost personifies, the
second is more probably the correct interpretation. Cf. ver. 12,
ἀπ' αὐτῆς τῆς ἀληθείας.

υπολαμβανειν ℵ A B C* 13, 16. 27. 29. 46. 66**. 68. 73. 126ᵐᵍ Oecᶜᵒᵈ]
post τοιουτους *l*ᵃ ⁵⁶ (316) : απολαμβανειν Cᶜᵃᵛ K L P al. pler. cat. Thphyl.
| γινωμεθα] post αληθεια *l*ᵃ ²⁵¹ (326) : γενωμεθα K 42. 69. 105 al. fere.¹⁰
cat. Thphyl : γινομεθα C 100 | αληθεια] εκκλησια ℵ* A.

9. ἔγραψα] The addition of αν is clearly an attempt to
remove the (supposed) difficulty of admitting that a letter
written by an Apostle has not been preserved, or could have
failed in its object. It must have been added at a time when
the supposed reference to the Second Epistle was unknown, or
at any rate not accepted.

τι] Cf. Mt. xx. 20, αἰτοῦσά τι ἀπ' αὐτοῦ. It must be taken
as strictly indefinite. It suggests neither something great
(Gal. ii. 6, τῶν δοκούντων εἶναί τι) nor something insignificant.
Its omission in the *Textus Receptus* is probably due to error.

τῇ ἐκκλησίᾳ] The local Church of which Gaius and Diotrephes
were members. Cf. S. Paul's usage in his earlier Epistles
(1, 2 Th.; Gal.; 1, 2 Co.) and the usage of the Apocalypse
(i. 4, ii. 1, etc.).

In spite of the close resemblance in form between the

Second and Third Epistles, which certainly favours the view
that they are companion Epistles, and the many points of
similarity in the circumstances of the Churches to which, or to
members of which, they are addressed, the context of ver. 9
makes it almost impossible to see in the words ἔγραψά τι τῇ
ἐκκλησίᾳ a reference to the Second Epistle. (Cf. Introduction,
lxxxiii.) It must, of course, be admitted that Diotrephes probably
favoured, or at least condoned, the Gnostic or other teaching
which the writer condemns in the Second Epistle. And in
spite of what Harnack has said, it is doubtful whether that
Epistle "must have contained a reference to the sins of Diotrephes if it had been addressed to the Church of which he was
a member." But ver. 9 must be read as it stands, between verses
8 and 10. The reception, or the refusal to receive, the Missionary brethren is the subject of both these verses. The letter to
which reference is made in the intermediate verse, and which
the writer fears that Diotrephes will suppress or persuade his
Church to neglect, if, indeed, he has not already done so, *must*
have contained some reference to the question of the hospitable
reception of these brethren. If we add to this the totally
different aim of the two letters, on which Harnack rightly lays
stress, the warning *not* to receive false brethren in the Second,
and the exhortation to welcome the true brethren in the Third
Epistle, the case against the supposed reference is convincingly
strong. The most natural interpretation of the words is that
the Elder wrote to the Church a letter of similar content to the
private letter to Gaius, exhorting them to show hospitality to
Demetrius and the brethren whom he commends to their care:
but knowing the power of Diotrephes to oppose his wishes he
wrote a private letter to Gaius, a member of the Church on
whose loyalty he could thoroughly depend. The Second Epistle,
with its sharply expressed prohibition of any intercourse with
those who claimed the rights of brethren, but who had forfeited
them by their false teaching, fails altogether to correspond to
the requirements of the case.

ἀλλ'] The letter had been written, but the writer feared that
it would fail to secure the carrying out of his wishes.

φιλοπρωτεύων] not found elsewhere, except in Patristic writings, where it is derived from this passage. A *scholion* in
Matthaei (p. 162) explains it as equivalent to ὁ ὑφαρπάζων τὰ
πρωτεῖα. The cognate φιλόπρωτος and φιλοπρωτεία are both
found. Of the passages quoted by Wettstein in illustration of
the word two will suffice: Plutarch, *Alcibiad.* p. 192, φύσει δὲ
πολλῶν ὄντων καὶ μεγάλων παθῶν ἐν αὐτῷ τὸ φιλόνεικον ἰσχυρότα-
τον ἦν καὶ τὸ φιλόπρωτον: *Agesil.* 596 D, φιλονεικότατος γὰρ ὢν
καὶ θυμοειδέστατος ἐν τοῖς νέοις καὶ πάντα πρωτεύειν βουλόμενος.

The word expresses ambition, the desire to have the first place
in everything. It should not be pressed either to prove or dis-
prove the possession by Diotrephes of an "episcopal" position.
It certainly does not suggest "aspiring to a place *not* already
obtained."

αὐτῶν] The members of the Church to which the Elder
had written. For the construction, cf. 1 Co. i. 2, τῇ ἐκκλησίᾳ τοῦ
θεοῦ . . . ἡγιασμένοις ἐν Χριστῷ Ἰησοῦ.

οὐκ ἐπιδέχεται ἡμᾶς] ἐπιδέχεσθαι is not found in the N.T.,
except here and in the following verse, where it is used in a
somewhat different sense. Diotrephes refuses to recognize the
authority of the Elder and those who side with him. Cf.
1 Mac. x. 1, κατελάβετο Πτολεμαΐδα καὶ ἐπεδέξαντο αὐτὸν καὶ ἐβασί-
λευσεν ἐκει : xii. 8, ἐπεδέξατο . . . τὸν ἄνδρα . . . ἐνδόξως : xii. 43,
xiv. 23. In papyri it is used for "accepting" the terms, of a
lease, etc. (esp. ἐπιδέχομαι μισθώσασθαι). For its use in ver. 10
we may compare Oxyrh. Pap. ii. 281 (p. 272), ἐγὼ μὲν οὖν ἐπι-
δεξαμένη αὐτὸν εἰς τὰ τῶν γόνεων μου οἰκητήρια λειτὸν παντελῶς ὄντα.

εγραψα] εγραψας B sah. :+αν אᶜ 13. 15. 18. 26. 29. 33**. 36. 40. 49.
66**. 73. 180 dˢᶜʳ cat. vg. syrᵇᵒᵈˡ ᵉᵗ ᵖ | τι א A B C 7. 29. 66**. 68 sah. cop.
arm.] om. K L P al. pler. vg. syrᵇᵒᵈˡ ᵉᵗ ᵖ aeth. Thphyl. Oec. | αλλ] *quia*
sah. | ο] οτι Iᵃ ¹⁰⁶. ³⁹⁷ (179) | αυτων] pr. τη αληθεια Iᵃ ¹⁷³ (156) | Διοτρεφης]
Διοτροφης Iᵃ ²⁶⁴ (233) boh-cod. : Διατρεφης H¹⁶² (61) | οτρεφης H ⁸⁶ (Ψ)
| ουκ] ουδε H¹⁶² (61) | αποδεχεται Iᵃ ³⁹⁷ᶠ (96).

10. διὰ τοῦτο] Because of his refusal to recognize our
authority, and the lengths to which he has gone in opposing
us in consequence.

ἐὰν ἔλθω] Those who find in the Second Epistle the letter
to which ver. 9 refers naturally see in these words a reference
to ver. 12 of that Epistle (ἐλπίζω γενέσθαι πρὸς ὑμᾶς). They
are equally well explained by the expectation expressed in ver. 14
of this letter. The writer perhaps speaks somewhat less confidently (ἐάν) of his coming than he does of the arrival of false
teachers in the Church to which 2 Jn. is addressed (εἴ τις
ἔρχεται). But the difference between the two constructions
cannot be pressed.

ὑπομνήσω] Cf. Jn. xiv. 26, ὑπομνήσει ὑμᾶς πάντα ἃ εἶπον ὑμῖν
ἐγώ. The Elder will recall to them the whole conduct of their
leader and show it in its true light.

τὰ ἔργα] Cf. Jn. iii. 19 ff. (ἵνα μὴ ἐλεγχθῇ τὰ ἔργα αὐτοῦ . . .
ἵνα φανερωθῇ αὐτοῦ τὰ ἔργα). The writer is confident that the
conduct of Diotrephes will not stand the light of truth, and
that the Church will recognize the fact.

λόγοις πονηροῖς κ.τ.λ.] Two accusations are brought against
Diotrephes : his boastful opposition to the Elder and his friends,
and his harsh action in the matter of the Missionaries.

φλυαρῶν] Cf. 1 Ti. v. 13, οὐ μόνον δὲ ἀργαὶ ἀλλὰ καὶ φλύαροι (*uerbosae*, vg.) καὶ περίεργοι, λαλοῦσαι τὰ μὴ δέοντα. Oecumenius interprets ἀντὶ τοῦ λοιδορῶν, κακολογῶν. The word is not found elsewhere in the N.T. It emphasizes the emptiness of the charges which Diotrephes brings against the Elder in so many words.

μὴ ἀρκεσθεὶς ἐπὶ τούτοις] Cf. 1 Ti. vi. 8, τούτοις ἀρκεσθησόμεθα : He. xiii. 5, ἀρκούμενοι τοῖς παροῦσιν. The construction with ἐπί is not found elsewhere in the N.T. The nearest parallel to this passage is, perhaps, 2 Mac. v. 15, οὐκ ἀρκεσθεὶς δὲ τούτοις κατετόλμησεν εἰς τὸ . . . ἱερὸν εἰσελθεῖν.

οὔτε . . καί] For the construction, cf. Jn. iv. 11, οὔτε ἄντλημα ἔχεις καὶ τὸ φρέαρ ἐστὶν βαθύ.

ἐπιδέχεται τοὺς ἀδελφούς] Cf. note on ver. 9. This refusal to receive the brethren probably has special reference to some former visit of the Missionaries, when Diotrephes refused to receive them in spite of the commendatory letter which they brought with them. But the present indicates a general practice rather than a particular incident. The words *may* simply mean that D. will not recognize as true Christians the brethren who side with the Presbyter. He will recognize neither the Presbyter nor his followers. It is better, however, not to exclude the reference to Diotrephes' former ill-treatment of those whom the Elder now commends to Gaius. The question of the welcome to be given to those who went from place to place ὑπὲρ τοῦ ὀνόματος was an important one at the time, and probably for some time afterwards. Cf. Didache xii. 1, πᾶς δὲ ὁ ἐρχόμενος ἐν ὀνόματι Κυρίου δεχθήτω ἔπειτα δὲ δοκιμάσαντες αὐτὸν γνώσεσθε, and the whole chapter, esp. § 5, εἰ δ' οὐ θέλει οὕτω ποιεῖν, χριστέμπορός ἐστιν· προσέχετε ἀπὸ τῶν τοιούτων.

τοὺς βουλομένους] *sc.* ἐπιδέχεσθαι. His custom is to put every hindrance in the way of their carrying out their wishes, or he actually prevents them. The description of his action does not decide his position. The words used express action possible either in the case of a "monarchical" bishop, or of an influential and self-willed leader.

ἐκ τῆς ἐκκλησίας ἐκβάλλει] Jn. ix. 34 f. is rightly quoted in illustration. But the difference in tense should also be noticed (καὶ ἐξέβαλον αὐτὸν ἔξω). Again a policy or practice is described rather than a single incident. And the words cannot be used to determine the exact position of Diotrephes. Even if he had already obtained the "monarchical" position he could not have inflicted the penalty of excommunication without the concurrence of the whole Church. And a leading presbyter might well succeed in forcing his will on the community. The words, therefore, only indicate the position of power to which he had

attained. And they do not determine whether the sentence of
excommunication had been actually carried out, either in the
case of those who wished to receive the Missionaries to whom
reference is made in this Epistle, or in any other case.

The suggestion of Carpzov, revived by Poggel, to make τοὺς
ἀδελφούς the object of ἐκ τῆς ἐκκλησίας ἐκβάλλει, involves a construction which is intolerably harsh. The writer's love of
parenthesis, even if ὁ εἰπών is the true reading in Jn. i. 15,
hardly goes so far as this. And the arguments by which it is
supported are not convincing: (1) Diotrephes could not have
expelled those whose only offence was the desire to show
hospitality to the Missionaries; (2) if he succeeded in preventing
them from carrying out their wishes, why should he go further?

υπομνησω] ελεγξω O⁴⁶ (154) | εργα]+mala boh-cod. | πονηροις λογοις
Iᵃᵟ¹⁸⁰ (1319) | ημας] pr. εις C vg. : υμας H¹⁶² (61) Iᵃ ¹⁵³ (395) Iᵇ ⁶² (498) Iᶜ ²⁵⁸
(56) | επι] om. H¹⁶² (61) | επιδεχεται] υποδεχεται Iᶜ²⁰⁸. ¹⁷⁴ (307) : + uos neque
accipit sahʷ | βουλομενους ℵ A B K L P al. pler. cat. am. fu. cop. syrᵖ ᵗˣᵗ
aeth. Thphyl. Oec.] επιδεχομενους C 5. 7. 27. 29. 66** vg. demid. tol. sah.
syrᵇᵒᵈˡ ᵉᵗ ᵖ ᵐᵍ arm. :+suscipere boh. | εκ—εκβαλλει] εκβαλλει και κωλυει της
εκκλησιας 4 | εκ A B C K L P al. plu. Thphyl. Oec.] om. ℵ 2. 3. 15. 25. 26.
36. 43. 95*. 98. 99. 100 bˢᶜʳ hˢᶜʳ.

11. ἀγαπητέ] Cf. note on ver. 2.

μὴ μιμοῦ τὸ κακόν] Cf. He. xiii. 7 ; 2 Th. iii. 7, 9. The use of
φαῦλον is more frequent in this writer, but κακόν is found in Jn.
xviii. 23 (εἰ κακῶς ἐλάλησα μαρτύρησον περὶ τοῦ κακοῦ). It is not
necessary to limit the writer's meaning to the examples of evil
and good afforded by Diotrephes and Demetrius, especially as
the conduct of the latter would seem to have needed apology.
If two special examples are intended, they must be the action of
Diotrephes, and that of Gaius and his friends who wished to
show hospitality. But the writer's object is rather to set two
courses of action in the sharpest possible contrast, and to help
forward a right decision by showing the true character of the
point at issue in all its simplicity. Viewed rightly, it is simply a
matter of refusing the evil and choosing the good. There are
times when the simplest platitude in the mouth of authority is
the expression of the truest wisdom ; cf. Mk. iii. 4 (= Lk. vi. 9).

ὁ ἀγαθοποιῶν ἐκ τοῦ θεοῦ ἐστίν] Cf. 1 Jn. iii. 9, 10. He who
" does good " shows by his conduct that the inspiration which
dominates his life and work comes from God. He who " does
evil " shows similarly that he has not made even the first step
towards union with God ; cf. 1 Jn. iii. 6, πᾶς ὁ ἁμαρτάνων οὐχ
ἑώρακεν αὐτόν (Dr. Westcott's note) ; Jn. iii. 3, 5.

For the use of ἀγαθοποιεῖν, κακοποεῖν, and cognate words, cf.
1 P. iii. 17, ii. 15, 20, iii. 6, iv. 19, ii. 12, 14, iv. 15. Several
points of connection between 2 and 3 John and 1 Peter have

been noticed by Dom Chapman in his articles on the historical setting of these Epistles.

o 2° ℵ A B C K P h al. longe. plu. cat. d vg. **boh-codd.** sah. syrᴾ]
+ δε L 31 aˢᶜʳ al. mu. tol. **boh-ed.** arm. aeth. Did. Dam. Thphyl. Oec.

12. Δημητρίῳ] Nothing is known of Demetrius except what can be gathered from the Epistle itself. The conjecture that he should be identified with the Demas mentioned in the Pauline Epistles (Col. iv. 14; Philem. 24, and 2 Ti. iv. 10), and the less improbable suggestion of his identity with the Ephesian silver-smith whose opposition to S. Paul is recorded in Ac. xix. 21 ff., have been referred to in the Introduction. *Purely* conjectural identification is hardly a branch of serious historical study. But the mention of Demetrius here may be interpreted in different ways. (i.) It is possible to regard him as a member of the Church of Gaius and Diotrephes, whose conduct had somehow or other given cause for suspicion, even if we cannot follow the ingenious attempts of Weiss to show that he must have been the leader of the Church to whom under the special circumstances of the case the Elder had sent his letter to the Church (ver. 9), and of whose attitude Gaius was uncertain, as he stood between the two parties (Weiss, p. 210).

(ii.) With greater probability he has been regarded as the bearer of the Epistle (3 Jn.). Wilamowitz and others are probably right in finding in this Epistle a commendatory letter on behalf of Demetrius and his companions. The special emphasis of ver. 12 is most easily explained, as Dom Chapman, Mr. Bartlet and others have seen, by the supposition that Demetrius had fallen under suspicion, though the grounds for such suspicion are altogether unknown. On the whole, the hypothesis which best suits the facts of the case which are known to us is that he was one of the Missionaries, perhaps their leader. The main object of the letter is to commend them to the hospitality of the Church of Gaius. This the Elder had already attempted to do in a letter written to the Church. But his object had been frustrated by the machinations of Diotrephes, who had succeeded in forcing his will upon the Church. Probably Diotrephes had found his task the easier because of suspicions felt about Demetrius, which were not altogether unwarranted. We cannot, however, say more than that of several possible hypotheses this is the most probable.

ἀπ' αὐτῆς τῆς ἀληθείας] Cf. Papias' quotation of the words of the Elder (Eus. *H. E.* iii. 39. 3), ἀπ' αὐτῆς παραγινομένας τῆς ἀληθείας. The tendency to personify the Truth is clearly marked in the Johannine writings. The relation of the Truth, as thus personified, to Christ and to the Spirit is not so clearly defined.

In view of the language of the Farewell discourses in the Gospel
(cf. especially Jn. xvi. 13), and the statement of 1 Jn. v. 6, ὅτι τὸ
πνεῦμά ἐστιν ἡ ἀλήθεια, there is much to be said in favour of
Huther's view, that the expression αὐτὴ ἡ ἀλήθεια is not merely a
personification of Truth, but a description of the Holy Spirit.
Against this, however, must be set the language of Jn. xiv. 6,
ἐγώ εἰμι . . . ἡ ἀλήθεια. With this want of clearness we naturally compare the difficulty which is so often found in the First
Epistle of determining whether the writer is speaking of the
Father or the Son. The writer does not think in the terms of
modern conceptions of personality as applied to the Godhead, or
of the more precise definitions which were the result of the
Trinitarian controversies. His function is rather to provide the
material out of which later thought developed clearer definition.

In what manner the "Truth" is said to bear witness to
Demetrius is a different question. Probably it is in so far as his
life and conduct show those who know him that the ideal of
Christianity has been realized in him, that he "abides in the
truth."

ὑπὸ πάντων] If any qualification of the words is necessary, that
of Oecumenius will serve the purpose, τῶν τὴν ἀλήθειαν ἐχόντων.
And his further suggestion is appropriate, εἴ τις τὸ ὑπὸ πάντων καὶ
ἐπὶ τῶν ἀπίστων ἐκλάβοι διὰ τὸ περιληπτικὸν τοῦ πᾶς μορίου, οὐ
κακῶς οὗτος ὑπολαμβάνων φωραθείη, and also his comparison of
S. Paul's πάντα πᾶσιν ἀρέσκω. But the natural exaggeration of
this use of πάντων, where the meaning practically is "all whom
the matter may concern," or "all who might be expected to do
the thing spoken of," is common in all language, and is best left
to explain itself.

καὶ ἡμεῖς δέ] For the construction, and also for the combination of the witness of men with the higher witness, cf. Jn.
xv. 26 f. ἐκεῖνος μαρτυρήσει περὶ ἐμοῦ· καὶ ὑμεῖς δὲ μαρτυρεῖτε, ὅτι
ἀπ' ἀρχῆς μετ' ἐμοῦ ἐστέ. The meaning of ἡμεῖς in these Epistles
is often difficult to determine,—a difficulty which is unnecessarily
exaggerated by the attempt to discover one meaning which it
must have throughout. It is certainly unsatisfactory to find in
it an expression for the αὐτόπται of the Province of Asia as often
as Dr. Zahn suggests, a fact which his critics are never tired of
emphasizing. But there are several passages in which the writer
would certainly seem to mean by ἡμεῖς himself and all who can
speak with authority as to the truth of Christianity and the
teaching of Christ, and where he is, perhaps, thinking primarily
of a company, most of whose lives "have passed into the unseen."
At any rate, he means something more than "I and those who
are like-minded with me." It is not altogether fanciful to
suppose that the words of Jn. xv. 26 f. are in his mind as he

writes. In the present verse, however, there is nothing to suggest that he means more than "we who are personally acquainted with Demetrius."

οἶδας κ.τ.λ.] The close connection of this clause with Jn. xxi. 24, καὶ οἴδαμεν ὅτι ἀληθὴς αὐτοῦ ἡ μαρτυρία ἐστίν, is obvious. There is very little to determine which should be regarded as the echo of the other.

οἶδας] The plural of the *Textus Receptus* is not well supported, and the personal appeal to Gaius is more natural. Possibly the correction is due to the influence of the plural in Jn. xxi. 24.

The writer apparently makes his appeal to Gaius' knowledge of himself, and the trustworthy character of his witness in general. It is possible, however, that he is thinking of Gaius' knowledge of Demetrius, which would help him to judge of the truth of the Elder's witness in this particular case.

αυτης] om. **boh. sah.** | της αληθειας] pr. της εκκλησιας και C syr[bodl et p mg] **arm.** (om. αυτης) : της εκκλησιας A* | και οιδας ℵ A B C al. plus²⁰ cat. d vg. sah. **boh-ed.** arm.] και οιδατε K L P al. longe. plur. syr[bodl et p] aeth. Thphyl. Oec. : και οιδαμεν 14*. 38. 93. 104. 180 al.³ ˢᶜʳ **boh-codd.** : om. aˢᶜʳ : om. και H δ⁶ (Ψ) | η-εστιν] αληθης ημων εστιν (εστ. ημ. 68) η μαρτυρια C 68 : αληθης εστιν η μαρτ. ημ. 31 aeth.

13-15. The close of the Epistle.

13. γράψαι . . . γράφειν] This is probably the true text, though the variants γράφειν—γράψαι are found. The use of the tenses is correct. The "much" which he has to communicate is naturally regarded as a whole, the aorist being used. But he does not wish to go on using pen and ink (γράφειν).

μέλανος] Cf. 2 Jn. 12.

καλάμου] The reed, the pen of the ancients, here takes the place of the writing material mentioned in 2 Jn. Cf. Ps. xliv. (xlv.) 1, κάλαμος γραμμάτεως, Oxyrh. Pap. ii. 326 (p. 306) παρα- τέθεικα τῇ μητρὶ φιλουμένῃ τὸ βροχίον τοῦ μέλανος καὶ τοὺς καλάμους.

ειχον] η θελον I[b 157] (29) : *habens* **boh-ed** (?) | γραψαι σοι ℵ A B C al.¹⁰ d vg. sah. cop. syr[bodl et p] arm. (*uobis* **codd.**) aeth. Thphyl.] γραφειν K L P al. pler. cat. Oec. : συγγραψαι I[c δ²⁹⁹] (—) | ου θελω] ουκ εβουληθην A : ουκ ηθελον 27 : *nolui* vg. | δια—καλαμου] *per chartam et atramentum* arm. | σοι γραφειν ℵ B C 5. 27. 31. 33. 105] γραφειν σοι A 73 : σοι γραψαι K L P al. pler. cat. Thphyl. Oec. : om. σοι 4. 16 **arm.**

14. ἐλπίζω . . . ἰδεῖν] Cf. 2 Jn. 12, ἐλπίζω γενέσθαι πρὸς ὑμᾶς. The εὐθέως may possibly suggest that the intended journey is nearer than when 2 John was written. The action of Diotrephes, and perhaps of others in other places, may have brought matters to a crisis.

στόμα πρὸς στόμα] Cf. 2 Jn. 12 (notes).

εἰρήνη σοι] The Christian wish (cf. Jn. xiv. 27) takes the

place of the usual ἔρρωσο, or ἐρρῶσθαί σε εὔχομαι of ordinary correspondence.

ἀσπάζονται] In the private letter the private greetings are given instead of the general greeting of the members of the Church in the more formal Epistle (2 Jn. 13).

σε ιδειν A B C 5. 31. 73. d vg.] ιδειν σε ℵ K L P al. pler. cat. cop. Thphyl. Oec. : *uenire ad te* sah. | λαλησομεν] λαλησωμεν K 22. 26. 33. 41. 99 Thphyl. : λαλησαι H¹⁰³· ¹⁶² (25) I^{a 70. 200f} (505) : *loqui tibi* arm.

15. ἀσπάζου τοὺς φίλους κατ᾽ ὄνομα] These forms of greeting are part of the common stock of epistolary correspondence, and should not be pressed as evidence about the state of parties in the Church of Gaius. It is especially misleading to inter-pret κατ᾽ ὄνομα as a proof of the scanty following left to the Elder in it. Compare the greetings in the letter of Amon the soldier to his father (Berlin Museum : Deissmann, *Licht von Osten*, p. 118), ἄσπασαι Καπίτωνα πολλὰ καὶ τοὺς ἀδελφούς μου καὶ Σερήνιλλαν καὶ τοὺς φίλους μου : and Oxyrh. Pap. ii. 123, ἀσπάζομαι τὴν γλυκυτάτην μου θυγατέρα Μακκαρίαν, καὶ τὴν δεσποίνην μου μητέραν ὑμῶν καὶ ὅλους τοὺς ἡμῶν κατ᾽ ὄνομα : or Tebtunis Pap. ii. 299 (p. 422), ἀσπάζομαι τὴν γυναῖκάν μου καὶ τὰ παιδία μου καὶ Σεραπάμμωνα καὶ Ἀματίαν καὶ τοὺς ἐνοίκους πάντας κατ᾽ ὄι ομα.

ειρηνη σοι] om. I^{a 170} (303) | σοι] *uobis* arm-codd. | οι φιλοι ℵ B C K L P al. pler. d vg. sah. cop. syr^{bodl} syr^{p txt} arm. Thphyl. Oec.] οι αδελφοι A 3. 13. 31. 33. 65. 67 d^{scr} syr^{p mg} aeth^{utr} | ασπαζου] ασπασαι ℵ 40 | τους φιλους] τους αδελφους 33. 81. 160 boh-cod. syr^{p} :+σου H^{δ6· 162} (Ψ) :+ *nostros* arm. | κατ ονομα]+αμην L 15. 26 vg. mss. arm.

APPENDIX.

⸺✦⸺

THE OLD LATIN VERSION.

In the following pages an attempt has been made to show to
what extent the Old Latin Version, or Versions, of these Epistles
is known or can be recovered.   With the exception of the first
eight verses of 1 Jn. i., the whole of the First Epistle is contained
in MSS which are predominantly Old Latin in character.   The
Fleury Palimpsest, edited by M. Berger in 1889, and more
recently by Mr. Buchanan in Old Latin Biblical Texts, No. 5,
contains 1 Jn. i. 8–iii. 20; the Freisingen Fragments, edited by
Ziegler in 1876, contain 1 Jn. iii. 8 (apparuit filius) to the end
of the Epistle.   The *Tractates* of Augustine give us a complete
text as far as 1 Jn. v. 3.   For the first eight verses Augustine's
text has been given till the Fleury Palimpsest begins (i. 8 -rimus
quoniam).   This is followed till iii. 8 in hoc, after which Ziegler's
Freisingen Fragment is used.   In the case of the Fleury
Palimpsest, M. Berger's text has been used.   Where Mr.
Buchanan differs from M. Berger the readings of the former
are added *intra lineas*.[1]   This text is followed by an apparatus
criticus in which the attempt is made to give the variants from
this text which are found in the Vulgate (Vg.), in the text contained in Augustine's *Tractates* on the Epistles (**Aug.**, quotations
from other works of Augustine, which are only cited when they
differ from the *Tractates*, are quoted as Aug.), and in the
quotations from Latin writers whose works have been published
in the Vienna *Corpus*.   No quotations have been included from
works not available in that edition, except in the case of
Tertullian where Oehler has been used for treatises not yet
published in the new edition, and Irenaeus (Stieren).   The
readings of the Perpignan MS, Paris Bibl. Nat. Lat. 321, which

---

[1] This refers to words and letters which both editors treat as legible,
wholly or in part.

differ from the Old Latin text printed here and which are not Vulgate readings, have been added (under the symbol "p") in the Critical Notes from the text of the Catholic Epistles, published by the Rev. E. S. Buchanan in the *Journal of Theological Studies*, xii. 48 (July 1911). The agreements of this MS in the First Epistle of S. John with Augustine and with the *Speculum* are of considerable interest. The form in which it gives the text of 1 Jn. v. 7, 8 is very close to that of one of the quotations in the *Speculum*.

The use of an approximately Old Latin text as a basis, which ensures the presentation of variants which have a claim to be regarded as Old Latin, as the Vulgate readings are always given where they differ from the text printed, reduces the bulk in the case of those writers whose text is largely Old Latin in character. The amount of Patristic support for Old Latin readings would, of course, have been shown more clearly by the use of a Vulgate text as a basis. A table of Greek words and their renderings has been added which may serve to call attention to the more interesting renderings. The work is tentative in character and has not led to any very definite results.

It may, however, be noticed that the twelve verses of ch. iii., where we have the guidance of both MSS, show that the Freisingen text is closer to that of Augustine than is the Fleury MS, though the verses offer very little evidence that is decisive. The differences between h and Cyprian are noticeable, but they do not invalidate von Soden's judgment as to the African character of the text of the Fleury Palimpsest (von Soden, p. 241 f.). And the general agreement between Augustine and the Freisingen Fragment can be clearly seen, though their texts are by no means identical. The independence of the version used by Lucifer of Cagliari is also very clearly marked. The evidence adduced also confirms the view that the tendency to add interpretative and explanatory glosses to the text of the Epistle is both widespread and dates back to early times. In view of the importance of the gloss which found its way into so many texts of 1 Jn. v. 7 f., this fact is not without interest. The growth of that gloss can be traced back at least as early as Cyprian. The following instances of this tendency should be noticed:

ii. 5. + si in ipso perfecti fuerimus, **Aug.**

 9. odit] + homicida est et, Cyp.

16. ex concupiscentia saeculi, Cyp.

17. + quomodo et ipse (Deus) manet in aeternum, Cyp. Aug. Luc.

23. nec filium nec patrem, **Aug.**
  et filium et patrem, Cyp. Prisc. Spec. (Luc.).

iii. 1. propter hoc mundus non cognoscit nos quia non cognoscit
   eum et nos non cognoscit mundus, **Aug.**

 7. (?) + sicut et ille iustus est.

 10. patrem suum] patrem suum aut matrem suam, Cyp. cod.

iv. 3. Sed est de antichristi spiritu, Cyp.
   omnis qui soluit Iesum Christum et negat eum in carne
   uenisse, **Aug.** $^1/_8$.

   cf. Tert. *adv. Macc.* v. 16, negantes Christum in carne
   uenisse et soluentes Iesum, scilicet in deo creatore.

v. 1. deus in ipso est et ipse in deo, Spec.

 20. + et carnem induit nostri causa et passus est et resurrexit
   a mortuis adsumpsit nos, Spec.

   aeterna] + et resurrectio nostra, Spec.

1 JN. I.

Augustine, *Comm. in Ep. Ioann.*

1. Quod erat ab initio, quod audiuimus, et quod uidimus
oculis nostris, et manus nostrae tractauerunt de uerbo uitae.

2. Et ipsa uita manifestata est, et uidimus et testes sumus, et
annuntiamus nobis uitam aeternam, quae erat apud Patrem, et
manifestata est in nobis.

3. Quae uidimus et audiuimus nuntiamus uobis, ut et uos
societatem habeatis nobiscum, et societas nostra sit cum Deo
Patre, et Iesu Christo, filio eius.

4. Et haec scribimus uobis, ut gaudium uestrum sit plenum.

5. Et haec est annuntiatio quam audiuimus ab eo, et
annuntiamus uobis, quia Deus lux est et tenebrae in illo non
sunt ullae.

6. Quodsi dixerimus quia societatem habemus cum eo, et in
tenebris ambulamus, mentimur, et non facimus ueritatem.

7. Quodsi in lumine ambulamus, sicut et ipse est in lumine,
societatem habemus cum inuicem, et sanguis Iesu Christi, filii
eius, purgabit nos ab omni delicto.

Fleury Palimpsest, *ed.* Berger, Paris, 1889.[1]

1 Jn. i. 8. [si dixe] Rimus quoniam peccatum n habemus
ipsos nos de*cipimus*[2] et ueritas in nobis non est

9. Si confiteamur peccata nos*tra fide*lis et iustus ut remittam
nobis peccata et purget no*s ex om*ni iniquitate

---

[1] Italics are used where the MS is illegible.   M. Berger's text is followed
where the two editions "supply" different words.   Where the "supplies"
agree, italics are used only for what is regarded as illegible by *both* editors.
[2] ese*ducimus* Buch.

10. quod si dixerimus quod non pecca*uimus* mendacem faciemus eum et uerbum eius non est *in nobis*

ii. 1. fili mei haec iscribo uobis ne peccetis et si quis pecc*auerit* aduocatum abemus aput patrem ih͞u x͞p͞m iustu*m*

2. *et ipse* est exoratio pro peccatis nostris non pro nostr*is autem* tantum sed et pro totius saeculi

3. et in hoc iscimus q*uoniam* cognouimus eum si mandata eius seruemus

4. qui d*icit se nosce*re eum et mandata *ei*us non seruat mendax est in *hoc ueritas* non est

5. nam qui custodit uerbum *us* in hoc carit*as* d͞i *per*fecta est in hoc isceimus quoniam in eo sumus

6. qui d*icit se in ipso* manere debet quemadmodum ille ambulauit et *ipse am*bulare

7. Carissimi non no*uum mandatum* scribo *uobis sed* mandatum
    od
uetus quem habuistis ab initio manda*tum* uetus est uerbum quod audistis

                                erit   um
8. iterum manda*tum nouum* iscribo uobis quod est uere [1] in ipso
    nobis
et in uobis qu*ia tene*brae iam transeunt et lumen uerum iam luce*t*

9. *qui dicit se* in lumine esse et fratrem suum hodit in teneb*ris est usq. ad*huc

10. nam qui diligit fratrem suum in lumine perm*anet et* *scan*dalum in eo non est

11. qui autem hodit fratrem su*um in tene*bris est et in tenebris ambulat et non scit ubi ea*t quia te* | *neb*rae obscoecauerunt oculos eius

            fili *mei qui*a iam
12. scribo uobis filio*li quoniam* remittuntur uobis peccata propter nomen eius

13. *scribo* uobis patres quoniam cognouistis quod erat ab *initio* scribo uobis iuuenes quoniam uicistis malignum

                                quia
14. *Scribo* uobis pueri quoniam cognouistis patrem quod cognouist*f*is eum qui est ab initio scribo uobis adulescentes *quonia*m fortes estis et uerbum d͞i in uobis permanet et *uicistis* malignum

15. nolite diligere seculum nec ea quae sunt *in saecu*lo si quis diligit saeculum non est caritas patris in eo

16. *quonia*m omne quod est in seculo concupiscentia carnis
                        saeculi
*est et c*oncupiscentia oculorum et superbia *uitae est* quae *non est* *d*e
ex patre sed de seculo est

                         re
[1] ue (sic) Buch.

transiet
17. et saeculum transit et *concupi*scentia qui autem facit
b*it*
uoluntatem d̄i permanet *in aete*rnum

18. Pueri nouissima hora est et sicut au*distis qu*oniam
e _ e _
antixp̄s uenit nunc antixp̄i multi facti sunt *unde cogn*oscimus
quoniam nouissima hora est
produit
19. Ex nobis *exierunt* sed non erat ex nobis nam si fuisset
et
ex nobis per*mansissen*t forsitan nobiscum sed ut praesto fiat
quoniam *non sunt* omnes ex nobis

20. et uos unctionem accepistis a st̄o et *nostis omnia*

21. non scripsi uobis quasi ignorantib ueritate̅ s*ed scien*tibus
eam et quoniam omnem mendacium ex ueri*tate non est*__

22. quis est mendax nisi is qui negat quia is est xp̄s *hic est*
non
*anti*xp̄s qui negat patrem et filium

23. omnis qui *negat* filium [1] | Nec patrem habet qui confitetur
filium et pa*trem habet*

24. uos quod audistis ab initio permaneat in uo*bis quod si* in
uobis permanserit quod ab initio audistis e*t uos in filio* et patre
permanebitis
uobis
25. et haec est promissio *quam ipse pol*licitus est *no*bis uitam
aeternam.
ese
26. Haec scri*psi uobis de* eis qui seducunt uos.

27. et uos untionem quam *accepistis* ab eo permaneat in
uobis et necesse non habe*tis ut aliquis* doceat uos sed sicut untio
eius docet uos de om*nib et uerum* est et non est mendum [2] et
man*ete*
sicut docuit uos *permanete in eo*
i
28. et nunc fili*o* manete in eo ut cum uenerit fidu*ciam*
*habea*mus et non confundamur ab eo In praes*entia eius*
si nostis eum qui fidelis est
29. *si scimus quonia*m *iust*us *est* scitote quoniam om*nis qui*
ueritatem de eo natus
*facit institiam ex ipso nat*us est

iii. 1. ecce qualem caritate*m dedit* uobis pater ut filii dei
egnorat
uocaremur et sumus propter*ea seculum nos inh*on*o*rat

habet
[1] negat filium] n̄ filium   (sic) Buch.
aci
[2] mendum (sic) Buch.

2. Carissimi nunc filii d̄i sumus et nondu*m* *manifesta*tum est qui futuri sumus scimus quoniam cum *apparuerit* similes erimus ei quoniam uidebimus eum sic*uti est*

3. *et om*nis qui habet spem hanc in eo castificat se sicut *et ille castus* est

4. omnis qui facit peccatum et iniquitatem fa*cit et peccatum* est iniquitas

5. et scitis quoniam ille apparuit ut p*eccata tolleret* et peccatum in illo non est

6. omnis qui in eo perma*net non peccat* omnis qui peccat non uidit eum nec cognouit e*um*

7. *filioli* nemo nos seducat qui facit iustitiam iustus est
      omnis qui fa

8. *qui autem fa* | *cit pecc*atum de diabolo est quia ab initio diabolus *peccat in* hoc.[1]

1 JN. III.

Freisingen Fragment.

8. apparuit filius d̄i ut soluat opera diaboli

9. Omnis qui natus est ex D̄o peccatum non facit quia semen eius in ipso manet et non potest peccare quoniam de D̄o natus est

10. Ex hoc manifesti sunt fil*ii* d̄i et filii diaboli omnis qui non facit iustitiam non est de d̄o et qui non diligit fratrem suum

11. Quoniam̄ hoc est mandatum quod audistis ab initio ut diligamus imuicē

12. Non sicut cain qui ex maligno erat et occidit fratrem suum et cuius rei gratia occidit eum quia opera eius maligna erant fratris autem eius iusta

13. et nolite mirari fratres si odit nos hic mundu*s*

14. Nos scimus quoniam transimus de morte ad uitam quia diligimus fratres qui non diligit permanet in mortem

15. omnis qui odit fratrem suum homicida est et scitis quia omnis homicida non habet uitam aeternam in se manentem

16. in hoc cognoscimus caritatem quia ille pro nobis animam suam posuit et nos debemus pro fratribus animas ponere.

17. qui autem habuerit substantiam huius mundi et uiderit

---

[1] The MS continues as far as ver. 20 (d̄s corde nostro et), so that for vv. 8–20 we have both the Fleury and the Freisingen text. The variations of the Fleury Palimpsest are henceforward noted, the text being taken from the Freisingen Fragment.

fratrem suum egere et clauserit uiscera sua ab eo quomodo
caritas dī manet in eo

18. filioli non diligamus tantum uerbo neque lingua sed
operae et ueritate

19. et in hoc cognoscimur q̄m ex ueritate sumus et coram
ipso suademus cordi nostro

20. q̄m si reprehendat nos cor nostrum maior est d̄s cordi
nostro et nouit omnia

21. k̄mi si cor n̄m non nos reprehendat fiduciam habemus
aput d̄m

22. et quidquid petierimus accipiemus ab eo q̄m mandata
eius seruamus et quae sunt placita in conspectu eius faci*m*us

23. et hoc est mandatum eius ut credamus nom*ini filii e*ius
ĪHŪ X̄PĪ et diligamus inuicem sicut dedit n*obis man*datum

24. et qui seruat mandatum eius in illo manebit et ipse in eo
et in hoc scimus q̄m permanet in nobis de s̄pu quem dedit nobis

iv. 1. K̄mi nolite omni s̄pu credere sed p*ro*bate s̄ps si ex d̄o
sunt q̄m multi pseudoprophetae prodierunt in hoc saeculo

2. hinc cognoscitur s̄ps d̄i omnis s̄ps qui confitetur ĪHM̄
X̄PM̄ in carne uenisse ex d̄o est.

3. et omnis s̄ps qui non confitetur ĪHM̄ ex d̄o non est et
hoc est illius antixpisti quem audistis quia uenturus est et nunc
in saeculo est

4. iam uos ex d̄o estis filioli et uicistis eos q̄m maior est qui
in uobis est quam hic qui in saeculo est

5. hii de saeculo sunt propterea de saeculo locuntur et
saeculum audit eos

6. nos ex do sumus qui cognoscit d̄m audit nos qui non est
ex d̄o non nos audit hinc cognoscimus s̄pm ueritatis et s̄pm
erroris

7. k̄mi diligamus inuicem q̄m caritas ex d̄o est et omnis qui
diligit fratrem suum ex do natus est et cognoscit d̄m

8. qui non diligit ignorat d̄m quia d̄s caritas est

9. in hoc apparuit caritas d̄i in nobis q̄m filium suum unicum
misit d̄s in saeculo ut uiuamus per eum

10. in hoc est caritas non quod nos dil*e*xerimus d̄m sed q̄m
ipse dilexit nos et misit filium suum propitiatorem pro peccatis
nostris.

11. k̄mi si sic d̄s dilexit nos et nos debemus diligere
imuicem

12. d̄m *ne*mo uidit umquam quodsi diligamus imuicem d̄s in
nobis manet et caritas eius perfecta est in nobis

13. in hoc cognoscimus q̄u̅m̅ in ipso manemus et ipse in nob*is* qm de s̄pu suo dedit nobis

14. et nos uidimus e*t* testamur qm̄ pater misit filium suum sal*uator*em saeculi

15. quicumque confessus fue*rit* q̄m̄ ī̅h̅s̅ est filius di d̄s in eo manet et ipse in d̄o

16. Et nos cognouimus et credidimus in *caritate* quam habet d̄s in nobis d̄s caritas e*st* *et qui ma*net in caritate in d̄o permanet et d̄s *in eo manet*

17. in hoc perfecta est Karitas in nobis . . . *fi*duciam habemus in diem iudicii quia *sicut ille est* et nos sumus in hoc mundo

18. timor n*on est in ca*ritate sed perfecta caritas foras m*ittit timore* qm timor poenam ha*b*et qui autem t*imet non est* perfectus in caritatem

19. *no*s ergo d*iligamus* q̄m̅ ipse prior dilexit nos

20. si quis dix*erit diligo* dm et fratrem suum odit mendax est *qui enim* non diligit fratrem suum quem uide*t* d̄m̅ *quem* non uidet quomodo potest diligere

21. *et hoc man*datum habemus a d̄o ut qui diligit dm̄ *diligat et fra*trem suum

v. 1. omnis qui credit quia Ī̅H̅s *est xps ex* d̄o natus est et omnis qui diligit genitor*em diligit* eum qui genitus est ex eo

2. hinc cog*noscimus* q̄m̄ diligimus filios di˙ cum diligimus dm̄ *et mandata* eius facimus

3. haec est enim c*ari*tas *ut manda*ta eius seruemus et manda*ta ei*us g*rauia non sunt*

4. quia omne quod natum est ex d̄o *uincit saeculum et* haec est uictoria quae uincit sa*ceulum fides nostra*

5. quis est autem qui uincit saeculu*m nisi qui cre*dit quia Ī̅H̅S̅ est filius d̄i

6. hic es*t qui uenit per aquam* et sanguinem Ī̅H̅S̅ X̅P̅S̅ et non ta*ntum in aqua sed* in aqua et sanguine et s̄ps e*st testi-monium* quia sps est ueritas

7. qm tre*s sunt qui testificantur* in terra · s̄ps et aqua et sa*nguis et tres sunt qui tes*tificantur in caelo pa*t*er e*t uerbum et s̄p̅s̅ scs et hi* tres unum sunt

9. si testim*onium hominum ac*cipimus testimonium d̄i *maius est quia hoc est* testimonium d̄i quia tes*tificatus est de filio suo*

10. *qui credit* in filio d̄i habet testimonium d̄i in se *qui non cr*edit in d̄o mendacem facit eum quia *non credi*t in testimonium eius quod testifica*tus est d̄s* de filio suo

11. et hoc est testimonium q̅m̅ *uitam aeter*nam dedit nobis d̅s̅ et haec uita in fi*lio eius e*st

12. qui habet filium d̅i̅ uitam habet *qui non ha*bet filium d̅i̅ uitam non habet

13. haec *scribo uob*is ut sciatis quia uitam habetis aeter*nam qui cre*ditis in n̅e̅ fili d̅i̅

14. et haec est fiducia *quam habe*mus ad eum quia quidquid petierimus *secundum u*oluntatem eius audit nos

15. et si scimus *quia audit no*s quidquid petierimus scimus q̅m̅ *habemus pe*titiones quas petiuimus ab eo

16. *si quis scit f*ratrem suum peccare peccatum no̅ *ad mortem* postulabit et dabit ei uitam his qui *peccat non* usque ad mortem est enim pecca*tum usque* ad mortem non pro illo dico ut pos*tulet*

17. *omn*is iniustitia peccatum est et est *peccatum ad* mortem

18. scimus q̅m̅ omnis qui *natus est ex* d̅o̅ no̅n peccat sed natiuitas d̅i̅ con*seruat eum* et *m*alignus non tangit eum

19. scim' q̅m̅ *ex d̅o̅ sum*us et totus mundus in maligno *positus est*

20. *et* scimus q̅m̅ filius d̅i̅ uenit et de*dit nobis intell*ectum ut sciamus quod est ueru̅ *et simus in uero fi*lio eius I̅H̅U̅ X̅P̅O̅ hic est uerus d̅s̅ *et vita aeterna*

21. filioli custodite uos ab idolis.

. . . .: CC·LXXIIII. I̅N̅C̅P̅EIUSDEM · II.

In the following critical notes differences of order have not, as a rule, been noted except for the Vulgate, and the text found in Augustine's *Tractates* on the Epistle. An attempt has been made to indicate by fractions the proportion which the evidence for any particular variant in any writer bears to the whole evidence on the point in question to be found in his quotations of the passage. This has not been attempted in the case of Augustine, except for the *Tractates* (**Aug.**), where different readings have been noted in this way, when, as sometimes happens, more than one rendering is found in the text.

i. 1. erat] fuit Vg. Cass. | quod 2°—uitae] quod uidimus quod audiuimus oculis nostris uidimus et manus nostrae contrectauerunt de sermone uitae Tert. ²/₂ | quod 2°—nostris] quae uidimus oculis nostris et auribus audiuimus Mur. Fr. | et 1°] *om.* Vg. Cass. | quod 3°] *om.* Amb. ¹/₃ | oculis nostris] *pr.* quod Amb-codd. ¹/₃ : *pr.* et Amb-codd. ¹/₃ : om. Amb-cod. ¹/₃ : + quod perspeximus Vg. Cass. : + perspeximus Amb. ²/₃-ed. ¹/₃ | et 2°] + quod Amb-codd. ¹/₃ | tractauerunt] contrectauerunt Vg. : palpauerunt Mur. Fr. Cass. : perscrutatae sunt Amb. ¹/₃ : scrutatae sunt Amb. ²/₃.

2. ipsa] *om.* Vg. Cass. Amb. ²/₂ | manifestata est 1°] apparuit Amb. ²/₂ | testes sumus] testamur Vg. Cass. Amb. ²/₂ : testificamur p. | uitam aeternam] de uita Amb. | manifestata est 2°] apparuit Vg. Cass. Amb-ed. : paruit Amb-cod. | in] *om.* Vg. Cass. Spec.

3. quae] quod ergo p. | annunciamus Vg. | et 3°—eius] ut communio sit nobis cum patre et filio eius Iesu Christo Tert. | sit] est p. | cum deo patre] apud patrem Spec. | Iesu—eius] cum filio eius Iesu Christo Vg. Spec.

4. scribimus] scripsimus Mur. Fr. (uid.) | uobis] pr. ut gaudeatis p.—gaudium] pr. gaudeatis et Vg. | uestrum] nostrum p.

5. quia societatem habemus] nos societatem habere p. | quia] quoniam Vg. | illo] eo Vg. Aug. Vict.Vit.

6. quodsi] si Vg. | quia] quoniam Vg. | societatem] communionem Tert. | ambulamus] incedamus Tert. | ueritatem non facimus Vg.

7. quod si] si autem Vg. : si uero Tert. | lumine 1°, 2°] luce Vg. | ambulamus] incedamus Tert. | sicut—lumine 2°] om. Tert. | societatem] communionem Tert. | cum inuicem] ad inuicem Vg. : cum eo Tert. : cum deo p. | filii eius] domini nostri Tert. | purgabit] emundat Vg. Tert. : mundat p. | delicto] peccato Vg.

8. dixerimus] dicamus Tert. | quoniam—habemus] nos delictum (peccatum Gel.) non habere Tert. Gel-Ep. $^{1}/_{3}$ | quoniam] quod Aug-codd. : quia p. Cyp. $^{2}/_{3}$-ed. $^{1}/_{3}$ **Aug.** Cass. $^{2}/_{3}$-ed. $^{1}/_{3}$ Gel-Ep. $^{2}/_{2}$ Opt. $^{1}/_{2}$-codd. $^{1}/_{2}$ Luc. Spec. | peccata Faust | ipsos nos decipimus] ipsi nos seducimus Vg. Aug. Paul-Oros. Cass. $^{2}/_{3}$-codd. $^{1}/_{3}$: nos ipsos seducimus **Aug.** Gel-Ep. $^{1}/_{3}$ Spec. : nos ipsos decipimus Cyp. $^{3}/_{3}$ (decepimus cod. $^{3}/_{3}$) : seducimus nosmet ipsos Tert. Aug. Gel-Ep. $^{1}/_{3}$: ipsi nos decipimus Cass-ed. $^{1}/_{3}$ Faust. | et] quia Gel-Ep. $^{1}/_{3}$ | ueritas] uerbum eius Cass. $^{1}/_{3}$ (cf. ver. 10).

9. si] quod si **Aug.** Gel-Ep. : +autem p. Cyp. | confitemur] confitemur Tert. : confessi fuerimus **Aug.** Cyp. Gel-Ep. | peccata 1°] delicta Tert. Aug. Gel-Ep. | fidelis]+est Vg. **Aug.** Gel-Ep. | iustus] : +est dominus Cyp. +est Spec. | ut—peccata 2°] qui nobis peccata dimittat Cyp. | ut] qui Spec. Gel-Ep. | remittam] remittat Vg. : dimittat Tert. **Aug.** Spec. Gel-Ep. | nobis peccata] ea nobis Tert. | peccata 2°] delicta nostra **Aug.** : +nostra Vg. Aug. | purget] emundet Tert. Vg. : mundet **Aug.** $^{1}/_{2}$ Spec. Gel-Ep. | ex] ab Tert. **Aug.** $^{1}/_{2}$ Vg. Spec. Gel-Ep. | iniquitate] iniustitia Tert.

10. quod si] si Tert. Vg. Gel-Ep. $^{1}/_{2}$ Cass. | dixerimus] dicamus Tert. | quod non peccauimus] nos non deliquisse Tert. | quod] quoniam Aug. Vg. : quia **Aug.** Gel-Ep. $^{2}/_{2}$ Cass-ed. | facimus Tert. **Aug.** Vg. Cass. | eum] illum Tert. : deum Cass-cod. | uerbum] sermo Tert. | est] erit Gel-Ep. $^{2}/_{2}$.

ii. 1. fili mei] filioli mei Cyp. **Aug.** Vg. : filioli Tert. Aug. : fratres Aug. | haec] ista Cyp. (ita-cod.) | scribo] scripsi Tert. Cyp-cod. | ne] ut non **Aug.** Vg. Gel-Ep. $^{2}/_{2}$ Vict. Vit. | peccatis] delinquatis Tert. Cyp. | et] pr. sed Vg. Vict.Vit-cod. : sed Gel-Ep. $^{2}/_{2}$ Vict.Vit-ed. | quis peccauerit] deliqueritis Tert. : qui deliquerit Cyp. (quis codd.) | aduocatum] paracletum Vict.Vit. Faust. | apud] ad Aug. | patrem] pr. deum Tert. ad-Vigil (dn̄m cod.) | Iesum Christum) om. Gel-Ep. $^{2}/_{2}$: om. Iesum ad-Vig. (uid.) : om. Christum Aug. | iustum] suffragatorem Cyp-cod. $^{1}/_{2}$: om. Vict.Vit. Faust.

2. et] om. Cyp-cod. Aug. | exoratio] propitiatio Vg. Faust. Paul-Nol. Hier. : propitiator **Aug.** : satisfactio et placatio ad-Vig. (uid.) : placatio Tert. Hil.: deprecatio Cyp. | pro 1°—tantum] peccatorum nostrorum non tantum nostrorum **Aug.** | peccatis] delictis Tert. Cyp. $^{1}/_{3}$ | non—tantum] om. Faust. | et 2°] etiam Vg. | pro 3°] om. **Aug.** | saeculo] mundi **Aug.** Vg. Faust.

3. in] ex Luc. | iscimus] intelligimus Cyp. Luc. : cognoscimus **Aug.** | quoniam cognoscimus] om. **Aug.** | quoniam] quia Cyp. | mandata] praecepta Cyp. | seruemus] seruauerimus **Aug.** : custodiamus Cyp. : obseruemus Vg.

4. qui]+autem Luc. | se noscere] se nosse Vg. : quia cognouit **Aug.** Cyp-codd. quia cognoui Aug : qui cognouit Aug. : quia nouit Ambr. : quoniam cognouit Cyp. (nouit cod.) : quoniam cognoui Cyp-cod. Luc. $^{2}/_{2}$ | eum] dm p. | mandata] praecepta Ambr. | seruat] custodit Vg. Luc. $^{2}/_{2}$ | in hoc ueritas] et ueritas in illo Cyp. | in hoc] et in eo Luc. $^{2}/_{2}$ | ueritas—(5) hoc 1°] om. p*.

5. nam qui custodit] qui autem custodit Vg. : qui autem seruauerit **Aug.**

Luc. $^2/_2$ | in hoc 1°] pr. uere Vg. **Aug.** : uere ab eis Luc. $^1/_2$: uere . . . apud illos Luc. $^1/_2$ | caritas] dilectio **Aug.** | perfecta] consummata Luc. $^2/_2$ | in 2°] pr. et. Vg. | iscimus] cognoscimus **Aug.** | quoniam] quia **Aug.** | eo] ipso Vg. **Aug.** | sumus]+si in ipso perfecti fuerimus p. **Aug.**

6. in ipso] in Christo Cyp. $^4/_4$ (*om.* in cod. $^1/_4$) Hier. | quemadmodum] sicut Vg. **Aug.** Paul-Nol. : quomodo Cyp. $^4/_4$ Hier. $^2/_2$ | et] pr. sic Salv.

7. carissimi] dilectissimi **Aug.** | mandatum nouum Vg. **Aug.** | quem] quod h^a Vg. **Aug.** | habebatis **Aug.**

8. est uere] erit uerum h^a : uerum est Vg. **Aug.** | quia] q̅m̅ p. | iam] om. Vg. **Aug.** | transierunt Vg. **Aug.** | lumen uerum] uerum lumen Vg. : lux uera **Aug.**

9. esse in lumine **Aug.** $^1/_2$ | lumine] luce Vg. **Aug.** $^1/_2$ Cyp. $^2/_3$: lucem Cyp-cod. $^1/_2$ Spec-cod. | odit]+homicida est et Cyp-cod. $^2/_2$ | est] ambulat Cyp-cod. $^1/_2$.

10. nam qui] qui autem Spec. Luc. : *om.* nam Vg. **Aug.** | diligit] amat Luc. | permanet] manet Vg. **Aug.** Spec. Euch.

11. qui autem] nam qui Aug. | est-tenebris 2°] om. Luc. $^2/_2$ | non scit] nescit Vg. Cyp-cod. **Aug.** Faust. Luc. | ubi eat] quo eat Vg. **Aug.** Cyp. Luc. : quo uadit Faust. | quia] quoniam **Aug.** Cyp. | obscoecauerunt] excaecauerunt **Aug.** Cyp. : obscurauerunt Luc. | oculos] cor Luc.

12. scribo] dico Prisc. | quoniam] quia **Aug.** Prisc. | propter] per **Aug.**

13. scribo 1°—initio] om. p. | quoniam 1°] quia **Aug.** Faust. | quod—initio] eum qui ab initio est Vg. Faust. : eum qui a principio est **Aug.** | iuuenes] adolescentes Vg. | quoniam 2°] quia **Aug.** Faust.

14. pueri] infantes Vg. | quoniam 1°] quia **Aug.** | quod—initio] om. Vg. | quod] scribo nobis patres quia p. **Aug.** | est ab initio] a principio est **Aug.** | adulescentes] iuuenes Vg. **Aug.** Euch. | quoniam 2°] quia p. **Aug.** Euch. | in uobis permanet] manet in uobis Vg. | permanet] manet **Aug.** Euch.

15. Nolite diligere mundum neque ambitum eius Claud. | Nolite quaerere quae in hoc mundo sunt Paul-Nol. | nolite] pr. filioli Cass. | seculum 1°] mundum Vg. **Aug.** Cyp. $^3/_3$ De duod-abus. Faust. $^2/_2$ Cass. | saeculo] mundo Vg. **Aug.** Cyp. $^2/_3$-ed. $^1/_3$ De d. a. Faust. $^2/_2$ Cass. : hoc mundo Cyp-cod. $^1/_3$ | si quis] quisquis Aug-ed. : qui enim Faust. : +autem p : +enim Aug-cod. | quis] qui Cyp. $^1/_3$-ed. $^2/_3$ | diligit] dilexerit **Aug.** Cyp. $^3/_3$ | saeculum 2°] mundum Vg. Cyp. $^2/_3$-ed. $^1/_3$ Aug. Faust. Cass. : hunc mundum Cyp-cod. $^1/_3$ | non—eo] dilectio patris non est in ipso **Aug.** (eo Aug-cod.) | caritas] dilectio Aug. | patris] Dei Cass. | eo] illo Aug. Cyp. $^3/_3$ Cass.

16. quoniam] quia **Aug.** Cyp. $^1/_4$ Faust. Cass. | omne—seculo] omnia quae in mundo sunt Aug. | est in saeculo] est in mundo Vg. Aug. Cass. Gel-Ep. Faust. : in mundo est **Aug.** Cyp. $^4/_4$ | concupiscentia carnis est] desiderium est carnis **Aug.** | concupiscentia 1°] pr. aut Aug-cod. | est 2°] om. Faust. | concupiscentia 2°] uoluntas Prisc. $^2/_2$ | superbia uitae] ambitio saeculi **Aug.** Cyp. $^3/_4$-ed. $^1/_4$ Gel-Ep. : ambitio mundi Cyp-codd. $^1/_4$: ambitio humanae uitae Prisc. :+humanae Faust. | est 3°] om. Vg. **Aug.** Cyp-cod. $^1/_4$ Faust. Prisc. Cass. : sunt Cyp-ed. $^1/_4$ | quae] et ubique Aug-cod. : om. Prisc. | est 4°] sunt **Aug.** Prisc. | ex] a Aug. Cyp. $^4/_4$ Gel-Ep. : de Aug-codd. Faust. Prisc. | de saeculo] ex mundo Vg. **Aug.** Cyp-cod. $^1/_4$ Gel-Ep. Cass. : de hoc mundo Prisc. : ex concupiscentia saeculi Cyp. $^1/_4$-ed. $^1/_4$-cod. $^1/_4$ (a *pro* ex cod. $^1/_4$) : ex concupiscentia mundi Cyp. $^1/_4$-cod. $^1/_4$ | est 5°] sunt **Aug.** Prisc. : om. Cyp. $^3/_4$-ed. $^1/_4$ cf. v. Sod. 225.

17. saeculum] mundus Vg. **Aug.** Cyp. $^4/_4$ Gel-Ep. Cass. Faust. Prisc. Luc. | transit] transibit Cyp. $^3/_4$-ed. $^1/_4$ Aug. : praeterit Prisc. : perit Cass. (-iit codd.) | concupiscentia]+eius Vg. Cyp. $^4/_4$ Aug. Faust. Prisc. Luc. : desideria eius **Aug.** | facit] fecerit **Aug.** Cyp. $^5/_5$ Gel-Ep. Faust. Luc. | dei] domini Gel-Ep. | permanet] manet Vg. **Aug.** Cyp. $^2/_5$-ed. $^1/_5$-cod. $^1/_5$ Gel-Ep. Cass. Faust. Luc. : manebit Cyp. $^1/_5$-ed. $^1/_5$-cod. $^1/_5$ | aeternum]+quomodo et ipse manet in aeternum p. **Aug.** (sicut) Cyp. $^5/_5$ (om. cod. $^2/_5$)

Luc. ⟦[quomodo et ipse] sicut et deus Aug. | et ipse] et deus p. Cyp. $^2/_5$·ed. $^1/_5$-cod. $^1/_5$ Luc. : deus Cyp-cod. $^1/_5$: om. et Cyp-codd. $^1/_5$ | manet] manebit Cyp-ed. $^1/_5$⟧.

18. pueri] filioli Vg. Iren. Euch. | sicut] quemadmodum Iren. : quoniam 1°] quia Vg. Cyp. $^2/_2$ Luc. : quod Aug. | uenit] sit uenturus Aug. | nunc] *pr.* et Vg. : + autem p. Cyp. $^2/_2$ Aug. Luc. | multi] om. Cyp-cod. $^1/_2$ | facti] om. Luc. | cognoscimus] scimus Vg. | quoniam 2°] quod Vg. Aug. : quia Cyp. $^2/_2$ | nouissima hora Vg. | hora est] sit hora Aug.

19. Cf. quia non erant nostri, nam si nostri essent, mansissent nobiscum Opt. | exierunt] prodierunt Vg. Tert. | erat] erant Vg. Aug. Iren. Amb. : fuerunt Tert. Cyp. $^5/_5$: sunt Petilianus ap. Aug. | ex 2°] de Pet-ap-Aug. | nam —nobis 3°] si enim ex nobis essent Amb. | nam si] quod si Aug. : si enim Cyp. $^5/_5$ Iren. : si Tert. | fuisset] fuissent Vg. Aug. Tert. Cyp. $^5/_5$ Iren. : essent Pet-ap-Aug. | ex 3°] de Pet-ap-Aug. | permansissent] mansissent Cyp. $^2/_5$-ed. $^2/_5$·cod. $^1/_5$ Aug. Amb. : mansisset Cyp-cod. $^1/_5$ | forsitan] utique Vg. Aug. Tert Cyp-ed. $^1/_5$-cod. $^4/_5$ Iren. Pet-ap-Aug. : om. Cyp-ed. $^4/_5$-cod. $^1/_5$ Amb. | praesto fiat] manifesti sint Vg. : manifestarentur Aug. Iren. | quoniam] quod Aug. | sunt omnes] omnes erant Aug. : *om.* omnes Iren.

20. et] sed Vg. | accepistis] habetis Vg. Aug. | et nostis omnia] ut *ipsi manifesti sites* Aug.

21. Cf. Cognoscite ergo quoniam omne mendacium extraneum est et non est de ueritate Iren. | non 1°—scientibus] scribo uobis non quod nescieritis sed quia nostis Aug. | scientibus] pr. quasi Vg. | quoniam] quia Aug. | omne Aug. Spec. | non est ex ueritate Aug. | ex] de Spec-ed.

22. qui autem negat I͞m X͞m in carnem (-ne $^1/_2$) uenisse hic antechristus estPrisc. $^2/_2$ | is] om. Iren. | quia is] quod Iesus Aug. | quia] quoniam Vg. Iren. | est 2°] pr. non p. Aug. Iren. | hic—filium] om. Aug.

23. negat filium] non filium (+ habet h͞a) h. (Buch.) | om. et h. (Buch.) | cf. qui non habet filium nec patrem habet qui autem habet filium et patrem habet Cass. $^1/_2$ | omnis]? om. Cyp. cf. von Soden, 225 | negat] non crediderit in Luc. | nec] *pr.* nec filium Aug. | qui 2°] pr. et Aug. : + autem p. Prisc. Spec. : + uero Luc. | confitetur] credit in Luc. | et patrem] pr. et filium Cyp. $^2/_2$ Prisc. Spec-ed. : + et filium Luc.

24. uos] pr. ergo Aug. : + autem p. | ab initio audistis Aug. | permaneat in uobis] in uobis permaneat Vg. : in uobis maneat Aug. | quod si] si Vg. | permanserit] manserit Aug. | audistis ab initio Aug. | manebitis Vg. Aug.

25. et] om. Aug. | promissio] repromissio Vg. : pollicitatio Aug.

26. eis] his Vg. Aug. | seducunt uos] uos seducunt ut sciatis quia unctionem habetis Aug.

27. uos unctionem] unctio Aug. | accepimus Aug. | permaneat] maneat Vg. | uobis] nobis Aug. | necesse non habetis] non necesse habetis Vg. : non habetis necessitatem Aug. | uos doceat Aug. | sed sicut] quia Aug. | eius] ipsius Aug. | uerum] uerax Aug. | mendum] mendacium h͞a Vg. : mendax Aug. | et 3°] om. Aug. | manete Vg. | eo 2°] ipsa Aug.

28. filioli Vg. | uenerit] apparuerit Vg. : manifestatus fuerit Aug. | fiduciam habeamus] habeamus fiduciam Vg. : habeamus fiduciam in conspectu eius Aug. | et] ut Aug. | praesentia] aduentu Vg. Aug.

29. scimus] scitis Vg. Aug. | quoniam 1°, 2°] quia Aug. | omnis] pr. et Vg. | est natus Aug.

iii. 1. ~~ecce~~] uidete Vg. | ~~caritatem~~] dilectionem Aug. | ~~uocaremur~~] nominemur Vg. : uocemur Aug. : appellamur Aug. | sumus] simus Vg. Aug. | propterea—inhonorat] propter hoc mundus non nouit nos quia non nouit eum Vg. p. (et ipsum ignorabat *pro* non nouit eum) : propter hoc mundus non cognoscit nos quia non cognouit eum et nos non cognoscit mundus Aug.

2. carissimi] dilectissimi Aug. | nunc.] om. Aug. | et nondum] necdum Hier. $^1/_2$ | manifestatum est] apparuit Vg. Aug. : revelatum est Amb. : *cf.* nescimus Hier. $^1/_2$ | qui futuri sumus] quid erimus Vg. Aug. Amb. : quod

erimus Aug. | qui] quid Tert. Hier. $^1/_2$: quales Hier. $^1/_2$ | scimus] *pr.* sed
Amb. : nouimus autem Hier. | quoniam] quia **Aug.** Tert. Amb. Hier. | cum
apparuerit] si manifestauerit Tert. (manifestatus fuerit cod.) | apparuerit]
reuelatum fuerit Amb. : ille reuelatus fuerit Hier. | ei erimus **Aug.** | ei] illi
Aug-codd. : eius Tert. | quoniam uidebimus] uidebimus enim Hier. $^1/_2$.

3. habet—eo] spem istam in illo habet Tert. | hanc spem Vg. | eo] ipso
Aug. : eum Aug. | castificat] sanctificat Vg. Aug. | se] semet ipsum **Aug.** |
sicut] quia Tert. | et 2°] om. p. | ille] ipse **Aug.** Tert. | castus] sanctus Vg.
Aug.

4. peccatum 1°] delictum Aug. | et 1°] om. Aug. Amb. | et 2°] om. Aug.
| peccatum 2°] delictum Tert.

5. quoniam] quia Vg. **Aug.** | apparuit] manifestatus est **Aug.** Tert.
(sit) | peccata tolleret] auferat delicta Tert. | peccata]+nostra Vg. : peccatum
Aug. $^1/_2$ | tolleret] auferat **Aug.** | et 2°—est] om. Aug. (uid.) | illo] eo Vg. :
ipso **Aug.**

6. in eo permanet] in eo manet Vg. Aug. : in ipso manet **Aug.** : manet
in illo Tert. | peccat 1°] delinquit Tert. | omnis 2°] pr. et Vg. | peccat 2°]
delinquit Tert. | non 2°] neque Tert. | uidit] uidet p. | eum 1°] om. Tert.

7. filii Luc. | seducat] fallat Luc | qui] pr. omnis Tert. | est]+sicut et
ille iustus est Vg. **Aug.** Tert. Spec. (*om.* et cod.).

8. *Cf.* omnis qui peccat non est de deo sed de diabolo est et scitis quoniam
ideo uenturus est ut perdat filios diaboli De aleat. | autem] *om.* Vg. Tert.
Spec. | peccatum] delictum Tert. | de] ex Vg. Tert. : a Luc. Spec-ed. | quia]
quoniam Vg. Tert. Luc. | ab—peccat] diabolus a primordio delinquit Tert. |
ab initio] origine Luc. | in hoc] pr. et Spec. : idcirco Luc. $^1/_2$: ad hoc enim
Luc. $^1/_2$: +enim Tert. | apparuit] *inc.* Cod-Freis. (ed. Ziegler): manifestatus
est **Aug.** Tert. : declaratus est Luc. $^2/_2$ | soluat] dissoluat Vg. : solueret Luc.
$^2/_2$ Spec. | opera] operas Luc-cod. $^1/_2$.

9. ex] de h. | natus 1°—d̄o 1°] ex deo nascitur Tert. | peccatum non
facit] non peccat **Aug.** $^1/_2$ Spec. | peccatum] delictum Tert. | quia] quoniam
Vg. | semen] sensus Spec-codd. | eius] ipsius Vg. Aug. Cass. : dei Tert. |
ipso] eo h. Vg. Aug. Cass. : illo Tert. | manet] est Cass. | peccare] delinquere
Tert. | quoniam] quia **Aug.** Tert. Cass-cod. Spec. | de] ex Vg. **Aug.** Tert.

10. ex hoc] in hoc h. Vg. **Aug.** Tert. Cyp. : hinc Spec. | manifesti sunt]
manifestati sunt **Aug.** : apparent Cyp. Luc. Spec. | et filii] *bis scr.* h. | omnis]
om. Tert. Spec-cod. | facit iustitiam] est iustus Vg. **Aug.** Tert. Cyp. Luc $^2/_2$
Spec. | de] ex Vg. Tert. Luc. $^2/_2$ Spec. : a **Aug.** | diligit] amat Luc. $^2/_2$ |
fratrem suum] patrem suum aut matrem suam Cyp-cod.

11. quoniam] quia **Aug.** | hoc—quod] haec est annunciatio quam Vg.
Aug. haec est (om. est $^1/_2$) repromissio quam Luc. $^2/_2$ | audiuimus **Aug.** |
initio] origine Luc $^1/_2$ | diligamus] amemus Luc. $^2/_2$ | inuicem] alterutrum Vg.
Luc. $^2/_2$.

12. non]pr. et Luc. $^2/_2$ | qui] *om.* h. Aug-ed. Luc. $^2/_2$ | erat] fuit Luc. $^2/_2$ |
occidit 1°] interfecit Luc. $^2/_2$ | cuius sei gratia] propter quid Vg. Luc. $^2/_2$ |
occidit 2°] interfecit Luc. $^2/_2$ | eum] *om.* **Aug.** | quia] quoniam h. (Buch.) Vg.
Luc. $^2/_2$ | eius 1°] illius Luc. $^1/_2$: ipsius Luc. $^1/_2$ | erant] erat h.* : fuerunt Aug.
Luc. $^2/_2$ | autem] uero **Aug.** | eius 2°] ipsius Aug-cod. : sui Luc. $^2/_2$: *om.*
Aug-codd.

13. et] om. h. Vg. **Aug.** Luc. $^1/_2$ | fratres] om. p. | nos] uos Vg. | hic
mundus] om. hic Vg. **Aug.** : saeculum Luc $^2/_2$.

14. quoniam] quia h. (Ber.) **Aug.** | transimus] translati sumus Vg. :
[translati s]umus h. (Buch.): transiuimus p. (-ibi-) **Aug.** : transitum fecimus
Luc. $^2/_2$ | de] a Luc. $^2/_2$ | ad] in h. p. | quia] quoniam Vg. Luc. $^2/_2$ | diligimus]
amamus Luc. $^2/_2$ | qui—mortem] omnis qui fratrem suum non diligit manebit in
morte Faust. | qui]+autem Luc. $^2/_2$ | diligit] amat Luc. $^2/_2$ | permanet] manet
Vg. **Aug.** Luc. $^2/_2$ | mortem] morte h. cett.

15. omnis qui] quicunque Hier. | omnis 1°] ? om. Cyp. $^3/_3$ | qui]+enim

14

Cyp-cod. $^1/_2$ | quia] quoniam h. Vg. Cyp-cod. $^1/_2$ | uitam—se] in se uitam Cyp-ed. $^2/_2$: *om.* aeternum Luc. $^1/_2$ | se] semet ipso Vg. | manentem] om. Cyp-cod. $^1/_2$.

16. in hoc] et quia ex hoc Spec. (*om.* et codd.) | cognoscimus] cognouimus h. (Buch.) Vg. | caritatem]+Dei Vg. : dilectionem **Aug.** : +ipsius Spec. | quia] quoniam Vg. Spec. | pro nobis] *post* suam Vg. : propter nos Luc. | pro fratribus] *post* animas **Aug.** : +nostris Spec-ed. | pro 2°] de h. | animas] animam h. Vict.Vit. : +nostras Luc. Spec-ed.

17. qui] quicunque Spec. | autem] om. Vg. Cyp. $^2/_2$ | substantiam] facultates **Aug.** | huius] om. **Aug.** Cyp. $^2/_2$ Spec. | suum egere] cui opus [est] h. (Buch.) | egere] necessitatem habere Vg. : esurientem **Aug.** : desiderantem Cyp. (+aliquid cod.) $^2/_2$ | ab eo] om. Cyp. $^1/_2$-ed. $^1/_2$ | Caritas dei manet] poterit caritas (dilectio **Aug.**) dei manere **Aug.** Cyp-cod. $^1/_2$ | caritas] agape Cyp-cod. $^1/_2$: dilectio Cyp-cod. $^1/_2$ | dei] om. Cyp-cod. $^1/_2$ | permanet h. | eo] illo Cyp. $^2/_2$ Spec-ed.

18. filioli]+mei Vg. | tantum] om. Vg. : post uerbo p. **Aug.** | uerba h.* | neque] et hp. **Aug.** Spec.

19. et] om. h. Vg. | cognoscimus h. Vg. | coram ipso] in conspectu eius Vg. | suadebimus h. Vg. | corda nostra Vg.

20. si]+non p. | reprehenderit Vg. | corde h. | et] *expl.* h.

21. reprehenderit nos Vg. | nos] *om.* Aug-cod. | reprehendit Cyp-codd. Ep-Sev-ad-Claud. | habemus] habebimus Aug-cod. : habeamus Luc. | apud] ad Vg. Cyp. Aug. Luc. Ep-Sev.

22. quidquid] quodcunque p. Cyp. : quaecunque Aug. Ep-Sev. | accipiamus Cyp-cod. | eius 1°] *om.* Luc. | seruamus] custodiimus p. : custodimus Luc. | quae] pr. ea Vg. | sunt placita] ei placent Luc. | in conspectu eius] coram eo Vg. : ante conspectum eius Luc. | faciamus Luc.

23. et 1°—credamus] om. Luc. | nomini] in nomine Vg. Luc. | eius 2°] ipsius Luc. | diligamus] amemus nos Luc. | inuicem] alterutrum Vg. | mandatum nobis Vg.

24. mandata Vg. | manebit] manet Vg. | permanet] manet Vg.

iv. 1. K̄m̄i] dilectissimi **Aug.** | sps 1°—sunt] spiritum qui ex deo est Aug. $^1/_2$ | ex] a Spec-codd. | sint Vg. Cass. | q̄m̄] quia **Aug.** | prodierunt] exierunt Vg. Iren. Luc. $^2/_2$ Spec. | in hoc saeculo] in mundum Vg. : in istum mundum **Aug.** : de saeculo Iren. : in hunc mundum p. Spec. : om. hoc Luc.

2. hinc] in hoc Vg. **Aug.** Iren. : ex hoc Luc. | cognoscitur sps] cognoscite spiritum Iren. : intellegite spiritum Luc. | Christum Iesum Prisc. $^2/_3$ | IH̄M] om. Prisc. $^1/_3$ | X̄P̄M] om. Cass. | in carne uenisse] om. Prisc. $^2/_3$ | carnem Prisc. $^2/_3$ | ex. de Cyp. Prisc. $^3/_3$ Amb.

3. Cf. Qui autem negat in carne uenisse de deo non est sed est de anti-christi spiritu (antichristus cod.) Cyp. (cf. etiam Epist. 73. 15) : et omnis spiritus qui soluit Christum in carne uenisse non est ex deo **Aug.** $^1/_3$: omnis qui soluit Iesum Christum et negat eum in carne uenisse non est ex deo **Aug.** $^1/_3$ | omnis sps qui] quicunque sps Amb. $^1/_2$ (uid.) : omnis qui Amb. $^1/_2$ (uid.) Cass. $^4/_4$ | non confitetur] soluit p. Vg. Tert. $^1/_2$ (uid.) Iren. Prisc. $^1/_2$ Cass. $^4/_4$: negat Tert. $^1/_2$ Prisc. $^1/_2$ Amb. $^1/_2$ (cf. Cyp.) : destruit Luc. | IH̄M] Iesum Christum in carne uenisse **Aug.** Tert. $^1/_2$ (om. Iesum) Amb. $^2/_2$ | non est ex dō **Aug.** | ex] de Amb. $^1/_2$ Prisc. $^2/_2$ | et 2°—antixp̄isti] et hic anti-christus est Tert. $^1/_2$ Prisc. Cass-cod. $^1/_3$: sed de antichri-to est Iren. : et hoc est antichristi Cass. $^2/_3$-ed. $^1/_3$ | hoc] hic p. Vg. **Aug.** | illus antixp̄isti p.] antichristus Vg. **Aug.** | illius] quod est Luc. | quem] de quo Vg. **Aug.** : quod Cass. | quia] quoniam Vg. | uenturus est] uenit Vg. Cass. | nunc]+iam Vg. Cass. | saeculo] mundo Vg.

4. iam] om. Vg. | et uicistis eos] uincite illos De sing. cler. | eos] eum Vg. **Aug.** | q̄m̄] quia **Aug.** Paul-Nol. $^3/_3$ | maior] potior Paul-Nol. $^1/_3$ | est in

uobis Aug. | uobis] nobis Cass. Paul-Nol. $^{3}/_{3}$ | hic—est 3°] qui in mundo Vg. :
qui in hoc mundo est Aug. : qui in hoc mundo Cyp. $^{1}/_{2}$ Cass. Paul-Nol. $^{2}/_{3}$:
qui in isto mundo Cyp. $^{1}/_{2}$.

5. hii] ipsi Vg. : isti Luc. | saeculo 1°] mundo Vg. Aug. | propterea] ideo
Vg. Aug. | saeculo 2°] mundo Vg. Aug. | saeculum audit eos] mundus eos
audit Vg. Aug.

6. nos 1°]+autem Luc. | cognoscit] nouit Vg. Aug. | qui 2°]+autem
Luc. | nos audit] audit nos Luc. | hinc] in hoc Vg. : ex hoc Aug. Luc. |
cognoscimus s͞p͞m] cognoscitur spiritus Aug. : intellegimus spiritum Luc.

7. km͞i] dilectessimi Aug. | diligamus] amemus Luc. | inuicem] *pr.* nos
Vg. : nos alterutrum Luc. | q͞m] quia Vg. Aug. | fratrem suum] om. Vg.
Aug. De rebap. | suum] om. p. | cognoscit] cognouit Aug.

8. qui—dm] om. Aug. (uid.) De rebap. (uid.) | qui] quicunque Luc. |
diligit]+fratrem Luc. | ignorat] non nouit Vg. Aug. Luc. | quia] quoniam
Vg. Luc. | caritas] dilectio Aug. De rebap. Claud. Mam.

9. in] ex Luc. Spec. | apparuit] manifestata est Aug. Spec. (manifesta
cod.): declarata est Luc. | caritas] dilectio Aug. | di] Domini Spec-ed. |
nobis] uobis Spec-ed. | q͞m] quia Aug. : quod Spec. | unicum] unigenitum
Vg. Aug. | ds͞] om. Aug. Spec. | saeculo] mundum Vg. : hunc mundum p.
Aug. Spec. : saeculum Luc. | eum] ipsum Aug. Spec-ed.

10. caritas] dilectio Aug. | quod] quasi Vg. : quia Aug. | nos 1°] *om.*
Aug. | dilexerimus] dileximus Aug. : amauerimus Luc. | dm] *om.* Aug. :
dnm. Aug-cod. | q͞m] quia Aug. : quod Luc. | ipse dilexit nos] prior nos ille
dilexit Cass. | ipse]+prior Vg. Aug. | dilexit] amauerit Luc. | misit] miserit
Luc.] propitiaiorem] propitiationem Vg. : litatorem Aug. : expiatorem Luc.
| pro peccatis nostris] peccatorum nostrorum Luc. | .

11. Km͞i] dilectissimi Aug. | si sic] sicut p. | si]+ergo] Luc. | sic] ita
Aug. | dilexit] amauit Luc.] debemus et nos Aug. | et] sic p. | diligere
inuicem] alterutrum diligere Vg. : inuicem diligere Aug. : alterutrum
amare Luc.

12. quod si] si Vg. Aug. | diligimus p. | manebit Aug. | caritas] dilectio
Aug. | perfecta—nobis] in nobis perfecta est Vg. : erit perfecta in nobis
Aug.

13. in 1°] ex Vict.Vit. | cognoscimus] scimus Vict.Vit. : intellegimus
p. | qn͞m] quia Aug. Vict.Vit. | in 2°—ipse] om. Vict.Vit. | ipso] eo Vg. |
q͞m] quia Aug. Vict.Vit. | suo] dei p. : sancto Vict.Vit.

14. testamur] testificamur Vg. : testes sumus Aug. | q͞m] quia p.
Aug. | pater misit] misit deus Cass. | saeculi] mundi Vg. Aug.

15. quicunque] quisquis Vg. Cass-cod. : qui Aug. $^{1}/_{2}$ Tert. Cass-cod. :
quisque Cass-ed. | confessus fuerit] crediderit Cass. | q͞m] quod Aug.] ih͞s]
Christus Tert. (uid.) | eo] ipso Aug. : illo Tert. Cass. | ipse in d͞o] caritas dei
in eo perfecta est Cass. (?).

16. credimus p. | in 1°—ds͞ 1°] quam dilectionem deus habet Aug. | in
caritate 1°] caritati Vg. | caritas] dilectio Aug. Cyp. $^{1}/_{2}$ Paul-Nol. : agape
Cyp-cod. $^{1}/_{2}$ | et 3°] *om.* Cyp. $^{1}/_{2}$ Cass-ed. | in 3°—do͞] in deo in dilectione
Cyp-codd. $^{1}/_{2}$ | caritate 2°] dilectione Aug. Cyp. $^{1}/_{2}$: agape Cyp. $^{1}/^{2}$ |
permanet] nanet Vg. Aug. Cyp. $^{2}/_{2}$ Cass. | eo] illo Aug. $^{1}/_{2}$ Cyp. $^{2}/_{2}$:
ipso Cass. | manet 2°] *om.* Vg. Cyp-codd. $^{1}/_{2}$ Aug. Cass.

17. karitas in nobis] dilectio (+eius $^{1}/_{3}$) in nobis Aug. $^{2}/_{3}$: in nobis
dilectio Aug. $^{1}/_{3}$ | karitas]+Dei Vg. | in nobis] nobiscum Vg. | . . .] ut
Vg. Aug. | habeamus Vg. Aug. Cass. | die Aug. Cass-ed.

18. caritate] dilectione Aug. $^{1}/_{2}$ Tert. | sed]+enim Tert. | perfecta] con-
summata Aug. | caritas] dilectio Aug. $^{1}/_{2}$ Tert. $^{3}/_{3}$ Amb. Salv. Tyr. Ruf.
Hier. | foras mittit] foras abicit Tert. $^{1}/_{2}$: excludit foras Amb. | foris Aug-

cod. | q̅m̅]quia Aug. Tert. ¹/₂ | poenam] tormentum **Aug**. : suppliciamentum
Tert. ¹/₂ | qui autem] et qui Tert. ¹/₂ | caritatem] dilectione **Aug**. Tert. ²/₂.

19. ergo] om. **Aug**. | diligamus]+deum Vg. | q̅m̅] quia Aug. Cass. |
ipse] deus Vg. Cass. (?) | nos dilexit **Aug**. ¹/₂.

20. quis] qui Cyp-ed. | dicit Luc. | diligo d̅m̅] *pr.* quoniam Vg. : quoniam
diligit d̅m̅ Cyp. : quia diligit d̅m̅ Luc. : <de>se quod deum diligit Faust. |
odit—suum 2°] om. p.* | oderit Vg. | enim]autem Luc. | diligit] amat Luc. |
quem uidet] om. Cyp-cod. Luc. | d̅m̅ 2°] dominum Aug.-codd. | quomodo]
non Cyp-ed. Luc.

21. hoc]+ergo p. | a do̅] ab ipso **Aug**. Luc. : ab eo p. | diligit] amat
Luc. | diligat]amet Luc.

v. 1 quia] quoniam Vg. : quod **Aug**. | est 1°] sit **Aug**. : om. Spec. | est
2°]+deus in ipso est et ipse in deo Spec. | genitorem] eum qui genuit Vg. :
qui genuit eum **Aug**. | eum] pr. et Vg. | genitus—eo] ex deo (eo p.) natus est
p. Spec-ed. : natus est ex ipso Spec-codd. | genitus] natus Vg.

2. hinc] in hoc Vg. **Aug**. | cognoscimus] intellegimus Luc. | q̅m̅] quia
Aug. | diligimus 1°] amamus Luc. | filios] natos Vg. | cum] quia **Aug**. :
quando Luc. | diligimus d̅m̅] deum diligamus Vg. : deum diligimus **Aug**. :
amamus d̅m̅ Luc. | mandata] praecepta **Aug**. | eius] ipsius Luc. | facimus]
faciamus Vg. : seruauimus p.

3. caritas]+dei Vg. Aug. Luc. : dilectio dei **Aug**. | ut—seruemus] om.
Luc. | mandata 1°] praecepta **Aug**. | seruemus] explic. **Aug**. : custodiamus
Vg. : obseruemus Aug. | eius] ipsius Luc.

4. quia] quoniam Vg. | saeculum 1°, 2°] mundum Vg.

5. quis] qui p. | autem] *om.* Vg. | saeculum] mundum Vg. | credidit p. |
quia] quoniam Vg.

6. et 2°] om. Vg. De rebap. | tantum in aqua] in aqua solum Vg. | testi-
monium] qui testificatur Vg. : qui testimonium perhibet De rebap. : qui
testimonium reddit Spec. | quia] quoniam Vg. | sp̅s̅] Christus p. Vg.

7, 8. quoniam tres sunt qui testimonium dant in caelo Pater uerbum et
spiritus sanctus et hi tres unum sunt et tres sunt qui testimonium dant in terra
spiritus et aqua et sanguis et hi tres unum sunt Vg. : cf. *et iterum de patre et
filio et spiritu sancto scriptum est* et tres unum sunt Cyp. : quia tres testimonium
perhibent spiritus et aqua et sanguis et isti tres unum sunt De rebap. ²/₂ (in
unum cod. ¹/₂, cf. von Soden, *Das lateinische NT. in Afrika*, p. 280) : tres
testes sunt aqua sanguis et spiritus Amb. : tria sunt quae testimonium
perhibent aqua sanguis (+et ¹/₂) Spiritus Euch. ²/₂ : tria sunt qui testimonium
dicunt in terra aqua caro et sanguis et haec tria in unum sunt et tria sunt
quae testimonium dicunt in caelo pater uerbum et spiritus et haec tria unum
sunt in Christo Iesu Prisc. : tres sunt qui testimonium perhibent (dant cod.)
in caelo pater uerbum (et filius codd.) et spiritus sanctus (*om.* sanctus cod.) et
hi tres unum sunt Vict.Vit. : tres sunt qui testimonium dicunt in caelo pater
uerbum et spiritus et hii tres unum sunt Spec. ¹/₂ : quoniam (quia p. Spec-
cod.) tres sunt qui testimonium dicunt (dant p.) in terra spiritus aqua et
sanguis et hi tres unum sunt in Christo Iesu et tres sunt qui testimonium
dicunt (dant p.) in caelo pater uerbum et (*om.* et p.) spiritus (+sanctus p.
Spec-cod.) et hii tres unum sunt p. Spec. ¹/₂.

9. accepimus p. | quia 1°—di 2°] om. p. | quia 1°] quoniam Vg. | quia
2°] quod maius est quoniam Vg. | testatus est Tert.

10. filio 1°] filium Vg. | di 2°] eius Spec. | se] semet ipso Spec. | qui 2°]
+autem Spec. | in do̅] filio Vg. : Iesu Christo Spec. | eum] deum Spec. |
quia non credit] quoniam non credidit p. | in testimonium] testimonio p.
Spec. | eius] om. Vg. Spec. | d̅s̅] om. Spec.

12. Cf. qui filium non habet nec uitam habet Tert. | di 1°] om. Vg.

Prisc. : + in se p. | uitam habet] habet uitam p.(+ eternam) **Vg.** | dī 2⁰] om.
Vg. Prisc.

13. haec] pr. carissimi p. | scripsi p. | quia] quoniam **Vg.**

14. ad eum] apud d̄m̄ p. | quidquid] quodcumque **Vg.**

15. si] om. **Vg.** | quia] q̄m p. | petiuimus] postulamus **Vg.**

16. si quis] qui **Vg.** Cass. : omnis qui p. | peccare] delinquere **Tert.** ²/₂
Hil. | peccatum 1⁰] delictum **Tert.** ²/₂ : *om.* Hil. | no̅] pr. sed Hil. |
postulabit] petat **Vg.** Hil. : petat pro eo p. | dabit ei uitam] dabitur ei uita **Vg.**
Tert. ¹/₂ Cass-codd. ¹/₂ : + deus p. Cass-codd. ²/₂ | ei] illi deus Hil. | his—
mortem 2⁰] peccanti non ad mortem p. **Vg.** Cass. (pr. sed p. cod. ¹/₂ :
peccantibus ed. ¹/₂) : qui (quia ¹/₂) non ad mortem delinquit **Tert.** ²/₂ : *om.*
Hil. | enim] *om.* **Vg.** **Tert.** ¹/₂ | peccatum 2⁰] delictum **Tert.** ²/₂ | usque 2⁰] *om.*
Vg. **Tert.** ²/₂ Hil. Cass. | non 3⁰] pr. sed Hil. | pro] de **Tert.** ¹/₂ | ut postulet]
om. Hil. (uid.) | postulet] roget quis **Vg.** : *pr.* quis **Tert.** ²/₂ : roget Cass.
(rogent Codd.) Aug. (+ quis cod.).

17. iniustitia] iniquitas **Vg.** | peccatum 1⁰, 2⁰] delictum **Tert.**

18. q̄m] quia **Vg.** : quod **Tert.** | est] sit **Tert.** | peccat] delinquit **Tert.** |
natiuitas] generatio **Vg.** Aug. Cass.

19. totus—est] saeculum totum in malo positum est Salv. | mundus totus
Vg. | totus] omnis Prisc. | mundus] pr. hic Paul-Nol. (uid.) | positus est] iacet
Paul-Nol.

20. uenit] + et carnem uiduit nostri causa et passus est et resurrexit a
mortuis adsumpsit nos p. Spec. | et 1⁰—XPO] Cf. et nos dedit sensum per quem
sciremus quod est uerbum in Christo Iesu Paul.Oros. | intellectum] sensum
Vg. Paul.Oros. Spec. | sciamus] cognoscamus **Vg.** : cognosceremus Spec. |
quod est uerum] uerum deum **Vg.** : eum qui (quia cod.) uerus est Spec. | et
3⁰] ut Spec-cod. | uero] uerbum Spec-codd. | IH̄U XP̄O] *om.* **Vg.** | hic]
ipse Aug. | d̄s̄] *om.* Spec. | aeterna] + et resurrectio nostra Spec.

21. filioli] fratres Aug. | custodite uos] cauete Aug. | ab idolis] a simulacris
Vg. Aug. Spec. + Amen **Vg.**

ἀγαπᾶν . . .	diligere h q **Vg.** **Aug.** (iii. 14) amare Luc.
	,, q **Vg.** **Aug.** (iii. 23) ,, Luc.
	dilexerimus q **Vg.** (iv. 10) amauerimus Luc.
	dileximus **Aug.**
	diligere q **Vg.** **Aug.** De rebap. (iv. 7, 11) amare Luc.
	,, q **Vg.** **Aug.** (iv. 20) ,, Luc.
	,, q **Vg.** **Aug.** (v. 2) ,, Luc.
ἀγάπη . . .	caritas h **Vg.** (ii. 5) dilectio **Aug.**
	,, h q **Vg.** (iii. 16) ,, **Aug.**
	,, h q **Vg.** (iii. 17) ,, **Aug.** Cyp-cod. ¹/₂ agape Cyp-cod. ¹/₂.
	,, q **Vg.** (iv. 8) ,, **Aug.** De rebap.
	,, q **Vg.** (iv. 9, 10, 12, 17) dilectio **Aug.** agape Cyp. ¹/₂.
	,, q **Vg.** (iv. 16) dilectio **Aug.** Cyp. ¹/₂.
	,, q **Vg.** Aug. (v. 3) ,, **Aug.** Luc.
	,, **Vg.** (3 Jn. 6) ,, Hier.
ἀγαπητός . .	carissimus h **Vg.** (ii. 7) dilectissimus **Aug.**
	,, q **Vg.** (iv. 7, 11) ,, **Aug.**
	,, **Vg.** (3 Jn. 1) ,, Aug.
ἀγγελία . . .	mandatum h q (iii. 11) annunciatio **Vg.** **Aug.** repromissio Luc.
ἀγνίζειν . . .	castificare h (iii. 3) sanctificare **Vg.** **Aug.**
ἀγνός	castus h (iii. 3) sanctus **Vg.** **Aug.**
ἀδικία . . .	iniquitas h **Vg.** **Aug.** (i. 9) iniustitia **Tert.**

ἀδικία . . . iniquitas Vg. (v. 17) iniustitia q.
αἴρειν . . . . tollere h Vg. (iii. 5) auferre **Aug.**
αἰτεῖν . . . . petere, petere q (v. 15) petere, postulare **Vg.**
         postulare q Tert. (v. 16) petere Vg. Hil.
ἐρωτᾶν . . . postulare q Tert. (v. 16) rogare Vg. Aug. **Cass.**
ἀλαζονία τοῦ βίου (ii. 16) superbia uitae h Vg.
         ambitio saeculi Cyp. **Aug.**
            ,,   mundi Cyp-cod. ¹/₄.
            ;,   humanae uitae Prisc.
ἀλλήλους . . . inuicem q **Aug.** (iii. 23) alterutrum Vg.
            ,,   q **Aug.** (iv. 7) nos inuicem Vg. nos alterutrum **Luc.**
            ,,   q **Aug.**   alterutrum Vg. Luc.
            ,,   **Aug.** (2 Jn. 5   ,,   Vg.
ἁμαρτάνειν . . peccare h Vg. **Aug.** (i. 10) delinquere Cyp. **Tert.**
            ,,   q Vg. (v. 16)   ,,   Tert. Hil.
ἁμαρτία . . . peccatum h Vg. Cyp. (i. 9) delictum Tert. **Aug.**
            ,,   h Vg. (iii. 5)   ,,   Tert. **Aug.**
ἄν . . . . . forsitan h (ii. 19) utique Vg. Aug. Cyp. (*om.* ed. ¹/₅ cod.¹/₅).
ἀφιέναι . . . remittere h Vg. (i. 9) dimittere Cyp. Tert. **Aug.** Spec.
βίος . . . . substantia h q Vg. Cyp. facultates **Aug.**
τὸν γεννήσαντα . genitorem q (v. 1) eum qui genuit Vg. qui genuit eum
         Aug.
τὸν γεγεννημένον qui genitus est q **Aug.** (v. i.) qui natus est Vg. Spec.
ὁ γεννηθείς . . natiuitas q (v. 18) generatio Vg. **Aug.** Cass.
γινώσκειν . . scire h Vg. (ii. 5) cognoscere **Aug.**
         cognoscere q Vg. **Aug.** (v. 2) intelligere **Luc.**
διὰ τοῦτο . . . propterea q (iv. 5) ideo Vg. **Aug.**
δίκαιον . . . iustum h Vg. Cyp. **Aug.** (ii. 1)? suffragatorem **Cyp.**
         cod. ¹/₂.
εἴδωλον . . . idolum q (v. 21) simulacrum Vg. Aug. Spec.
ἐντολή . . . mandatum h Vg. **Aug.** (ii. 3) praeceptum Cyp.
            ,,   q Vg. (v. 2)   ,,   **Aug.**
            ,,   q Vg. (v. 3)   ,,   **Aug.**
            ,,   Vg. Luc. (2 Jn. 5)   ,,   Aug.
ἐξεληλύθασιν . prodierunt q **Aug.** (iv. 1)   exierunt Vg. Luc. Spec.
ἐξῆλθαν . .   ,,   Vg. Tert. (ii. 19)   ,,   h Cyp. **Aug.**
         (prodiit h (Buch.).
         profecti sunt Vg (3 Jn. 7)   ,,   Hier.
ἔξω βάλλει . . (iv. 18) foras mittit q Vg. **Aug.** Tert. ²/₃.
         foras abicit Tert. ¹/₃.
         excludit foras Amb.
ἐπιθυμία . . . concupiscentia h Cyp. Vg. (ii. 16) desiderium **Aug.**
         uoluntas Prisc.
            ,,   h Cyp. Vg. (ii. 17) desideria **Aug.**
ἱλασμός . . . (ii. 2) exoratio h.
         propitiatio Vg.
         propitiator **Aug.**
         placatio Tert. Hil.
         deprecatio Cyp.
         ~~? satisfactio et placatio Ad Vigil.~~
         (iv. 10) propitiator q.
         propitiatio Vg.
         litator **Aug.**
         expiator Luc.
καθαρίζειν . . purgare h (i. 9) emundare Vg. Tert. mundare **Aug.** Spec.
καθώς . . . . quemadmodum h (ii. 6) sicut Vg. **Aug.** quomodo **Cyp.**
         Hier.

κληθῶμεν . . uocaremur h (iii. 1) nominemur Vg. appellemur **Aug.**
uocemur **Aug.**

κόλασις . . . poena q Vg. Tert. ¹/₂ (iv. 18) tormentum **Aug.** supplicia-
mentum Tert. ¹/₂.

κόσμος . . . saeculum h (ii. 2)   mundus Vg. **Aug.**
     ,,   h Cyp. (ii. 16)   ,,   Vg. **Aug.** Cyp.
     ,,   h (ii. 17)   ,,   Vg. **Aug.** Cyp.
     ,,   Luc. (iii. 13)   ,,   hq Vg. **Aug.**
     ,,   q (iv. 1, 5, 14)   ,,   Vg. **Aug.**
     ,,   q Luc. (iv. 9)   ,,   Vg. **Aug.** Spec.
     ,,   (2 Jn. 7) Luc.   ,,   Vg.

λόγος . . . . uerbum h Vg. (i. 10) sermo Tert,

μαρτυροῦμεν . (iv. 14) testamur q.
testificamur Vg.
testes sumus **Aug.**

μαρτυρεῖν . . (v. 7, 8) testimonium dare Vg.
testificari q.
testimonium perhibere De rebap. **Euch. Vict.Vit.**
testis esse Amb.
testimonium dicere Prisc. Spec.

μεταβεβήκαμεν . (iii. 14) transimus h q.
translati sumus Vg. h (Buch.).
transiuimus **Aug.**
transitum fecimus Luc.

μονογενής . . unicus q (iv. 9) unigenitus Vg. **Aug.**
νεανίσκος . . . iuuenis h **Aug.** (ii. 13)   adolescens **Vg.**
     ,,   Vg. Aug. (ii. 14)   ,,   h.

ὅτι ἔγνωκα . . (ii. 4) se noscere h.
se nosse Vg.
quia cognouit (-ui) Cyp. **Aug.**

παιδία . . . pueri h **Aug.** (ii. 14) infantes Vg.
παράκλητος . . aduocatus h Vg. Cyp. **Aug.** (ii. 1) paracletus Faust. Vict.
Vit.

παρουσία . . . praesentia h (ii. 28) aduentus Vg. **Aug.**
ἔσφαξεν . . . occidit h q Vg. **Aug.** (iii. 12) interfecit.
ταῦτα . . . . haec h Vg. **Aug.** (ii. 1) ista Cyp.
τέκνα . . . . filii q **Aug.** (v. 2) nati Vg.
τεκνία . . . . fili h (ii. 1) filioli Vg. Cyp. **Aug.** Tert. fratres Aug.
τέλειος . . . perfectus q Vg. **Aug.** (iv. 18) consummatus Aug.
πηρεῖν . . . seruare h **Aug.** (ii. 3) obseruare Vg. custodire Cyp. Luc.
     ,,   **Aug.** Luc. (ii. 5)   ,,   h Vg.
     ,,   q Vg. **Aug.** (iii. 22)   ,,   Luc.
     ,,   q **Aug.** (v. 3) obseruare Luc.   ,,   Vg.

τυφλοῦν . . . obscoecare h Vg. (ii. 11) excaecare Cyp. **Aug.** obscurare
Luc.

φανεροῦσθαι . . manifestus esse Vg. (ii. 19).
manifestari **Aug.** (ii. 19, 28, iii. 2), h (iii. 2), **Tert.** (iii. 2),
Tert. **Aug.** (iii. 8), **Aug.** Spec. (iv. 9).
praesto esse h (ii. 19).
uenire h (ii. 28).
apparere Vg. (ii. 28) Vg. Aug. (iii. 2) h q Vg. (iii. 8) q Vg.
(iv. 9).
reuelari Amb. (iii. 2).
declarari Luc. (iii. 8. iv. 9).

φῶς . . . . lumen h Vg. (ii. 7) lux **Aug.**
     ,,   h **Aug.** (¹/₂) (ii. 9) lux Vg. **Aug.** (¹/₂) Cyp.
(**Spec.**).

χρείαν ἔχειν . . (iii. 17) egere q.
(cui) opus [est] h (Buch.).
necessitatem habere **Vg**.
desiderantem Cyp.
esurientem **Aug**.

Collation of the Old Latin Text with the Greek (ed. Nestle).

I. **1.** ο 3°] pr. et.
    om. ο εθεασαμεθα.
  2. η ζωη] ipsa uita.
    μαρτυρουμεν] testes sumus.
    ημιν] in nobis.
  3. ο] quae.
    και υμιν] uobis.
    μετα 1°] pr. sit.
    μετα του πατρος] cum Deo Patre.
    μετα 2°] om.
    του υιου αυτου] post Χριστου.
  4. ημεις] uobis.
    ημων] uestrum.
  6. εαν] quodsi.
  7. αυτος] et ipse.
    καθαριζει] purgabit.
    Ιησου] + Χριστου = Vg.
  8. ουκ εστιν] post ημιν = **Vg**.
  9. εστιν] om.
    απο] ex.
  10. εαν] quod si : si **Vg**.
    ποιουμεν] faciemus.

II. **2.** ιλασμος] post εστιν = Vg.
  4. οτι εγνωκα] se noscere : se nosse ᵛg.: quia cognoni
      Cyp.
    και 2°] om.
  5. ος δ᾿ αν] nam qui.
    αυτου] post λογον = Vg.
    αληθως] om.
  6. ουτως] om.
  7. εντολην] post καινην.
    ειχετε] habuistis.
  8. αληθες] uere.
    παραγινεται] iam transeunt : transierunt **Vg**.
  10. ο] pr. nam.
  13. τον απ αρχης] quod erat ab initio.

14. εγραψα 1°, 3°] *scribo.*
    εγραψα υμιν πατερες] om.
16. σαρκος] + *est.*
    βιου] + est (uid.).
    ουκ] pr. *quae.*
17. αυτου] om.
18. και 2°] om.
19. εξηλθαν] ? prodiit.
    ησαν 1°] erat.
    ησαν 2°] fuisset.
    μεμενηκεισαν] permansisset.
    φανερωθωσιν] praesto fiat.
20. εχετε] accepistis.
    παντες] *omnia.*
21. οτι ουκ οιδατε] *quasi ignorantibus.*
    αλλ' οτι οιδατε] *sed* (+ quasi Vg.) *scientibus.*
22. ουκ εστιν] *est.*
24. εν υμιν 1°] post μενετω.
    εαν] quod si.
27. μενει] permaneat : maneat Vg.
28. εαν] cum.
    φανφωθη] uenerit : apparuerit Vg.
    σχωμεν] post παρρησιαν.

III. 1. ιδετε] ecce.
    ου γινωσκει ημας] nos inhonorat (Ber.) : nos egnorat (Buch.).
    οτι—αυτον] om.
  2. τι] qui.
    εαν] *cum.*
    αυτω] post εσομεθα.
  3. επ αυτω] *in eo.*
    εκεινος] *et ille.*
  7. καθως—εκεινος] om.
  8. ο 1°] + autem.
 10. εν τουτω] ex hoc q : *in hoc* h Vg. Aug.
 11. αυτη—αγγελια] hoc est mandatum h q.
 12. εκ] pr. *qui* q.
 13. μη] pr. et.
    υμας] nos h q.
 16. εγνωκαμεν] cognoscimus.
 17. χρειαν εχοντα] egere h q ; necessitatem habere **Vg.**
 18. λογω] tantum uerbo h (uerba) q.
 19. εν] pr. et.
    γνωσομεθα] *cognoscimus* h : cognoscimur q.

πεισομεν] suademus q : suadebimus h **Vg.**

20. η καρδια] *cor nostrum* h ꞵ.
οτι 2°] om. h q Vg.

21. η καρδια μη] *cor nostrum non nos.*

22. λαμβανομεν] *accipiemus.*

23. εντολην] post ημιν.

24. τας εντολας] mandatum.
ημιν] post εδωκεν = Vg.

IV. 2. εν τουτω] hinc.
γινωσκετε] *cognoscitur.*
εληλυθοτα] *uenisse.*

3. μη ομολογει] non confitetur : soluit **Vg.**
ερχεται] uenturus est.

4. ο 2°—κοσμω] his qui in saeculo est.

5. αυτοι] hii.
αυτων] post ακουει.

6. ακουει 2°] post ημων 2°.

7. αγαπαν] + fratrem suum = De rebap**t.**

8. ουκ εγνω] ignorat.

10. ιλασμον] propitiatorem.
αλληλους] post αγαπαν.

12. πωποτε] post τεθεαται = **Vg.**
εν ημιν] post εστιν.

14. τον υιον] *filium suum.*

17. μεθ' ημων] in nobis.
εχωμεν] habemus.

19. πρωτος] *prior.*

20. οτι] om.
εωρακεν (bis)] *uidet.*
ου] *quomodo.*

21. απ αυτου] a deo.

V. 2. εν τουτω] hinc.
τον θεον] post αγαπωμεν **2°.**

3. γαρ] post εστιν = Vg.
του θεου] om.

4. η νικησασα] *quae uincit.*

5. εστιν] + autem.

6. ουκ] pr. et.
εν τω υδατι] post μονον.
το μαρτυρουν] testimonium.

7. μαρτυρουντες] + in terra.
αιμα] + et tres sunt qui testificantur in **caelo pater et**
uerbum et sps scs.
οι τρεις] hi tres.

εις το εν] unum.

10. μαρτυριαν 1°] + *di.*

τω θεω] in do: filio Vg.

μαρτυριαν 2°] + eius.

11. ο θεος] post ημιν = Vg.

12. τον υιον 1°] + *di.*

13. εγραψα] ? *scribo.*

14. οτι εαν τι] quia quidquid : quia quodcunque Vg.

16. ιδη] *scit.*

αμαρτανοντα] *peccare.*

εστιν] + enim.

17. ου] om. = Vg.

18. ο γεννηθεις εκ του θεου] natiuitas di : generatio Dei Vg.

19. ο κοσμος] post ολος.

20. οιδαμεν δε] et scimus : scimus Vg.

τον αληθινον] quod est uerum : uerum Deum Vg.

εσμεν] *simus.*

εν τω υιω] *filio.*

In the above collation the Greek has been underlined when the Latin supports a Greek reading which differs from that contained in Nestle's text. The differences between the Old Latin and Vulgate have also been marked. When the Old Latin agrees with the Vulgate the rendering has been printed in Italics, or the agreement has been noted by the symbol " = Vg."; when the Vulgate differs from both the Greek and the Old Latin its rendering has been added ; in all other cases the Vulgate agrees with the Greek against the Old Latin. For the " Vulgate," Nestle's printed text has been used. The amount of help to be obtained from the Old Latin in determining the Greek text is not great. There are, of course, but few passages in which there is serious doubt as to the true reading. But the collation brings out at least one interesting fact, in the number of instances where Greek variants are not involved, but where the Vulgate agrees with the Greek against the Old Latin. This shows the extent to which the Vulgate has revised a not very accurate translation into far closer conformity with the Greek text. The facts are of some interest in connection with the tendency which is clearly marked in the Old Latin to add interpretative glosses. In two passages the textual evidence of the Old Latin is of special interest. In iv. 3 the reading " non confitetur " supports the view which is suggested by the evidence of Cyprian and Tertullian that the original reading in Greek has μὴ ὁμολογεῖ and that the λύει (represented by the Vulgate "soluit" and apparently known to Tertullian) came into the Latin text as an

interpretative gloss.   In the more famous passage **v. 7, 8** the
Old Latin gives us the gloss in its earlier form in which the
earthly witnesses precede the heavenly, as in the text of
Priscillian, whose quotation of the passage is the earliest known
evidence for the insertion.   It is unfortunate that in both these
verses we are dependent for our Old Latin text on Ziegler's
Freisingen Fragments, and have not the help of the Fleury
Palimpsest, which, though not pure African, undoubtedly
approaches nearer to the earlier forms of the Old Latin text.

In the case of the two shorter Epistles we have no help from
MSS, except the last few verses (11b–end) of the Third Epistle,
which are extant in the Latin (only) of Codex Bezae, where they
are found between the Fourth Gospel and the Acts, a position
which perhaps suggests, as has been pointed out, that in this MS
the Johannine Epistles were treated as an appendix to the Gospel.

It has therefore been possible to reproduce only the quotations of the Epistles which follow the Old Latin text or at
least afford information about it.   The words in these quotations
which do not agree with the Vulgate have been printed in
Clarendon type, in order to show how far the citations yield Old
Latin evidence.   A few have been added which are not contained in the Volumes already published in the Vienna *Corpus*.
In their case the reference to Migne has been given with the
number of the volume in his edition of the Father quoted.   It
may be worth while to tabulate the following renderings, in
addition to those already given, which they attest :

	O. L.	Vulgate.
ἀπολαμβάνειν	recipere (Luc.)	accipere.
ἐθνικός	gentilis (Hier.)	gens.
ἐνώπιον	coram (,,)	in conspectu.
ἔργον	factum (Cyp.)	opus (Luc.).
καθώς	sicut (Luc.)	quemadmodum
	quasi (Aug.)	
λαμβάνειν	admittere (Cyp.)	recipere.
	accipere (Luc.)	
πλάνος	fallax (Luc. Spec.)	seductor.
προπέμπειν	praemittere (Hier.)	deducere.
ὡς	sicut (Luc.)	tanquam.

So far as it goes this evidence supports that which has been
collected in connection with the First Epistle.   The Bezan
fragment, which has been collated with the Vulgate and also
with the Greek (Nestle's text has been used in both cases)
again shows the usual Vulgate accommodation to the Greek, but
suggests a Greek text further removed from that which Jerome
made the basis of his Vulgate.

The *Speculum* quotation of 2 Jn. 11 affords another instance of the addition of glosses. The words (ecce praedixi uobis ne in diem domini condemnemini) are found in some MSS of the Vulgate.

The text of the Perpignan MS in the two minor Epistles is mainly Vulgate. The following readings may, however, be noted :

2 Jn. 4 gauisus] pr. Karissimi | 7 prodierunt | 8 custodite ne perdatis | estis]+in Dn̄o | 9 doctrina]+eius | 12 per chartam et atramentum] per atramentum et in epistola | futurum] uenturum | electae]+ecclesie 3 Jn. 2 | egit | 4 gratiam] gaudium | 6 benefacis deducens | profecti sunt] peregrinantur | huiusmodi]+participes | 14 te uisurum (cf. d) | saluta tu amicos nominatos.

2 Jn. 10, 11—Cypr. *Sent. Episc.* 81. "Si quis ad uos[1] uenit et doctrinam Christi non habet, nolite eum admittere in domum uestram et aue[2] illi ne dixeritis[3] qui enim dixerit[4] illi aue[2] communicat factis eius malis."

[1] eos A.	[2] haue SL habe T[1].
[3] dixeris S.	[4] om. qui enim dixerit S.

2 Jn. 7–8—Irenaeus, III. xvi. 8 (ed. Stieren). "Multi seductores exierunt in hunc mundum qui non confitentur Iesum Christum in carne uenisse. Hic est seductor et Antichristus."

2 Jn. 11. "Qui enim dicit eis Aue communicat operibus ipsorum nequissimis."

2 Jn. 7—Priscillian, p. 30. "Qui non confitentur Christum Iesum in carne uenisse, hi sunt seductores et antichristi."

2 Jn. 4–11—Lucifer, p. 28 (ed. Hartel). 4. "Gauisus sum valde quod inueni de filiis tuis ambulantes in ueritati sicuti mandatum accepimus a patre.

5. "Oro te, domina, non sicut mandatum nouum scribens tibi, sed quod habuimus ab initio, ut diligamus nos alterutrum ;

6. "et haec est caritas ut ambulemus secundum mandata eius. hoc est mandatum sicut audistis ab initio ut in eo ambuletis.

7. "quoniam multi fallaces progressi sunt in saeculo[1] qui non confitentur Iesum Christum uenisse in carnem ; isti sunt fallaces et antichristi.

[1] seclo.

8. "uidete eos, ne perdatis quod operati estis, sed ut mercedem plenam recipiatis.

9. "omnis qui recedit et non manet in doctrina Christi deum non habet ; qui autem manet in doctrina eius ille et patrem et filium habet.

et 1°—christo] a doctrina eius Luc. ¹/₃.

10. "si quis uenerit ad nos et hanc doctrinam non adfert, nolite accipere eum in domum et aue nolite dicere ei ;

11. "qui enim dicit ei aue communicat operibus eius malignis.

2 Jn. 7—ad Petrum Fullonen. Ep. Imp. p. 198. "Multi exierunt in mundum seductores, qui non confitentur Christum Iesum in carne uenisse."

2 Jn. 7—Gelasius i. ad Ep. Dardaniae.　Ep. 79, p. 221. "Qui negat Christum in carne uenisse hic est antichristus."

2 Jn. 3—Augustine, *ad Rom.* c. 12 (Migne, iii. 2096). "Sit uobiscum gratia misericordia pax a Deo Patre et Jesu Christo Filio Patris."

2 Jn. 5—Augustine, *De gratia et libero arbitrio*, c. 35 (Migne, x. 903). "Non quasi praeceptum nouum scribam tibi sed quod habuimus ab initio ut diligamus inuicem."

3 Jn. 1—Augustine, *ad Rom.* c. 12 (Migne, iii. 2096). "Senior Gaio dilectissimo quem ego diligo in ueritate."

3 Jn. 5–7—Jerome, *In Titum*, Lib. i. 701 (Migne, vii. 568). "Charissime fideliter facis quodcumque operaris in fratribus et hoc peregrinis qui testimonium dederunt dilectioni tuae coram ecclesia quos optime facies si praemiseris Deo digne pro nomine enim Domini exierunt nihil accipientes a gentilibus."

2 Jn. 7—Spec. 315, 6, ed. Weihrich.　7. "Quoniam multi fallaces[1] prodierunt in hunc mundum, qui non confitentur iesum christum dominum nostrum[2] in carne[3] uenisse hii[4] fallaces et antichristi[5] sunt."

[1] fallaces S.　　　　　　　　[2] d̄n̄m̄ nrm īh̄m̄ x̄p̄m̄ M V L C.
[3] om. in carne C.　　　　　　[4] hi L.
[5] antecris | tii S anticristi V.

2 Jn. 10, 11—Spec. 517, 4.　10. "Si quis uenit ad uos et hanc doctrinam non adfert, nolite eum recipere in domum[1] et aue[2] ne dixeritis ei.[3]

11. "qui enim dicit illi aue[4] communicat operibus eius malignis. ecce praedixi uobis ne in diem[5] domini condemnemini.[6] "

3 Jn. 4*b*—end.

[1] in domo M.　　　　　　　　[2] habe S M[1] aue M[2] L C.
[3] illi ne dixeritis M L C.　　　[4] habe S abe M[1].
[5] diem S M L C.　　　　　　　[6] condempnemini M C.

CODEX BEZAE (f. 415).

　　　qui malefacit non uidit d̄m̄
demetrio testimonium exhibetur ab omnibus
　　　et ab ipsa ueritate
　　　et nos uero testimonium perhibemus
[5] et scis testimonium nostrum uerum est
plura habui scribere tibi

sed nolo per atramentum
et calamum scribere tibi
spero enim protinus te uisurum
10 et os ad os locuturum pax tecum
Salutant te amici tui
saluta amicos nomatim.

Epistulae Iohanis III.

Explicit
incipit
Actus Apostolerum.

2. exhibetur] redditur Vg.

4. et nos uero] sed et nos Vg.
5. scis] nosti quoniam Vg.
6. plura] multa Vg.
7. nolo] nolui Vg.
9. enim] autem Vg.
   uisurum] uidere Vg.
10. locuturum] loquemur **Vg.**
    tecum] tibi Vg.
11. tui] om. **Vg.**

12. μεμαρτυρηται] testimo-
    nium exhibetur.
    οτι] om.
13. πολλα] plura.
    σοι 2⁰] post γραφειν.
14. δε] enim.
    λαλησομεν] locuturum
15. σοι] tecum.
    οι φιλοι] amici tui.

INDICES.

—⸰—

A. GENERAL.
B. AUTHORS AND WORKS.
C. GREEK WORDS AND PHRASES.
D. WORDS USED IN THE EPISTLES.
E. WORDS USED IN GOSPEL BUT NOT IN EPISTLES.

Roman figures refer to the Introduction.

A. GENERAL.

ABSOLUTE statements, writer's use of, 53.
Anointing, 55.
Antichrist, 49 ff., 59, 69 ff.
Antinomianism, 1 f., 84.
Antiochus IV., 73.
Aorist, Epistolary, 42, 179.
  meaning of, 82, 131.
Apodosis, introduced by καί, 63.
Article, absence of, 51.
  use of double, 6.
Assurance, xxviii., 98, 121, 141.
Atonement, Day of, 28.

Babylonian Myth, 69 ff.
Barkochba, xviii.
Belief, 103.
Blood, meaning of, in Jewish thought, 15.
Brotherhood, author's conception of, 39, 94.

Cain, interpretation of history of, 92.
Chiliasm, lxxv ff.
Christology of Epistles, xvi, xx, 8.
Commandment, Old and New, meaning of, 33 ff.

Demas, lxxxiii.
Demetrius, lxxxii f., 192 f.
Demonstrative, use of, for emphasis, vi.
Diotrephes, lxxxii, 187 f.
Docetism, xliv ff., lxxvi.

Eschatology, xviii, xxi, 37, 51.
Ethical teaching of opponents, l.
Eye-witnesses, 2.

False Teachers, the, xxxviii ff., 58 f.
Fellowship, 8, 15, 104, 120.
First person plural, use in these Epistles, 9, 13, 93, 122, 193.
Forgiveness, meaning of ἄφεσις in N.T., 20.

Genitive, after substantives, 5.
Glosses, 49, 138, 179.
Gnosticism, xxviii f., 29, 31 f., 83, 85.
Gospel and Epistles—
  Common types of sentences, v.
  Differences in minor points, xi.
  External attestation, xxii.
  Ideas common to both, viii f.
  Limitations of Vocabulary, vii.
  'Originality' of Author, x, xxiii.

15

Gospel and Epistles—
    Parallels in Epistles to the Last
        Discourses, xxiv.
    Peculiarities of Epistles, xiii.
    Phrases Common to both, i ff.
    References in Epistles to Gospel,
        xxiv ff.
    Similarity and differences of style,
        v, xxii.

Heavenly Witnesses, the history of
    the Gloss, 154 ff.
Hospitality, duty of, lxxix, lxxxi,
    178, 184.

Intercession, 145, 147.
Itacism, 108.

Judaism, xli ff.

Knowledge, meaning in S. John, 29.

Love, teaching of Epistle on, 117 ff.,
    122, 125.

Monarchian tendencies in Epistles,
    xvi, xix.
Monarchical Episcopate, development
    of, lxxxviii.
Marduk, 70 ff.

Name, meaning of, in Jewish thought,
    44.
Nominative absolute, use of, 60, 62.

Organization of Asiatic Churches,
    lxxxix f.

Paraclete, xx ff., 23 ff.
Parenthesis, 6, 80.
Parousia, 37, 66, 81.
Polemical aim of Epistles, xxvii,
    xxxviii ff.
Prayer, teaching on, 102, 144.
Propitiation, xviii, xxi, 28, 119.

Relative, infrequent use of, v.
Repetition, writer's fondness for,
    60.

Second and Third Epistles—
    Relation to the First, lxxiv ff. ; his-
        torical background of, lxxxiv ff.
Second Epistle—
    Circumstances under which written,
        lxxix.
    Comparison with the Didache,
        lxxx.
    Destination, lxxx.
Sin, meaning of ἁμαρτίαν ἔχειν in
    Gospel and Epistle, 17.
    universality of, 22.
Sin unto death, 145 ff.

Third Epistle—
    Circumstances under which written,
        lxxxi.
    Relation to the Second, lxxxiii,
        187 f.
Tiâmat, 69 ff.
Titles of Christ, 8, 16, 27, 58, 105,
    131, 175.

World, the, meaning of, in S. John,
    47, 92 f., 107.

B. AUTHORS AND WORKS.

Addai, Doctrine of, lix.
Apocalypse, use of Antichrist Legend,
    77 f.
Athanasius, lxii.
Augustine, xxx, lxi, 3, 27, 43, 86,
    113, 156.

Babut, 160.
Bacon, lii.
Bartlet, lxxxiii, lxxxv, 172, 182.
Baruch, Apocalypse of, 75.
Basilides, xliii.
Bede, 88 f., 133.
Bengel, 33.

Berger, 156 ff., 197 ff.
Bousset, 69.
Briggs, 3, 44.
Buchanan, 197 ff.
Burkitt, lxi.

Caius of Corinth, lxxxi, lxxxiv.
Carpocrates, xlvi ff.
Cassiodorus, xxx.
Cerinthus, xxv, xxxix, xlv ff., lxxvi,
    58.
Chapman, Dom, lxxxii, lxxxiv, 169,
    172, 181, 185.
Chrysostom, 25.

Clemen, xxxix, xlii, 2, 59.
Clement of Alexandria, xxxi f., lvi, lx f., 111, 159, 169.
Clement of Rome, lii.
Coenen, 181.
Cyprian, lix, 155.

Daniel, Book of, 73, 75.
Deissmann, 27, 66, 151, 183, 195.
Didache, liv, lxxx, 107, 186.
Diognetus, liv.
Dittenberger, 67.

Ebrard, xxv.
Enoch, Book of, 27, 36, 74.
Epiphanius, xliii, xlvi ff.
Eusebius, lix f.
Ezra, Fourth Book of, 75.

Findlay, 3, 12, 55, 100.
Fulgentius, 161.

Gaius, 181.
von der Goltz, 111 ff.
Gunkel, 69 ff.

Häring, xxxiv ff.
Harnack, lxxxvii ff., 182.
Hermas, liv.
Hilgenfeld, xlviii.
Hippolytus, xlvi ff.
Holtzmann, i, xix, xxix, 118, 153, 168, 176.
Hort, xxxvii f.
Huther, xxix, 193.

Ignatius, xlv.
Irenaeus, xliii, xlv ff., lv, lix, 3, 111.

Jerome, lxi, 169.
Jülicher, lxxvi, lxxxi, 164.
Justin, lv, 81, 89.

Karl, 3, 42 f., 89.
Knopf, xlvi.
Künstle, 155 ff.

Law, xxxvi f., 17, 42, 128.
Lietzmann, lxi.
Lightfoot, xviii, xxii, xxv.
Lipsius, xlviii f.
Lücke, xxviii, xxxii, 168.
Lyons and Vienne, Letter, lv.

Mommsen's Canon, lix.
Muratorian Fragment, lvii.

Oecumenius, 115, 193.
Origen, lvii, lix, lxi, 25, 38, 112, 181.

Papias, liv, lxxv, lxxvii, 192.
Paul, S. Eschatological Teaching, 76 f.
Peshitta, lix, lxi.
Pfleiderer, xliii, lxxv.
Philaster, xlvi.
Photius, lx.
Pirqe Aboth, 80.
Poggel, 191.
Polycarp, xliv, lii, lxxv.
Priscillian, 158.

Rendel Harris, lxxxvi, 155, 165, 167, 176.
Réville, xx, lxxvii.
Rönsch, 26.
Rothe, xxix, 1, 44, 88, 139.

Sabatier, lxi.
Sanday, xxvii.
Schlatter, 30, 40, 45, 92, 95.
Schmiedel, xliv, 30.
Schöttgen, 148.
Schwartz, xxii, lxxvi.
Sibylline Books, 74.
Socrates, 113.
von Soden, xxxii, lxiv, 60, 198.
Solomon, Psalms of, 75.
Spitta, 96.

Tacitus, 3.
Talmud (see Schlatter), 25.
Tertullian, lvii, 113, 133.
ps-Tertullian, xlvi.
Thoma, lxxxvi.

Weiss, B., li, 8, 83, 86.
Wellhausen, xxvi.
Westcott, xxxvii f., 23, 88, 113, 165.
Wettstein, 23, 47, 176, 184.
Wilamowitz, lxxxii, 183, 192.
Windisch, 3, 89 f., 177.
Wohlenberg, 89, 100, 149.
Wurm, xxxix, xlii, l, 36, 59, 114.

Zahn, xxx f., xlvi, lx, lxxiii, 7, 112, 168, 193.
Ziegler, 164, 197 ff.
Zimmern, 27.

C. GREEK WORDS AND PHRASES EXPLAINED.

ἀγαθοποιεῖν, 191.
ἀγαπητοί, 34, 81, 117.
ἀγγελία, 11, 91,
ἅγιος, ὁ, 56.
ἁγνίζειν, 84.
ἁγνός, 84.
ἀδελφός, 38, 90.
αἴρειν, 85.
αἰσχύνεσθαι, 66.
αἰτεῖν, 147.
αἰώνιος, 6.
ἀλήθεια, 19, 170.
ἀληθινός, 151.
ἁμαρτίαν ἔχειν, 17.
ἀρχή, 2, 34, 45, 60, 88, 91.
ἀσπάζεσθαι, 195.
ἀφιέναι, 20.

βαρύς, 130.
βίος, 97.

γεννᾶσθαι, 68 f., 148.
γράφω, ἔγραψα, 41 ff., 46, 142, 187.

διδαχή, 177.
δοκιμάζειν, 107.

ἐάν, c. indic., 144.
εἶναι ἐκ, 115.
ἐκεῖνος, iv, 33, 84 f., 87, 124.
ἐκλεκτή, lxxx, 180.
ἐκλεκτῇ Κυρίᾳ, 167.
ἐλθών, ὁ, 132, 134.
ἐντολὴν λαβεῖν, 172.
ἐπιδέχεσθαι, 189 f.
ἔρχεσθαι, 178.
ἐρωτᾶν, 147, 173.
εὐοδοῦσθαι, 182.

θαυμάζειν, 93.
θεᾶσθαι, 4.

ἱλασμός, 119.
ἵνα, definitive, 19, 80, 124, 130.
    elliptic, vii, 54.
    c. indic., 150.

καθαρίζειν, 16, 21.
καί . . . δέ, 8.
καὶ νῦν, 64.
κατ᾽ ὄνομα, 195.
κοινωνεῖν, 8.
κόλασιν ἔχειν, 125.
κόσμος, 47.
Κυρία, lxxx, 167.

λαμβάνειν, 178.
λόγος, 35.
λόγος τῆς ζωῆς, 1, 5.
λύειν, 89, 111 ff.

μαρτυρεῖν, 135, 138 f
μένειν, 33, 39, 53, 61, 64, 86, 123.
μισεῖν, 38.
μονογενής, 119.

ὁμολογεῖν, 108, 121.
ὅστις, 7.
οὗτος, 31, 134, 152, 178.
    ἐκ τούτου, 116.
    ἐν τούτῳ, 9, 100, etc.

παιδία, 43.
πάλιν, 36.
πᾶς, 16, 21, 83 f.
    c. negat., 54, 57, 94.
    c. partic., vi.
παρρησία, 65, 102.
πείθειν, 99.
περιπατεῖν, 13 f., 174, 183.
πιστεύειν, 104 f., 128.
πλανᾶν, 18.
πλάνος, 175.
ποιεῖν, τὴν ἀλήθειαν, 14.
    καλῶς ποιεῖν, 185.
    πιστὸν ποιεῖν, 183.
ποταπός, 80.
πρεσβύτερος, ὁ, 166.
πρός, 7.

σάρξ, l, 48.
    ἐν σαρκὶ ἐλθεῖν, 109, 175.
σκάνδαλον, 39.
σκοτία, 12.
σκότος, 14.
σπλάγχνα, 97.
συνεργός, 187.

τεκνία, 43, 87.
τηρεῖν, 30.

φανεροῦν, 65, 82, 85.
φιλοπρωτεύειν, 188.
φλυαρεῖν, 190.
φῶς, 11.

ψηλαφᾶν, 4.
ψυχὴν τιθέναι, 95 f.

χρίσμα, 55.

ὥρα, 51.

D. GREEK WORDS USED IN THE EPISTLES.

The figure in brackets after each word gives the number of times the word is used in the Johannine Epistles. The figure after each capital gives the number of times the word is used in the Book or Group of Books represented by the Capital.

J = Gospel according to John, M = Matthew and Mark, L = Luke, A = Acts, P = Pauline Epistles (excluding the Pastoral Epistles), Pa = Pastoral Epistles, H = Hebrews, C = Catholic Epistles (excluding 1–3 John), R = Apocalypse.

ἀγαθοποιέω (1) M¹ L³ C⁴ : III. 11.
ἀγαθός (1) J³ M¹⁶ L¹⁵ A³ P³⁸ Pa¹⁰ H³ C⁹ : III. 11.
ἀγαπάω (31) J³⁴ M¹³ L¹² P²⁹ Pa² H² C⁹ R⁴ : I. ii. 10, 15 (*bis*), iii. 10, 11, 14 (*bis*), 18, 23, iv. 7 (*bis*), 8, 10 (*bis*), 11 (*bis*), 12, 19 (*bis*), 20 (*ter*), 21 (*bis*), v. 1 (*bis*), 2 (*bis*), II. 1, 5, III. 1.
ἀγάπη (21) J⁷ M¹ L¹ P⁶⁴ Pa¹¹ H² C⁷ : I. ii. 5, 15, iii. 1, 16, 17, iv. 7, 8, 9, 10, 12, 16 (*ter*), 17, 18 (*ter*), v. 3, II. 3, 6, III. 6.
ἀγαπητός (10) M⁶ L³ A¹ P²⁴ Pa² H¹ C¹⁴ : I. ii. 7, iii. 2, 21, iv. 1, 7, 11, III. 1, 2, 5, 11.
ἀγγελία (2) : I. i. 15, iii. 11.
ἅγιος (1) J⁶ M¹⁷ L²⁰ A⁵⁴ P⁷⁵ Pa⁴ H¹⁸ C¹⁶ R²⁴ : I. ii. 20.
ἁγνίζω (1) J¹ A² C² : I. iii. 3.
ἁγνός (1) P³ Pa² C² : I. iii. 3.
ἀδελφή (1) J⁶ M⁸ L³ A¹ P⁵ Pa¹ C¹ : II. 13.
ἀδελφός (18) J¹⁴ M⁵⁵ L²³ A⁵⁷ P¹²⁸ Pa⁴ H¹⁰ C²³ : I. ii. 9, 10, 11, iii. 10, 12 (*bis*), 13, 14, 15, 16, 17, iv. 20 (*bis*), 21, v. 16, III. 3, 5, 10.
ἀδικία (2) J¹ L⁴ A² P¹⁰ Pa¹ H² C³ : I. i. 9, v. 17.
αἷμα (4) J⁶ M¹⁵ L⁸ A¹¹ P¹² H²¹ C² R¹⁹ : I. i. 7, v. 6 (*bis*), 8.
αἴρω (1) J²⁵ M³⁹ L²⁰ A⁹ P⁴ R² : I. iii. 5.
αἰσχύνομαι (1) L¹ P² C¹ : I. ii. 28.
αἰτέω (5) J¹⁰ M²³ L¹² A¹⁰ P⁴ C⁵ : I. iii. 22, v. 14, 15 (*bis*), 16.
αἴτημα (1) L¹ P¹ : I. v. 15.
αἰών (2) J¹⁸ M¹³ L⁷ A² P²⁶ Pa⁵ H¹³ C⁶ R¹⁴ : I. ii. 17, II. 2.
αἰώνιος (6) J¹⁷ M⁹ L⁴ A² P¹³ Pa⁸ H⁶ C⁴ R¹ : I. i. 2, ii. 25, iii. 15, v. 11, 13, 20.

ἀκούω (16) J⁵⁹ M¹⁰⁴ L⁶⁰ A⁹⁰ P²⁹ Pa⁵ H⁸ C⁴ R⁴⁶ : I. i. 1, 3, 5, ii. 7, 18, 24 (*bis*), iii. 11, iv. 3, 5, 6 (*bis*), v. 14, 15, II. 6, III. 4.
ἀλαζονία (1) C¹ : I. ii. 16.
ἀλήθεια (20) J²⁵ M⁴ L³ A³ P³⁴ Pa¹⁴ H¹ C⁶ : I. i. 6, 8, ii. 4, 21 (*bis*), iii. 18, 19, iv. 6, v. 6, II. 1 (*bis*), 2, 3, 4, III. 1, 3 (*bis*), 4, 8, 12.
ἀληθής (3) J¹⁴ M² A¹ P³ Pa¹ C² : I. ii. 8, 27, III. 12.
ἀληθινός (3) J⁹ L¹ P¹ H³ R¹⁰ : I. ii. 8, v. 20 (*bis*).
ἀληθῶς (1) J⁷ M⁵ L³ A¹ P¹ : I. ii. 5.
ἀλλά (20).
ἀλλὰ καί (2) J³ M¹ L³ A⁴ P²⁶ Pa³ H¹ C¹ : I. ii. 7, II. 1.
ἀλλ' οὐ (2) J³ M⁴ L² A¹ P¹⁵ Pa² H² : I. ii. 19, III. 13.
ἀλλήλων (7) J¹⁵ M⁷ L¹¹ A⁸ P³⁹ Pa¹ H¹ C⁷ R² : I. i. 7, iii. 11, 23, iv. 7, 11, 12, II. 5.
ἁμαρτάνω (10) J³ M² L⁴ A¹ P¹⁵ Pa² H² C² : I. i. 10, ii. 1 (*bis*), iii. 6 (*bis*), 8, 9, v. 16 (*bis*), 18.
ἁμαρτία (16) J¹⁷ M¹³ L¹¹ A⁸ P⁵¹ Pa³ H²⁵ C¹⁵ R³ : I. i. 7, 8, 9 (*bis*), ii. 2, 12, iii. 4 (*bis*), 5 (*bis*), 8, 9, iv. 10, v. 16 (*bis*), 17.
ἄν (5) J²⁷ M⁶³ L³⁸ A¹⁸ P²⁵ H⁶ R² : I. ii. 5, 19, iii. 17, 22, iv. 15.
ἀναγγέλλω (1) J⁵ M¹ A⁵ P² C¹ : I. i. 5.
ἀνθρωποκτόνος (2) J¹ : I. iii. 15 (*bis*).
ἄνθρωπος (2) J⁵⁹ M¹¹³⁺⁵³ L⁹⁵ A⁴⁶ P¹⁰⁶ Pa²⁰ H⁹ C¹⁷ R²⁴ : I. v. 9.
ἀνομία (2) M⁴ P⁵ Pa¹ H² : I. iii. 4 (*bis*).
ἀντίχριστος (5) I. ii. 18 (*bis*), 22, iv. 3, II. 7.
ἀξίως (1) III. 6.
ἀπαγγέλλω (2) J¹ M¹³ L¹¹ A¹⁶ P² H¹ : I. i. 2, 3.

ἀπολαμβάνω (1) M¹ L⁵ P³ : II. 8.
ἀπόλλυμι (1) J¹⁰ M³⁰ L²⁸ A² P¹² H¹
C⁶ R¹ : II. 8.
ἀποστέλλω (3) J²⁸ M⁴² L²⁵ A²⁶ P³ Pa¹
H¹ C¹ R³ : I. iv. 9, 10, 14.
ἅπτομαι (1) J¹ M²⁰ L¹³ A¹ P³ : I. v. 18.
ἀρεστός (1) J¹ A² : I. iii. 22.
ἀρκέω (1) J² M¹ L¹ P¹ Pa¹ H¹ : III.
10.
ἀρνέομαι (3) J⁴ M⁶ L⁴ A⁴ Pa⁶ H¹ C²
R² : I. ii. 22 (bis), 23.
ἄρτι (1) J¹² M⁷ P¹² C² R² : I. ii. 9.
ἀρχή (10) J⁸ M⁸ L³ A⁴ P¹¹ Pa¹ H⁶ C²
R³ : I. i. 1, ii. 7, 13, 14, 24 (bis),
iii. 8, 11, II. 5, 6.
ἀσπάζομαι (3) : II. 13, III. 15 (bis).
αὐτός (10) J¹⁸.
  αὐτοῦ (61).
  αὐτῆς (1).
  αὐτῷ (24).
  αὐτῇ (1).
  αὐτόν (12).
  αὐτήν (1).
  αὐτοί (1).
  αὐτῶν (2).
  αὐτούς (1).
αὐτός ὁ (1) J⁵ M⁴ L¹¹ A² P¹³ H⁴ R¹ :
III. 12.
αὐτοῦ (1) J⁴ M¹ L⁴ A¹ P⁴ R² : I. v. 10.
ἀφίημι (2) J¹⁴ M⁸⁵ L³² A³ P⁵ H² C¹
R⁸ : I. i. 9, ii. 12.

βάλλω (1) J¹⁷ M⁵¹ L¹⁹ A⁵ C¹ R²⁸ : I.
iv. 18.
βαρύς (1) M² A² P¹ : I. v. 3.
βίος (2) M¹ L⁵ Pa² : I. ii. 16, iii. 17.
βλέπω (1) J¹⁵ M³² L¹⁵ A¹⁴ P²⁸ H⁸ C¹
R¹⁷ : II. 8.
βούλομαι (2) J¹ M³ L² A¹⁴ P⁵ Pa⁴ H¹
C⁵.

Γάϊος (1) A² P² : III. 1.
γάρ (6) J⁽⁶⁶⁾ : I. ii. 19, iv. 20, v. 3,
II. 11, III. 3, 7.
γεννάω (10) J¹⁸ M⁴⁵⁺¹ L⁶ A⁷ P⁶ Pa¹
H⁴ C¹.
γίνομαι (3) J⁵³ M⁷³⁺⁵⁵ L¹³² A¹²⁴ P¹²⁷
Pa⁹ H³¹ C²² R³⁶ : I. ii. 18, II.
12, III. 8.
γινώσκω (25) J⁵⁶ M³³ L²⁸ A¹⁶ P⁴⁵ Pa³
H⁴ C⁵ R⁴.
γλῶσσα (1) M³ L² A⁶ P²⁴ C⁶ R⁸ : I.
iii. 18.
γράφω (18) J²⁰ M²⁰ L²⁰ A¹² P⁶² Pa¹
H¹ C⁶ R²⁹ : I. i. 4, ii. 1, 7, 8,
12, 13 (ter), 14 (bis), 21, 26, v.
13, II. 5, 12, III. 9, 13 (bis).

Δημήτριος (1) A² : III. 12.
διά, c. gen. (4) J¹⁵ M³⁸ L¹⁴ A⁵⁵ P¹⁷⁹
Pa¹⁴ H⁴⁰ C²² R² : I. iv. 9, v. 6,
II. 12, III. 13, c. acc. (5) J⁴⁴
M⁵⁵ L²⁶ A¹⁹ P⁸⁵ Pa⁶ H¹⁷ C⁸ R¹⁷ :
I. ii. 12, iii. 1, iv. 5, II. 2, III.
10.
διάβολος (4) J³ M⁶ L⁵ A² P² Pa⁶ H¹
C³ R³ : I. iii. 8 (ter), 10.
διάνοια (1) M² L² P³ H² C².
διδάσκω (3) J⁹ M³² L¹⁷ A¹⁶ P¹⁰ Pa⁵ H²
R² : I. ii. 27 (ter).
διδαχή (3) J³ M⁸ L¹ A⁴ P⁴ Pa² H²
R³ : II. 9 (bis) 10.
δίδωμι (7) J⁷⁴ M⁵⁶⁺³⁷ L⁵⁹ A³⁴ P⁶² Pa¹⁰
H⁶ C⁹ R⁵⁶ : I. iii. 1, 23, 24, iv.
13, v. 11, 16, 20.
δίκαιος (5) J³ M¹⁹ L¹¹ A⁶ P¹⁴ Pa³ H³
C⁹ R⁵ : I. i. 9, ii. 1, 29, iii. 7, 12.
δικαιοσύνη (3) J² M⁷ L¹ A⁴ P⁵² Pa⁵
H⁶ C⁹ R² : I. ii. 29, iii. 7, 10.
Διοτρέφης (1) : III. 9.
δοκιμάζω (1) L³ P¹⁶ Pa¹ C¹ : I. iv. 1.
δύναμαι (2) J³⁰ M⁶⁰ L²⁶ A²¹ P³² Pa⁶
H⁹ C⁷ R¹⁰ : I. iii. 9, iv. 20.

ἐάν (23) J⁴¹ M⁵⁶⁺²⁸ L²⁸ A⁷ P⁷⁷ Pa⁵ H⁶
C⁷ R⁵ : I. i. 6, 7, 8, 9, 10, ii. 1,
3, 15, 24, 28, 29, iii. 2, 20, 22,
iv. 12, 15, 20, v. 14, 15 (bis), 16,
III. 5, 10.
ἐὰν μή (1) J¹⁸ M¹⁰⁺⁶ L³ A⁴ P¹³ Pa¹ C²
R⁴ : I. iii. 21.
ἑαυτοῦ (6) J²⁸ M⁶⁰ L⁵⁹ A²³ P¹¹⁰ Pa¹⁰
H¹⁴ C¹⁹ R⁸ : I. i. 8, iii. 3, 15
(bis), v. 21, ii. 8.
ἐγώ (3) J¹²⁴ M²⁹⁺¹⁷ L²⁴ A⁴⁶ P⁶⁰ Pa⁷
H⁷ C² R¹⁴ : II. 1 (bis), III. 1.
μοῦ (1).
ἡμεῖς (12) J¹⁸ M⁸ L⁵ A²¹ P⁵⁶ Pa²
H⁵ C¹ : I. i. 4, iii. 14, 16, iv. 6,
10, 11, 14, 16, 17, 19, III. 8,
12.
ἡμῶν (25).
ἡμῖν (18).
ἡμᾶς (8).
ἐθνικός (1) M³ : III. 7.
εἰ (5) J³¹ M³⁵⁺¹³ L³² A³⁰ P⁹⁸ Pa⁸ H¹⁴
C¹⁸ : I. ii. 19, iii. 13, iv. 1, 11,
v. 9.
εἰ μή (2) J¹⁵ M¹⁹⁺¹⁷ L¹⁶ A² P²⁸ Pa¹ H¹
R⁸ : I. ii. 22, v. 5.
εἴ τις (1) M⁹ L³ A⁴ P⁴² Pa⁸ C⁷ R⁸ :
II. 10.
εἶδον (3) J³⁶ M⁵⁸⁺⁴⁴ L⁶⁸ A⁴⁹ P¹⁷ Pa²
H⁴ C³ R⁵⁶ : I. iii. 1, v. 16, III.
14.

οἶδα (16) J^{82} M^{25+23} L^{26} A^{19} P^{92} Pa^{11} H^3 C^{11} R^{12} : I. ii. 11, 20, 21 (*bis*), 29, iii. 2, 5, 14, 15, v. 13, 15 (*bis*), 18, 19, 20, III. 12.

εἴδωλον (1) A^2 P^7 R^1 : I. v. 21.

(εἰμί) ἐστίν (78).

ἐσμέν (8) J^4 M^1 L^2 A^8 P^{25} H^4 : I. ii. 5, iii. 1, 2, 19, iv. 6, 17, v. 19, 20.

ἐστέ (2) J^{17} M^{13} L^9 A^4 P^{44} H^2 C^1 : I. ii. 14, iv. 4.

εἰσίν (5) J^{13} M^{33} L^{18} A^{13} P^{32} Pa^6 H^5 C^5 R^{25} : I. ii. 19, iv. 5, v. 3, 7, 8.

ὦ (2) J^{17} M^9 L^6 A^1 P^{28} Pa^5 C^2 : I. i. 4, II. 12.

εἶναι (1) J^3 M^{14} L^{23} A^{21} P^{42} Pa^{12} H^3 C^5 R^2 : I. ii. 9.

ἤμην (6) J^{112} M^{40+55} L^{99} A^{86} P^{30} Pa^1 H^7 C^5 R^{12} : I. i. 1, 2, ii. 19 (*bis*), iii. 12 (*bis*).

ἔσομαι (3) J^6 M^{67} L^{49} A^9 P^{22} Pa^6 H^7 C^5 R^{14} : I. iii. 2, II. 2, 3.

εἶπον (4) J^{203} M^{83+85} L^{298} A^{129} P^{14} Pa^1 H^6 C^6 R^6 : I. i. 6, 8, 10, iv. 20.

εἰρήνη (2) J^6 M^5 L^{14} A^7 P^{38} Pa^4 H^4 C^8 R^2 : II. 3, III. 15.

εἰς (13).

εἷς (1) J^{35} M^{59+39} L^{44} A^{21} P^{28} Pa^6 H^5 C^6 R^{23} : I. v. 8.

ἐκ, ἐξ (35).

ἐκβάλλω (1) J^6 M^{28+18} L^{20} A^5 P^1 C^1 R^1 : III. 10.

ἐκεῖνος (7) J^{69} M^{54+22} L^{32} A^{22} P^{20} Pa^1 H^8 C^3 R^2 : I. ii. 6, iii. 3, 5, 7, 16, iv. 17, v. 16.

ἐκκλησία (3) M^2 A^{23} P^{59} Pa^3 H^2 C^1 R^{20} : III. 6, 9, 10.

ἐκλεκτός (2) J^1 M^8 L^2 P^3 Pa^3 C^4 R^1 : II. 1, 13.

ἔλεος (1) M^3 L^6 P^5 Pa^5 H^1 C^5 : II. 3.

ἐλπίζω (2) J^1 M^1 L^3 A^2 P^{15} Pa^4 H^1 C^2 : II. 12, III. 14.

ἐλπίς (1) A^8 P^{27} Pa^4 H^5 C^3 : I. iii. 3.

ἐμός (1) J^{36} M^7 L^3 P^{22} C^1 R^1 : III. 4.

ἔμπροσθεν (1) J^5 M^{18+2} L^{10} A^2 P^7 R^3 : I. iii. 19.

ἐν (90).

ἐντολή (18) J^{11} M^{12} L^4 A^1 P^{12} Pa^2 H^4 C^2 R^2 : I. ii. 3, 4, 7 (*ter*), 8, iii. 22, 23 (*bis*), 24, iv. 21, v. 2, 3 (*bis*), II. 4, 5, 6 (*bis*).

ἐνώπιον (2) J^7 L^{23} A^{13} P^8 Pa^8 H^2 C^2 R^{32} : I. iii. 22, III. 6.

ἐξέρχομαι (4) J^{29} M^{45+39} L^{44} A^{30} P^8 H^5 C^1 R^{14} : I. ii. 19, iv. 1, II. 7, III. 7.

ἔξω (1) J^{13} M^{19} L^9 A^{11} P^5 H^3 R^2 : I. iv. 18.

ἐπαγγελία (1) L^1 A^8 P^{24} Pa^2 H^{14} C^2 : I. ii. 25.

ἐπαγγέλλομαι (1) M^1 A^1 P^2 Pa^3 H^4 C^3 : I. ii. 25.

ἐπί, c. dat. (2) J^5 M^{18+17} L^{34} A^{27} P^{48} Pa^5 H^{10} C^3 R^{16} : I. iii. 3, III. 10.

ἐπιδέχομαι (2) : III. 9, 10.

ἐπιθυμία (3) J^1 M^1 L^1 P^{13} Pa^6 C^{12} R^1 : I. ii. 16 (*bis*), 17.

ἐργάζομαι (2) J^7 M^5 L^1 A^3 P^{18} H^1 C^2 R^1 : II. 8, III. 5.

ἔργον (5) J^{27} M^8 L^2 A^{10} P^{48} Pa^{20} H^{11} C^{20} R^{20} : I. iii. 8, 12, 18, II. 11, III. 10.

ἔρχομαι (8) J^{153} M^{113+87} L^{111} A^{55} P^{64} Pa^9 H^5 C^2 R^{35} : I. ii. 18, iv. 2, 3, v. 6, II. 7, 10, III. 3, 10.

ἐρωτάω (2), J^{28} M^7 L^{16} A^7 P^4 : I. v. 16, II. 5.

ἔσχατος (2) J^7 M^{12} L^5 P^8 Pa^1 H^1 C^6 R^6 : I. ii. 18 (*bis*).

εὐθέως (1) J^3 M^{12} L^6 A^9 P^1 C^1 R^1 : III. 14.

εὑρίσκω (1) J^{19} M^{27+10} L^{46} A^{34} P^{14} Pa^2 H^4 C^4 R^{13} : II. 4.

εὔχομαι (1) A^2 P^3 C^1.

ἔχω (32) J^{86} M^{73+68} L^{74} A^{46} P^{133} Pa^{22} H^{39} C^{20} R^{100} : I. i. 3, 6, 7, 8, ii. 1, 7, 20, 23 (*bis*), 27, 28, iii. 3, 15, 17 (*bis*), 21, iv. 16, 17, 18, 21, v. 10, 12 (*bis*), 13, 14, 15, II. 5, 9 (*bis*), 12, III. 4, 13.

ἕως, prep. (1) J^5 M^{36} L^{13} A^{17} P^{10} H^1 C^1 R^1 : I. ii. 9.

ζάω (1) J^{16} M^9 L^9 A^{12} P^{48} Pa^6 H^{12} C^8 R^{13} : I. iv. 9.

ζωή (13) J^{37} M^{11} L^5 A^8 P^{28} Pa^8 H^2 C^6 : I. i. 1, 2 (*bis*), ii. 25, iii. 14, 15, v. 11 (*bis*), 12 (*bis*), 13, 16, 20.

ἤ (quam) (1) I. iv. 4.

ἤδη (2) J^{17} M^{15} L^{10} A^3 P^9 Pa^3 C^1 : I. ii. 8, iv. 3.

ἥκω (1) J^4 M^5 L^5 P^1 H^3 C^1 R^6.

ἡμέρα (1) J^{31} M^{44+28} L^{82} A^{95} P^{43} Pa^6 H^{18} C^{16} R^{21} : I. iv. 17.

ἡμέτερος (2) L^2 A^3 P^1 Pa^2 : I. i. 3, ii. 2.

θάνατος (5) J^8 M^{13} L^7 A^8 P^{44} Pa^1 H^9 C^2 R^{19} : I. iii. 14 (*bis*), v. 16 (*bis*), 17.

θαυμάζω (1) J^6 M^{11} L^{13} A^5 P^2 C^1 R^4 : I. iii. 13.

θεάομαι (3), J⁶ M⁶ L³ A³ P¹ : I. i. 1,
iv. 12, 14.
θέλημα (2) J¹¹ M⁷ L⁵ A³ P²² Pa² H⁵
C⁵ R¹ : I. ii. 17, v. 14.
θέλω (1) J²² M⁴²⁺²⁵ L²⁸ A¹⁶ P⁵⁷ Pa⁴
H⁴ C⁵ R⁵ : III. 13.
θεός (66) J⁸⁰ M⁵¹⁺⁴⁵ L¹²⁰ A¹⁷² P⁴⁹⁷ Pa⁵⁰
H⁶⁶ C⁶⁵ R⁹⁶ : I. i. 5, ii. 5, 14,
17, iii. 1, 2, 8, 9 (bis), 10 (bis),
17, 20, 21, iv. 1, 2 (bis), 3, 4, 6
(ter), 7 (ter), 8 (bis), 9 (bis), 10,
11, 12 (bis), 15 (bis), 16 (quater),
20 (bis), 21, v. 1, 2 (bis), 3, 4, 5,
9 (bis), 10 (ter), 11, 12, 13, 18
(bis), 19, 20, (bis), II. 3, 9, III.
6, 11 (bis).
θεωρέω (1) J²³ M⁹ L⁷ A¹⁴ H¹ R².

Ἰησοῦς (14) J²³⁹ M⁵²⁺⁸² L⁸⁷ A⁶⁹ P⁸⁸ Pa³²
H¹³ C²⁷ R¹⁴ : Ἰησοῦς I. i. 7, ii.
22, iv. 3, v. 1, 5 : Ἰησοῦς Χριστός
I. i. 3, ii. 1, iii. 23, iv. 2, 15, v.
6, 20, II. 3, 7.
ἱλασμός (2) I. ii. 2, iv. 10.
ἵνα (25) J¹²⁷ M³³⁺⁵⁸ L³⁹ A¹² P¹⁷⁹ Pa²⁸
H¹³ C¹⁶ R³² : I. i. 3, 4, 9, ii. 19,
27, 28, iii. 1, 5, 8, 11, 23, iv. 9,
17, 21, v. 3, 13, 16, 20, II. 5, 6
(ter), 12, III. 4, 8.
ἵνα μή (3) J¹⁸ M⁸⁺⁶ L⁹ A³ P³⁵ Pa⁵ H⁷
C³ R¹¹ : I. ii. 1, 28, II. 8.
ἰσχυρός (1) M⁷ L⁴ P⁵ H³ R⁹ : I. ii.
14.

καθαρίζω (2) M¹¹ L⁷ A³ P² Pa¹ H⁴
C¹ : I. i. 7, 9.
καθώς (13) J³¹ M¹¹ L¹⁷ A¹¹ P⁸⁴ Pa¹ H⁸
C³ : I. ii. 6, 18, 27, iii. 2, 3, 7,
12, 23, iv. 17, II. 4, 6, III. 2, 3.
Κάϊν (1) H¹ C¹ : I. iii. 12.
καινός (3) J² M¹¹ L⁵ A² P⁷ H³ C¹ R⁸ :
I. ii. 7, 8, II. 5.
κακοποιέω (1) M¹ L¹ C¹ : III. 11.
κακός (1) J² M⁵ L² A⁴ P²¹ Pa³ H¹ C⁶
R² : III. 11.
κάλαμος (1) M⁷ L¹ R³ : III. 13.
καλέω (1) J² M²⁹ L⁴³ A¹⁸ P³¹ Pa² H⁶
C⁸ R⁷ : I. iii. 1.
καλῶς (1) J⁴ M⁸ L⁴ A³ P⁸ Pa⁴ H¹ C⁴ :
III. 6.
καρδία (4) J⁶ M²⁷ L²² A²¹ P⁵⁰ Pa² H¹⁰
C¹⁰ R³ : I. iii. 19, 20 (bis), 21.
κατά, c. acc. (3) J⁸ M²¹⁺¹⁵ L³⁷ A⁷⁵
P¹⁵⁰ Pa¹⁹ H³⁷ C¹⁶ R⁶ : I. v. 14,
II. 6, III. 15.
καταγινώσκω (2) P¹ : I. iii. 20, 21.

κεῖμαι (1) J⁷ M³ L⁶ P⁴ Pa¹ R² : I. v.
19.
κλείω (1) J² M³ L² A² R⁶ : I. iii. 17.
κοινωνέω (1) P⁴ Pa¹ H¹ C¹ : II. 11.
κοινωνία (4) A¹ P¹³ H¹ : I. i. 3 (bis),
6, 7.
κόλασις (1) M¹ : I. iv. 18.
κόσμος (23) J⁷⁶ M¹² L³ A¹ P⁴³ Pa³ H⁵
C¹³ R³ : I. ii. 2, 15 (bis), 16
(bis), 17, iii. 1, 13, 17, iv. 1, 3,
4, 5 (ter), 9, 14, 17, v. 4 (bis), 5,
19, II. 7.
κρίσις (1) J¹¹ M¹² L⁴ A¹ P¹ Pa¹ H² C⁹
R⁴ : I. iv. 17.
Κυρία (2) : II. 1, 5.
κωλύω (1) M⁴ L⁶ A⁶ P³ Pa¹ H¹ C¹ :
III. 10.

λαλέω (3) J⁵⁹ M²⁶⁺²¹ L³¹ A⁶¹ P⁵⁵ Pa³
H¹⁶ C⁹ R¹² : I. iv. 5, II. 12, III.
14.
λαμβάνω (6) J⁴⁴ M⁵⁶⁺²⁰ L²³ P⁶⁰ Pa²
H¹⁶ C⁹ R²³ : I. ii. 27, iii. 22, v.
9, II. 4, 10, III. 7.
λέγω (6) J²⁶⁴ M²⁸⁶⁺¹⁹⁹ L²¹⁸ A¹⁰¹ P⁹⁰
Pa⁷ H³² C¹⁰ R⁹⁵ : I. ii. 4, 6, 9,
v. 16, II. 10, 11.
λίαν (2) M⁸ L¹ Pa¹ : II. 4, III. 3.
λόγος (7) J⁴⁰ M³⁴⁺²⁴ L³³ A⁶⁵ P⁶³ Pa²⁰
H¹² C¹⁶ R¹⁸ : I. i. 1, 10, ii. 5, 7,
14, iii. 18, III. 10.
λύω (2) J⁶ M⁹ L⁶ A⁶ C³ R⁶ : I. iii. 8
[iv. 3].

μαρτυρέω (10) J³³ M¹ L¹ A¹¹ P⁶ Pa²
H⁸ R⁴ : I. i. 2, iv. 14, v. 6, 7,
9, 10, III. 3, 6, 12 (bis).
μαρτυρία (7) J¹³ M³ L² A¹ Pa² R⁹ : I.
v. 9 (ter), 10 (bis), 11, III. 12.
μείζων (11) J¹³ M¹² L⁷ P⁴ H⁴ C³ : I.
iii. 20, iv. 4, v. 9, III. 4.
μέλας (2) M¹ P¹ R² : II. 12, III. 13.
μένω (26) J⁴⁰ M⁵ L⁷ A¹³ P¹³ Pa⁴ H⁶ C²
R¹ : I. ii. 6, 10, 14, 17, 19, 24
(ter), 27 (bis), 28, iii. 6, 9, 14,
15, 17, 24 (bis), iv. 12, 13, 15,
16 (bis), II. 2, 9 (bis).
μετά, c. gen. (9) J⁴¹ M⁶⁰⁺⁴⁶ L⁵¹ A³⁶
P⁵¹ Pa¹⁸ H¹⁴ C¹ R³⁸ : I. i. 3 (ter),
6, 7, ii. 19, iv. 17, II. 2, 3.
μεταβαίνω (1) J³ M⁵ L¹ A¹ : I. iii. 14.
μή (21) J⁴⁹ M⁷⁵⁺³⁸ L⁹⁹ A⁵² P²²² Pa³²
H²⁸ C⁴¹ R¹² : I. ii. 4, 15, iii. 10
(bis), 13, 14, 18, iv. 1, 3, 8, 20,
v. 10, 12, 16 (bis), II. 7, 9, 10
(bis), III. 10, 11.

μηδέ (2) J² M¹⁶ L⁸ A² P¹⁸ Pa⁶ H¹ C³ :
    I. ii. 15, iii. 18.
μηδείς (2) M¹⁴ L⁹ A²¹ P²⁵ Pa⁹ H¹ C⁴
    R² : I. iii. 7, III. 7.
μιμέομαι (1) P² H¹ : III. 11.
μισέω (5) J¹¹ M⁶ L⁷ P³ Pa¹ H¹ C¹ R³ :
    I. ii. 9, 11, iii. 13, 15, iv. 20.
μισθός (1) J¹ M¹⁰⁺¹ L³ A¹ P⁵ Pa¹ C⁴
    R² : II. 8.
μονογενής (1) J⁴ L³ H¹ : I. iv. 9.
μόνον (2) J⁵ M⁹ L¹ A⁸ P³³ Pa³ H² C³ :
    I. ii. 2, v. 6.
μόνος (3) J⁹ M¹² L⁹ A¹ P¹⁰ Pa⁴ H¹ C²
    R¹ : I. ii. 2, v. 6, II. 1.

νεανίσκος (2) M⁴ L¹ A⁴ : I. ii. 13,
    14.
νικάω (6) J¹ L¹ C³ R¹⁵ : I. ii. 13, 14,
    iv. 4, v. 4 (bis), 5.
νίκη (1) : I. v. 4.
νῦν (5) J²⁸ M⁷ L¹⁴ A²⁵ P⁴⁷ Pa⁵ H⁶ C¹¹ :
    I. ii. 18, 28, iii. 2, iv. 4, II. 5.

ξένος (1) M⁵ A² P³ H² C¹ : III. 5.

ὅθεν (1) M⁴ L¹ A³ H⁶ : I. ii. 18.
οἰκία (1) J⁵ M⁴⁴ L²⁴ A¹² P⁵ Pa³ : II.
    10.
ὅλος (2) J⁶ M⁴⁰ L¹⁷ A²⁰ P¹³ Pa¹ H² C⁴
    R⁵ : I. ii. 2, v. 19.
ὅμοιος (1) J² M⁹ L⁹ A¹ P¹ C¹ R²¹ : I.
    iii. 2.
ὁμολογέω (6) J⁴ M⁴ L² A³ P² Pa² H²
    R¹ : I. i. 9, ii. 23, iv. 2, 3, 15,
    II. 7.
ὄνομα (5) J²⁵ M³⁷ L³⁴ A⁵⁹ P¹⁹ Pa² H⁴
    C⁵ R³⁶ : I. ii. 12, iii. 23, v. 13,
    III. 7, 15.
ὁράω (8) J³⁰ M²⁰ L¹³ A¹⁶ P⁹ Pa¹ H⁶ C²
    R⁷ : I. i. 1, 2, 3, iii. 2, 6, iv. 20
    (bis), III. 11.
ὅστις (2) J⁷ M²⁸⁺⁶ L²³ A²⁴ P³⁷ Pa⁷ H¹⁰
    C⁴ R⁹ : I. i. 2, iii. 20.
ὅταν (1) J¹⁴ M⁴⁰ L²⁹ A² P²¹ Pa² H¹ C¹
    R⁹ : I. v. 2.
ὅτι (78).
οὐ (57).
οὐδέ (2) J¹⁵ M²⁷⁺¹⁰ L²¹ A¹² P³² Pa³ H⁶
    C² R¹¹ : I. ii. 23, iii. 6.
οὐδείς (2) J⁵¹ M⁴⁵ L³³ A²⁷ P⁴¹ Pa⁷ H⁶
    C² R¹².
οὔπω (1) J¹³ M⁷ L¹ P³ H² R² : I. iii.
    2.
οὔτε (1) J⁹ M¹⁰ L¹⁷ A¹⁴ P³⁴ C¹ R¹⁷ :
    III. 10.
οὗτος (5) J⁵¹ M³³⁺¹² L³⁹ A³⁶ P⁵ H⁴ C⁵
    R¹ : I. ii. 22, v. 6, 20, II. 7, 9.

οὗτος—
    αὕτη (12) J⁷ M¹⁸ L¹⁴ A⁷ P⁹ Pa¹ H² C²
        R¹ : I. i. 5, i i. 25, iii. 11, 23, v.
        3, 4, 9, 11 (bis), 14, II. 6 (bis).
    τοῦτο (6).
    τούτου (1).
    τούτῳ (15).
    ταύτην (3).
    ταῦτα (4).
    τούτοις (1).
οὕτως (2) J¹⁵ M³³⁺¹⁰ L²¹ A²⁷ P⁷¹ Pa¹
    H⁹ C¹⁰ R⁷ : I. ii. 6, iv. 11.
ὀφείλω (4) J² M⁶ L⁵ A¹ P¹⁴ H³ : I. ii.
    6, iii. 16, iv. 11, III. 8.
ὀφθαλμός (3) J¹⁷ M²²⁺⁷ L¹⁷ A⁶ P¹¹ H¹
    C² R¹⁰ : I. i. 1, ii. 11, 16.

παιδίον (3) J³ M¹⁸⁺¹² L¹³ P¹ H³ : I.
    ii. 13, 18, iii. 7.
παλαιός (2) M³⁺³ L⁵ P⁶ : I. ii. 7
    (bis).
πάλιν (1) J⁴⁶ M¹⁶⁺²⁸ L³ A⁵ P²⁸ H¹⁰ C²
    R² : I. ii. 8.
παρά, c. gen. (3) J²⁵ M⁶⁺⁷ L⁹ A¹³ P⁸
    Pa⁴ C³ R² : II. 3 (bis), 4.
παράγω (2) J² M³⁺³ P¹ : I. ii. 8, 17.
παράκλητος (1) J⁴ : I. ii. 1.
παρουσία (1) M⁴ P¹⁴ C⁵ : I. ii. 28.
παρρησία (4) J⁶ M¹ A⁵ P⁷ Pa¹ H⁴ : I.
    ii. 28, iii. 21, iv. 17, v. 14.
πᾶς (31) J⁶⁶ M²⁵⁺⁶⁶ L¹⁵⁸ A¹⁷⁰ P²⁷⁰ Pa⁵⁵
    H⁵² C⁴¹ R⁵⁴ : I. i. 7, 9, ii. 16,
    19, 20, 21, 23, 27, 29, iii. 3, 4,
    6 (bis), 9, 10, 15 (bis), 20, iv. 1,
    2, 3, 7, v. 1 (bis), 4, 17, 18, II.
    1, 9, III. 2, 12.
πατήρ (18) J³⁴ M⁶³⁺¹⁹ L⁵⁴ A³⁵ P⁶⁰ Pa⁴
    H⁹ C¹⁰ R⁵ : I. i. 2, 3. ii. 1, 13
    (bis), 14, 15, 16, 22, 23 (bis), 24,
    iii. 1, iv. 14, II. 3 (bis), 4, 9.
πείθω (1) M³⁺¹ L⁴ A¹⁷ P²⁰ Pa² H⁴
    C¹ : I. iii. 19.
περί, c. gen. (10) J⁶⁴ M²⁰⁺¹³ L³⁸ A⁶³
    P⁴³ Pa⁴ H²¹ C¹¹ : I. i. 1, ii. 2
    (ter), 26, 27, iv. 10, v. 9, 10, 16.
περιπατέω (10) J¹⁷ M⁷⁺⁹ L⁵ A⁸ P³¹ H¹
    C¹ : I. i. 6, 7, ii. 6 (bis), 11, II.
    4, 6 (bis), III. 3, 4.
πιστεύω (9) J⁹⁴ M¹¹⁺¹⁴ L⁹ A³⁹ P⁴⁸ Pa⁶
    H² C⁴ : I. iii. 23, iv. 1, 16, v. 1,
    5, 10 (ter), 13.
πίστις (1) M⁹⁺⁵ L¹¹ A¹⁵ P¹⁰⁷ Pa³³ H³²
    C²⁵ R⁴ : I v. 4.
πιστός (2) J¹ M⁵ L⁵ A⁴ P¹⁶ Pa¹⁷ H⁵
    C³ R⁸ : I. i. 9, III. 5.
πλανάω (3) J² M⁸⁺⁴ L¹ P³ Pa² H³ C⁴
    R⁸ : I. i. 8, ii. 26, iii. 7.

πλάνη (1) Μ¹ P⁴ C⁴ : I. iv. 6.
πλάνος (2) Μ¹ P¹ Pa¹ : II. 7 (*bis*).
πλήρης (1) J¹ Μ²⁺² L² A⁸ : II. 8.
πληρόω (2) J¹⁵ Μ¹⁶⁺³ L⁹ A¹⁶ P²² Pa¹
    C¹ R² : I. i 4, II. 12.
πνεῦμα (11) J²³ Μ¹⁹⁺²³ L³⁶ A⁷² P¹³⁶
    Pa⁷ H¹² C¹³ R¹⁸ : I. iii. 24, iv. I
    (*bis*), 2 (*bis*), 3, 6, 13, v. 6 (*bis*), 8.
ποιέω (15) J¹⁰⁴ Μ⁸⁶⁺⁵¹ L⁸⁸ A⁷⁰ P⁷³ Pa⁶
    H¹⁹ C²⁰ R²⁹ : I. i. 6, 10, ii. 17,
    29, iii. 4, 7, 8, 9, 10, 22, v. 2,
    10, III. 5, 6, 10.
πολύς (5) J³⁶ Μ⁵²⁺⁵⁵ L⁴⁹ A⁴⁹ P⁷⁰ Pa⁹
    H⁷ C⁵ R¹⁴ : I. ii. 18, iv. I, II. 7,
    12, III. 13.
πονηρός (8) J³ Μ²⁴⁺² L¹² A⁸ P¹⁰ Pa³
    H² C² R¹ : I. ii. 13, 14, iii. 12
    (*bis*), v. 18, 19, II. 11, III. 10.
ποταπός (1) Μ¹⁺¹ L² C¹ : I. iii. 1.
ποῦ (1) J¹⁹ Μ⁴⁺³ L⁷ P⁷ H¹ C² R¹ : I.
    ii. 11.
πρεσβύτερος (2) J⁽¹⁾ Μ¹²⁺⁷ L⁵ A¹⁸ Pa⁴
    H¹ C³ R¹² : II. 1, III. 1.
προάγω (1) Μ⁶⁺⁵ L¹ A⁴ Pa² H¹ : II. 9.
προπέμπω (1) A³ P⁴ Pa¹ : III. 6.
πρός, c. acc. (12) J⁹⁸ Μ⁴²⁺⁶⁴ L¹⁶⁶ A¹³³
    P¹²⁸ Pa¹⁶ H¹⁹ C⁷ R⁷ : I. i. 2, ii.
    1, iii. 21, v. 14, 16 (*ter*), 17, II.
    10, 12 (*bis*), III. 14.
πρῶτος (1) J⁸ Μ¹⁶⁺¹⁰ L¹⁰ A¹² P⁷ Pa⁵
    H⁹ C¹ R¹⁷ : I. iv. 19.
πώποτε (1) J⁴ L¹ : I. iv. 12.
πῶς (2) J²⁰ Μ¹⁴⁺¹⁵ L¹⁶ A⁹ P²⁵ Pa² H¹
    R¹ : I. iii. 17, iv. 20.

σάρξ (3) J¹² Μ⁵⁺⁴ L² A³ P⁸⁹ Pa¹ H⁶
    C¹² R⁶ : I. ii. 16, iv. 2, II. 7.
σκάνδαλον (1) Μ⁵ L¹ P⁶ C¹ R¹ : I.
    ii. 10.
σκοτία (5) J⁸ Μ² L¹ : I. i. 5, ii. 8, 9,
    11 (*bis*).
σκότος (1) J¹ Μ⁷⁺¹ L⁴ A³ P¹¹ C³ : I. i. 6.
σπέρμα (1) J³ Μ⁷⁺⁵ L² A⁴ P¹⁷ Pa¹ H³
    R¹ : I. iii. 9.
σπλάγχνον (1) L¹ A¹ P⁸ : I. iii. 17.
στόμα (2) J¹ Μ¹¹ L⁹ A¹² P¹² Pa¹ H²
    C⁴ R²¹ : II. 12, III. 14.
σύ¹ (1) J⁶¹ Μ¹⁸⁺¹⁰ L²⁸ A¹⁷ P¹³ Pa⁸ H⁸
    C⁵ R⁴ : III. 3.
ὑμεῖς (6) J⁶⁸ Μ³¹⁺¹¹ L²¹ A²⁵ P⁶⁹ C⁷ :
    I. i. 3, ii. 20, 24 (*bis*), 27, iv. 4.
συνεργός (1) P¹² : III. 8.
σφάζω (1) R⁸ : I. iii. 12.
σωτήρ (1) J¹ L² A² P² Pa¹⁰ C⁶ : I. iv.
    14.

τεκνίον (7) J¹ P¹ : I. ii. 1, 12, 28, iii.
    7, 18, iv. 4, v. 21.
τέκνον (9) J³ Μ¹⁴⁺⁹ L¹⁴ A⁵ P²⁸ Pa⁹ C³
    R³ : I. iii. 1, 2, 10 (*bis*), v. 2, II.
    1, 4, 13, III. 4.
τέλειος (1) Μ³ P⁸ H² C⁵ : I. iv. 18.
τελειόω (4) J⁵ L² A¹ P¹ H⁹ C¹ : I. ii.
    5, iv. 12, 17, 18.
τηρέω (7) J¹⁸ Μ⁶⁺¹ A⁸ P⁴ Pa² C¹¹ R¹¹ :
    I. ii. 3, 4, 5, iii. 22, 24, v. 3, 18.
τίθημι (2) J¹⁸ Μ⁵⁺¹² L¹⁶ A²³ P¹³ Pa³
    H³ C³ R³ : I. iii. 16 (*bis*).
τίς (4) J⁷⁵ Μ⁹²⁺⁷¹ L¹¹³ A⁵⁵ P¹⁰⁵ Pa² H¹¹
    C³ R⁹ : I. ii. 22, iii. 2, 12, v. 5.
τις (8) J⁵² Μ²⁰⁺³⁴ L⁷⁷ A¹¹⁴ P¹²⁸ Pa²²
    H²¹ C²⁵ R¹³ : I. ii. 1, 15, 27, iv.
    20, v. 14, 16, II. 10, III. 9.
τοιοῦτος (1) J³ Μ³⁺⁶ L² A⁴ P³¹ Pa¹ H⁵
    C¹ : III. 8.
τρεῖς (2) J⁴ Μ¹²⁺⁸ L¹⁰ A¹⁴ P⁶ Pa¹ H¹
    C¹ R¹¹ : I. v. 7, 8.
τυφλόω (1) J¹ P¹ : I. ii. 11.

ὕδωρ (4) J²⁵ Μ⁸⁺⁵ L⁶ A⁷ P¹ H² C⁴ R¹⁸ :
    I. v. 6 (*ter*), 8.
υἱός (24) J⁵⁷ Μ⁸⁸⁺³⁵ L⁷⁵ A²² P³⁹ H²⁴ C³
    R⁸ : I. i. 3, 7, ii. 22, 23 (*bis*), 24,
    iii. 8, 23, iv. 9, 10, 14, 15, v. 5,
    9, 10 (*bis*), 11, 12 (*bis*), 13, 20
    (*bis*), II. 3, 9.
ὑπάγω (1) J³² Μ¹⁶⁺¹⁹ L⁵ C¹ R⁶ : I. ii.
    11.
ὑπέρ, c. gen. (3) J¹³ Μ¹⁺² L³ A⁷ P⁸⁶ Pa⁴
    H¹⁰ C³ : I. iii. 16 (*bis*), III. 7.
ὑπό, c. gen. (1) J¹ Μ²⁴⁺⁹ L²⁴ A³⁹ P⁴⁵
    Pa¹ H⁹ C¹³ R² : III. 12.
ὑπολαμβάνω (1) L² A² : III. 8.
ὑπομιμνήσκω (1) J¹ L¹ Pa² C² : III. 10.

φανερόω (9) J⁹ Μ³ P¹⁹ Pa³ H² C² R² :
    I. i. 2 (*bis*), ii. 19, 28, iii. 2 (*bis*),
    5, 8, iv. 9.
φέρω (1) J¹⁶ Μ⁶⁺¹⁵ L⁴ A¹¹ P¹ Pa¹ H⁵
    C⁶ R² : II. 10.
φιλοπρωτεύω (1) : III. 9.
φίλος (2) J⁶ Μ¹ L¹⁵ A³ C² : III. 15 (*bis*).
φλυαρέω (1) : III. 10.
φοβέομαι (1) J⁵ Μ¹⁸⁺¹² L²³ A¹⁴ P⁹ H⁴
    C³ R⁶ : I. iv. 18.
φόβος (3) J³ Μ³⁺¹ L⁷ A⁶ P¹³ Pa¹ H¹
    C⁶ : I. iv. 18 (*ter*).
φυλάσσω (1) J³ Μ¹⁺² L⁶ A⁸ P³ Pa⁵ C³ :
    I. v. 21.
φῶς (6) J²² Μ⁶⁺¹ L⁷ A¹⁰ P¹² Pa¹ C¹
    R³ : I. i. 5, 7 (*bis*), ii. 8, 9, 10.

---

¹ The use of the nominative only, sing. and plur., has been recorded.

χαίρω (4), J⁹ M⁶⁺² L¹² A⁷ P²⁵ C² R² :
II. 4, 10, 11, III. 3.
χαρά (3) J⁹ M⁶⁺¹ L⁸ A⁴ P²¹ Pa¹ H⁴ C³.
χάριν (1) L¹ P³ Pa² C¹ : I. iii. 12.
χάρις (2) J⁴ L⁸ A¹⁷ P⁸⁷ Pa¹² H⁸ C¹⁵
R² : II. 3, II. 4.
χάρτης (1) : II. 12.
χείρ (1) J¹⁵ M²⁴⁺²⁷ L²⁶ A⁴⁶ P¹³ Pa⁴ H⁶
C² R¹⁶ : I. i. 1.
χρεία (2) J⁴ M⁶⁺⁴ L⁷ A⁵ P¹³ Pa¹ H⁴
R³ : I. ii. 27, iii. 17.
χρίσμα (1) : I. ii. 20, 27 (bis).
Χριστός (12) J¹⁹ M¹⁷⁺⁸ L¹² A²⁸ P³⁵⁵ Pa³²
H¹² C³⁸ R⁸ : I. ii. 22, v. 1, II.
9 : Ἰησοῦς Χριστός I. i. 3, ii. 1,
iii. 23, iv. 2, 15, v. 6, 20, ii. 3, 7.

ψεύδομαι (1) M¹ A¹ P⁴ Pa¹ C¹ R¹ :
I. i. 6.
ψευδοπροφήτης (1) M³⁺¹ L¹ A¹ C¹
R³ : I. iv. 1.
ψεῦδος (2) J¹ P⁴ R³ : I. ii. 21, 27.
ψεύστης (5) J² P¹ Pa² : I. i. 10, ii. 4,
22, iv. 20, v. 10.
ψηλαφάω (1) L¹ A¹ H¹ : I. i. 1.
ψυχή (3) J¹⁰ M¹⁶⁺⁸ L¹⁴ A¹⁵ P¹³ H⁶ C¹⁰
R⁷ : I. iii. 16 (bis), III. 2.

ὥρα (2) J²⁶ M²¹⁺¹² L¹⁶ A¹² P⁷ R¹⁰ : I.
ii. 18 (bis),
ὡς (sicut) (3) J¹³ M⁴⁰⁺²⁰ L²⁹ A³¹ P¹³⁰
Pa¹⁰ H²¹ C⁴³ R⁷⁰ : I. i. 7, ii. 27,
II. 5.

E. WORDS USED IN THE GOSPEL BUT NOT IN THE EPISTLES OF S. JOHN.

Ἀβραάμ (10).
ἀγαλλιάω (2).
ἀγγέλλω (2).
ἄγγελος (4).
ἁγιάζω (4).
ἀγοράζω (3).
ἄγω (12).
ἀγωνίζομαι (1).
ἀθετέω (1).
αἰγιαλός (1).
Αἰνών (1).
αἰτία (3).
ἄκανθαι (1).
ἀκάνθινος (1).
ἀκοή (1).
ἀκολουθέω (19).
ἀλείφω (2).
ἀλέκτωρ (2).
ἁλιεύω (1).
ἀλλαχόθεν (1).
ἅλλομαι (1).
ἄλλος (34).
ἀλλότριος (2).
ἀλόη (1).
ἁμαρτωλός (4).
ἀμὴν ἀμήν (25).
ἀμνός (2).
ἄμπελος (3).
ἀνά (1).
ἀναβαίνω (16).
ἀναβλέπω (4).
ἀναγινώσκω (1).
ἀνάκειμαι (4).

ἀναπίπτω (5).
ἀνάστασις (4).
ἀναστρέφω (1).
ἀνατρέπω (2).
ἀναχωρέω (1).
Ἀνδρέας (5).
ἄνεμος (1).
ἀνέρχομαι (1).
ἀνήρ (8).
ἀνθρακία (2).
ἀνίστημι, trans. (4), intrans. (4).
Ἄννας (2).
ἀνοίγω (11).
ἀντί (1).
ἀντιλέγω (1).
ἀντλέω (4).
ἄντλημα (1).
ἄνω (4).
ἄνωθεν (5).
ἄξιος (1).
ἀπάρτι (2).
ἅπας (1).
ἀπειθέω (1).
ἀπέρχομαι (21).
ἄπιστος (1).
ἀποβαίνω (1).
ἀποθνήσκω (28).
ἀποκαλύπτω (1).
ἀποκόπτω (2).
ἀποκρίνομαι (78).
ἀπόκρισις (2).
ἀποκτείνω (12).
ἀπολύω (5).

ἀπορέω (1).
ἀπόστολος (1).
ἀποσυνάγωγος (3).
ἀπώλεια (1).
ἄραφος (1).
ἀριθμός (1).
Ἀριμαθαία (1).
ἀριστάω (2).
ἀρνίον (1).
ἁρπάζω (4).
ἀρτός (24).
ἀρχιερεύς (21).
ἀρχιτρίκλινος (3).
ἄρχω (1).
ἄρχων (7).
ἄρωμα (1).
ἀσθένεια (2).
ἀσθενέω (9).
ἀτιμάζω (1).
αὐλή (3).
αὐξάνω (1).
αὐτόφωρος (1).

βαθύς (1).
βαίον (1).
βαπτίζω (13).
βάπτω (1).
Βαραββᾶς (2).
βασιλεία (5).
βασιλεύς (16).
βασιλικός (2).
βαστάζω (5)
[Βηθαβαρά (1)].
Βηθανία (4).
Βηθζαθά (1).
Βηθλεέμ (1).
Βηθσαιδά (3).
βῆμα (1).
βιβλίον (2).
βιβρώσκω (1).
βλασφημέω (1).
βλασφημία (1).
βοάω (1).
βόσκω (2).
βουλεύομαι (2).
βοῦς (2).
βραχίων (1).
βραχύς (1).
βροντή (1).
βρῶμα (1).
βρῶσις (4).

Γαββαθά (1).
γαζοφυλάκιον (1).
Γαλιλαία (17)
Γαλιλαῖος (1).
γάμος (3).

γε (καίτοιγε) (1).
γείτων (1).
γεμίζω (2).
γενετή (1).
γέρων (1).
γεύομαι (2).
γεωργός (1).
γῆ (9).
γηράσκω (1).
γλωσσόκομον (2).
γνωρίζω (2).
γνωστός (2).
γογγύζω (4).
γογγυσμός (1).
Γολγοθά (1).
γονεῖς (6).
γράμμα (2).
γραφή (12).
γυμνός (1).
γυνή (18).

δαιμονίζομαι (1).
δαιμόνιον (6).
δακρύω (1).
δάκτυλος (2).
Δαυείδ (2).
δεῖ (10).
δεικνύω (7).
δειλιάω (1).
δεῖπνον (4).
δεκαπέντε (1).
δέκατος (1).
δεξιός (2).
δέρω (1).
δεῦρο (1).
δεῦτε (2).
δεύτερος (4).
δέχομαι (1).
δέω (4).
δηνάριον (2).
δήποτε (1).
διαδίδωμι (1).
διαζώννυμι (3).
διακονέω (3).
διάκονος (3).
διακόσιοι (2).
διαμερίζω (1).
διασκορπίζω (1).
διασπορά (1).
διατρίβω (2).
διδακτός (1).
διδάσκαλος (7).
Δίδυμος (3).
διεγείρω (1).
διέρχομαι (3).
δίκτυον (4).
διψάω (6).

διώκω (2).
δοκέω (8).
δόλος (1).
δόξα (17).
δοξάζω (22).
δουλεύω (1).
δοῦλος (11).
δύο (13).
δώδεκα (6).
δωρεά (1).
δωρεάν (1).

ἕβδομος (1).
Ἑβραιστί (5).
ἐγγύς (11).
ἐγείρω (13).
ἔθνος (5).
ἔθος (1).
εἰ οὐ (2).
εἴκοσι (1).
εἰμί (53).
  εἶ (26).
  ὤν (26).
εἰσάγω (1).
εἰσέρχομαι (15).
εἶτα (3).
ἕκαστος (3).
ἑκατόν (2).
ἐκδέχομαι (1).
ἐκεῖ (22).
ἐκεῖθεν (2).
ἐκκέντεω (1).
ἐκλέγομαι (4).
ἐκμάσσω (3).
ἐκνεύω (1).
ἐκπορεύομαι (2).
ἐκτείνω (1).
ἕκτος (2).
ἐκχέω (1).
ἐλάσσων (1).
ἐλαττόω (1).
ἐλαύνω (1).
ἐλέγχω (3).
ἐλεύθερος (2).
ἐλευθερόω (2).
ἔλιγμα (1).
ἑλκύω (5).
Ἕλλην (3).
Ἑλληνιστί (1).
ἐμαυτοῦ (16).
ἐμβαίνω (4).
ἐμβλέπω (2).
ἐμβριμάομαι (2).
ἐμπίμπλημι (1)
ἐμπόριον (1).
ἐμφανίζω (2).
ἐμφυσάω (1).

ἐνθάδε (2).
ἐνιαυτός (3).
ἐνκαίνια (1).
ἐνταφιάζω (1).
ἐνταφιασμός (1)
ἐντέλλομαι (4).
ἐντεῦθεν (5).
ἐντυλίσσω (1).
ἕξ (3).
ἐξάγω (1).
ἔξεστιν (2).
ἐξετάζω (1).
ἐξηγέομαι (1).
ἐξουσία (8).
ἐξυπνίζω (1).
ἑορτή (17).
ἐπαίρω (4).
ἐπάνω (2).
ἐπάρατος (1).
ἐπσύριον (5).
ἐπεί (2).
ἔπειτα (1).
ἐπενδύτης (1).
ἐπερωτάω (2).
ἐπί, c. gen. (7).
  c. acc. (21).
ἐπιβάλλω (2).
ἐπίκειμαι (2).
ἐπιλέγομαι (1).
ἐπιπίπτω (1).
ἐπιστρέφω (1).
ἐπιτίθημι (3).
ἐπιτρέπω (1).
ἐπιχρίω (2).
ἐπουράνιος (1).
ἐραυνάω (2).
ἔρημος (5).
ἑρμηνεύω (3)
ἐρῶ (6).
ἐσθίω (15).
ἔσω (1).
ἕτερος (1).
ἔτι (8).
ἑτοιμάζω (2).
ἕτοιμος (1).
ἔτος (3).
εὐθύνω (1).
εὐθύς (3).
εὐλογέω (1).
εὐχαριστέω (3).
Ἐφραίμ (1).
ἐχθές (1).
ἕως, conj. (5).

Ζεβεδαῖος (1).
ζῆλος (1).
ζητέω (34).

ζήτησις (1).
ζώννυμι (2).
ζωοποιέω (3).

Ἠλείας (2).
ἡλικία (2).
ἧλος (2).
ἤπερ (1).
Ἠσαίας (4).

θάλασσα (9).
θαρσέω (1).
θαυμαστός (1).
θεοσεβής (1).
θεραπεύω (1).
θερίζω (4).
θερισμός (2).
θερμαίνομαι (3).
θήκη (1).
θλίψις (2).
θνήσκω (2).
θρέμμα (1).
θρηνέω (1).
θρίξ (2).
θυγάτηρ (1).
θύρα (7).
θυρωρός (3).
θύω (1).
Θωμᾶς (7).

Ἰακώβ (3).
ἰάομαι (3).
ἴδε (15).
ἴδιος (15).
ἰδού (4).
ἱερεύς (1).
ἱερόν (10).
Ἱεροσόλυμα (12).
Ἱεροσολυμεῖται (1).
ἱμάς (1).
ἱμάτιον (6).
ἱματισμός (1).
Ἰορδάνης (3).
Ἰουδαία (6).
Ἰουδαῖος (71).
Ἰούδας (Iscariot) (8).
Ἰούδας (1)
Ἰσκαριώτης (6).
ἴσος (1).
Ἰσραήλ (4).
Ἰσραηλείτης (1).
ἴστημι (18).
ἰσχύω (1).
ἰχθύς (3).
Ἰωάνης (Baptista) (18).
Ἰωάνης (4).
Ἰωσήφ (filius Israel) (1).

Ἰωσήφ (Mariae maritus) (2).
Ἰωσήφ (1).

κἀγώ (31).
καθαίρω (1).
καθαρισμός (2).
καθαρός (4).
καθέζομαι (4).
κάθημαι (4).
καθίζω (2).
Καιάφας (5).
καιρός (4).
Καῖσαρ (3).
καίτοιγε (1).
καίω (2).
κἀκεῖ (1).
κἀκεῖνος (6).
κακῶς (1).
καλός (7).
κἄν (4).
Κανά (4).
καρπός (10).
κατά, c. gen. (1).
καταβαίνω (18).
καταβολή (1).
κατάγνυμι (3).
κατάκειμαι (2).
καταλαμβάνω (3).
κατεσθίω (1).
κατηγορέω (2).
κατηγορία (1).
κάτω (1).
Καφαρναούμ (5).
Κέδρος (1).
κειρία (1).
κέρμα (1).
κερματιστής (1).
κεφαλή (5).
κῆπος (4).
κηπουρός (1).
Κηφᾶς (1).
κίνησις (1).
κλαίω (8).
κλάσμα (2).
κλέπτης (4).
κλέπτω (1).
κλῆμα (4).
κλῆρος (1).
κλίνω (1).
Κλωπᾶς (1).
κοιλία (2).
κοιμάομαι (2).
κοίμησις (1).
κόκκος (1).
κολλυβιστής (1).
κόλπος (2).
κολυμβήθρα (4).

κομψότερον (1).
κοπιάω (3).
κόπος (1).
κόφινος (1).
κράβαττος (4).
κράζω (4).
κρανίον (1).
κρατέω (1).
κραυγάζω (6).
κρίθινος (2).
κρίμα (1).
κρίνω (19).
κρυπτός (3).
κρύπτω (1).
κυκλεύω (1).
κυκλόω (1).
κύριος (52).
κώμη (3).

λαγχάνω (1).
Λάζαρος (11).
λάθρα (1).
λαλιά (2).
λαμπάς (1).
λαός (2).
λατρεία (1).
λέντιον (2).
λευείτης (1).
λευκός (2).
λῃστής (3).
λιθάζω (4).
λίθινος (1).
λίθος (6).
λιθόστρωτος (1).
λίτρα (2).
λογίζομαι (1).
λόγχη (1).
λοιδορέω (1).
λούω (1).
λύκος (2).
λυπέω (2).
λύπη (4).
λύχνος (1).

Μαγδαληνή (3)
μαθητής (78).
μαίνομαι (1).
μακάριος (2).
μακράν (1).
μᾶλλον (4).
Μάλχος (1).
μανθάνω (2).
μάννα (2).
Μάρθα (9).
Μαρία ἡ Μαγδαληνή (5).
Μαριάμ, Μαρία (Laz. soror) (9).
μαστιγόω (1).

μάχαιρα (2).
μάχομαι (1).
μέγας (5).
μεθερμηνεύομαι (2).
μεθύω (1).
μέλει (2).
μέλλω (12).
μέν (8).
μέντοι (5).
μέρος (3).
μέσος (5).
μεσόω (1).
Μεσσίας (2).
μεστός (3).
μετά, c. acc. (16).
μεταξύ (1).
μέτρον (1).
μετρητής (1).
(μή), οὐ μή (17).
μηκέτι (1).
μήποτε (1).
μήτηρ (11).
μήτι (3).
μιαίνω (1).
μίγμα (1).
μικρόν (9).
μικρός (2).
μιμνήσκομαι (3).
μισθωτός (1).
μνημεῖον (14).
μνημονεύω (3).
μύρον (4).
Μωυσῆς (11).

Ναζαρέτ (2).
Ναζωραῖος (3).
Ναθαναήλ (6).
ναί (3).
ναός (3).
νάρδος (1).
νεκρός (8).
νέος (1).
νεύω (1).
Νικόδημος (5).
νιπτήρ (1).
νίπτω (13).
νοέω (1).
νομή (1).
νόμος (13).
νόσημα (1).
νύμφη (1).
νυμφιός (3).
νύξ (6).
νύσσω (1).

ξηραίνω (1).
ξηρός (1).

ὁδηγέω (1).
ὁδός (4).
ὄζω (1).
ὀθόνιον (4).
οἰκοδομέω (1).
οἶκος (3).
οἶμαι (1).
οἶνος (6).
ὀκτώ (2).
ὁμοίως (3).
ὁμοῦ (3).
ὅμως (1).
ὀνάριον (1).
ὄνος (1).
ὄξος (3).
ὀπίσω (7).
ὅπλον (1).
ὅπου (30).
ὅπως (1).
ὀργή (1).
ὄρος (4).
ὀρφανός (1).
ὅσος (10).
ὀστέον (1).
ὅτε (21).
οὔ (3).
οὐδέποτε (1).
οὐδέπω (3).
οὐκέτι (12).
οὐκοῦν (1).
οὐρανός (20).
οὗτοι (5).
οὐχί (7).
ὄφις (1).
ὄχλος (20).
ὀψάριον (5).
ὀψία (2).
ὄψις (2).

παιδάριον (1).
παιδίσκη (1).
παῖς (1).
παίω (1).
πάντοτε (7).
παρά, c. dat. (9).
παραγίνομαι (2).
παραδίδωμι (15).
παρακύπτω (1).
παραλαμβάνω (3).
παραμυθέομαι (2).
παρασκευή (3).
πάρειμι (2).
παρίστημι (2).
παροιμία (4).
πάσχα (10).
πατρίς (1).
Πειλᾶτος (20).

πεινάω (1).
πειράζω (2).
πέμπω (32).
πενθερός (1).
πεντακισχίλιοι (2).
πέντε (5).
πεντήκοντα (2).
πέραν (8).
περί, c. acc. (1).
περιβάλλω (1).
περιδέομαι (1).
περιίστημι (1).
περισσεύω (2).
περισσός (1).
περιστερά (3).
περιτέμνω (1).
περιτίθημι (1).
περιτομή (2).
Πέτρος (34).
πηγή (3).
πηλός (5).
πῆχυς (1).
πιάζω (8).
πίνω (11).
πιπράσκω (1).
πίπτω (3).
πιστικός (1).
πλείων (5).
πλέκω (1).
πλευρά (4).
πλῆθος (2).
πλήρωμα (1).
πλησίον (1).
πλοιάριον (4).
πλοῖον (8).
πνέω (2).
πόθεν (13).
ποιμαίνω (1).
ποιμήν (6).
ποίμνη (1).
ποῖος (4).
πόλις (8).
πολλάκις (1).
πολύτιμος (1).
πορεύομαι (17).
πορνεία (1).
πορφύρεος (2).
πόσις (1).
ποταμός (1).
ποτέ (1).
πότε (2).
πότερον (1).
ποτήριον (1).
πούς (14).
πραιτώριον (4).
πράσσω (2).
πρίν (3).

πρό (9).
προβατικός (1).
προβάτιον (2).
πρόβατον (19).
πρός, c. dat. (3).
προσαιτέω (1).
προσαίτης (1).
προσέρχομαι (1).
προσκόπτω (2).
προσκυνέω (10).
προσκυνητής (1).
προσφάγιον (1).
πρότερος (3).
προτρέχω (1).
πρόφασις (1).
προφητεύω (1).
προφήτης (14).
πρωί (2).
πρωία (1).
πρῶτον (8).
πτέρνα (1).
πτύσμα (1).
πτύω (1).
πτωχός (4).
πυνθάνομαι (1).
πῦρ (1).
πυρετός (1).
πωλέω (2).
πῶλος (1).
πωρόω (1).

ῥαββεί (8).
ῥαββουνεί (1).
ῥάπισμα (2).
ῥέω (1).
ῥῆμα (12).
Ῥωμαῖος (1).
Ῥωμαϊστί (1).

σάββατον (14).
Σαλείμ (1).
Σαμαρείτης (4).
Σαμαρεῖτις (2).
Σαμαρία (3).
Σατανᾶς (1).
σεαυτοῦ (9).
σημαίνω (3).
σημεῖον (17).
Σιλωάμ (1).
Σίμων (Πέτρος) (22).
Σίμων (3).
σῖτος (1).
Σιών (1).
σκανδαλίζω (2).
σκέλος (3).
σκεῦος (1).

σκηνοπηγία (1).
σκηνόω (1).
σκληρός (1).
σκορπίζω (2).
σμύρνα (1).
Σολομών (1).
σός (6).
σουδάριον (2).
σπεῖρα (2).
σπείρω (2).
σπήλαιον (1).
σπόγγος (1).
στάδιος (2).
σταυρός (4).
σταυρόω (10).
στέφανος (2).
στῆθος (2).
στήκω (2).
στοά (2).
στρατιώτης (6).
στρέφω (4).
συγγενής (1).
συκῆ (2).
συλλαμβάνω (1).
συμφέρω (3).
σύν (3).
συνάγω (7).
συναγωγή (1).
συνέδριον (1).
συνεισέρχομαι (2).
συνέρχομαι (2).
συνήθεια (1).
συνμαθητής (1).
συνσταυρόω (1).
συντελέω (1).
συντίθεμαι (1).
συντρίβω (1).
συνχράομαι (1).
σύρω (1).
Συχάρ (1).
σφραγίζω (2).
σχίζω (2).
σχίσμα (3).
σχοινίον (1).
σώζω (6).
σῶμα (6).
σωτηρία (1).

ταράσσω (7).
ταραχή (1).
τάχειον (2).
ταχέως (1).
ταχύ (1).
τε (3).
τελευτάω (1).
τελευτή (2).
τέλος (1).

τέρας (1).
τέσσαρες (2).
τεσσεράκοντα (1).
τεταρταῖος (1).
τετράμηνος (1).
Τιβεριάς (3).
τίκτω (1).
τιμάω (6).
τιμή (1).
τίτλος (2).
τολμάω (1).
τόπος (17).
τοσοῦτος (4).
τότε (10).
τράπεζα (1).
τρέχω (2).
τριάκοντα (3).
τριακόσιοι (1).
τρίς (1).
τρίτον (4).
τρίτος (1).
τροφή (1).
τρώγω (5).
τύπος (1).
τυφλός (16).

ὑγιής (7).
ὑδρία (3).
ὑμέτερος (3).
ὑπαντάω (4).
ὑπάντησις (1).
ὑπέρ, c. acc. (1).
ὑπηρέτης (9).
ὕπνος (1).
ὑπό, c. acc. (1).
ὑπόδειγμα (1).
ὑπόδημα (1).
ὑποκάτω (1).
ὕσσωπος (1).
ὑστερέω (1).
ὕστερον (1).
ὑφαντός (1).
ὑψόω (5).

φανερῶς (1).
φανός (1).
Φαρισαῖος (20).
φαῦλος (2).
φεύγω (3).
φημί (4).
φιλέω (13).
Φίλιππος (12).
φοῖνιξ (1).
φραγέλλιον (1).
φρέαρ (2).
φυλακή (1).
φωνέω (13).
φωνή (15).
φωτίζω (1).

χαμαί (2).
χείμαρρος (1).
χειμών (1).
χείρων (1).
χιλίαρχος (1).
χιτών (2).
χολάω (1).
χορτάζω (1).
χόρτος (1).
χρόνος (4).
χωλός (1).
χώρα (3).
χωρέω (3).
χωρίον (1).
χωρίς (3).

ψύχος (1).
ψωμίον (4).

ὧδε (5).
ὡς, conj. (21).
ὡσαννά (1).
ὥσπερ (2).
ὥστε (1).
ὠτάριον (1).
ὠτίον (1).
ὠφελέω (2).